MATLAB – A FUNDAMENTAL TOOL FOR SCIENTIFIC COMPUTING AND ENGINEERING APPLICATIONS – VOLUME 1

Edited by **Vasilios N. Katsikis**

MATLAB – A Fundamental Tool for Scientific Computing and Engineering Applications – Volume 1
http://dx.doi.org/10.5772/2557
Edited by Vasilios N. Katsikis

Contributors

A.B. Campo, Tomas Vydra, Daniel Havelka, Christophe Batard, Frédéric Poitiers, Christophe Millet, Nicolas Ginot, Jacques Fanjason Ramahaleomiarantsoa, Eric Jean Roy Sambatra, Nicolas Héraud, Jean Marie Razafimahenina, Ergin Kosa, Levent Trabzon, Umit Sonmez, Huseyin Kizil, Kosol Oranpiroj, Worrajak Moangjai, Wichran Jantee, Sven Fagerstrom, Nagy Bengiamin, Khalid Chikh, Mohamed Khafallah, Abdallah Saâd, Konrad Urbanski, Adel Aktaibi, M. Azizur Rahman, Mostefa Ghassoul, Octavio Ramos-Leaños, Jose Luis Naredo, Jose Alberto Gutierrez-Robles, M. Ould Ahmedou, M. Ferfra, M. Chraygane, M. Maaroufi, Viliam Fedák, Tibor Balogh, Pavel Záskalický, S. Chountasis, V.N. Katsikis, D. Pappas, Mohammed Z. Al-Faiz, Abbas H. Miry, Ramy Saad, Sebastian Hoyos, Samuel Palermo, Momoh-Jimoh E. Salami, Ismaila B. Tijani, Abdussamad U. Jibia, Za'im Bin Ismail, David Ernesto Troncoso Romero, Gordana Jovanovic Dolecek, Nur Diyana Kamarudin, Kamaruddin Abd. Ghani, Siti Noormiza Makhtar, Baizura Bohari, Noorlina Zainuddin

Published by InTech

Janeza Trdine 9, 51000 Rijeka, Croatia

Copyright © 2012 InTech

Notice

Publishing Process Manager Ivona Lovric
Technical Editor InTech Prepress, Novi Sad
Cover InTech Design team

Additional hard copies can be obtained from orders@intechopen.com

MATLAB – A Fundamental Tool for Scientific Computing and Engineering Applications – Volume 1, Edited by Vasilios N. Katsikis
p. cm.
ISBN 978-953-51-0750-7

For EU product safety concerns:
IN TECH d.o.o., Prolaz Marije Krucifikse Kozulić 3, 51000 Rijeka, Croatia,
info@intechopen.com or visit our website at intechopen.com.

Meet the editor

Dr Vasilios N. Katsikis received his Diploma of Mathematics from the University of Athens, his M.Sc. in Applied Mathematics and his Ph. D. in Mathematics from the National Technical University of Athens. He also worked as a post-doc researcher in Applied and Computational Mathematics under the financial support of the State Scholarship Foundation (IKY). During the years 1999-2009 he worked in several Greek universities and Technological Education Institutes and from September 2009 he belongs to the teaching and research stuff of the Department of Mathematics at the Technological Education Institute of Piraeus as an assistant professor of Mathematics. His research interests lie in the areas of Computational Mathematics, Functional Analysis, Computational Finance, Matrix Analysis and Applied Linear Algebra, Image and Signal Processing. He has published several articles in high quality journals concerning the above areas and he serves as a reviewer for many journals and congresses while he belongs to the editorial board of three journals.

Contents

Preface

"If you would be a real seeker after truth, it is necessary that at least once in your life you doubt, as far as possible, all things."
Rene Descartes

It is well known that MATLAB is a numerical computing environment that not only provides numerical calculations but also facilitates analytical calculations in most engineering applications of computers.

This is the first book in a three-volume series deploying MATLAB-based applications in almost every branch of science. The present textbook contains a collection of 20 high quality articles. In particular, the book consists of two sections, the first one is devoted to MATLAB applications in engineering and the second is devoted to image and signal processing. In what follows, we present a short summary focusing on the key concepts of each chapter.

Section 1: MATLAB applications in engineering

In **chapter 1** some script MATLAB codes and Simulink models about the PID structure applied to closed loop systems are presented. The closed loop control is used at several industrial applications. The most used control structure is the Proportional-Integral-Derivative (PID) controller. The MATLAB software offer several resources to analyzes dynamical systems and to tune the parameters of this kind of controller.

Chapter 2 should give readers overall information about processing of rough data obtained from numeric simulator of electromagnetic field (EM). Many possibilities of visualization are be discussed with regard to practical use and with concrete examples from researcher's practice. Part of this chapter is dedicated to processing of multisource simulations, while the main purpose is to aid many researchers and students in the vast field of EM research. The authors present, in detail, their knowledge and tips which they have gathered through their studies and research activities.

In **chapter 3** the ability to simulate power converters is presented by using only Simulink. Traditionally two approaches are used to simulate power electronic systems:

- The first, so called fixed topology, where semiconductors are impedances with low or high values based on their on-state or off-state. Equations system does not depend on the state of the semiconductor. Despite its simplicity, this approach raises problems of compromise between accuracy of the results and stability of numerical integration methods.

- The second, so called variable topology, assimilates the switches to open-circuits or short-circuits. The system equations then depend on the state of the semiconductor. There are no accuracy problems but writing the equations of different configurations can be laborious as well as obtain switching conditions of the semiconductor.

In this chapter, the authors propose a method for simulating static converters with Simulink based on the variable topology approach where switching conditions of semiconductor are realized by switching functions.

Chapter 4 deals with the faults diagnosis of a wound rotor synchronous machine (WRIM) by the principal component analysis (PCA) method. This work intends to show the strength of the PCA method in the faults diagnosis of systems, using the WRIM as the application device. To do this, the authors propose an accurate analytical model of the WRIM without or in the presence of faults. This model provides the matrix data of the several characteristic quantities of the machine. These data are included as input variables of the PCA method. Then, the authors present a complete approach of the PCA method based on the study of residues. Simulation results show the efficiency of the detection but require a good choice of the number of principal components. All of above work has been then implemented in the MATLAB software.

In **chapter 5** position, quasi-static behavior, velocity, acceleration and dynamic simulations are modelled and run by MATLAB/Simulink in order to analyze the dynamic and quasi-static behavior of the compliant MEMS amplifier.

Chapter 6 proposes the SagWave software as a visual interactive capability to generated data for the dsPIC controller. The SagWave software can show the waveform and the phasor of the three-phase voltage. The simulation and experimental results have shown the simple control algorithm for generating the sag signal for testing. The SagWave software is based on MATLAB graphic user interface (GUI) and the hardware is based on dsPIC microcontroller.

In **chapter 7** the authors use the capabilities of MATLAB and its associated SimPower and Simulink toolboxes in the modeling and simulation of power electronics devices. Design and analysis steps were illustrated using MATLAB and Simulink as an engineering tool. The effectiveness of the SimPower toolbox was demonstrated via typical examples which lead the way for further investigation. The presented methodologies facilitate analysis, characterization, and design of efficient buck/boost converters. Researchers and practicing engineers should find practical value in the presented material. The chapter is self-contained in the sense of providing sufficient background and theoretical development on the subject.

Chapter 8 discusses Permanent Magnet Synchronous Motors (PMSM's). In particular, another solution has been presented to overcome the problems associated to DTC for PMSM in case of motor parameters variation and/or nonlinear operating conditions, which utilize speed FLC and an independent stator resistance estimator.

In **chapter 9** the authors deal with the problem of estimation the rotor position and speed in sensorless PMSM drive. At low speed range position estimation is particularly difficult due to the small value of the input and estimated signals, which are covered by measured noises and disturbances. Additional problem is to obtain high dynamic of the proposed drive system in the observer presence in control loop. The research was realized using MATLAB/Simulink.

In **chapter 10** it is explained how to simulate a digital differential relay using MATLAB. The following major sections are featured: a) General explanation about the differential protection algorithm, b) The problems that is aimed to be solved using the differential protection, c) General idea about the digital algorithms used to implement the differential protection, d) Explanation how to implement some of the digital algorithms using MATLAB.

Chapter 11 develops a PH control strategy using MATLAB interfaced to NI acquisition card. The control strategy was developed using MATLAB Block Sets for fuzzy logic. To enhance the validity of this technique, a tuned Proportional-Integral-Derivative (PID) controller was developed and the results obtained were nowhere near those discussed in this chapter no matter how the fine tuning of the PID.

In **chapter 12** a detailed analysis and description of a line and cable model that is based on the principles of the Universal Line Model (ULM) is discussed. Moreover, a comprehensive description of the theoretical basis of ULM, phase domain line model is presented. The model structure being implemented in MATLAB is provided as well while the included application examples illustrate the model capabilities and provide benchmarks for further model development by readers interested in the subject.

Chapter 13 presents a new approach for modeling the non-linear inductances by an analytic expression under the MATLAB/Simulink code. The current representation is based on the introducing point by point, by a Lookup Table bloc in Simulink, the values of its characteristic Φ(i) outcome deduced from the values of the magnetizing curve B-H and the geometric parameters of the corresponding portion of the magnetic circuit. This approach can solve many problems of modeling, simulation and optimization of the electrical networks and electric machines.

In **chapter 14** the principles of development virtual models in GUI MATLAB for chosen electrical machines and controlled drives are discussed. Moreover, it discusses methodology and results at design of a unified series of virtual models for electrical machines and drives, virtual models for analysis of dynamical properties of electrical machines, virtual models applied for synthesis of drive systems and experiences with utilization of virtual models.

Section 2: Image and Signal Processing

In **chapter 15** the authors introduced a novel computational method based on the calculation of the Moore-Penrose inverse of full rank rectangular matrix, with particular focus on problems arising in image processing. The motivation here relies on the problem of restoring blurry and noisy images via well developed mathematical methods and techniques based on the inverse procedures in order to obtain an approximation of the original image. By using the proposed algorithm, the resolution of the reconstructed image remains at a very high level, although the main advantage of the method was found on the computational load that has been decreased considerably compared to the other methods and techniques. The efficiency of the generalized inverse is evidenced by the presented simulation results in MATLAB.

Chapter 16 presents the anatomy of Electromyography (EMG) signal, measurement, analysis, and it's processing. Moreover, the motion classification simulations are carried out, in order to evaluate classification performance of the human arm movements recognition based on K-Nearest Neighbor (K-NN) algorithm. The simulated data were generated from an EMG signal simulator. The results illustrate that the recognition using K-NN presents better results than artificial neural network in term of recognition accuracy. This chapter also presents the simulation of human arm motion in virtual reality to test the algorithm of EMG recognition. It can be concluded that, the virtual reality is useful to test the viability of designs before the implementation phase on a virtual reality prototype. It found that, MATLAB a convenient platform for development of computational algorithms, and with the visualization functions of MATLAB Ver.R2009a a reasonable amount of visualization techniques are available.

In **chapter 17** it is provided a comprehensive background and study for the effects of clock-jitter in the sampling-clocks of delta-sigma modulators. The study includes detailed analysis for the effects of clock-jitter on various waveforms and signals provided by different types of DACs used in delta-sigma modulators. Also, efficient MATLAB/Simulink models for additive errors induced by clock-jitter in delta-sigma modulators are shown so that to help designers characterize the sensitivities of various types of delta-sigma architectures to clock-jitter. The robustness of the adopted models is demonstrated through illustrative examples based on system-level simulations using MATLAB/Simulink.

Chapter 18 Generally, a multiexponential transient signal is represented by a linear combination of exponentials of the form $S(\tau)=\sum_{k}^{M} A_k e^{-\lambda_k \tau}+n(\tau)$, where M is the number of components, A_k and k, respectively, correspond to the amplitude and real-valued decay rate constants of the kth component and n(τ) is the additive white Gaussian noise with variance σ_n^2. This chapter reports the development of a computationally efficient algorithm for high resolution estimates the signal parameters (M, A_k and λ_k) using MATLAB.

The proposed algorithm involves modification of Gardner transform as well as a systematic approach for selecting the optimal truncation point which is required for real-time analysis. Furthermore, an integrated MATLAB--Labview software interface is proposed for real-time deployment of the algorithm. The analytical strength of MATLAB together with simplicity and user-friendly benefits of the National Instrument (NI) Labview design platforms are explored in developing an efficient, user-friendly algorithm for analysis and real-time implementation of multiexponential transient signal.

In **chapter 19** the basic fundamentals on digital Finite Impulse Response (FIR) Hilbert transformers are covered by reviewing the characteristics of analytic signals. The main connection between Hilbert transformers and half-band filters are highlighted. The methods to design low-complexity FIR filters, namely Frequency-Response Masking (FRM), Frequency Transformation (FT) and Piecewise Polynomial-Sinusoidal (PPS), as well as the Pipelining-Interleaving (PI) architecture, are introduced in a simplified and concise way. These methods are the cornerstone of the efficient techniques to design Hilbert transformers. Finally, with such background, an extensive revision of the aforementioned methods to design low--complexity efficient FIR Hilbert transformers is given, providing MATLAB routines for every method.

Chapter 20 proposes a new method in order to detect craters on optical images by using MATLAB. Moreover, the chapter focuses on identification of craters in terms of its characteristics and detection of these visual features of the moon to determine a safe landing site for a lunar Lander. This is achieved by using autonomous crater detection on image using MATLAB image processing tools.

At this point, I would like to thank the authors for their great contribution in this series of scientific books regarding MATLAB applications in Sciences. Also, I thank the InTech team for their significant support during the preparation of this book.

Vasilios N. Katsikis
Department of Mathematics,
Technological Education Institute of Piraeus,
Greece

Section 1

MATLAB Applications in Engineering

Chapter 1

PID Control Design

A.B. Campo

Additional information is available at the end of the chapter

http://dx.doi.org/10.5772/48497

1. Introduction

Many industrial applications have digital closed loop control systems and the main algorithm used at these applications is the Proportional Integral Derivative structure (PID). This chapter presents some useful MATLAB commands that might be used as an instrument to analyze the closed loop and also to help the control system design. The first part presents the general standard structure of this controller, whereas MATLAB/SIMULINK programs are used to illustrate some design aspects. Script codes are used to describe the dynamic systems through the Laplace Transform and time response analysis of the system with time delays. Block diagram descriptions employed to represent the distillation process are used to analyses the Proportional Integral controller (PI) applied to the system. Performance analysis is conducted to implement an exhaustive searching algorithm applied in tuning PI parameters. At the second part a Smith Predictor structure is designed and presented to enhance the system performance. Some common feedback structures are presented and the classical literature will be referenced to present the main topics.

Along the chapter the tuning algorithms and the system analyses tools are presented through a specific application. This example is related to the tuning of PI control system applied to the temperature and pressure control in a distillation process designed to obtain the anhydrous ethanol and the hydrated ethanol from the sugarcane fermentation and distillation.

2. PID structures

In the literature, several works has describing the PID structure (Åström & Hägglund, 1995), (Ang, 2008), (Mansour, 2011) and (Alfaro, 2005). According to the authors the three term form is the standard PID structure of this controller. The structure is also known as parallel form and is represented by:

$$G(s) = K_p + K_I \frac{1}{s} + K_D s = K_p \left(1 + \frac{1}{T_I s} + T_D s \right) \tag{1}$$

Where:

K_P : proportional gain;
K_I : integral gain;
K_D : derivative gain;
T_I : integral time constant and
T_D : derivative time constant.

In MATLAB, the script code of parallel form may be represented by:

```
s = tf('s');
% PID Parallel form
Kp=10;
Td=0.1;
Ti=0.1;
G=Kp*(1+(1/(Ti*s))+Td*s);
```

The control parameters are:

- The proportional term: providing an overall control action proportional to the error signal through the constant gain factor.
- The integral term: the action is to reduce steady-state errors through low-frequency compensation by an integrator.
- The derivative term: improves transient response through high-frequency compensation by a differentiator.

The very same system may be designed at SIMULINK Toolbox, represented in figure 1.

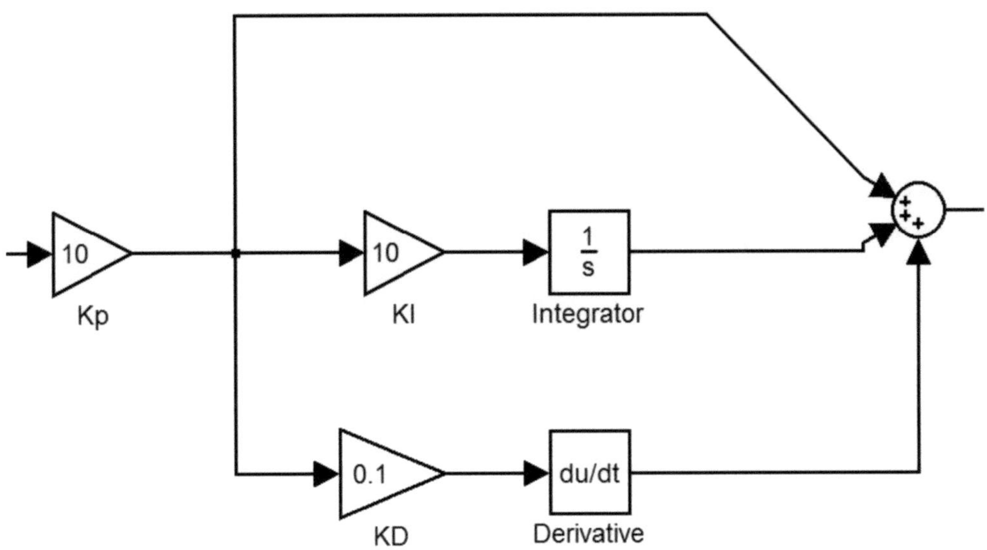

Figure 1. Simulink PID Control

To minimize the gain at high frequencies, the derivative term is usually modified to:

$$G(s) = K_p\left(1 + \frac{1}{T_I s} + \frac{T_D s}{1 + \alpha T_D s}\right) \tag{2}$$

Where α is a positive parameter adjusted between 0.01 and 1. This formulation is also used to obtain a causal relationship between the input and the output of the controller. Another usual structure employed at the PID controller is presented in figure 2.

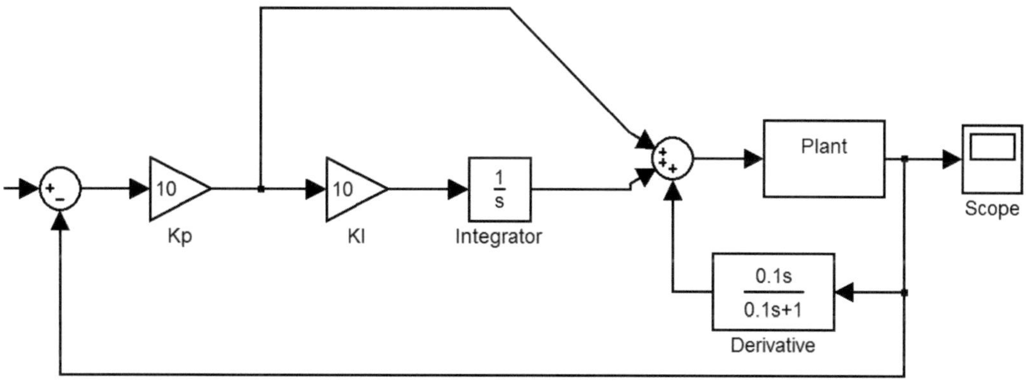

Figure 2. PID Controller with derivative term at the feedback branch.

According to this configuration, the derivative term is inserted out of the direct branch. The structure is carried to minimize the effect of set-point changes at the output of the control algorithm. By using this configuration only variations at the output signal of the plant will be added with the integral and proportional actions.

2.1. Tuning methods

Several tuning methods are described in (Åström & Hägglund, 1995) and in (Ang, 2007). The tuning methods are employed to obtain the stability of the closed-loop system and to meet given objectives associated with the following characteristics:

- stability robustness;
- set-point following and tracking performance at transient response, including rise-time, overshoot, and settling time;
- regulation performance at steady-state, including load disturbance rejection;
- robustness against plant modelling uncertainty;
- noise attenuation and robustness against environmental uncertainty.

In (Ang, 2007), the PID controllers tuning methods are classified and grouped according to their nature and usage. The groups that describe each tuning method are:

- Analytical methods—at these methods the PID parameters are calculated through the use of analytical or algebraic relations based in a plant model representation and in some design specification.

- Heuristic methods—These methods are evolved from practical experience in manual tuning and are coded trough the use of artificial intelligence techniques, like expert systems, fuzzy logic and neural networks.
- Frequency response methods—the frequency response characteristics of the controlled process is used to tune the PID controller. Frequently these are offline and academic methods, where the main concern of design is stability robustness since plant transfer function have unstructured uncertainty.
- Optimization methods—these methods utilize an offline numerical optimization method for a single composite objective or use computerised heuristics or, yet, an evolutionary algorithm for multiple design objectives. According to the characteristics of the problem, an exhaustive search for the best solution may be applied. Some kind of enhanced searching method may be used also. These are often time-domain methods and mostly applied offline. This is the tuning method used at the development of this work.
- Adaptive tuning methods—these methods are based in automated online tuning, where the parameters are adjusted in real-time through one or a combination of the previous methods. System identification may be used to obtain the process dynamics over the use of the input-output data analysis and real time modelling.

2.2. Measures of controlled system performance

A set of performance indicators may be used as a design tool aimed to evaluate tuning methods results. These performance indicators are listed from (3) to (6) equations.

Integral Squared Error (ISE)

$$J_{ISE} = \int_0^T \left(e(t)\right)^2 dt \tag{3}$$

Integral Absolute Error (IAE)

$$J_{IAE} = \int_0^T \left|e(t)\right| dt \tag{4}$$

Integral Time-weighted Absolute Error (ITAE)

$$J_{ITAE} = \int_0^T t\left|e(t)\right| dt \tag{5}$$

Integral Time-weighted Squared Error (ITSE)

$$J_{ITSE} = \int_0^T t\left(e(t)\right)^2 dt \tag{6}$$

These indicators can help the design engineer to decide about the best adjustment for the PID control parameters. In (Cao, 2008) it is presented some MATLAB codes to obtain these indicators.

3. Distillation column dynamics

In Brazil approximately 50% of vehicle fleet is composed of flex vehicles, resulting in 30 million of vehicles. This kind of vehicle uses fossil fuel and/or ethanol. The ignition system is adjusted automatically depending of the proportion of each fuel kind. To attend the national ethanol demand there are several ethanol distillation facilities across the country. In each of these facilities the fermented sugarcane is distilled, obtaining two products: the anhydrous ethanol and the hydrated ethanol.

The hydrated ethanol is obtained from link between the second and the third column. The anhydrous ethanol is obtained at the base of the third column, see Figure 3. The production process is composed of a series of columns where two variables are controlled to generate the hydrated ethanol and the anhydrous ethanol at the standardized specification: the pressure at the column A and the temperature at the distillation tray A20 (Santos et al., 2010). The hydrated ethanol has to have a concentration of 92,6 ºINPM (ºINPM is a measurement of the weight of pure ethanol fuel in 100g of ethanol fuel – water mixture). So as near the concentration is about this value, the best will be the quality of the hydrated ethanol and the anhydrous ethanol.

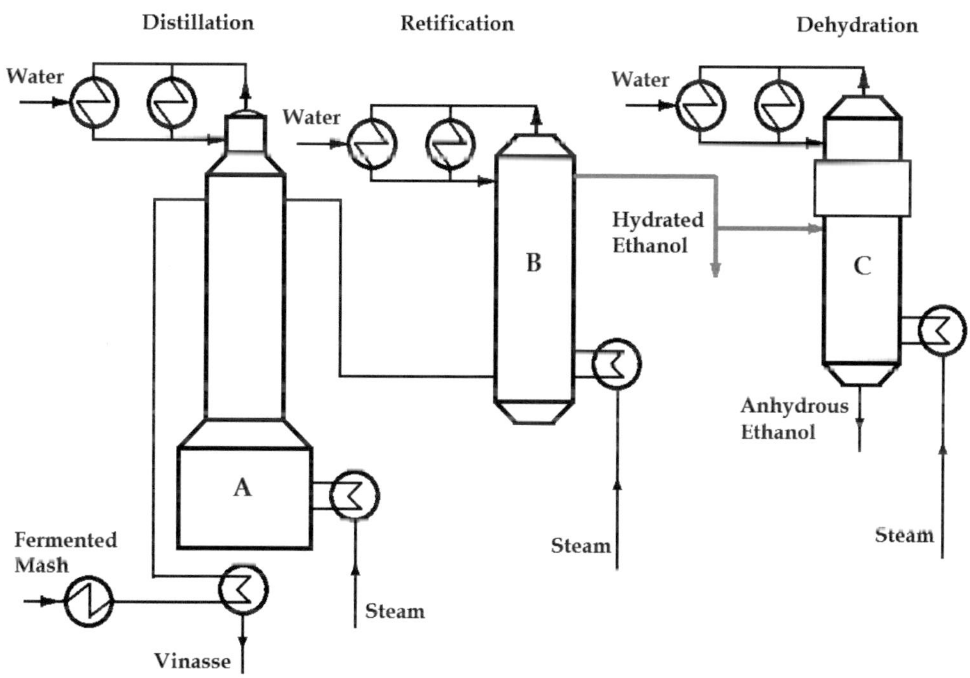

Figure 3. Distillation process to produce anhydrous ethanol and the hydrated ethanol.

These variables depend respectively on the steam flow at the basis of the column A and on the flow of fermented mash applied at the column A. The minimization of the variability of the alcoholic content according the brazilian standard NBR 5992-80 is the main design objective of the control system.

The distillation process is characterized by a high coupling through the system variables and by a non-linear relationship between them. According (Santos, 2010) the models that represent the relationship between the main process variables is FOTD (First Order with Time Delay).

$$G(s) = \frac{Ke^{-\theta s}}{\tau s + 1} \tag{7}$$

In this work the modeling procedure was developed and the following equation was obtained from the relationship of the pressure variation at the A column and the steam flow valve actuation:

$$\begin{aligned} K &= \frac{\Delta PV}{\Delta MV} = \frac{(0,36 - 0,44).110\%}{55 - 85,91} \\ K &= 0,26\%bar / \%opennig \\ \theta &= t_1 - t_0 = 3s \\ \tau &= t_2 - t_1 = 23s \end{aligned} \tag{8}$$

Where MP is the Manipulated Variable e PV is the Process Variable.

So, the FODT representation is:

$$G(s) = \frac{0,26e^{-3s}}{23s + 1} \tag{9}$$

The same modeling procedure was developed to obtain the relationship among the variation of the temperature at the distillation tray A20 and the variation of the flow of fermented mash applied at the column A:

$$\begin{aligned} K' &= \frac{\Delta PV}{\Delta MV} = \frac{\frac{(97,8 - 95,8)}{150}.110\%}{23\% - 33\%} \\ K' &= -0,133\%^{o}C / \%_{opennig} \\ \theta' &= t_1 - t_0 = 85s \\ \tau' &= t_2 - t_1 = 174s \end{aligned} \tag{10}$$

So, the FODT representation is:

$$G(s) = \frac{-0,133e^{-85s}}{174s + 1} \tag{11}$$

3.1. Tuning methods

The above systems were described in (Santos, 2010) and at that work there also were described and applied four tuning methods of the PI control: Ziegler-Nichols (First Method), CHR, Cohen-Coon and IMC (Internal Model Control).

Each method was analyzed through the use of Integral Absolute Error (IAE) and the best results are described at Table 1.

	Method	Kp	TI	IAE	Overshoot (%)
Pressure Control Loop	IMC	13	24	7,5	0%
Temperature Control Loop	Ziegler-Nichols	13.8	283	190	18%

Table 1. PI Tuning parameters

The simulation results presented (Santos, 2010) were used at the real process and another manual calibration was made. The new tuning parameters are presented at Table 2.

	Kp	T_I
Pressure Control Loop	13	2
Temperature Control Loop	12	30

Table 2. Manual PI Tuning parameters adjusted at the process.

The process where the temperature and pressure loops were modelled is described at figure 4 (Santos, 2010).

3.2. Exhaustive search solution

Both transfer functions represent a First Order plus Dead Time (FODT). So, for both systems it was applied the same procedure to tune the PI parameters. A Pade approximation is applied to generate a polynomial approximation to the delay time and a MATLAB program was designed to search the PI parameters.

The delay time of the system may be represented as a polynomial ratio according the Pade approximation. MATLAB has a specific function to generate this ratio, given the time delay and the order of the desired polynom. This function is:

[num,den] = pade(T,N)

Using this function and the transfer function of the pressure variation at the A column and the steam flow valve actuation, it was built an exhaustive searching algorithm to obtain the minimum Integral Absolute Error (IAE) using a Proportional Integral (PI) control system. At the next program it may be seen that the Pade approximation was built with two second order polynomial ratio.

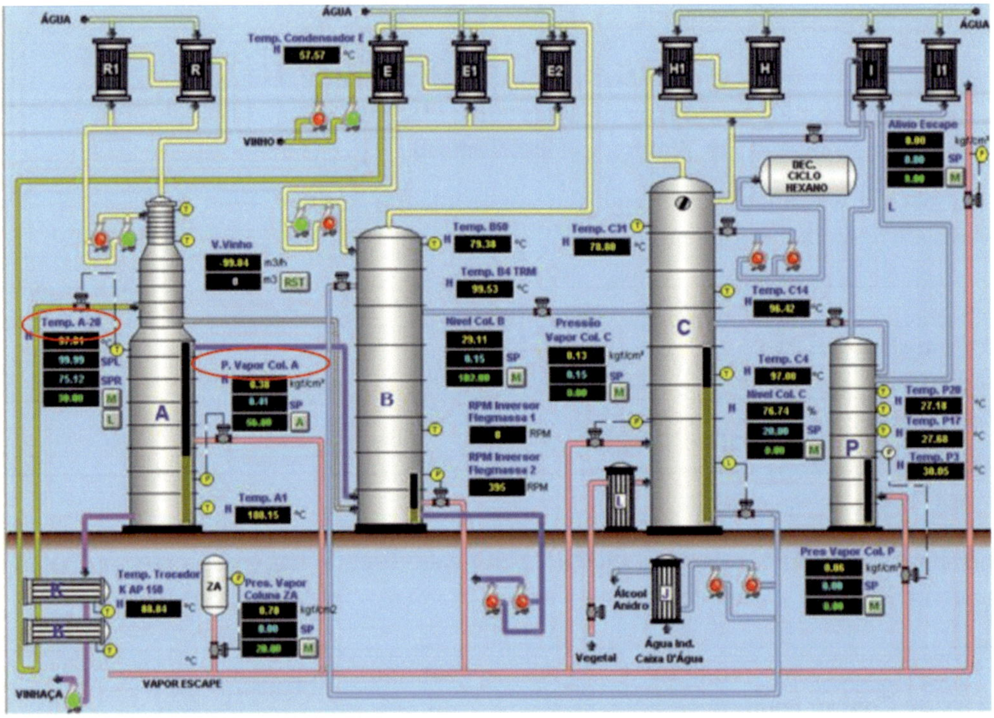

Figure 4. Piping and instrumentation diagram.

At the end of the execution, the minimum K_P obtained was equal to 17.3 and the minimum T_i was 23, and IAE equal 6.35. This is a better result than that presented at (Santos, 2010).

MATLAB program uses a Transfer Function representation for the Dead Time and for the plant. Both are associated in series through a specific MATLAB function and a unitary feedback loop is calculated to analyses the system response to several pairs of K_P and T_i values.

```
clc
close all
s = tf('s')
t=0:0.1:1000; tam=length(t);
T = 3;
% Plant - Transfer Function
plant = (0.26*((1-(T/2)*s+((T*s)^2)/12)/(1+(T/2)*s+((T*s)^2)/12)))/(23*s+1)
Kc = 12.00:0.01:18.00;
Ti = 22.00:0.01:25.00;
tamKp = length(Kp);
tamTi = length(Ti);
count = 1;
for i = 1:tamKc,
        for j = 1:tamTi,
```

```
            PI = Kp(i)*(1+1/(Ti(j)*s));
            H=series(PI,plant);
            L=feedback(H,1);
             [output, t] = step(L,t);
            MP = Calcul_MP(output);
            IAE = IAE_U_Step(output,0.1);
            result(count,1) = Kp(i);
            result(count,2) = Ti(j);
            result(count,3) = MP;
            result(count,4) = IAE;
            count = count+1;
        end
        count
end
% Search for minimum Kc and minimum Ti
tam = length(result)
minimumIAE = 1000
for i=1:tam(1),
        if  minimumIAE > result(i,4)
            minimumIAE = result(i,4);
            minimumKp = result(i,1);
            minimumTi = result(i,2);
        end
end
minimumIAE
minimumKp
minimumTi
```

At the program listed above, two other functions were developed: *Calcul_Mp* and *IAE_U_Step*.

These functions are listed below:

```
function [MP] = CalculMP(output)
        tam = length(output);
        MP = (max(output)-output(tam))/output(tam)*100;
end
```

At the function CalculMP the output length is obtained to take the last value of the output variable to the step response. It is used to calculate the overshoot of the system.

At the next function the Integral Absolute Error (IAE) is numerically obtained using the output generated at the main mathscript code.

```
function [IAE_Value] = IAE_U_Step(output,int_T)
        Tam = length(output);
        IAE_Value = 0;
```

```
        for i=1:Tam,
                if output(i) < 1
                   IAE_Value = IAE_Value + (1-output(i))*int_T;
                else
                   IAE_Value = IAE_Value + (1-output(i))*(-1)*int_T ;
                end
        end
end
```

The closed loop system model with a PI control was built at SIMULINK as represented at figure 5.

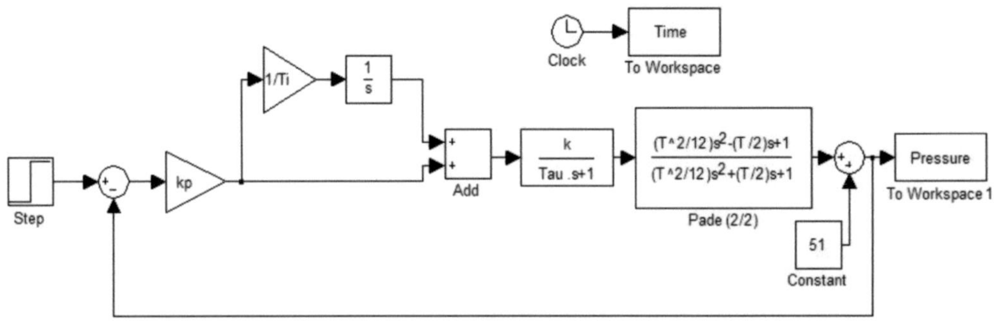

Figure 5. Closed loop Pressure Control with Pade approximation.

Applying a step function from 51 bar to 85 bar at the input of the system presented at figure 5, the output is presented at figure 6 for the tuning parameters obtained at the exhaustive search algorithm.

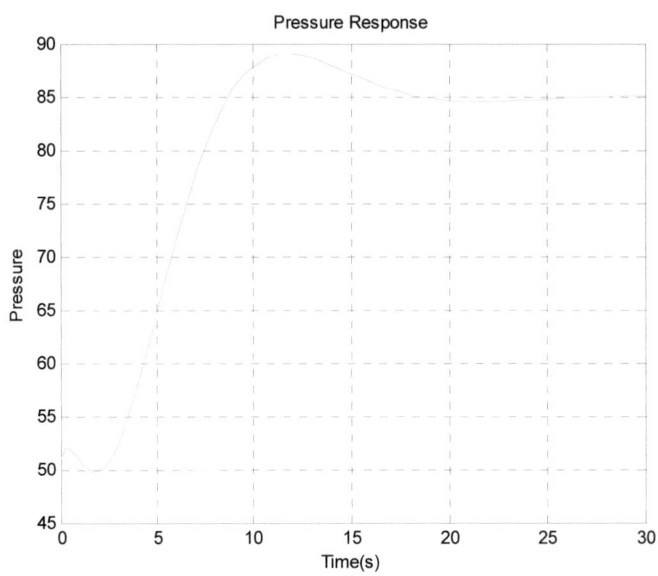

Figure 6. Step response of the closed loop pressure control system.

The step response presented at Figure 6 represents a fast response with low overshoot than that presented at (Santos, 2010). It is possible to verify the delay time at the output signal.

The same procedure was used to design the control algorithm to the temperature loop and best results were obtained when compared with those presented at (Santos, 2010). In both closed loops the exhaustive search for the best response was executed near the initial solution obtained through the experimental tuning procedure.

4. Smith Predictor design

A design tool very useful to control engineers when it is necessary to design a control system with delay at time response is the Smith Predictor (Ogata, 2009). At the distillation plant both SISO systems are represented by transfer functions with time delays. At this item it is done some considerations about the use of this technique to generate better results for the time response of the system. The control structure of the Smith Predictor is presented at figure 7.

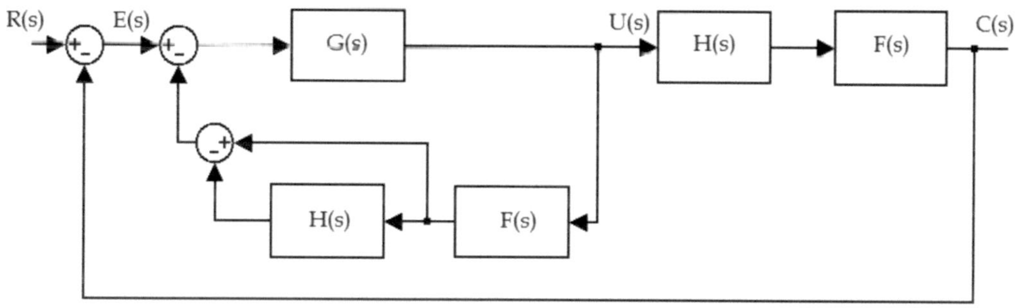

Figure 7. Smith Predictor Structure.

In the system presented at figure 7, H(s) represents the pure delay time and F(s) represents the plant transfer function without delay. Analysing as separated parts, it is proposed a controller with input E(s) and output U(s) that has the delay time transfer function H(s) and F(s) modelled in its structure. It is possible to analyse the system proposed and verify that its transfer function C(s)/R(s) is equal to the transfer function of the system presented at figure 8.

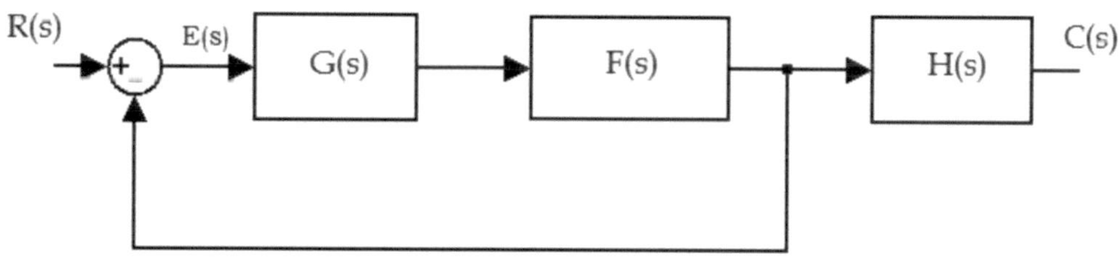

Figure 8. Equivalent system.

At figure 8 it is possible to verify that G(s) may be designed considering the transfer function F(s) without the time-delay. The transfer function of the complete system has the design specification plus the dead time present at the original plant.

4.1. MATLAB code implementing Smith Predictor

To analyse the system performance with a Smith Predictor structure it was developed a MATLAB code and a SIMULINK model. The mathscript code is presented below, with a Pade approximation to represent the time delay. The polynomial ratio used at the next code represents a delay of 3 seconds with the ratio of two second order polynomials. The block association was developed through the use of the association commands *series* and *feedback*.

Representing the Smith Predictor in a MATLAB code:

```
% Smith Predictor

clc
clear all
close all

s=tf('s')

% Delay with Pade aproximation
[num_d,den_d]=pade(3,2)

% PI Control System
Kp=2;
Ti=15;
G=Kp*(1+(1/(Ti*s)));

H=tf(num_d,den_d)
Gc=feedback(G,series((1-H),(0.26/(23*s+1))))

CL=feedback(series(Gc,series(tf(num_d,den_d),0.26/(23*s+1))),1)

figure(1)
step(CL,200)
grid
```

It is possible to see that the association G_c represents the control algorithm, where G is the Proportional Integral controller designed to the plant without delay. The system designed with SIMULINK model is presented at figure 9.

At the next figure the step response obtained at the end of the program. It is possible to see that the stationary error is equal to zero and that the control parameters could be adjusted to obtain a small overshoot.

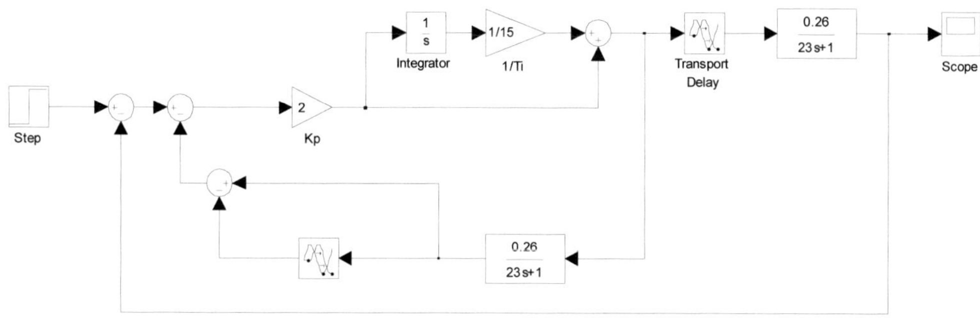

Figure 9. Smith Predictor in SIMULINK model.

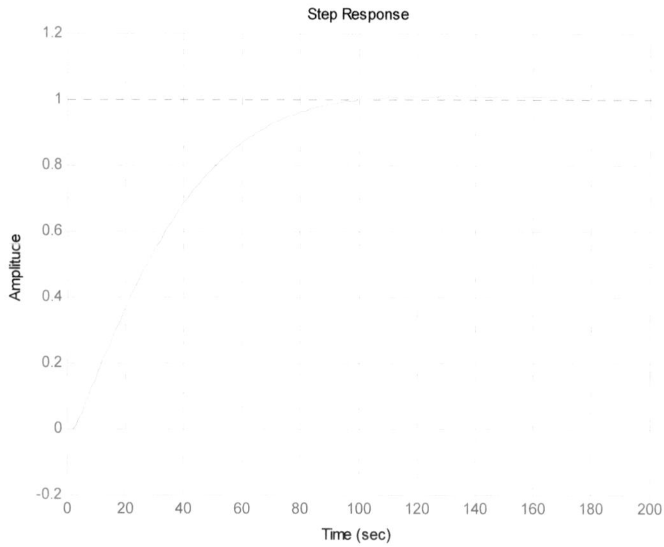

Figure 10. Closed loop system response.

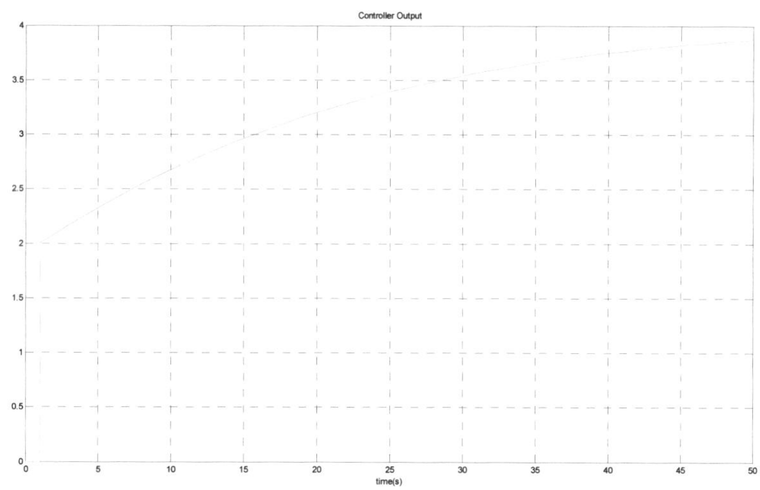

Figure 11. Controller output.

The output of the controller must be verified after the control system design to avoid the saturation of the actuators.

4.2. Digital control design

The control algorithm designed through the Smith Predictor may be described in a digital form, using the Z-Transform representation. The MATLAB script code below represents this transfer function.

```
% Digital Smith Predictor

clc
clear all
close all

s=tf('s')

Kp=2;
Ti=15;
G=Kp*(1+(1/(Ti*s)));

T=0.1;

Gz=c2d(G,T,'tustin')

n=3/T;

z=tf('z',0.1)

Hz=c2d(0.26/(26*s+1),T,'tustin')
Gcz=feedback(Gz,series(Hz,1-z^(-n))
```

The G transfer function represents the Proportional Integral algorithm and Gz is its discrete form using the Bilinear (Tustin) approximation. The sample time was adjusted in 0.1 s, since the dimension of time delay is about 30 times greater than this value. The time delay verified at the system may be easily modelled measuring how many samples the system measure along the total time delay. This measurement is represented at n=3/T.

The digital controller designed is represented by:

```
Transfer function:
                        2.007 z^32 – 3.992 z^31 + 1.986 z^30
-----------------------------------------------------------------------------------------------------
1.001 z^32 – 1.996 z^31 + 0.9952 z^30 – 0.001001 z^2 – 6.654e-006 z + 0.0009948

Sampling time: 0.1
```

The result presented above may be used to generate the difference equation:

$$\begin{aligned} u(k) &= 2.007e(k) - 3.992e(k-1) + 1.986e(k-2) + 1.996u(k-1) - 0.9952u(k-2) + \ldots \\ &\ldots 0.001u(k-30) + 0.000006u(k-31) - 0.00099u(k-32) \end{aligned} \tag{12}$$

This equation implements the control algorithm at the digital system. The control algorithm designed to the temperature plant may also be described in a digital form, using the Z-Transform representation. At the next mathscript code this design procedure was applied, but at this case the sample frequency was adjusted to 1Hz, since the time response of the temperature system is very larger than the pressure system.

```
% Digital Smith Predictor - Temperature

G=Kp*(1+(1/(Ti*s)));

T=1;

Gz=c2d(G,T,'tustin')

n=85/T;

z=tf('z',T)

Hz=c2d(-0.133/(174*s+1),T,'tustin')
Gcz=feedback(Gz,series(Hz,1-z^(-n))
```

Better results also were obtained using the Smith Predictor structure applied to the temperature loop control.

5. Conclusion

The analyses of two closed loops at a distillation process were presented at this chapter. The design specification presented at the references was attended through the use of an exhaustive search algorithm to obtain the best response according to the performance indices Integral Absolute Error (IAE). MATLAB code used to apply this algorithm is effective and generated a better response than that presented at references. Using MATLAB and SIMULINK it was designed a Smith Predictor algorithm and an enhanced control system was obtained. The MATLAB toolboxes used to analyse the control system was very useful to enhance the control system design. The digital representation of the control system was calculated with digital control systems commands.

Author details

A.B. Campo
Instituto Federal de Educação, Ciência e Tecnologia de São Paulo, Brazil

Acknowledgement

The author would like to thanks Instituto Federal de Educação, Ciência e Tecnologia de São Paulo for the MATLAB license and hardware resources used at the development of this work.

6. References

Alfaro, V. M., Vilanova, R. Arrieta O. Two-Degree-of-Freedom PI/PID Tuning Approach for smooth Control on Cascade Control Systems, *Proceedings of the 47th IEEE Conference on Decision and Control Cancun*, Mexico, Dec. 9-11, 2008.

Ang, K.H., Chong G. LI, Yun PID Control System Analysis, Design, and Technology, In: *IEEE Transactions on Control Systems Technology*, vol. 13, no. 4, july, 2005.

Åström, K.J. , Hägglund, T. (1995) *PID controllers Setting the standard for automation* 2nd Edition, 343 p., International Society for Measurement and Control.

Åström, K. J. , Hägglund, T. (1995) *PID Controllers: Theory, Design, and Tuning*, 2nd Edition ISBN 978-1-55617-516-9.

Cao, Yao. (January 2008). Learning PID Tuning III: Performance Index Optimization, In: *MATLAB CENTRAL File Exchange*, 08.04.2012, Available from http://www.mathworks.com/matlabcentral/fileexchange/18674-learning-pid-tuning-iii-performance-index-optimization

Mannini, P. ; Mello, V.F.; Santos, D.S.; Araújo, G.C.; Campo, A.B (2012) Projeto de controle PID em uma coluna de destilação de álcool, *Revista Sinergia* (submitted).

Mansour,T. (2011) *PID Control, Implementation and Tuning*, 238 p., InTech, ISBN 978-953-307-166-4, Rijeka, Croatia.

Ogata, K. (2009) *Modern Control Engineering*, 912p., 5nd. Edition, Prentice Hall ISBN-13: 978-0136156734,

Seborg, D.E.; Edgar, T.F., Mellichamp, D.A. *Process Dynamics and Control*, John Wiley & Sons, Singapore, 717p., 1989.

Santos, J.C. dos S.; Santos, R.P. dos; Salles, J.L.F. *Redução da Variabilidade do Teor Alcoólico na Indústria Sucroalcooleira*, ISA Show, Brazil, 2010.

Yurkevich, V. D. (2011) *Advances in PID Control*, InTech, ISBN 978-953-307-267-8, Rijeka, Croatia.

Chapter 2

Post Processing of Results of EM Field Simulators

Tomas Vydra and Daniel Havelka

Additional information is available at the end of the chapter

http://dx.doi.org/10.5772/46452

1. Introduction

In this chapter we shall focus on the needs that many researchers, scientists and even students have very often. When using commercial simulation software for numerical simulation of electromagnetic field we frequently encounter many insufficiencies which those software products have. Usually, main aim of computational software developers is to optimize and refine so called core of these programmes – EM field solver. After that CAD (Computer Assisted Design) and post processing parts of EM simulators are dealt with. Mainly this can be an issue with newer, short-time in development products but one's own post processing using Matlab can be greatly beneficial even when using well established simulators of EM field. This is largely due to its flexibility which cannot be overcome by any EM field simulator.

Throughout this chapter we will show you many ways of post processing which we use in our research of EM field in industrial and medical applications (Vrba et al., 2008; Vydra et al., 2011) and in primary research of EM field around living cells and structures inside cell bodies (Cifra et al., 2011; Havelka et al., 2011).

We hope that this chapter will aid many researchers and students in the vast field of EM research. Here, we present our knowledge and tips which we have gathered through our studies and our research.

1.1. Technical introduction

Generally, rough results we obtain using simulators of electromagnetic field - or from analytical solution of systems described by discrete elements - are in the form of complex vector components of intensity of electric and magnetic field (i.e. time dependent – periodical – components in the directions of coordinate axes). We process these results using Matlab and interpret them to draw conclusions. In this chapter we would like to present basic processing of rough data, calculation of specific absorption rate and other parameters in particular regions of simulation domain, visualization of results in many ways (pcolor, slices, histograms, multiple iso-surface, surf interpretation on various shapes according to specific task etc.). We will provide detailed examples with practical applications and explanation of advantages provided by presented solutions.

2. Rough results from EM field simulator

As mentioned above, in this chapter we suppose that we have obtained rough data from any numerical simulator of EM field and now we want to interpret them. First of all we should look at how the structure of this data looks like. To get the full understanding we shall briefly go through some EM field basics.

2.1. EM field basics

Electromagnetic Field can be described using well known Maxwell's equations (for more information on Maxwell's equations please refer to any book dealing with EM field theory).

$$\left.\begin{aligned} &\oint\!\!\oint DdS = Q \\ &\oint\!\!\oint BdS = 0 \\ &\oint Edl = -\frac{d\phi}{dt} \\ &\oint Hdl = I_0 + I_c \end{aligned}\right\} \tag{1}$$

Simply by solving those equations EM field can be completely described at all points of space and time. This leads us to complete description of EM field using only phasors of intensity of electric and magnetic field $\boldsymbol{E}$ and $\boldsymbol{H}$ (or $\boldsymbol{D}$ and $\boldsymbol{B}$ where $\boldsymbol{D} = \varepsilon\boldsymbol{E}$ and $\boldsymbol{B} = \mu\boldsymbol{H}$). This means that output of conventional commercial simulator is in the form of time dependent vectors that have components in axis x, y and z. These vectors are defined for each part of computational domain (e.g. when using FDTD (Thomas et. al., 1994), vectors are defined for each voxel – block discretizing computational domain).

We can see that this type of data can be extracted in form of matrices (multi-dimensional, e.g. 4D). Now, we shall look closer at those matrices.

2.2. Data structure

As we mentioned in previous chapter, results from simulators of EM field are represented as matrices, which directly predestines them to be processed in Matlab, which is the perfect tool for matrix operations.

There is a sample of data obtained from simulation in the following table. It depicts x-component of vector of intensity of electric field [V/m] in y-axis section in a part of some model.

X/Z [mm]	1	2	3	4	5	6	7	8	9	10
1	10	10	11	12	13	14	12	9	8	7
2	10	10	11	12	13	14	11	10	9	8
3	11	11	11	12	13	14	13	11	10	9
4	12	12	12	12	13	14	13	12	11	10
5	13	13	13	12	13	14	12	12	12	11
6	14	14	13	13	13	14	13	13	13	12
7	13	14	13	13	13	14	14	14	14	12
8	13	14	14	14	14	14	15	15	14	13
9	13	13	13	14	15	15	16	15	14	13
10	12	13	13	14	14	15	15	15	14	13

Table 1. X-component of vector of intensity of electric field [V/m]

Following graphical representation can help us shed some more light on the structure of data we obtained. These data are represented as four dimensional matrices (for phasors ***E*** and ***H*** separately) depicting whole computational domain and they are time dependent.

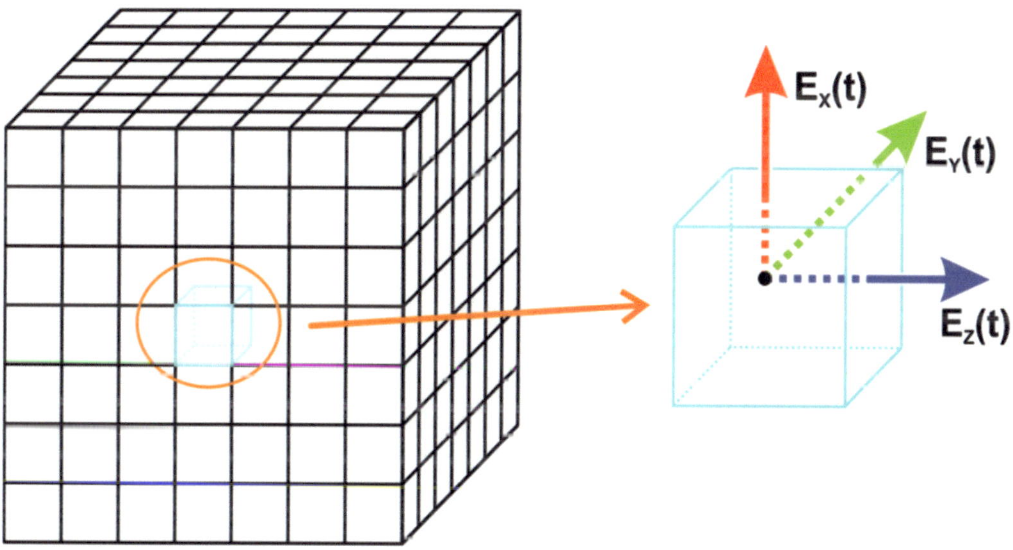

Figure 1. Data structure

Generally we can describe phasors as follows.

$$\widehat{V}_{(x,y,z,t)} = V_{(x,y,z)} e^{j\omega t} \tag{2}$$

Note: It may be necessary to convert data to suitable matrix form (e.g. rough data are in the form of a row vector with axial information for each element). We will look into it in the chapter 3.

Now that we know what our data source looks like we can simply process it to view the results and highlight some of their aspects according to our needs (see Table 2. for axial information).

```
actualAxisX(1) = loadedVectorX(1);
for a = (2:length(loadedVectorX))
    if loadedVectorX(a) == loadedVectorX(1)
        break;
    else
        actualAxis(a) = loadedVector(a);
    end;
end;

d = 2;
actualAxisY(1) = loadedVectorY(1);
for b = (2:length(loadedVectorY)-1)
    if loadedVectorY(b+1) ~= loadedVectorY(b)
        actualAxis(d) = loadedVector(b+1);
        d = d + 1;
    else
        if loadedVector(b+1) == loadedVector(1)
            break;
        end;
    end;
end;

e = 2;
actualAxisZ(1) = loadedVectorZ(1);
for c = (2:(length(loadedVectorZ)-1))
    if loadedVectorZ(c+1) ~= loadedVectorZ(c)
        actualAxisZ(e) = loadedVectorZ(c+1);
        e = e + 1;
    end;
end;
```

Figure 2. Extraction of Axes (in our example)

3. Viewing the results

In this section we are going to show some examples of how obtained data can be viewed, how to interpret those results, what type of projection should we use etc. We shall illustrate this on some practical examples of EM field applications.

3.1. Basic transformation of rough data

As mentioned above we might obtain rough data in the form of a row vector. Let us illustrate this in this simple example. Our computational domain is 2 by 2 by 2 thus obtained row vector (x-component, apmlitude) has 8 elements. See Table 2.

x axis	1	2	1	2	1	2	1	2
y axis	1	1	2	2	1	1	2	2
z axis	1	1	1	1	2	2	2	2
Vector of values	8	6	5	2	5	6	8	9

Table 2. Amplitude of x-component of intensity of electric field [V/m]

From this we can extract axis. As long as we do not know the length of each axis we need to utilize this method to find actual axial data (see Figure 2.).

Note that actual axis arrangement can be different in your case (e.g. x and y axis arrangement may be commuted). Thus it is vital to get familiar with axial arrangement in your exporter from EM field simulator.

Furthermore, `actualAxis` vectors are underlined because they are growing on every loop iteration. Since axial vectors are not usually very long, this poses only mild concern. They cannot be preallocated because we generally do not know their actual length. If you are expecting very long axial vectors you may consider preallocating them safely longer than your expectations and then just using part of them which is non-zero (you may select this part of a vector using `find` – please refer to Matlab documentation).

Now that we know the length of each axial vector we may sort the vector of exported values and transform it to a matrix which will better represent three dimensional nature of our computational domain and will allow us to plot data with axial information. In this case we can very well utilize `reshape` which is built in Matlab.

MATRIX = reshape(vector_of_values,lenght(X),lenght(Y),lenght(Z))

Thanks to this process we now have every component of each vector (i.e. ***E*** and ***H***) represented as three dimensional matrix and we can utilize it further.

3.2. Basic plotting of data

First of all, we need to bear in mind that we have time-dependent data. The most basic process is to plot actual situation (distribution of intensity of electric or magnetic) at a given time, or amplitude of vector. (In some applications we may need to plot just one component of this vector. This is even simpler because then we can disregard following method.)

Phasor of intensity of electric or magnetic field can be represented by modulus and phase or real and imaginary part. We need to merge all the components of the vector and obtain real and imaginary part. This can be simply done (i.e. vector adding component matrices together). Then we have one matrix of complex numbers. We can choose specific time in which we need EM field to be plotted simply by adding $<0,2\pi>$ to the phase of each vector and then we can plot real and imaginary modulus of the vector in specified time. Or we take just the amplitude of vectors and plot them.

It is very usual to plot RMS (i.e. Root Mean Square) value of vectors which is defined as follows.

$$RMS|E| = \frac{|E|}{\sqrt{2}} \tag{3}$$

This can be again obtained very simply from amplitude of intensity of electric field. (Note that this same procedure can be used also in the case of intensity of magnetic field ***H***, usually in applications involving heating and/or drying we deal only with intensity of electric field ***E***, because it is the source of heat generation in exposed samples.)

Now that we have three dimensional matrix of values of $RMS|E|$ we can plot it to see what our results look like. In the following section there is an example we prepared to illustrate how the results can be viewed and interpreted.

3.2.1. Example of basic data plotting

In this section we shall extract data from a simulation which has setup according to the Figure 3. Please note that this is just an example without any practical use, it serves only as an illustration.

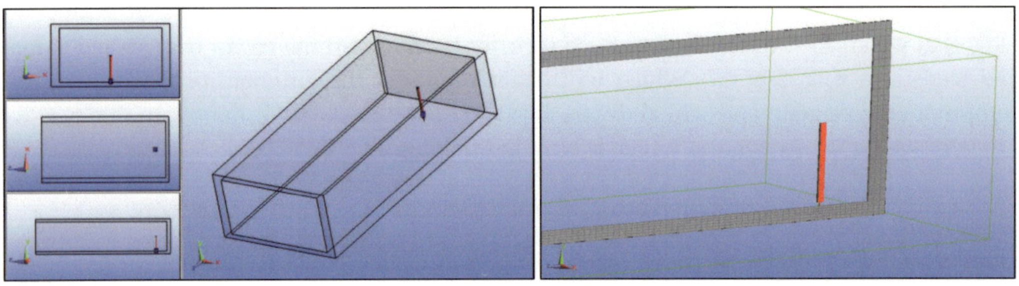

Figure 3. Model Setup and Its Voxel Representation (waveguide section with excitation probe at 2.45 GHz, voxels shown in section)

We simulated simple section of a waveguide (inner dimensions 100x50x200 mm) with one side shorted (there is an excitation probe in form of a cylinder in the distance of 17 mm from the shorted end) and the other side open (absorbing boundary condition – absorbs 99.9% of incident power). We extracted the data and plotted them using Matlab.

As you can see (Fig 4ab.) we used several colormaps which enable us to highlight different aspects in our results interpretation. Sometimes it is needed to have contrast colormap (jet, lines – for more information see Product Help of Matlab), at other circumstances you may need to use fine and moderate colormaps (hot, gray, bone, pink – for more information see Product Help of Matlab). In the fourth graph in Fig. 4 we used different shading – faceted. This enables us to highlight structure of computational grid. In many commercial simulators of EM field parts of a model need to be meshed finer than others (e.g. in our case the excitation probe needs to be meshed four times more than the rest of the waveguide to be voxeled sufficiently). In other examples we used shading interp to get more clear view.

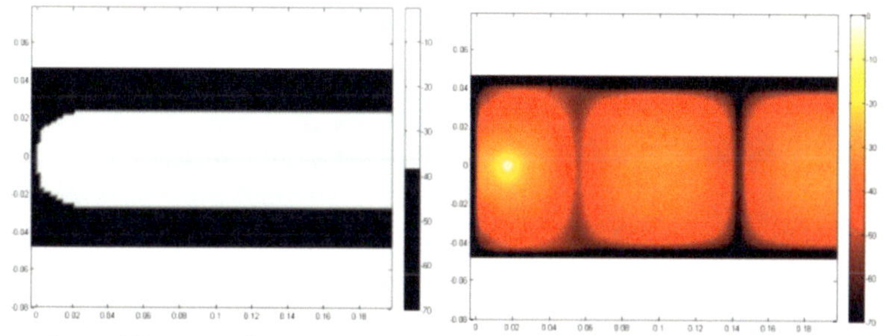

a - Interpretation of Extracted Data (Y-plane, middle section of the waveguide) [dB]

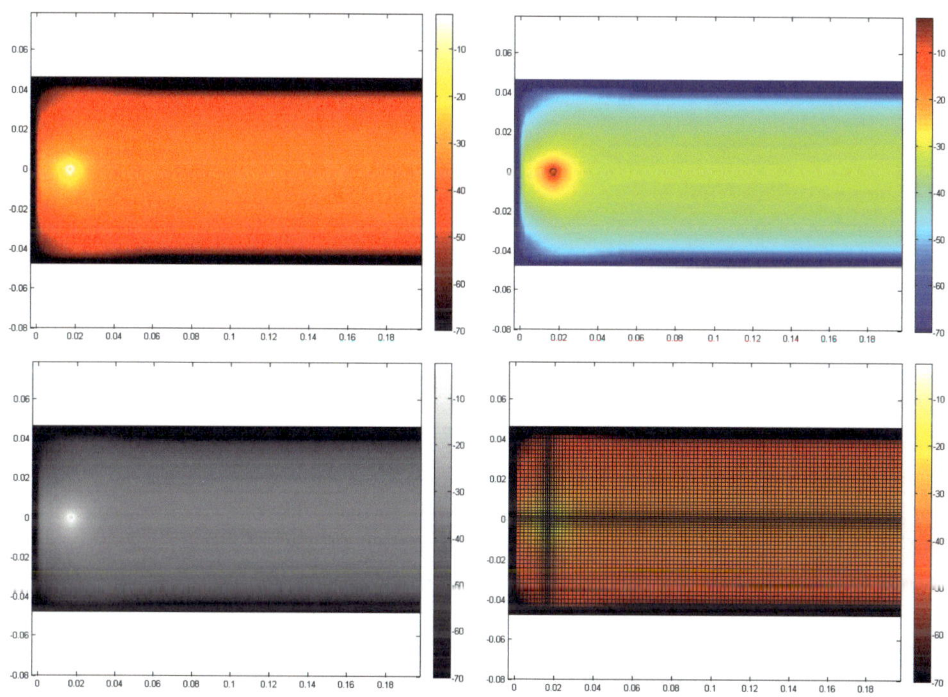

b - Interpretation of Extracted Data (Y-plane, middle section of the waveguide) [dB]

Figure 4. a - (*RMS*|*E*| colormap-Custom, real modulus E in phase 0° colormap-Hot)
b - (from left upper corner to right lower corner: *RMS*|*E*| colormap-Hot, *RMS*|*E*| colormap-Jet, *RMS*|*E*| colormap-Gray, *RMS*|*E*| shading faceted)

We can also utilize custom colormaps. This can be exceptionally beneficial in applications where we need to find out where values are at some critical level or higher. We illustrated this feature in the first image in Fig. 4a. In Fig. 5. there is an Colormap Editor which can be accessed through: Figure – Edit – Figure Properties – Colormap pull-down menu – Custom.

In our example we set segment in the middle to black colour and segment next to it to white colour. This resulted in the graph as seen in Fig. 4a. For more information on colormaps please refer to the Product Help of Matlab.

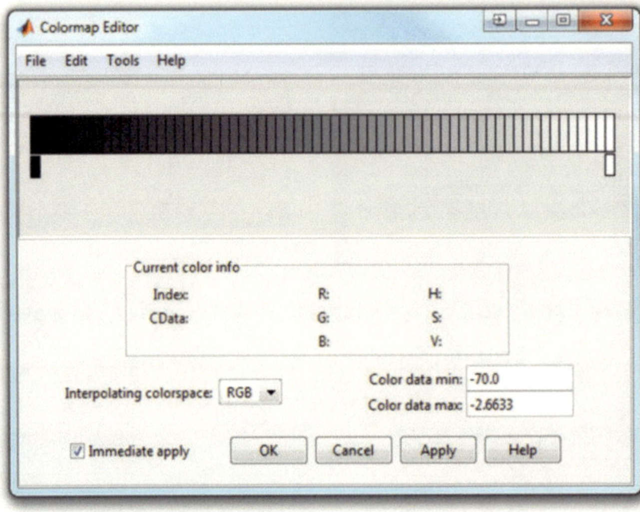

Figure 5. Colormap Editor Window

Furthermore, we illustrated how real modulus of vector of intensity of electric field at phase 0° is interpreted using Matlab (second image in Fig. 4a.). This is the most basic interpretation of obtained data we can do.

Note that this kind of results interpretation is much more flexible than the interpretation allowed by post processing tools in commercial EM simulators. In the following example we shall show how to work with time dependency of phasors. Since the results of EM field simulator are extracted when the steady state is reached time dependency is reduced to angle of phasors depicting the field of vectors. Through the following method we can alter phase of those phasors and show real part and imaginary part through one period. The results can be seen in Fig. 6. Figure 7. shows example of data processing to achieve this.

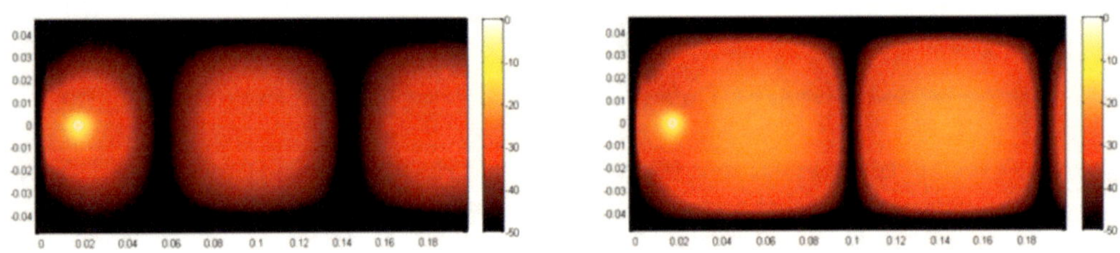

Figure 6. Phase Shifted Data – real part of vector E [dB] (left phase = 0°, right phase = 90°)

Note: In many EM field simulators you may encounter various errors. Pay special attention to the data structure of your exported data since it may not be useful in the way we have shown here (e.g. real and imaginary parts are exported as absolute values so the vital information about phase is lost).

Note: In the part of the script (Fig. 7.) where lowerThan variable is used we are changing the range of values. Since there are parts of model where values of intensity of electric or magnetic field are very near to zero, minimum of these values in dB would be around -400 dB. This renders produced images useless (value range is huge but most of the relevant values are in the region <-50,0>). Using function find we identify indexes of elements with values lower than -50 dB and we replace those elements with value -50 dB. For more information on function find please refer to the Product Help of Matlab.

Note: In this example we use function subaxis which has similar usage as function subplot but allows users to set the layout of plots in the figure more accurately (options Padding, Spacing, Margin etc.). For more information on subaxis please see internet documentation.

3.2.2. Treatment efficiency analysis

In the following example we will go through one of many useful applications of EM simulators today – evaluation of hyperthermia cancer treatment. Generally, hyperthermia is a method through which tissue is overheated (usually using microwave energy) and cells die (principle of this method is that energy is focused into the cancerous tissue which is less perfused and thus it is more heated – temperature in treated area rises above levels that trigger cell apoptosis). For more information on microwave hyperthermia see for example (Vrba & Oppl., 2008).

Model of simulated experiment can be seen in Figure 8. In this example we use waveguide applicator which is fed by coaxial line ending in protruding inner wire which is located near the shorted end of the waveguide section. There is a horn aperture which helps focus microwave energy to the desired area.

Relatively complex and complicated structure of human body is replaced with so called "phantom" that represents simple muscle tissue. In the model there is a tumor located 1 cm below the surface of phantom. This tumor has the same dielectric parameters as the surrounding muscle tissue (usually the only difference in simulations between muscle tissue and tumorous tissue is in their perfusion, heat transfer rate and heat generation rate – generated heat in tumorous tissue is usually transferred slower than in physiological surrounding tissue).

Additionally there is a water bolus which serves as a coolant body protecting the surface tissue of patient and moving the maximum of temperature to the lower layers. In this example we use source at 434 MHz and the applicator is filled with water (required dimensions of the applicator are effectively lower and impedance matching between waveguide-bolus and body are much better). For more information on waveguide hyperthermia applicators please refer to (Vera et al., 2006).

In this simulation we again extract rough data from EM simulator and we process them further using Matlab. We again have intensity of electric and magnetic field defined in every element of the model. For effective analysis of the treatment we need to evaluate SAR (Specific Absorption Ratio) which describes how much power is absorbed in a weight unit [W/kg]. For more information on SAR see http://www.ets-lindgren.com/pdf/sar_lo.pdf.

```


% In previous process we separated only one slice from the 3D matrices
complexMatrix = exportedRealPart + 1i.*exportedImaginaryPart;
phi = [0,pi/2]; % variable phase shift
cMatrixDimensions = size(complexMatrix);

logMatrix = zeros(cMatrixDimensions(1),cMatrixDimensions(2),length(phi));

for k = (1:length(phi))
    phaseShiftedMatrix = complexMatrix.*exp(1j.*phi(k));

    realMatrix = real(phaseShiftedMatrix);

    hValue = max(max(abs(realMatrix)));

    logMatrix(:,:,k) = 20.*log10(abs(realMatrix)./hValue);

    lowerThan = find(logMatrix < -50);
    logMatrix(lowerThan) = -50;
end;

d=figure(k); clf;
subaxis(1,2,1,'Padding',0.001,'Spacing',0.001,'Margin',0.03); hold on;
pcolor(osaY,osaX,logMatrix(:,:,1));
colormap(hot);
shading interp;
axis image;
colorbar;
subaxis(1,2,2,'Padding',0.001,'Spacing',0.001,'Margin',0.03); hold on;
pcolor(osaY,osaX,logMatrix(:,:,2));
colormap(hot);
shading interp;
axis image;
colorbar;

```

Figure 7. Method of phase shifting results

To determine how SAR is distributed we need to use this formula.

$$SAR = \frac{\sigma}{2\rho}|E|^2 \tag{4}$$

As we see, in this case we can very well utilize $RMS|\mathbf{E}|$. From formula (3) we can say that SAR is defined by following equation.

$$SAR = \frac{\sigma}{\rho}RMS|E|^2 \tag{5}$$

SAR is thus depending on RMS value of intensity of electric field, on conductivity of a material and on its density. We need to obtain those values somehow. In our case whole phantom has homogeneous density and electric conductivity thus we can only mask matrix of $RMS|E|$ and multiply each element by coefficient produced by ratio of σ and ϱ.

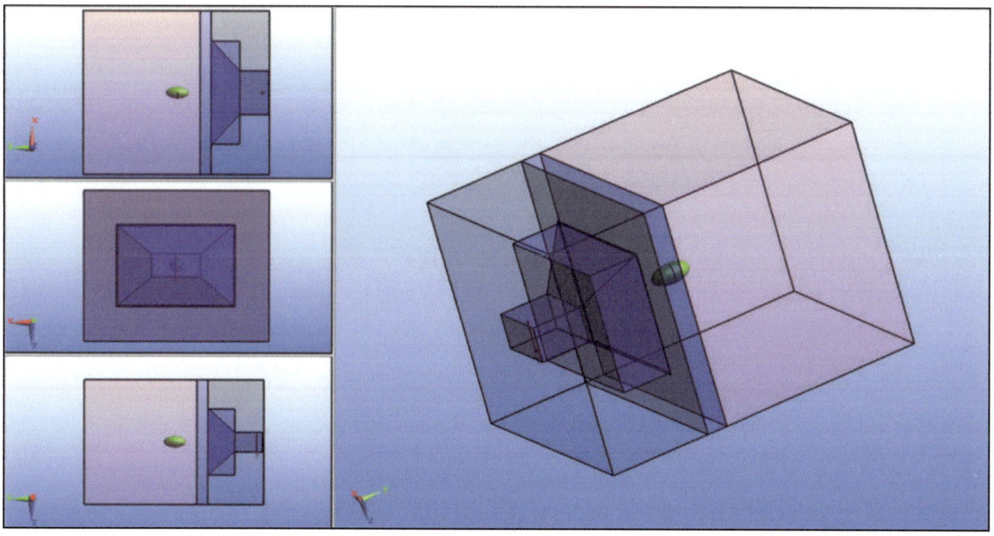

Figure 8. Model of microwave hyperthermia at 434 MHz

Note: There are other options how to do that. For example some EM simulator allow users to export matrix of dielectric parameters of a model (this will produce similar matrix to our masking matrix).

Now we should look into how to produce masking matrix efficiently. From our model we know that every element of the voxelized model is phantom if its value of y axis is higher than 120 mm (we can find out this in CAD part of EM simulator). We can prepare our three dimensional matrix of $RMS|E|$ according to previous sections. We also have actual axis of this matrix which we obtained from exported file as well. We simply need to identify which element is at the 120 mm value and then we shall mask the elements with lower value of y axis.

An elegant way to find the index at y axis of element which has the value nearest to 120 mm (note that the value is not usually exactly 120 so if we looked for the exact match we would probably fail) is to use function `min`. Example of this method is as follows.

```
lookFor = 120;
[min_difference, array_position] = min(abs(araay-lookFor));
% Minimal difference shows us the difference between the closest element
% and our looked for value. Array position then indicates the position of
% such element.
```

Figure 9. Example of finding the closest element position

In this example, we can illustrate one other useful feature of Matlab processing of EM simulator results. We can instantly normalize obtained results. Usually it is possible to extract actual power in the source which was simulated (e.g. 0.002496 W) and we can utilize this to obtain normalization coefficient. Power normalization coefficient is given by the following formula.

```
if min_difference > 0
      values(:,((position-1):-1:1),:) = 0;
      values(:,(position:length(actualAxisY)),:)...
      = (values(:,(position:length(actualAxisY)),:)).^2.*sigma./rho;
else
    values(:,((position+1):-1:1),:) = 0;
    values(:,(position:length(actualAxisY)),:)...
    = (values(:,(position:length(actualAxisY)),:)).^2.*sigma./rho;
end;
```

Figure 10. Covering Field of *RMS*|*E*| with Mask

$$coef\, f_{power} = \frac{Power\, to\, which\, we\, want\, to\, normalize}{Actual\, Simulated\, Power} \tag{6}$$

Since this is the coefficient of power ratio we need to use coefficient of intensity of electric field ratio which is the square root of coefficient of power (see the equation below).

$$coef\, f_{power} \approx \frac{E^2{}_{norm}}{E^2{}_{acctual}} \Rightarrow coef\, f_E = \sqrt{coef\, f_{power}} \tag{7}$$

Simply by multiplying the matrix of data by this coefficient we obtain normalized data to the desired value of delivered power.

Now we can show several interpretations of results we obtained (Z section in the middle of the model). Thanks to Matlab's flexibility and versatility we can highlight the results in the way that is far more efficient than by using post processing of the EM field simulator. In the following figures we show intensity of electric field and SAR in the treated area.

As you can see in figure 11. each colour scheme highlights different thing (as for the first three). In the fourth graph we used custom colormap to show some kind of a critical zone. In this example we expected that higher values of SAR than 1000 W/kg are considered to be dangerous in some regions (note that these critical limits differ significantly in every application – many factors contribute, e.g. vital or sensitive organs near the treated area etc.) and thus we highlighted the zone with higher values using bright red colour. This may be very important but commercial simulation software generally omits such option.

It may be also very useful to show obtained data only in the region of the tumour or to show values in form of several slices, semi-transparent layers or iso-surface view. Now we shall show how to prepare masking matrix for some simple geometrical objects representing tumours. For more information on the mentioned advanced techniques of results representation please see section 4. Advanced Viewing Techniques.

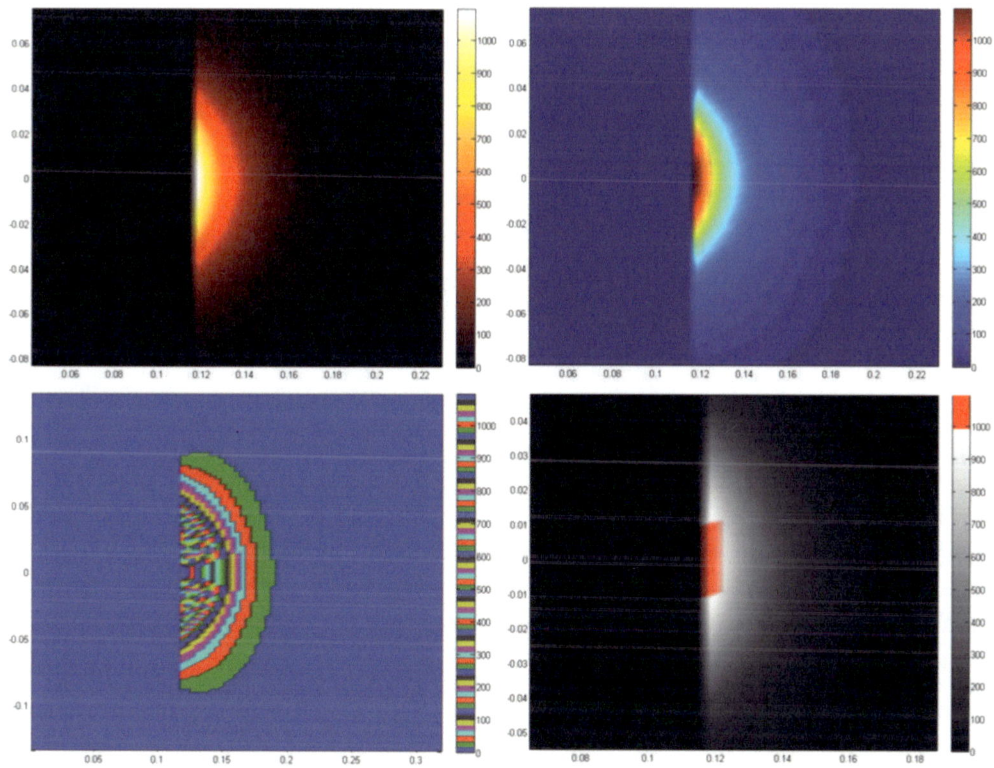

Figure 11. SAR [W/kg] in Different Colour Schemes (from left upper corner to right lower corner: hot, jet, lines, custom)

3.2.3. Preparation of masking matrix

Very simple masking (i.e. when the region that needs to be masked is in the form of a cuboid) was shown in previous section. Now we should look into masking regions round in shape (i.e. spheres, ellipsoids and other common shapes that parts of model can be represented by).

Spheres are case of ellipsoid and we shall treat them as such. So our main aim now is to mask region generally in ellipsoidal form. Equation defining an ellipsoid (with its origin at x_c, y_c, z_c) in the three dimensional coordinate system is shown below.

$$\frac{(x-x_c)^2}{a^2}+\frac{(y-y_c)^2}{b^2}+\frac{(z-z_c)^2}{c^2}\leq 1 \qquad (8)$$

The graphical representation of a general ellipsoid can be seen in figure 12. There we can see that a, b and c are semi-principal axes of ellipsoid and define its dimensions.

Albeit there is a built-in function designed to generate ellipsoid (see the Product Help of Matlab) we shall show you an easy way which allows you to generate desired masking matrix (e.g. with values 0 or 1).

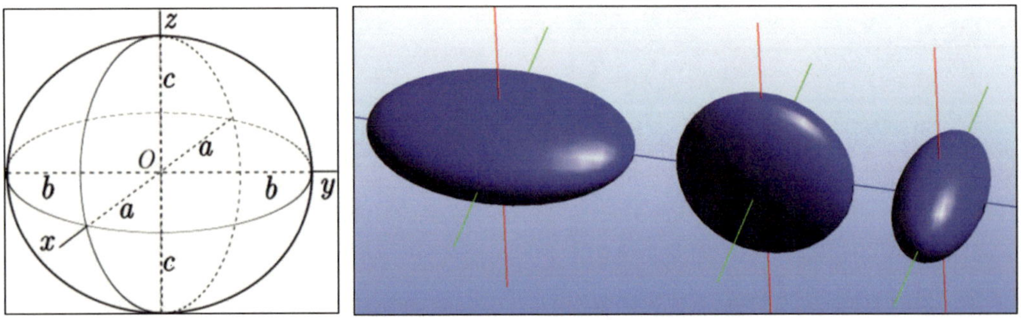

Figure 12. Representation of Ellipsoid (from left: scheme, tri-axial, oblate, prolate)

As you can see in Fig. 13. we simply utilized the formula representing ellipsoid and all elements whose coordinates meet the given restrictions are filled with ones. The other elements remain zero. Constants `elementsX`, `elementsY` or `elementsZ` define the length of axis of computational domain (i.e. `actualAxisX` and so on). Variables `xc`, `yc` and `zc` define centre of our ellipsoid.

```
maskingMatrix = zeros(elementsX,elementsY,elementsZ);
% Note that the size of a maskingMatrix will be the same as the size of
% matrix containing the results. We can use this to our advantage and
% define maskingMatrix using size[resultsMatrix].
for x = (1:elementsX)
    for y = (1:elementsY)
        for z = (1:elementsZ)
            if (((actualAxisX(x)-xc)^2/a^2)+...
                    ((actualAxisY(y)-yc)^2/b^2)+...
                    ((actualAxisZ(z)-zc)^2/c^2)) <= 1;
                maskingMatrix(x,y,z) = 1;
            end;
        end;
    end;
end;
```

Figure 13. Defining Ellipsoid in the Masking Matrix

Now we can simply use generated masking matrix and multiply every element of result matrix by according element of masking matrix. Then we can look how our results are interpreted in detailed view in the tumour.

From masked matrix of SAR we can also easily extract total power radiated to the tumorous region. Total power lost in the healthy tissue is than given by the difference between total power (in the case of perfectly matched source) and power lost in the tumour.

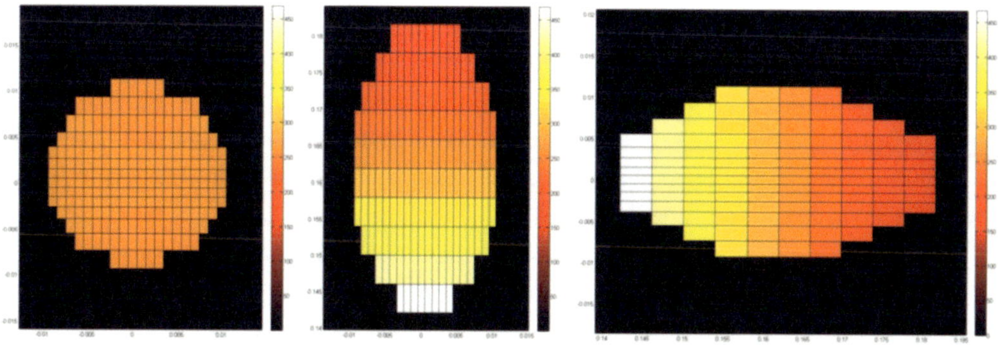

Figure 14. SAR [W/kg] in Tumour (from left: Y-slice, X-slice, Z-slice)

Note: In some cases it might be beneficial to set the colorbar range the same in all pictures (as shown in Fig. 14.). The simplest way to do this is to set value of [1,1] element of displayed matrix (i.e. a slice) to the maximum value of the whole three dimensional matrix (if needed, the minimum value should be set to element [max,max] of displayed matrix).

Additional information that we can obtain from masked result matrix is total absorbed power in the tumour. Since we know the dimensions of the tumour we can easily calculate its volume and use following formula.

$$P_{absorbed} = Volume \sum_{all\, voxels} RMS\left|E\right|^2 \sigma \tag{9}$$

The volume of standard ellipsoid is given as follows.

$$V = \frac{3}{4}\pi abc \tag{10}$$

For example in our case tumour has volume only 8.37766e-6 m^3. Information on total absorbed power may be very efficient way of preliminary evaluation for the treatment planning. Through this method we can determine power lost in any part of a simulated model. There may be some intricate volumes which are not as easily described as ellipsoid. Then we need to export their volume or masking matrix from the EM simulator (if possible).

We can determine the volume of such complicated shapes by summing elementary volumes of voxels representing those shapes. This may be unnecessary in some more advanced EM field simulators since they allow us to export model data in many suitable forms for Matlab processing. But the method presented in the following text is universal and can serve for better understanding of the model, its grid and working principals of EM simulations.

First of all we need to define which voxels are occupied by the model we want to evaluate. For this example we shall use our previously generated ellipsoid. As you can see in Fig. 14. generally grid of a simulation does not have to be symmetrical (i.e. voxels are not cubes but they are in the form of general cuboids). This means that each element may be representing different volume. We have our matrix of zeros and ones which we generated in Fig. 13. Now we need to apply this matrix to the actual coordinate system.

We can use built-in function `meshgrid` to produce three dimensional matrices which contain coordinates for specified element (for more information on function `meshgrid` please refer to the Product Help of Matlab). Now we can easily determine exact coordinates of elements occupied by our model (see Fig. 15.).

```
oldValue = 1;
for k = 1:length(actualAxisZ)
    [D,E] = find(valuesMasked(:,:,k) > 0);
    if isempty(D) == 0
        C(oldValue:(oldValue + length(D) - 1)) = k;
        oldValue = oldValue + length(D);
    end;
    if k == 1
        A = D';
        B = E';
    else
        A = [A D'];
        B = [B E'];
    end;
end;

completeVolume = abs(actualAxisX(A + 1) - actualAxisX(A)).*...
    abs(actualAxisY(B + 1) - actualAxisY(B)).*...
    abs(actualAxisZ(C + 1) - actualAxisZ(C));

sum(completeVolume)
```

Figure 15. Determination of Coordinates of Model Elements

At this moment we need to get better understanding of how models are defined. Since the values (in this case ones) are located in the nodes of the grid not in the centers we need to determine how the model actually looks like. See the following figure for better understanding (2D-plane is used to illustrate).

As you can see there will be an error caused by this node to cell transformation. When the simulation grid is defined appropriately (i.e. it is fine enough) the error will be only marginal. If such error is unacceptable more advanced techniques of node to cell transformation should be used. But for purposes of this example this method is more than sufficient. For example, volume of previously defined ellipsoid determined voxel by voxel is 8.5302e-6 m^3. This means that the relative error is 1.8 % (and this error includes error caused by voxelization itself – this means that node to cell transformation really brings only marginal error in simulations with fine grid).

In the Fig. 16. you can see that node to cell transformation can be done in a few (precisely 8) ways. We can easily determine which way is the most precise (i.e. [(A+1) – A] or [(A-1) – A] and its combinations with B and C). Since our model is voxelized symmetrically there is almost no difference between volumes computed accordingly to various node to cell transformations (ranging between 8.5302e-6 and 8.5304e-6).

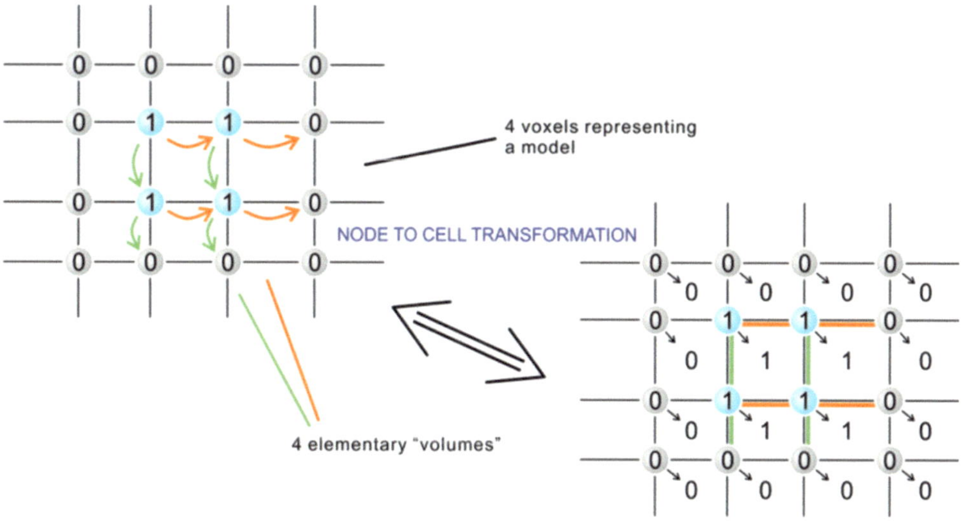

Figure 16. Actual Model Dimensions

4. Advanced viewing techniques

This section deals with some examples of advanced viewing of results that we have found useful during our work. As you have noticed, up to this point we have represented 3D results only in 2D graphs. This is because usually these 2D representations are clearer and easier to interpret. But for overviewing or demonstrational purposes we might need to show whole situation in 3D. For doing this we shall use multiple sections of a computational domain (`slice` or `surf`) and iso-surfaces.

4.1. Multiple layer viewing

We can display results in multiple 2D sections with variable transparency. This method of results visualization can give us much better overview of how a situation looks like.

It can be also beneficial to use surface view as semi-transparent layers to view results in semi-masked way. Through this we can highlight some regions of model without completely blocking visual output from other regions. For example, in our case, we can use one surface view of *RMS|E|* in agar phantom and semi-mask it with alphamap of tumour (values 1) and the rest of tissue (values 0.5).

Figure 19. shows us how this graph is plotted and how `transparencyMatrix` is prepared.

Note that when using this type of transparency mapping maximum and minimum values must be present in `transparencyMatrix` (i.e. one edge of transparencyMatrix is set to 0 to denote the minimum value of transparency).

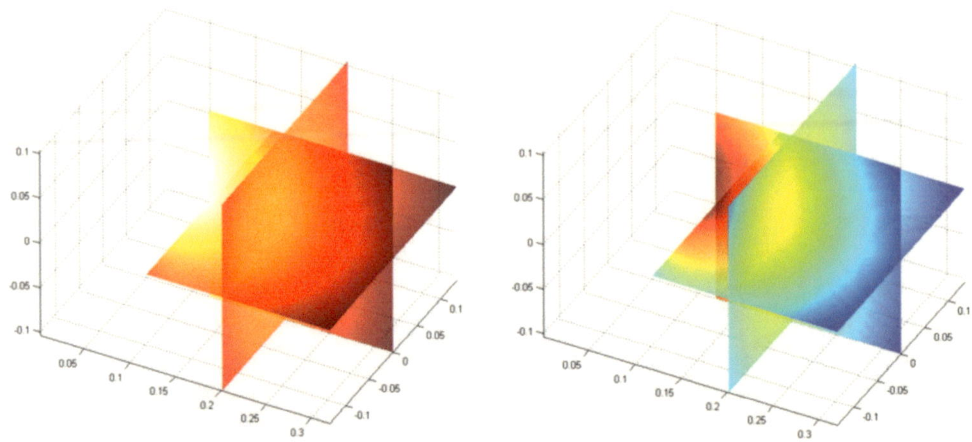

Figure 17. Sliced View of $RMS|E|$ [dB] (only in agar phantom, colormap hot, jet, alpha 0.7)

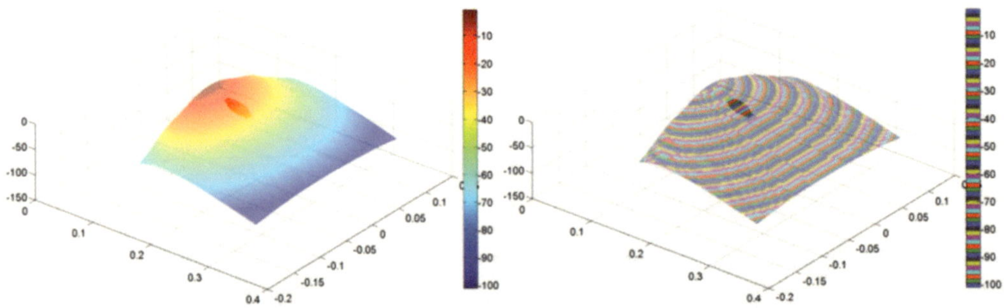

Figure 18. Surface View of RMS|E| in [dB] (transparency of tumour region set to 1 – opaque, transparency of other regions set to 0.5 – semi-transparent; colormap – jet and lines)

Through this method we can produce much more intricate visualizations of results which are unseen in commercial EM simulators. For example we can mask results in uninteresting regions (immediate vicinity of power source etc.) almost entirely, semi-mask results in exposed tissue and left results in tumour unmasked, vital organs and other key regions of simulation domain. Note that masking results with transparency matrix does not alter presented values.

This may pose a problem when values around a power source are extreme and render the rest of results unclear. For this purpose you may consider utilizing simmilar approach as presented in Figure 7. Instead of finding values lower than some value you may find values higher than some reasonable value and lower all higher values to this level.

Many more possibilities are offered thanks to post processing of EM results in Matlab. As mentioned before, the greatest advantage is that it is extremely flexible and can meet very specific requirements which can arrise with various applications of EM field. In the following section we shall demonstrate some results obtained during our primary research of EM field of microtubules (nanostructures in living cells which serve as a crude frame of a cell and have other important roles in life cycle of a cell).

```
transparencyMatrix = zeros(elementsX,elementsY,elementsZ);
% Note that the size of a transparencyMatrix will be the same as the
% size of matrix containing the results. We can use this to our
% advantage and define maskingMatrix using size[resultsMatrix].
for x = (1:elementsX)
    for y = (1:elementsY)
        for z = (1:elementsZ)
            if (((actualAxisX(x)-xc)^2/a^2)+...
                    ((actualAxisY(y)-yc)^2/b^2)+...
                    ((actualAxisZ(z)-zc)^2/c^2)) <= 1;
                transparencyMatrix(x,y,z) = 1;
            else
                transparencyMatrix(x,y,z) = 0.5;
            end;
        end;
    end;
end;

transparencyMatrix(length(actualAxisX),:,:) = 0;

figure(1);clf;
surf(actualAxisY(40:end),actualAxisX,valuesLog(:,40:end,51),...
    'FaceAlpha','flat','AlphaDataMapping','scaled',...
    'AlphaData',transparencyMatrix(:,40:end,51));
colorbar;
shading interp;
set(gca,'FontSize',14)
```

Figure 19. Fig. 19. Generation of Overalaying Transparency Matrix and Its Utilization

4.2. Iso-surface viewing

In this section we are going to show several results of EM field around microtubule. This structure is generally consisting of protofilaments which are polymerized tubulin heterodimers. Thirteen protofilaments bound together form a microtubule structure which resembles a long hollow tube (see Fig. 20).

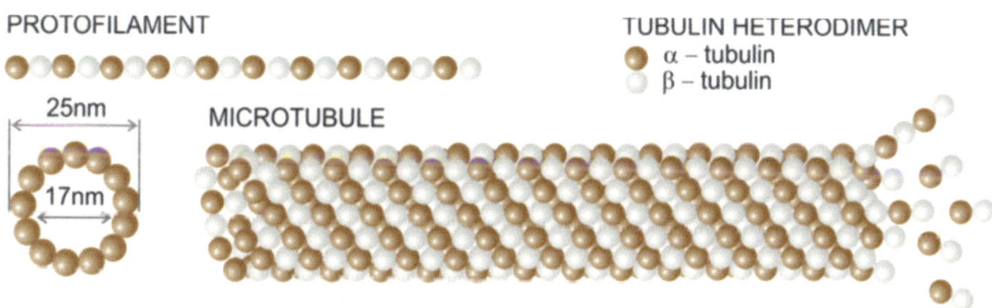

Figure 20. Microtubule Structure Visualization

Tubulin heterodimers (i.e. basic building block of microtubules) are highly polar structures and provided some form of external energy (movement of microtubules, mechanical vibrations etc.) they may produce EM field around themselves (Pohl, 1981; Fröhlich, 1978).

In our work EM field simulations of microtubule model were entirely conducted using Matlab. Tubulin heterodimers were represented as vibrating elementary electrical dipoles (EED) and EM field was determined for each of these EEDs. Combining the results led to unravelling the EM field produced by these complicated structures at whole (Havelka, 2009).

For the purpose of this text we shall look at visualization of these results we used to present obtained EM field. Because microtubules are symmetrical structures we have found out that representing its field by iso-surface view is very clear and easy to interpret.

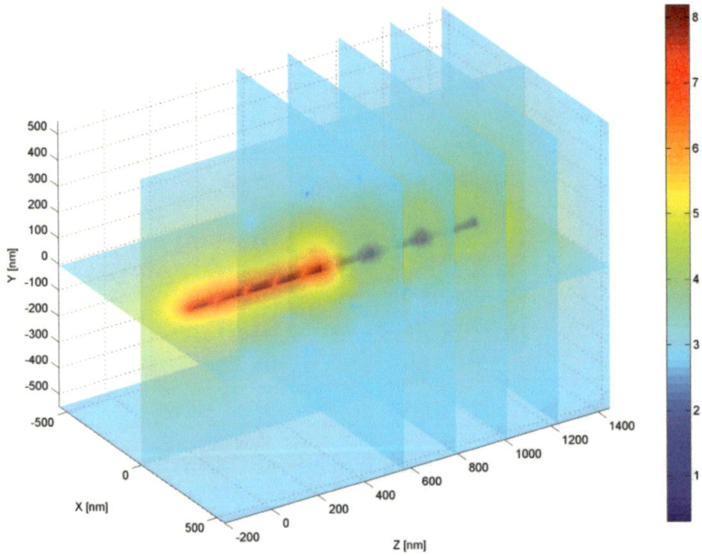

Figure 21. Sliced Semi-transparent View of Electric Field around Microtubule (see 4.1)

In the figure 23. you can see part of the code used to generate such visualization. More information on isosurface can be found in the Product Help of Matlab. In this particular example we wanted to view results in the form of several iso-surfaces. First of all we determined the range of data obtained through Matlab analysis of EM field around our sample microtubule.

Then we need to choose which values we want to be visualized as iso-surfaces (in this case, values range is extremely wide therefore we choose only exponents – 7, 5, 2). Then we need to find which positions at colour scale are lower than our actually viewed value (we generate the colour scale using function `jet(length of colour scale)`). Then we simply use function `patch` (to build 3D wire model of locations with desired values – i.e. 1e2, 1e5, 1e7) and we set its colour which we choose accordingly from our generated colour scheme.

Additionally you can choose lighting (particularly useful in this case is `gouraud` lighting which does not produce any glances on multiple iso-surfaces). It is also beneficial to use alpha which is lowered with each loop (to retain clarity of the visualization).

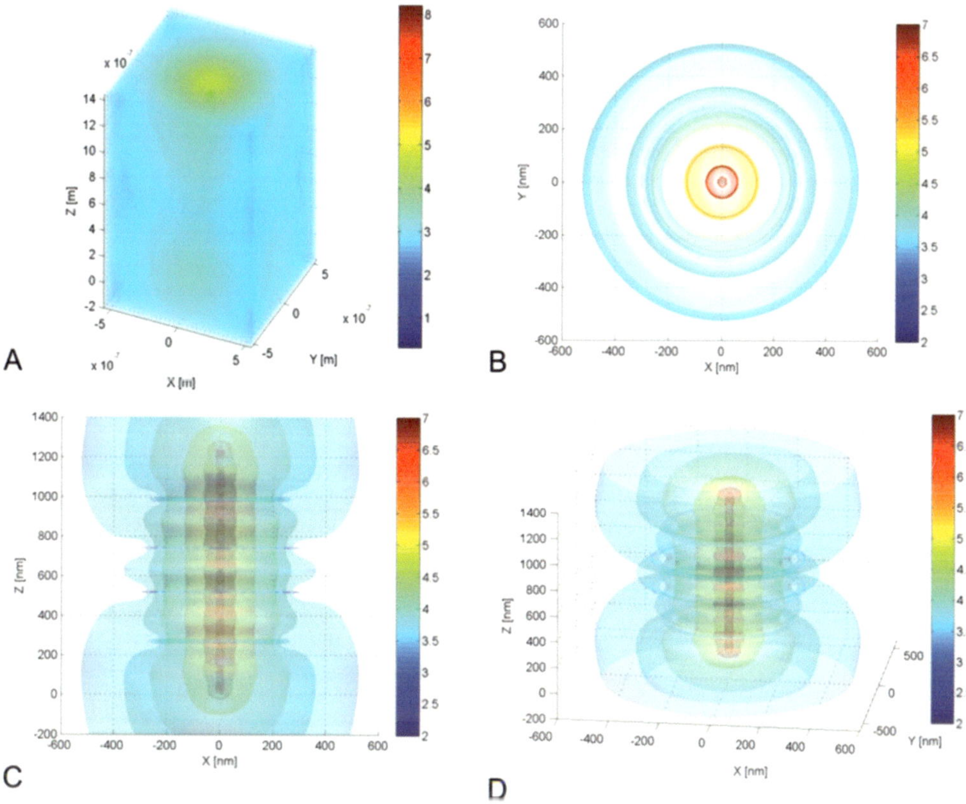

Figure 22. Iso-surface View of Electric Field around Microtubule [-] (A – rough data, B – iso-surface view from above, C – iso-surface view from enface, D – iso-surface view – general angle)

Last part is generating tiny triangle which is concealed in the middle of viewed data and contains the minimum and the maximum values which allows us to show colorbar appropriately for all the iso-surfaces .

5. Conclusion

In this work we have presented basic methods of how to process obtained rough data from commercial EM simulators or even process data from our own simulations done in Matlab. We show how Matlab processing can be greatly beneficial in highlighting results in many ways that are unseen in commercial EM simulators.

We present very simple way to modify data in the form suitable for further processing and then we illustrate how to view these data in ways highlighting specific aspects (i.e. values in specific regions (tumorous tissue), evaluation of treatment efficiency, utilization of Matlab in primary research, 3D viewing etc.). These innovative ways of combination of specialized software with researcher's versatile tool, such as Matlab is, yield in very productive and efficient way of scientific exploration of the vast field of electromagnetism.

```
max_E = log10(max(max(max(E_matrix)))); % Range of values in imported data
min_E = log10(min(min(min(E_matrix)))); % Range of values in imported data
ISOsurfaces = [7 5 2]; % Which values should be visualized
color_scale = 1000; % Refinement of colorbar
for u = 1:size(ISOsurfaces,2)

  T_vp = find(ISOsurfaces(u) >=...
         linspace(min(ISOsurfaces),max(ISOsurfaces),color_scale));
  color_all = jet(color_scale);

  figure(3);hold on
    p = patch(isosurface...
        (Xcoord*1e9,Ycoord*1e9,Zcoord*1e9,E_matrix,10^ISOsurfaces(u)));
    set(p,'FaceColor',color_all(T_vp(1,end),:),'EdgeColor','none');

    title({'Intensity of electric filed around model of microtubule';...
        'log_{10}(V/m)'});
    xlabel('X [nm]'); ylabel('Y [nm]'); zlabel('Z [nm]');
    grid on;
    camlight; lighting gouraud
    alpha(0.5 - 0.05*u)
    hold on;
    a = [1,1;0,0]*1e-9; b = [0,1;1,0]*1e-9; c = [0,0;0,0]*1e-9;
    d = [max(ISOsurfaces) max(ISOsurfaces) ;...
         min(ISOsurfaces) min(ISOsurfaces)];
    surf(a,b,c,d)
    colorbar;
end;
```

Figure 23. Generation of Iso-surface View of EM Field around Microtubule

The results that are obtained in our research of EM field around living cell help us understand crucial facts about this part of our lives which has to be truly discovered yet. Matlab in this instance allows us to visualize result so we can support or on the other hand disapprove many theories (e.g. transportation of particles around microtubule via EM field).

Author details

Tomas Vydra and Daniel Havelka
Czech Technical University in Prague, FEE, Department of Electromagnetic Field, Czech Republic

Acknowledgement

This research is supported by the Grant Agency of the Czech Republic by project 102/08/H081: "Non Standard Applications of Physical Fields" and by CTU project SGS12/071/OHK3/1T/13: "Advanced techniques in the processing of industrial materials and biopolymers using electromagnetic field - multi-frequency processing ". Further it is supported also by research program MSM6840770012: "Transdisciplinary Research in the Area of Biomedical Engineering II" of the CTU in Prague, sponsored by the Ministry of Education, Youth and Sports of the Czech Republic.

6. References

Cifra, M.; Pokorný, J.; Havelka, D. & Kučera, O. (2010). Electric field generated by axial longitudinal vibration modes of microtubule, *BioSystems*, ISSN 0303-2647, vol.100, no.2 (May 2010), pp. 122-131, Oxford, GB

Fröhlich, H.; (1978). Coherent electric vibrations in biological systems and the cancer problem, *IEEE Transactions on Microwave Theory and Techniques*, Vol.26, No.8 (August 1978), pp. 613-618, ISSN 0018-9480

Havelka, D.; Cifra, M. (2009). Calculation of the Electromagnetic Field Around a Microtubule. *Acta Polytechnica*, Vol.49, No.2 (2009), pp. 58-63. ISSN 1210-2709.

Havelka, D.; Cifra, M.; Kučera, O.; Pokorný, J. & Vrba, J. (2011). High-frequency electric field and radiation characteristics of cellular microtubule network, *Journal of Theoretical Biology*, ISSN 0022-5193, vol. 286, no. 1, p. 31-40, London, GB

Pohl, H.A. (1981). Electrical oscillation and contact inhibition of reproduction in cells, Journal of Biological Physics, Vol.9, No.4 (1981), pp. 191-200, ISSN 0092-0606

Thomas, V.A.; Ling, K.; Jones, M.E.; Toland, B.; Lin, J. & Itoh, T. (1994). FDTF analysis of an active antenna, *IEEE Microwave Guided Wave Lett.*, Vol 4, No 9 (September 1994), pp. 296-298, ISSN 1051-8207

Vera, A.; Valentino, A.; Baez, A.; Trujillo, C.J.; Zepeda, H. & Leija, L. (2006). Rectangular Waveguide for Electromagnetic Oncology hyperthermia: Design, Construction and Characterization, *Proceedings of 3rd International Conference on Electrical and Electronics Engineering 2006*, pp. 1-4, ISBN 1-4244-0402-9, Veracruz, Mexico, September 6-8, 2006

Vrba, J.; Oppl, L.; & Vrba, D. (2008). Microwave Medical Imaging and Diagnostics, *Proceedings of EuMC 2008 38th European Microwave Conference*, pp. 408-411, ISBN 978-2-87487-006-4, Amsterdam, Netherlands, October 28-31, 2008

Vrba, J. & Oppl, L. (2008). Prospective Applications of Microwaves in Medicine, *Proceedings of COMITE 2008 14th Conference on Microwave Techniques*, pp. 1-4, ISBN 978-1-4244-2138-1, Prague, Czech Republic, April 23-24, 2008

Vydra, T.; Vorlicek, J. & Vrba, J. (2011). Measurement and analysis of microwave processing of biopolymers, *Proceedings of 21th International Conference Radioelektronika 2011*, pp. 1-4, ISBN 978-1-61284-325-4, Brno, Czech Republic, April 19-20, 2011

Chapter 3

Simulation of Power Converters Using Matlab-Simulink

Christophe Batard, Frédéric Poitiers, Christophe Millet and Nicolas Ginot

Additional information is available at the end of the chapter

http://dx.doi.org/10.5772/46419

1. Introduction

A static converter is an electrical circuit which can control the transfer of energy between a generator and a receiver. The efficiency of a converter should be excellent. The components constituting a converter are:

- Capacitors, inductors and transformers with minimum losses,
- Power semiconductors operating as switches.

The design of power converter consumes time with a significant cost. Performance is generally determined after testing converters at nominal operating points. Thus, simulation can substantially reduce development cost.

The development of specific software dedicated to simulation of power electronic systems (PSIM, SABER, PSCAD, "SimPowerSystems" toolbox of Simulink…) allows simulating fast and accurately the converter behavior. Unfortunately, the designers of converters don't always have such available software. In many cases, they have to simulate power electronics devices for occasional need. So they don't want to buy the SimPowerSystems toolbox in addition to Matlab and Simulink. The purpose of this chapter is to present the ability to simulate power converters using only Simulink. Simulink is a graphical extension to MATLAB for representing mathematical functions and systems in the form of block diagram, and simulate the operation of these systems.

Traditionally two approaches are used to simulate power electronic systems:

- The first, so called fixed topology, where semiconductors are impedances with low or high values based on their on-state or off-state. Equations system does not depend on the state of the semiconductor. Despite its simplicity, this approach raises problems of compromise between accuracy of the results and stability of numerical integration methods.

- The second, so called variable topology, assimilates the switches to open-circuits or short-circuits. The system equations then depend on the state of the semiconductor. There are no accuracy problems but writing the equations of different configurations can be laborious as well as obtain switching conditions of the semiconductor.

In this chapter, we propose a method for simulating static converters with Simulink based on the variable topology approach where switching conditions of semiconductor are realized by switching functions.

2. Linear load modeling in Simulink

This paragraph deals with the modelling of linear elements commonly encountered in the electrical energy conversion. Elementary linear dipoles are described by a system of linear differential equations. There are several different ways to describe linear differential equations. The state-space representation (SSR) is the most easy to use with Matlab. The SSR is given by equations (1) and (2).

$$\dot{X} = A\,X + B\,U \tag{1}$$

$$Y = C\,X \tag{2}$$

where X is an n by 1 vector representing the state (commonly current through an inductance or voltage across the capacitance), U is a scalar representing the input (voltage or current), and Y is a scalar representing the output. The matrices A (n by n), B (n by 1), and C (1 by n) determine the relationships between the state and input and output variables.

The commonly elementary dipoles encountered in power electronics are:

- RL series dipole
- RLC series dipole
- RC parallel dipole
- L in series with RC parallel dipole

2.1. RL series dipole

The variation of the current through the dipole is governed by equation (3).

$$v(t) = R\,i(t) + L\,di/dt \;\Rightarrow\; i(t) = \frac{1}{L}\int\left(v(t) - R\,i(t)\right)dt \tag{3}$$

The RL series dipole is modelled by the scheme illustrated in figure 1.

2.2. RLC series dipole

The variation of the current through the dipole is governed by equation (4) and the variation of the voltage across the capacity is governed by equation (5).

$$v(t) = R\,i(t) + v_C(t) + L\,di/dt \;\Rightarrow\; i(t) = \frac{1}{L}\int\left(v(t) - Ri(t) - v_C(t)\right)dt \tag{4}$$

$$i(t) = C\,dv_C/dt \;\Rightarrow\; v_C(t) = \frac{1}{C}\int i\,dt \tag{5}$$

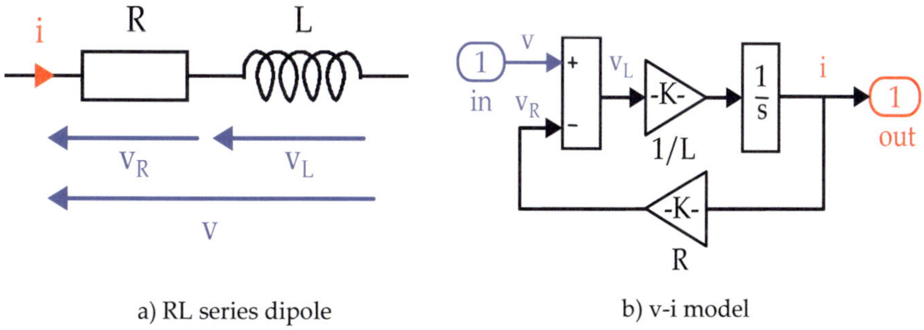

Figure 1. Model of a RL series dipole

The RLC series dipole is modelled by the scheme illustrated in figure 2.

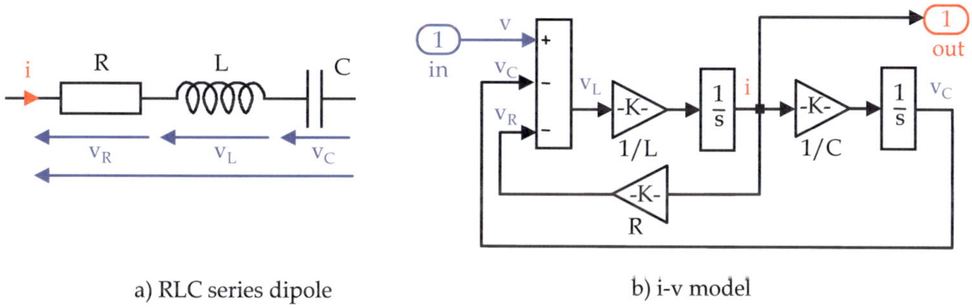

Figure 2. Model of a RLC series dipole

2.3. RC parallel dipole

The variation of the voltage across the dipole is governed by equation (6).

$$i(t) = C\,dv/dt + v(t)/R \;\Rightarrow\; v(t) = \frac{1}{C}\int\left(i(t) - v(t)/R\right)dt \tag{6}$$

The RC parallel dipole is modelled by the scheme illustrated in figure 3.

2.4. L in series with RC parallel dipole

In a L in series with RC parallel dipole, the variation of the current through the inductance is governed by equation (7) and the variation of the voltage across the capacity is governed by equation (8).

$$v_i(t) = v_o(t) + L\frac{di_L}{dt} \Rightarrow i_L(t) = \frac{1}{L}\int\left(v_i(t) - v_o(t)\right)dt \tag{7}$$

$$i_L(t) = i_R(t) + C\frac{dv_o}{dt} \Rightarrow v_o(t) = \frac{1}{C}\int\left(i_L(t) - i_R(t)\right)dt \tag{8}$$

$$i_R(t) = v_o(t)/R \tag{9}$$

The L in series with RC parallel dipole is modelled by the scheme illustrated in figure 4.

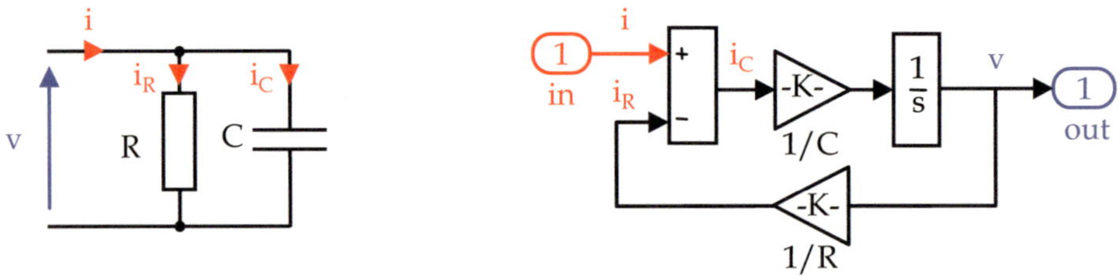

a) RC parallel dipole

b) i-v model

Figure 3. Model of a RC parallel dipole

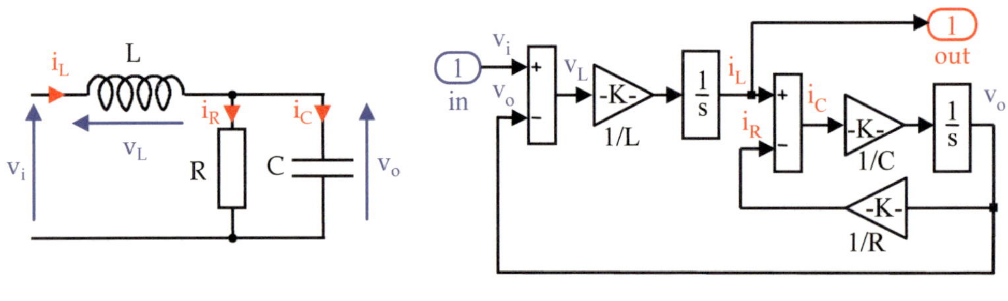

a) L series with RC parallel dipole

b) v-i model

Figure 4. Model of a L in series with RC parallel dipole

3. DC-DC converter model in Simulink

This part will be dedicated to the DC-DC converter modelling with Simulink. The input generator is a DC voltage source and the output generator is also a DC voltage source. The output voltage is always smoothed by a capacitor. Only the non-isolated DC-DC converters are studied in this paragraph. The switches are assumed ideal, as well as passive elements (L, C)

3.1. Buck converter

3.1.1. Operating phases

The buck converter circuit is illustrated in figure 5a. The most common strategy for controlling the power transmitted to the load is the intersective Pulse Width Modulation (PWM). A control voltage v_m is compared to a triangular voltage v_t. The triangular voltage v_t determines the switching frequency f_t. The switch T is controlled according to the difference $v_m - v_t$ (figure 5b). Three operating phases are counted (figure 5c):

- T state-on and D state-off
- T state-off and D state-on
- T and D state-off

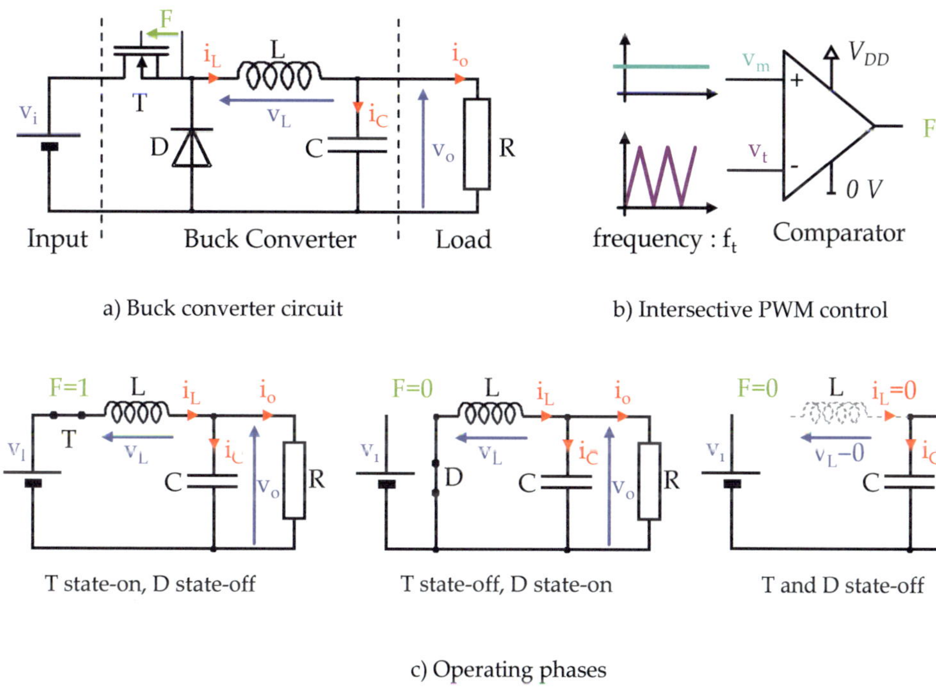

Figure 5. Buck converter

The variation of the current through the capacitor C is governed by equation (*10*). The variation of the voltage across the capacity is governed by equation (*11*). Equation (*12*) describes the variation of the voltage across the inductance which depends on the operating phase. F is a logical variable equal to one if v_m is greater than or equal to v_t, F equal to zero if v_m is less than v_t. Sign(i_L) is also a logical variable which is equal to one if i_L is positive, sign (i_L) equal to zero if i_L is zero.

$$i_C(t) = i_L(t) - i_o(t) = C\frac{dv_o}{dt} \tag{10}$$

$$v_o(t) = \frac{1}{C}\int i_C(t)\,dt = \frac{1}{C}\int\left(i_L(t) - i_o(t)\right)dt \tag{11}$$

$$v_L(t) = \left(v_i(t) - v_o(t)\right) * F - v_o(t) * \overline{F} * sign(i_L) \tag{12}$$

3.1.2. Open-loop buck converter

Simulink model of the open-loop buck converter is shown in figure 6a. The Buck block is illustrated in figure 6c. Equation (*12*) is modelled by blocks addition, multiplication and logic. The structure of the converter requires a current i_L necessarily positive or zero. Also, the inductance current is modelled by an integrator block that limits the minimum value of i_L to zero.

The PWM control block is illustrated in figure 6b.

In the case of a resistive load, the load block is constituted by a gain block (value 1/R).

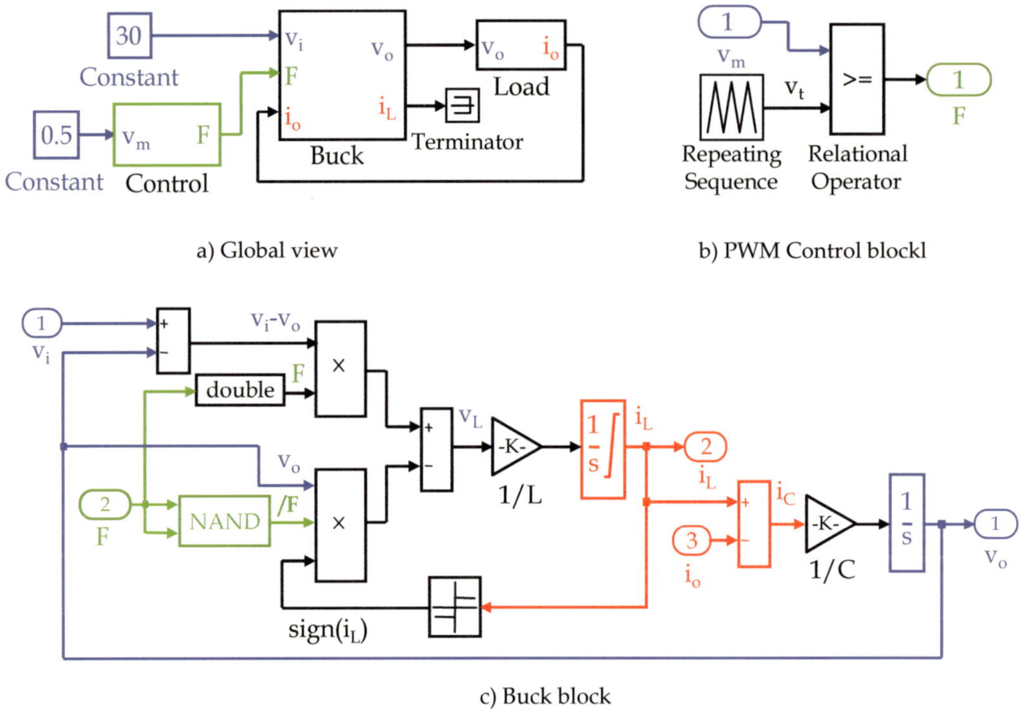

Figure 6. Buck converter described in Simulink

3.1.3. Closed-loop buck converter

A closed-loop buck converter circuit is illustrated in figure 7a. The measurement of the output voltage is realized by 2 resistances R_1 and R_2. The regulation is achieved by a PID controller. Simulink model of the closed loop converter is shown in figure 7b. Simulink PID control block is illustrated in figure 7c .

The parameters used for the closed-loop simulation are :

$V_i = 12$ V	$L = 300\ \mu H$	$C = 5\ \mu F$	$R = 3\ \Omega$	$f_t = 50$ kHz
Output voltage measurement:		$R_1 = 10\ k\Omega$	$R_2 = 10\ k\Omega$	
PID block :		$K_p = 10$	$T_i = 0.2$ ms	

The voltage reference was fixed to 2.5 V. The simulation of the closed-loop buck converter is illustrated in figure 7d. The list of configuration parameters used for is:

Start time : 0
Type : Variable-step
Max step size : 1e-6
Min step size : auto

Stop time : 0.5 e-3
Solver : ode15s (stiff/NDF)
Relative tolerance : 1e-3
absolute tolerance : auto

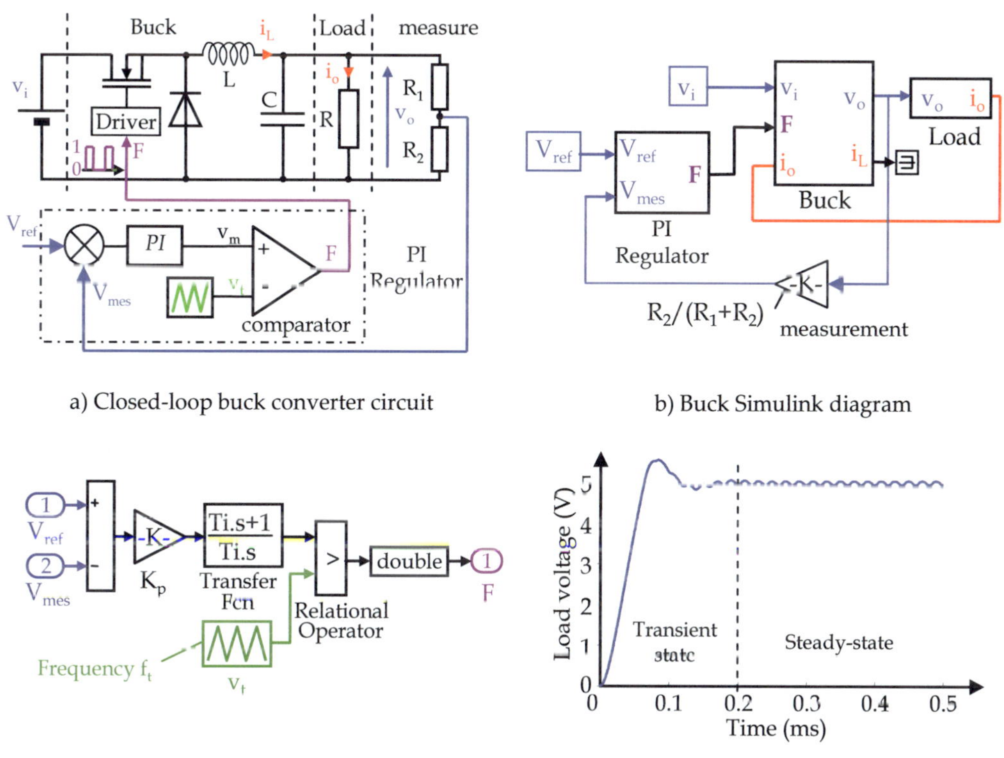

a) Closed-loop buck converter circuit

b) Buck Simulink diagram

c) Simulink PI regulator

d) Output voltage of the buck converter

Figure 7. Modeling a closed loop DC / DC converter

In steady-state, $V_{ref} = V_{mes} = 2.5$ V. From figure 7a, we deduce the theoretical value of V_o:

$$V_o\Big|_{steady-state} = \frac{R_1 + R_2}{R_2} V_{ref} = 5\ V \tag{13}$$

Simulation is in good agreement with theoretical value. From figure 7d, we deduce that the transient state last roughly 0.2 ms.

3.2. Boost converter

3.2.1. Operating phases

The boost converter circuit is illustrated in figure 8a. The principle of the switch control is described in figure 5b Three operating phases are counted (figure 8c) :

- T state-on and D state-off
- T state-off and D state-on
- T and D state-off

The variation of the voltage across the inductance L (equation *14*) and the current through the capacity (equation *15*) depend on the operating phase.

$$v_L(t) = v_i(t) * F + \left(v_i(t) - v_o(t)\right) * \overline{F} * sign(i_L) \tag{14}$$

$$i_C(t) = -\,i_o(t) * F + i_L(t) * \overline{F} * sign(i_L) = C\,\frac{dv_o}{dt} \tag{15}$$

$$v_o = \frac{1}{C}\int i_C(t)\,dt = \frac{1}{C}\int\left(-i_o(t)\,.\,F + i_L\,.\,\overline{F}\,.\,sign(i_L)\right)dt \tag{16}$$

3.2.2. Open-loop operation

Simulink model of a open-loop boost converter is shown in figure 9a. The Boost block is illustrated in figure 9b. Equation (14), (15) and (16) are modeled by addition blocks, multiplication blocks and logic blocks. The structure of the converter requires a current i_L necessarily positive or zero. Also, the inductance current is modeled by an integrator block that limits the minimum value of i_L to zero.

The PWM control block is illustrated in figure 6b.

In the case of a resistive load, the load block is constituted by a gain block (value 1/R).

Simulation example:

The parameters used for of an open-loop simulation are :

$V_i = 12$ V	L = 200 µH	C = 50 µF	R = 5 Ω	$f_t = 50$ kHz
Control blok:	$V_{t\,max} = 1$ V		$V_{t\,min} = -1$ V	$V_m = 0$

The simulation of the open-loop boost converter is illustrated in figure 9c. The list of configuration parameters used is:

Start time : 0
Type : Variable-step
Max step size : 1e-6
Min step size : auto

Stop time : 7 e-3
Solver : ode15s (stiff/NDF)
Relative tolerance : 1e-3
absolute tolerance : auto

Knowing that v_t varies from – 1 V to + 1 V and $v_m = 0$, we deduce that the duty cycle α is equal to 0.5. In steady-state, we deduce theoretical value of V_o :

$$V_o\big|_{steady-state} = \frac{V_i}{\alpha} = 24\ V \tag{17}$$

Simulation is in good agreement with theoretical value. From figure 9c, we deduce that the transient state last roughly 2.5 ms.

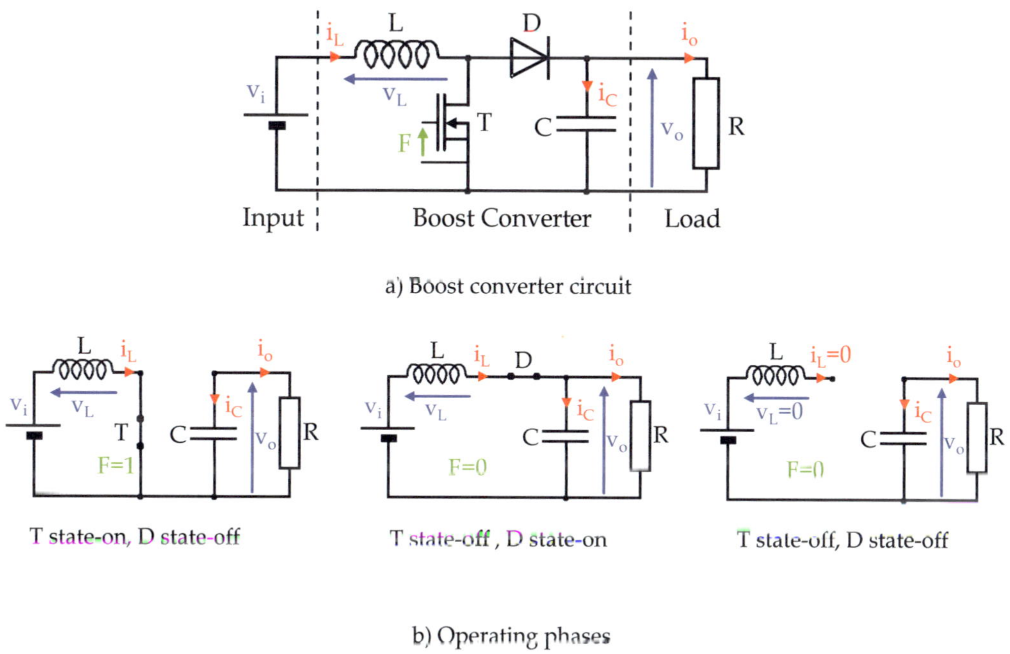

Figure 8. Boost converter

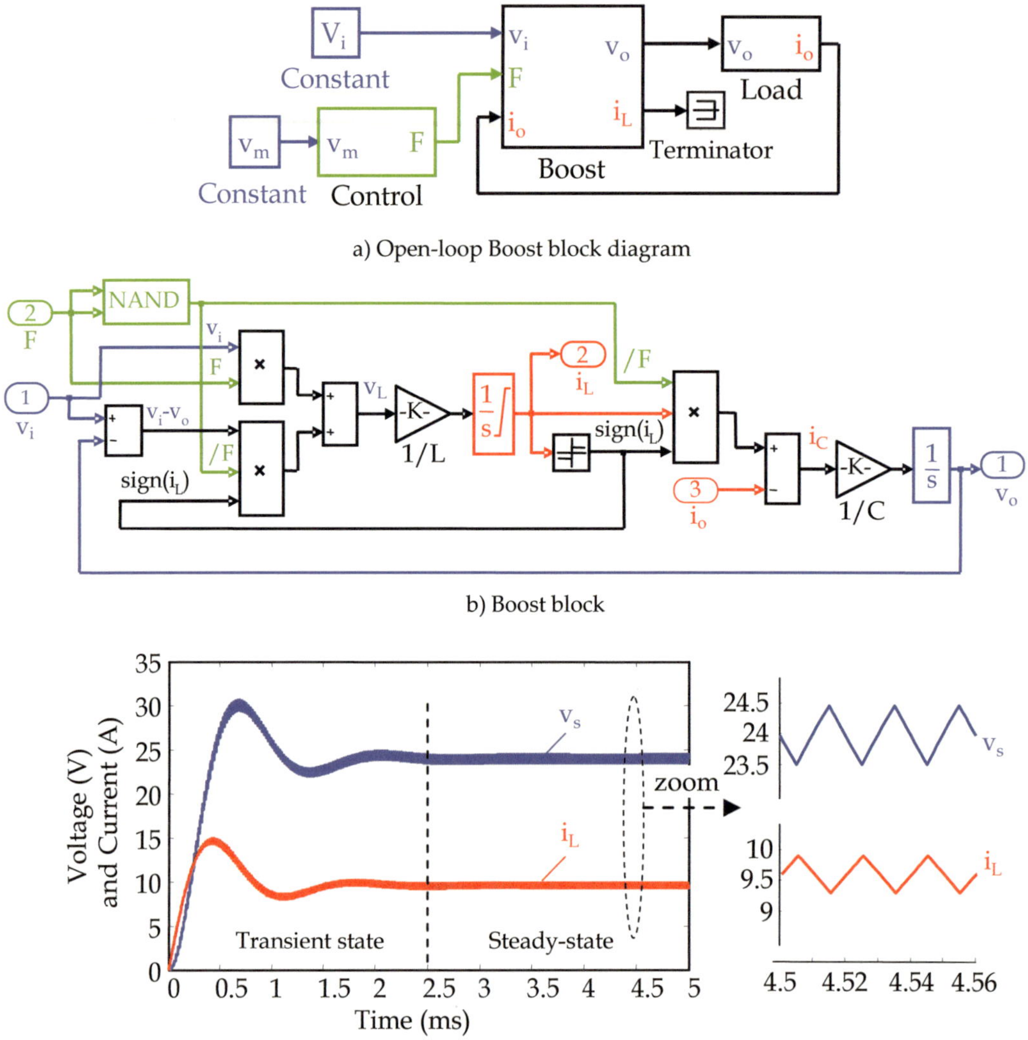

a) Open-loop Boost block diagram

b) Boost block

c) Open-loop Boost simulation

Figure 9. Boost converter described in Simulink

4. DC-AC converter model in Simulink

An inverter is a DC – AC power converter. This converter obtains AC voltage from DC voltage. The applications are numerous: power backup for the computer systems, variable speed drive motor, induction heating... In most cases, the dead times introduced into the control of the switches do not change the waveform of the inverter.

This paragraph is dedicated to the simulation of a three-phase inverter without taking into account the dead times introduced into the control of the switches.

4.1. Electrical circuit

A variable speed drive for AC motor is shown in figure 10. It consists on a continuous voltage source and a three-phase inverter feeding an AC motor.

In order to simplify the modelling, the electrical equivalent circuit of the AC motor is described by an inductance L_M in series with a resistance R_M. The motor runs with delta connection of the stator.

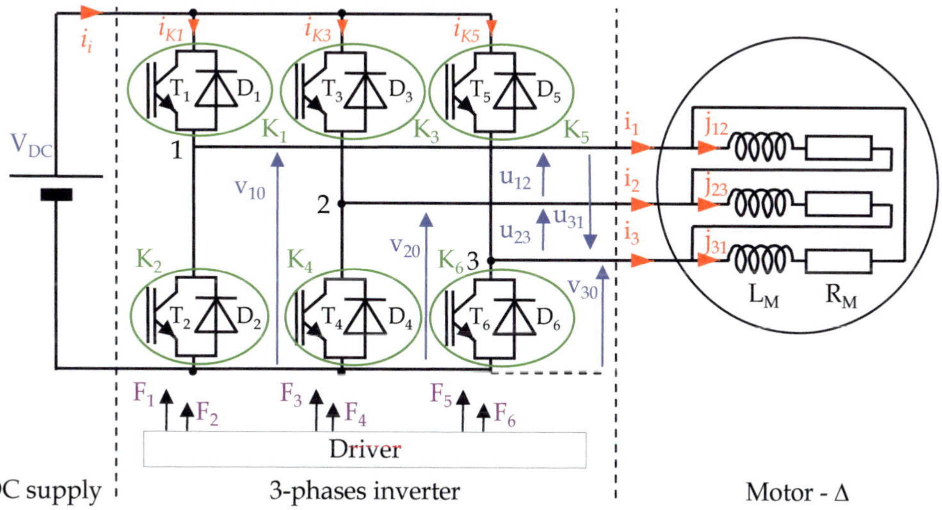

Figure 10. Electrical circuit

There are many strategies for controlling the switches. The most common control strategy is the intersective PWM. Its principle is reminded in figure 11. The switch control signals are generated by comparing three sinusoidal voltages (modulating) which are phase-shifted through 2π/3 [rad] with a same triangular voltage waveform (carrier).

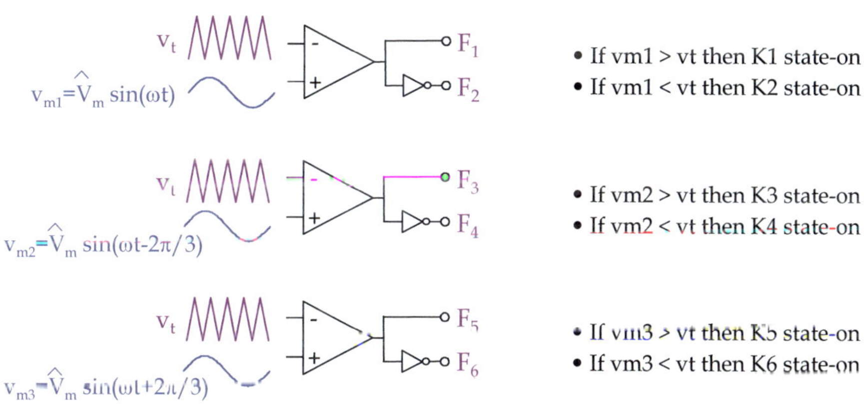

Figure 11. Three phase PWM control

Knowing the conduction intervals of the switches, it is then possible to determine the waveform of different voltages and currents.

The line to neutral voltage v_{10}, v_{20} et v_{30} are dependent on the state of the switches. Examples:

K_1 state-on and K_2 state-off: $v_{10} = + V_{DC}$

K_3 state-on and K_4 state-off: $v_{20} = + V_{DC}$

K_5 state-on and K_6 state-off: $v_{30} = + V_{DC}$

K_1 state-off and K_2 state-on: $v_{10} = 0$

K_3 state-off and K_4 state-on: $v_{20} = 0$

K_5 state-off and K_6 state-on: $v_{30} = 0$

The phase-phase voltage can be deduce from the line to neutral voltage:

$$u_{12} = v_{10} - v_{20} \tag{18}$$

$$u_{23} = v_{20} - v_{30} \tag{19}$$

$$u_{31} = v_{30} - v_{10} \tag{20}$$

The input current i_i is deduced from the current of switches K_1, K_3 and K_5:

$$i_i = i_{K1} + i_{K3} + i_{K5} = F_1 \,.\, i_1 + F_3 \,.\, i_2 + F_5 \,.\, i_3 \tag{21}$$

4.2. Simulink model

Simulink model of the three-phase inverter is shown in figure 12a. The control block is illustrated in figure 12b. It models a three phases PWM control. The inverter block is illustrated in figure 12c.

In the case of a resistive load, the load block is constituted by a gain block (value 1/R).

4.3. Simulation example

The parameters used for of an open-loop simulation are :

Power Circuit :	$V_{DC} = 400$ V	$L_M = 10$ mH	$R_M = 5\ \Omega$
Control blok:	$f_t = 20$ kHz	$V_{t\,max} = 1$ V	$V_{t\,min} = -1$ V
	$f_m = 50$ Hz	$V_{m\,max} = 0.5$	

The simulation of the open-loop three-phase inverter is illustrated in figure 13. The list of configuration parameters used is:

Start time: 0

Type: Variable-step

Max step size: 1e-5

Min step size: auto

Stop time: 1.5

Solver: ode15s (stiff/NDF)

Relative tolerance: 1e-3

absolute tolerance: auto

The relation between the amplitude of the sinusoidal voltage and the triangular voltage determines the maximum value of the fundamental line-line voltage of the inverter:

$$U_{\max} = \frac{\sqrt{3}}{2}\frac{V_{m\max}}{V_{t\max}}V_{DC} = \frac{\sqrt{3}}{2}\frac{0.5}{1}400 = 173\,V \qquad (22)$$

Neglecting the current harmonics, the maximum value of the line current is deduced from equation (22) :

$$I_{1\max} = \sqrt{3}\,J_{12\max} = \frac{\sqrt{3}\,.\,U_{\max}}{\sqrt{R_M{}^2 + (L_M\,2\,\pi\,f_m)^2}} = \frac{\sqrt{3}\,.\,173}{\sqrt{4^2 + (10^{-2}\,2\,\pi\,50)^2}} = 59\text{ A} \qquad (23)$$

Simulations are in good agreement with theoretical values.

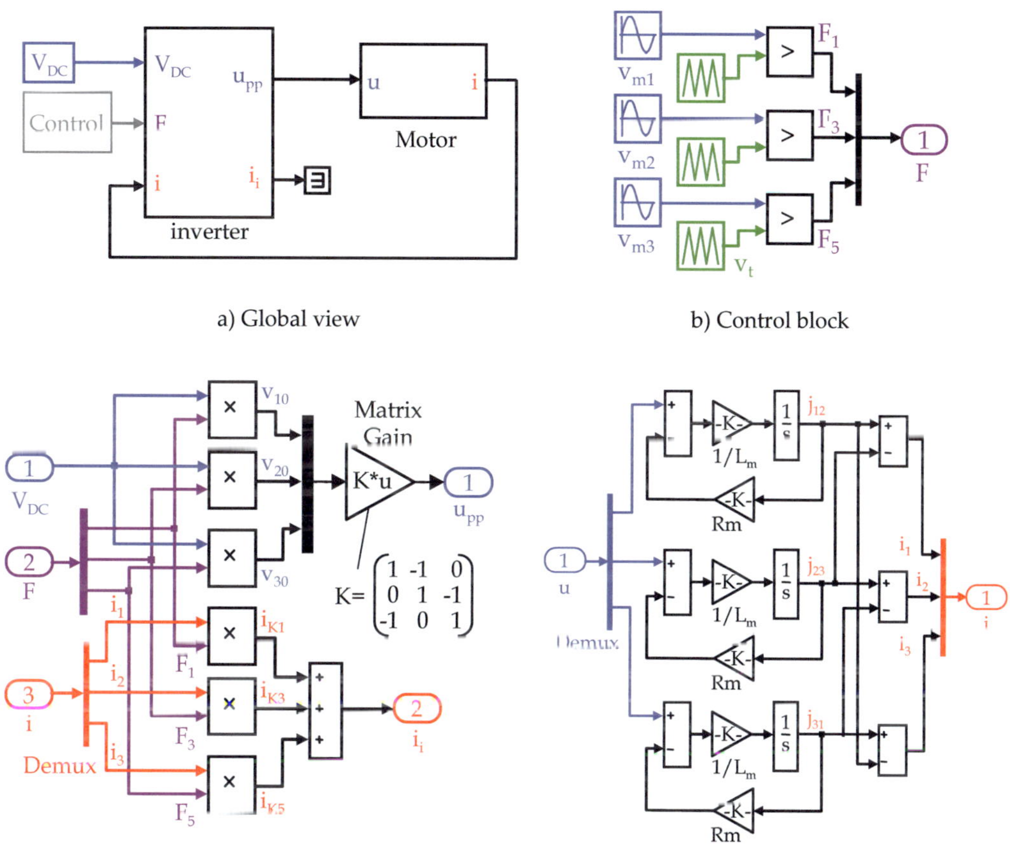

a) Global view b) Control block

c) Inverter Block d) Motor block

Figure 12. Three phase inverter

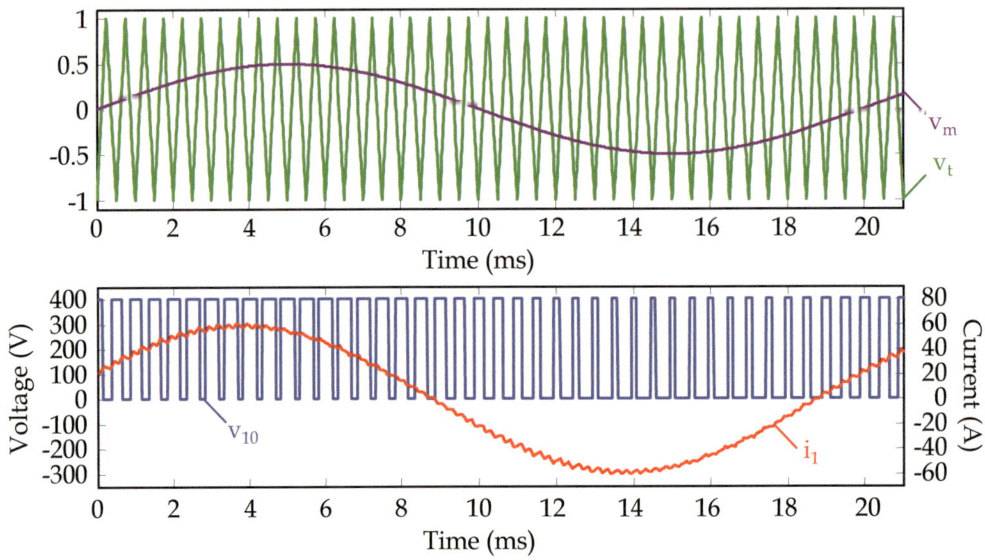

Figure 13. Simulation example of a three-phase inverter with PWM control

5. Modeling and simulation of diode rectifiers

Three-phase AC to DC converters are widely used in many industrial power converters in order to obtain continuous voltage using a classical three-phase AC-line. These converters, when they are used alone or associated for specific applications, can present problems due to their non-linear behaviour. It is then important to be able to model accurately the behaviour of these converters in order to study their influence on the input currents waveforms and their interactions with the loads (classically inverters and AC-motors).

Several studies have shown the importance to have tools to simulate the behaviour of complex power electronics systems (Ladoux et al., 2005), (Qijun et al. 2007), (Zuniga-Haro & Ramirez, 2009) and several methods have been also presented in order to reduce the simulation time or to improve the precision. Although constant topology methods have been developed (Araujo et al., 2002), variable topology methods seem to be very suitable for simulation of power-electronics converters (Terrien et al., 1999).

In this chapter, an original and simple method is developed to model and simulate AC-DC converters taking into account overlap phenomenon with continuous and discontinuous conduction modes using Matlab-Simulink. The diodes are assumed ideal ($v_d = 0$ when the diode is state-on, $i_d = 0$ when the diode is state-off)

If the electrical network is considered as ideal (no line inductance) and the conduction is maintained continuous, ($i_d>0$), the modelling of the converters can be realised very simply by a functional approach (commutation functions) where the switches are opened or closed. An example is presented in figure 14.

$v_o = F_1 \cdot v_i - F_2 \cdot v_i$ With : $F_1 = 1$ if $v_i > 0$ and $F_1 = 0$ if $v_i < 0$
$F_2 = 0$ if $v_i > 0$ and $F_2 = 1$ if $v_i < 0$

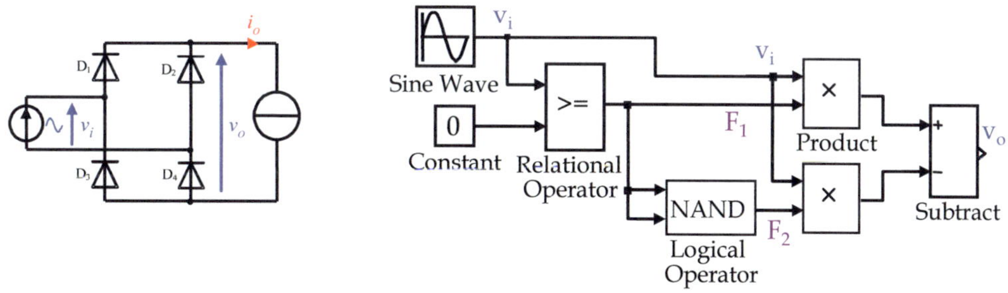

a) Electrical circuit   b) Simulink equivalent circuit

Figure 14. Basic model of a single-phase rectifier.

In this chapter, the proposed approach is completely different from the approach based on commutation functions. It permits to simulate accurately the commutation in the six-pulse AC-DC converter, even under unbalanced supply voltages (the influence of voltages unbalances on AC harmonic magnitudes currents has been demonstrated (de Oliveira & Guimaraes, 2007) or line impedances conditions.

The overlap phenomenon and the unbalance of line impedances can be taken into account by modifying the commutation functions to correspond to the real behaviour of the rectifiers in these conditions. Indeed, the commutations are not instantaneous. Several contributions have already been proposed in scientific literature to refine the modelling of rectifiers. Most of these contributions show good simulation results but the analytical models used are complex and not reflecting precisely the real behaviour of the converter (Hu & Morrison, 1997), (Arrillaga et al., 1997). Some methods have been developed in order to model and simulate power factor corrected single-phase AC-DC converters (Pandey et al., 2004).

5.1. Electrical model

The six-pulse AC-DC converter is illustrated in figure 15a. Inductances L_i characterize the line inductances and L_o characterizes the output inductance. The AC-DC converter modelling is based on the variable topology approach. The diodes are modelled by an ideal model which traduces the state of the switch:

- $v_D = 0$ when the diode is state-on;
- $i_D = 0$ when the diode is state-off.

There are 13 operating phases:

- 1 phase of discontinuous conduction mode (P_0)

All the diodes are state-off (figure 15b)

- 6 phases of classical conduction P_1 to P_6 (figure 15c)

P_1 : D_1 and D_5 state-on P_2 : D_1 and D_6 state-on P_3 : D_2 and D_6 state-on

P_4 : D_2 and D_4 state-on P_5 : D_3 and D_4 state-on P_6 : D_3 and D_5 state-on

- 6 phases of overlap O_1 to O_6 (figure 15d)

O_1 : D_1, D_5 and D_6 state-on O_2 : D_1, D_2 and D_6 state-on O_3 : D_2, D_4 and D_6 state-on

O_4 : D_2, D_3 and D_4 state-on O_5 : D_3, D_4 and D_5 state-on O_6 : D_1, D_3 and D_5 state-on

For an operating phase, we determinate the di/dt through each inductance (L_i and L_o) and the voltage across each diode. In order to simplify results presentation, we consider that the line is balanced (same RMS voltages and line inductances L_i) and have no resistive part.

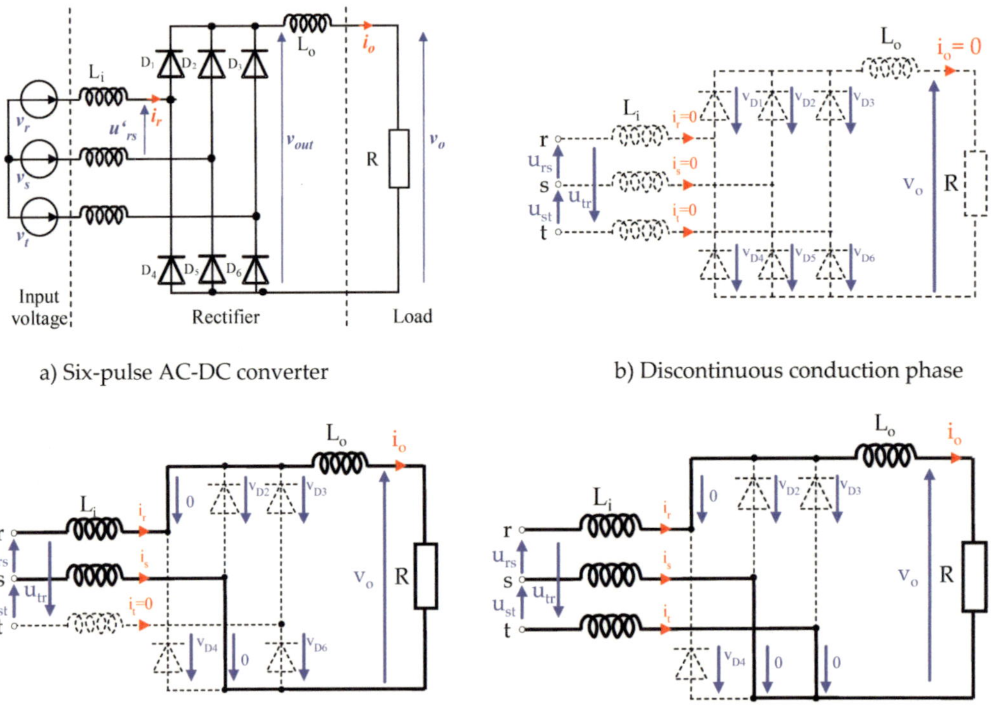

a) Six-pulse AC-DC converter b) Discontinuous conduction phase

c) Conduction phase P1 : D1 et D5 state-on d) Overlap phase O1 : D1 D5 et D6 state-on

Figure 15. Six-pulse diode rectifier.

Naturally, the method is equivalent under unbalanced conditions but the mathematical expressions of the different variables are more complex.

As an example, we will consider the following succession of phases: P_0, P_1, O_1, P_2, O_2, P_3…:

To shift from phase P_0 (diodes state-off) to phase P_1 (D_1 D_5 state-on), the voltage across diodes D_1 and D_5 have to be equal to zero.

To shift from phase P_1 (D_1 D_5 state-on) to overlap phase O_1 (D_1 D_5 D_6 state-on), the voltage across the diode D_6 has to be equal to zero.

To shift from overlap phase O_1 (D_1 D_5 D_6 state-on) to phase P_2 (D_1 D_6 state-on), the current through the diode D_5 has to be equal to zero.

And so forth …

5.1.1. Discontinuous conduction mode

This mode corresponds to the case where $i_o = 0$ (figure 15b). In this case, all diodes are opened. Equation (24) describes this mode.

$$\frac{di_r}{dt} = \frac{di_s}{dt} = \frac{di_t}{dt} = 0 \tag{24}$$

5.1.2. Continuous conduction mode

Let's take example of the continuous conduction mode P_1. From the figure 15c, we can write equations (25), (26) and (27) :

$$\frac{di_r}{dt} = -\frac{di_s}{dt} = \frac{di_o}{dt} = \frac{u_{rs} - v_o}{2L_i + L_o} \tag{25}$$

$$\frac{di_t}{dt} = 0 \tag{26}$$

$$v_{D6} = u_{st} \frac{L_i}{2L_i + L_o} \left(u_{rs} - v_o\right) \tag{27}$$

We obtain the di/dt corresponding to the other continuous conduction modes by making circular permutations of indexes. For example, for conduction mode P_2: D_1 and D_6 are state-on. The indexes s and t are permuted as presented below:

$$\frac{di_r}{dt} = -\frac{di_t}{dt} = \frac{di_o}{dt} = \frac{u_{rt} - v_o}{2L_i + L_o} \tag{28}$$

$$\frac{di_s}{dt} = 0 \tag{29}$$

5.1.3. Overlap phases

Let's take example of the overlap phase O_1. From the figure 15c, we can write equations (30) and (31) :

$$\frac{di_r}{dt} = \frac{di_o}{dt} \tag{30}$$

$$i_s + i_t = -i_0 \Leftrightarrow -\frac{di_s}{dt} - \frac{di_t}{dt} = \frac{di_o}{dt} \tag{31}$$

The expression of the di/dt as a function of the device parameters is more complicated to obtain here than in the case of a classical operating phase. Equations have been detailed in (Batard et al., 2007) and the final result is recalled below:

$$\frac{di_r}{dt} = \frac{di_o}{dt} = \frac{1}{3\,L_i + 2\,L_o}\left[u_{rs} + u_{rt} - 2\,v_o\right] \tag{32}$$

$$\frac{di_s}{dt} = \frac{1}{3\,L_i + 2\,L_o}\left(-\frac{2\,L_i + L_o}{L_i}u_{rs} + \frac{L_i + L_o}{L_i}u_{rt} + v_o\right) \tag{33}$$

$$\frac{di_t}{dt} = \frac{1}{3\,L_i + 2\,L_o}\left(\frac{L_i + L_o}{L_i}u_{rs} - \frac{2\,L_i + L_o}{L_i}u_{rt} + v_o\right) \tag{34}$$

We obtain the di/dt corresponding to the other overlap modes by making circular permutations of indexes. For example, for overlap mode O_2: D_1, D_2 and D_6 are state-on. The indexes r and t are permuted and the sign of v_s and di_o/dt are changed:

$$\frac{di_r}{dt} = \frac{1}{3\,L_i + 2\,L_o}\left(\frac{L_i + L_o}{L_i}u_{ts} - \frac{2\,L_i + L_o}{L_i}u_{tr} - v_o\right) \tag{35}$$

$$\frac{di_s}{dt} = \frac{1}{3\,L_i + 2\,L_o}\left(-\frac{2\,L_i + L_o}{L_i}u_{ts} + \frac{L_i + L_o}{L_i}u_{tr} - v_o\right) \tag{36}$$

$$\frac{di_t}{dt} = -\frac{di_o}{dt} = \frac{1}{3\,L_i + 2\,L_o}\left[u_{ts} + u_{tr} + 2\,v_o\right] \tag{37}$$

5.2. Simulink model

The simulink model of the six-pulse diode rectifier is illustrated in figure 16a. The resistive load is modelled as a gain. The internal structure of the diodes rectifier block is presented in figure 16b. Four different blocks can be seen on this scheme.

The first one called MF1 is a Matlab function which computes each diode voltage. The inputs of this block are the initial phase and the three-phase network voltages.

The second one called MF2 is also a Matlab function which computes the new operating phase and each inductance di/dt. Its computing algorithm is shown in figure 16d. The new operating phase depends on the initial phase, the diode voltages and currents.

The third, called "Initial Phase" extract the operating phase of the MF2 block, this operating phase becomes the initial phase of the next calculation step (the Simulink block "memory" is used).

The Current block computes each diode current which permits to obtain the DC current and the line currents.

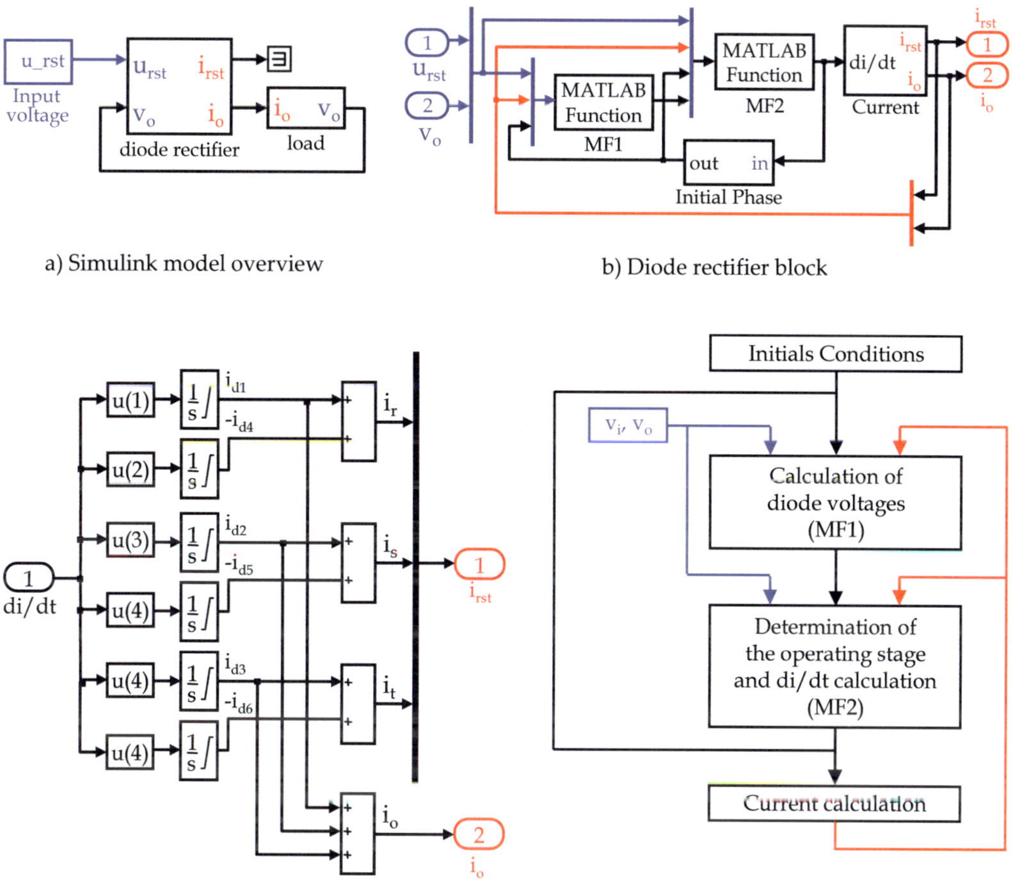

a) Simulink model overview

b) Diode rectifier block

c) Diode current block

d) Computing algorithm

Figure 16. Diode rectifier model

The internal structure of the Current block is shown in figure 16c. The originality of our approach is the calculation of the values of each diode current with the values of di/dt of inductances L_i and L_o. We use then six integrator blocks (one for each diode). The integrator blocks are set to limit their minimal output value to zero (lower saturation limit), this feature permits to avoid the problem of accurate determination of the instant when diodes currents reach to zero.

It is then possible to determinate the output current of the rectifier ($i_o = i_{D1} + i_{D2} + i_{D3}$) and the input line currents ($i_r = i_{D1} - i_{D4}$, $i_s = i_{D2} - i_{D5}$, $i_t = i_{D3} - i_{D6}$).

5.3. Experimental validation

Simulations and experimental waveforms related to figure 15 are shown in figure 17. The simulation parameters are adjusted as follows:

$$U_{RMS} = 230\ \text{V}\ ;\ R = 58\ \Omega\ ;\ L_i = 800\ \mu\text{H}\ ;\ L_o = 800\ \text{mH}$$

It can be seen that the simulated waveforms are very close to the experimental ones. The overlap interval υ_1 is equivalent for simulation and experimental results ($\upsilon_1 \cong 0.7$ ms).

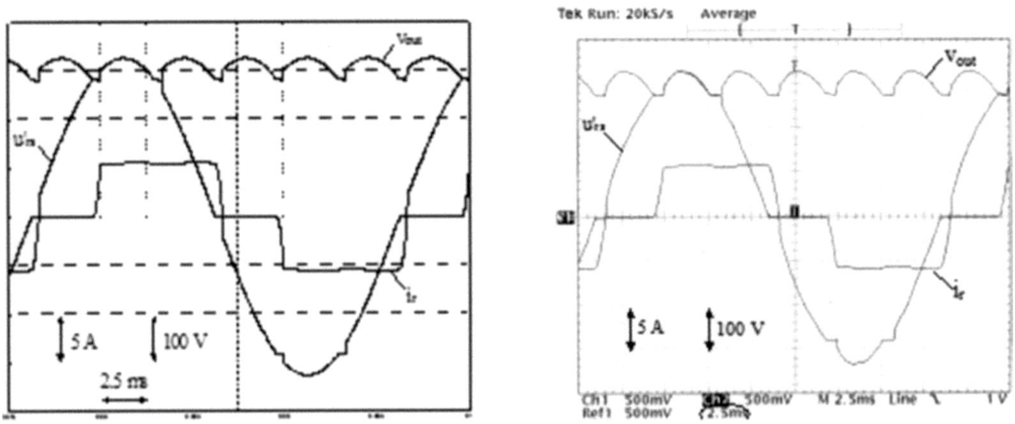

a) Simulation b) Experimental result

Figure 17. Comparison of Simulation and Experimental Waveforms in a six-pulse diode rectifier

The list of configuration parameters used for Matlab simulation is:

Start time : 0	Stop time : 0.2s
Type : Variable-step	Solver : ode15s (stiff/NDF)
Max step size : 1e-4	Relative tolerance : 1e-5
Min step size : auto	absolute tolerance : auto

Using a PC with an Intel core 2 duo CPU running at 2.19 GHz with 1 Go de RAM, the simulation time was 4 s.

This model has also been tested with a load constituted of an inverter and an induction machine. The results of this test have validated operations for discontinuous conduction mode. For the same configuration parameters, the simulation time was 5 s.

6. Modeling and simulation of thyristor rectifiers

The Simulink model of the controlled rectifier is very close to the Simulink model of the diode rectifier. Only the condition to turn the thyristor on is different to the condition to turn the diode on. For an ideal thyristor, it is recalled that the thyristor turn-on if its voltage is positive and if a current pulse is sent to the gate.

To illustrate the modelling of controlled rectifier with Simulink, let's look at one of the principles of speed control of DC machines.

6.1. Electrical model

Let us consider the electrical scheme presented on figure 18a. It represents a DC motor fed by a six-pulse rectifier. The electrical equivalent circuit of the DC motor is described by an inductance L_a in series with a resistance R_a in series with an induced voltage V_a which characterizes the electromotive force, as illustrated in figure 18b.

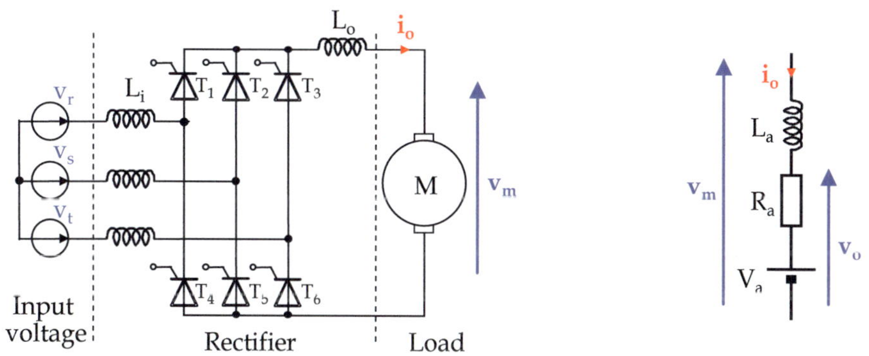

a) Electrical circuit b) Simplified electrical circuit of a DC motor

Figure 18. Controlled rectifier with inductive load

The thyristor are modelled by an ideal model which traduces the state of the switch:

- $V_T = 0$ when the thyristor is state-on
- $I_T = 0$ when the thyristor is state-off

Similar to the diode rectifier, there are 13 operating phases to describe:

- 1 phase of discontinuous conduction mode (P_0)

All the thyristor are state-off

- 6 phases of classical conduction P_1 to P_6 (figure 15c)

P_1 : T_1 and T_5 state-on P_2 : T_1 and T_6 state-on P_3 : T_2 and T_6 state-on

P_4 : T_2 and T_4 state-on P_5 : T_3 and T_4 state-on P_6 : T_3 and T_5 state-on

- 6 phases of overlap O_1 to O_6 (figure 15d)

O_1 : T_1, T_5 and T_6 state-on O_2 : T_1, T_2 and T_6 state-on O_3 : T_2, T_4 and T_6 state-on

O_4 : T_2, T_3 and T_4 state-on O_5 : T_3, T_4 and T_5 state-on O_6 : T_1, T_3 and T_5 state on

The different operating phases are illustrated in figure 15. The equations that governs an operating phase are the same whatever we work on a diode rectifier or a controlled rectifier.

6.2. Simulink model

The simulink model of the controlled rectifier with inductive load is presented in figure 19. It consists of four blocks:

- Input Voltage block characterizes the mains supply,
- teta_r block models the thyristor control,
- Controlled rectifier block computes the different operating phases.
- The load block represents the motor resistance R_a and the induced voltage V_a.

The motor inductance L_a is regrouped with the output line inductance L_o to have a single output inductor L_{oeq}.

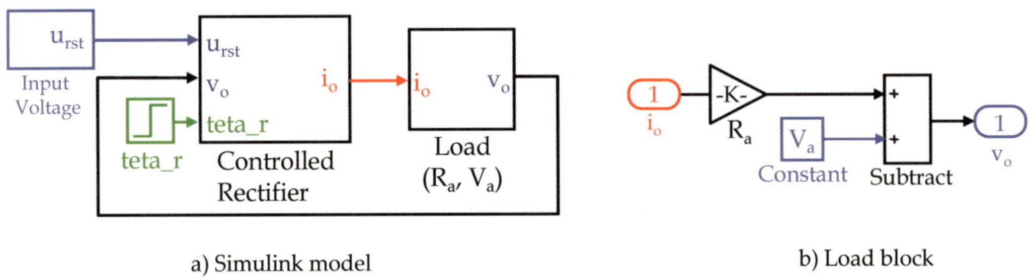

Figure 19. Simulink model of the controlled rectifier with inductive load

6.2.1. Internal structure of the rectifier block

The structure of the rectifier block is presented on figure 20a. Four different blocks can be seen on this scheme: the first one called "Control T" is used for the control of the thyristor gate. The second one called MF1 is used to compute the inductances state and voltage. The third called Current computes inductances currents. Then, the Initial Phase block computes the initial state for next computing phase.

The computing algorithm has been created in accordance with figure 20b. For each computing step, the new operating phase is calculated. This phase is a function of the initial phase, the sign of the inductance currents and the diode voltages. For each operating phase, the value of each inductance di/dt is calculated and permits to know the diodes currents with the integrator function.

The current block is strictly identical to the current block shown in figure 16.

6.2.2. Thyristor control

The control device for thyristor T_1 is presented in figure 21. The switch-on of T_1 is delayed of θ_r after u_{rt} has reached to zero (block "Delay 1"). The control thus carried out is a pulse train (the width of a pulse is computed by block "Delay 2").

The same principle is applied to the other thyristor.

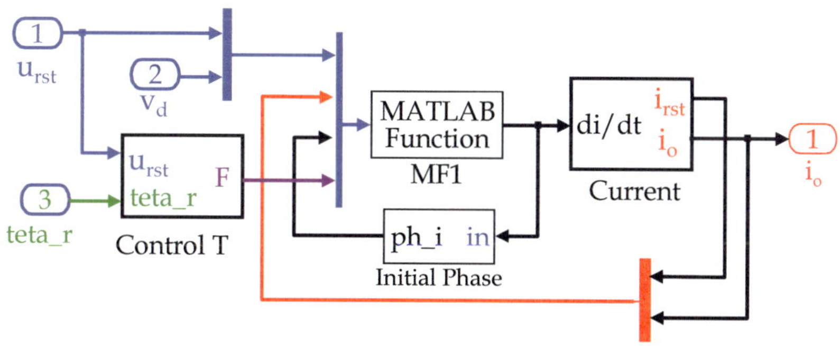

a) Structure of the rectifier block

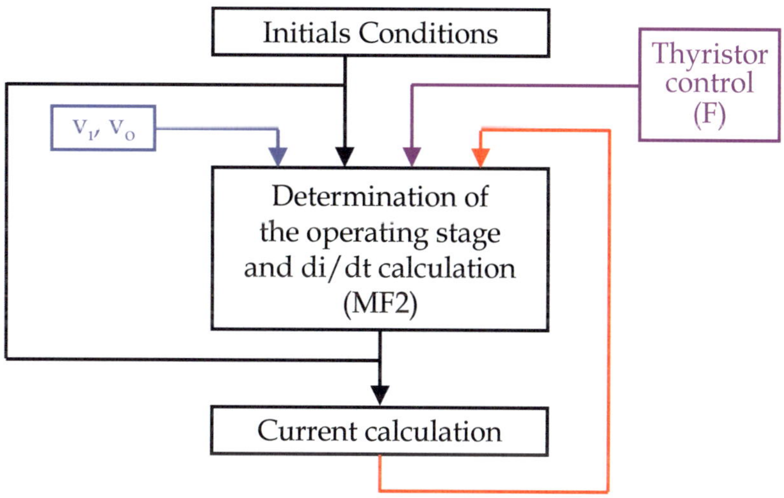

b) Computing algorithm

Figure 20. Structure of the rectifier block

6.3. Experimental validation in continuous conduction mode

Simulations and experimental waveforms related to the electrical circuit presented in figure 18 are shown in figure 22. The simulation parameters are adjusted as follows:

$$U_{RMS} = 230\ V\ ;\ R_a = 4\ \Omega\ ;\ V_a = 145\ V;\ L_i = 800\ \mu H\ ;\ L_{oeq} = 800\ mH$$

The list of configuration parameters used for Matlab simulation is:

Start time : 0	Stop time : 0.2s
Type : Variable-step	Solver : ode15s (stiff/NDF)
Max step size : 1e-4	Relative tolerance : 1e-5
Min step size : auto	absolute tolerance : auto

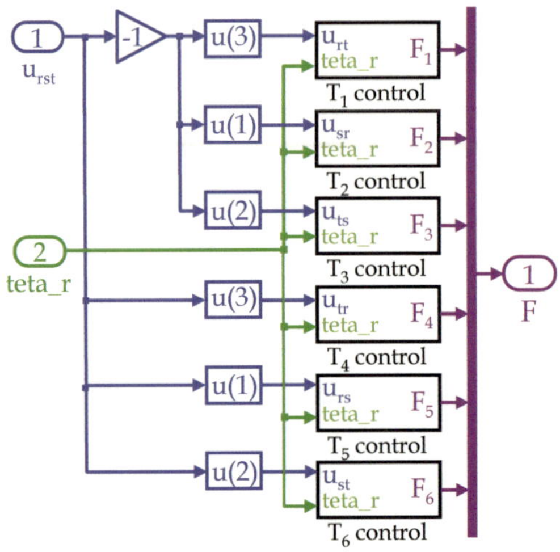

a) Control T block

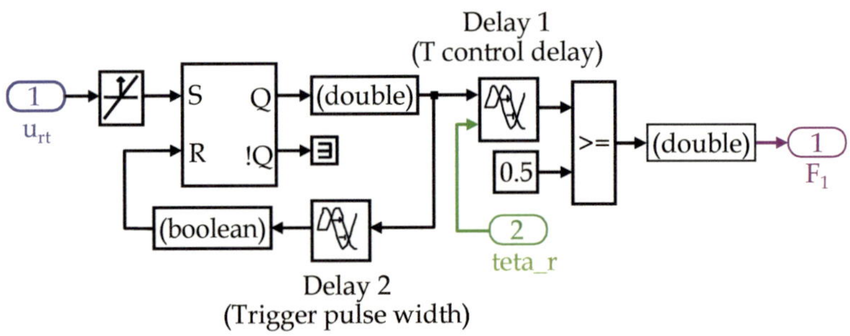

b) T_1 Control block

Figure 21. Control of thyristor T_1

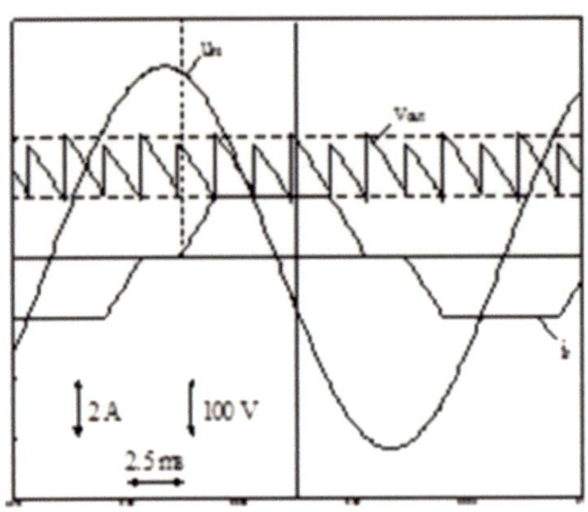

a) Simulation

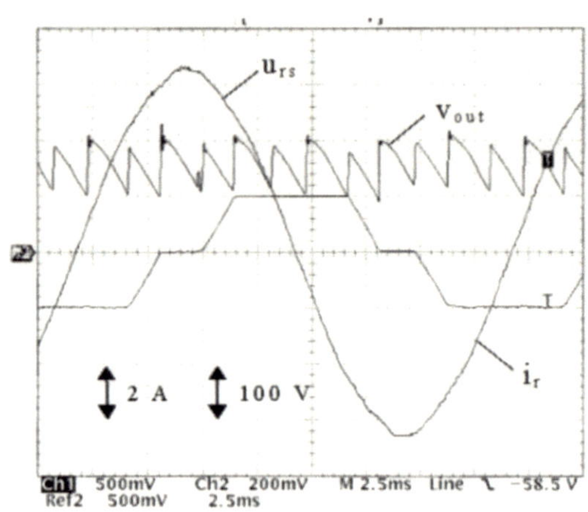

b) Experimental result

Figure 22. Comparison of Simulation and Experimental Waveforms

We can see that simulation results are in good agreement with experimental waveforms. The overlap delays are equivalent for simulation and experimental results.

7. Conclusion

This chapter has shown that it is possible to simulate many electrical power converters only using Simulink toolbox of Matlab, thus avoiding the purchase of expensive and complex dedicated software. The simulation method is based on the variable topology approach where switching conditions of semiconductor are realized by switching functions.

The first part of this chapter is dedicated to the modelling of linear loads: RL series, RLC series and L in series with RC parallel dipoles are considered. The second part deals with the simulation of DC-DC converters. The buck converter is first studied: after describing the operating phases, open-loop and closed-loop models are presented. A simulation is realised for closed-loop model showing good agreement with theoretical values. The third part shows how to model three-phases DC-AC converters. The electrical circuit and his complete Simulink model are presented and simulation results on RL series load with PWM control are shown. The fourth part presents the modelling of a six-pulse AC-DC converter which is frequently used in industrial applications. The complete model of this converter and his Simulink equivalent circuit are accurately described taking into account overlap phenomenon. A simulation result on RL series load is presented and compared to experimental result. The similarity of the two results shows the validity of the proposed model. The fifth part extends the method to controlled rectifier. The structure studied here is a six-pulse thyristor rectifier feeding a DC motor. The difference with the diode rectifier is presented with the introduction of a thyristor control block in the simulation. Simulations results are showed in continuous condition mode and are in good agreement with experimental results.

Many of the results presented in this chapter are computed with short simulation times (few seconds). This can be achieved thanks to the simplicity of the proposed method. The power electronics converters presented are used alone but the method can be easily extended to cascaded devices allowing the simulation of complex power electronic structures such as, for example, active filters with non-linear loads.

Author details

Christophe Batard, Frédéric Poitiers, Christophe Millet and Nicolas Ginot
Lunam University - University of Nantes, UMR CNRS 6164 ,
Institut d'Electronique et de Télécommunications de Rennes (IETR), France

8. References

Ladoux, P.; Postiglione, G.; Foch, H.; & Nuns, J.; "A Comparative Study of AC/DC Converters for High-Power DC Arc Furnace," *IEEE Trans. Indus. Electron.*, vol. 52, no. 3, pp. 747-757, June 2005.

Qijun, P.; Weiming, M.; Dezhi, L.; Zhihua, Z. & Jin, M.; "A New Critical Formula and Mathematical Model of Double-Tap Interphase Reactor in a Six-Phase Tap-Changer Diode Rectifier," *IEEE Trans. Indus. Electron.*, vol. 52, no. 1, pp 479-485, Feb. 2007.

P. Zuniga-Haro, J. M. Ramirez, "Multi-pulse Switching Functions Modeling of Flexible AC Transmission Systems Devices", Electric Power Components and Systems, Volume 37, Issue 1 January 2009 , pages 20 – 42.

R. E. Araujo, A. V. Leite and D. S. Freitas, "Modelling and simulation of power electronic systems using a bond graph formalism," *Proceedings of the 10th Mediterranean Conference on Control and Automation* - MED2002 Lisbon, Portugal, July 9-12, 2002.

F. Terrien, M. F. Benkhoris and R. Le Doeuff, "An Approach for Simulation of Power Electronic Systems," *Electrimacs' 99,* Saint Nazaire, France, vol. 2, pp 201-206.

S. E. M. de Oliveira and J. O. R. P. Guimaraes, "Effects of Voltage Supply Unbalance on AC Harmonic Current Components Produced by AC/DC Converters", *IEEE Trans. on Power Delivery*, vol. 22, no. 4, pp. 2498-2507, Oct. 2007.

L. Hu and R. E. Morrison "The use of modulation theory to calculate the harmonic distorsion in HVDC systems operating on an unbalanced supply," *IEEE Trans. on Power Delivery.*, vol. 12, no. 2, pp. 973-980, May 1997, Letters to editor.

J. Arrillaga, B. C. Smith, N. R. Watson and A. R. Wood, "Power system harmonic analysis," ed *John Wiley & Sons, 1997.*

A. Pandey, D. P. Kothari, A. K. Mukerjee, B. Singh, "Modelling and simulation of power factor corrected AC-DC converters", International Journal of Electrical Engineering Education, Volume 41, Issue 3, July 2004, pp 244-264.

C. Batard, F. Poitiers and M. Machmoum, "An Original Method to Simulate Diodes Rectifiers Behaviour with Matlab-Simulink Taking into Account Overlap Phenomenon," *IEEE International Symposium on Industrial Electronics 2007, ISIE 2007*, pp 971-976, Vigo, Spain, 4-7 June 2007

Chapter 4

Performances of the PCA Method in Electrical Machines Diagnosis Using Matlab

Jacques Fanjason Ramahaleomiarantsoa, Eric Jean Roy Sambatra, Nicolas Héraud and Jean Marie Razafimahenina

Additional information is available at the end of the chapter

http://dx.doi.org/10.5772/46449

1. Introduction

Nowadays, faults diagnosis is almost an inevitable step to be maintained in the optimal safety operating of every physical system. Electrical machines, main elements of every electromechanical system, are among the research topics of many academic and industrial laboratories because of the importance of their roles in the industrial process. Lots of technologies of these machines are old and well controlled. However, they remain the seat of several electrical and mechanical faults [1-4]. Thus, this article deals with faults detection of a wound rotor synchronous machine (WRIM) by the principal component analysis (PCA) method.

Several diagnostic methods have been proposed and used in the literature for the electrical machines diagnosis [1-4]. The PCA method, which showed his effectiveness in the fault detection and isolation (FDI), was implemented recently for the system diagnosis [5-8].

This work is then to prove the strength of PCA method in faults diagnosis of systems using WRIM as application device.

To proceed with, in the first, we propose an accurate analytical model of the WRIM without or in the presence of faults [1, 9]. This model provides the matrix data of several characteristic quantities of the machine. These data will be included as input variables of the PCA method.

Then, we present a complete approach of PCA method based on the study of residues [10]. Special attention has been paid for the choice of the number of principal components to be maintained [11, 12].

These models are then implemented in the Matlab software. Simulation results of several variables (stator and rotor currents, shaft rotational speed, electrical power, electromagnetic torque and other variables issued from mathematical transformations) of healthy and faulted WRIM are analyzed. Comparisons of simulation results with those of other diagnostic methods are performed to show the effectiveness and importance of the PCA method in fault diagnosis systems [9].

The following are the different steps of the approach:

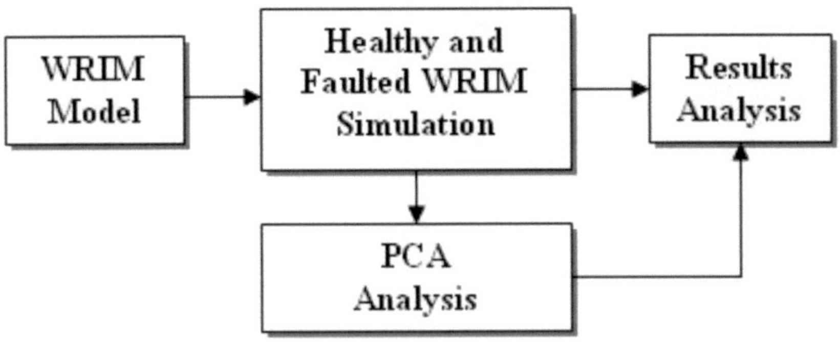

Figure 1. Synoptic diagram of the different steps of the data treatment

The Figure 1 shows that the proposed approach is divided in four blocs:

- WRIM modeling: mathematical equations calculation and simulation.
- Simulation :graph showing the output states of the system (healthy and faulted operation)
- Results Analysis: system diagnosis.
- PCA: data treatment.

2. WRIM modeling

In the process of faults survey and diagnosis, an accurate modeling of the machine is necessary. In this paper, three phases model based on magnetically coupled electrical circuits were chosen.

The aim of the modeling is to highlight the electrical faults influences on the different state variables of the WRIM. For that, some modeling assumptions given in the following section are necessary.

2.1. Modeling assumptions

In the proposed approach, we assumed that:

- the magnetic circuit is linear, and the relative permeability of iron is very large compared to the vacuum,
- the skin effect is neglected,

- hysteresis and eddy currents are neglected,
- the airgap thickness is uniform,
- magnetomotive force created by the stator and the rotor windings is sinusoidal distribution along the airgap,
- the stator and the rotor have the same number of turns in series per phase,
- the coils have the same properties,
- the WRIM stator and rotor coils are coupled in star configuration and connected to the considered balanced state grid.

2.2. Differential equation system of the WRIM

We note that the voltage vectors ($[V_S]$, $[V_R]$), the current vectors ($[I_S]$, $[I_R]$) and the flux vectors ($[\Phi_S]$, $[\Phi_R]$) of the stator and rotor are respectively:

$$[V_S] = \begin{bmatrix} V_A \\ V_B \\ V_C \end{bmatrix}; \ [I_S] = \begin{bmatrix} I_A \\ I_B \\ I_C \end{bmatrix}; \ [\phi_S] = \begin{bmatrix} \phi_A \\ \phi_B \\ \phi_C \end{bmatrix}$$

$$[V_R] = \begin{bmatrix} V_a \\ V_b \\ V_c \end{bmatrix}; \ [I_R] = \begin{bmatrix} I_a \\ I_b \\ I_c \end{bmatrix}; \ [\phi_R] = \begin{bmatrix} \phi_a \\ \phi_b \\ \phi_c \end{bmatrix}$$

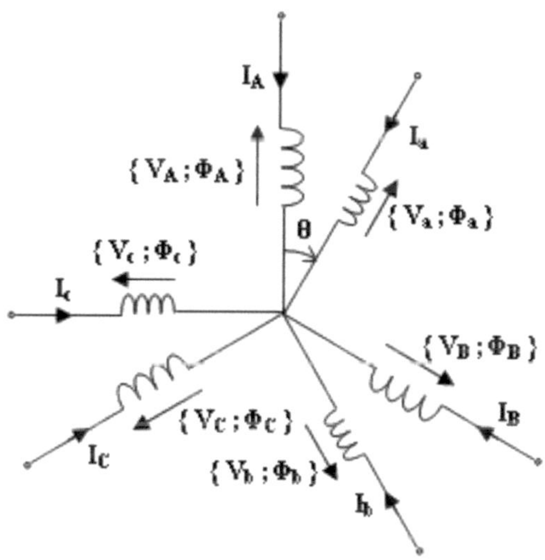

Figure 2. Equivalent electrical circuit of the WRIM

V_j, I_j and Φ_j (j : A, B, C for the stator phases and a, b, c, for the rotor phases) are respectively the voltages, the electrical currents and the magnetic flux of the stator and the rotor phases, θ is the angular position of the rotor relative to the stator.

The Figure 2 shows the equivalent electrical circuit of the WRIM. Each coil, for both stator and rotor, is modelised with a resistance and an inductance connected in series configuration (Figure 3).

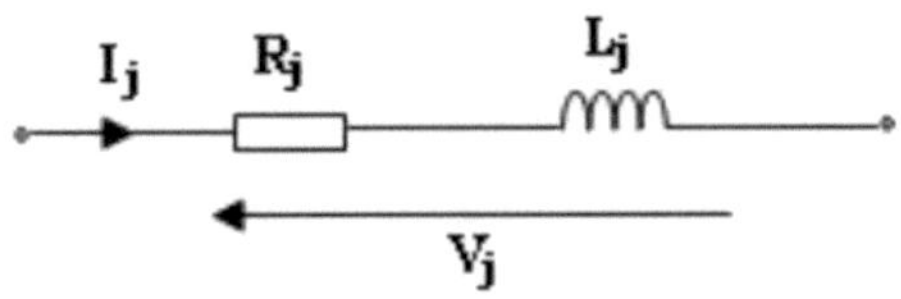

Figure 3. Equivalent electrical circuit of the WRIM coils

$$[V_S]=[R_S]\,[I_S]+\frac{d[\phi_S]}{dt} \tag{1}$$

$$[V_R]=[R_R]\,[I_R]+\frac{d[\phi_R]}{dt} \tag{2}$$

$$[\phi_S]=[L_S]\,[I_S]+[M_{SR}]\,[I_R] \tag{3}$$

$$[\phi_R]=[L_R]\,[I_R]+[M_{RS}]\,[I_S] \tag{4}$$

$[R_S]$ and $[R_R]$ are the resistance matrices, $[L_S]$ and $[L_R]$ the self inductance matrices, and $[M_{SR}]$ and $[M_{RS}]$ the mutual inductances matrix between the stator and the rotor coils.

With (3) and (4), (1) and (2) become:

$$[V_S]=[R_S]\,[I_S]+\frac{d\{[L_S]\,[I_S]\}}{dt}+\frac{d\{[M_{SR}]\,[I_R]\}}{dt} \tag{5}$$

$$[V_R]=[R_R]\,[I_R]+\frac{d\{[L_R]\,[I_R]\}}{dt}+\frac{d\{[M_{RS}]\,[I_S]\}}{dt} \tag{6}$$

By applying the fundamental principle of dynamics to the rotor, the mechanical motion equation is [13]:

$$J_t\frac{d\Omega}{dt}+f_v\Omega=C_{em}-C_r \tag{7}$$

$$\Omega=\frac{d\theta}{dt} \tag{8}$$

with:

$$C_{em}=\frac{1}{2}[I]^t*\frac{d([L])}{d\theta}*[I] \tag{9}$$

is the total inertia brought to the rotor shaft, the shaft rotational speed, $[I]=[I_A\ I_B\ I_C\ I_a\ I_b\ I_c]^t$ the current vectors, the viscous friction torque, the electromagnetic torque, the load torque, the angular position of the rotor relative to the stator and $[L]$ the inductance matrix of the machine.

Introducing the cyclic inductances of the stator and the rotor $L_{SC}=\frac{3}{2}L_S$ and $L_{RC}=\frac{3}{2}L_R$ (L_S is the self inductance of each phase of the stator and L_R is the self inductance of each phase of the rotor), the mutual inductances between the stator and the rotor coils M_{SR} and pole pair number p, the inductance matrix of the WRIM can be written as follow:

$$[L]=\begin{bmatrix} L_{SC} & 0 & 0 & M_{SR}f_1 & M_{SR}f_2 & M_{SR}f_3 \\ 0 & L_{SC} & 0 & M_{SR}f_3 & M_{SR}f_1 & M_{SR}f_2 \\ 0 & 0 & L_{SC} & M_{SR}f_2 & M_{SR}f_3 & M_{SR}f_1 \\ M_{SR}f_1 & M_{SR}f_3 & M_{SR}f_2 & L_{RC} & 0 & 0 \\ M_{SR}f_2 & M_{SR}f_1 & M_{SR}f_3 & 0 & L_{RC} & 0 \\ M_{SR}f_3 & M_{SR}f_2 & M_{SR}f_1 & 0 & 0 & L_{RC} \end{bmatrix} \tag{10}$$

$$f_1=\cos(p\theta) \tag{11}$$

$$f_2=\cos(p\theta+\frac{2\pi}{3}) \tag{12}$$

$$f_3=\cos(p\theta-\frac{2\pi}{3}) \tag{13}$$

By choosing the stator and rotor currents, the shaft rotational speed and the angular position of the rotor relative to the stator as state variables, the differential equation system modeling the WRIM is given by:

$$[\dot{X}]=[A]^{-1}([U]-[B][X]) \tag{14}$$

with:

$$[X]=[I_A\ I_B\ I_C\ I_a\ I_b\ I_c\ \Omega\ \theta]^t$$

$$[A]=\begin{bmatrix} [L] & 0 & 0 \\ 0 & J_t & 0 \\ 0 & 0 & 1 \end{bmatrix};\ [U]=\begin{bmatrix} [V] \\ -C_r \\ 0 \end{bmatrix};$$

$$[V]=[V_A\ V_B\ V_C\ V_a\ V_b\ V_c]^t;$$

$$[B]=\begin{bmatrix} [R]+\Omega\frac{d[L]}{d\theta} & 0 & 0 \\ -\frac{1}{2}[I]^t\frac{d[L]}{d\theta} & f_v & 0 \\ 0 & -1 & 0 \end{bmatrix}$$

This model of the WRIM will be used to simulate both the healthy and the faulted configuration of the stator and the rotor.

2.3. WRIM faults

Despite the constant improvements on technical design of reliable machine, different types of faults still exist. The faults can be resulted by normal wear, poor design, poor assembly (misalignment), improper use or combination of these different causes.

Figure 4 and Figure 5 show the faults distribution carried out by a German company on industrial systems. The Figure 4 shows the faults of the low and medium power machines (50KW to 200KW), and the Figure 5 those of the high power machines (from 200KW) [1-2].

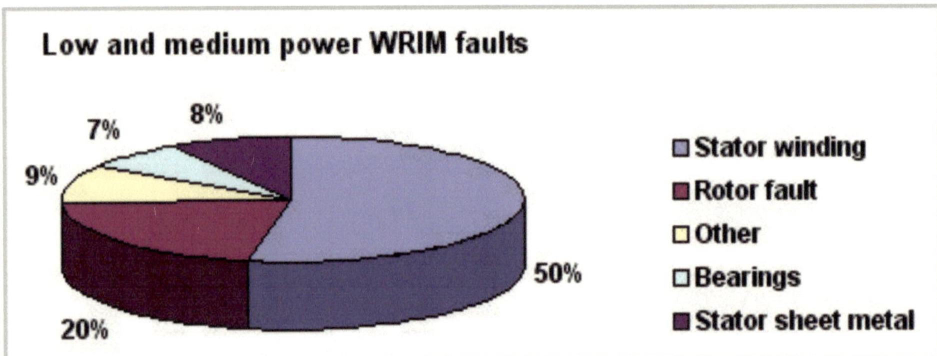

Figure 4. Low and medium power induction machines faults [1-2]

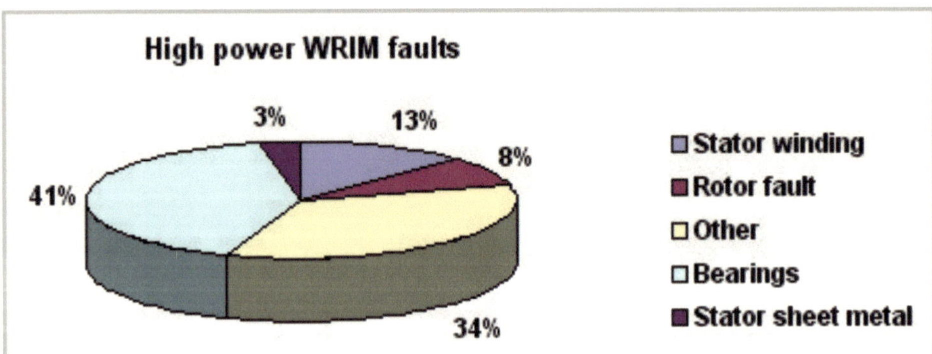

Figure 5. High power induction machines faults [1-2]

Figure 4 shows that the most encountered faults of the low and medium power on the induction machines are the stator faults and the Figure 5 shows that the faults due to mechanical defects give the highest percentage. The induction machine faults can be classified into four categories [2]:

The stator faults can be found on the coils or the breech. In most cases, the winding failure is caused by the inter-turns faults. These last grow and cause different faults between coils, between several phases or between phase and earth point before the deterioration of the machine [3]. The breech of electrical machines is built with insulated thin steel sheets in order to minimize the eddy currents for a greater operational efficiency. For the medium and great power machines, the core is compressed before the steel sheets emplacement to minimize the rolling sheets vibrations and to maximize the thermal conduction. The core problems are very low, only 1% if compared to winding problems [4].

The rotor faults can be bar breaks, coils faults or rotor eccentricities.

The bearings faults can be caused by a poor choice of materials during the manufacturing steps, the problems of rotation within the breech caused by damaged, chipped or cracked bearing and can create disturbance within the machines.

The other defaults might be caused by flange or shaft defaults. The faults created by the machine flange are generally caused during the manufacturing step.

2.4. Considered faults

The considered faults are on the resistance values which increase due to the rise of their temperature. In normal operation, a resistance value variation compared to its nominal value (in ambient temperature, 25°C) is a faulted machine due to machine overload or coils fault [1,9]. The resistance versus the temperature is expressed as:

$$R = R_0(1 + \alpha \Delta T) \tag{15}$$

R_0 is the resistance value at T_0 = 25°C, α the temperature coefficient of the resistance and ΔT the temperature variation.

3. PCA methodology

The PCA method is based on simple linear algebra. It can be used as exploring tool, analyzing data and models design. The PCA method is based on the transformation of the data space representation. The new space dimension is smaller than that the original space dimension. It is classified as without model method, [5] and it can be considered as full identification method of physical systems [6]. The PCA method allows providing directly the redundancy relations between the variables without identifying the state representation matrix of the system. This task is often difficult to achieve.

3.1. PCA method formulation

We note by $x_i(j) = [x_1\ x_2\ x_3 \ldots x_m]$ the measurements vector. « *i* » represents the measurement variables that must be monitored (*i* = *1 to m*) and « *j* » the number of measurements for each variable « *m* », *j* = *1 to N*.

The measurements data matrix ($X_d \in R^{N*m}$) can be written as follows:

$$X_d = \begin{pmatrix} x_1(1) & \dots & x_m(1) \\ \dots & \dots & \dots \\ x_1(N) & \dots & x_m(N) \end{pmatrix} \tag{16}$$

The data matrix is described by a smallest new matrix, that is an orthogonal linear projection of a subspace of m dimension on a less dimension subspace l ($l<m$). The method consists in identifying the PCA model and it is based on two steps [10]:

- Determination on the eigenvalues and the eigenvectors of the covariance matrix R.
- Determination of the structure of the model, which consists in calculating the component number « l » to be retained in the PCA model.

3.2. Eigenvalues and eigenvectors determination

The first step is the data normalization. The variables must be centered and reduced. Then, the obtained normalized matrix is:

$$X = [X_1 \dots X_m] \tag{17}$$

And the covariance matrix R is given by:

$$R = \frac{1}{N-1} XX^T \tag{18}$$

By decomposing R, (17) can be expressed as:

$$R = P \Lambda P^T \tag{19}$$

With

$$PP^T = P^T P = I_m \tag{20}$$

Λ is the diagonal matrix of the eigenvectors of R and their eigenvalues are ordered in descending order with respect to magnitude values ($\lambda_1 \geq \lambda_2 \geq \dots \geq \lambda_m$).

The eigenvectors matrix P is expressed as:

$$P = [p_1, p_2, \dots, p_m] \tag{21}$$

p_i is the orthogonal eigenvectors corresponding to the eigenvalue λ_i. Then, the principal components matrix can be calculated using:

$$T = XP \tag{22}$$

$$T \in \Re^{N*m}$$

3.3. PCA model construction

To obtain the structure of the model, the components number « l » to be retained must be determined. This step is very important for PCA construction. The component number can be determined by using the following:

$$\left(\frac{\sum_{i=1}^{l} \lambda_i}{\sum_{k=1}^{m} \lambda_k} \right) * 100 \geq thc, l < m \tag{23}$$

Where "*thc*" is an user defined threshold expressed as percentage. Now, user should retain only the components number « l » which was associated in the first term of (23). By reordering the eigenvalues, the minimum numbers of components are retained while still reaching the minimum variance threshold [14].

By taking into account the number of components to be retained and by partitioning the principal component matrix T, the eigenvectors matrix P and the eigenvalues matrix Λ [12], the constructed PCA model is given by:

$$T = \left[T_p^{N*l} T_r^{N*(m-l)} \right] \tag{24}$$

$$P = \left[P_p^{N*l} P_r^{N*(m-l)} \right] \tag{25}$$

$$\Lambda = \begin{bmatrix} \Lambda^{l*l} & \cdots & 0 \\ \vdots & \ddots & \vdots \\ 0 & \cdots & \Lambda^{(m-l)(m-l)} \end{bmatrix} \tag{26}$$

T_p and T_r are respectively the principal and residual parts of T, P_p and P_r are respectively the principal and residual parts of P.

With this PCA model, the centered and reduced matrix X can be written as:

$$X - P_p T_p^T + P_r T_r^T \tag{27}$$

By considering:

$$X_p = P_p T_p^T = \sum_{i=1}^{l} P_i T_i^T \tag{28}$$

$$E = P_r T_r^T - \sum_{i=l+1}^{m} P_i T_i^T \tag{29}$$

The centered and reduced data matrix is given by:

$$X = X_p + E \qquad (30)$$

X_p is the principal estimated matrix and E the residues matrix which represents information losses due to data matrix X reduction. It represents the difference between the exact and the approached representations of X. This matrix is associated with the lowest eigenvalues $\lambda_{l+1},...,\lambda_m$. Therefore, in this case, the data compression preserves all the best information that it conveys.

4. PCA method application on WRIM

4.1. Simulation conditions

Nine state variables (m=9) have been chosen to be monitored and 10000 measures (N=10000) during 4s are considered. The WRIM faults are introduced from the initial time (t=0s) to the final time (t=4s) of the different simulations. The machine is coupled to a mechanical load torque (10Nm) at t=2s. The considered faults are respectively, increases from 10% to 40% of the resistance value of both stator and rotor coils.

4.2. Choice of the number of principal components

The Figure 6 and the Figure 7 represent the residues variation of the WRIM stator current versus time and show impact of the « l » number in the diagnosis approach.

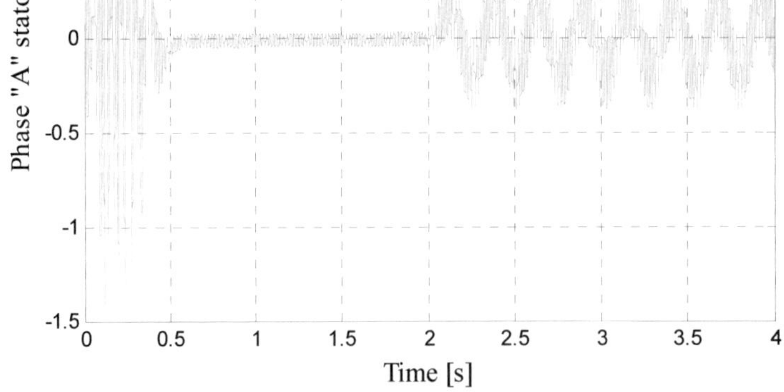

Figure 6. Stator current residue for $l = 5$

Figure 6 show that the chosen number of components is too high then the residual space dimension is reduced. Some faults are projected in the principal space and the stator current residues can not be detectable.

However, with the Figure 6, the number of components is well chosen. Faults can be detected and localized and the PCA model is well reconstructed.

Generally, the detection approach in the case of diagnosis based on analytical model is linked with the residues generation step. From these residues analysis, the decision making step must indicate if faults exist or not. The residues generation approach can be the state estimation approach or the parameter estimation approach.

The residue indicates the information losses given by the matrix dimension reduction of the state variables matrix data to be monitored. Indeed, a small residue means that the estimated value tends to approach the exact value in healthy operation case.

In our case, the eigenvalues corresponding to the number of the retained principal components represent 93% of the total sum of eigenvalues. Only 7% of the total represent the residues subspace. One can conclude that the PCA model has been well constructed.

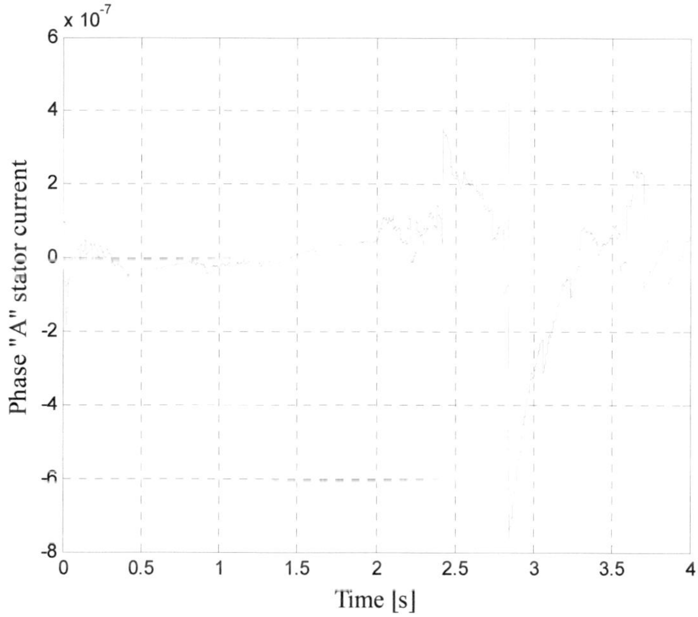

Figure 7. Stator current residue for $l = 6$

5. Simulation results

The different simulation results have been performed with respect to the simulation conditions mentioned earlier.

Figure 8 to Figure 13 and Figure 16 represent the real variations without PCA method, and Figure 14, Figure 15 and Figure 17 represent the residue variations with PCA application of the faulted WRIM state variables in considering the stator defaults.

With the WRIM state variables, other quantities obtained by their transformations have been calculated:

- quadrature axis and direct axis currents with Park transformation,
- α axis and β axis currents with Concordia transformation.

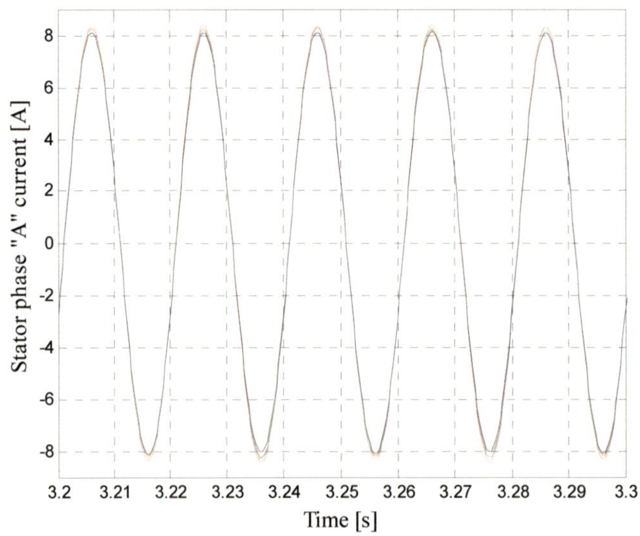

Figure 8. Real variations versus time of the stator current of the healthy and faulted WRIM

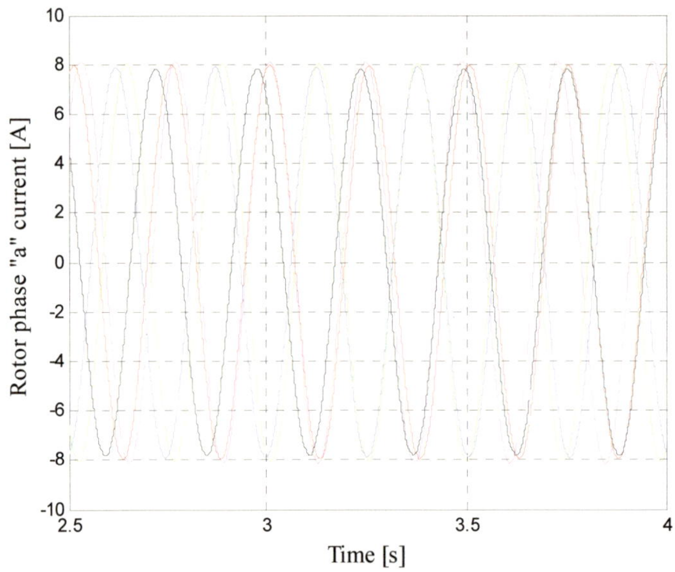

Figure 9. Real variations versus time of the rotor current of the healthy and faulted WRIM

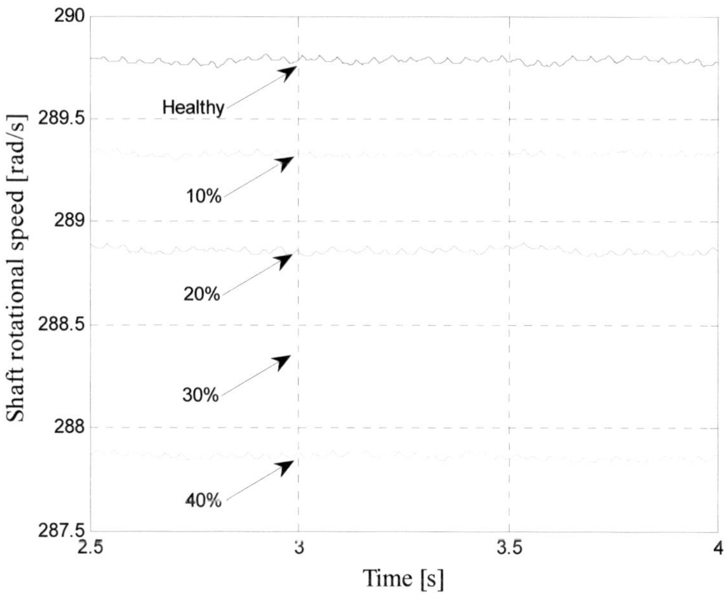

Figure 10. Real variations versus time of the shaft rotational speed of the healthy and faulted WRIM

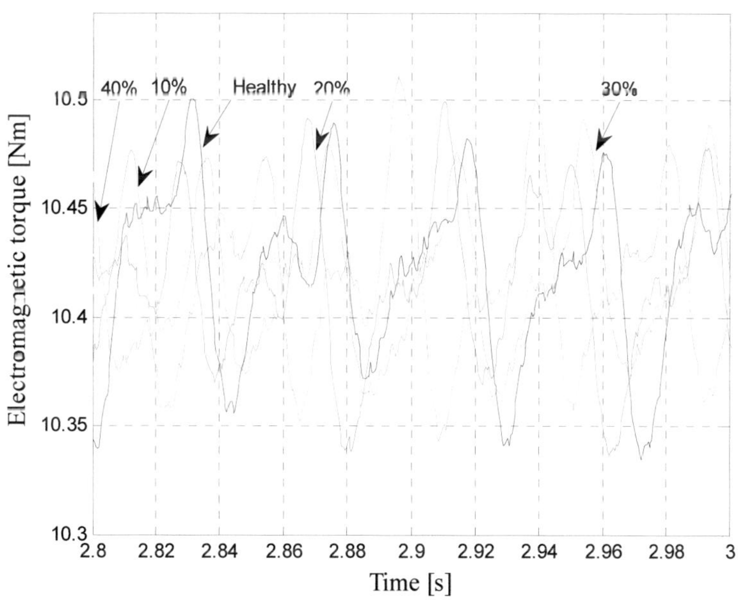

Figure 11. Real variations versus time of the electromagnetic torque of the healthy and faulted WRIM

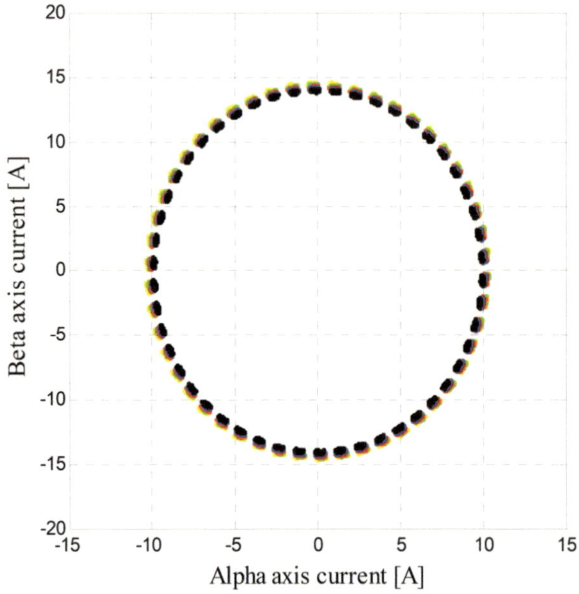

Figure 12. Real variations of β axis current versus the phase α axis current of the stator phase

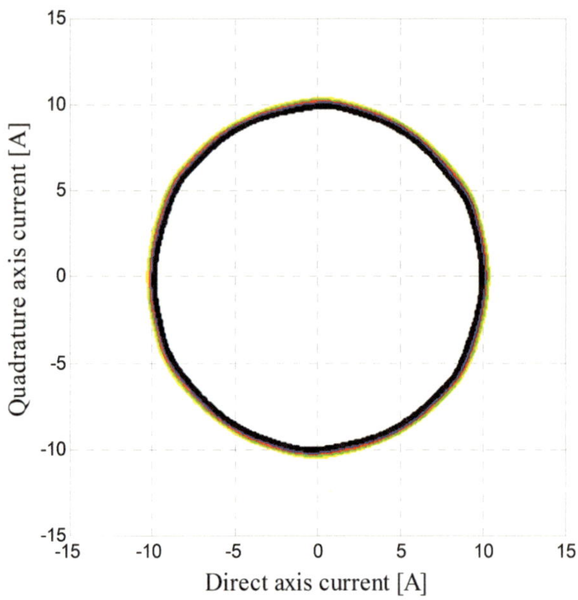

Figure 13. Real variations of the quadrature axis current versus the phase direct axis current of the stator phase

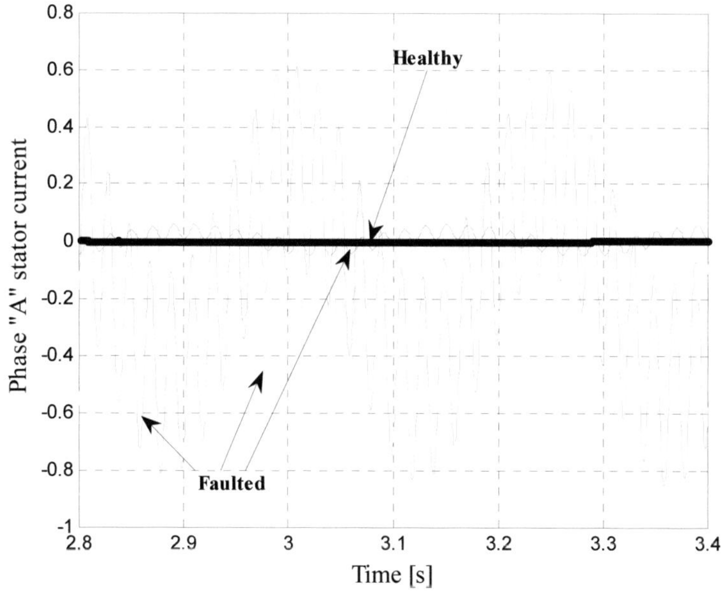

Figure 14. Variations of the stator phase "A" current residues versus time of the healthy and faulted WRIM

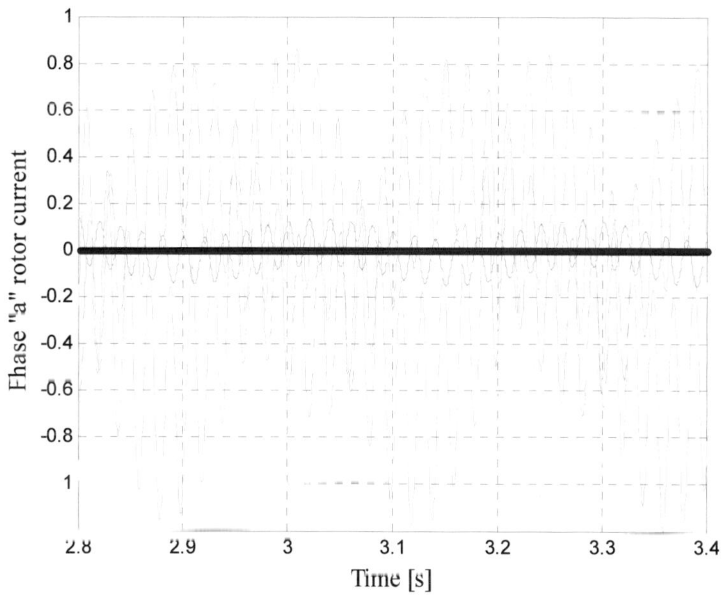

Figure 15. Variations of the rotor phase "a" current residues versus time of the healthy and faulted WRIM

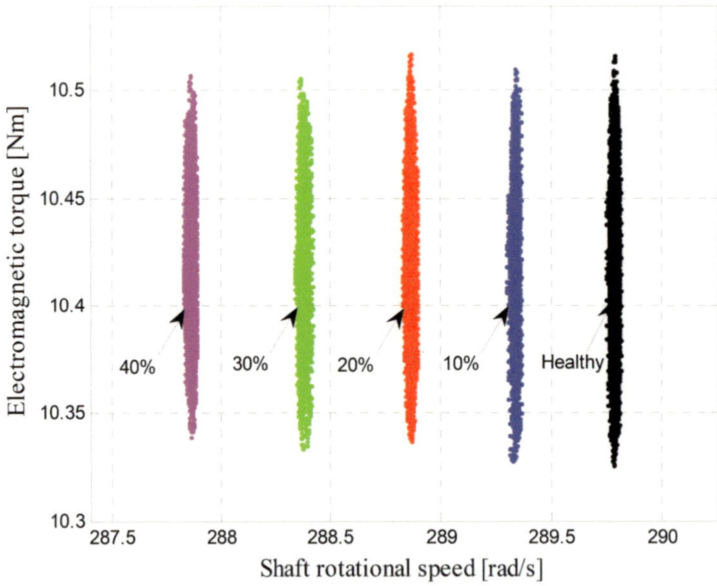

Figure 16. Real variations of electromagnetic torque versus the shaft rotational speed of the WRIM

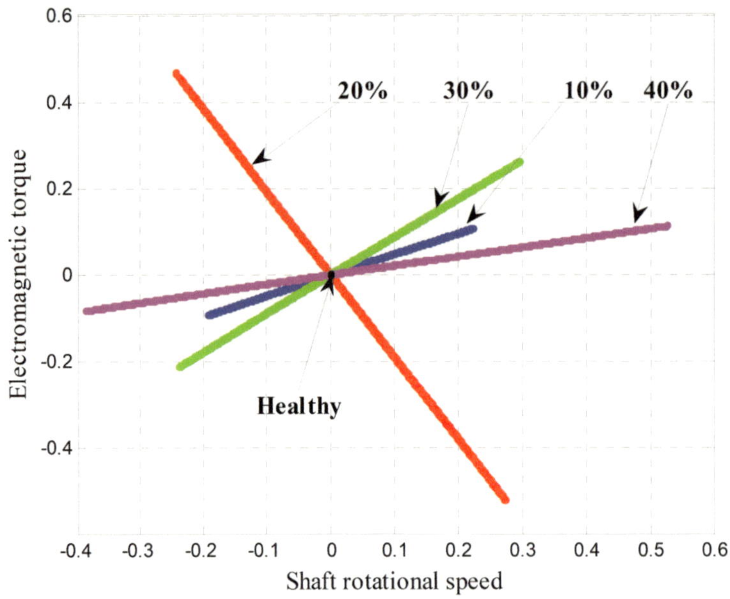

Figure 17. Variations of electromagnetic torque residues versus the shaft rotational speed residues of the WRIM

6. Discussion

Several types of representations are used in the signals processing domain, especially for the electrical machines diagnosis. We can mention the temporal representation (Figure 8 to Figure11, Figure 14 and Figure 15) and the signal frequency analysis. Although they have proved their efficiency, the state variable representations between them also show their advantages. They can be performed without mathematical transformation (Figure 16) and with mathematical transformation (Figure 12 and Figure 13).

The latter representation type and the temporal representation are confronted with the PCA method application results (Figure 14, Figure 15 and Figure 17). Only the simulation results with stator faults are presented because the global behavior of the state variables in both rotor and stator faults are almost similar.

For the temporal variations case, the rotor currents (Figure 9) and the shaft rotational speed (Figure 10) are the variables which produce the most information in presence of defaults. The defaults occur on the rotor current frequency and the shaft rotational speed magnitude.

The electromagnetic torque variations versus the shaft rotational speed also show clearly the WRIM operation zone in the presence of defaults (Figure 16). On the opposite, the representations with mathematical transformations (Figure 12 and Figure 13) do not provide significant information due to the fact that the stator currents remain almost unchanged in the presence of defaults (Figure 8).

With PCA method application, every representation type shows precisely the differences between healthy and faulted WRIM (Figure 14, Figure 15 and Figure 17). In the healthy case, residues are zero. When defaults appear, the residue representations have an effective value with an absolute value superior to zero.

In the figure 17, the healthy case is represented by a point situated on the coordinate origins. Therefore, one can show several right lines corresponding to the faulted cases. This behavior is due to the proportional characteristic of the considered faults.

PCA method proved to be very effective in electrical machines faults detection. This requires a good choice of the number of the principal components to be retained so that information contained in residues is relevant.

7. Implementation of the WRIM and the PCA models in the Matlab software

The differential equations system governing the WRIM is composed of linear differential equation which has the following form:

$$\frac{dy}{dt} = f(y) \tag{31}$$

Pre-programmed solvers are available in the Matlab software to solve easily this type of equation. These pre-programmed functions (ode45, ode113 ...) proposed by the software helped to solve correctly with scalable computation time by the number of data to be processed. We adopted *"ode45"*, solver based on the Runge-Kutta 4, 5 numerical resolution method. After creating a function detailing the differential equation system, we have to use it in the chosen solver to calculate numerically the equations governing the WRIM.

The following extract lines of code illustrate the use of the pre-programmed function *"ode45"* (Figure 18):

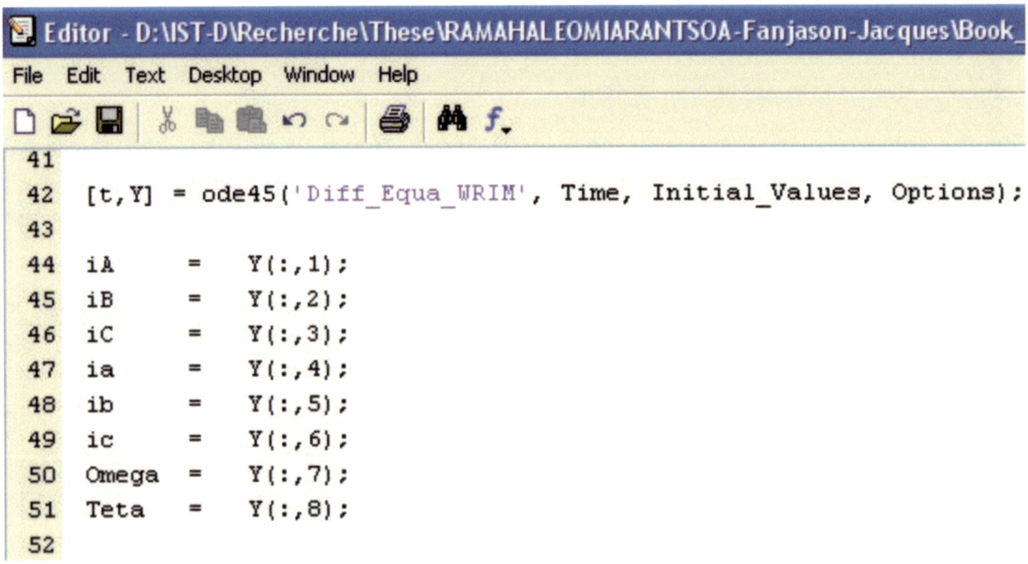

Figure 18. Use of ode45 solver to solve the differential equations system of the WRIM

The differential equations system is established in the *"Diff_Equa_WRIM"* function.

One of the major strengths of Matlab is the matrix manipulation. With the amount of data in matrix form that we consider in this paper, this feature of the software allows us to treat easily and without complexity these data. Thus, for the ACP method, matrix manipulations are done by simple operations because all variables in Matlab are intrinsically represented by matrix forms. In addition, pre-programmed functions are available to perform some precise operations such as the descendant sorting with *"descend"* function.

And finally, Matlab offers a multitude of possibilities for graphic representations. At the end of the PCA process, the original data and those from the treatment are represented graphically. This allowed more comparative studies as well as quantitative and qualitative analysis of the entire device. A function was reserved to the automatic superposition of curves of the same variables for the different considered defaults.

To summarize, three major functions have been developed to carry out the approach:

- resolution of de differential equations system governing the WRIM,

- resolution of the PCA method,
- visualization of comparative curves.

We would like to note that each approach has been developed as a separate function, but our program runs automatically. These functions are executed automatically, one after the other, in another function.

8. Conclusion

PCA method based on residues analysis has been established and applied on WRIM diagnosis.

An accurate analytical model of the machine has been proposed and simulated to perform the healthy and faulted data for PCA approach need.

Several representations of nine state variables of the machine have been analyzed. For the temporal variation without PCA, the rotor current and the shaft rotational speed are the more affected by the considered fault type. The representations of the electromagnetic torque versus the shaft rotational speed in both with and without PCA approach show clearly the presence of defaults. Indeed, PCA method is interesting for all types of representation compared to some other signal processing types.

Simulation results show the efficiency of the detection but require a good choice of the number of principal components.

Author details

Jacques Fanjason Ramahaleomiarantsoa and Nicolas Héraud
Université de Corse, U.M.R. CNRS 6134 SPE, BP 52, Corte, France

Eric Jean Roy Sambatra
Institut Supérieur de Technologie, BP 509, Antsiranana, Madagascar

Jean Marie Razafimahenina
Ecole Supérieure Polytechnique, BP O, Antsiranana, Madagascar

Acknowledgement

This research was supported by MADES/SCAC Madagascar project. We are grateful for technical and financial support.

9. References

[1] Benbouzid M. E. H (2000) A Review of Induction Motors Signature Analysis as a Medium for Faults Detection, IEEE Transactions On Industrial Electronics, vol. 47, N° 5, pp. 984-993.

[2] Chia-Chou Y & al. (2008) A reconfigurable motor for experimental emulation of stator winding interturn and broken bar faults in polyphase induction machines, 01, IEEE transactions on energy conversion, vol.23, n°4. pp. 1005-1014.
[3] Sin M.L, Soong W.L, Ertugrul N (2003) Induction machine on-line condition monitoring and fault diagnosis – a survey, University of Adelaide.
[4] Negrea M.D (2006) Electromagnetic flux monitoring for detecting faults in electrical machines, PhD, Helsinki University of Technology, Department of Electrical and Communications Engineering, Laboratory of Electromechanics, TKK Dissertations 51, Espoo Finland.
[5] Liu L (2006) Robust fault detection and diagnosis for permanent magnet synchronous motors, PhD dissertation, College of Engineering, The Florida State University, USA.
[6] Benaïcha A, GuerfeL M, Bouguila N, Benothman K (2010) New PCA-based methodology for sensor fault detection and localization, 8th International Conference of Modeling and Simulation, MOSIM'10, "Evaluation and optimization of innovative production systems of goods and services", Hammamet, Tunisia.
[7] Ku W, Storer R.H, Georgakis C (1995) Disturbance detection and isolation by dynamic principal component analysis. Chemometrics and Intelligent Laboratory Systems, 30. pp. 179-196.
[8] Huang B (2001) Process identification based on last principal component analysis, Journal of Process Control, 11. pp. 19-33.
[9] Ramahaleomiarantsoa J. F, Héraud N, Sambatra E. J. R, Razafimahenina J. M (2011) Principal Components Analysis Method Application in Electrical Machines Diagnosis, ICINCO'08, Noordwykerhout, Pays Bas.
[10] Li W, Qin S.J (2001) Consistent dynamic pca based on errors-in-variables Subspace identification, Journal of Process Control, 11(6). pp. 661-678.
[11] Valle S, Weihua L, Qin S.J (1999) Selection of the number of principal components: The variance of the reconstruction error criterion with a comparison to other methods, Industrial and Engineering Chemistry Research, vol. 38. pp. 4389-4401.
[12] Benaïcha A, Mourot G, Guerfel M, Benothman K, Ragot J (2010) A new method for determining PCA models for system diagnosis, 18th Mediterranean Conference on Control & Automation Congress Palace Hotel, Marrakech, Morocco June 23-25. pp. 862-867.
[13] Wieczorek M, Rosołowski E (2010) Modelling of induction motor for simulation of internal faults, Modern Electric Power Systems, MEPS'10, paper P29, Wroclaw, Poland.
[14] Halligan R.G, Jagannathan S (2009) PCA Based Fault isolation and prognosis with application to Water Pump, paper1, thesis, Fault detection and prediction with application to rotating machinery, Missouri University of Science and Technology.

Chapter 5

Dynamic and Quasi-Static Simulation of a Novel Compliant MEMS Force Amplifier by Matlab/Simulink

Ergin Kosa, Levent Trabzon, Umit Sonmez and Huseyin Kizil

Additional information is available at the end of the chapter

http://dx.doi.org/10.5772/46450

1. Introduction

MEMS are micro electromechanical systems having component sizes varying from 1 micrometer to 1 millimeter and provide specific engineering operations. MEMS are used as a micro sensor, micro actuator, micro accelerometer etc. and also have tendency to function rapidly due to having low inertia moment and affected less by disturbances coming from environment due to their small size (Hsu, 2002).

Compliant mechanisms having an ability to transmit motion and energy via their flexible hinges and/or flexible components instead of joints and rigid components, perform large deflections (Sreekumar et al, 2008). The large deflections of compliant mechanisms instead of rigid-body mechanisms depend on applied force that causes a much more complexity to nonlinear analysis (Ashok, 2000). Moreover, the geometry of several flexure hinges are modeled as torsion springs in its pseudo-rigid-body mechanisms (Howell, 2001). Flexible segments of compliant mechanism store and transfer energy when it is functioning (Howell, 2001; Tantanawat & S. Kota, 2007). Flexible links having small cross sections instead of traditional joints provide acting of mechanism due to its very low moment of inertia (Howell, 2001; Lobontiu et al, 2001).

Compliant four-link mechanism is designed as seen in Fig. 1 achieving force or displacement application according to the output spring constant and also, studied on size optimization to achieve maximum mechanical or geometric benefit at specific spring constants (Parkinson et al, 2001). Large displacement amplifier integrated with comb drive achieves 100 times amplifying of comb drive displacement by means of its design is modeled (Li et al, 2005).

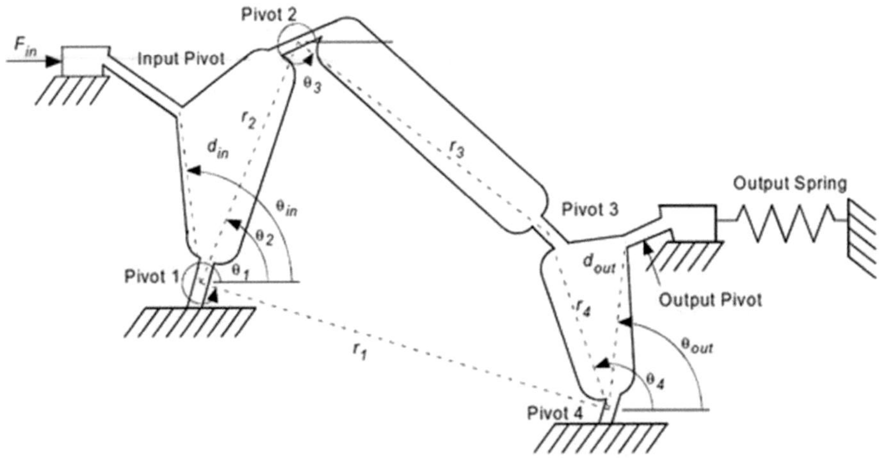

Figure 1. Schematic view of force or displacement amplifier' mechanism

Compliant MEMS have been used as a force amplifier in micro actuators and micro-mechanisms (Parkinson et al, 2001).

They are preferred since there is no need for assembly, no energy loss due to absence of friction, thus requiring no need for lubrication all of which providing high precision (Kosa et al, 2010). Besides, compliant micro mechanisms could be activated by mechanically (Han et al, 2007; Krishnan & Ananthasuresh, 2008), electro statically (Français et al, 2005; Millet et al, 2004), thermally (Lai et al, 2004; Terre & Shkel, 2004) or electrical (Gomm et al, 2002; Huang & Lan, 2006) induced forces.

Moreover, compliant MEMS having two or three clear stable states as named bi-stable or tri-stable behavior respectively were used in micro valve, micro switch, micro clasps applications (Chen et al, 2009; Jensen et al, 2001; Jensen & Howell, 2003; Nathan & Howell, 2003; Wilcox & Howell, 2005). For instance, Jensen designed several mechanisms such as double slider crank, slider-rocker mechanisms and explained the theory of bi-stable behavior (Jensen et al, 2004).

Recent studies on compliant mechanisms are focused on novel designs (Kosa et al, 2010), new developed methodologies and optimization in topology (Chour & Jyhjei, 2006; Krishnan & Ananthasuresh, 2008; Pedersen & Seshia, 2004), size and shape (Krishnan & Ananthasuresh, 2008) or the use of finite element methods (Jensen et al, 2001). Compliant micro mechanisms enable mechanical or geometric benefit meaning that the ratio of output force to input force and the ratio of output displacement to input displacement, respectively, and both mechanical and geometric advantage (MA and GA, respectively) are formulized as follows;

$$MA=F_{out}/F_{in} \tag{1}$$

$$GA=d_{out}/d_{in} \tag{2}$$

The energy is conserved during the motion transfer of compliant micro mechanism indicating that the increase in the output force causes decrease in the output displacement and vice versa. So, both mechanical and geometric benefits are significant to provide input to the micro actuators in MEMS applications (Kosa et al, 2010).

Optimization of compliant mechanisms such as topology and size optimization is a challenging issue. In topology optimization, it is critical to design a suitable functional configuration of the mechanism to provide desired output motion under applied forces while in size optimization, it is important to achieve desired force or displacement amplification so as to operate under maximum loads (Kota et al, 2001).

In this study, novel compliant MEMS force amplifier is designed and simulated by modeling its rigid body mechanism by Matlab/Simulink to determine the dynamic and quasi-static behavior. Kinematic approach is investigated and kinematic equations are derived and velocity and acceleration analysis of the micro mechanism are modeled. Dynamic response of MEMS amplifier is validated at a constant angular velocity and it is concluded that force amplification reaches to infinity at zero-crank angle. It is achieved that force amplification ratio reaches 5093, as the first stage crank angle, Θ_2 passes from 0° in quasi-static simulation.

2. Mechanism design

Compliant MEMS force amplifier's configuration is schematically shown in Fig. 2. Micro amplifier is composed of two slider-crank mechanisms. The two stage slider-crank amplifier provides force amplifying by means of its novel design. Its aim is to perform high output force at point B under low input forces. Two stages provide much more amplification compare to one stage. For both stages, rigid beams are linked by single thin flexible beams having a width of 3 μm. These flexible beams make the micro mechanism motion possible under operating forces. The micro mechanism stores energy and transfers force by elastic deformation of flexible beams linking rigid beams as both stage-slider cranks get close zero degree crank angle. Afterwards, input force is removed and micro amplifier springs back to its original position by means of flexible links having large deflections.

The beams in first stage have a length of 100 μm and width of 25 μm as the beams in second stage have a length of 800 μm and width of 25 μm, as all beams have rectangular cross sectional area. The depths of all beams are chosen as 25μm limited by SOI-MUMPs (Silicon on Insulator Multi User MEMS Process) manufacturing technology (Cohen et al, 2009).

2.1. Grashof theorem

In rigid body model of the MEMS amplifier, four-bar configuration is attained after vector loop equations are derived. Grashof theorem becomes significant to demonstrate the act of micro mechanism. Grashof theorem takes three cases into consideration and states that when both of beams are rocked it is called a double-rocker when both of beams are able to revolve, then it is called double-crank, when the short beam is able to rotate as the long one is rocked, then it is called a crank-rocker mechanism. To determine the moving limit of the micro mechanism, the relation between the lengths of beams turns out to be an important issue. Therefore, selecting the length of a beam plays a crucial role for the micro mechanism.

Due the fact that, x1, x2 are assumed as length of the shortest beam and length of the longest beam, respectively, as x3, x4 are the mean lengths of the beams. If x1+x2<= x3+x4, at least one of the beams can rotate and If x1+x2= x3+x4, the mechanism is activated and crank has limited rotation this feature enables beams to pass horizontal positions closely to each other achieving a high force amplifying.

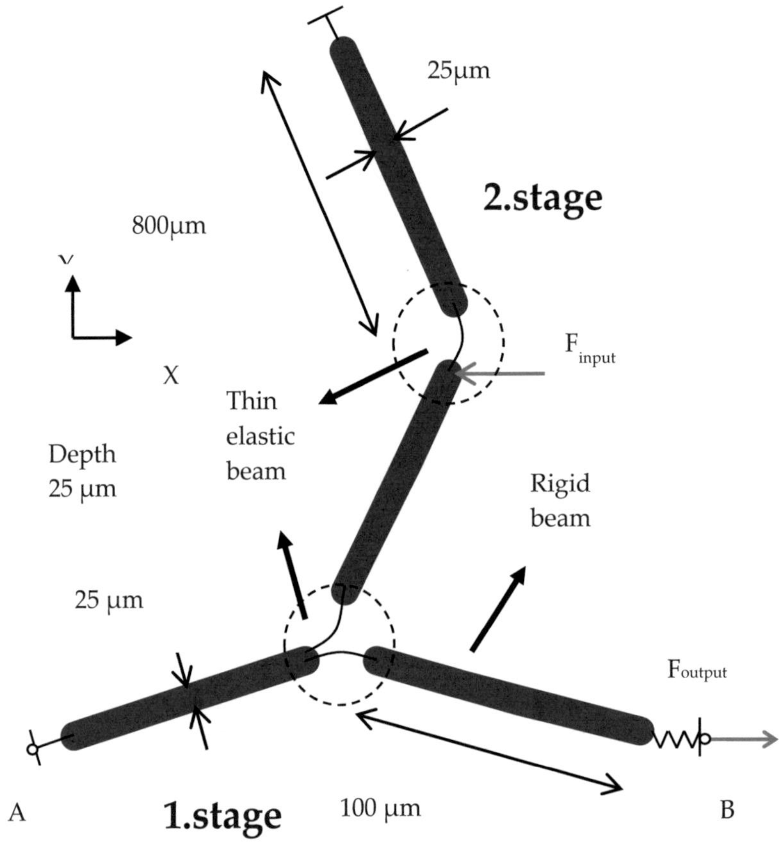

Figure 2. Novel compliant MEMS Force Amplifier

3. Analysis of quasi-static behavior

3.1. Force and moment equation derivation

Rigid body model of the compliant micro mechanism is considered. Free body diagram of each beam is sketched and a typical beam model is schematically shown in Fig. 3. Forces acting on each beam is broken down into x and y components as follows;

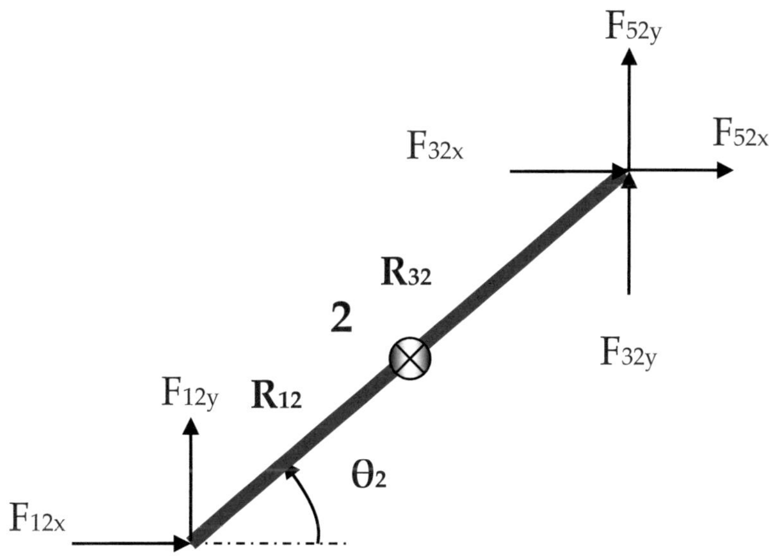

Figure 3. Free body diagram of beam 2

The static force and moment equations of beam 2 is typically shown and derived as; Equation derivation of forces acting on beam 2 along x axis;

$$\sum F_x = 0 \quad (3)$$

$$F_{12x} + F_{32x} + F_{52x} = 0 \quad (4)$$

Equation derivation of forces acting on beam 2 along y axis;

$$\sum F_y = 0 \quad (5)$$

$$F_{12y} + F_{32y} + F_{52y} = 0 \quad (6)$$

Equation derivation of moments acting on beam 2 along z axis;

$$\sum M_z = 0 \quad (7)$$

$$R_{12x} * F_{12y} - R_{12y} * F_{12x} + R_{32x} * F_{32y} - R_{32y} * F_{32x} + R_{52x} * F_{52y} - R_{52y} * F_{52x} = 0 \quad (8)$$

Free body diagram of beam 3 is shown in Fig. 4 and equation derivation of forces acting on beam 3 along x axis;

$$\sum F_x = 0 \quad (9)$$

$$F_{23x} + F_{43x} = 0 \tag{10}$$

Equation derivation of forces acting on beam 3 along y axis;

$$\sum F_y = 0 \tag{11}$$

$$F_{23y} + F_{43y} = 0 \tag{12}$$

Equation derivation of moments acting on beam 3 along z axis;

$$\sum M_z = 0 \tag{13}$$

$$R_{23x} * F_{23y} - R_{23y} * F_{23x} + R_{43x} * F_{43y} - R_{43y} * F_{43x} = 0 \tag{14}$$

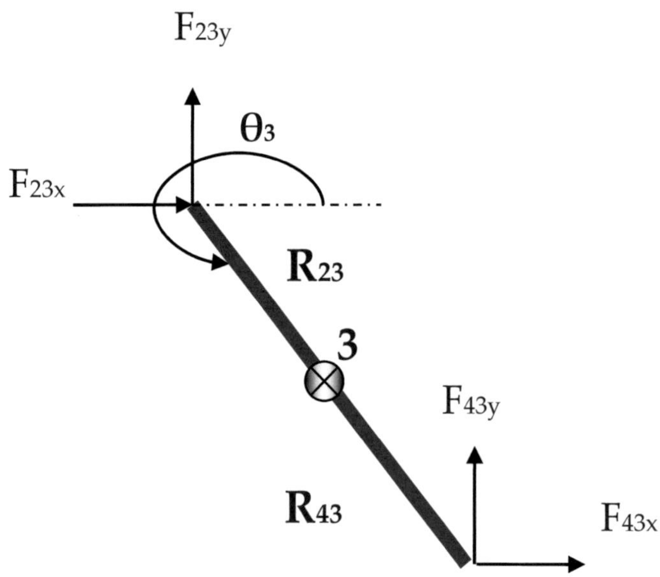

Figure 4. Free body diagram of beam 3

Free body diagram of beam 5 is shown in Fig. 5 and equation derivation of forces acting on beam 5 along x axis;

$$\sum F_x = 0 \tag{15}$$

$$F_{65x} + F_{25x} = 0 \tag{16}$$

Equation derivation of forces acting on beam 5 along y axis;

$$\sum F_y = 0 \tag{17}$$

$$F_{65y} + F_{25y} = 0 \tag{18}$$

Equation derivation of moments acting on beam 5 along z axis;

$$\sum M_z = 0 \tag{19}$$

$$R_{65x} * F_{65y} - R_{65y} * F_{65x} + R_{25x} * F_{25y} - R_{25y} * F_{25x} = 0 \tag{20}$$

Free body diagram of beam 6 is shown in Fig. 6 and equation derivation of forces acting on beam 6 along x axis;

$$\sum F_x = 0 \tag{21}$$

$$F_{g6x} + F_{56x} = 0 \tag{22}$$

Equation derivation of forces acting on beam 6 along y axis;

$$\sum F_y = 0 \tag{23}$$

$$F_{g6y} + F_{56y} = 0 \tag{24}$$

Equation derivation of moments acting on beam 6 along z axis;

$$\sum M_z = 0 \tag{25}$$

$$R_{g6x} * F_{g6y} - R_{g6y} * F_{g6x} + R_{56x} * F_{56y} - R_{56y} * F_{56x} = 0 \tag{26}$$

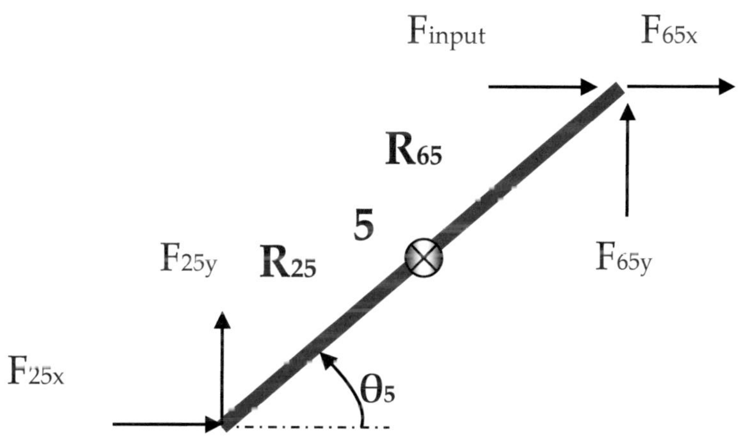

Figure 5. Free body diagram of beam 5

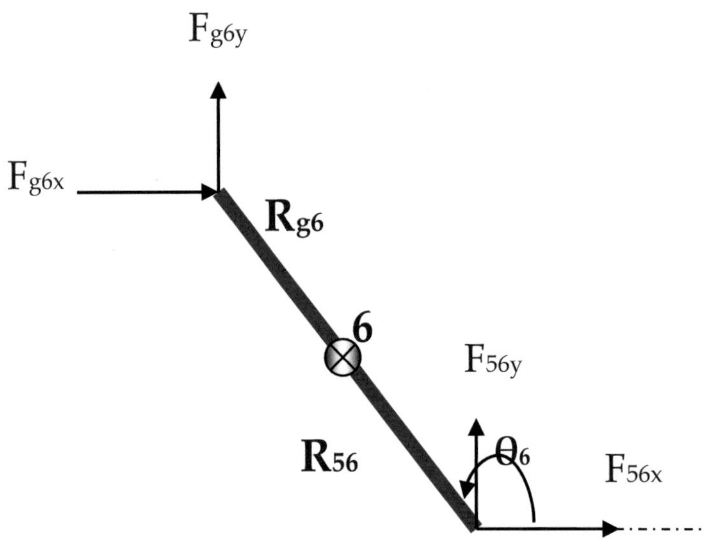

Figure 6. Free body diagram of beam 6

Free body diagram of slider is shown in Fig. 7 and equation derivation of forces acting on slider along x- and y- axes;

$$\sum F_x = 0 \tag{27}$$

$$F_{output} + F_{34x} = 0 \tag{28}$$

$$\sum F_y = 0 \tag{29}$$

$$F_{s4y} + F_{34y} = 0 \tag{30}$$

Thus, 14 force and moment equations are derived. Equations of relation between internal forces of beams;

$$F_{32x} = F_{23x} \tag{31}$$

$$F_{32y} = F_{23y} \tag{32}$$

$$F_{43x} = F_{34x} \tag{33}$$

$$F_{43y} = F_{34y} \tag{34}$$

$$F_{52x} = F_{25x} \tag{35}$$

$$F_{52y} = F_{25y} \tag{36}$$

$$F_{65x} = F_{56x} \tag{37}$$

$$F_{65y} = F_{56y} \tag{38}$$

8 equations are derived from the relations between internal forces of beams.

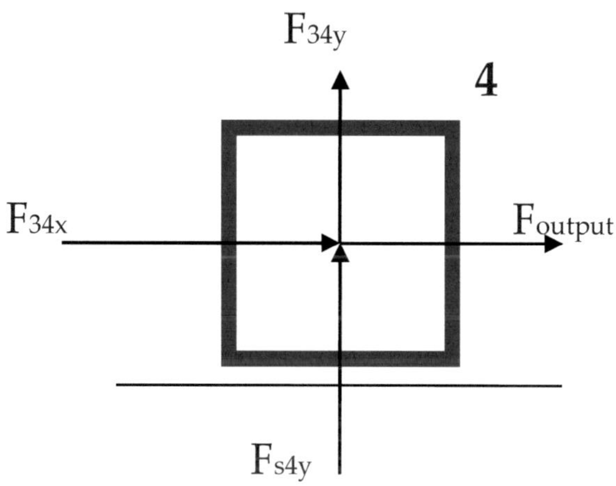

Figure 7. Free body diagram of slider

3.2. Equations and initial conditions

The vector loop equations are derived and broken down into x and y components as force and moment equations. It is seen that linear matrix method could not be used to solve the position problem. To analyze the position behavior of the micro mechanism, nonlinear and transcendental equations should be solved by Matlab and in quasi-static run, initial conditions of Θ_2 and (Θ_6-90°) are chosen as 10° and 20°, respectively.

3.3. Position analysis

The micro mechanism is a single degree of freedom mechanism and position analysis provides to inform the positions of other links and points as one of the links moves or rotates.

To find out position problem of the micro mechanism, nonlinear and transcendental vector loop equations that are derived and solved.

The vector loops are schematically shown in Fig. 8. There are two vector loop equations such as;

First vector loop equation:

$$R_2 + R_3 = R_1 \tag{39}$$

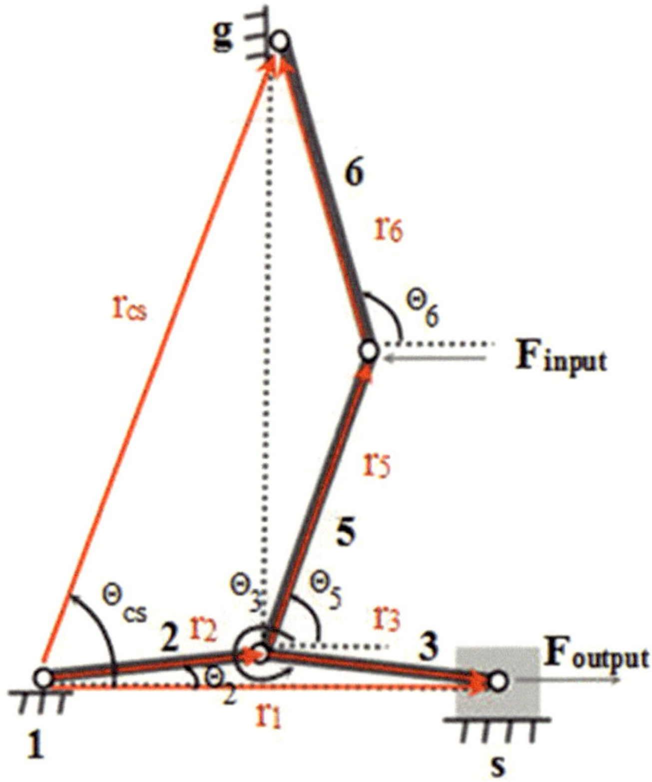

Figure 8. Vector loops for the force amplifier

Deriving equations according to coordinates of x and y:

$$r_2 * \cos\theta_2 + r_3 * \cos\theta_3 = r_1 \tag{40}$$

$$-r_2 * \sin\theta_2 - r_3 * \sin\theta_3 = 0 \tag{41}$$

Second vector loop equation:

$$R_2 + R_5 + R_6 = R_{cs} \tag{42}$$

Vector loop equations along x--axis

$$r_2 * \cos\theta_2 + r_5 * \cos\theta_5 + r_6 * \cos\theta_6 = r_{cs} * \cos\theta_{cs} \tag{43}$$

Vector loop equations along y--axis

$$r_2 * \sin\theta_2 + r_5 * \sin\theta_5 + r_6 * \sin\theta_6 = r_{cs} * \sin\theta_{cs} \tag{44}$$

By quasi-static analysis, it is claimed that (360°-Θ_3) and Θ_2 decreases linearly and are equal to each other during both quasi-static and dynamic simulations run by Matlab/Simulink. As seen in Fig. 9, it is calculated that as Θ_5 goes from 70° to 74.0248°, Θ_6 reduces from 110° to

105.9756°. Thus, as Θ_2 rotates 20°, both Θ_5 and Θ_2 rotates approximately 4.02° and slightly different from each other. The relation both between Θ_5 and Θ_2, Θ_6 and Θ_2 are linear.

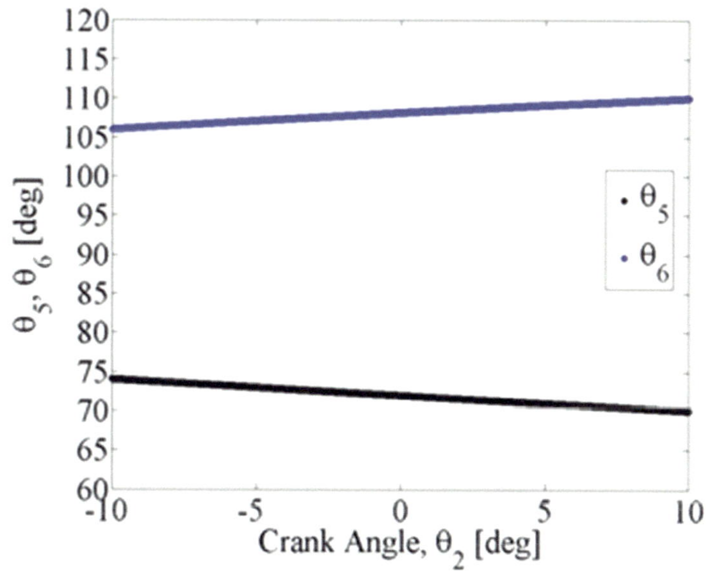

Figure 9. Plot of Θ_5 and Θ_6 according to first stage crank angle, Θ_2

Displacement ratio is defined as U_{output}/U_{input}. As the micro mechanism operates under an input force along – x direction, the first stage crank angle starts decreasing and pass from 0° and again starts increasing in an opposite direction and the ratio of output displacement to input displacement decreases as shown in Fig. 10. Beams 5 and 6 moves along –x and –y directions and the length of beams 5 and 6 are 8 times of beams 2 and 3. So, the input displacement increases rapidly than output displacement at close to zero degree crank angles. At negative crank angle values defining opposite directions, the slider gets close to initial position on contrast, beams 5 and 6 continue to get close to their vertical positions meaning that input displacement goes on to increase whereas output displacement begin to decrease. Therefore, after zero-crank angle, the displacement ratio continues to decrease according to Θ_2.

As the micro mechanism displays, both the second stage crank angle, (Θ_6-90°) and the first stage crank angle, Θ_2 get close to zero degree, the force amplification defined as F_{output}/F_{input} starts increasing and when Θ_2 is 0° and (Θ_6-90°) is at about small values, the micro mechanism provides high output force and force amplifying sharply increases as seen in Fig. 11 under $1.7*10^{-7}$ in [N]. Also, there are two peaks in force amplification by quasi-static run. As, the first crank angle is close to zero but at still positive value, the force amplifying reaches 5093 and after that step first crank angle gets negative value but it is still close to zero, the force amplification ratio is 4830 at negative direction due to the fact that the slider motion begin to move in opposite direction and also, output force is in opposite direction. It is claimed that the toggle position of the micro mechanism is a very crucial issue meaning that if the initial conditions such as crank angles are adjusted properly to enable both crank angle pass 0° at the same time, the ratio of the output to the input force applied to the mechanism goes to infinity at zero degree crank angles.

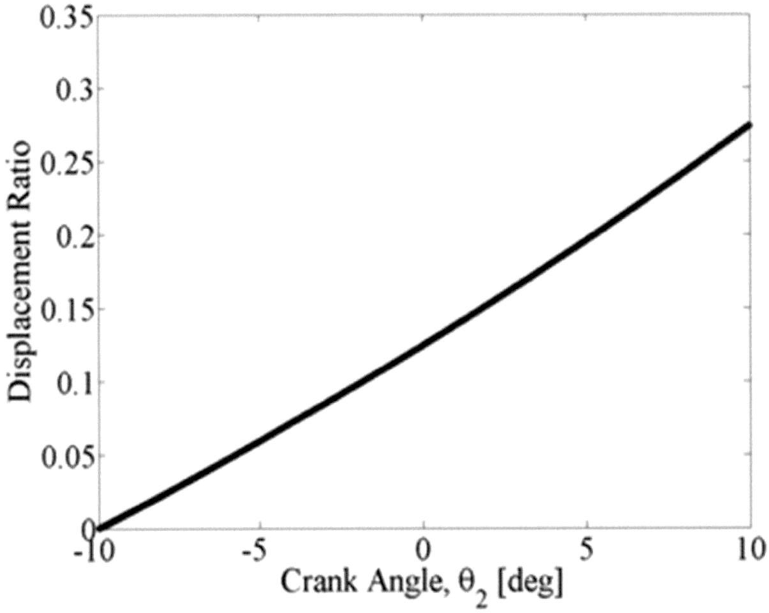

Figure 10. Plot of displacement ratio according to first stage crank angle, Θ_2

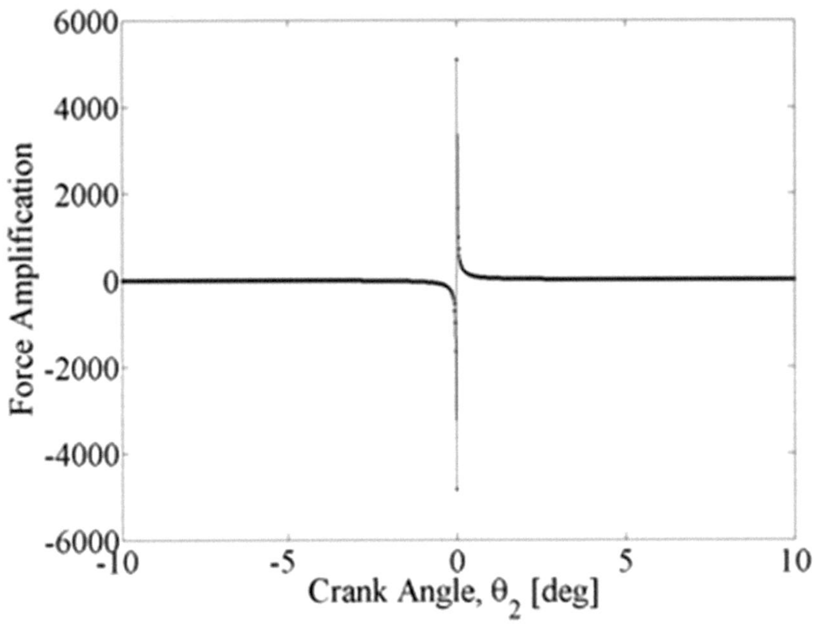

Figure 11. Plot of force amplifying according to first stage crank angle, Θ_2

4. Dynamic behavior of a novel MEMS amplifier

4.1. Inertial and geometric parameters:

It is assumed that micro mechanism is made up of silicon having a density of 2.33 g/cm^3. For short length of beams, lengths are 100 micron, widths and heights are 25 micron. The mass of short beams is;

$$M_s=2.33*100*25*25*10^{-15}=145625*10^{-18}\ [kg] \tag{45}$$

For long length of beams, lengths are 800 micron, widths and heights are 25 micron. The mass of short beams is;

$$M_l=2.33*800*25*25*10^{-15}=1165000*10^{-18}\ [kg] \tag{46}$$

The mass of the slider is accepted as $145625*10^{-18}$ in kilograms.

The mass moments of inertia of the beams are calculated as follows;

For short beams;

$$I_s = M_s*(L^2+a^2)/12=145625*10^{-18}*(100^2+25^2)/12=128938802.1*10^{-18}\ [kg*\mu m^2] \tag{47}$$

For long beams;

$$I_l = M_s*(L^2+a^2)/12=1165000*10^{-18}*(800^2+25^2)/12=6.219401042*10^{-8}[kg*\mu m^2] \tag{48}$$

4.2. Kinematic behavior

4.2.1. Velocity analysis

Kinematic simulation is used to calculate and to plot the velocities and acceleration of the beam of the MEMS amplifier.

To understand kinematic behavior of the mechanism, first of all, derivatives of vector loop equations derived in position analysis are taken with respect to time and the velocity equations are arranged as follows;

$$-r_2*\sin\theta_2*w_2-r_3*\sin\theta_3*w_3=r1 \tag{49}$$

$$r_2*\cos\theta_2*w_2+r_3*\cos\theta_3*w_3=0 \tag{50}$$

$$-r_2*\sin\theta_2*w_2-r_5*\sin\theta_5*w_5-r_6*\sin\theta_6*w_6=0 \tag{51}$$

$$r_2*\cos\theta_2*w_2+r_5*\cos\theta_5*w_5+r_6*\cos\theta_6*w_6=0 \tag{52}$$

The beam 6 are rotated at a constant speed, 0.01 rad/s, in clockwise direction and the initial conditions of w_2, w_3, w_5, $\dot{r}_1$ are -0.059378175917485 [rad/s], 0.059378175917485 [rad/s], 0.011371580426033 [rad/s], 2.062182408251533 [μm/s], respectively.

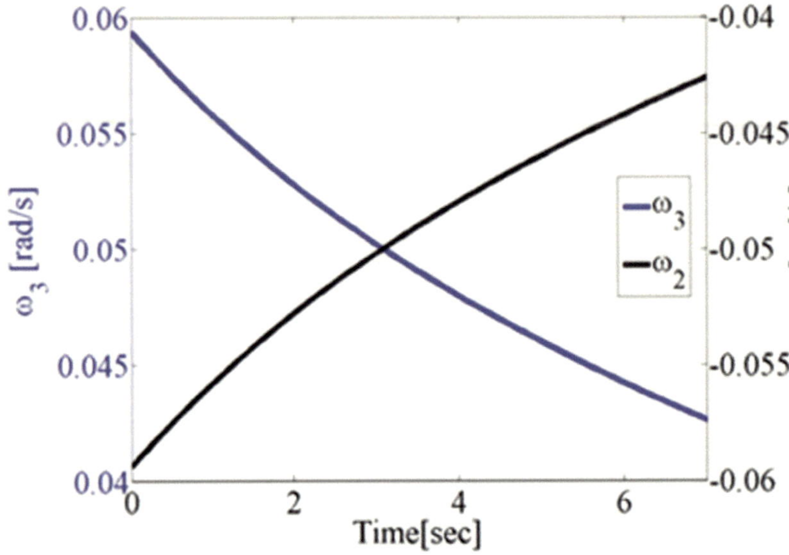

Figure 12. Plot of angular velocity of beam 2 and beam 3 versus time for simulation of force amplifier

The angular velocities of beams 2 and 3 in 1 stage are equal to each other in magnitude. As w_3 rotate counter clockwise direction, w_2 rotate clockwise direction and the absolute values of the changes in w_3 and w_2 equal to each other according to time as shown in Fig. 12.

Slider slows down until the first stage crank angle, Θ_2 pass from 0°. When first stage beams are fully open, as having horizontal position, slider velocity is equal to zero. Then the slider moves to along -x direction and angular velocity of beam 5 decreases according to time as in Fig. 13.

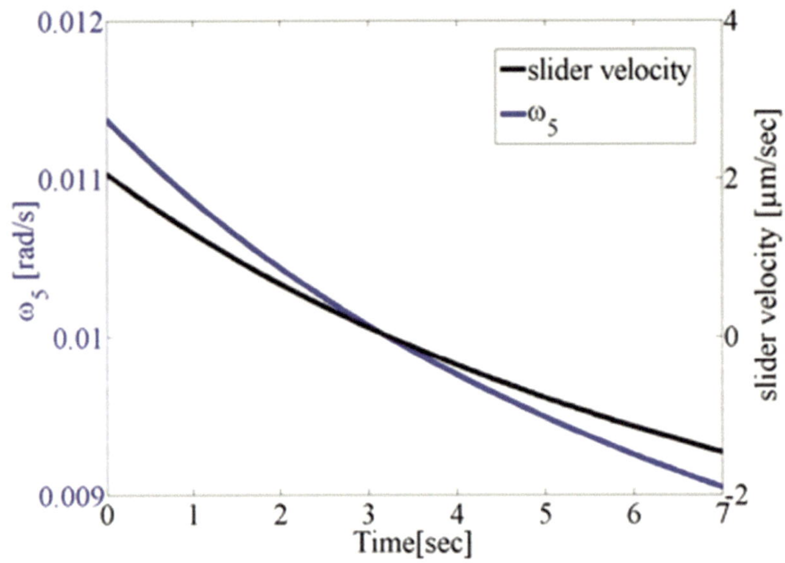

Figure 13. Plot of angular velocity of beam 5 and slider velocity versus time for simulation of force amplifier

4.2.2. Acceleration analysis

To analyze the acceleration of the beams, second derivatives of the terms must be handled. The second derivatives of the vector loop equations for the micro mechanism are as follows;

$$-r_2 * \cos\theta_2 * w_2^2 - r_2 * \sin\theta_2 * \alpha_2 - r_3 * \cos\theta_3 * w_3^2 - r_3 * \sin\theta_3 * \alpha_3 - \ddot{r}_1 = 0 \quad (53)$$

$$-r_2 * \sin\theta_2 * w_2^2 + r_2 * \cos\theta_2 * \alpha_2 - r_3 * \sin\theta_3 * w_3^2 + r_3 * \cos\theta_3 * \alpha_3 = 0 \quad (54)$$

$$\begin{aligned} &-r_2 * \cos\theta_2 * w_2^2 - r_2 * \sin\theta_2 * \alpha_2 - r_5 * \cos\theta_5 * w_5^2 \\ &-r_5 * \sin\theta_5 * \alpha_5 - r_6 * \cos\theta_6 * w_6^2 - r_6 * \sin\theta_6 * \alpha_6 = 0 \end{aligned} \quad (55)$$

$$\begin{aligned} &-r_2 * \sin\theta_2 * w_2^2 + r_2 * \cos\theta_2 * \alpha_2 - r_5 * \sin\theta_5 * w_5^2 \\ &+r_5 * \cos\theta_5 * \alpha_5 - r_6 * \sin\theta_6 * w_6^2 - r_6 * \cos\theta_6 * \alpha_6 = 0 \end{aligned} \quad (56)$$

In acceleration simulation by Simulink, the velocities such as w_2, w_3, w_5, $\dot{r}_1$, w_6 are considered as known. The beam 6 rotates at a constant speed meaning that acceleration of beam 6 is zero.

Acceleration of beam 2 and beam 3 are shown in fig. 14. Both acceleration of beams decrease as the micro mechanism operates under constant w_6, angular velocity. The magnitude of acceleration of beam 2 and beam 3 are equal to each other during simulation. Also, as seen in Fig. 15, acceleration of beam 5 and slider decrease as function of time.

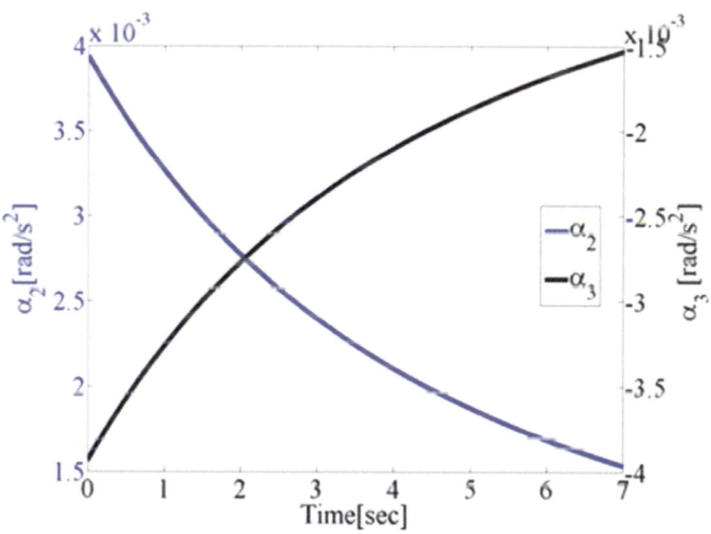

Figure 14. Acceleration of beam 2 and beam 3 under constant angular acceleration, α_2

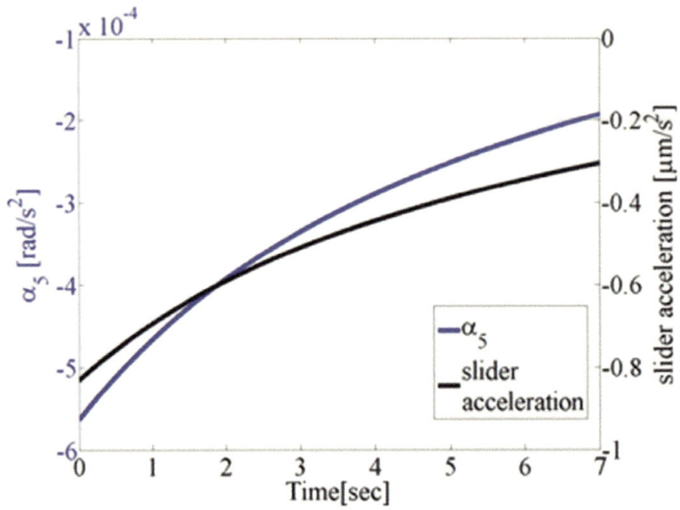

Figure 15. Acceleration of beam 5 and slider under constant angular acceleration, α_2

4.3. Acceleration vector equations according to center of mass

The linear acceleration of the center of mass equations are not present in vector loop equations that are previously derived. So, there must be equations relating to the acceleration of the center of mass of beams. Equation derivation is as follows and schematic representation of the center of mass acceleration in first and second loops is shown in Fig. 16 and Fig. 17, respectively.

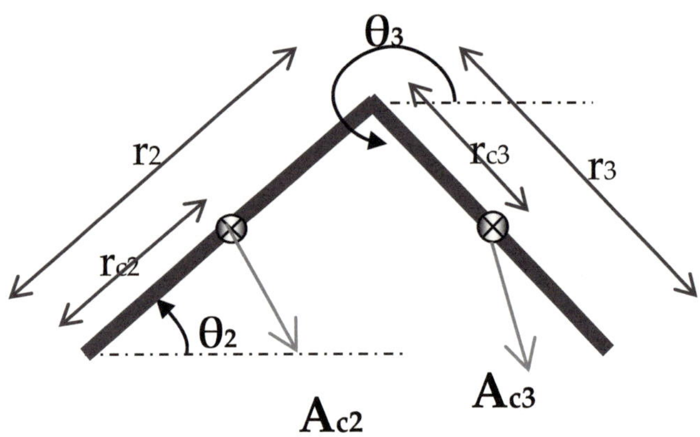

Figure 16. The center of mass acceleration in first loop

The center of mass acceleration of beam 2 along x and y direction;

$$A_{c2} = \ddot{R}_{c2} \tag{57}$$

$$A_{c2x} = -r_{c2} * \sin\theta_2 * \alpha_2 - r_{c2} * \cos\theta_2 * w_2^2 \tag{58}$$

$$A_{c2y} = r_{c2} * \cos\theta_2 * \alpha_2 - r_{c2} * \sin\theta_2 * w_2^2 \tag{59}$$

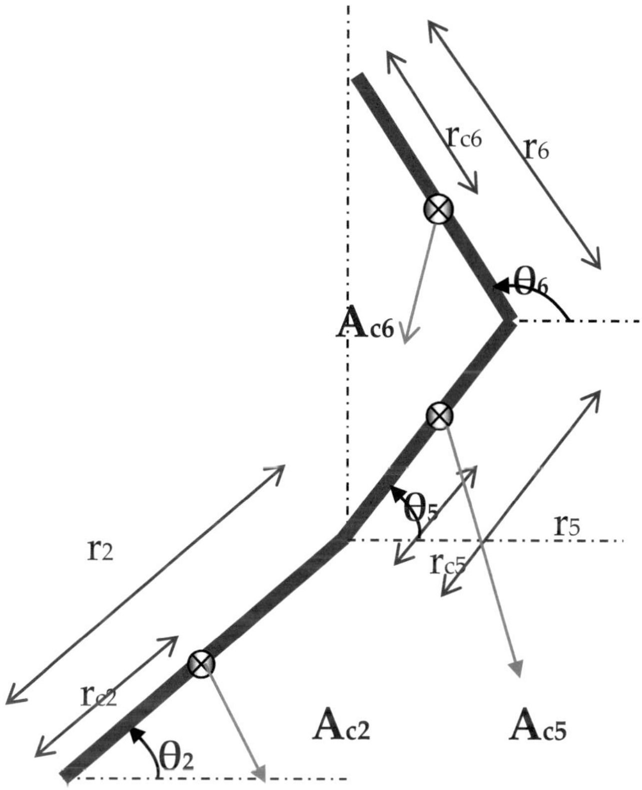

Figure 17. The center of mass acceleration in second loop

The center of mass acceleration of beam 3 along x and y direction;

$$A_{c3} = \ddot{R}2 + \ddot{R}c3 \tag{60}$$

$$A_{c3x} = -r_2 * \sin\theta_2 * \alpha_2 - r_{c2} * \cos\theta_2 * w_2^2 - r_{c3} * \sin\theta_3 * \alpha_3 - r_{c3} * \cos\theta_3 * w_3^2 \tag{61}$$

$$A_{c3y} = r_2 * \cos\theta_2 * \alpha_2 - r_{c2} * \sin\theta_2 * w_2^2 + r_{c3} * \cos\theta_3 * \alpha_3 - r_{c3} * \sin\theta_3 * w_3^2 \tag{62}$$

The center of mass acceleration of beam 6 along x and y direction;

$$A_{c6} = \ddot{R}c6 \tag{63}$$

$$A_{c6y} = r_{c6} * \sin\theta_6 * \alpha_6 + r_{c6} * \cos\theta_6 * w_6^2 \quad (64)$$

$$A_{c6x} = -r_{c6} * \cos\theta_6 * \alpha_6 + r_{c6} * \sin\theta_6 * w_6^2 \quad (65)$$

The center of mass acceleration of beam 5 along x and y direction;

$$A_{c5} = \ddot{R}_2 + \ddot{R}_{c5} \quad (66)$$

$$A_{c5y} = r_6 * \sin\theta_6 * \alpha_6 + r_6 * \cos\theta_6 * w_6^2 + r_{c5} * \sin\theta_5 * \alpha_5 + r_{c5} * \cos\theta_5 * w_5^2 \quad (67)$$

$$A_{c5x} = -r_6 * \cos\theta_6 * \alpha_6 + r_6 * \sin\theta_2 * w_2^2 - r_{c5} * \cos\theta_5 * \alpha_5 - r_{c5} * \sin\theta_5 * w_5^2 \quad (68)$$

4.4. Force and dynamic analysis of the micro mechanism

The micro mechanism operates under constant angular velocity, 0.01 [rad/s], the slider crank starts increasing and reaches to its maximum value, 200 micron, meaning that the first stage slider crank is fully opened at 3.20 sec. then the first crank angle pass from 0° and slider begins to get close to its initial position and R_1 decreases as shown Fig. 18. According to both crank angles, Θ_2 and (90-Θ_6), the output force increases or decreases. In the first section of the F_{output} vs. time curve, first, both crank angles decrease, and two slider cranks start to open and at small crank angles, F_{output} sharply increase and at 3.20 sec Θ_2 is equal to 0.0013°

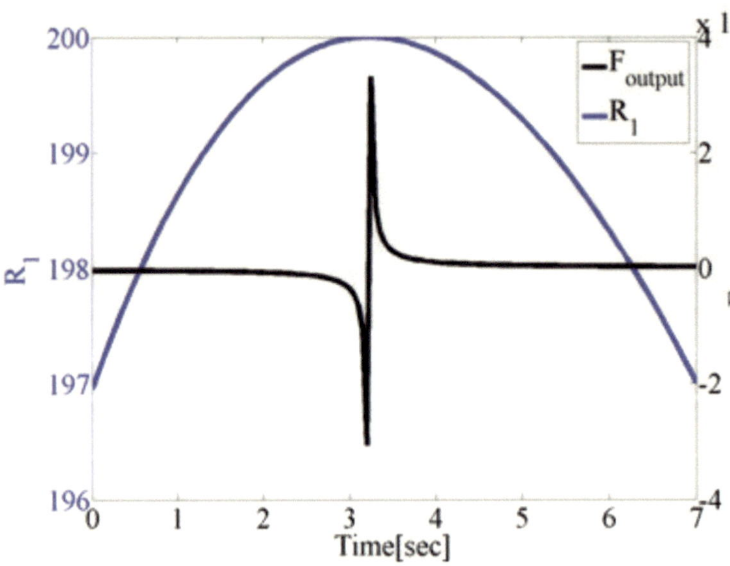

Figure 18. Displacement of slider and output force versus time

and at 3.25sec. Θ_2 is equal to -0.0012° and at Θ_2 these values, F_{output} goes to its peak values such as -3.07*10^4 µN at 3.20 sec. and 3.32*10^4 µN at 3.25 sec. Θ_2 decreases until 3.20 sec. and then it increases, whereas 90°-Θ_6 decreases and gets close to small values during the simulation. The magnitude of first peak of F_{output} at 3.25 sec. is higher than the magnitude of second peak of F_{output} at 3.20 sec. due to the fact that (90°-Θ_6) at 3.25 sec. is smaller than the value of (90°-Θ_6) at 3.20 sec., meaning that small crank angle value of (90°-Θ_6) contributes to get much more output force.

5. Conclusion

The MEMS force amplifier designed in this study is shown to provide high output to input ratio.

By quasi-static analysis, 5090 force amplifying is achieved as the first crank angle, Θ_2, rotates 10° and passes from its horizontal position and (90°-Θ_6) rotates 1.85° and continues to decrease.

The maximum amplifying ratio changes based on the initial position of the micro mechanism. So, the toggle of the micro mechanism has a crucial role to get high force output and high force amplification. If the mechanism's initial position is adjusted properly as both crank angles pass 0° at the same time, the force output and consequently force amplification go to infinity.

If pseudo rigid body of the compliant MEMS force amplifier having elastic hinges is modeled as a further study, it would provide us to get much more close response to the micro mechanism's real behavior. This novel MEMS amplifier design achieves high force amplifying due to its geometric design.

By dynamic analysis, high output force is achieved as the micro mechanism operates under 0.01 [rad/s] constant angular velocity of beam 6 at 3.20 sec and at about fully open position of first crank angle.

By Simulink, the simulation displays dynamic behavior of the micro compliant mechanism and it is claimed that second stage crank angle rotates 4.01°, whereas first stage crank angle, Θ_2, rotates 19.92°.

5.1. Nomenclature

R_1, r_1	vector of beam 1
R_2, r_2	vector of beam 2
R_3, r_3	vector of beam 3
R_5, r_5	vector of beam 5
R_6, r_6	vector of beam 6
R_{cs}, r_{cs}	vector of beam cs
F_{12x}	force of beam ground acting on link 2 along x direction
F_{12y}	force of beam ground acting on link 2 along y direction

F_{23x}	force of beam 2 acting on link 3 along x direction
F_{23y}	force of beam 2 acting on link 3 along y direction
F_{32x}	force of beam 3 acting on link 2 along x direction
F_{32y}	force of beam 3 acting on link 2 along y direction
F_{43x}	force of beam 4 acting on link 3 along x direction
F_{43y}	force of beam 4 acting on link 3 along y direction
F_{34x}	force of beam 3 acting on link 4 along x direction
F_{34y}	force of beam 3 acting on link 4 along y direction
F_{52x}	force of beam 5 acting on link 2 along x direction
F_{52y}	force of beam 5 acting on link 2 along y direction
F_{25x}	force of beam 2 acting on link 5 along x direction
F_{25y}	force of beam 2 acting on link 5 along y direction
F_{65x}	force of beam 6 acting on link 5 along x direction
F_{65y}	force of beam 6 acting on link 5 along y direction
F_{56x}	force of beam 5 acting on link 6 along x direction
F_{56y}	force of beam 5 acting on link 6 along y direction
F_{g6x}	force of ground acting on link 6 along x direction
F_{g6y}	force of ground acting on link 6 along y direction
A_{c2x}	center of mass acceleration of beam 2 along x direction
A_{c2y}	center of mass acceleration of beam 2 along y direction
A_{c3x}	center of mass acceleration of beam 3 along x direction
A_{c3y}	center of mass acceleration of beam 3 along y direction
A_{c5x}	center of mass acceleration of beam 5 along x direction
A_{c5y}	center of mass acceleration of beam 5 along y direction
A_{c6x}	center of mass acceleration of beam 6 along x direction
A_{c6y}	center of mass acceleration of beam 6 along y direction
α_2	angular acceleration of beam 2
α_3	angular acceleration of beam 3
α_5	angular acceleration of beam 5
α_6	angular acceleration of beam 6
F_{in}	input force
F_{out}	output force
M_z	moment acting on a beam along z axis
w_2	angular velocity of beam 2
w_3	angular velocity of beam 3
w_5	angular velocity of beam 5
w_6	angular velocity of beam 6
$\dot{R}_1, \dot{r}_1$	velocity of slider
$\ddot{R}_1, \ddot{r}_1$	acceleration of slider
Θ2	first stage crank angle
Θ3	angle of beam 3 from +x axis in counter clockwise direction
Θ5	angle of beam 5 from +x axis in counter clockwise direction
Θ6	angle of beam 6 from +x axis in counter clockwise direction

Author details

Ergin Kosa* and Levent Trabzon
Mechanical Engineering, Istanbul Technical University, Istanbul, Turkey

Umit Sonmez
Mechanical Engineering, Sharjah University, Dubai, United Arab Emirates

Huseyin Kizil
Metallurgical and Materials Engineering, Istanbul Technical University, Istanbul, Turkey

6. References

Ashok, M.; Howell, L. L. & Norton, T. W. (2000). Limit Positions of Compliant Mechanisms Using the Pseudo-Rigid-Body Model Concept. Mechanism and Machine Theory, Vol. 35, pp. 99-115

Chen, G.; Wilcox, D. L. & Howell L. L. (2009). Fully Compliant Double Tensural Tristable Micromechanisms (DTTM), *Journal of Micromechanics and Microengineering,* Vol., 19, pp. 1-8

Cohen, A.; Hames, G.; Monk, D., Wilcenski, S. & Hardy B. (2009). Soimumps Design Handbook, MEMSCAP Revision 5.

Français, O.; Rousseau, L., Bourouina, T., Haussy, J. & Tissot, A. (2005). MEMS Memory Based on Bi-stable Mechanical Structures, Proceedings of DTIP of MEMS and MOEMS, ISBN 2-84813-0357-1, Montreux, Switzerland, June, 2005

Gomm, T.; Howell, L. L. & Selfridge, R. H. (2002). In-plane Linear Displacement Bistable Microrelay, *Journal of Micromechanics and Microengineering,* Vol. 12, pp. 257–264

Han, J. S.; Müller, C., Wallrabe, U. & Korvink, J. G. (2007). Design, Simulation, and Fabrication of a Quadstable Monolithic Mechanism with *X*- and *Y*-Directional Bistable Curved Beams. *Journal of Mechanical Design,* Vol. 129, pp. 1198-2003

Hsu, Tai Ran. (2002). *MEMS & Microsystems Design and Manufacture,* McGraw Hill (1st edition), ISBN 0-07-113051, USA

Huang, S. C. & Lan, G. J. (2006). Design and Fabrication of a Micro Compliant Amplifier with a Topology Optimal Compliant Mechanism Integrated with a Piezoelectric Microactuator. *Journal of Micromechanics and Microengineering,* Vol. 16, pp. 531–538. ISSN 0960-1317

Jensen, B. D.; Parkinson, Matthew B., Kurabayashi, Katsuo, Howell, Larry L. & Baker, Michael S. (2001). Design Optimization of a Fully-Compliant Bistable Micromechanism, Proceedings of 2001 ASME International Mechanical Engineering Congress and Exposition, New York, November, 2001

Jensen, B. D. & Howell, L. L. (2003). Identification of Compliant Pseudo-Rigid-Body Four-Link Mechanism Configurations Resulting in Bistable Behavior. *Journal of Mechanical Design,* Vol. 125, pp. 701-708

* Corresponding Author

Jensen, B. D. & Howell, L. L. (2004). Bistable Configurations of Compliant Mechanisms Modeled Using Four Links and Translational Joints. *Journal of Mechanical Design*. Vol. 126 , pp. 657-666

Kosa, E.; Sonmez, U., Kizil, H. & Trabzon L. (2010). The Design and Analysis of a Novel MEMS Force Amplifier. *Turkish Journal of Engineering & Environmental Sciences*, Vol. 34, pp. 253–259

Kota, S.; Joo J., Li Z., Rodgers, S. M. & Sniegowski J. (2001). Design of Compliant Mechanisms: Applications to MEMS. *Analog Integrated Circuits and Signal Processing*, Vol. 29, pp. 7-15

Krishnan , G. & Ananthasuresh G. K. (2008). Evaluation and Design of Displacement-Amplifying Compliant Mechanisms for Sensor Applications. *Journal of Mechanical Design*, Vol. 130, pp. 1-9

Lai, Y.; McDonald , J., Kujath, M. & Hubbard, T., (2004). Force, Deflection and Power Measurements of Toggled Microthermal Actuators. *Journal of Micromechanics and Microengineering*, Vol. 14, pp. 49–56

Larry, H. L. (2001). *Compliant Mechanisms*, John Wiley & Sons, ISBN 0-471-38478-X, USA.

Li, J.; Liu, Z. S., Lu, C., Zhang, Q. X. & Liu, A. Q. (2005). A Self Limited Large Displacement Ratio Micromechanical Amplifier. *Proceedings of The 13th International Conference on Solid-State Sensors, Actuators and Microsystems*, ISBN 0-7803-8952-2, Seoul, Korea, June, 2005

Lobontiu, N.; Paine, J. S. N., Garcia, E. & Goldfarb, M. (2001). Corner-Filleted Flexure Hinges. *Journal of Mechanical Design*, Vol. 123, pp. 346-352

Millet, O.; Bernardoni, P., Régnier, S., Bidaud, P., Tsitsiris, E., Collard, Dominique. & Buchaillot, Lionel. (2004). Electrostatic Actuated Micro Gripper using an Amplification Mechanism, *Sensors and Actuators A*, Vol. 114, pp. 371–378

Nathan, D. & Howell, Larry L. (2003). A Self-Retracting Fully Compliant Bistable Micromechanism. *Journal of Microelectromechanical Systems*, Vol. 12, pp. 273-280

Parkinson, M. B.; Jensen, B. D. & Kurabayashi K. (2001). Design of Compliant Force and Displacement Amplification Micro-Mechanisms. *Proceedings of DETC'01 ASME, Design Engineering Technical Conferences and Computers and Information in Engineering Conference*, Pittsburgh, Pennsylvania, September, 2001

Pedersen, C. B. W. & Seshia, A. A. (2004). On the Optimization of Compliant Force Amplifier Mechanisms for Surface Micromachined Resonant Accelerometers. *Journal of Micromechanics and Microengineering*, Vol. 14, pp. 1281–1293

Sreekumar, M.; Nagarajan, T. & Singaperumal, M. (2008). Experimental Investigations of the Large Deflection Capabilities of a Compliant Parallel Mechanism Actuated by Shape Memory Alloy Wires. *Smart materials and structures*, Vol. 17, pp. 1-12

Tantanawat , T. & Kota, S. (2007). Design of Compliant Mechanisms for Minimizing Input Power in Dynamic Applications. *Journal of Mechanical Design*, Vol. 129, pp. 1064-1075

Terre, J. C. & Shkel, A. (2004). Dynamic Analysis of a Snap-Action Micromechanism, *IEEE*, pp. 1245-1248

Wilcox, D. L. & Howell, L. L. (2005). Fully Compliant Tensural Bistable Micromechanisms (FTBM). *Journal of Microelectromechanical Systems*, Vol. 14, pp. 1-8

Chapter 6

Voltage Sag Waveform Using SagWave GUI

Kosol Oranpiroj, Worrajak Moangjai and Wichran Jantee

Additional information is available at the end of the chapter

http://dx.doi.org/10.5772/46448

1. Introduction

A recent survey attributes that 92% of all disturbances in power system is caused by voltage sags. Three-phase voltage sag can be classified in seven types as shown in Fig.1 (Bollen MHJ, 2000). The electrical sensitive load often trips of shunts down when voltage sag occur. It's very important to know how these sensitive equipment works when the voltage sag occur. This is the reason to develop the voltage sag generator that can created varied type of voltage sag waveform. The purpose of voltage sag generator is use to test the immunity of equipment against the voltage sag.

The magnitude and angle of three phase voltage sag can calculate form equation 1 to equation 7(Bollen MHJ, 2000).

Type A

$$\left.\begin{aligned} V_a &= V \\ V_b &= -\frac{1}{2}V - j\frac{1}{2}\sqrt{3}V \\ V_c &= -\frac{1}{2}V + j\frac{1}{2}\sqrt{3}V \end{aligned}\right\} \quad (1)$$

Type B

$$\left.\begin{aligned} V_a &= V \\ V_b &= -\frac{1}{2} - j\frac{1}{2}\sqrt{3} \\ V_c &= -\frac{1}{2} + j\frac{1}{2}\sqrt{3} \end{aligned}\right\} \quad (2)$$

Type C

$$\left.\begin{aligned} V_a &= 1 \\ V_b &= -\frac{1}{2} - j\frac{1}{2}\sqrt{3}V \\ V_c &= -\frac{1}{2} + j\frac{1}{2}\sqrt{3}V \end{aligned}\right\} \tag{3}$$

Type D

$$\left.\begin{aligned} V_a &= V \\ V_b &= -\frac{1}{2}V - j\frac{1}{2}\sqrt{3} \\ V_c &= -\frac{1}{2}V + j\frac{1}{2}\sqrt{3} \end{aligned}\right\} \tag{4}$$

Type E

$$\left.\begin{aligned} V_a &= 1 \\ V_b &= -\frac{1}{2}V - j\frac{1}{2}\sqrt{3}V \\ V_c &= -\frac{1}{2}V + j\frac{1}{2}\sqrt{3}V \end{aligned}\right\} \tag{5}$$

Type F

$$\left.\begin{aligned} V_a &= V \\ V_b &= -j\frac{\sqrt{3}}{3} - \frac{1}{2}V - j\frac{\sqrt{3}}{6}V \\ V_c &= +j\frac{\sqrt{3}}{3} - \frac{1}{2}V + j\frac{\sqrt{3}}{6}V \end{aligned}\right\} \tag{6}$$

Type G

$$\left.\begin{aligned} V_a &= \frac{2}{3} + \frac{1}{3}V \\ V_b &= -\frac{1}{3} - \frac{1}{6}V - j\frac{\sqrt{3}}{2}V \\ V_c &= -\frac{1}{3} - \frac{1}{6}V + j\frac{\sqrt{3}}{2}V \end{aligned}\right\} \tag{7}$$

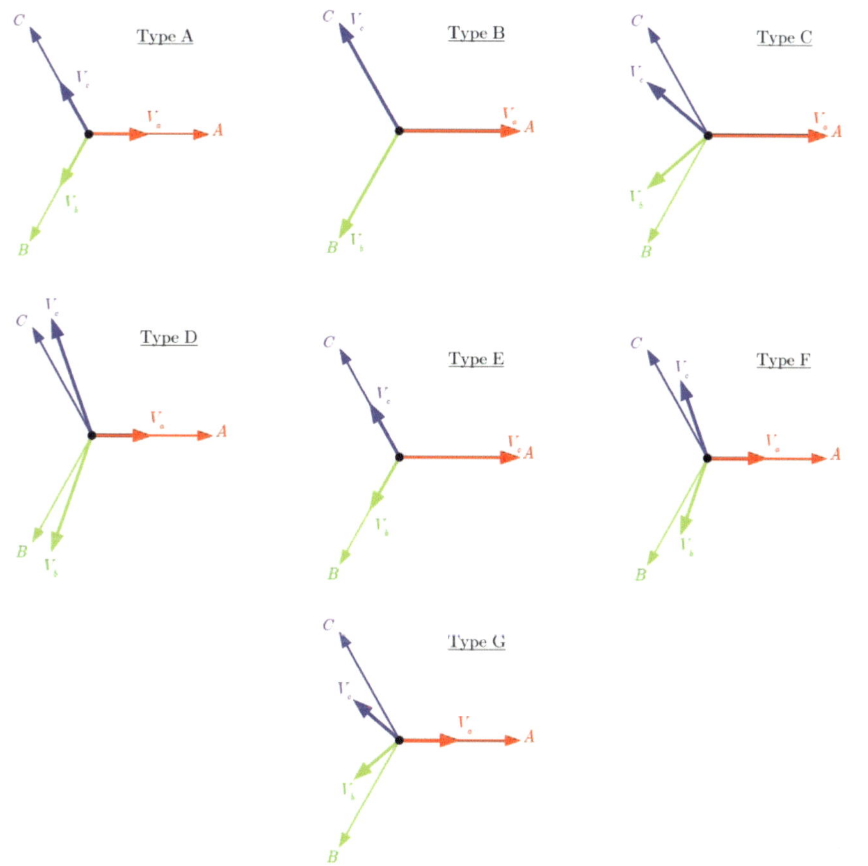

Figure 1. The seven type of voltage sag (Bollen MHJ, 2000).

2. Voltage sag generator

Previous works (Takahashi *et al.*, 2008; Rylander *et al.*, 2007; Bhavar *et al.*, 2008; Teke *et al.*, 2008; Ma and Karady, 2008), have developed voltage sag generator which can be simply classified into 4 types. These four types of voltage sag generator are transformer, switching-impedance, generator and amplifier. The transformer type uses a switch to adjust both pre-sag voltage and sag magnitudes. The switching-impedance type creates voltage sags by switching impedance into a power system by using a thyristor-controlled reactor (TCR). The generator type uses a synchronous generator to give controlled 3-phase voltage sags. The amplifier type uses a waveform generator to create controlled 3-phase voltage sags.

An autotransformer is used as the 1-phase voltage sag generator as demonstrated (Rylander *et al.*, 2007, Bhavar *et al.*, 2008); Rylander, *et al* .used MOSFET to turn-on/turn-off for changing between the primary source and the secondary source. Bhavsar, *et al.* used motorized variac with multi tapping transformer, the position of the variac is changed using a signal generated by the PIC. The main disadvantage of this method is that the non-conducting pairs connected to the unselected taps dissipate power due to the taps. It has a complex structure and requires control of signal processors. The TCR type creates a difference in voltage by firing the TCR at different angles. The disadvantages of TCR are the generation of low frequency harmonic current components and higher losses when working in the inductive region (Teke *et al.*, 2008). The generator type uses a synchronous generator that provides voltage sag by changing the exciting current of the generator. The control of sag generator's operation and monitoring of the system under test in performed by the Visual Basic programming (Collins and Morgan, 1996). The software of this paper had not displayed the waveform of voltage sag and disadvantages of this type are that it needs more space to install and is more expensive (Ma & Karady, 2008). The amplifier type can provide voltage sags with varying magnitude, duration, frequency and harmonics. After defining the desired waveform data is passed to power amplifier, at which outputs of adequate voltage levels of voltage sag are produced. This type is more convenient than others types, because it enables more precise control of all voltage sag characteristics and also allows testing of equipment in context of frequency variations and harmonic distortions. Therefore, a power amplifier type of voltage sag generator is selected for designing the voltage sag generator in this study. This chapter presents a 3-phase 4-wire voltage sag generator based on an *abc* algorithm((Oranpiroj *et al.*, 2009). Voltage sag generator has been created waveform by SagWave software. The actual voltage sag is created by the 3-phase 4-wire inverter which is controlled by low-cost dsPIC.

3. Graphic user interface (GUI) waveform generator

The graphic user interface (GUI) "SagWave" (Oranpiroj *et al.*, 2010, Oranpiroj *et al.*, 2011) is designed for easy input of the designed waveform. The user can create sag magnitude, sag duration, phase angle jump and point on wave for a designed sag waveform from the front panel of GUI. Users can verify the desired waveform in time domain or vector form as shown in windows. Then, parameters of desired sag waveform can be sent to dsPIC microcontroller directly from GUI to control voltage sag generator. From the requirement, the SagWage GUI had designed consisted of:

1. The window for showing the 3-phase voltage.
2. The window for showing vector of A, B and C phase.
3. Magnitude of Voltage (A, B and C phase), user had used value box or slider bar.
4. Phase angle jump of voltage sag on A, B or C phase.
5. Sag type for selected the voltage sag type (single-phase, two-phase and three-phase).
6. Display normal or repeat mode of voltage sag.
7. Point on wave in degree.
8. Sag duration time for period time of voltage sag.
9. Number of repeat of voltage sag.
10. The button "Plot" for generated the voltage sag waveform.
11. The button "Send" for send the data from SagWave to the dsPIC microcontroller.
12. The button "Refresh" for clear the value and graphic display.

The layout of GUI "SagWave" designed as shown in Fig.2. The SagWave development on MATLAB's Graphical User interface Development Environment (GUIDE)(Patrick Marchand & O. Thomas Holland., 2003).

3.1. The window for showing the 3-phase voltage

This is an "Axes" object in component palette (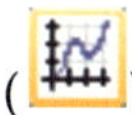) on the left-side of window. The "Axes" can move and resize by drag it with the mouse. This "Axes" to shown the 3-phase voltage of voltage sag, then we assigned name to "Time_Plot" in Property inspector by double click on "Axes1" as shown in Fig. 3.

3.2. The window for showing vector of A, B and C phase

This "Axes2" to shown the vector of A, B and C of voltage sag, then we assigned name to "Com_pass" in Property inspector by double click on "Axes2" as shown in Fig. 4.

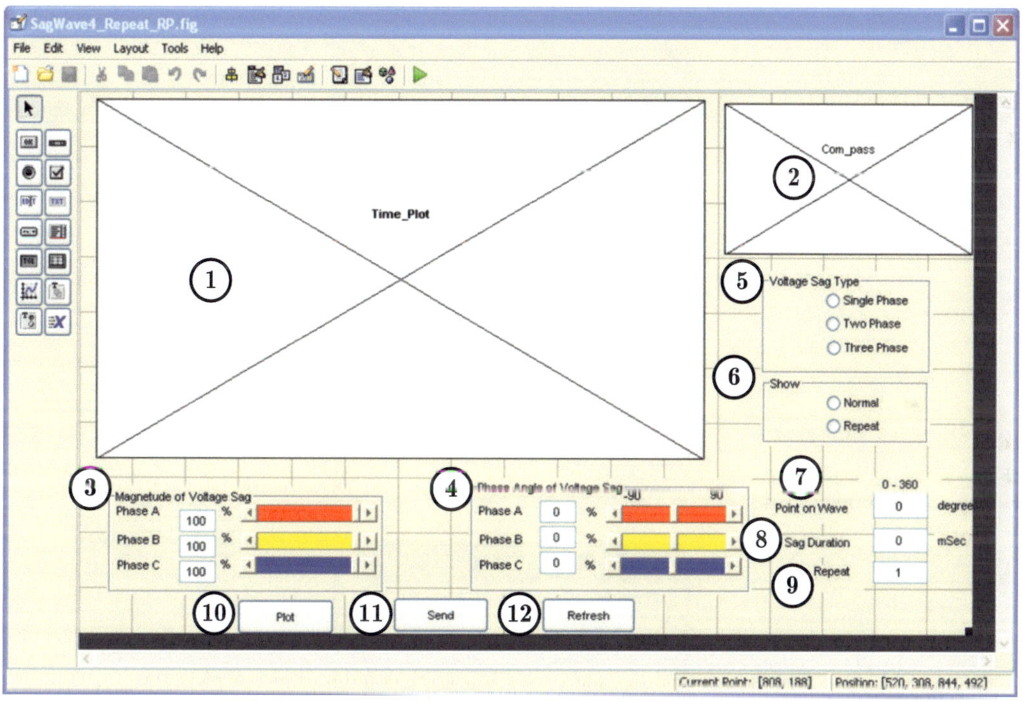

Figure 2. GUI "SagWave" designed.

3.3. Magnitude of Voltage (A, B and C phase), user had used value box or slider bar

This group used the Edit Text and Slider object. The Edit Text and Slider object set the default value as 100%. In the property inspector of three Edit Text changed the String to "100", Max to "1.0" and Min to "0.0", as shown in Fig. 5. The String in Edit Text property to changed to the number value in m-file. In the property inspector of three Slider changed the Value to "[100.0]", Max to "100.0" and Min to "0.0", as shown in Fig. 6.

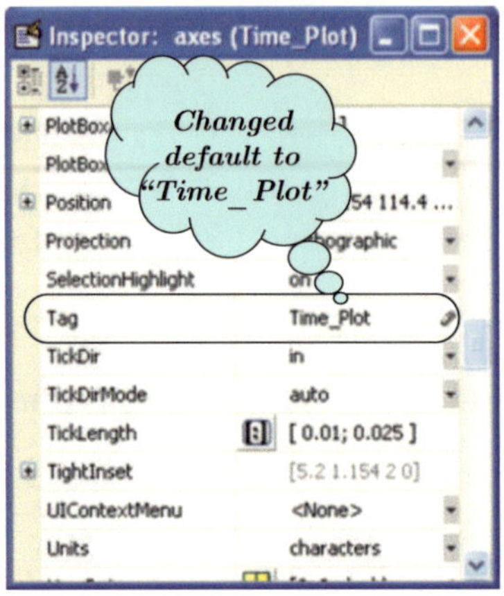

Figure 3. The property inspector of Axes1 assigned name to "Time_Plot".

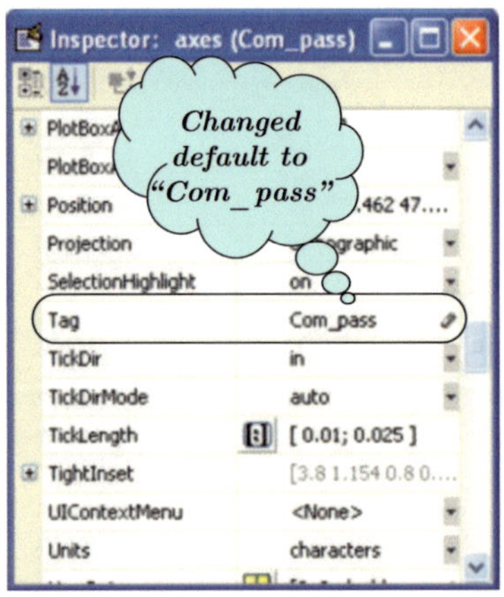

Figure 4. The property inspector of Axes2 assigned name to "Com_pass".

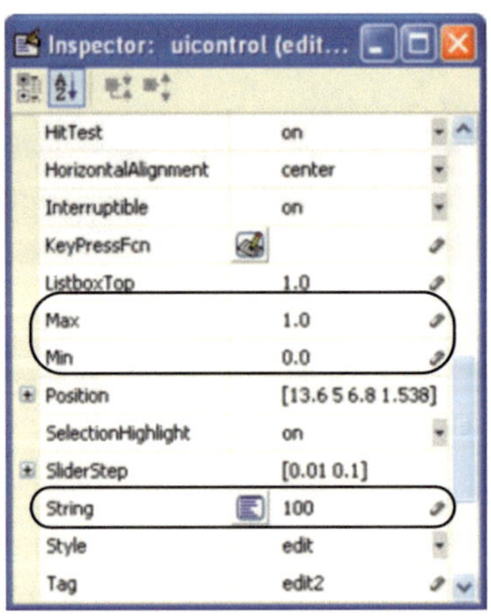

Figure 5. The property inspector of Edit Text (Magnitude) set Max and Min. (Magnitude) set Max and Min.

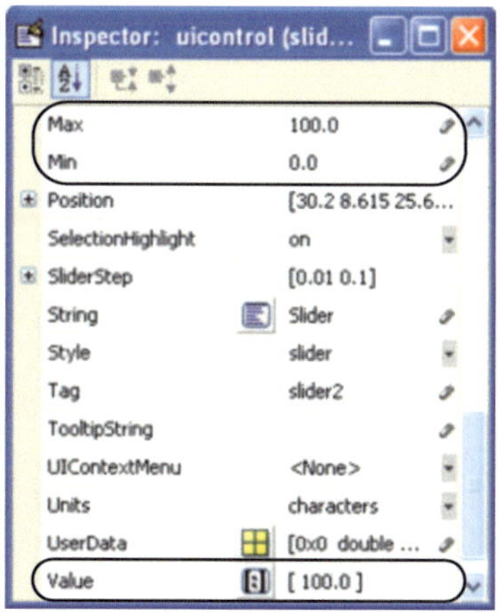

Figure 6. The property inspector of Slider.

3.4. Phase angle jump of voltage sag on A, B or C phase

This group used the Edit Text () and Slider () object, that the same as Magnitude group. In the property inspector of three Edit Text changed the String to "0", Max to "1.0" and Min to "0.0", as shown in Fig. 7. The String in Edit Text property to changed to the number value in m-file. In the property inspector of three Slider changed the Value to "[0,0]", Max to "90.0" and Min to "-90.0", as shown in Fig. 8.

3.5. Sag type for selected the voltage sag type (single-phase, two-phase and three-phase)

This group are "Radio Button" objects in component palette () on the left-side of window. The Radio Button of this group used to select the voltage sag type, Single-phase, Two-phase and Three-phase type. The property inspector was shown in Fig. 9.

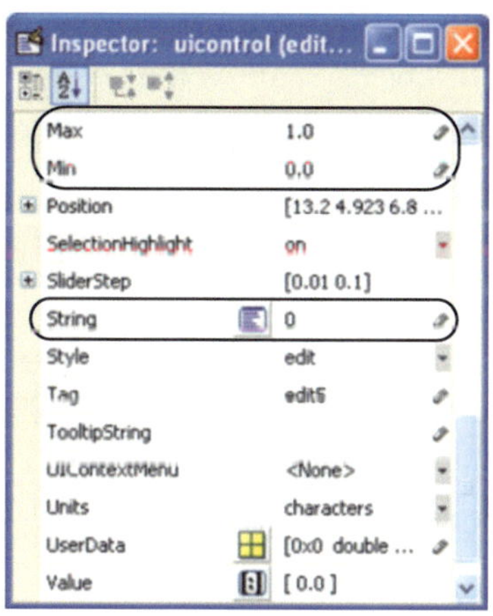

Figure 7. The property inspector of Edit Text of the Magnitude group.

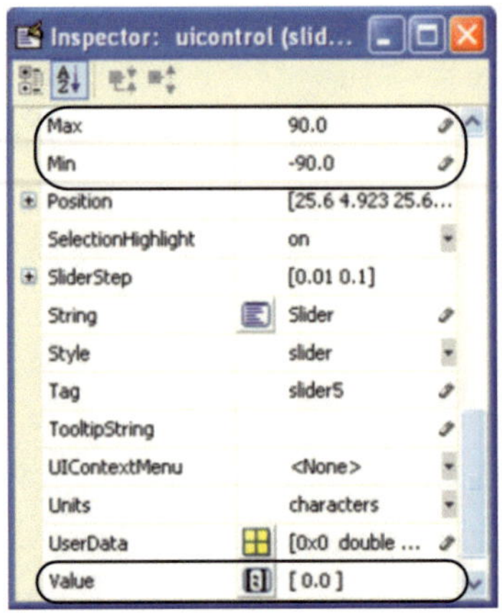

Figure 8. The property inspector of Slider of the Magnitude group.

Figure 9. The property inspector of Radio Button of voltage sag type group.

3.6. Display normal or repeat mode of voltage sag

These groups are "Radio Button" objects same as the voltage type group. The Radio Button of this group used to select the graph to shown normal and repeat mode of voltage sag. The property inspector was shown in Fig. 10.

3.7. Point on wave in degree

This object is the Edit Text for input degree of voltage on wave. The property inspector was shown in Fig.11.

3.8. Sag duration time for period time of voltage sag

This object is the Edit Text for input time duration of voltage sag. The property inspector was shown in Fig.11.

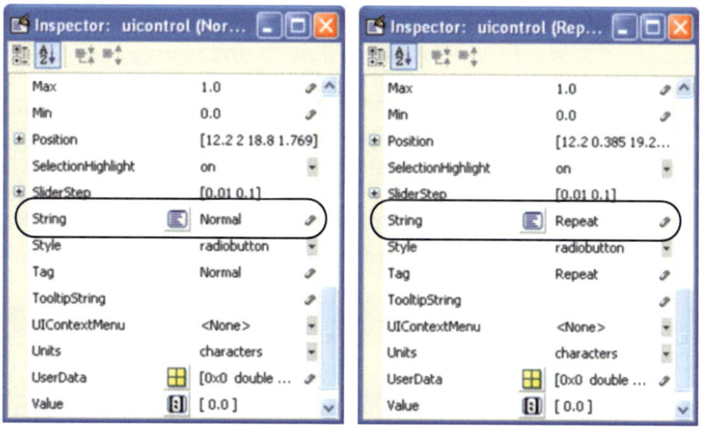

Figure 10. The property inspector of Radio Button of show group set to Normal and Repeat.

3.9. Number of repeat of voltage sag

This object is the Edit Text for input the repeated number of voltage sag. The property inspector was shown in Fig.11.

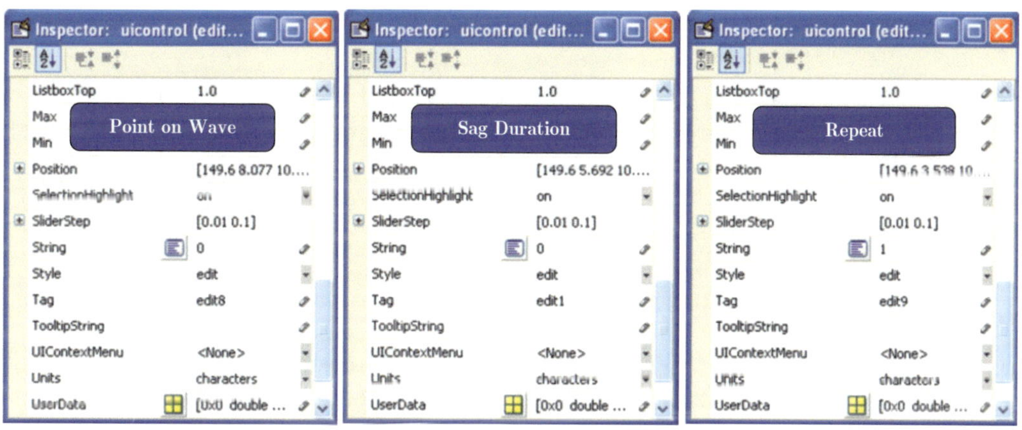

Figure 11. The property inspector of Point on Wave, Sag Duration and Repeat.

3.10. The button "Plot" for generated the voltage sag waveform

This object is "Button" objects in component palette () on the left-side of window. The "Plot" button is the main object of the GUI "SagWave", this button used to calculate and showed the graph of voltage sag. The property inspector was shown in Fig.12.

3.11. The button "Send" for send the data from SagWave to the dsPIC microcontroller

The "Send" button used to send the wave form data of voltage sag to dsPIC microcontroller. The property inspector was shown in Fig.12.

3.12. The button "Refresh" for clear the value and graphic display

The "Refresh" button used to clear the graphic, all of the value in program to provide the new value. The property inspector was shown in Fig.12.

Figure 12. The property inspector of Plot, Send and Refresh Button.

Finally users are ready to let GUIDE create the Fig-file and M-file. They are two options to create; one, simply select menu File → Save As.., or users can run GUI by select menu Tools → Run or click on tool bar. GUIDE will save user's GUI to file with the name as gave by user with extension *.fig and *.m of the same name.

4. SagWave programming

The concept of SagWave programming shown in Fig. 13. Form the 3th topic, GUIDE will create an M-File with callback function prototypes. The callback function was response to an event by MATLAB code. There must be a callback to implement the function of each graphical component on the GUI. Now we must be programming the callback to implement the function of each component on the SagWave.

4.1. Magnitude of Voltage Sag

These groups to input the magnitude of the voltage sag. There are two ways to input the magnitude;

1. Edit Text (Phase A, Phase B, Phase C Magnitude)

The Edit Text is an element that user to enter a text string(0 to 100). The program of this element is shown in Fig.14, in this program shown how to converse string to numeric.

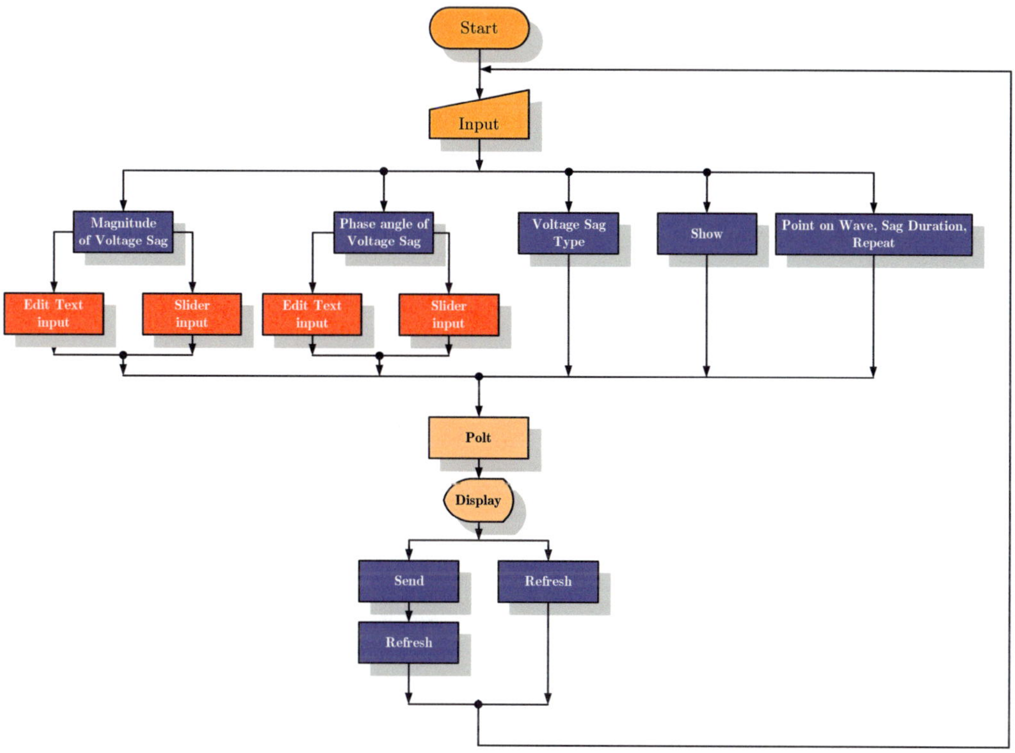

Figure 13. The main concept of SagWave programming.

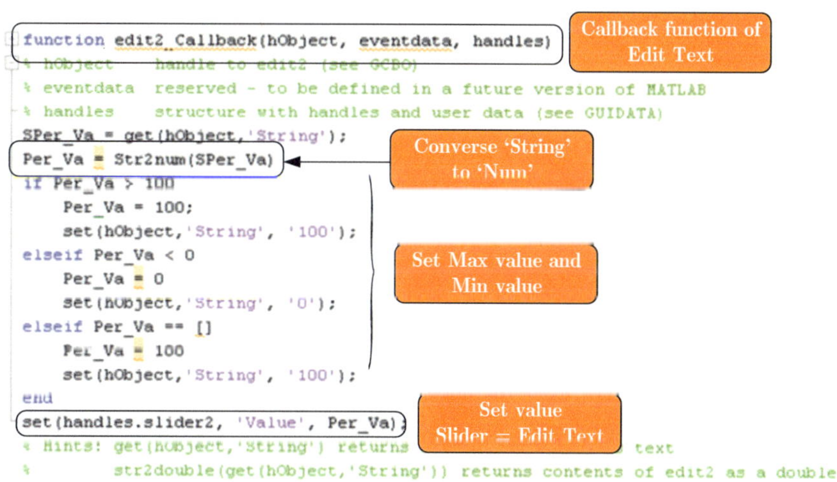

Figure 14. Program on Edit Text(Magnitude) callback function for input Magnitude.

2. Slider (Phase A, Phase B, Phase C Magnitude)

The Slider is the element that user to select values from continuous range between a specified minimum and maximum value by moving a bar with mouse. The program of this element is shown in Fig.15.

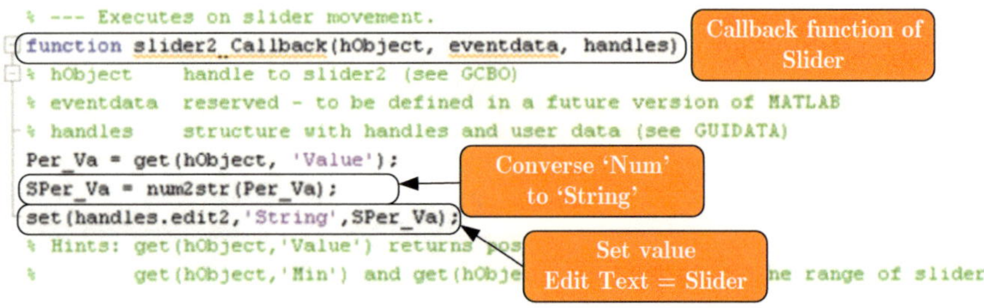

Figure 15. Program on Slider(Magnitude) callback function for input Magnitude.

4.2. Phase angle of Voltage Sag

These groups to input the phase angel of voltage sag. There are two ways to input the magnitude;

1. Edit Text (Phase A, Phase B, Phase C Phase angle)

The Edit Text is an element that user to enter a text string (-90 to +90). The program of this element is shown in Fig.16, in this program shown how to converse string to numeric.

2. Slider (Phase A, Phase B, Phase C Phase angle)

The program of this element is shown in Fig.17.

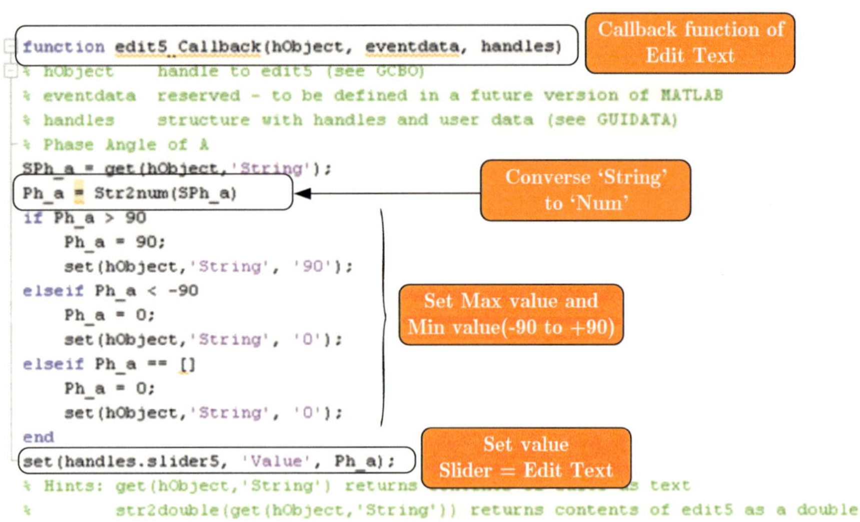

Figure 16. Program on Edit Text(Phase angle) callback function for input phase angle.

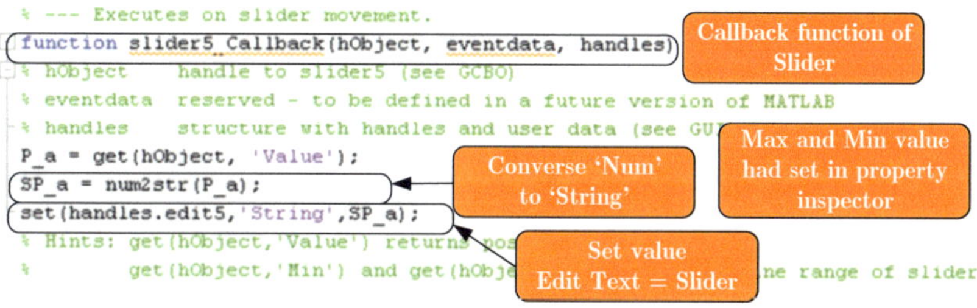

Figure 17. Fig. 17. Program on Slider(Phase angle) callback function for input phase angle.

4.3. Voltage Sag Type

These groups to select the voltage sag type, the program of this element shown in Fig. 18.

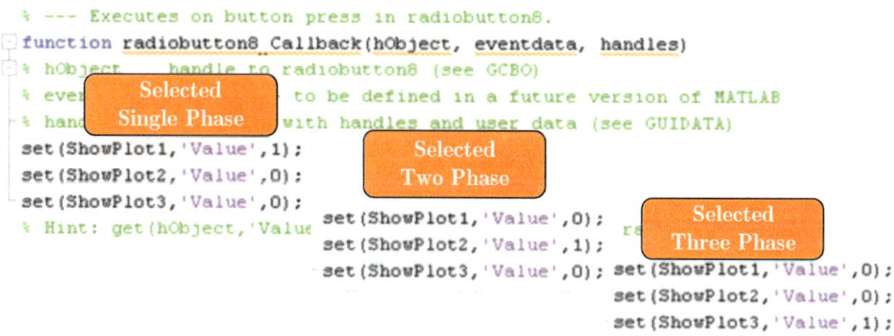

Figure 18. Program on Radio Button callback function for select voltage sag type.

4.4. Show

These groups to select the program to show single or repeat of voltage sag, program of this element shown in Fig. 19.

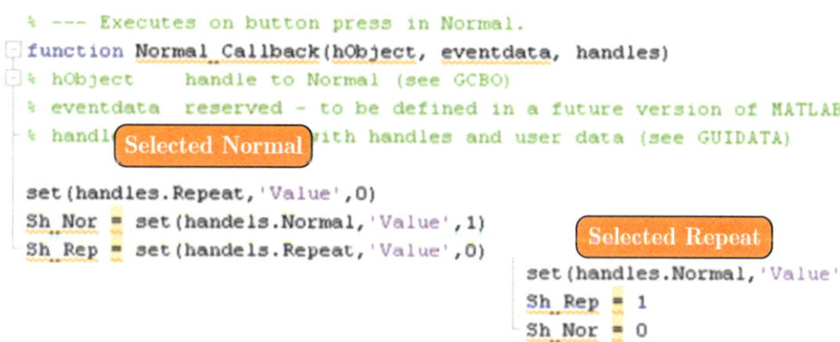

Figure 19. Program on Radio Button callback function for show Normal and Repeat.

4.5. Point on Wave, Sag Duration and Repeat

These groups to enter the value of Point on Wave, Sag duration and Repeat of voltage sag, the program of this element shown in Fig. 20.

4.6. Send Button

The Send Button is the button for user to send the data from SagWave to dsPIC microcontroller. The Duty.dat was generated by SagWave. The user clicked the "Send" button to send the Data.dat to dsPIC microcontroller by a RS-232 port. The program of this element shown in Fig. 21.

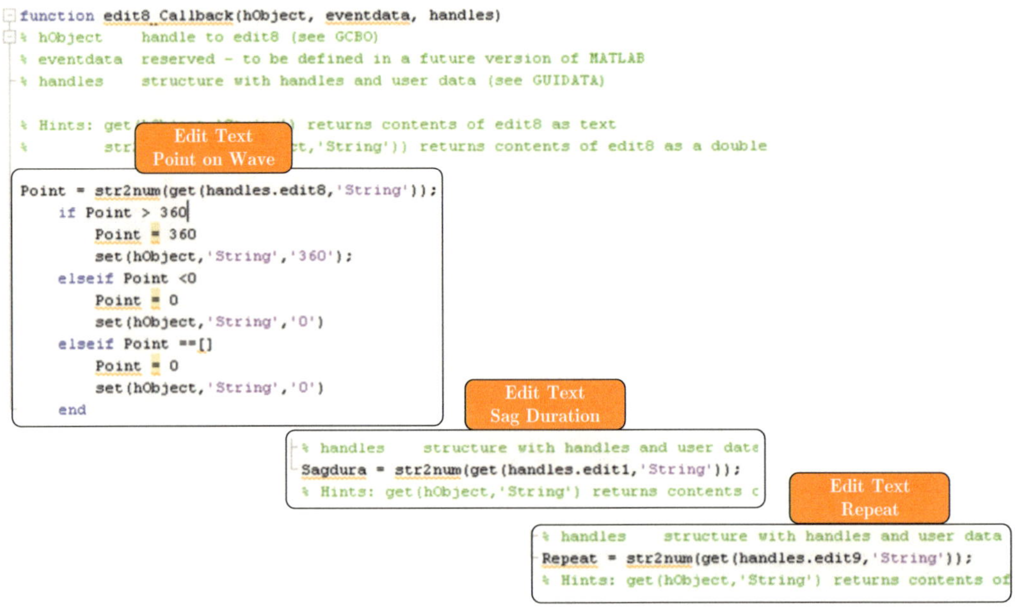

Figure 20. Program on Edit Text(Point on Wave, Sag Duration and Repeat) callback function.

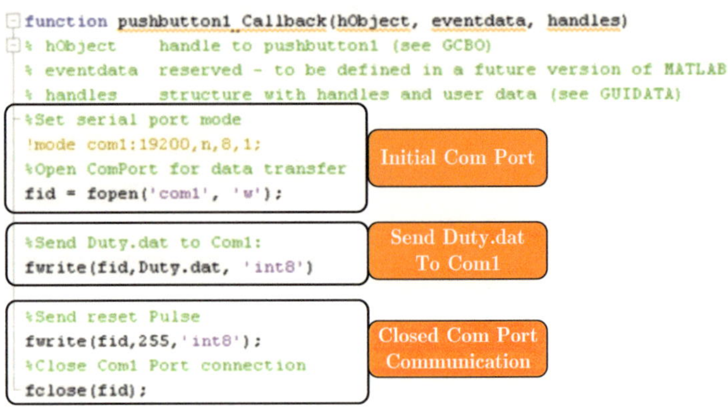

Figure 21. Program on "Send" Button callback function for open communication port and send file.

4.7. Refresh Button

The Refresh Button is the button for user to clear the parameter and graph in SagWave for the next simulation. The program of this element shown in Fig. 22.

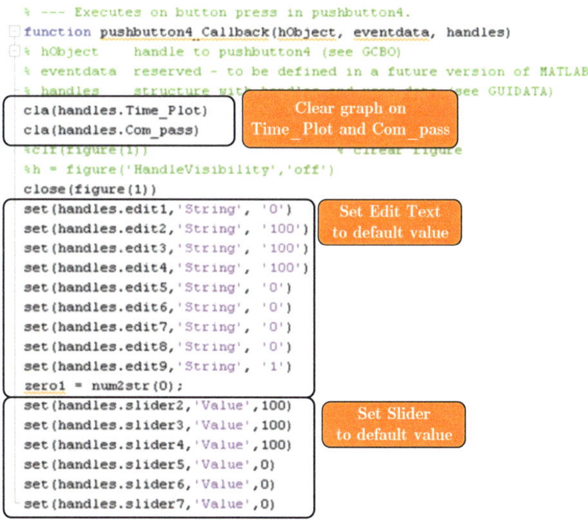

Figure 22. Program on "Refresh" Button callback function to clear all parameter.

4.8. Plot Button

The Plot Button is a main element of the SagWave, when user clicked this button the callback program calculated and plot graph of voltage sag. The program of this element shown in Fig. 23 to Fig. 25.

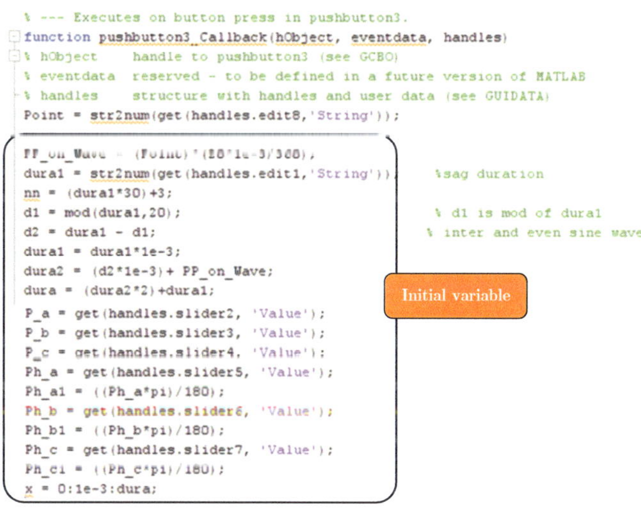

Figure 23. Initial variable sections of Plot button.

5. Simulation result

From equation 1 to equation 7 in Topic 1, if we need 60%(V = 0.6) voltage sag there can be calculate and result in Table. 1. The operation of this program with the user designing the voltage sag wave form SagWave software. Then the user clicks the "Send" button to send the parameters to dsPIC microcontroller. The actual voltage sag is created by a 3-phase 4-leg 4-wire inverter based on an *abc* algorithm.

```
plot(handles.Time_Plot,x4,Va4,'r','LineWidth',2)
grid on
hold on
plot(handles.Time_Plot,x4,Vb4,'b','LineWidth',2)
plot(handles.Time_Plot,x4,Vc4,'g','LineWidth',2)
axis(handles.Time_Plot,[0 dura -1.2 1.2]);
```

Plot voltage sag graph

```
        axes(handles.Com_pass)

        VecA = (P_a/100)*exp(i*Ph_a1);
        VecB = (P_b/100)*exp(i*(-(2*pi/3)+Ph_b1));
        VecC = (P_c/100)*exp(i*((2*pi/3)+Ph_c1));

compass(handles.Com_pass,VecA,'r')
hold on;
compass(handles.Com_pass,VecB,'k')
set(findobj('type','line'),'linewidth',3)
compass(handles.Com_pass,VecC,'b')
set(findobj('type','line'),'linewidth',3)

compass(handles.Com_pass,1,'r')
text(1.3,0,'Va')
compass(handles.Com_pass,(1*exp(i*(-(2*pi/3)))),'k')
text(-0.75,-1.1,'Vb')
compass(handles.Com_pass,(1*exp(i*(2*pi/3))),'b')
text(-0.75,1.1,'Vc')
```

Plot voltage sag Phasor

Figure 24. The program of graph and vector of phase voltage plotting section.

For example, the designed waveforms have parameters as found in "Bollen, (2000)". The parameters in Table 1. are used to generate seven types of voltage sag. Users can verify waveforms through graphic display windows as shown in Fig. 24.

Voltage Sag Type	Phase Voltage									
	A		B				C			
	Magnitude	Phase	Magnitude	Phase	Lag	Lead	Magnitude	Phase	Lag	Lead
A	*V*	0°	0.6	–120°	-	-	0.6	120°	-	-
B	*V*	0°	1	–120°	-	-	1	120°	-	-
C	1	0°	0.72	–133.9°	-13.39°	-	0.72	133.9°	-	13.39°
D	0.6	0°	0.92	–109.1°	-	10.9°	0.92	109.1°	-10.9°	-
E	1	0°	0.6	–120°	-	-	0.6	120°	-	-
F	*V*	0°	0.808	–111.79°	-	8.21°	0.808	111.79°	-8.21°	-
G	0.867	0°	0.6	–129.83°	-9.83°	-	0.6	129.83°	-	9.83°

Table 1. Parameter for seven type of voltage sag.

SagWave software can create point on wave single-phase(phase A) voltage sag, the parameters are shown in Table 2. The display of waveforms was is in Fig. 25. The parameters of single-phase(phase A) repeated voltage sag is shown in Table 3, and the simulation waveform in Fig.26.

```
if Sh_Nor == 1 & Sh_Rep == 0                    % Normal Show
        dura = (dura2*2)+dura1;
        axes(handles.Time_Plot);
        %set(findobj('type','line'),'linewidth',0.5)

        plot(handles.Time_Plot,x4,Va4,'r','LineWidth',2)
        grid on
        hold on
        plot(handles.Time_Plot,x4,Vb4,'b','LineWidth',2)
        plot(handles.Time_Plot,x4,Vc4,'g','LineWidth',2)
        axis(handles.Time_Plot,[0 dura -1.2 1.2]);
        %title(200,1000,'Phase Voltage Va, Vb, Vc');

elseif Sh_Rep == 1 & Sh_Nor == 0                % if 1 show sag wave RP and duty cycl

Repeat = str2num(get(handles.edit9,'String'));
```

Normal Display

```
case 3
    dura = 4*dura2 + 3*dura1 - (3*d1*1e-3);
    x3 = (dura2+dura1):0.01e-3:(dura2+dura1)+(dura2-d1*1e-3);
    Va2 = sin(pi*2*50*x3);
    x5 = (dura2+dura1)+(dura2-d1*1e-3):0.01e-3:(dura2+dura1)+(dura2-d1*1e-3)+dura1;
    x6 = ((dura2+dura1)+(dura2-d1*1e-3)+dura1): 0.01e-3 :((dura2+dura1)+(dura2-(d1*1e-3))+ dura1 + (dura2-(d1*1e-3)));
    y3 = 1*x3;
    y3(:)=1;
    y5 = 1*x5;
    Va5 = sin((pi*2*50*x5)+Ph_a1);
    y5(:) = P_a/100;
    y6 = 1*x6;
    y6(:)= 1;
    Va6 = sin(pi*2*50*x6);
    x7 = (3*dura2)+(2*dura1)-((d1*1e-3)*2): 0.01e-3 : (3*dura2)+(3*dura1)-((d1*1e-3)*2);
    x8 = (3*dura2)+(3*dura1)-((d1*1e-3)*2): 0.01e-3 : (4*dura2) + (3*dura1) - ((d1*1e-3)*3);
    Va7 = sin((pi*2*50*x7)+Ph_a1);
    Va8 = sin(pi*2*50*x8);
    y7 = 1*x7;
    y7(:) = P_a/100;
    y8 = 1*x8;
    y8(:)= 1;
    ya1 = [y1 ya y3 y5 y6 y7 y8];
    x4 = [x1 x2 x3 x5 x6 x7 x8];
    Va3 = [Va Va1 Va2 Va5 Va6 Va7 Va8];
    Va4 = Va3.*ya1;
    axes(handles.Time_Plot);
    plot(handles.Time_Plot,x4,Va4,'r','LineWidth',0.5)
    grid on
    axis(handles.Time_Plot,[0 dura -1.2 1.2]);
    figure(1)
    plot(x4,Va4)
    axis([0 dura -1.2 1.2]);
    grid on
```

Repeat Display
Repeat = 3

Figure 25. The program of Normal and Repeat as Repeat = 3.

Case	Manitude(%)	Duration(ms)	Point on Wave (degree)
1	5	60	45
2	25	60	45
3	25	60	270

Table 2. Parameter of point on wave voltage sag.

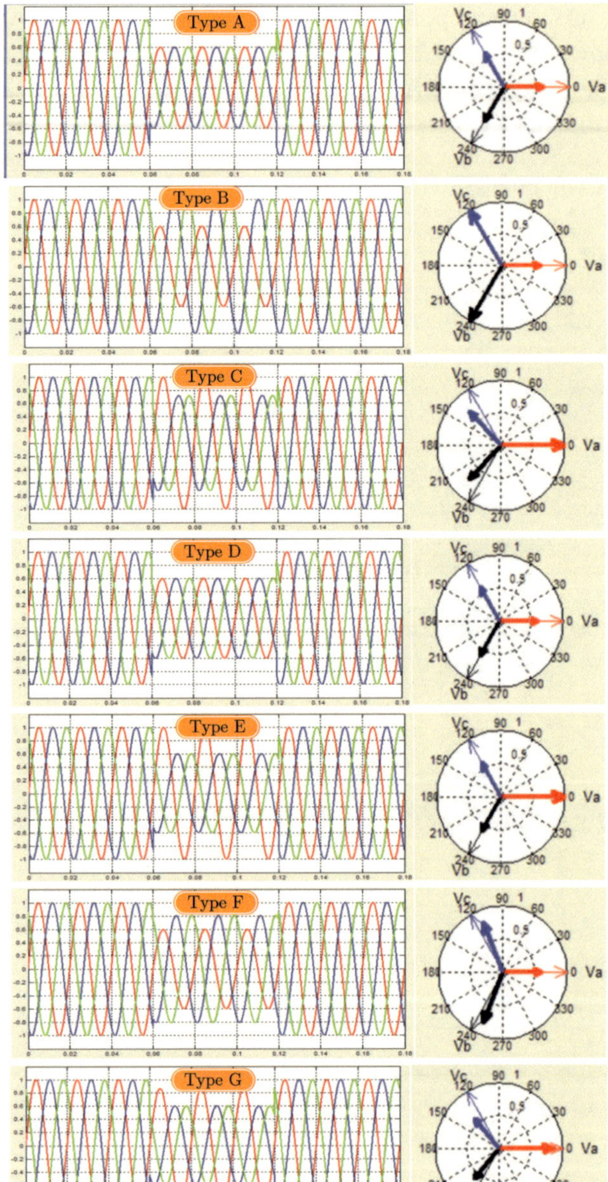

Figure 26. The seven types of voltage sag created using SagWave software.

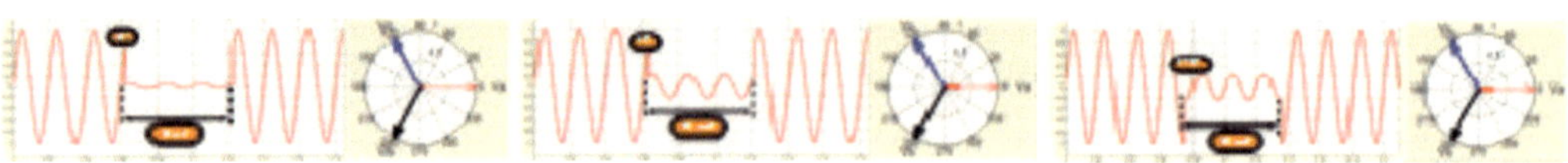

a) b) c)

Figure 27. a) The point on wave at $45°$; b) The point on wave at $45°$; c) The point on wave at $270°$

Case	Manitude(%)	Duration(ms)	Number of repeated
1	60	60	4
2	60	60	6

Table 3. Parameter of repeated voltage sag.

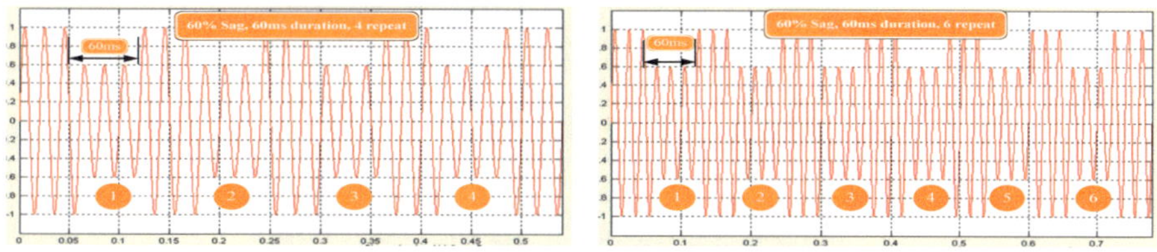

Figure 28. The simulation of single-phase voltage sag repeated.

6. Experimental of 3-phase 4-wire voltage sag generator

From section 3 the SagWave software generates the parameter file and sends it to the dsPIC microcontroller. The dsPIC uses this file to control the 3-phase 4-leg 4-wire inverter in order to create the actual waveform. Experimental results for voltage sag types A, B and E are shown in Fig. 27-29, respectively.

The experimental results in Fig. 27 are according with simulation results in Fig.24 (Type A). Fig.27 shows the 3-phase voltage and 3-phase current of voltage sag Type A. During voltage sag, the voltage on phase A (V_a), phase B (V_b) and phase C (V_c) are reduced to 60%. The current on phase A (I_a), phase B (I_b) and phase C (I_c) also are reduced to 60%. Before voltage sag occurs, the neutral current (I_n) has zero currents due to the balanced load condition. However during voltage sag transition, the unbalance load currents causes non-zero in the neutral current (I_n).

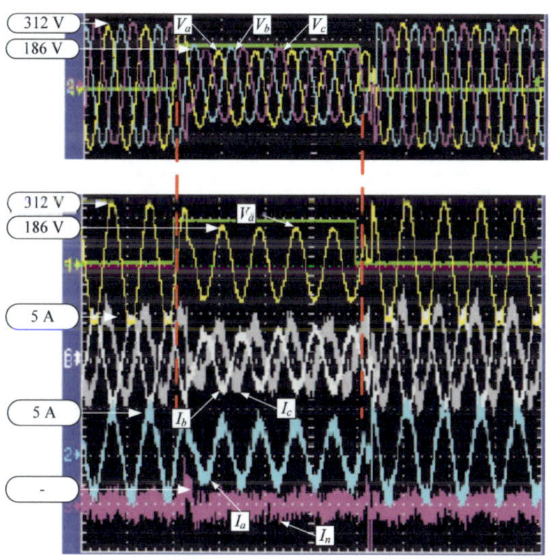

Figure 29. Voltage sag Type A.

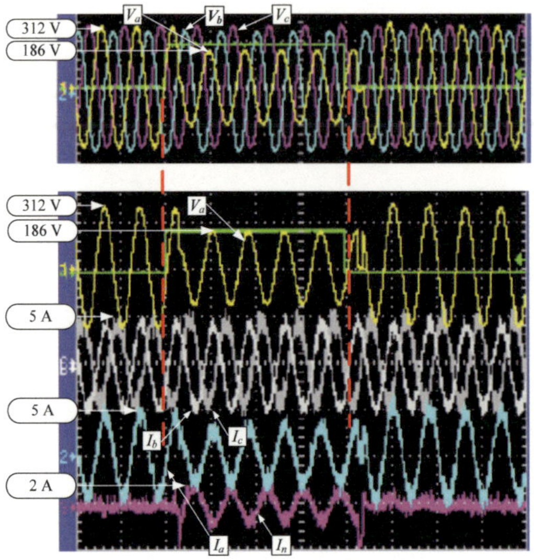

Figure 30. Voltage sag Type B.

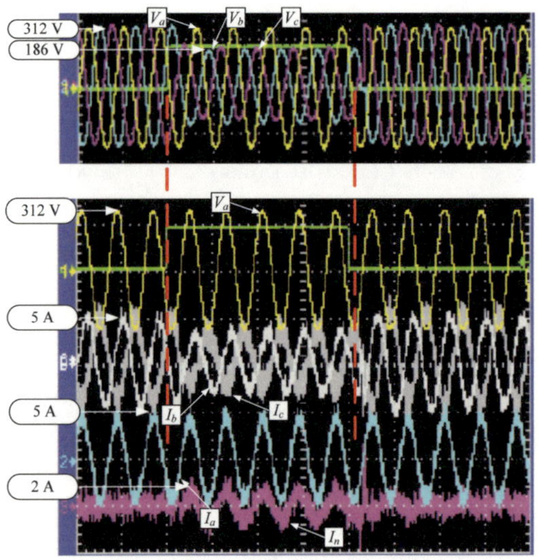

Figure 31. Voltage sag Type E.

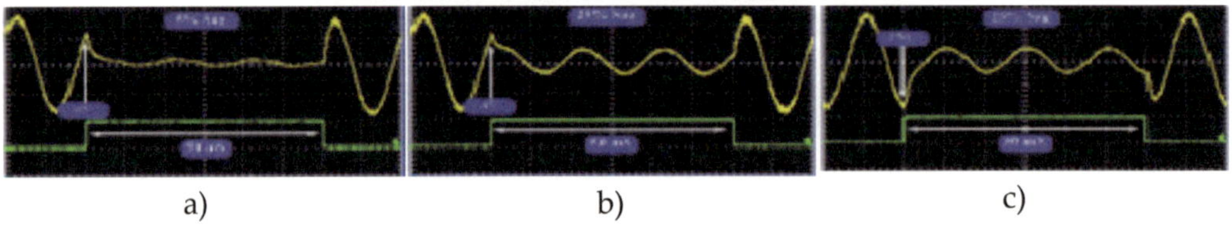

Figure 32. Experimental result: a) point on wave at 45° b) point on wave at 45° c) point on wave at 270°

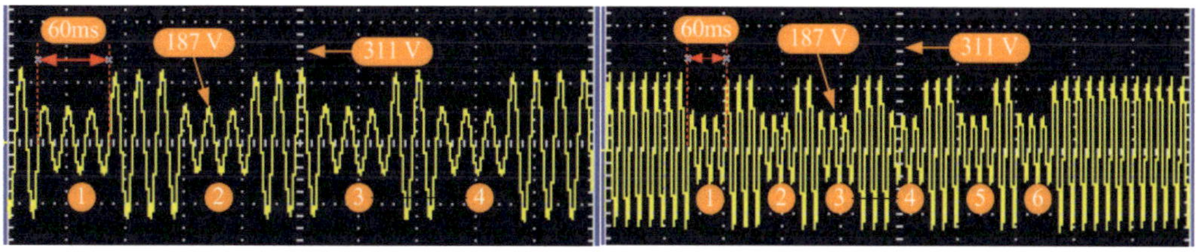

a) b)

Figure 33. Experimental results: a) 4 repeated voltage sag b) 6 repeated voltage sag

The experimental results in Fig. 28 are according with simulation results in Fig.24(Type B). Fig.28 shows the 3-phase voltage and 3-phase current of voltage sag Type B. During voltage sag, the voltage on phase A (V_a) is reduced to 60%. The current on phase A (I_a) also is reduced to 60%. Before voltage sag occurs, the neutral current (I_n) has zero currents due to the balanced load condition. However during voltage sag, the unbalance load causes an increase in the neutral current (I_n) that the return current in fourth leg of inverter.

The experimental results in Fig. 29 are according with simulation results in Fig.24 (Type E). Fig. 29 shows the 3-phase voltage and 3-phase current of voltage sag Type E. During voltage sag, the voltage on phase B (V_b) and phase C (V_c) are reduced to 60%. The current on phase A(I_a) is constant, while current on phase B (I_b) and current on phase C (I_c) are reduced to 60%. Before voltage sag occurs, the neutral current (I_n) has zero currents due to the balanced load condition. However during voltage sag, the unbalance load causes an increase in the neutral current (I_n) that the return current in fourth leg of inverter.

The experimental results of point on wave are shown in Fig. 30. The sag generator can generate waveform at any point of wave of sine wave as desired.

The experimental results of repeated voltage sags are shown in Fig. 31. The sag generator can generate repeated voltage sag waveform as many as desired.

7. Conclusions

This chapter has proposed the use of GUI SagWave software to provide a visual interactive capability generating data for the dsPIC controller. SagWave software can show the waveform and the phasor of the three-phase voltage. The simulation and experimental results have shown a simple control algorithm for generating the sag signal for testing. The experimental results have shown the main advantages of this prototype: point on wave, sag duration, magnitude of voltage sag and varied type of voltage sag. A future study will design software for the dsPIC microcontroller to generate all seven types of voltage sag and to test the dynamic and nonlinear loads.

Author details

Kosol Oranpiroj, Worrajak Moangjai and Wichran Jantee
Rajamangala University of Technology Lanna Chiangmai, Thailand

8. References

Bollen MHJ (2000). Understanding Power quality problems voltage sags and interruption. New York, IEEE Press. 193 – 196.

Bhavsar S, Shah VA, Gupta V. "Voltage dips and short interruption immunity test generator as per IEC 61000-4-11". *in Proc. of 15th National Power Systems Conference. Bombay, India,* 2008.

Collins ER, Morgan RL. "A Three-Phase Sag Generator for Testing Industrial Equipment". *IEEE Transaction on Power Delivery.* 11(1): 526 – 532, 1996.

Ma Y, Karady GG . "A single-phase voltage sag generator for testing electrical equipments". *in Proc. of Transmission and Distribution Conference and Exposition, Chicago IL,* pp 1 – 5, 2008.

Oranpiroj K, Premrudeepreechacharn S, Ngoudech M, Muangjai W, Yingkayun K, Boonsai T. "The 3-phase 4-wire voltage sag generator based on three dimensions space vector modulation in abc coordinates". *In Proc. of International Symposium on Industrial Electronics ISIE2009,* 275 – 280, 2009.

Oranpiroj K, Premrudeepreechacharn S, Ngoudech M, Muangjai W, Yingkayun K, Boonsai T. "The 3-phase 4-wire voltage sag generator based on abc algorithm". *in Proc. of Electrical Engineering/Electronics, Computer, Telecommunications and Information Technology ECTI-CON 2009,* 82 – 85, 2009.

Oranpiroj K, Premrudeepreechacharn S, Higuchi K. "SagWave for the 3-phase 4-wire voltage sag generator prototype". *in Proc. of IEEE International conference on Control Applications CCA 2010,* 2209 – 2212, 2010.

Oranpiroj K, Premrudeepreechacharn S,Muangjai W, C.V. Nayar., "Development of the 3-phase 4-wire voltage sag generator". *Scientific Research and Eassys,* 6(23): 4960 – 4974, 2011.

Patrick Marchand, O.Thomas Holland, *Graphics and GUIs with MATLAB.* (CHAPMAD & HALL/CRC, LTD, 2003)

Rylande M, Grady WM, Arapostathis A. "Enhancement and application of a voltage sag station to test transient load response". *in Proc. of IEEE Electric Ship Technology Symposium, Arlington VA.* pp. 428 – 433, 2007.

Takahashi R, Cortez JA, da Silva VF, Rezek AJJ. "A prototype implementation of a voltage sag generator". *VIII Conferencia Internacional de Aplicacoes Industriais, Poços de Caldas, Brazil,* 2008

Teke A, Meral ME, and Tümay M. "Evaluation of available power quality disturbance generators for testing of power quality mitigation devices". *Int. J. of Sciences and Techniques of Automatic Control and Computer Engineering, (special issue),* pp. 624 – 635, 2008

Modelling and Characterization of Power Electronics Converters Using Matlab Tools

Sven Fagerstrom and Nagy Bengiamin

Additional information is available at the end of the chapter

http://dx.doi.org/10.5772/48544

1. Introduction

Advances in semiconductor technologies to produce high power devices have facilitated numerous applications where high power density is a key for practical and sophisticated solutions. Instead of being limited to the traditional low power electronics applications, high power devices opened a broad frontier for engineering design. These devices are now embedded in systems that span the full range from small electric motor drives to very high voltage transmission lines where hundreds of amperes are regulated while the devices are exposed to thousands of volts. Compared to the traditional rotating electric machine based (dynamic) energy conversion, these devices made static conversion from one form of electricity to another so seamless that employing a certain form of electric power (AC, DC, or a combination) has become an engineering design option rather than a forced solution. Application areas like in motor drives, fuel cells, solar panels, wind turbines, electric cars, and high speed transportation systems are only a few of the major beneficiaries of advances in power electronics. Emphases on energy conservation motivated the design for improved system efficiency where power electronics devices are utilized in their most desirable mode. These efforts resulted in increased portability of high power density systems and affected the design of the full range of power systems including those for small electronic equipment which are becoming more demanding on power for their ever increasing features and capabilities. Like all advanced engineering design applications, mathematical developments and supporting software tools for modeling, simulation and analysis are critical (Shaffer, 2007; Assi, 2011). In addition to introducing some of the fundamental concepts in power electronics and related applications, this chapter exploits the capabilities of Matlab and its associated SimPower and Simulink toolboxes as an effective relevant engineering tool.

When dealing with an alternating current, changing voltage levels, at the same frequency, is achieved simply by utilizing AC transformers where the principle of mutual induction exists between two magnetic coils with the proper turns-ratio. Mutual induction is possible due to the rate at which the magnetic lines cut the wires of the transformer coils and the produced electromotive force that is capable of producing current in closed electric loops. This fundamental concept is not applicable to DC voltage and current due to the absence of the alternating nature of the produced magnetic fields. Therefore, changing DC voltage from one level to another must be achieved using different methodologies. One possible methodology is to modulate DC voltages by switching them on and off at proper rates and durations such that the average produced voltage is controlled. The key concept here is to store energy then release it at the proper time with the proper rate needed for the desired load. Energy storage elements like inductors and capacitors facilitate this methodology. Therefore, a combination of energy storage elements and switching schemes provide the basic ingredients for the design of DC-DC conversion devices. Such devices are referred to as power electronic DC-DC converters. The modes of operation of these devices are dependent on the shape of the produced voltage waveform which is manipulated by the switching scheme and the size of the energy storage elements. Compared to AC transformers which usually exhibit linear characteristics for its most modes of operation, DC transformers (DC-DC converters) possess highly non-linear characteristics which require more intensive analysis and design schemes.

Optimization of power electronics systems' design and operation is important to accommodate the growing need for energy efficiency in portable electronic devices to extend their battery life and respond to their increasing functionality and features. These features demand more electric power while the devices must reduce in size and weight; i.e. increased energy density. DC-DC converters are embedded in numerous electronic equipment and they have become an integral part of many commercial and industrial products. These converters are employed to lower (buck) or raise (boost) DC voltage levels as needed by the application. Buck and boost converters are emphasized in this chapter for their different topologies and modes of operation. The presented methodologies facilitate analysis, characterization, and design of efficient DC-DC converters. Sufficient background and theoretical development are provided for completeness.

2. Static power converters

Static power converters can take numerous topologies which enable AC-AC, AC-DC, DC-AC, and DC-DC conversion. AC-AC converters vary in complexity from the crude chopping of the AC waveform in order to regulate the delivered average power like in light dimmers and electric stove burners to varying the produced frequency like in Variable Speed Drives (VSD) for AC motors. AC-DC converters usually utilize the simple rectifier bridge configuration. They are popular in windmill applications as a front stage before converting to AC for interface with the utility grid. This last stage employs the DC-AC converter which is also popular in applications like solar panels interface with the utility grid. In addition to the AC-DC converter, most household and commercial electronic equipment use DC-DC converters. These converters produce the multiple DC voltage levels necessary for the operation of the equipment. DC-DC converters are also critical for battery powered portable electronic devices where power density is high and efficiency of converters is critical to the charging cycle of the device.

2.1. AC-AC converter

Converting AC at the same frequency is most effectively achieved using induction transformers. This is particularly true for high frequency/low-power applications where the magnetic core is relatively small. Applications that require converting to different frequencies, however, can be achieved in several configurations. One configuration may utilize an intermediate stage of AC-DC back-to-back with DC-AC as is the case for wind energy conversion for example; assuming that the wind turbine is coupled to an AC electric generator. Cycloconverters (Rashid, 2004) on the other hand, don't require an intermediate stage as they utilize chopping techniques to shape the waveform directly. Conversion from three-phase to either single-phase or three-phase is usually possible with the proper control scheme. One crude application to regulate power at the same frequency using waveform chopping is that of the light-dimmer (Paul, 2001); used here to illustrate some of the basic concepts. Although light dimmers usually regulate power consumption without altering the fundamental frequency of the source, they provide a more economical solution compared to tap-changing induction type transformers.

Fig. 1 depicts the circuit configuration for a simple light dimmer where the primary power control device is the Triac whose gate firing device is the Diac (Skvarenina, 2002). The Diac is a fixed break-over voltage device compared to the Triac that permits a variable firing angle through its gate terminal. Compared to the Silicon Controlled rectifier (SCR) which is also gate controlled, the Triac permits device firing on the positive and negative half cycles of the AC waveform. The SCR has a similar characteristic to that of a rectifier (unidirectional) but with an adjustable conduction angle (Rashid, 2004). Both devices are self-commutated, i.e. they turn off naturally at the zero crossings of the waveform. The triggering circuit for the Triac is comprised of R_1, R_2, and C where the potentiometer R_2 represents the adjustable resistor which is usually operated by the dial (or slide switch) on the operating plate of the light dimmer. The value of R_2 controls the conduction phase of the Triac. As the capacitor charges to a voltage higher than the break-over voltage of the Diac, a pulse is produced at the gate of the Triac to turn it on. In the conduction mode, the internal resistance of the Triac becomes small causing the flow of current through the light bulb. A higher value of R_2 elongates the charging time of C (longer time constant $\tau = C(R_1+R_2)$), causing a delayed triggering pulse and a shorter conduction period for the Triac. The average power transmitted to the light bulb becomes less, resulting in a dimmer light. The same logic works for both halves of the source's waveform cycle. This application will be analyzed using Matlab in Section 4 to demonstrate some of the capabilities of the SimPower and Simulink tool boxes.

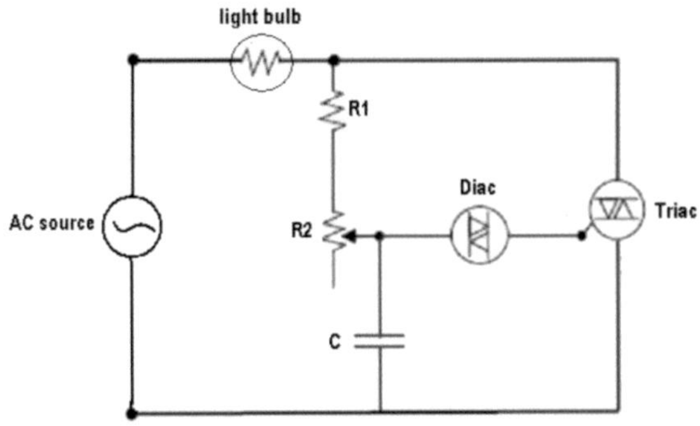

Figure 1. Light Dimmer Circuit

Several practical notes relative to the circuit in Fig. 1 are due,

1. While it may seem that the Diac is an unnecessary device in this application since the voltage of the capacitor may trigger the gate of the Triac directly, it must be noticed that Triacs are notorious for not firing symmetrically. Lack of symmetry in triggering at the same voltage level for both polarities of a full cycle produces unnecessary additional harmonics that negatively affect the efficiency of the circuit. The symmetrical characteristic if the Diac provides accurate timing that enhances the firing symmetry of the Triac.
2. One may use two SCRs back-to-back to implement the power control device in place of the Triac.
3. The firing time through the RC circuit is perfectly synchronized with the conduction cycle of the Triac because they are both powered by the same AC source.

2.2. DC-DC converter

Converting DC voltage to the proper levels from a single energy source that might be depleting, like in battery applications, requires employing energy storage elements (inductors) with associated power electronics devices. When switched ON-OFF at a certain rate, stored energy gets released to the load at the proper time to maintain the desired voltage level. Pulse-Width-Modulation (PWM) techniques are most popular in this application. Converters of this type are suited for boosting or bucking the source voltage; commonly known as switching power supplies. Since the current is DC and zero crossing is not one of the steady cyclic features like in AC circuits, self-commutation is not possible. Therefore, Gate-Turn-Off (GTO) devices are required (Skvarenina, 2002). These devices are turned off with a negative pulse on the gate terminal. MOSFETs and BJTs also provide a viable option in low power applications. Feedback loop methodologies are an integral part of DC-DC converters to regulate the load voltage, compensating for load variations and irregularities in the source voltage.

Current and voltage ripples, and high frequency harmonic distortion are common byproducts of switching techniques. Capacitors are usually employed to insure acceptable ripple content. Harmonics negatively affect the efficiency of the converter and produce losses in the form of heat. While the produced load current is regulated for a desired average value, the cyclic behavior produces current fluctuations in the energy storage elements. Operating at zero current for energy storage elements during part of the cycle results in a highly nonlinear characteristic, where the converter is known to be in its Discontinuous Conduction Mode (DCM). The Continuous Conduction Mode (CCM), however, insures nonzero current during the full cycle of switching (Rashid, 2004; Shaffer, 2007). Each mode of operation has certain implications on the ripples and harmonics content which affects the efficiency of the converter.

2.2.1. Buck converter

In low power applications, voltage bucking is usually achieved using voltage divider resistors. This simple solution is acceptable because the current is usually too small to cause significant losses in the resistors. Employing this approach in high power applications is unrealistic because the losses of the resistors may exceed the useful power consumed by the load; that is in addition to the associated heat dissipation issues that must be resolved to insure sufficient ventilation. The DC-DC converter provides a more practical solution in spite of its associated design complexities at times.

Bucking DC source voltages can be achieved using a topology like the one shown in Fig. 2. The energy storage element (L) is to be sized for the desired mode of operation (CCM or DCM). The power device (GTO in this case) switches On-OFF using PWM where the duty-ratio ($D=T_{on}/T$) determines the average load voltage; T is the time of one period of the switching frequency (f). The diode facilitates inductor current wheeling during the OFF time of the GTO. The capacitor is usually sized to reduce the load current ripples. The inherent inductor current ripples (usually in the range of about 30%) are then facilitated by the capacitor while blocking it from flowing through the load. Snubber circuits are installed across the power devices for protection and to minimize the stress on the device that may result from opening the circuit while the current cannot be stopped instantaneously due to the nature of the energy storage element. Current and voltage waveforms will be shown in Section 4 for illustration.

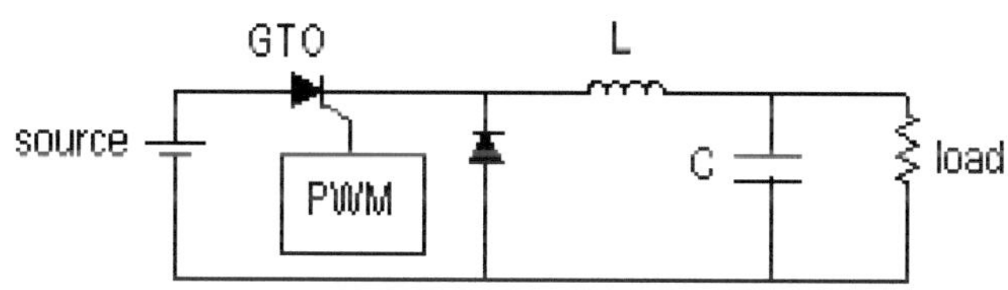

Figure 2. DC-DC Buck Converter

Design of the DC-DC converter centers around determining the size of the energy storage element (L) which achieves predetermined V_{source}, V_{load}, ΔV_{load} (load voltage ripple), and I_{ripple}. Knowing that $I_{ripple}=\Delta I_L$, $D=V_{load}/V_{source}$ assuming CCM, $T=1/f$, and $V_L=V_{source}-V_{load}$ during T_{on} (Rashid, 2004), Eq. (2) can be obtained.

Since,

$$V_L = L\frac{di_L}{dt} \tag{1}$$

therefore,

$$\begin{aligned} L&=V_L\frac{\Delta T}{\Delta i_L} \\ &= (V_{sourse}-V_{load}).(\frac{D}{f}).(\frac{1}{I_{ripple}}) \\ &= (V_{load}-\frac{V_{load}^2}{V_{source}}).(\frac{1}{f.I_{ripple}}) \end{aligned} \tag{2}$$

Notice that L is charging during T_{on} only, which means that ΔT=D/f. The calculated "L" is usually well above the minimum inductance needed to insure CCM in many applications. Only very light load conditions may force DCM.

The capacitor "C" is sized to reduce load current ripple while providing a pass for the inductor current ripples (I_{ripple}). It is worth noting that the inherent Effective Series Resistance (ESR) of the capacitor plays a major role in determining the size of the capacitor.

Since,

$$i_C=C\frac{dV_C}{dt} \tag{3}$$

but,

$$\Delta V_C=\Delta i_C(ESR+\frac{\Delta T}{C}) \text{ and } \Delta V_C=\Delta V_{load} \tag{4}$$

therefore,

$$\begin{aligned} C&=\frac{\Delta i_C.\Delta T}{\Delta V_{load}-ESR.\Delta i_C} \\ &=\frac{I_{ripple}.D}{f(\Delta V_{load}-ESR.I_{ripple})} \end{aligned} \tag{5}$$

Eq. (5) shows that the capacitor's ESR rating can have a significant effect on the size of the capacitor knowing that the tolerated ΔV_{load} is usually small in sophisticated applications. Therefore, the ESR rating shouldn't be overlooked when selecting the capacitor. The Effective Series Inductance (ESL) rating of the capacitor is also relevant but it is usually considered for very high switching frequencies only (>1 MHz). By then, inductive effect of board tracings can start to be critical as well.

2.2.2. Boost converter

While bucking the source voltage for low power applications can be achieved with resistor voltage dividers (passive components), boosting the voltage requires active devices like Operations-Amplifiers (OpAmps). Power OpAmps are also available for low-voltage medium power (500 Watt) applications but they usually exhibit high power loss and they need active cooling (fans) in addition to passive cooling via heat sinks. OpAmps are also analog devices which are usually controlled with analog control voltages, while PWM controlled power devices can be easily interfaced with digital controllers. Real-time load voltage regulation is achieved most effectively with embedded digital controllers.

By rearranging the components of the buck converter as shown in Fig. 3, it becomes possible to boost the source voltage. The underlying principle of operation is in the fact that the polarity of the inductor (L) voltage reverses instantaneously when the rate of change in the inductor current (i_L) reverses pattern; i.e. di_L/dt changes sign. During the ON time (T_{on}) of the GTO, the inductor charges with its voltage taking the opposite polarity of the source. When the GTO turns OFF during T_{off}, the inductor current starts to drop and accordingly its polarity reverses direction to become in the same direction like the source. The load, then, becomes supported by V_{source} plus V_L which signifies the higher load voltage compared to the source voltage. The role of the capacitor is similar to that of the buck converter, that is to reduce the ripples of the load voltage as it supports the load voltage during T_{on} in this case. It must be noted that V_L is equal to $L(di_L/dt)$ which means that the inductor voltage can rise significantly if the current is allowed to change at a high rate, resulting in load voltages much higher than that of the source. The inductor, however, must be sized properly and allowed to charge enough by increasing the duty-ratio (D) of the PWM scheme such that it stores enough energy to feed the load during T_{off}. The ratio V_{load}/V_{source} is determined by 1/(1-D) which implies that V_{load} can rise well above V_{source} as the duty ratios gets closer to 100% (Rashid, 2004). The physical limit of the employed components is usually the determining factor for how high V_{load} may be attained.

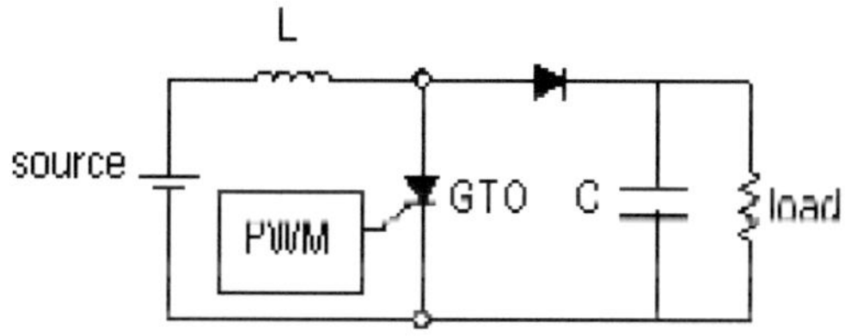

Figure 3. DC-DC Boost Converter

2.2.3. Buck-boost converter

Rearranging the components as shown in Fig. 4 provides the flexibility to buck or boost the source voltage by adjusting the duty-ratio (D) of the PWM. A 50% duty-ratio provides the load with the same source voltage while a lower duty-ratio bucks the voltage and a higher duty ratio boosts the voltage (Rashid, 2004). It was proven that V_{load}/V_{source} is determined by

D/(1-D). The orientation of the diode is such that the load current is blocked while the inductor is charging during T_{on}. During T_{off} the inductor releases its energy to the load through the diode loop resulting in an opposite voltage polarity compared to that of the buck or boost configurations. The size of the storage element (L) is critical to facilitating the boost mode. To insure CCM, the inductor must be of a certain minimum size (Rashid, 2004). Current and voltage waveforms will be shown in Section 4 for illustration.

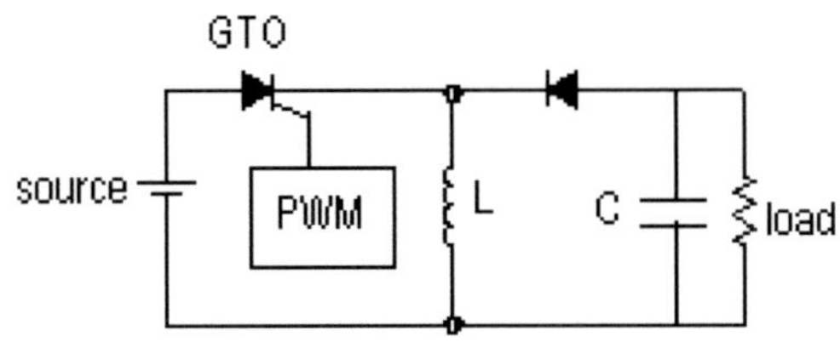

Figure 4. DC-DC Buck-Boost Converter

2.3. Voltage control

Control of switching power converters requires modulating the width of the pulse provided to the power devices' gate, based on feedback from the load voltage and the inductor's current. Fig. 5 illustrates the basic components of an analog control scheme; where the output voltage provides the desired feedback. This scheme is identified as the "voltage-mode" control. The low-pass filter (R_3, C_3) of the error amplifier along with R_1 provide feedback gain and reduce harmonics. The PWM hardware can be a typical controllable IC and the Schmitt-trigger is to produce sharp edges for the power device's gate. Needed high gate current usually requires current amplification as well.

The compensator can be implemented with Op-Amps to realize desired dynamic characteristics for voltage recovery and regulation. Traditional compensators like PID, lead-lag, and Sliding Mode Control (SMC) are all applicable. Digital control, however, provides flexibility in implementing sophisticated control schemes and mixed mode operations to achieve power saving and to possibly automatic controller tuning. Digital schemes also reduce magnetic interference effects which would most probably exist in applications that require DC-DC power conversion. Digital Signal Processors (DSPs), microcontrollers, and Field Programmable Gate Arrays (FPGAs) together with the Analog-to-Digital Converter (ADC) are widely used to implement digital controllers. However, high-speed high-resolution ADCs are expensive and they are not easy to consolidate into an integrated circuit.

Design of the compensator requires transient analysis and solving the differential equations that describe each waveform. Retaining the instantaneous detailed characteristic of the circuit requires analysis of each mode of the switching cycle. This level of detail is usually not necessary for the design of the compensator. Averaging over a number of switching cycles provides viable approximate models (Forsyth & Mollov, 1998) which simplify the compensator design significantly. In this technique, the state equations for the RC circuit are written for both modes of the converter (ON and OFF). A combined state equations model is then formed using the weighted average of the state matrices of the ON and OFF models according to the duty ratio (D). The produced model is a set of two linear time-variant state equations which ignore ripple components. The time-variant effect is due to the presence of the control variable "D(t)" (varying duty-ratio) in the state matrices rather than being part of the input control variables vector. Since solving time-variant equations is difficult, further simplifications are required. Linearization techniques are then employed for specific operating conditions, resulting in small-signal state-space models (Johansson, 2004). These models facilitate frequency and time domain design methodologies.

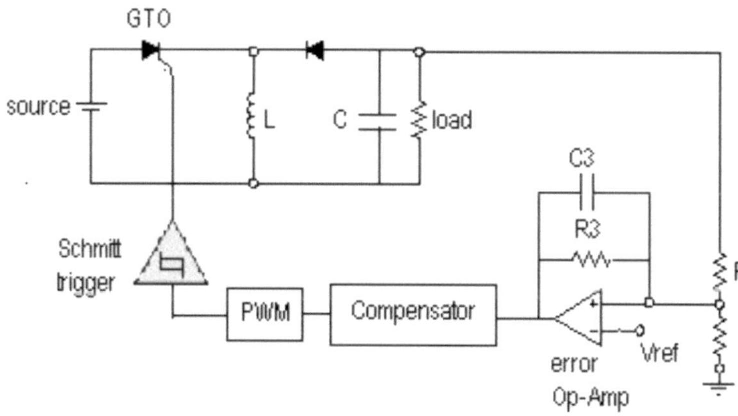

Figure 5. Voltage Control of Buck-Boost Converter

In addition to the above explained voltage-mode control scheme, current-mode control can also be achieved by sensing the current of the switching power device or the energy storage element and integrating it into the main voltage control loop (Johansson, 2004). In this scheme, the output of the voltage compensator acts are the reference voltage for the current feedback loop which controls the PWM and adjusts the gate pulse for the power device. This scheme usually improves the stability of the converter in high performance applications. Controlling the peak inductor current is one of the popular schemes employed. Current sensing can also be used to determine when to switch between CCM and DCM which facilitates implementing high efficiency schemes for operation.

2.4. Power saving and improved efficiency

Minimization of DC-DC converter power losses is important to accommodate the growing need for a longer battery life and reduced size and weight of portable electronic devices. Power losses are usually dependent on the type of power devices and their conduction losses, the effective series resistance of inductors and capacitors, mode of operation of the converter, switching scheme, and the switching frequency. While diodes are simple in their use, they may reduce the efficiency of the converter due to their high losses in certain modes of operation. The same function of a diode can be achieved by using a switching power device similar to the main energy transfer device of the converter (e.g. GTO or MOSFET).

This will require applying switching logic to multiple devices in the same converter. Synchronizing the switching of the devices introduces an additional control challenge and the converter topology is therefore referred to as the "synchronous" topology. The diode topology is then called "asynchronous". A detailed characterization of power losses in DC-DC converters is offered by Gildersleeve, et.al., (2002).

Various techniques were proposed in the literature to reduce power losses in DC-DC converters, including soft-switching (Zhou & Rincon-Mora, 2006), synchronous rectification (Djekic & Brkovic, 1997; Arbetter et al., 1995), mode hopping between CCM and DCM (Wang et al., 1997), Zero-Voltage Switching (Stratakos, 1998), mixed synchronous-asynchronous control (Saggini et al., 2007), variable switching frequency (Djekic & Brkovic, 1997; Arbetter et al., 1995), and Hybrid Mode Hopping combined with variable frequency (Wang et al., 1997). These techniques are summarized and compared by Zhou (2003). Djekic et al. (1997) compared synchronous and asynchronous rectification buck converters for efficiency at various loads and switching frequencies. This work was extended to the buck-boost converter recently (Fagerstrom & Bengiamin, 2011). The methodologies herein build on that latest work.

The basic asynchronous and synchronous converter topologies are given in Figs. 6.a and 6.b, respectively. Table 1 lists the sources of losses considered assuming a MOS switching device.

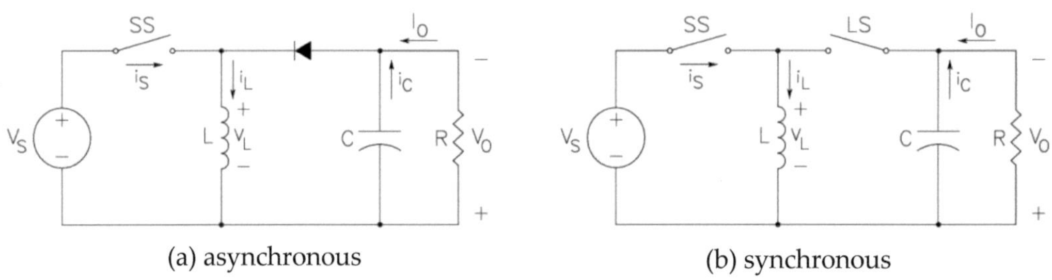

Figure 6. Buck-Boost Converter Architecture

Synchronous	*Asynchronous*
PMOS Conduction	PMOS Conduction
PMOS Switching	PMOS Switching
PMOS Gate Drive	PMOS Gate Drive
NMOS Conduction	Diode Conduction
NMOS Switching	Diode Leakage
NMOS Gate Drive	Diode Junction Capacitance
NMOS Body Diode	
Dead Time	

Table 1. Buck-Boost Converter Losses Considered

Extensive lists of DC-DC converter losses may be found in Zhou, S. (2003) and Djeki, O. & Brkovic, M. (1974). Buck-boost converter losses considered in this work are given in Table 1, as itemized and developed analytically in the following subsections. The PMOS is used for the Source Switch (SS) and NMOS is used for the Load Switch (LS), respectively.

a. PMOS Source Switch Conduction Loss

When the PMOS transistor is in forward conduction there is a resistive loss in accordance with Eq.(6). PMOS conduction loss is associated with both asynchronous and synchronous converters (Gildersleeve et al, 2002; Klien, J., 2006).

$$\text{PMOS Conduction Loss} \triangleq SScL = I_{SS}^2 R_{DS} D \tag{6}$$

Where, I_{SS}=PMOS current (Amp) R_{DS}=PMOS forward conduction ON resistance (Ohm), D=duty ratio

b. PMOS Source Switch Switching Loss

During the transition of voltage rising or falling between the maximum and minimum steady-state values across either switch, and similarly the rise or fall transition of current through the same switch, losses occur. Much work has been done in an effort to correctly model this behavior (Klein, 2006; Xiong et al, 2009), without a highly accurate model still as yet developed. A combination of the work of Klein, (2006) and Xiong et al, (2009) are presented here to develop the switch model loss. The development starts with the following power loss equation.

$$P_{SW} = \frac{1}{2} I_{SW} V_{SW} f_s \left(t_{s(off)} + t_{s(on)} \right) \tag{7}$$

Where, P_{SW}=MOSFET switching loss power (Watt), I_{SW}=current through MOSFET (Amp), V_{SW}=drain to source voltage across the MOSFET, f_s=switching frequency (Hertz), $t_{s(off)}$=MOSFET switching time transitioning off, $t_{s(on)}$=MOSFET switching time transitioning on. All parameters of Eq. (7) are readily measurable in a physical circuit except the switching time terms t_{off} and t_{on} which are developed in the following equations.

$$t_{s(on)} = \frac{Q_{G(SW)}}{I_{Driver(L\text{-}H)}} \tag{8}$$

$$t_{s(off)} = \frac{Q_{G(SW)}}{I_{Driver(H\text{-}L)}} \tag{9}$$

$$I_{Driver(L\text{-}H)} = \frac{V_{DD} - V_{SP}}{R_{Driver(Pull\text{-}up)} + R_G} \tag{10}$$

$$I_{Driver(H-L)} = \frac{V_{SP}}{R_{Driver(Pull-up)} + R_G} \quad (11)$$

$$V_{SP} \approx V_G + \frac{I_{SW}}{G_m} \quad (12)$$

Where, $Q_{G(SW)}$=MOSFET switching-point gate charge (Coulomb), $I_{Driver(L-H)}$=MOSFET gate current while switching on (Amp), $I_{Driver(H-L)}$=MOSFET gate current while switching off, V_{DD}=gate drive controller voltage, V_{SP}=MOSFET gate voltage at switching point, $R_{Driver(Pull-up)}$=gate drive controller internal resistance, R_G=MOSFET gate resistance, V_G=MOSFET gate switching voltage, G_m=MOSFET transconductance.

Combining Eqs. (7) through (12) gives the combined switching loss Eq. (13).

$$P_{sw} = \frac{1}{2} I_{SW} V_{SW} f_s Q_{G(SW)} G_m \left(R_{Driver(Pull-up)} + R_G\right)\left(\frac{1}{V_G G_m + I_{SW}} + \frac{1}{V_{DD} G_m - V_G G_m - I_{SW}}\right) \quad (13)$$

c. PMOS Source Switch Gate Drive Loss

Gate drive loss accounts for the energy dissipated by the MOSFET to drive the gate for the switching operation. The loss equation is given in Eq. (14). PMOS gate drive loss is associated with both converters.

$$\text{PMOS Gate Drive Loss} \triangleq gdL = Q_{G(SW)} V_G f_s \quad (14)$$

d. NMOS Load Switch Conduction Loss

Load switch conduction loss is similar to that of the source switch shown in Eq. (6), differing by the (1-D) factor as this loss occurs during the latter portion of the switching period. This loss is represented in Eq. (15). NMOS conduction loss is associated with only the synchronous converter.

$$\text{NMOS Conduction Loss} \triangleq LScL = I_{LS}^2 R_{DS}\left(1\text{-}D\right) \quad (15)$$

Where, I_{LS}=load switch drain to source voltage.

e. NMOS Load Switch Switching Loss

The load switch MOSFET switching loss is calculated with the same model as the source switch shown in Eq. (14). NMOS switching loss is associated with only the synchronous converter.

f. NMOS Load Switch Gate Drive Loss

NMOS gate drive loss is accounted for by simply doubling the gate drive loss Eq. (15) for the synchronous case. NMOS gate drive loss is associated with only the synchronous converter.

g. NMOS Load Switch Body Diode Loss

The load switch body diode loss occurs only in the load switch due to the reverse bias during the ON portion of the period (Djekic et al., 1997). The reverse-bias voltage and leakage current dissipate power according to the equation shown in Eq. (16). NMOS body diode loss is associated with only the synchronous converter.

$$\text{NMOS Body Diode Loss} \triangleq \text{LSbdL}= i_{\text{leakage}} V_{LS} D \tag{16}$$

Where, $i_{leakage}$=reverse bias leakage current, V_{LS}=load switch drain to source voltage.

h. Synchronous Switching Dead-Time Loss

Dead-time loss occurs through the load switch when neither transistor is on as the load switch is in forward conduction (Klien, 2006). A period of dead-time must exist to prevent current "shoot-through" whereby current flows through both switches simultaneously to the load. The value of t_{dead} is assumed to be 60 ns as is typical for DC-DC converter controllers (Djekic & Brkovic, 1997). The dead-time loss representation is shown in Eq. (17). Synchronous switching dead-time loss is associated with only the synchronous converter.

$$\text{Dead-Time Loss} \triangleq \text{deadL}=I_{\text{load}} V_{LS} f_s t_{\text{dead}} \tag{17}$$

Where, I_{load}=load current, t_{dead}=time where both switches are off.

i. Diode Conduction Loss

Diode forward conduction losses are found with the equation shown in Eq. (18). Diode conduction loss is associated with only the asynchronous converter.

$$\text{Diode Conduction Loss} \triangleq \text{DcL}=I_D V_f (1\text{-}D) \tag{18}$$

Where, I_D=current through diode, V_f=diode forward voltage.

j. Diode Reverse Bias Loss

During the portion of the period *d*, the diode has a reverse bias across it. There is a certain amount of leakage current under this condition that is listed by the manufacturer on the data sheet. This value is used to calculate diode reverse bias leakage loss in Eq. (19). Diode reverse bias loss is associated with only the asynchronous converter.

$$\text{Diode Reverse Bias Loss} \triangleq DrbL = V_D i_{leakage} D \tag{19}$$

Where, V_D=voltage across diode.

k. Diode Junction Capacitance Loss

Diodes have a certain capacitance associated with changing voltages across them (Klein, J., 2006). The charging and discharging of this capacitance creates a power loss as modeled by Eq. (20). Diode junction capacitance loss is associated with only the asynchronous converter.

$$\text{Diode Capacitive Loss} \triangleq \text{DcapL}=\frac{CV_D^2 f_s}{2} \tag{20}$$

3. Matlab capabilities

The Matlab simulation platform (by MathWorks, Inc.) offers a versatile and robust option in design and simulation of power electronic converter systems. Matlab is matrix based, offering diverse options in data manipulation, preparation, and presentation. Simulink, a sub-program of Matlab included in the standard software package, offers a relatively high-level programming language utilizing drag-and-drop function blocks that mask embedded functions. These icons can be incorporated into yet larger models and again masked into new system blocks. This modular block-symbol based modeling system allows ease of construction and programming of large complex systems while maintaining the ability to edit and control internal systems all the way down to the most base-level functions.

The power electronic system designer upon starting Simulink, then, is entering the design process at the phase of assembly of power electronic, measurement, and signal routing components into larger more complex systems to accomplish a desired task. The designer may from time to time wish to delve into base Simulink models to change component characteristics and behavior, add base-level monitoring of characteristics, change signal routing, confirm calculation methods, or even develop system models from scratch.

This section is intended for the Matlab user who possesses basic workspace programming knowledge. Many resources are available to learn or refresh on Matlab workspace programming, including the help files included with the Matlab software. Matlab help files are an invaluable resource in workspace and Simulink programming and are recommended for perusal.

3.1. SimPowerSystems toolbox

Simulink provides a rich suite of toolboxes applicable to wide areas in engineering applications. The power electronics devices discussed in this chapter are simulated using "SimPowerSystems", a versatile toolbox for modeling electro-mechanical systems. In addition to popular power electronics devices, this toolbox provides a wide range of simulation apparatuses such as transformers, rotating machines, hydraulic turbine & governor, and wind turbines, as well as basic electric circuit components. Detailed characteristic parameters can be configured for these components to represent typical performance scenarios. To monitor the performance of constructed models, a host of measurement blocks are available for discreet, continuous, and phasor based measurements. Relevant variables like active & reactive power, total harmonic distortion, and power factor can be monitored with ease. Custom functions can also be set up with simple manipulations. Since this chapter deals with power electronics applications, attention is focused on the Power Electronics block-set which includes several power electronics semiconductor simulation blocks relevant to industry, Table 2. Devices shown in Table 2 are modeled into systems with other standard Simulink and SimPower devices, some of which are presented in Table 3.

Type	Schematic Symbol	SimPower Device	Commutation	Characteristics	Typ. Application
SCR		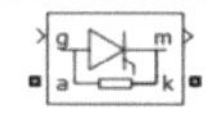 Thyristor	Line	Pass current in one direction, active control	Simple power control circuits, overcurrent protection circuits (crowbar)
DIAC		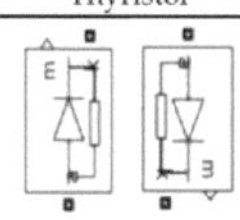 Opposing Diodes	Line	Pass current in both directions, A/C waveforms, passive control (forward voltage)	Light dimmer, symmetrical firing of TRIACs
GTO		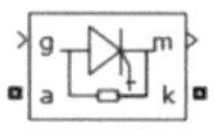 Gto	Forced	High power applications, active control, extended switch-off time (tail-time)	HVDC Systems, applications with low switching frequencies
Diode		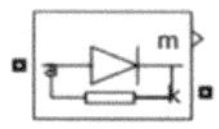 Diode	Line	Pass current in one direction, passive control (forward voltage)	Rectifier, protection circuitry (free-wheel)
IGBT		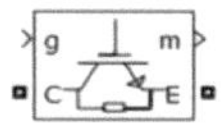 IGBT	Forced	Fast switching, medium or high power applications	Electric Heater, audio amplifier
MOSFET		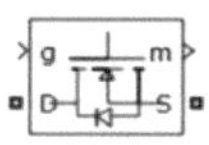 Mosfet	Forced	Low power capablities	Signal amplifier, electronic switching

Table 2. SimPower Power Electronics Models

3.2. Simulation parameters and data presentation

For proper numerical computations Matlab provides various simulation options including the specific numerical method (solver), the allowed tolerance, and mode of computation. Since some numerical methods are more computationally intensive than others, the user may choose a less intensive method for simulations that don't require solving highly nonlinear differential equations, for example. This improves the efficiency of the simulation and accelerates obtaining results. Some trial and error may be necessary to achieve a successful simulation. However, the default simulation options can typically be used for most simulations. If the simulation takes too long to execute or the computed data is incomplete, is at an unacceptable resolution, or has errors, it will be necessary to change simulation parameters. Highly complex simulations may require some time invested in finding the correct solver for the application in order to achieve a good balance between accuracy and computation times. The Configuration Parameters dialog box is found under the Simulation tab in Simulink, Fig. 7. Usually the best choice is to leave these set to "auto" to allow Simulink to determine simulation parameters automatically, based on the model.

SimPower Device	Notes	SimPower Device	Notes	SimPower Device	Notes
Parallel RLC Branch	Can be reduced to any combination of R, L, C	Display	Numerical readout in a variety of formats	From, Goto	Signal routing tags for complex models to avoid confusing model interconnections
Ground	Constant zero voltage reference	RMS	Similar functions available such as mean, THD, fourier, active power, etc.	Demux, Mux	Multiplexers, settable number of inputs/outputs
AC Voltage Source	Programmable source, DC, current, battery, etc. also available	Gain	Multiply input by constants, functions, or variables	Current, Voltage Measurements	Impedance, multimeter, 3-phase, etc. also available
Math Function	Other fxns: log, exp, square, power, conjugate, etc.	Logical Operator	Configurable as OR, NAND, NOR, XOR, NXOR, NOT	Rational Operator	Compare 2 signals rationally: greater, less, equal, etc.
Constant	Constant value independent of all variables	Integrator	Transfer functions also available	Saturation	Model effects of saturation
Scope	Used to view waveforms	Sine Wave	Other sources such as step, ramp, pulse, stair, etc.	First order hold	An array of discreet-time functions available

Table 3. Common SimPower Power Electronics Models

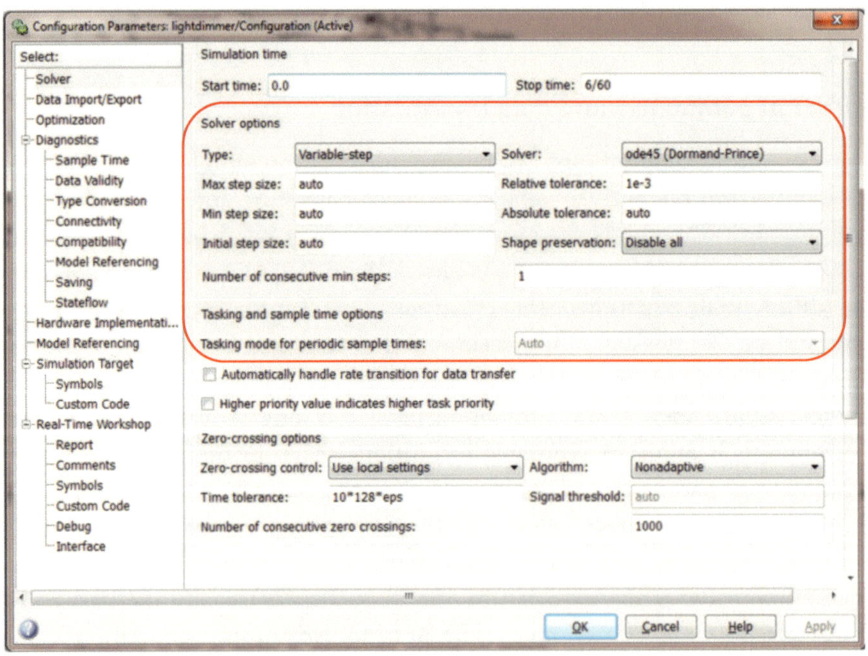

Figure 7. Configuration Parameters Dialog Box

The solvers are categorized into two general types: Fixed step, and Variable step. Fixed step simulations evaluate in user-set time steps that are constant throughout simulation. Variable step solvers dynamically change the simulation step size to optimize simulation time vs. accuracy. Therefore, the goal in choosing the solver is to find the least computationally intensive method that yields the level of accuracy required. Solver types are summarized in Table 4.

Step	Solver Type	Order of Accuracy	Method	Trial Order	Notes
Variable (continuous)	Discrete				Settable maximum step size
	ode45	Fifth, Medium	Runge-Kutta	1	Default
	ode23	Low	cubic Hermite interpolation	2	
	ode113	Low to High	Adams-Bashforth-Moulton PECE		Models with stringent error tolerances or computationally intensive
	ode15s	Variable order (1-5), Medium to Low	Numerical Differentiation	3	Try if ode45 fails, limit order to 2 initially, and increase as needed
	ode23s	Second, Low	Modified Rosenbrock	4	Try if ode15s is not effective
	ode23t	Low	Trapezoidal rule with "free" interpolant	5	Try if ode15s is not effective
	ode23tb	Second, Low	TR-BDF2, trapezoidal with second order backward differentiation	5	Try if ode15s is not effective
Fixed (discreet)	Discrete				Settable fixed step size
	ode1	First	Euler's Method		No error control, accuracy & simulation time depend on step size, small steps yield higher accuracy and higher simualation time, and vice-versa
	ode2	Second	Heun's Method		
	ode3	Third	Bogacki-Shampine		
	ode4	Fourth	Runge-Kutta RK4		
	ode5	Fifth	Dormand-Prince RK5		
	ode8	Eighth	Dormand Prince RK8		
	ode14x	Variable	Newton's method/ extrapolation		Settable Jacobian method, Newton's iterations, extrapolation order

Table 4. Solver Types

3.3. Configuration of SimPowerSystems blocks

Simulation of any SimPower circuit involves parameter configuration within model blocks after circuit is constructed. This is achieved by double-clicking on the circuit block to reveal block parameters. Table 5 shows the possible block configuration parameters for common SimPower power electronic devices. A user may also elect to use typical values provided by default.

Abbreviation	Parameter	SCR (Thyristor)	Diode	GTO	IGBT	Mosfet
Ron	Conduction resistance	X	X	X	X	X
Lon	Conduction capacitance	X	X	X	X	X
Vf	Forward voltage drop	X	X	X	X	X
Ic	Initial current	X	X	X	X	X
Rs	Snubber resistance	X*	X*	X*	X*	X*
Cs	Snubber capacitance	X*	X*	X*	X*	X*
Il	Latching current	X				
Tq	Turn-off Time	X				
Tf	Current 10% fall-time			X	X	
Tt	Current tail-time			X	X	
Rd	Internal diode resistance					X

* set Rs=inf or Cs=0 to eliminate snubber, or Cs=inf for resistive snubber

Table 5. SimPowerSystems Block Configuration Parameters

The parameters of Table 5 can be classified according to the following: R_{on}, L_{on}, V_f are applicable during forward conduction of current, current 10% fall time and current tail time are applicable during shut-off, and snubber resistance and snubber capacitance affect the circuit during the OFF condition.

The definitions of R_{on}, L_{on}, and V_f are evident by inspection of the typical power electronic device circuit diagram shown in Fig. 8.

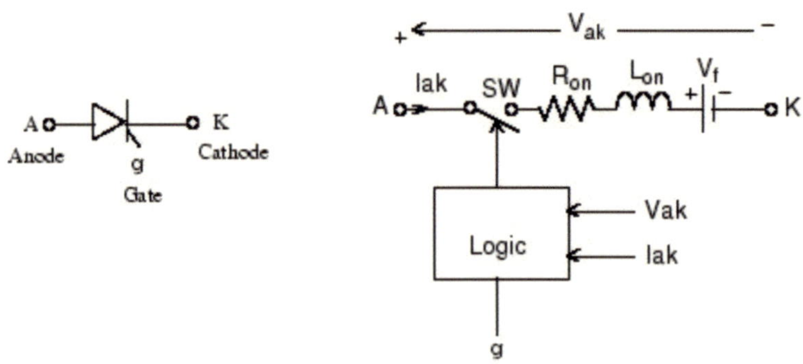

Figure 8. Example SimPower Power Electronic Device Equivalent Circuit

Initial current is the amount of current in amperes flowing through device at the start of simulation. Snubber resistance and capacitance (Rs and Cs) are self-evident for snubber circuits. Latching current (Il) is defined as the amount of current required for thyristor to become self-commutated. Turn-off time (Tq) is defined as the minimum amount of time required for the voltage across anode and cathode to be zero or less to avoid the device automatically turning on again when a forward voltage is seen. Current fall-time and tail time are explained in waveform shown in Fig. 9 (from Matlab help file).

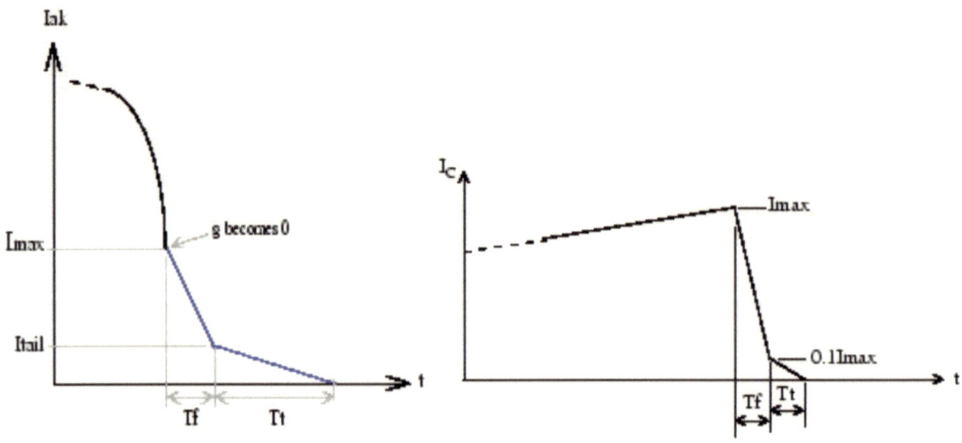

Figure 9. SimPower GTO and IGBT Fall-Time and Tail-Time Waveform, Respectively

Internal diode resistance of the MOSFET (Rd) is explained in Fig. 10.

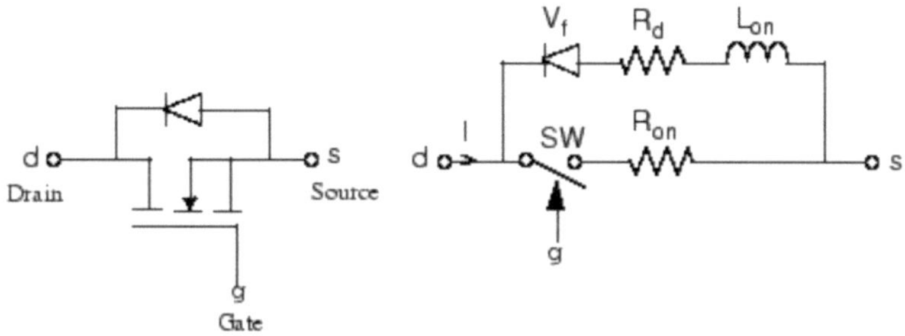

Figure 10. SimPower MOSFET Equivalent Circuit

4. Simulation, analysis, and design

A Matlab script file can accompany simulations performed in the Simulink environment. Script files provide ease in defining and computing variables from a single location which allows the model to be general and applicable to many different cases as well as maintain uniformity in plotting and results presentation. If modification of parameters is desired, the changes are easily accomplished by changing the numbers in the workspace and repeating the simulation. This general-modeling functionality is a distinct advantage of Matlab over Multisim.

Simulink offers a simple and versatile platform for equation modeling. Practically any equation can be implemented in Simulink following an easy and direct method. Consider Eq. (1), the inductor voltage as a function of inductor current – these are the input and output variables of what can be implemented as a small subsystem in Simulink. The first modeling step can be to introduce variable routing tags for each input and output variable as shown in Fig. 11 (a). Next, consider the intermediate mathematics of the function. It is observed that the equation involves multiplication by a constant and a derivative – therefore drag these function blocks into the Simulink workspace and connect appropriately, Fig. 11 (b). For example Eq. (1) is simulated as in Fig. 11 (b). Following the signal step-by-step as shown in Fig. 11 (c) reveals that the subsystem output is the voltage of the inductor based on the input current to the inductor. The equation is therefore successfully modeled. It is well to mention that the model shown in Fig. 11 is an analytical exercise only; physically implementing the model shown is not recommended as the differentiator will amplify noise in a real system.

As an exercise to bring together the concepts discussed of blocks performing functions based on embedded subsystems and equation modeling, consider the non-linear signal created with the Matlab program shown in Fig. 12.

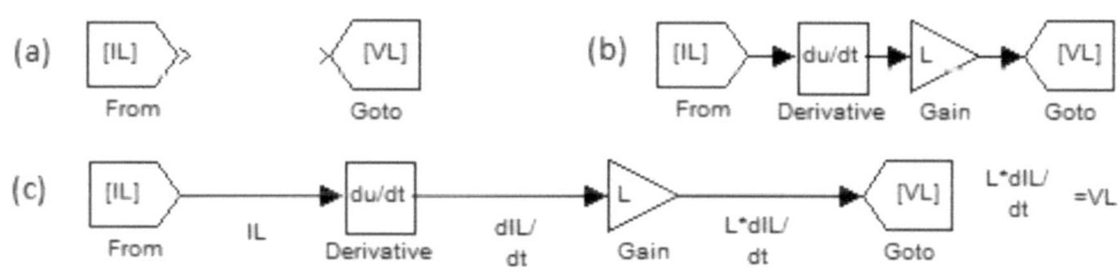

Figure 11. Equation Modeling: Inductor Voltage as a Function of Current

```
%% non-linear current signal
clear; close; %intialize
workspace
t=0:0.0001:0.016; %Defines
time array for one period
i=10*sin(377*t)+3*sin(754*t)
+2*cos(1131*t); %defines
array for current signal
plot(t,i); grid;
xlabel('time (s)');
ylabel('current (A)');
%plots signal
vv=[t' i'] %defines 2-column
array containing both t and
i values for one period
```

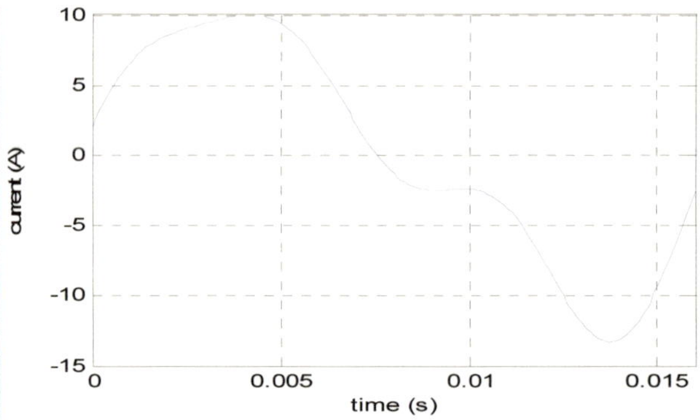

Figure 12. Sinusoidal Signal Generation with Harmonic Content

The signal shown in Fig. 12 can be imported into the Simulink model with the "From Workspace" block and evaluated for total harmonic distortion (21) as shown in Fig. 13.

$$THD = \frac{I_{Harmonic}}{I_{1_{RMS}}} = \frac{\sqrt{I_{RMS}^2 - I_{1_{RMS}}^2}}{I_{1_{RMS}}} \tag{21}$$

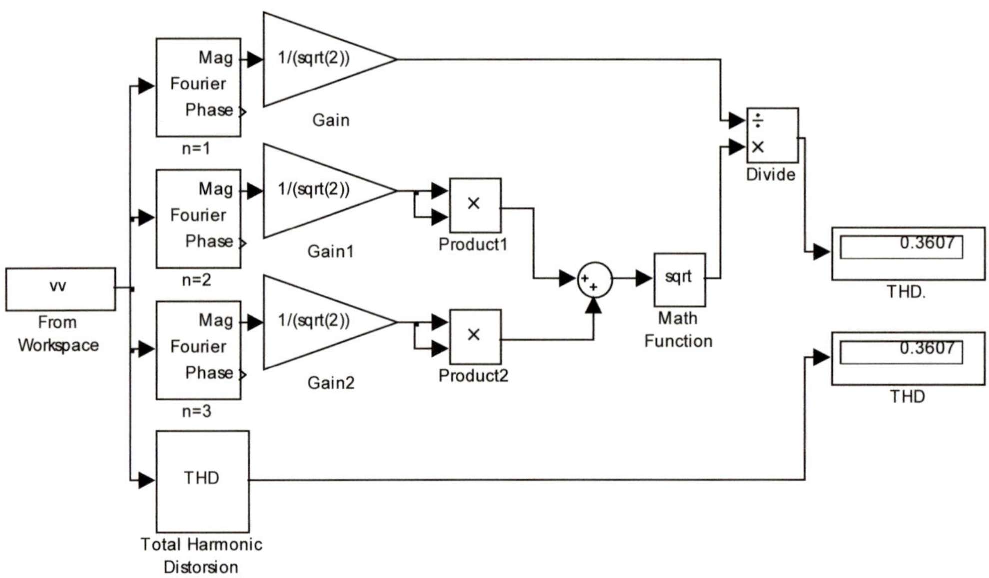

Figure 13. Total Harmonic Distortion Analysis of Signal with Harmonic Content

Compare the top three forward paths of the block diagram in Fig. 13 to Eq. (21). It can be seen that the signal has been successfully evaluated for Total Harmonic Distortion (THD) of the given signal (neglecting harmonic content beyond the 3rd). Now consider the fourth forward path of the block diagram and compare the THD measurement blocks at the right – the results are identical illustrating the embedded mathematical functionality contained in Simulink blocks. To explore further, right-click on the Simulink THD block, choose "Look Under Mask", and compare mathematical functionality.

Applying the same modeling techniques shown in the THD example in an effort to aid in optimization of power electronic converters and to exemplify the block modeling concepts discussed, the loss equations introduced in section 2.4 have been modeled in Simulink (Fig. 14) for the buck-boost converter and combined into a Simulink model block (Fig. 15). The Buck-Boost Converter Power & Efficiency block is used in section 4.3 for converter optimization.

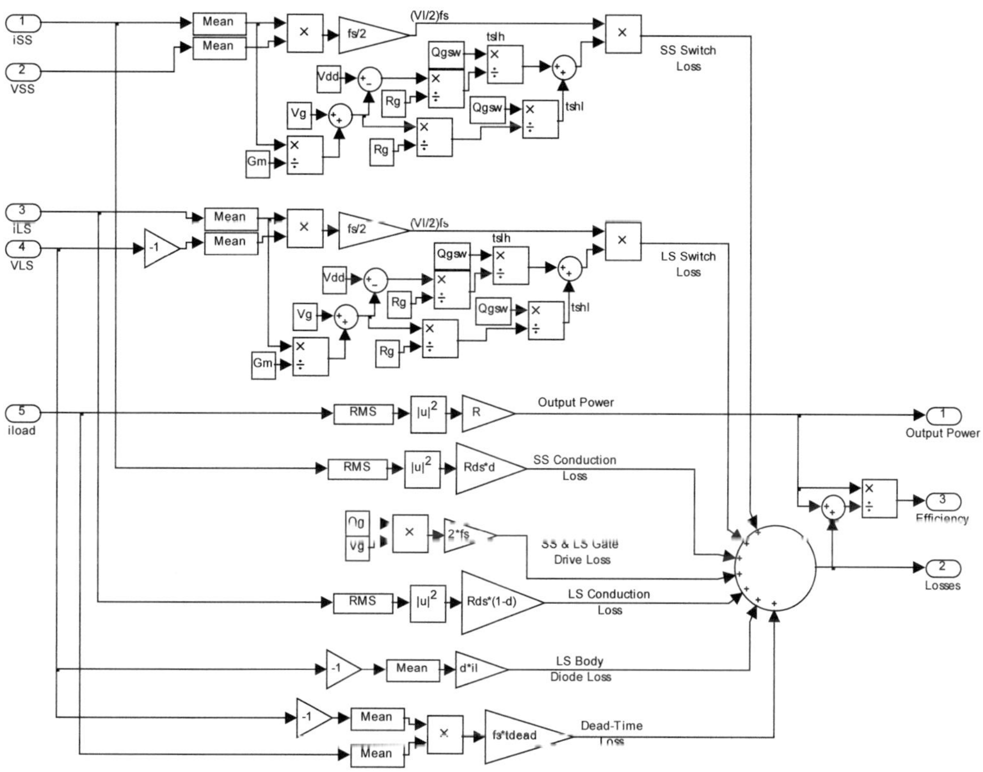

Figure 14. Buck-Boost Power & Efficiency Block Embedded Calculations

4.1. Light dimmer

Consider the light dimmer circuit introduced in section 2.1. A good first step in simulation of this circuit is to understand the range of available output voltage and power as controlled by varying the potentiometer R2. As R2 is adjusted between its minimum and maximum resistance values, Matlab can be used to plot the waveforms to illustrate the output characteristics of the circuit. The light dimmer TRIAC is self-commutating as introduced in section 2.1. This behavior in general is plotted as shown in Fig. 16, where alpha represents the firing angle of the TRIAC in the supplied waveform.

To find the output power of the light dimmer circuit, the light dimmer voltage waveform shown in Fig. 16 can be evaluated for RMS current over one-half period (as negative portion of waveform is symmetrical) giving,

$$I_{RMS} = \sqrt{\frac{1}{\pi}\int_{\alpha}^{\pi}\frac{V_m^2}{R^2}\sin^2(\theta)d\theta} = \frac{V_m}{R}\sqrt{1-\frac{\alpha}{\pi}+\frac{1}{2\pi}\sin(2\alpha)} \tag{22}$$

It follows that,

$$\mathrm{P}(\alpha)=\mathrm{I}_{RMS}^2 R = \frac{\mathrm{Vm}^2}{2\mathrm{R}}\left[1-\frac{\alpha}{\pi}+\frac{1}{2\pi}\sin(2\alpha)\right] \tag{23}$$

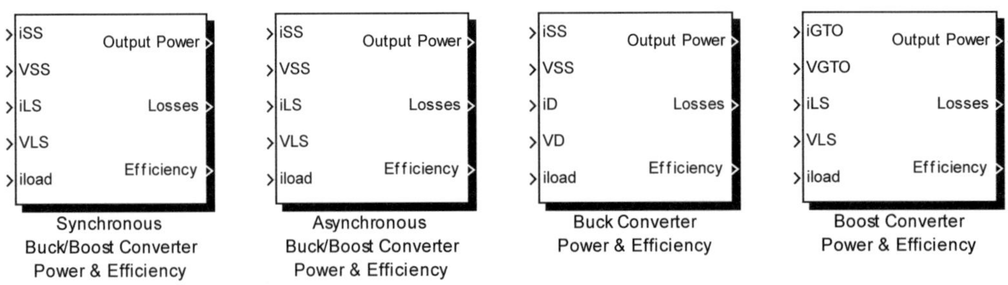

Figure 15. Developed DC/DC Converter Power & Efficiency Blocks – Buck, Boost, Buck-Boost

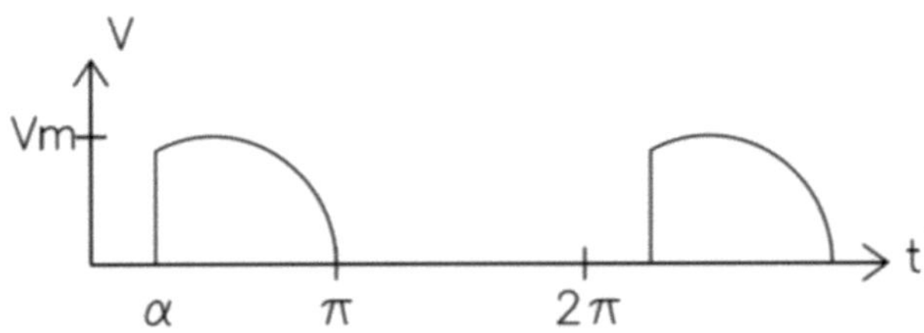

Figure 16. Self-Commutation at Firing Angle Alpha

and,

$$\mathrm{V}(\alpha)=\sqrt{[\mathrm{P}(\alpha)](\mathrm{R})} \tag{24}$$

where α = firing angle of TRIAC

The relationships shown in 23 and 24 can be plotted in the Matlab workspace as shown in Fig. 17, assuming a supply of 120V$_{RMS}$, 60 Hz, and light bulb impedance of 576Ω (purely resistive – inductive effects negligible).

```
%% Light Dimmer Power and Voltage as
a Function of Firing Angle
clear; close; %clear previous data
Vm=120*sqrt(2); %voltage signal
R=576; %ohm - bulb impedance (j0)
alpha=0:pi/180:pi; %scale output to
degrees in workspace

for m=1:length(alpha)
 P(m)=(Vm^2/(2*R))*(1-
(alpha(m)/pi)+(1/(2*pi))*(sin(2*alpha
(m)))); % SCR formula*2 for TRIAC &
resistive load
end

subplot(2,1,1);
plot(alpha*(180/pi),P); grid;
xlabel('degrees'); ylabel('Watts');
title('P vs. alpha'); %plot results

Vl=sqrt(P*R);
subplot(2,1,2);
plot(alpha*(180/pi),Vl); grid;
xlabel('degrees'); ylabel('Volts
RMS'); title('V vs. alpha');
```

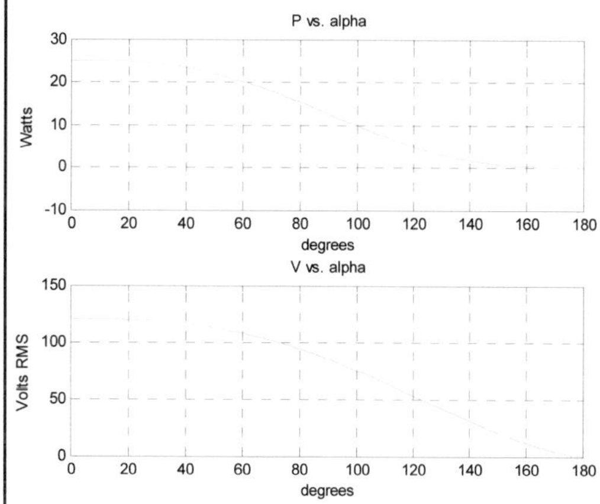

Figure 17. Power and Voltage as a Function of Firing Angle Alpha

Fig. 17 reveals power and voltage characteristics that can be expected from the light dimmer circuit. As expected, the power output is non-linear, i.e. proportional changes in potentiometer dial rotation do not result in proportional changes in lamp brightness. The graph also confirms the maximum voltage and power the lamp will experience for proper lamp sizing.

To examine light dimmer circuit behavior in more detail and observe waveforms, the circuit can be implemented in Simulink. The model can be constructed as shown in Fig. 18. Simulink blocks are added to the model simply by dragging-and-dropping from the Simulink Library Browser, while connections between blocks are accomplished by single-clicking and dragging to appropriate nodes. The blocks shown are color coded by type of block as organized within Simulink as follows: orange – SimPower sources, red – SimPower power electronic devices, magenta – SimPower elements, light blue – SimPower measurements devices, dark blue – standard Simulink blocks.

Some devices shown in Fig. 18 are identical to those introduced in Fig. 1, such as resistors and capacitors. The DIAC is represented by two diodes placed to conduct current in opposite directions (for AC) as diodes exhibit the same self-commutating behavior. The TRIAC is implemented using two thyristors to pass AC current in much the same way as the DIAC, the difference being the active control input at the gate. Thyristors are chosen in SimPower for their self-commutating behavior and representation of TRIAC characteristics. Double-click model blocks to set parameters according to those shown.

Note the block in Fig. 18 labeled "powergui" near the AC voltage source. This block automatically appears upon running a SimPower simulation, and is required. The powergui contains configuration functions such as initial states, machine initialization parameters, FFT analysis, and other useful tools, albeit none are utilized in this chapter.

The results of evaluating the light dimmer circuit in Simulink are shown in real time as the simulation progresses on the numerical readouts. After the simulation is completed, double-clicking on the "V_{load}" scope icon reveals a waveform similar to Fig. 19. The waveform of Fig. 19 shows the self-commutation behavior discussed earlier in that, once fired, the TRIAC passes current until the voltage across it drops to zero. Note the time that the gate voltage spikes to 1 is the exact time that the TRIAC fires and allows the source voltage waveform to pass until the current drops below the holding current IH which occurs in this ideal case at I=0. Also notice the waveform that fires at approximately 10ms is slightly distorted – this asymmetrical firing of the TRIAC's occurs for a brief period until the converter stabilizes.

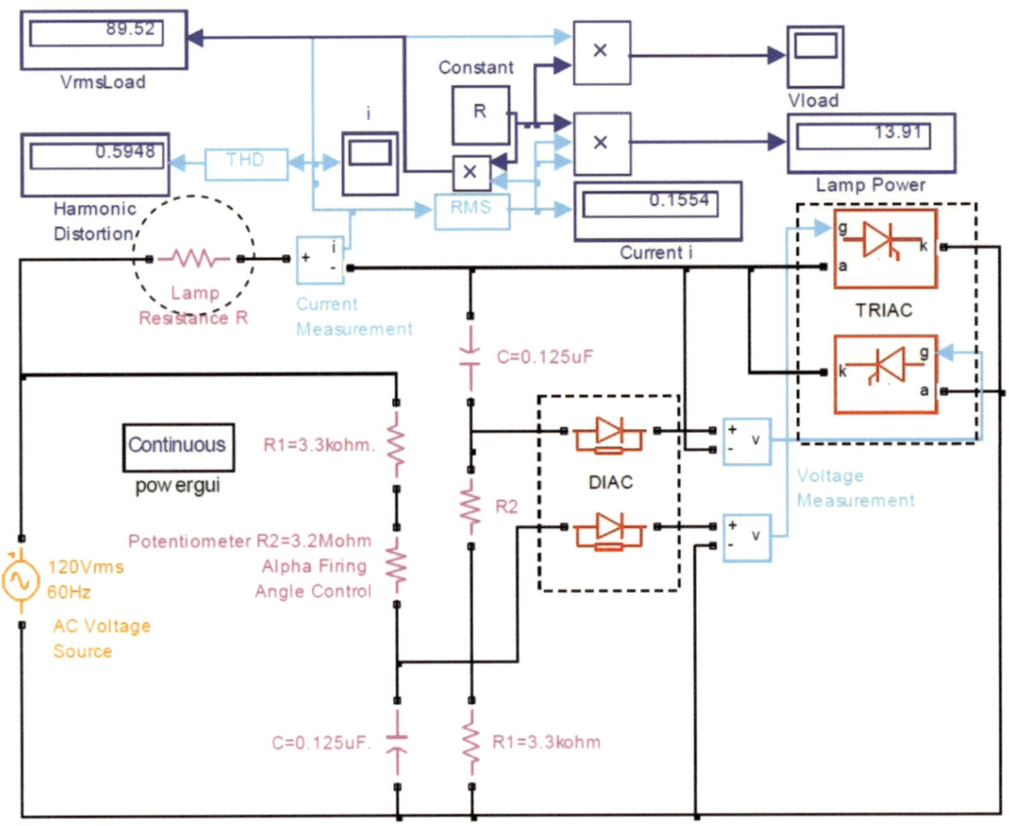

Figure 18. Light Dimmer Circuit

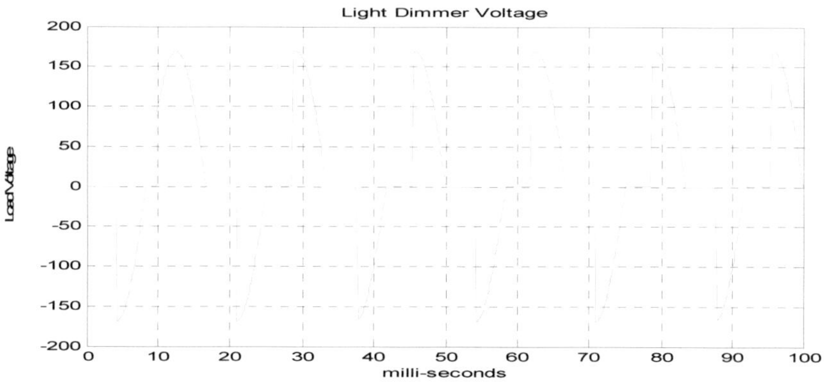

Figure 19. SimPower Light Dimmer Output Voltage Waveform - α=87°

The light dimmer circuit was also constructed using physical components and tested for validity. A 60 Watt light bulb was light controlled using the Littlefuse Q2015L5 TRIAC and the STMicroelectronics DB3 DIAC. The Fluke-41 Power Harmonics Analyzer was the primary waveform capturing device (Fig. 20).

Graphical comparison of simulated and experimental results shows very good agreement. Observe the symmetrical firing angle on both halves of the waveform as presented and discussed earlier – this provides confirmation of a successful design concerning firing angle symmetry. Simulated and experimental data were taken for firing angles ranging from 28° to 155° and recorded as presented in Table 6.

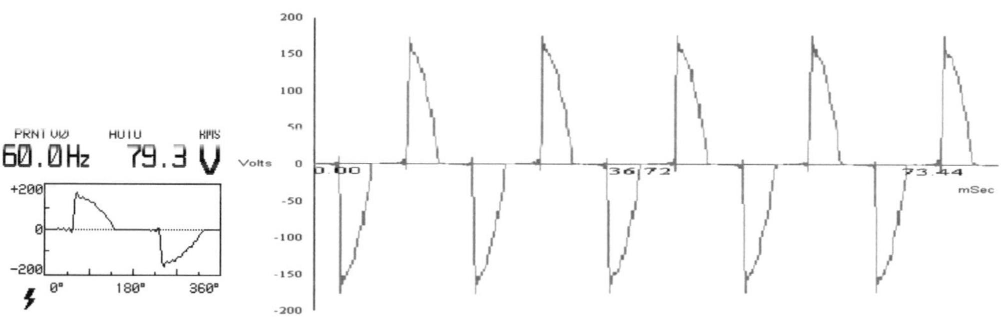

Figure 20. Experimental Light Dimmer Output Voltage Waveform - α=87°

	Simulated in Simulink			Experimental		
Firing Angle α(deg)	Vrms	Power (W)	THD(%)	Vrms	Power (W)	THD(%)
28	116.3	23.48	4.4	114.6	26	8.6
62	109.8	20.93	28.83	103.6	21	34.1
87	89.65	13.95	57.49	79.4	14	64.6
127	58.89	6.021	93.51	49.0	6	102.3
132	53.52	4.973	100.8	45.8	5	107.5
155	24.5	1.043	105.81	19.2	1	169.7

Table 6. Light Dimmer Characteristics – Experimental vs. Simulated Results

There is good agreement between the simulated and experimental data given in Table 6. The values diverge particularly toward the upper firing angles. Divergence and inconsistencies are expected due to variations in the load resistance due to thermal effects. THD is expected to be lower for low firing angles as less harmonic components are present in undisturbed waveforms closely resembling the smooth curve of the input sine wave. The more the voltage waveform is modified by the TRIAC firing at higher angles the more high frequency components are produced, and therefore the more total harmonic distortion.

4.2. DC-DC converter

A designer concerned with the behavior of DC-DC converters introduced in earlier sections may wish to consider the voltage gain of the buck, boost, and buck-boost converters as a starting point. The Matlab workspace can be used to plot V_{load}/V_{source} as introduced in section 2.2 for each converter to graphically represent the curves for consideration.

Recognizing that duty ratio ranges between 0 and 1 for all PWM converters, a Matlab workspace script program is used to create the plot shown in Fig. 21 to show output voltage of each type of DC-DC converter introduced in section 2 as a function of duty ratio. Note the asymptotic behavior of the boost and buck-boost at higher duty ratios.

4.3. Buck DC-DC converter

The buck converter was introduced in section 2.2.1 including equations 1 through 5 which describe buck converter behavior. To further develop tools in power electronics design in Matlab, consider the following design example.

It is desired to design a buck converter for a particular automotive application. The supply voltage in a typical automobile while running is 13.8 volts. The device to be powered is purely resistive at 100 ohms and requires a constant 5 volt supply. A maximum of 5% current and voltage ripple is desired. The design has physical size constraints, so a switching frequency of 100 kHz or above is decided upon to keep inductor size at a minimum. Analytically, minimum inductor size is given by Eq. (25) (Shaffer, 2007),

$$L_{CCM} = \frac{(V_S - V_O)R}{2fV_S} = \frac{(13.8-5)100}{2(100e3)(13.8)} = 318.8\mu H \qquad (25)$$

To account for current ripple, the scaling factor lambda is developed,

$$\lambda = \frac{2V_O}{R(\Delta I)} = \frac{2(5)}{100(0.05)} = 2 \qquad (26)$$

Inductor size accounting for current ripple follows with,

$$L = \lambda\left(L_{CCM}\right) = 2\left(318.8\right) = 637.6\mu H \tag{27}$$

Capacitor size determines output voltage ripple according to the relationship,

$$C = \frac{\left(1-\frac{V_O}{V_S}\right)}{8Lrf^2} = \frac{\left(1-\frac{5}{13.8}\right)}{8\left(637.6\mu\right)0.05\left(100e3\right)^2} = 250nF \tag{28}$$

```
%% Vload/Vsource as a function of duty
ratio
close; clear; %initialize workspace
d=0:0.01:0.9; %duty ratio ranges from 0 to
1

%buck
for x=1:length(d)
 Vbk(x)=d(x); %compute output voltage
end

%boost
for x=1:length(d) %intermediate variable
may be reused
 Vbst(x)=1/(1-d(x)); %compute output
voltage
end

%buck-boost
for x=1:length(d)
 Vbb(x)=d(x)/(1-d(x)); %compute output
voltage
end

%plot results
plot(d,Vbk); hold on; plot(d,Vbst,'r');
plot(d,Vbb,'g'); %hold allows plotting on
same graph
grid; xlabel('duty ratio');
ylabel('Vo/Vs'); %presentation
enhancements
legend('Buck','Boost', 'Buck-Boost',
'Location', 'NorthWest' )
```

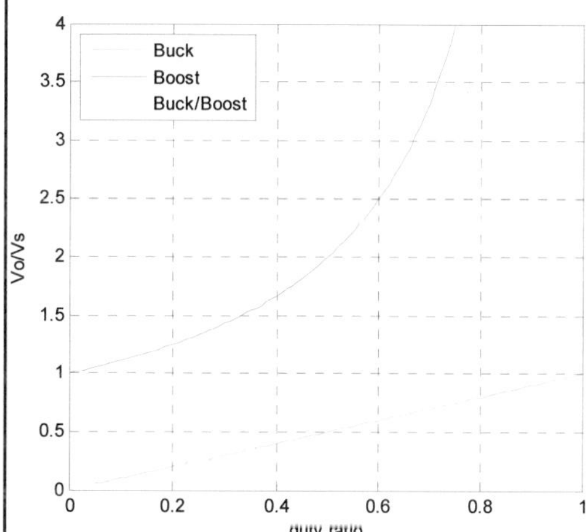

Figure 21. DC-DC Converter V_{load}/V_{source}

The analytic development of parameters may be used for simulation, but Matlab/Simulink offers another option. A Matlab program can be created to calculate and store system parameters, and used to support a Simulink simulation. First, the following script program is written to calculate system parameters (Fig. 22).

```
%Buck Evaluation Parameters
Vin=13.8; %Volt - Input Voltage, use highest value if source varies
Vout=5; %Volt - desired output voltage
fs=100e3; %1/Second - define switching frequency
vripple=0.05; %max acceptable voltage ripple
iripple=0.05; %max acceptable current ripple
R=100; %ohm - load resistance, purely resistive assumed (j0)
P=1/fs; %Second - switching period
d=Vout/Vin; %unitless ratio - duty ratio calculation
Lccm=(((Vin-Vout)*R)/(2*fs*Vin)); %Henry - minimum L value for CCM
Lambda=(2/iripple)*(Vout/R); %inductor scaling factor - intermediate
calculation
L=Lccm %Henry - inductor size at absolute minimum for CCM
%L=Lccm*Lambda %Henry - inductor size accounting for current ripple
C=(1-(Vout/Vin))/(8*L*vripple*fs^2) %Farad - capacitor calculation
```

Figure 22. Buck Converter Simulink Simulation

Merely by executing this program the values of C and L will be written to the Matlab workspace, and are also saved into temporary memory for use in a Simulink simulation. Such a simulation is constructed as shown in Fig. 23 for the buck converter.

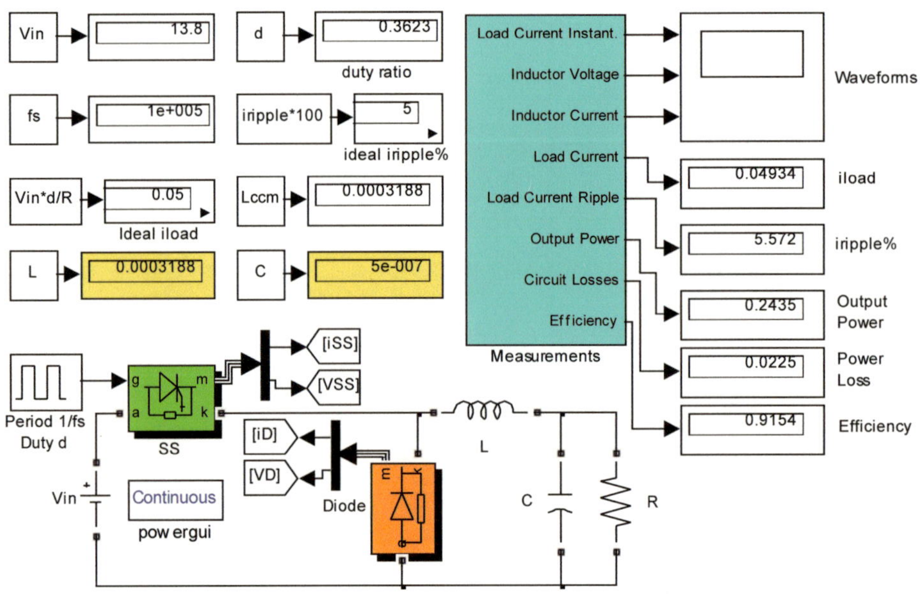

Figure 23. Buck Converter Simulink Simulation

Note the large red arrow in the script program which shows a command that is commented out. If we wished to evaluate this circuit with proper design considerations for current ripple, this line can be commented back in to the program. However, for the purpose of examining the behavior of the converter at the CCM/DCM borderline, the value of L_{CCM} is used for the following evaluation. The capacitor size automatically changes accordingly when the program is reevaluated, highlighting the great advantage that computer-based systems have over analytic calculations: the ability to modify parameters at will without having to perform additional calculations. The circuit is set to run over the duration of 0 to 100*P, with all simulation settings default except Max step size set to P/20 to increase resolution. Examine and consider the actual simulation values shown in the Simulink simulation diagram of Fig. 23, and waveforms shown in Fig. 24. Note the values of L and C and other values shown in the upper left of the Simulink diagram as calculated from the workspace program.

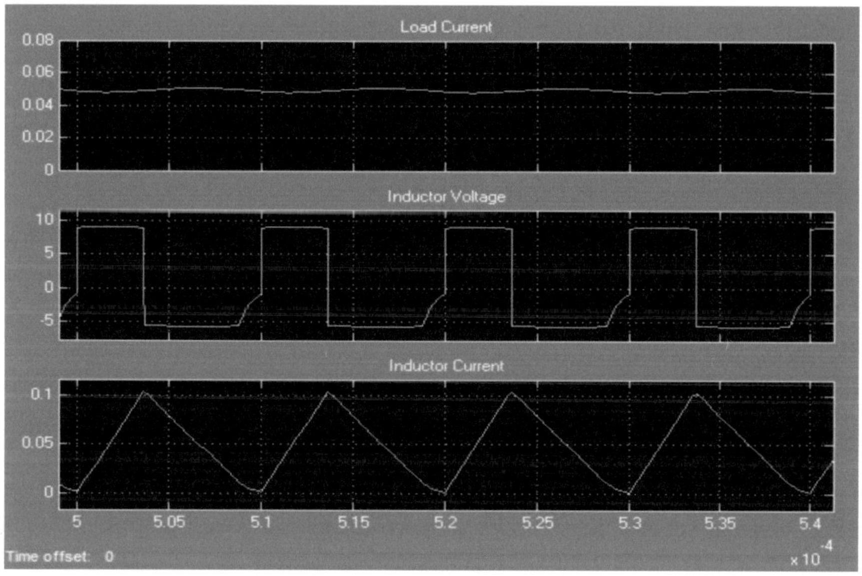

Figure 24. Buck Converter Voltage and Current Waveforms

Observe the buck converter's inductor current characteristics operating on the borderline of CCM and DCM behavior by nearly falling to zero. A related behavior is observed in the inductor voltage waveform as the energy contained in the inductor field exponentially decays nearly to zero before the source-switch closes and raises the voltage level. Also note the instantaneous voltage polarity change on the inductor – this capability is what makes power electronic converters possible (keep in mind that when the polarity across the inductor is negative, current is still flowing in the same direction through the load). The slight variation in load current is observed exhibiting ripple behavior. The circuit's efficiency is also evaluated at 92% with the loss model block developed in section 4.0.

4.4. Buck-boost DC-DC converter

Continuing with practical designs, consider an application for a portable electronic device that requires power such as a laptop or cellular phone. These devices require precisely controlled voltage levels for supply to sensitive electronics. Batteries, however, do not exhibit stable output voltage characteristics as illustrated in Fig. 25 for two typical battery types.

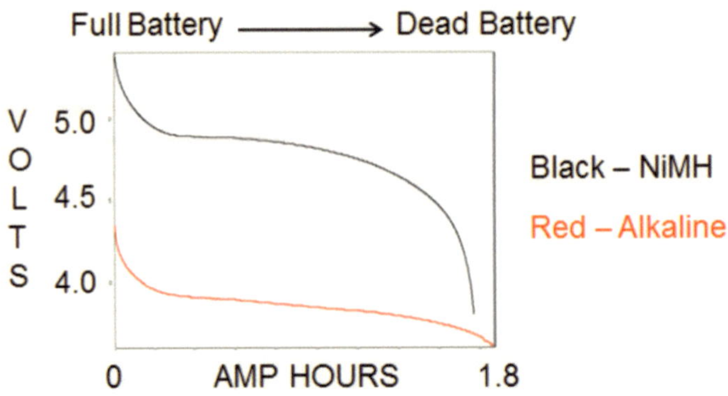

Figure 25. Typical Battery Output Voltage Discharge Characteristics

As the battery undergoes its normal discharge cycle, its supplied voltage varies significantly as Fig. 25 shows. A solution is required in order to provide a relatively constant input voltage to electronic devices fed from a source whose voltage varies. The buck-boost converter is very effective for this application as it can provide a well regulated load voltage, as discussed in Section 2.3.

Assume a designer wishes incorporate a converter for its voltage stability characteristics into a portable electronic device. Portable electronics require continuous current in order to retain information in volatile memory registers, therefore CCM mode is required. The designer will be concerned with minimizing the power losses of the converter in order to provide the maximum battery life possible. Simulink provides an effective option to determine optimal configuration of parameters to maximize efficiency. The synchronous converter as introduced earlier can be modeled in Simulink as shown in Fig. 26. The asynchronous converter is modeled by changing the active load switch to a diode, and changing the power & efficiency calculation block accordingly (see Fig. 15).

Parameters for simulation are defined in a workspace program according to data sheets for the IRFP450 MOSFET and SB245E Diode, as these are common devices. A median battery supply voltage of 5 volts is chosen as well as a 5 volt output from the converter as this is a common required voltage for electronic devices. Simulated buck-boost inductor behavior as described earlier is plotted in Fig. 27.

The synchronous and asynchronous buck-boost converters can be evaluated at various load currents in order to yield the overall efficiency of each in order to optimize power transfer. After some trial runs are executed to explore the range of load current that should be simulated, a minimum and maximum load current test range of 1mA to 1A are chosen. The converters are evaluated accordingly; efficiency data is recorded, and subsequently plotted in the Matlab workspace as shown in Fig. 28.

The curves shown in Fig. 28 can be used to select the appropriate buck-boost converter topology and design load current for various applications. If inductor size is not a consideration, the designer will elect to use a synchronous converter at a switching frequency of 10kHz as this configuration yields maximum efficiency for all loads examined (keep in mind that larger inductors allow lower switching frequencies). If perhaps size is a consideration and a minimum switching frequency of 50kHz must be used, the designer will choose a 50kHz asynchronous converter for loads ranging from 10mA to ~50mA, and a synchronous converter for loads above 50mA. Other considerations may regulate various switching frequencies, topologies, and load current such as harmonic considerations, available control circuitry for the load switch, etc. – Fig. 28 can be used for these various applications to choose the most efficient converter configuration.

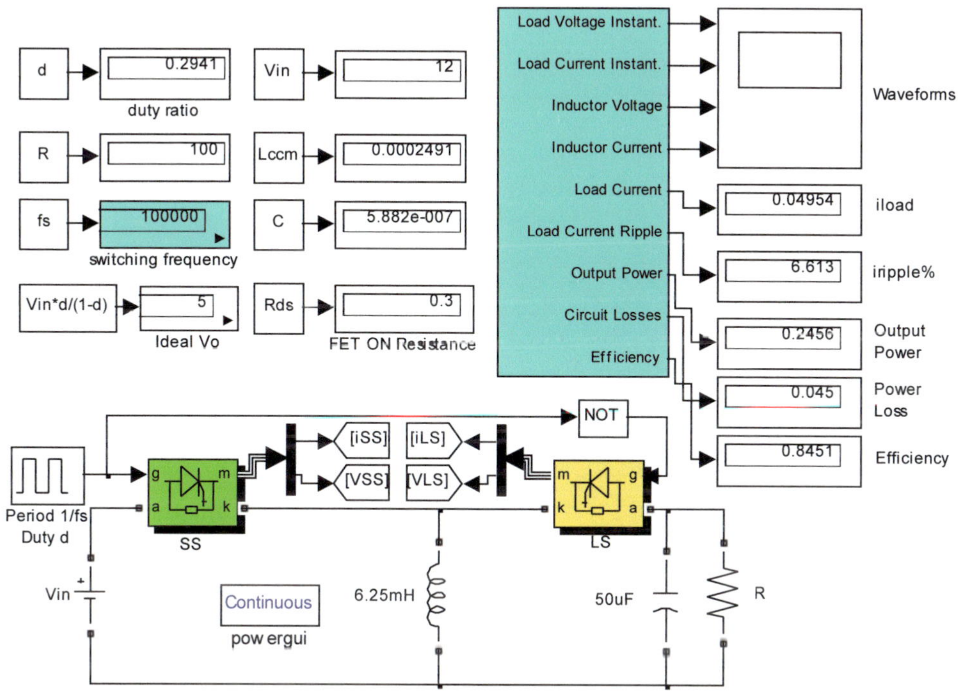

Figure 26. Buck-Boost Converter Simulation Diagram

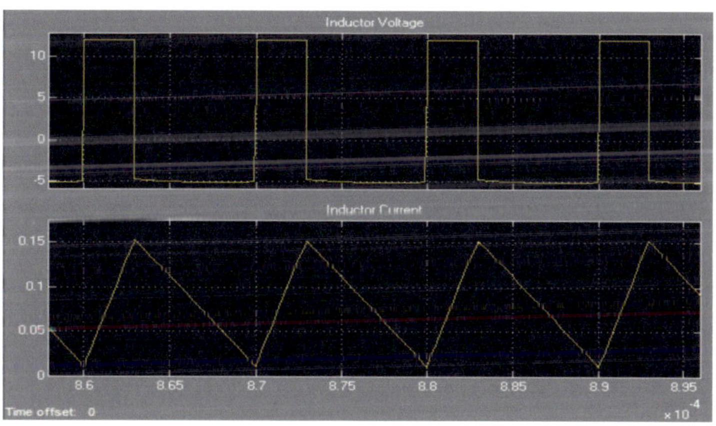

Figure 27. Buck-Boost Inductor Voltage and Current Waveforms

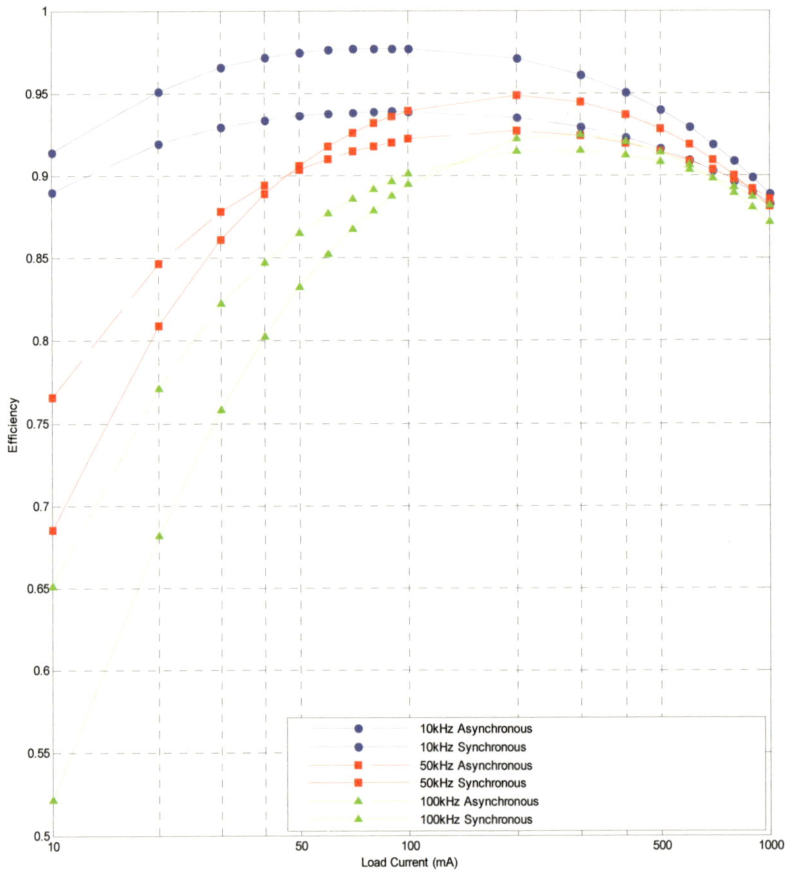

Figure 28. Buck-Boost Converter Synchronous and Asynchronous Efficiency

5. Conclusion

This chapter gave a general overview of AC and DC converters with special emphases on DC-DC converters and their applications. The different topologies were discussed and the importance of designing for efficiency and energy saving was emphasized. Design and analysis steps were illustrated using Matlab and Simulink as an engineering tool. The effectiveness of the SimPower toolbox was demonstrated via typical examples which lead the way for further investigation. The tools available for simulation were exploited to facilitate additional related studies.

Author details

Sven Fagerstrom
Pacific Gas and Electric (PG&E), Fresno, CA, USA

Nagy Bengiamin
California State University Fresno, Fresno, CA, USA

Acknowledgement

This work was supported partially by DPS Telecom, Inc. through a gift to enhance research and development projects in Electrical and Computer Engineering at California State University Fresno. DPS Telecom is located in Fresno, CA, USA.

6. References

Arbetter, B., Erickson, R., & Maksimović, D., (1995), *DC-DC Converter Design for Battery-Operated Systems*. University of Colorado at Boulder

Assi, A.H., (Ed.), (2011), *Engineering Research and Education using Matlab*. Capter *by* Carvalho, A., & Quterio, M.T., *Matlab in Model-based Design for Power Electronics Systems*, Intech, ISBN 978-953-307-656-0

Chen, Y., Lee, F.C., Amoroso, L., & Wu, H.P., (2000), *A Resonant MOSFET Gate Driver With Efficient Energy Recovery*, International Power Electronics and Motion Control (IPEMC) Conference

Djekic, O., & Brkovic, M., (1997), *Synchronous Rectifiers vs. Schottky Diodes in a Buck Topology for Low Voltage Applications*, Power Electronics Specialists Conference, Vol. 2, pp. 1974 1980.

Fagerstrom, S.E. & Bengiamin, N.N., (2011), *Buck/Boost Converter Modeling and Simulation*, IASTED Modeling and Simulation Conference (MS 2011), July 4-6, 2011, Calgary, Canada, paper # 735-059

Forsyth, A.J. &Mollov, S.V., (1998), *Modeling and Control of DC-DC Converters*, IEEE Power Engineering Journal, ISSN 0950-3366

Gildersleeve, M., Zadeh, H.P.F, & Mora, G.A.R, (2002), *A Comprehensive Power Analysis and a Highly Efficient, Mode-Hopping DC-DC Converter*, IEEE Asia-Pacific Conference on ASIC, pp. 153-156

Johansson, B., (2004),*DC-DC Converters – Dynamic Model Design and Experimental Verification*, Lund University, Sweden, ISBN 91-88934-34-9

Klein, J., (2006), *Synchronous buck MOSFET loss calculations with Excel Model*, Fairchild Semiconductor, www.fairchildsemi.com

Paul, B., (2001), *Industrial Electronics and Control, Prentice-Hall of India*, ISBN 81-203-1811-0

Rashid, M.H., (2004), *Power Electronics Handbook (third edition)*, Pearson Prentice Hall, ISBN 0 13-101140-5

Saggini, S., Trevisan, D., Mattavelli, P., Ghioni, M., (2007), *Synchronous-Asynchronous Digital Voltage-Mode Control for DC-DC Converters*, IEEE Transactions on Power Electronics, ISBN 0885-8993

Shaffer, R., (2007), *Fundamentals of Power Electronics with MATLAB*, Charles River Media, ISBN 1-58450-852-3

Skvarenina, T.L., (Ed.), (2002), *The Power Electronics Handbook*, CRC, ISBN-0-8493-7336-0

Stratakos, J., (1998), *High-Efficiency Low-Voltage DC-DC Conversion for Portable Applications*, University of California, Berkeley, Ph.D. Thesis

Wang, T.G., Zhou, X., & Lee, F.C., (1997), *A Low Voltage High Efficiency and High Power Density DC/DC Converter*, 28th Annual IEEE Power Electronics Specialists Conference, Vol. 1, pp. 240-245.

Xiong, Y., Sun, S., Jia, H., Shea, P., & Shen, Z.J., (2009), *New Physical Insights on Power MOSFET Switching Losses*, IEEE Transactions on Power Electronics, Vol. 24, No. 2

Zhou, S., (2003). *Fully Integrated Power-Saving Solutions for DC-DC Converters Targeted for the Mobile, Battery-Powered Applications*, Georgia Tech Analog Consortium Industry Research Review

Zhou, S. & Rincon-Mora, G.A., (2006),*A high Efficiency, Soft Switching DC-DC Converter with Adaptive Current-Ripple Control for Portable Applications*, IEEE Transactions on Circuits and Systems, Vol.53, No. 4

Chapter 8

Improved DTC Algorithms for Reducing Torque and Flux Ripples of PMSM Based on Fuzzy Logic and PWM Techniques

Khalid Chikh, Mohamed Khafallah and Abdallah Saâd

Additional information is available at the end of the chapter

http://dx.doi.org/10.5772/48503

1. Introduction

Permanent Magnet Synchronous Motors (PMSM's) are widely used in high-performance drives such as industrial robots, automotive hybrid drive trains and machine tools thanks to their advantages as: high efficiency, high power density, high torque/inertia ratio, and free maintenance. In the recent years, the magnetic and thermal capabilities of the Permanent Magnet (PM) have been considerably increased by employing the high-coercive permanent magnet material.

Direct Torque Control (DTC) method has been first proposed and applied for induction machines in the mid-1980s, by Takahachi and Noguchi, for low and medium power applications. This concept can also be applied to synchronous drives. Indeed, PMSM DTC has appeared in the late 1990s. However, for some applications, the DTC has become unusable although it significantly improves the dynamic performance (fast torque and flux responses) of the drive and is less dependent on the motor parameters variations compared to the classical vector control due to torque and flux ripples. Indeed, hysteresis controllers used in the conventional structure of the DTC generates a variable switching frequency, causing electromagnetic torque oscillations. Also this frequency varies with speed, load torque and hysteresis bands selected. In addition, a high sampling frequency is needed for digital implementation of hysteresis comparators and a current and torque distortion is caused by sectors changes.

In the last decade, several contributions have been proposed to overcome these problems by using the three level or the multilevel inverter: more voltage space vectors are available to control the flux and torque. However, more power switches are needed to achieve a lower ripple and almost fixed switching frequency, which increases the system cost and complexity. In order to improve the DTC performance and overcome the above cited problems, another solution combines basic DTC and fuzzy logic control advantages in one control strategy, named Fuzzy Direct Torque Control (FDTC). In this technique, the hysteresis comparator and the switching table used in basic DTC are replaced by a fuzzy logic switcher, which decides directly on the switches states of the Voltage Source Inverter (VSI). In addition, it's known that fuzzy control works as well for complex non-linear multi-dimensional system, system with parameter variation problem and/or cases where the sensor signals are not precise. The fuzzy control is basically nonlinear and adaptive in nature, giving robust performance under parameter variation and load disturbance effect. For all these reasons, a Fuzzy Logic Controller can be used instead of the speed PI controller in FDTC in order to achieve a complete fuzzy control for the PMSM. Also, much interest has been focused on the use of modified DTC structures to improve basic DTC performances by replacing the hysteresis controllers and the switching table by a PI regulator, predictive controller and Space Vector Modulation (SVM). Indeed, under DTC-SVM strategy, both torque and flux linkage ripples are greatly reduced when compared with those of the basic DTC, because the application of SVM guarantees lower harmonics current by eliminating the distortion caused by sector changes in case of DTC switching table and by fixing the switching frequency.

Moreover, the design of the speed controller used in basic DTC or in modified DTC strategies, greatly affects the performance of the drive. The PI controllers have a simple structure and can offer satisfactory performances over a wide range of operations. However, due to the uncertainties, the variations in the plant parameters and the nonlinear operating conditions, the fixed gains of the PI controller may become unable to provide the required control performance. In order, to realize a good dynamic behaviour of the PMSM, a perfect speed tracking with no overshoot and a good rejection of impact loads disturbance, the speed PI controller can be replaced by a PI-Fuzzy speed controller.

This chapter is organized as follows: PMSM modelling and simulation results of the basic DTC by using Matlab/Simulink environment with a simple speed PI corrector, will be presented and discussed in Section 2 and 3, respectively. Whereas in Section 4 a complete Fuzzy Direct Torque Control (FDTC), which uses a fuzzy switching table and a PI-Fuzzy speed controller, for PMSM is proposed to reduce the torque and flux ripples. In addition, the simulation results show the effectiveness of this strategy when compared with the basic DTC and a classical speed PI controller. Section 5 and 6 are devoted to presenting a fixed switching-frequency DTC with two approaches: Sinusoidal Pulse With Modulation (SPWM) and Space Vector Modulation (SVM). The objective, of these two strategies, is reducing the flux and torque ripples and fixing the switching-frequency. Of course, the simulation results of these two approaches will be discussed and compared with those of basic DTC and FDTC, in section 7. Section 8 is devoted to study DTC performances under PMSM parameters variation, also a solutions have been proposed to overcome this issue. Eventually, conclusion and simulation results interpretations are included in Section 9.

2. Modelling of the VSI and the PMSM

2.1. Voltage Source Inverter (VSI) for adjustable speed or torque drive

In large number of industries the PMSM's are required to be operated at different speeds or torques. In order to obtain variable speed or torque, these motors are fed from inverters with variable voltage and variable frequency supply. Figure 1 shows the VSI structure used to produce well the voltage waveforms at the terminal of the motor. The voltage control of this inverter is obtained by using switching table in case of basic DTC or by pulse width modulation (PWM) in case of modified DTC techniques.

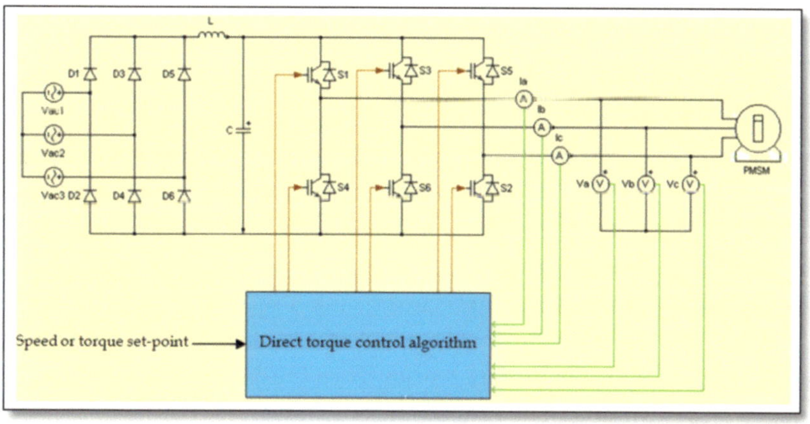

Figure 1. Three phase voltage source bridge inverter structure

The model of the VSI is given by:

$$\begin{bmatrix} V_a \\ V_b \\ V_c \end{bmatrix} = \frac{U_{dc}}{3} \begin{bmatrix} 2 & -1 & -1 \\ -1 & 2 & -1 \\ -1 & -1 & 2 \end{bmatrix} \begin{bmatrix} C_{s1} \\ C_{s3} \\ C_{s5} \end{bmatrix} \tag{1}$$

Where U_{dc} is the DC bus voltage and C_{s1}, C_{s3}, C_{s5} are the transistor states.

2.2. Modeling of the PMSM

The stator voltages equation for a PMSM in the rotor oriented coordinates d-q can be expressed as:

$$\begin{bmatrix} U_{sd} \\ U_{sq} \end{bmatrix} - \begin{bmatrix} R_s + s.L_d & -P.\omega_m.L_q \\ P.\omega_m.L_d & R_s + s.L_q \end{bmatrix} \begin{bmatrix} I_{sd} \\ I_{sq} \end{bmatrix} + \begin{bmatrix} 0 \\ P.\omega_m.\Phi_{PM} \end{bmatrix} \tag{2}$$

Where I_{sd} and I_{sq} are the d - q axis stator currents, R_s is the stator resistance, Ψ_{PM} is the flux linkage of the rotor magnets linking the stator, L_d and L_q are the d - q axis stator inductances, P is the number of pole pairs and ω_m is the mechanical speed.

And the electromagnetic torque equation in the rotor oriented coordinates d-q can be expressed as (3):

$$\Gamma_{em} = \frac{3}{2}P(\Phi_{sd}I_{sq} - \Phi_{sq}I_{sd}) = \frac{3}{2}P[\Phi_{PM}I_{sq} + (L_d - L_q)I_{sd}I_{sq}] \quad (3)$$

Where Φ_{sd} and Φ_{sq} are d - q components of the stator flux linkage, which are expressed as:

$$\begin{bmatrix}\Phi_{sd}\\ \Phi_{sq}\end{bmatrix} = \begin{bmatrix}L_d & 0\\ 0 & L_q\end{bmatrix}\begin{bmatrix}I_{sd}\\ I_{sq}\end{bmatrix} + \begin{bmatrix}\Phi_{PM}\\ 0\end{bmatrix} \quad (4)$$

Finally, when the dry friction torque is neglected; the motion equation is expressed as:

$$J\frac{d\omega_m}{dt} = \Gamma_{em} - \Gamma_{r-}f_r\omega_m \quad (5)$$

Where J moment of inertia, Γ_r motor load and f_r damping constant.

3. Basic direct torque control for PMSM

DTC is a vector control method used to control the torque and therefore the speed of the motor bycontrolling the switching sequence of the inverter transistors. Figure 2 shows the DTC for a PMSM block diagram. It can be seen that once one has the estimated and reference instantaneous values of electromagnetic torque and stator flux, we proceed to calculate the error between them; these errors are used as inputs for the hysteresis controllers, which aim to maintain the torque and flux errors within upper and lower limits allowed, so that when evaluating within these limits an output level is obtained to know the status of the variable. The output levels achieved in this stage of the control are input signals to the block that is responsible for finding the right vector to get rid of the speed error. This procedure is made for each sampling instant to drive the PMSM to the desired speed value.

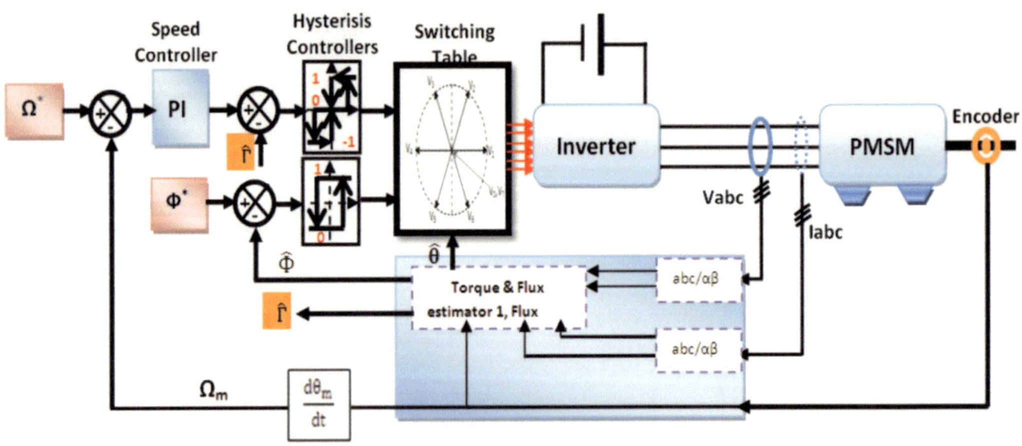

Figure 2. DTC scheme for PMSM with Classical Torque and Flux Estimator (CTFE)

In the DTC, the motor torque control is achieved with two hysteresis controllers, one for stator flux magnitude error and the other for the torque magnitude error. The selection of one switching vector per sampling time depends on the sign of these two controllers without inspections of the magnitude of the errors produced in the transient and dynamic situations per sampling time and level of the applied stator voltage.

3.1. Stator flux control

The stator voltage vector equation, in a stator reference frame, is given by:

$$\overline{V_s} = R_s . \overline{I_s} + \frac{d\overline{\Phi}_s}{dt} \tag{6}$$

Where R_s is the stator resistance and $\overline{V_s} = V_{s\alpha} + jV_{s\beta}$.

So

$$\overline{\Phi}_s = \overline{\Phi}_o + \int_0^t (\overline{V_s} - R_s . \overline{I_s})\, dt \tag{7}$$

For high speeds, the term $R_s . \overline{I_s}$ can be neglected, so the equation 7 is given by:

$$\overline{\Phi}_s \approx \overline{\Phi}_o + \int_0^t \overline{V_s}\, dt \tag{8}$$

$\overline{\Phi}_o$ is the initial stator flux at the instant t_0.

Because during one sampling period T_e the selected stator voltage vector is always constant, the last question becomes:

$$\overline{\Phi}_s(k+1) \approx \overline{\Phi}_s(k) + \overline{V_s} . T_e \tag{9}$$

$$\Delta\overline{\Phi}_s = \overline{V_s} . T_e = \overline{\Phi}_s(k+1) - \overline{\Phi}_s(k) \tag{10}$$

With: T_e is the sampling period.
$\overline{\Phi}_s$ (k) is the stator flux vector at the actual sampling period.
$\overline{\Phi}_s$ (k + 1) is the stator flux vector at the next sampling period.
$\Delta\overline{\Phi}_s$ is the variation of stator flux vector.

From equation 10, it is seen that the variation of the stator flux is directly proportional to the stator voltage; consequently the control is carried out by varying the stator flux vector by selecting a suitable voltage vector with the Voltage Source Inverter (VSI).

Figure 3 shows that the stator flux vector is varied in the same direction as the applied stator voltage vector. Therefore, applied a collinear stator voltage vector as the stator flux vector and in the same direction as it is a sufficiently condition to increase it, and vice versa. Indeed, to control the stator flux vector $\Phi_s(k)$ an estimator of its module $\widehat{\Phi}_s$ and its argument $\widehat{\theta}_s$ is needed; the stator flux can be estimated from the measure of stator currents and voltages and their transformation in the $\alpha\beta$ subspace, by integrating of difference between the input voltage and the voltage drop across the stator resistance as given by:

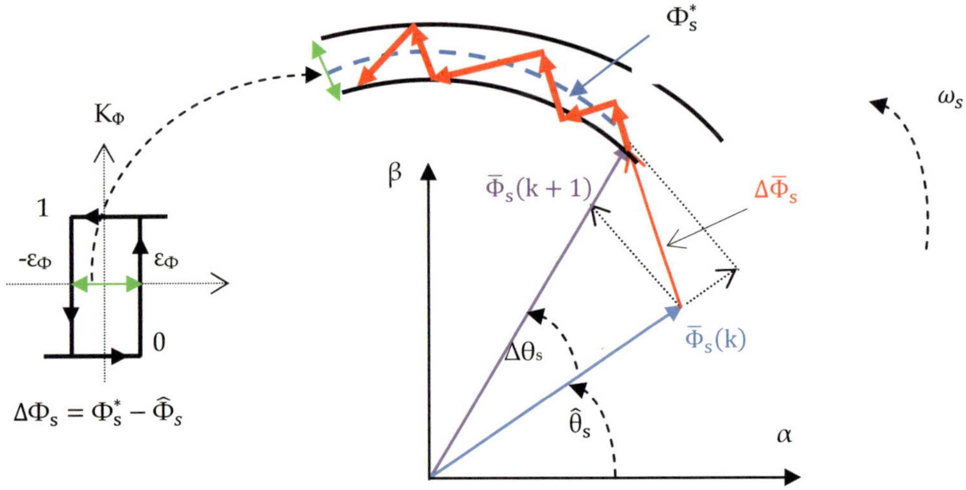

Figure 3. Stator flux vector evolution in the αβ subspace

$$\Phi_{s\alpha} = \Phi_{PM} + \int_0^t (V_{s\alpha} - R_s . I_{s\alpha})\, dt \tag{11}$$

$$\Phi_{s\beta} = \int_0^t \left(V_{s\beta} - R_s . I_{s\beta}\right) dt \tag{12}$$

Note that Φ_{PM} is the permanent magnet flux. From equations 11 and 12, the stator flux module and its argument are given by:

$$\widehat{\Phi}_s = \sqrt{{\Phi_{s\alpha}}^2 + {\Phi_{s\beta}}^2} \tag{13}$$

$$\widehat{\theta}_s = \tan^{-1}\left(\frac{\Phi_{s\beta}}{\Phi_{s\alpha}}\right) \tag{14}$$

A two level hysteresis controller, as indicated in figure 3, is used to control the stator flux, which compares the reference stator flux Φ_s^* with the estimated stator flux $\widehat{\Phi}_s$. The flux hysteresis comparator output is denoted by Boolean variable K_Φ which indicates directly if the amplitude of flux must be increased $K_\Phi = 1$ or decreased $K_\Phi = 0$: if $K_\Phi = 1$, it means that the actual value of the flux linkage is below the reference value and outside the hysteresis limit; so the stator flux must be increased, while if $K_\Phi = 0$, it means that the actual value of the flux linkages is above the reference value and outside the hysteresis limit; so the stator flux must be decreased.

The two level VSI, as shown in figure 1, is used to select proper voltage vectors from the output of flux and torque hysteresis controller (will be presented in the next part). The inverter has eight permissible switching states (V_0, V_1 … V_7), out of which six are active (V_1, V_2… V_6) and two zero or inactive states (V_0 and V_7). The voltage vector plane is divided into six sectors so that each voltage vector divides each region in two equal parts as shown in Figure 4. In each sector four of the six non-zero voltage vectors along with zero vectors may be used.

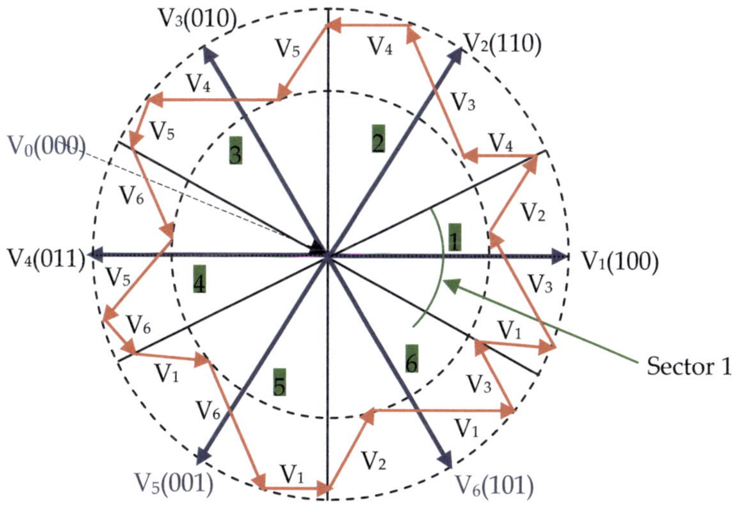

Figure 4. Control of stator flux by selection of the suitable voltage vector $V_{i(i=0,\ldots,7)}$

3.2. Torque control

The electromagnetic torque equation is defined as follows:

$$\Gamma = k.(\bar{\Phi}_s.\bar{\Phi}_r) = \|\bar{\Phi}_s\|.\|\bar{\Phi}_r\|.\sin\delta \tag{15}$$

Where δ is the angle between the rotor and the stator flux vectors and the constant k is expressed as (when $L_d = L_q$):

$$k = \frac{3P}{2L_q}$$

The equation 15 indicates that the electromagnetic torque depends to the rotor and stator amplitude, and the angle δ. So, if the stator flux vector is perfectly controlled, by mean of the stator voltage vector $\overline{V_s}$, in module and in position; consequently, the electromagnetic torque can be controlled by the same stator voltage vector.

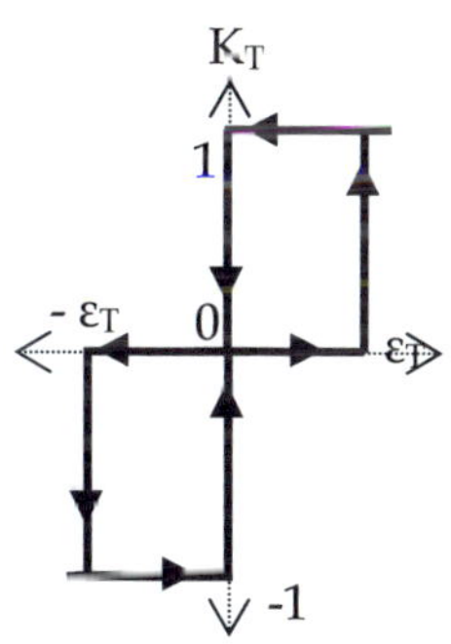

Figure 5. Three level hysteresis controller

Note that the electromagnetic torque can be controlled by mean of a two level comparator as the same as stator flux (see figure 3) or by using a three level comparator as shown in figure 5. In this work, a three level comparator has been used in order to minimize the switches commutation numbers and to have the two senses of the motor rotation. The output of this controller is represented by a Boolean variable K_T which indicates directly if the amplitude of the torque must be increased, maintained constant or decreased, respectively, when K_T is equal 1, 0 or -1. The goal of this controller is to maintain the torque variation $\Delta\Gamma$ in the bandwidth $[-\varepsilon_T, \varepsilon_T]$ chosen by the programmer of DTC algorithm. Indeed, this controller adjusts the torque variation generated by a comparator of electromagnetic torque reference (Γ^*)and the estimated torque ($\hat{\Gamma}$).

$$\Delta\Gamma = \Gamma^* - \hat{\Gamma} \quad (16)$$

3.3. Switching table for controlling flux and torque

According to the signal generated by the hysteresis controller of stator flux and electromagnetic torque presented in figure 3 and 5, respectively; just one voltage vector can be selected to adjust the torque and flux. The choice of this vector depends on the outputs of the torque and flux controller and the position of the stator flux vector, as shown in table 1.

K_Φ	K_T	θ_1	θ_2	θ_3	θ_4	θ_5	θ_6
1	1	V_2	V_3	V_4	V_5	V_6	V_1
	0	V_7	V_0	V_7	V_0	V_7	V_0
	-1	V_6	V_1	V_2	V_3	V_4	V_5
0	1	V_3	V_4	V_5	V_6	V_1	V_2
	0	V_0	V_7	V_0	V_7	V_0	V_7
	-1	V_5	V_6	V_1	V_2	V_3	V_4

Table 1. Takahashi and Noguchi switching table

3.4. Torque and flux estimator

In this chapter, two estimators of torque and stator flux will be presented.

3.4.1. Classical Torque and Flux Estimator (CTFE)

The figure 2 shows that the torque and stator flux can be estimated by measuring the mechanical position, stator voltages and currents. Indeed, the stator flux is estimated by using equations 11, 12 and 13. Whereas, the torque is estimated by using equation 17:

$$\hat{\Gamma} = \frac{3}{2} P \left[\Phi_{s\alpha} I_{s\beta} - \Phi_{s\beta} I_{s\alpha} \right] \quad (17)$$

Note that the stator voltages used in this estimator can be measured directly by mean of two or three sensors, or indirectly by combining the measured DC bus voltage and the transistor states (C_{s1}, C_{s3}, C_{s5}) of the VSI.

$$\begin{bmatrix} V_{s\alpha} \\ V_{s\beta} \end{bmatrix} = U_{dc}\sqrt{\frac{2}{3}}\begin{bmatrix} 1 & -\frac{1}{2} & -\frac{1}{2} \\ 0 & 1 & 1 \end{bmatrix}\begin{bmatrix} C_{s1} \\ C_{s3} \\ C_{s5} \end{bmatrix} \tag{18}$$

C_{s1}, C_{s3} and C_{s5} are the switching commands of each VSI leg and they are complementary. For the first leg (transistors S_1 and S_4), C_{s1} is 1 if the upper switch (S_1) is commanded to be closed and 0 if the lower one (S_4) in commanded to be closed first.

The drawbacks of this estimation technique are: In addition to stator current sensors, at least one voltage sensor is necessary. In addition, the estimated torque and stator flux dependent to the stator resistance.

3.4.2. Robust Torque and Flux Estimator (RTFE)

In order to estimate stator flux and electromagnetic torque with this estimator, just current components and rotor position are measured without measuring stator voltages directly or by using transistor states and DC bus voltage sensor. The bloc diagram of this estimation technique is shown in figure 6.

The advantages of this NTFE are: Any stator voltage sensor is necessary to estimate stator flux or electromagnetic torque and the estimated stator flux and electromagnetic torque are independent to the stator resistance variations, which can improve the performances of the drive and reduce the cost of this equipment.

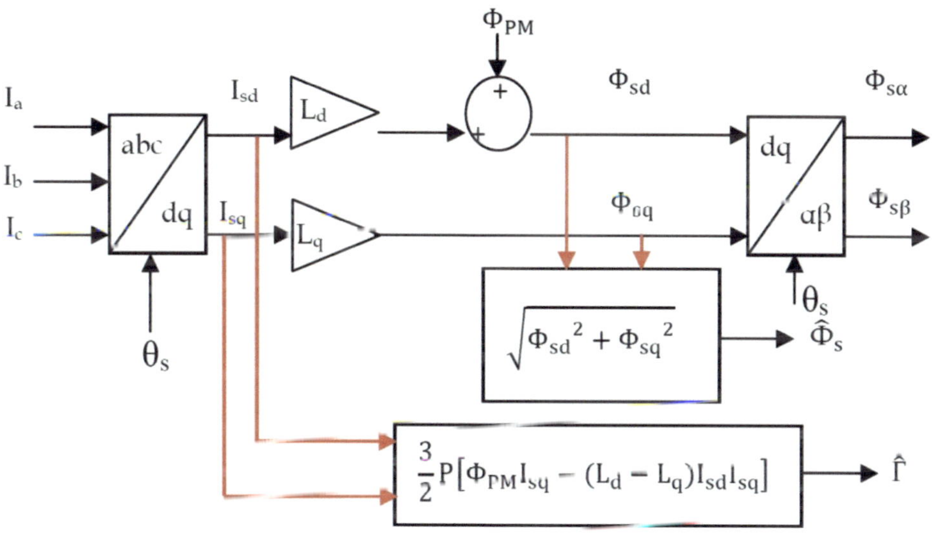

Figure 6. Robust Torque and Flux Estimator structure

3.5. Speed PI controller synthesis

The speed closed loop with the PI controller is presented by the bloc diagram in Figure 7. To eliminate the zero effect due to corrector, the compensation method is used to the corrector synthesis. In this case the regulator parameters are given by the relationships:

$k_p = \frac{J}{K_T.\tau_w}$ and $k_i = \frac{J}{K_T.\tau_w}$ where $\tau_w = 0.1$ second

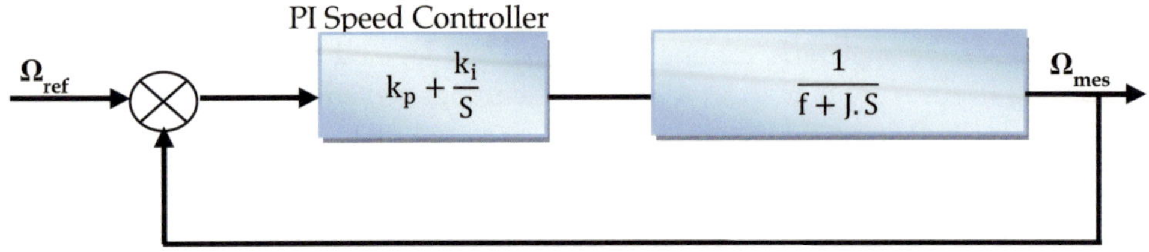

Figure 7. Closed loop PI speed controller

3.6. Simulation results

The PMSM parameters used in this simulation are shown in table II. These parameters will be used in all the simulations of this chapter.

Rated output power (Watt)	Rated phase voltage (Volt)	Magnetic flux linkage (Wb)
500	190	0.052
Rated torque (Nm)	Rated speed (r/min)	Maximum speed (r/min)
0.8	1000	6000
d-axis inductance (mH)	q-axis inductance (mH)	Inertia (Kg.m²)
3.3	3.3	0.003573
Poles	Stator resistance (Ω)	friction coefficient (Nm.s/rd)
3	1.59	0.00047

Table 2. PMSM parameters

The models of the PMSM, VSI and basic DTC algorithm are developed in Matlab/Simulink in order to examine the complete behaviour of the basic DTC. The sampling period has been chosen equal to 50 μs (20 KHz) for basic DTC. Various tests have been carried out in order to investigate the drive performance and to characterize the steady-state and transient behavior.

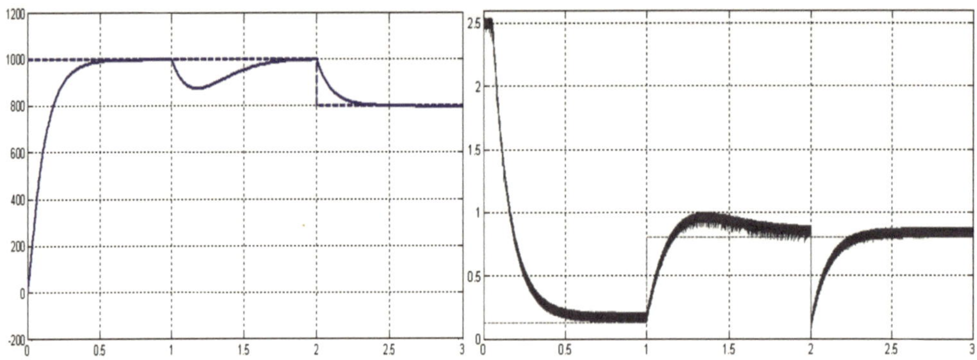

Figure 8. Mechanical speed (on the left) and electromagnetic torque (on the right) tracking performance under load variations in case of basic DTC

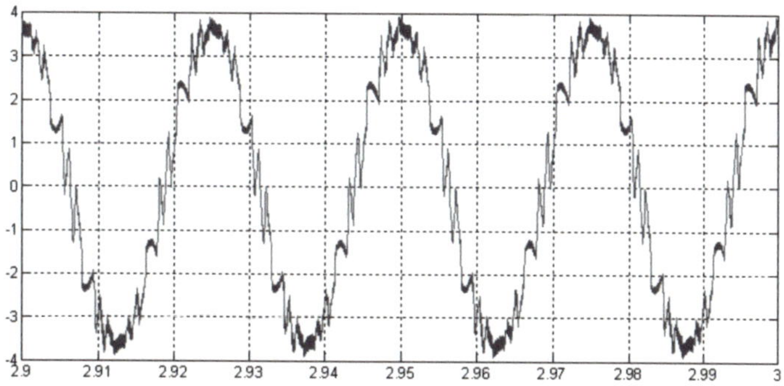

Figure 9. Stator current waveform at 800 rpm with nominal load under basic DTC

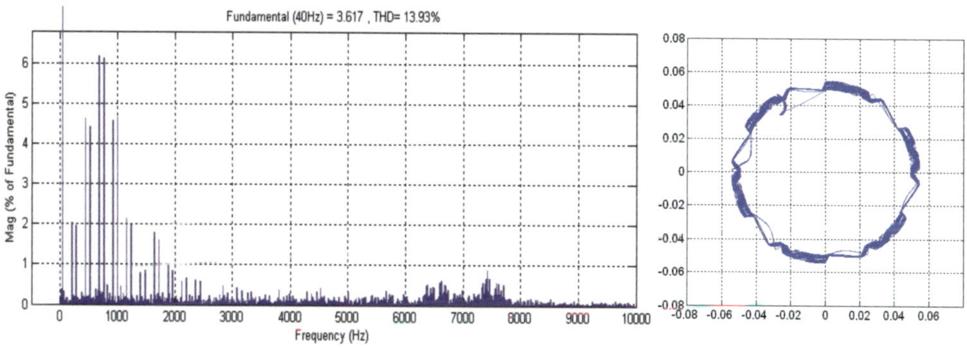

Figure 10. Stator current spectrum at 800 rpm with nominal load (on the left) and Stator flux in (α,β) axes under load variations (on the right) in case of basic DTC

4. Fuzzy direct torque control for PMSM

4.1. FDTC strategy

Figure 11 shows the complete FDTC structure which combines FDTC and PI-Fuzzy speed controller. Indeed, the switching table used in basic DTC and the hysterisis controllers are replaced by a fuzzy switching table, whose inputs are electromagnetic torque and stator flux errors denoted respectively $\Delta\Gamma$ and $\Delta\Phi_s$, and the argument $\theta_s$of the stator flux (should remain between $\pm\pi$).Whereas its outputs are the states of the VSI switches. In other hand, the classical speed PI corrector is replaced by a PI-Fuzzy speed controller in order to improve the dynamic performance of the DTC.

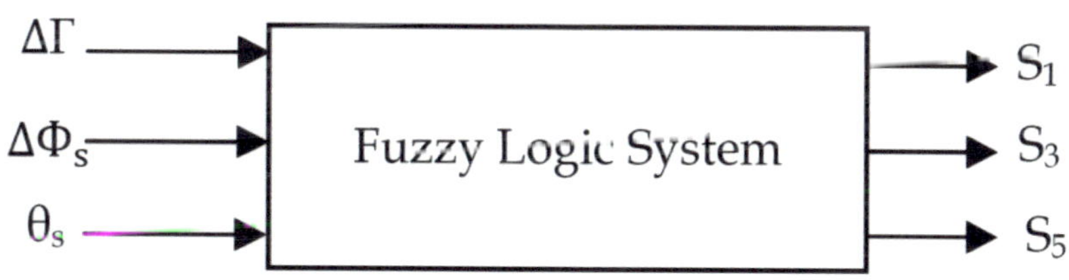

Figure 11. Fuzzy logic switching table used in FDTC

Figure 12 shows the design of this fuzzy logic system in Matlab/Simulink and also the configuration of its inputs and outputs as membership functions.

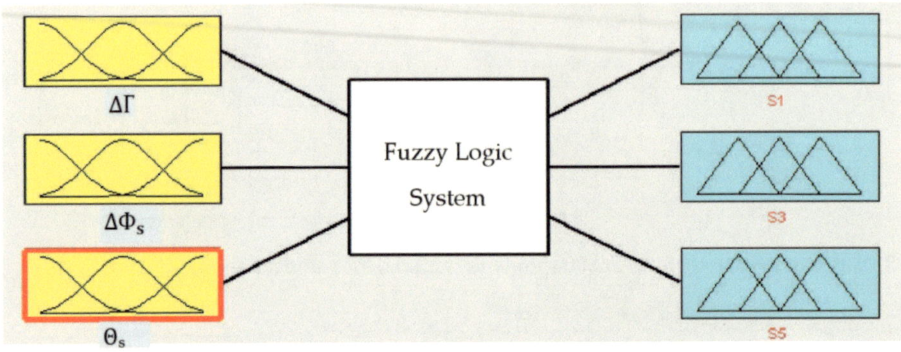

Figure 12. Matlab/Simulink design of the fuzzy logic switching table used in FDTC

4.2. Inputs fuzzification and outputs defuzzification

In order to examine the fuzzy logic contribution to DTC, the choice of the membership functions number for the fuzzification of flux and torque errors has been repected in this part, i.e two membership functions for $\Delta\Phi_s$, because a two level hysteresis controller was utilized to control the stator flux in basic DTC. Whereas three membership functions for the fuzzification of $\Delta\Gamma$ because a three level hysteris controller was used to adjust the torque.

4.2.1. Stator flux error fuzzification

Two trapezoidal membership functions are selected to fuzzify the stator flux error, so the following two fuzzy sets are used, N signify Negative and P for Positive. The parameters of these two functions are indicated in figure 13.

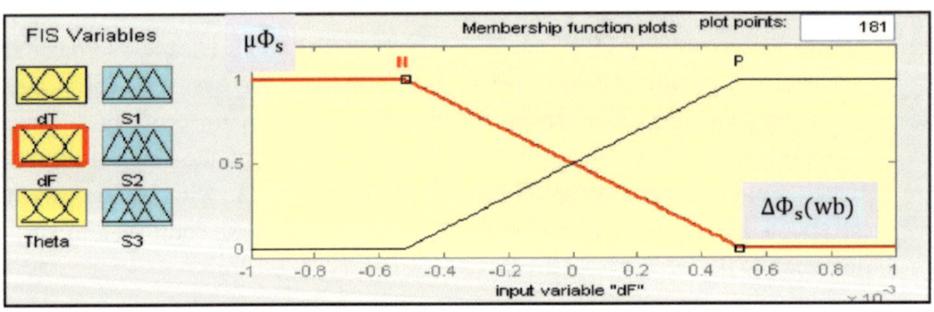

Figure 13. Membership functions for stator flux error

4.2.2. Electromagnetic torque error fuzzification

Three trapezoidal membership functions are selected to fuzzify the torque error as shown in figure 14, so the following three fuzzy sets are used, N signify Negative, EZ for Zero and P for Positive.

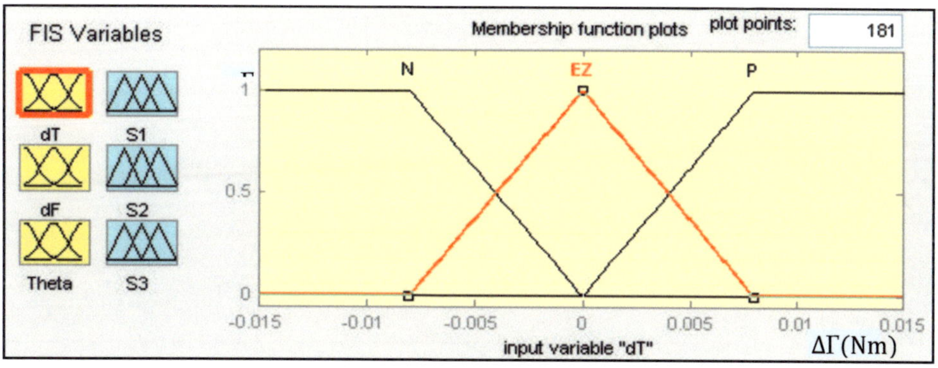

Figure 14. Membership functions for electromagnetic torque error

4.2.3. Stator flux angle fuzzification

The flux angle has a universe of discours equal 2π radians, as shown in figure 15. It is divided into six zones or sectors in order to be equivalent to that of the basic DTC. "thetai" means sector i, i.e "theta1" means sector 1 (θ_1) and so on.

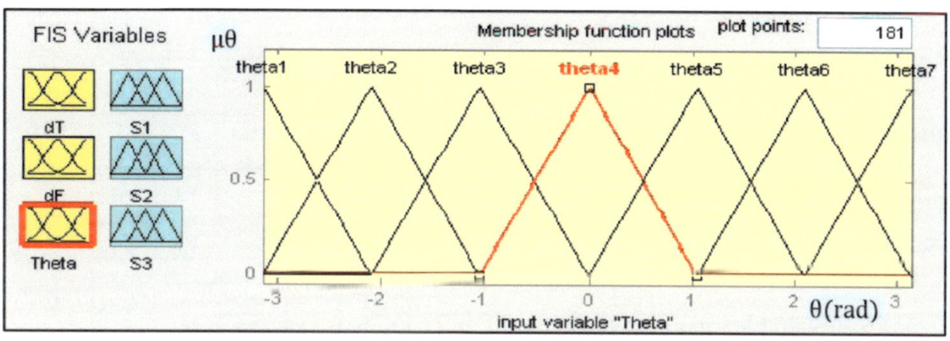

Figure 15. Membership functions for stator flux position

4.2.4. State switches defuzzification

The sole output control variable of fuzzy logic system is the inverter switching states S_1, S_3 and S_5 or the selected voltage vector. Figure 16, illustrates the suggested output fuzzy set as singletons. Indeed, the choice of the stator volt dge vector is based on the rules indicated in table 3. Each control rule can be described using the state variables ΔΦ, ΔΓ and θs and the control variables. The ith rule Ri can be written as:

$$Ri : \text{if } \Delta\Phi, \text{ is } A_i, \Delta\Gamma \text{ is } B_i \text{ and } \theta s \text{ is } C_i \text{ then } S_1 \text{ is } a, S_3 \text{ is } b \text{ and } S_5 \text{ is } c$$

Where a, b and c are a boolean variable. A_i, B_i and C_i denote the fuzzy set of the variables ΔΦ, ΔΓ and θs, respectively.whereas Ri is the control rule number i.

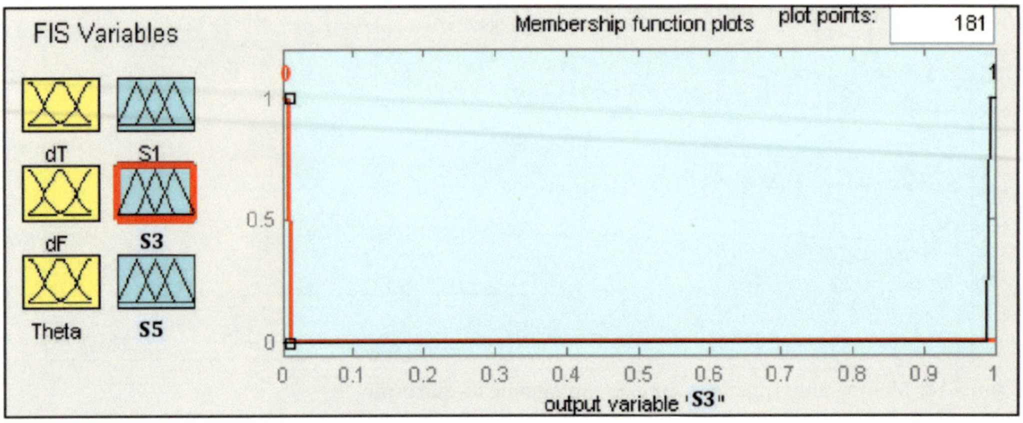

Figure 16. Membership functions for state switches as singletons

4.3. Fuzzy logic switcher rules

The most important part of designing the fuzzy controller (fuzzy logic system) is to design the rule base, because it gouverns the behiviour of fuzzy controller and stores the expert knowledge on how to control the plant. The fuzzy associative memory of Mamdani rule base model to develop DTFC is as shown in Table 3.

θ_1, θ_7		
ΔΓ\ΔΦ	**P**	**N**
P	V_5	V_6
Z	V_0	V_7

θ_2		
ΔΓ\ΔΦ	**P**	**N**
P	V_6	V_1
Z	V_7	V_0

θ_3		
ΔΓ\ΔΦ	**P**	**N**
P	V_1	V_2
Z	V_0	V_7

θ_4		
ΔΓ\ΔΦ	**P**	**N**
P	V_2	V_3
Z	V_7	V_0

θ_5		
ΔΓ\ΔΦ	**P**	**N**
P	V_3	V_4
Z	V_0	V_7

θ_6		
ΔΓ\ΔΦ	**P**	**N**
P	V_4	V_5
Z	V_7	V_0

Table 3. Fuzzy logic switcher rules

4.4. PI-Fuzzy speed controller synthesis

The speed closed loop with the PI-Fuzzy controller structure is shown in Figure 17. The inputs of this FLC are the normalized values of the speed error denoted "e" and its rate of change denoted "de" that should remain between ±1. Wherefore, two scaling factors (K_{ne} and $K_{\Delta ne}$) are used to normalize the actual speed error and its rate of change. The output of the controller is the normalized change of the motor torque command which generates the actual value of the motor torque demand when it's multiplied by a third scaling factor (K_{nc}).

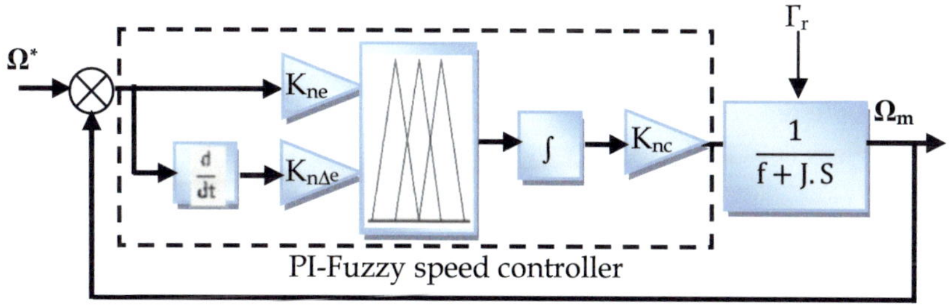

Figure 17. Closed loop PI-Fuzzy speed controller

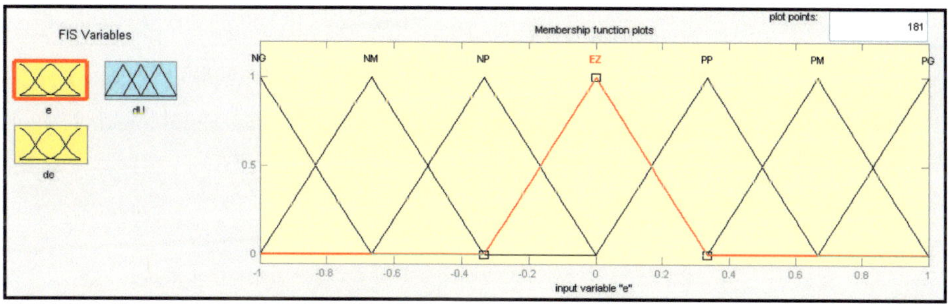

Figure 18. Membership functions for speed error

The membership functions used, in this chapter, for the inputs and the output are the same, as shown in figure 18. Where, the following fuzzy sets used in these membership functions: NG is negative big, NM is negative medium, NP is negative small, EZ is equal zero, PP is positive small, PM is positive medium and PG is positive big.

From the speed behavior analysis, the table 4 has been developed to obtain a good performance in the speed closed loop. Whereas, from the membership functions of inputs and the output, and the rules presented in this table, the FLC elaborates the electromagnetic torque reference to be developed by the PMSM.

e\Δe	NG	NM	NP	EZ	PP	PM	PG
PG	EZ	PP	PM	PG	PG	PG	PG
PM	NP	EZ	PP	PM	PG	PG	PG
PP	NM	NP	EZ	PP	PM	PG	PG
EZ	NG	NM	NP	EZ	PP	PM	PG
NP	NG	NG	NM	NP	EZ	PP	PM
NM	NG	NG	NG	NM	NP	EZ	PP
NG	NG	NG	NG	NG	NM	NP	EZ

Table 4. PI-Fuzzy speed controller rules

4.5. Simulation results

The sampling period has been chosen equal to 100 μs (10 KHz) for FDTC; in order to compare this strategy with basic DTC; despite the fact that the sampling time used to simulate DTC is less than that used in case of FDTC.

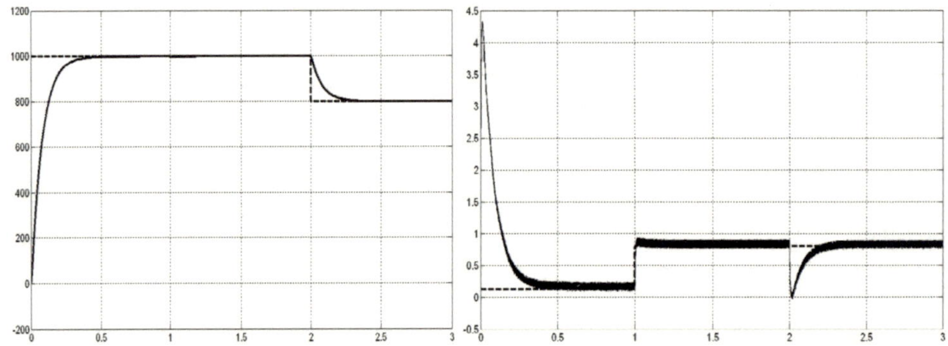

Figure 19. Mechanical speed (on the left) and electromagnetic torque (on the right) tracking performance under load variations in case of FDTC

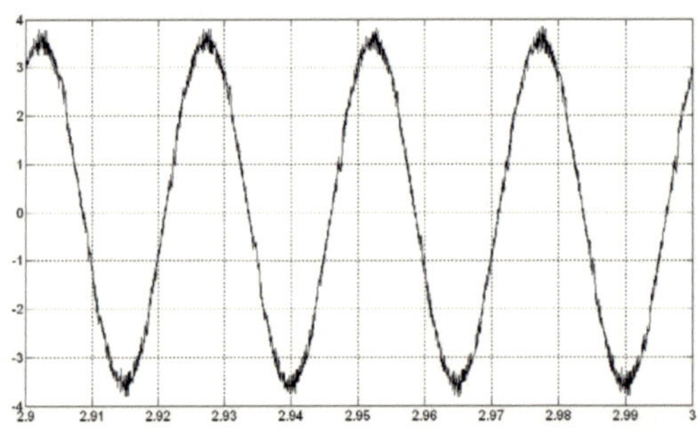

Figure 20. Stator current waveform at 800 rpm with nominal load under FDTC

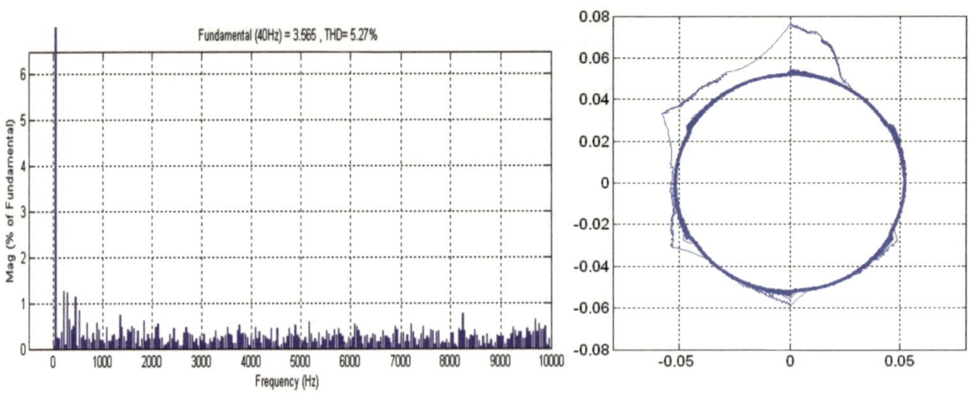

Figure 21. Stator current spectrum at 800 rpm with nominal load (on the left) and Stator flux in (α,β) axes under load variations (on the right) in case of FDTC

5. Direct Torque Control with Space Vector Modulation for PMSM

Figure 22 shows the DTC with SVM scheme for PMSM drive, this technique is a solution to overcome the drawbacks of the basic DTC by using the same torque and flux estimators and the same speed PI controller. In this modified DTC, torque and flux hysteresis controllers and the switching table used in basic DTC are replaced by a PI torque controller and a predictive calculator of vector voltage reference to be applied to stator coils of the PMSM.

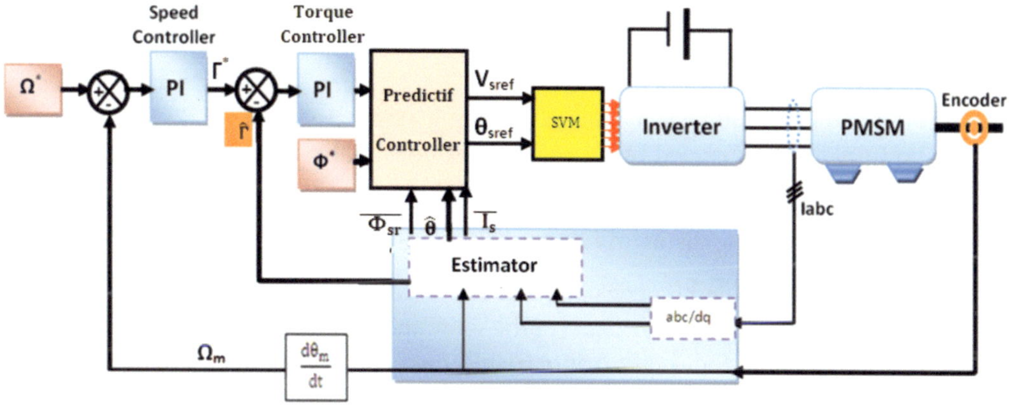

Figure 22. DTC-SVM scheme for PMSM drive

In the proposed scheme of DTC-SVM with speed loop control, shown in this figure, after correction of the mechanical speed through a PI controller, the torque PI controller delivers V_{sq} voltage to the predictive controller and also receives, more the reference amplitude of stator flux $\Phi^*=\Phi_{PM}$, information from the estimator namely, the position of the actual stator flux, estimated flux vector and measured current vector, where:

$$\overline{\Phi_s} = \Psi_{s\alpha} + j\Phi_{s\beta} \text{ and } \overline{I_s} = i_{s\alpha} + ji_{s\beta}$$

After calculation, the predictive controller determinates the polar coordinates of stator voltage command vector $\overline{V_{sref}} = [V_{sref}, \theta_{sref}]$ for space vector modulator, which finally generates the pulses S_1, S_3 and S_5 to control the VSI.

5.1. Torque and flux control by means of SVM

The electromagnetic torque of the PMSM can be expressed as:

$$\Gamma_{em} = \frac{3}{2}P\frac{\Phi_{sr}}{L_d L_q}\left[\Phi_{PM}L_q\sin\delta + \frac{1}{2}\Phi_{sr}(L_d - L_q)\sin\delta\right] \quad (19)$$

Where δ is the angle between the stator and rotor flux linkage (or the torque angle).

Above equation consist of two terms, the first is the excitation torque, which is produced by permanent magnet flux and the second term is the reluctance torque.

In the case where $L_d = L_q = L$, the expression of electromagnetic torque becomes:

$$\Gamma_{em} = \frac{3}{2} P \frac{\Phi_{sr}}{L} \Phi_{PM} \sin\delta \tag{20}$$

Under the condition of constant stator flux amplitude Φ_{sr} , by diffentiating equation 20 with respect to time, the rate of increasing of torque at t=0 can be obtained in equation 21.

$$\frac{d\Gamma}{dt} = \left(\frac{3}{2} P \frac{\Phi_{sr}}{L} \Phi_{PM} \cos\delta\right) \frac{d\delta}{dt} \tag{21}$$

From equations 20 and 21, it can be seen that for constant stator flux amplitude Φ_{sr} and flux produced by Permanent Magnets (PM) Φ_{PM}, the electromagnetic torque can be changed by control of the torque angle; quick dynamic reponse can be achieved by changing this angle as quickly as possible, this is the basis of DTC for PMSM (Tang et al., 2003). This is the angle between the stator and rotor flux linkage, when the stator resistance is neglected. The torque angle δ, in turn, can be changed by changing position of stator flux vector in respect to PM vector using the actual voltage vector supplied by PWM inverter.

When the PMSM drive, we distinguish between two cases:

- Steady state: the angle δ is constant and its value is the load torque of the machine, while the stator flux and rotor rotate at the same speed is the synchronous speed.
- The transient state, the angle δ is variable then the stator and rotor flux rotate at different speeds (see figure 23).

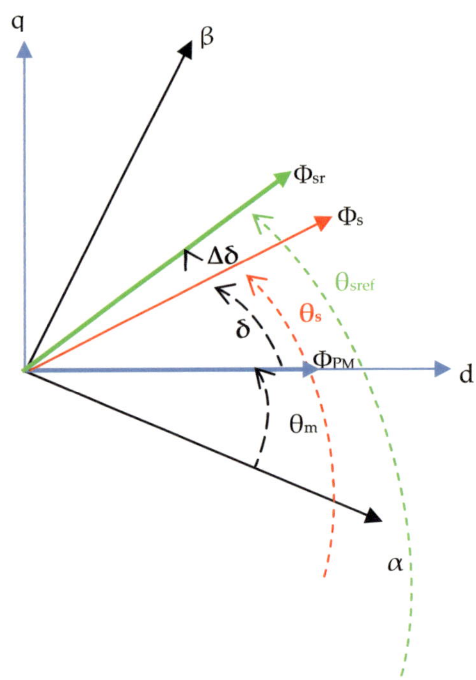

Figure 23. Vector diagram of illustrating torque and flux control conditions

The change of the angle δ is done by varying the position of the stator flux vector relative to the rotor flux vector with the vector V_{sref} provided by the predictive controller to the power of the SVM. The figure 23 above shows the evolution of the stator flux vector at the beginning and the end of a period vector modulation. At the beginning, stator flux vector is at the position δ with an amplitude Φ_s, it's at this moment that the predictive controller calculated the variation Δδ of the stator flux angle, it's also at this same moment that the space vector modulator receives the new position and amplitude of the voltage vector that must be achieved at the end of the modulation period. Of course, this vector will allow the stator flux to transit to the location as defined by the predictive controller to adjust the torque fluctuations, and this by calculating the time of application of the adjacent vectors V_1, V_2 and V_0 as well as their sequence that depends on the symmetry of the modulation vector.

The internal structure of the predictive torque and flux controller is shown in figure 24. So the average change Δδ of the angle δ is expressed as:

$$\Delta\delta = T_s \frac{d}{dt}\left[\text{Arcsin}\left(\frac{\Phi_{sr}}{L_q\, I_{sq}}\right)\right] \tag{22}$$

where: T_s is the sampling time.

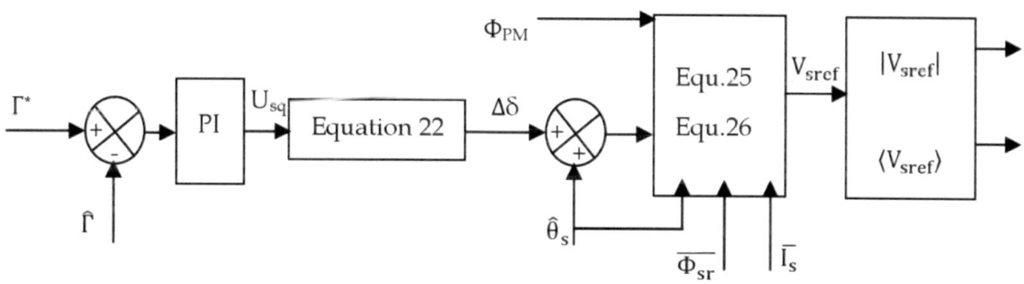

Figure 24. Internal structure of predictive controller used in DTC-SVM

From equation 22, the relation between error of torque and increment of load angle Δδ is non linear. In odrder to generate the load angel increment required to minimize the instantaneous error between reference and actual estimated torque; a PI controller has been applied as indicated in figure 24. The step change Δδ that corresponds to the torque error is added to the current position $\hat{\theta}_s$ of the stator flux vector to determine the new position of this vector at the next simple time.

The module and argument of the reference stator voltage vector is calculated by the following equations, based on stator resistance R_s, Δδ signal and actual stator flux argument:

$$|V_{sref}| = \sqrt{{V_{s\alpha\ ref}}^2 + {V_{s\beta-ref}}^2} \tag{23}$$

$$\langle V_{sref}\rangle = \arctan\left(\frac{V_{s\beta-ref}}{V_{s\alpha-ref}}\right) \# \tag{24}$$

Where:

$$V_{s\alpha-ref} = \frac{\Phi_{sr}\cos(\hat{\theta}_s+\Delta\delta)-\Phi_s\cos\hat{\theta}_s}{T_s} + R_s.\, I_{s\alpha} \tag{25}$$

$$V_{s\beta-ref} = \frac{\Phi_{sr}\sin(\widehat{\theta}_s+\Delta\delta)-\Phi_s\sin\widehat{\theta}_s}{T_s} + R_s.I_{s\beta} \tag{26}$$

The figure 25 shows the application sequence of the two adjacent vectors and zero vector in the first sector of the vector V_{sref}. Indeed, after the vector modulation algorithm computation times T_1, T_2 and T_0 successively apply the voltage vectors V_1, V_2 and V_0, we choose the symmetry in the schematic figure 25 of dividing each modulation period T_s into two sequences and transistor control of the upper arms of the VSI, in the second half of the period are an image of themselves in relation to the vertical axis passing through the point $T_s/2$.

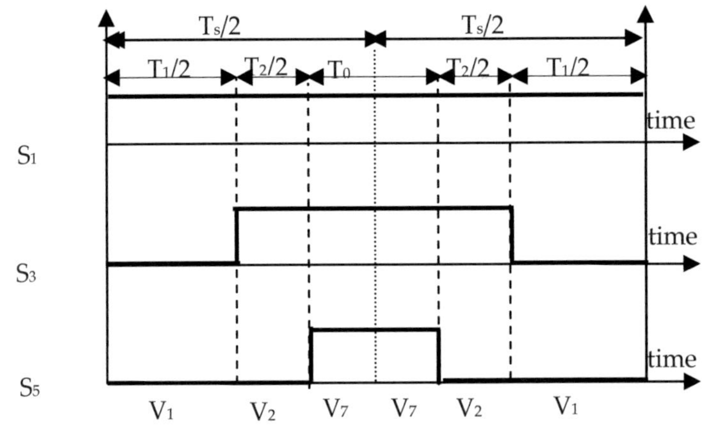

Figure 25. Time sequences and applications of adjacent vectors in the first sector

So to have a fast transit of stator flux vector, very low flux ripple and fast torque response, the space vector modulator generates a voltage vector V_{sref} governed by the following law:

$$V_{sref} = \frac{1}{T_s}\left[\left(\frac{T_1}{2}V_1 + \frac{T_2}{2}V_2 + \frac{T_0}{2}V_0\right) + \left(\frac{T_0}{2}V_0 + \frac{T_2}{2}V_2\ \frac{T_1}{2}V_1\right)\right] \tag{27}$$

So at each modulation period and in this case, the sequence of adjacent vectors in the first sector is applied (V_1-V_2-V_7-V_7-V_2-V_1) respectively during the time $\left(\frac{T_1}{2}, \frac{T_2}{2}, \frac{T_0}{2}, \frac{T_0}{2}, \frac{T_2}{2}, \frac{T_1}{2}\right)$ to rebuild the better the rotating vector.

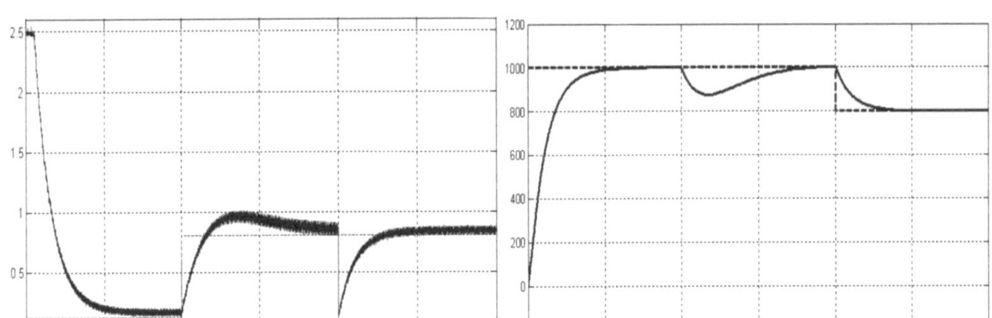

Figure 26. Stator current spectrum at 800 rpm with nominal load (on the left) and Stator flux in (α,β) axes under load variations (on the right) in case of DTC-SVM

5.2. Simulation results

The sampling period has been chosen equal to 100 μs (10 KHz) for DTC-SVM; in order to compare this strategy with basic DTC; despite the fact that the sampling time used to simulate DTC is less than that used in case of DTC-SVM. Whereas, the sampling frequencies used to simulate FDTC and DTC-SVM are equal; so as to compare these two techniques in the same conditions.

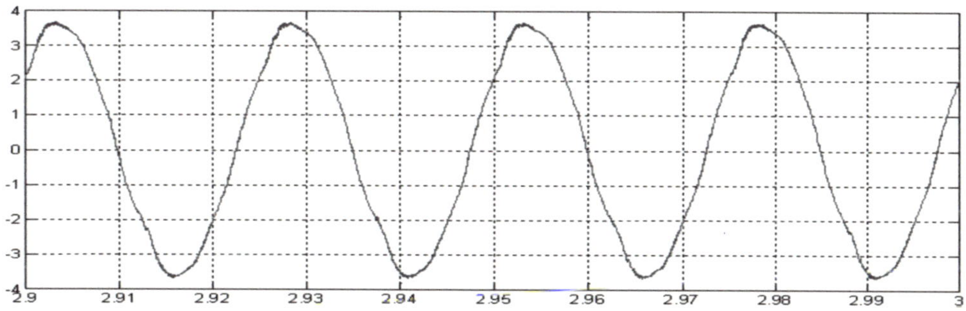

Figure 27. Stator current waveform at 800 rpm with nominal load under DTC-SVM

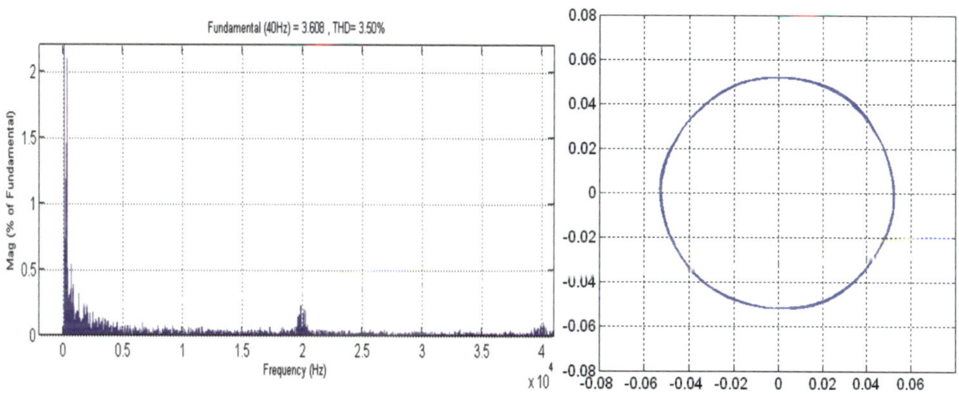

Figure 28. Stator current spectrum at 800 rpm with nominal load (on the left) and Stator flux in (α,β) axes under load variations (on the right) in case of DTC-SVM

6. Direct Torque Control with Sinusoidal Pulse with Modulation for PMSM

DTC-SPWM for PMSM is based on the same algorithm used in DTC-SVM already presented in figure 22, but instead of using SVM pulses generator, a simple and fast SPWM pulses generator is investigated to control the VSI. Indeed, after transformation of $V_{s\alpha-ref}$ and $V_{s\beta-ref}$ produced by the predictive controller (from the stator flux reference frame (α-β) to the (a-b-c) frame). These three signals, used as reference signals, will be compared with a triangular signal (figure 29); then the inverter is controlled by the SPWM.

In this proposed technique, the same flux and torque estimators and the predictive torque and flux controller as for the DTC-SVM are still used. Instead of the SVM generator, a SPWM technique is used to determine reference stator flux linkage vector. It is seen that the proposed scheme retains almost all the advantages of the DTC-SVM, such as no current control loop, constant switching frequency, low torque and flux ripple, etc. But, the main advantage of the DTC-SPWM is the simple algorithm of PWM (SPWM) used to control the VSI. Of course, the SVM algorithm needs more calculation time than SPWM and the same advantages of DTC-SVM will be obtained by using DTC-SPWM. Whatever is the load torque and speed variation, SPWM guarantees a constant switching frequency, which greatly improves the flux and torque ripples.

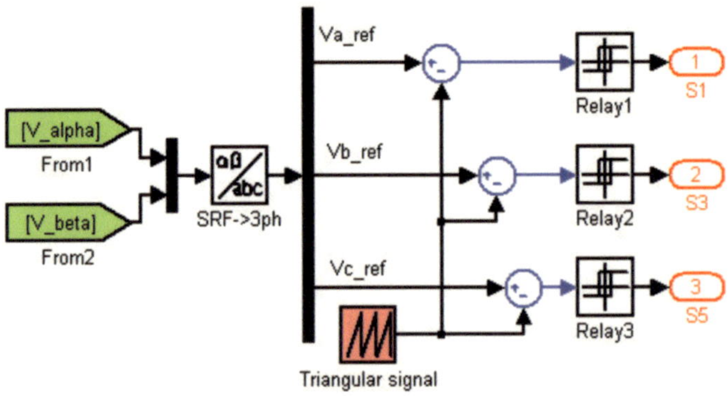

Figure 29. Sinusoidal PWM pulses generator scheme

6.1. Simulation results

The sampling period has been chosen equal to 100 μs (10 KHz) for DTC-SVM; in order to compare this strategy with basic DTC; despite the fact that the sampling time used to simulate DTC is less than that used in case of DTC-SVM. Whereas, the sampling frequencies used to simulate FDTC and DTC-SVM are equal; so as to compare these two techniques in the same conditions.

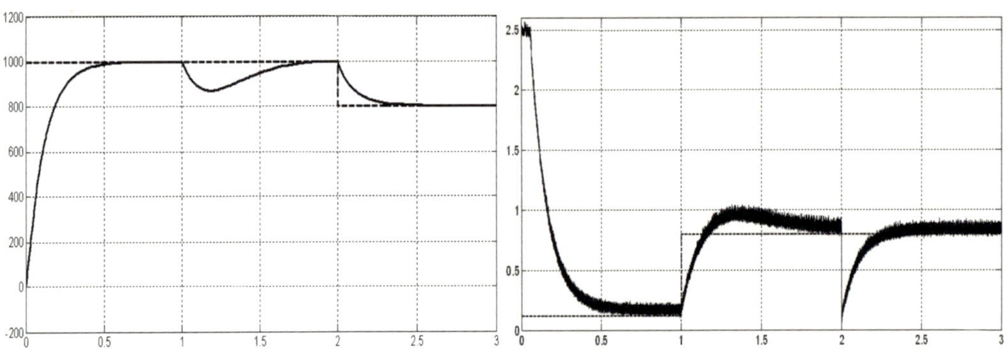

Figure 30. Stator current spectrum at 800 rpm with nominal load (on the left) and Stator flux in (α,β) axes under load variations (on the right) in case of DTC-SPWM

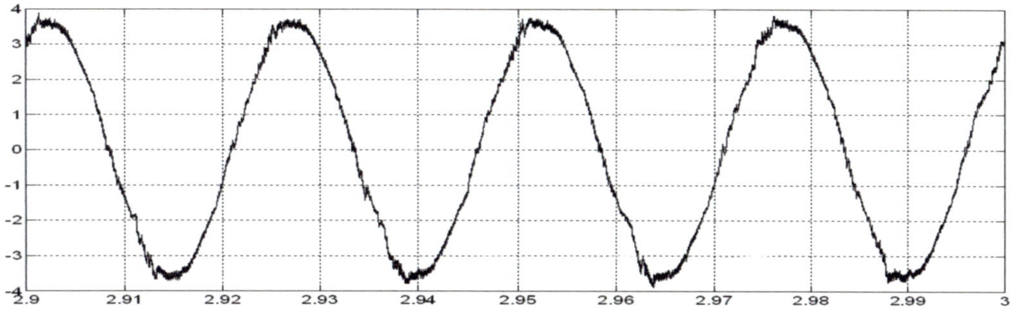

Figure 31. Stator current waveform at 800 rpm with nominal load under DTC-SPWM

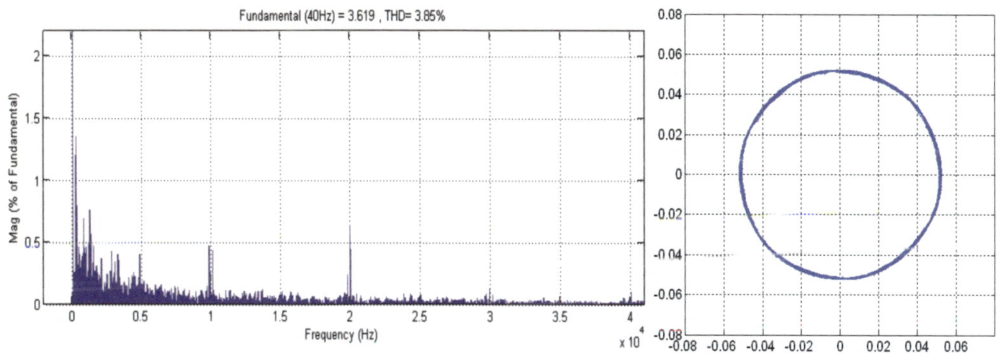

Figure 32. Stator current spectrum at 800 rpm with nominal load (on the left) and Stator flux in (α,β) axes under load variations (on the right) in case of DTC-SPWM

7. Comparison of DTC strategies

To verify and to compare the four DTC strategies proposed in this chapter, digital simulations have been carried out, by using the environment Matlab/Simulink, for the same PMSM parameters and conditions, except the sampling frequency utilized to simulate basic DTC which was taken equal to 20 KHz while for the FDTC, DTC-SVM and DTC-SPWM was taken equal to 10 KHz. Taking into consideration those conditions, the strategies' performances have been compared for both regimes dynamic and steady state.

Dynamic state: Figures 8, 26 and 30 shows that DTC, DTC-SVM and DTC-SPWM present the same speed and torque response time. Whereas, it's seen in figure 19 that torque and speed response time was greatly improved; at start time and at load toque or speed set-point variation. Indeed, speed FLC used in FDTC improves the dynamic state performances when compared to speed PI controller used in the other strategies.

Steady state: Figure 10 (on the left) show the spectral analysis of current presented in figure 10, it's seen that the Total Harmonic Distortion (THD) of the current waveform under basic DTC is 13.93 %. Whereas, figure 21 show that FDTC allows to decrease the THD value to 5.27 % with a variable switching frequency as indicated in the current spectral analysis. In addition, torque and stator flux ripple are reduced in case of FDTC in comparison with basic DTC, and also the current quality was improved. Figure 28 (on the left) shows that the current THD under DTC-SVM is 3.5 %, which is smother than that of basic DTC and FDTC. Also, it's seen that torque and flux ripples are greatly reduced under DTC-SVM when compared to DTC and FDTC (compare figures 26 and 28 with figures 8, 10, 19 and 21). Figure 32 shows that the THD of the current waveform under DTC-SPWM is 3.85%, which is almost the same as DTC-SVM, also DTC-SVM guarantees a constant switching frequency; as shown in figure 32 which allow to reduce torque and flux ripple as the same as DTC-SVM. Furthermore, the calculation time of the DTC-SPWM is much inferior to the DTC-SVM, this is because SPWM algorithm is very simple than SVM. Note that the SVM symmetry used in this work eliminates the harmonics which are around the uneven switching frequency (Chikh et al., 2011a). The same performances for DTC-SVM and DTC-SPWM can be obtained if an asymmetric SVM has been used instead of symmetrical SVM.

8. Effect of PMSM parameters variations and their compensation

This part is devoted to compare two speed controllers performances used in DTC under PMSM parameters variations. Also, a comparison between classical and novel torque and flux estimators has been developed in order to show their performances under PMSM parameters variations.

8.1. PI and FLC performances

Figure 33 shows the rotation speed and motor torque evolution for PMSM DTC strategy by using PI speed controller (green color) and speed FLC (red color). Indeed, the FLC has exhibited high performance in tracking the speed reference, as compared with speed PI controller. This figure confirms that the motor torque response with fuzzy controller is faster than PI controller during the start up regime and during a step change in load torque. The speed dynamic state imposes the motor torque response time because these two variables are regulated in cascade: the inner loop controls the motor electromagnetic torque and the outer loop regulates the motor rotation speed.

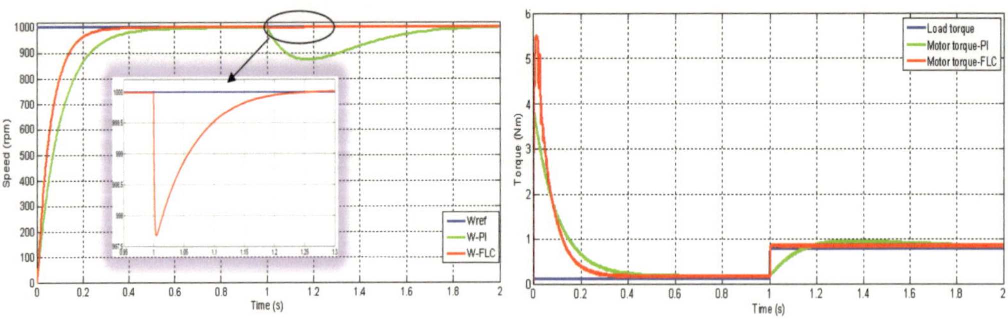

Figure 33. Rotation speed (on the left) and motor torque (on the right) performances under DTC for PMSM drive by using speed PI controller (green color) or speed FLC (red color)

8.2. Classical and novel estimators under stator resistance variation

The simulation results presented in this part shows the robustness of the classical and the novel flux and torque estimators, described at the beginning of this chapter, under stator resistance variation. Figure 34 shows the stator resistance variation applied to examine DTC for PMSM drive by using classical or novel estimator. In this case, the value of stator resistance was changed from the nominal value 1.59 Ω to the double of this value 3.18 Ω. Where, the reference stator flux and load torque are kept constant at 0.052 Wb and 0.8 Nm, respectively.

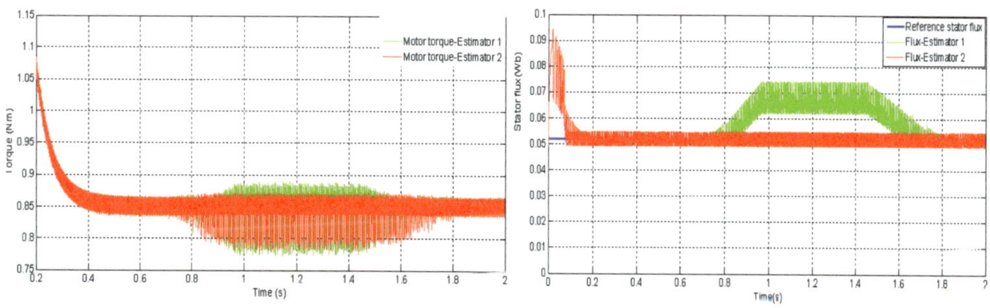

Figure 34. Stator resistance variation

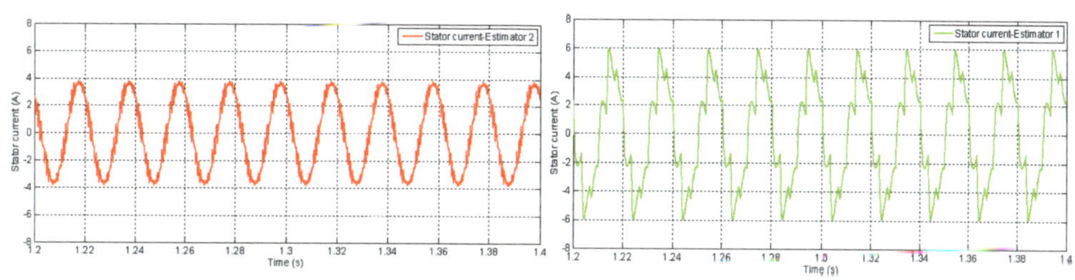

Figure 35. Motor torque (on the left) and stator flux (on the right) evolution by using classical estimator (green color) or by using novel estimator (red color)

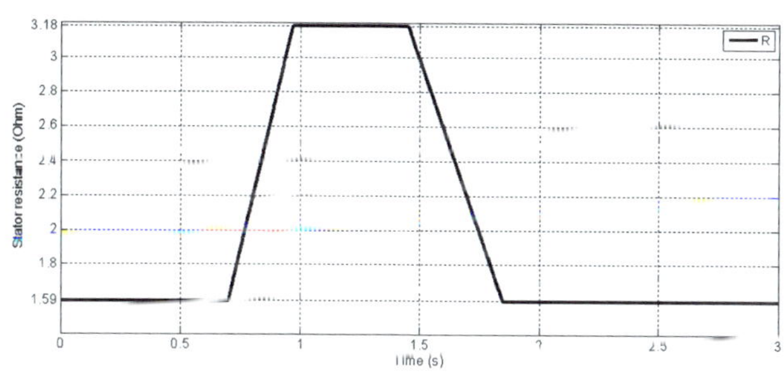

Figure 36. Stator current waveform in case of classical estimator (on the left) and novel estimator (on the right)

It's seen in figure 35 that the estimated stator flux was affected, when the stator resistance was changed at t=0.75 s; when the stator flux was estimated by using classical estimator.

This figure shows that, in spite of stator resistance variation, the stator flux was maintained constant when it is estimated by the novel estimator, because this estimator does not depends to the stator resistance variation. This stator flux deviation is normal and forecasted because the estimated flux value by using classical estimator depends on the stator resistance. When the PMSM stator resistance varies; while this classical estimator still uses the nominal stator resistance to estimate the actual stator flux; the estimated stator flux differ significantly from the real stator flux.

As shown in figure 35, the torque and flux ripples are increased when stator resistance varies in case of classical estimator, because the stator flux deviation causes the DTC algorithm to select a wrong switching state, which can result in unstable operation of the PMSM. Indeed, figure 36 shows that the stator current waveform in case of the novel estimator presents a good THD than the current in case of classical estimator, this is due to the wrong selection of the switching state.

8.3. Classical and Robust estimators under PMSM parameters variation

The simulation results below presents the DTC for PMSM performances in case of speed PI controller and Robust estimator, and speed FLC and this estimator under motor parameters variation, which are stator resistance, friction coefficient and motor inertia. Figure 37 (on the left) shows the variations, of these three parameters, applied to examine DTC robustness: the stator resistance was changed from the nominal value 1.59 Ω to the double of this value 3.18 Ω, the friction coefficient was changed from the nominal value f=0.00047 Nm.s/rd to f1=100*f and the motor inertia was changed from the nominal value J=0.003573 Kg.m^2 to J1=100*J.

It's seen in figure 37 (on the right) that the speed FLC allows to achieve a faster response and reject the perturbations (motor parameters variations), whereas the speed PI controller takes much time, in comparison with FLC, to reject these perturbations. Also, a faster motor torque response has been achieved with speed FLC compared to speed PI controller; as shown in figure 38 (on the left). Indeed, combining speed FLC and the novel estimator allow DTC for PMSM to reject stator resistance variation thanks to this estimator and reject motor inertia and friction coefficient thanks to speed FLC, which is shown in figure 38 (on the right).

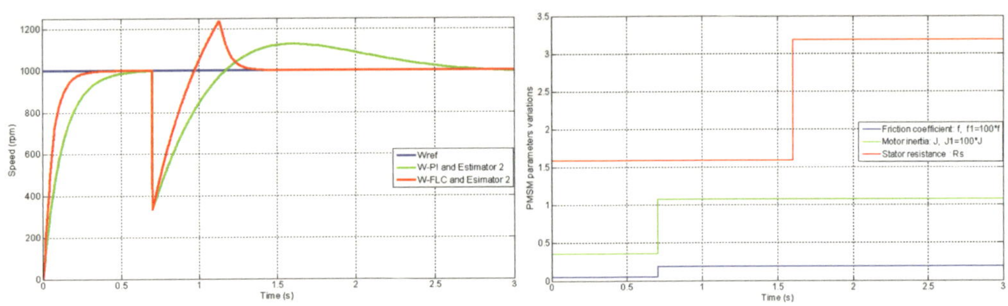

Figure 37. PMSM parameters variation (on the left) and rotation speed evolution (on the right) in case of DTC for PMSM drive using speed PI controller and novel estimator (green color), and speed FLC and novel estimator (red color)

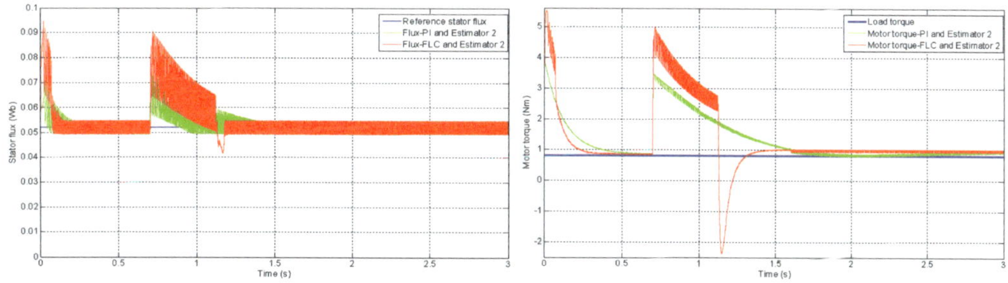

Figure 38. Motor torque (on the left) and stator flux (on the right) in case of DTC for PMSM drive using speed PI controller and novel estimator (green color), and speed FLC and novel estimator (red color)

9. Conclusion

Another solution has been presented to overcome the problems associated to DTC for PMSM in case of motor parameters variation and/or nonlinear operating conditions, which utilize speed FLC and an independent stator resistance estimator. Of course, FDTC allows rejecting the perturbations and minimizing torque and flux ripple. For all these reasons, a fixed switching frequency (DTC-SVM or DTC-SPWM) presented in this chapter can be combined with speed FLC and this independent stator resistance estimator to develop a robust DTC for PMSM.

Author details

Khalid Chikh, Mohamed Khafallah and Abdallah Saâd
Hassan II University, National Higher School of Electricity and Mechanics (ENSEM), Department of Electrical Engineering, Energy and Electrical Systems Research Group, Morocco

10. References

Chikh, K.; Saad, A.; Khafallah, M. & Yousfi, D. (2011a). PMSM Vector Control Performance Improvement by Using Pulse with Modulation and Anti-windup PI Controller, *Proceedings of IEEE 2011 2nd International Conference on Multimedia Computing and Systems*, pp. 1-7, ISBN 978-1-61284-730-6, Ouarzazate, MOROCCO, April 07-09, 2011

Chikh, K.; Khafallah, M.; Saad, A. & Yousfi, D. (2011b). Drive with Low Torque and Flux Ripple for PMSM by Using Direct Torque Control with Space Vector Modulation, *Proceedings of WASET 2011 International Conference on Computer, Electrical, and System Sciences, and Engineering*, pp. 1130-1137, ISSN 2010-3778, Paris, FRANCE, June 24-26, 2011

Chikh, K.; Khafallah, M.; Saad, A. & Yousfi, D. (2011c). A Novel Drive Implementation for PMSM by Using Direct Torque Control with Space Vector Modulation. *Canadian Journal on Electrical and Electronics Engineering*, Vol.2, No.8, (September 2011), pp. 400-408, ISSN 1923-0540

Lokriti, AS.; Zidani, Y. & Doubabi, S. (2011). Fuzzy Logic Control Contribution to the Direct Torque and Flux Control of an Induction Machine, *Proceedings of IEEE 2011 2nd International Conference on Multimedia Computing and Systems*, pp. 1-6, ISBN 978-1-61284-730-6, Ouarzazate, MOROCCO, April 07-09, 2011

Ningzhou, L.; Xiaojuan, W. & Xiaoyun, F. (2010). An Improved DTC algorithm for Reducing Torque Ripples of PMSM Based on Cloud Model and SVM, *Proceedings of International Conference on Multimedia Information Networking and Security*, pp. 274-277, ISBN 978-1-4244-8626-7, Nanjing, Jiangsu, November 04-06, 2010

Pujar, HJ. & Kodad, SF. (2009). Digital Simulation of Direct Torque Fuzzy Control of PMSM Servo System. *International Journal of Recent Trends in Engineering*, Vol.2, No.2, (November 2009), pp. 89-93, ISSN 1797-9617

Tang, L.; Zhong, L.; Fazlur Rahman, M. & Hu, Y. (2003). A Novel Direct Torque Control for Interior Permanent-Magnet Synchronous Machine Drive with Low Ripple in Torque and Flux- A Speed-Sensorless Approach. *IEEE Transactions on Industry Applications*, Vol.39, No.6, (November 2003), pp. 1748-1756, ISSN 0093-9994

Tlemcani, A.; Bouchhida, O.; Benmansour, K.; Boudana, D. & Boucherit, M.S. (2009). Direct Torque Control Strategy (DTC) Based on Fuzzy Logic Controller for a Permanent Magnet Synchronous Machine Drive, *Journal of Electrical Engineering & Technology*, Vol.4, No.1, (December 2009), pp. 66-78, ISSN 1975-0102

Ziane, H.; Retif, J.M. & Rekioua, T. (2008). Fixed-Switching-Frequency DTC Control for PM Synchronous Maching with Minimum Torque Ripples, *Canadian Journal on Electrical and Computer Engineering*, Vol.33, No.3/4, (December 2008), pp. 183-189, ISSN 0840-8688

Haque, M.E. & Rahman, M.F. (2002). Influence of Stator Resistance Variation on Direct Torque Controlled Interior Permanent Magnet Synchronous Motor Drive Performance and Its Compensation, *IEEE-Industry Applications Conference-Thirty Sixth IAS annual meeting*, Vol.4, (Aout 2002), pp. 2563-2569, ISSN 0197-2618

Chapter 9

Position Estimation of the PMSM High Dynamic Drive at Low Speed Range

Konrad Urbanski

Additional information is available at the end of the chapter

http://dx.doi.org/10.5772/48750

1. Introduction

Permanent Magnet Synchronous Motors (PMSM) are widely used in industrial drives due to their high power density, high torque-to- inertia ratio, small torque ripple and precise control at low speed range, possibility to torque control at zero speed, high efficiency and small size. To exploit presented advantages, a vector control should be used. Vector control allows the drive a good dynamic, effective performance especially during transients and prevents overload of the motor by controlling the torque. However, a motor shaft position sensor is required to enable the effective vector control of a PMSM. Such sensors increase the overall cost of the drive and decrease its reliability. That sensor occupies usually the end of the shaft, so elimination of the need for its installation allows new applications of such drive. This scientific problem remains an open question for and is the subject for extensive research in many scientific centers. Several approaches to this problem are reported in the literature, which are based on state observers [1,2], various versions of the Kalman filters [3,4], sliding-mode observers [5,6] or methods of applying motor saliency [7,8,9]. State observers and Kalman filters based on a motor model require complex computational operations to obtain proper accuracy, which always causes problems in real time operation. Several approaches apply motor magnetic saliency and detect the rotor position by measuring phase inductances. These methods provide a real solution at small speeds and during standstill operation, but requirements with respect to hardware and software are high. The additional scientific problem is to obtain high dynamic sensorless drive [10,11]. Assumption of the limitation the applications up to speed control (without position control) gives possibility to achieve well performance of high dynamic sensorless drive for low speed operating range.

A simple and effective structure of an observer is proposed in this paper. The presented observer structure is based on a modified concept of back EMF detection [5] and introduces a more complex corrector function which differs from the traditional one. The structure contains a corrector with a proportional-multi integral function (PII^2) instead of the proportional correction used in the Luenberger observer [12]. Prepared observer structure is applied to control structure presented at figure 1. The motor is fed by the PWM inverter, the control system includes vector control system of stator currents at *dq* independent axes (R_{iq} and R_{id}), speed controller (R_ω) and observer. The system is equipped with position and speed sensors which are used only to analysis of the estimation quality. The estimated value of the actual shaft position is used in transforming blocks of the coordinate system dq-$\alpha\beta$ and $\alpha\beta$-dq. The estimated value of the speed is used in control loop of the speed.

Presented structure gives possibility to test system in closed (observed values are used to control drive) and open (observed values are only considered) mode using manual switches as it is shown on figure 1. To achieve smooth observed values, a reference voltage can be used instead of measured ones.

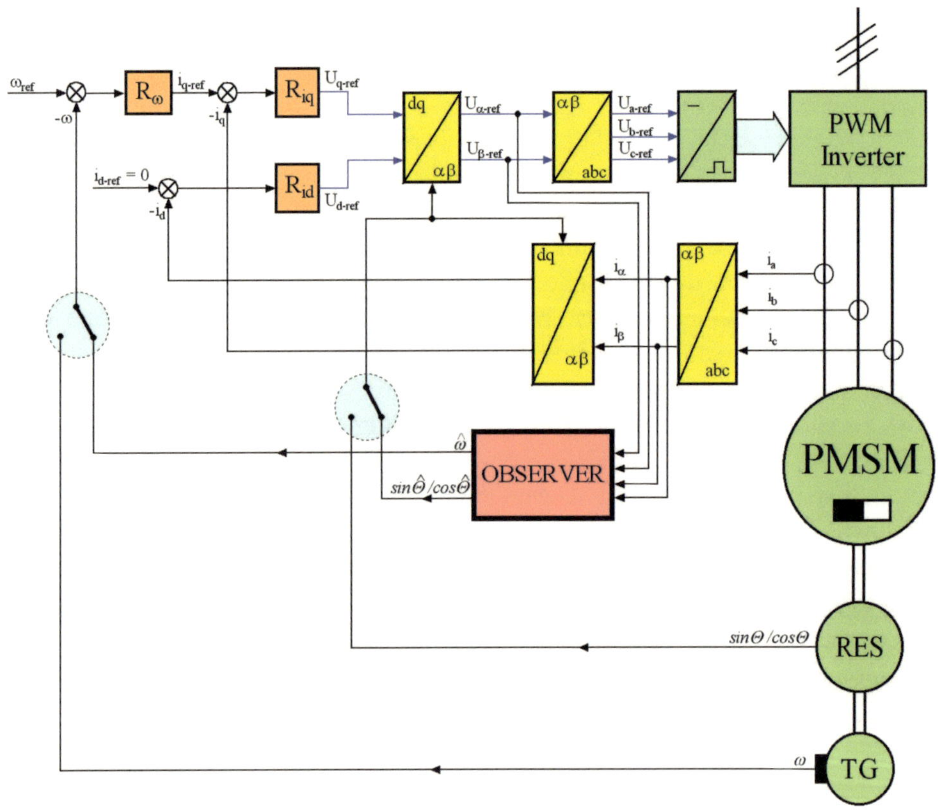

Figure 1. Structure of sensorless drive model

2. Inverter

For modeling the PWM converters can be used models with various complexity degrees. First approximation can be a usage of the inverter's transfer function equal to one. One can do that in the case of high carrier frequency of the inverter, since any significant delays occur in the measuring loops. At this case, the observer input signals may be smooth, and is easily obtained the proper observer performance. The other possibility to ease modeling transfer function of the inverter is zero order sample and hold block, usage the delay block or first order transfer function, which time constant or sampling interval is calculated depends on the proposed carrier frequency. These models do not require a very small simulation step size. In the case of the simulation where the effect of the inverter such as simply the impact the modulated voltage on generated state vector's waveforms and drive performance or inverter's dead time impact is taken into account, the more accurate model is inserted in place of the simplified one. Figure 3 presents used in this model simplified structure of the PWM inverter. Structure of this model is directly derived from the method of generating the states of the switches, the change of switch state is carried out at the intersection of the reference voltage and the carrier signal. This model does not take into account the dead time phenomenon.

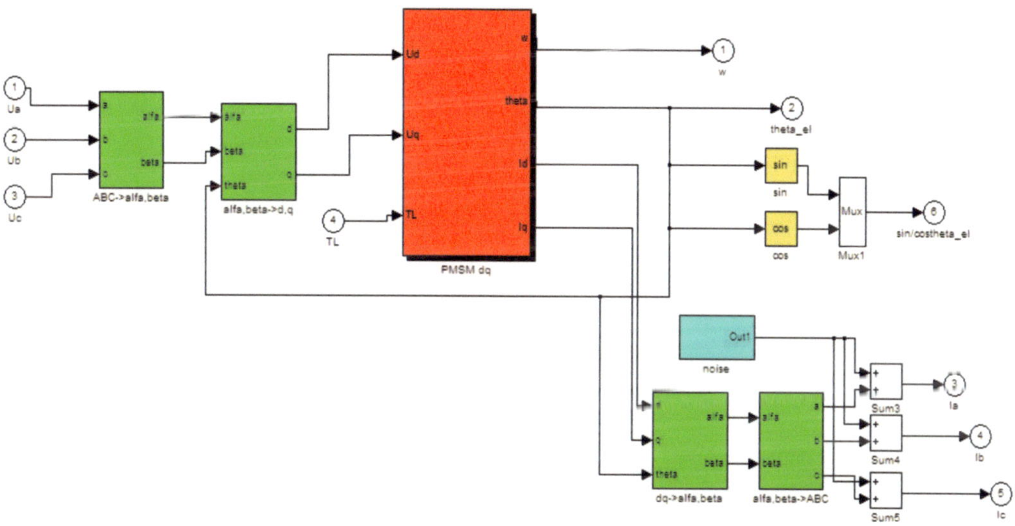

Figure 2. General view of PMSM model in *dq* axis expanded on *ABC* coordinates system inputs and outputs

The cost of the exact model of inverter usage is of course much smaller calculating step, from single microseconds up to dozens of nanoseconds (for range about 10 kHz carrier frequency) in place of dozens or hundreds microseconds for simple inverter model for presented drive parameters. The calculating step value is very important due to simulation time especially during optimization procedure (thousands or hundreds of thousands of repetitions). For example, the presented drive is simulated in normal mode, at 2.10 GHz dual core Intel processor at 8.3 s, (simulation stop time 0.12 s, fixed step size – 5 μs), but start simulation without opening the model (using only the command window), will reduce the simulation time to about 6.3 s.

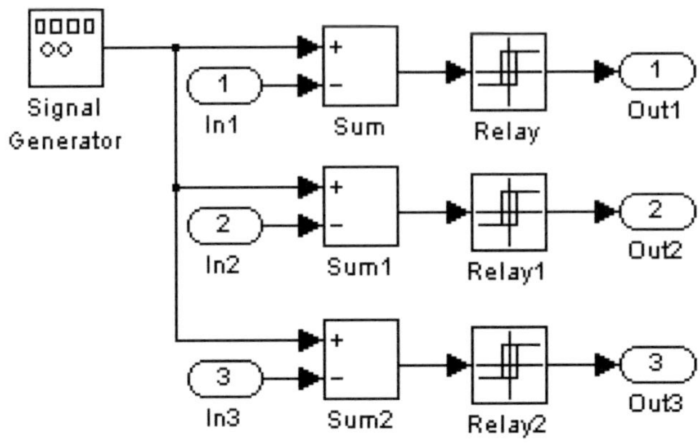

Figure 3. General view of simple PWM inverter model

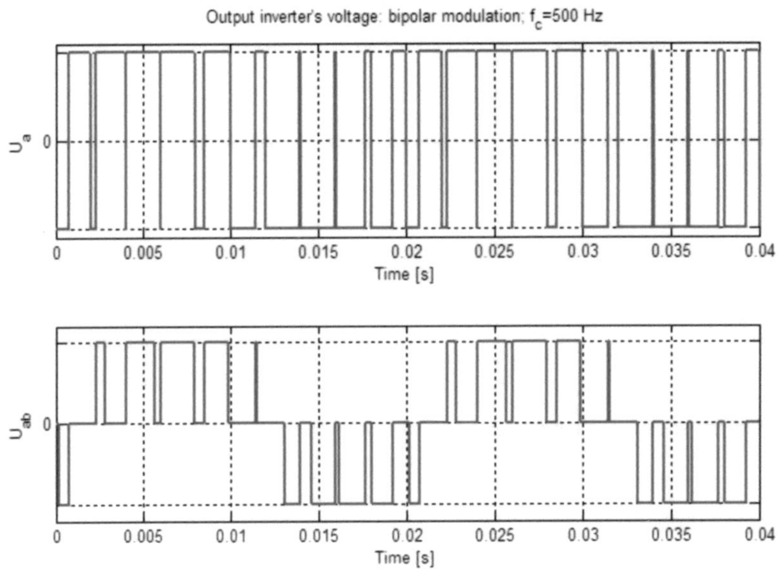

Figure 4. Testing output voltage waveforms of the inverter model

Presented at figure 3 inverter model generates the exemplary (for the ideal three-phase sinusoidal excitation) waveforms of the output voltage (the testing waveform obtained for carrier frequency f_c=500 Hz) for bipolar voltage modulation – as presented on figure 4. Figure 5 presents the carrier frequency influence for waveforms for the excited phase current for the stationary circuit.

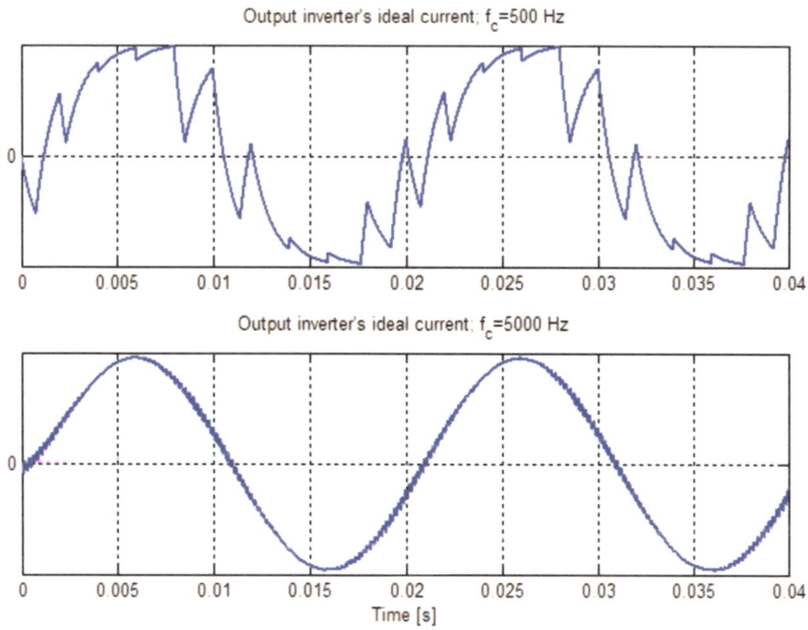

Figure 5. Carrier frequency influence for current I_a waveform

3. Speed controller structure

All the controllers and observer are implemented as a discrete structure. The used in this study structure of speed controller is shown in figure 6 (the currents controllers used in q and q axis are typical PI structure with anti wind-up and limited output). The signals used in a controller module are "Wref" – reference speed, "Wm" – measurement (or estimated) feed back speed value and speed controller output signal, "Iref" – reference current/torque. Choice of controller structure allows determining the impact of the control algorithm for ability to sensorless performance because of the transients. The tested structure of speed controller was the typical P/PI structure. To avoid integrator saturation for a controller with limited output level, a hard limit is imposed. It is easy and effective solution. The easiest way to set the integrator limit is to use the same value as in the output. Figure 6 shows the tested structure of PI controller. The structure is parallel. Block zero-order-hold in proportional gain branch is used to "synchronize" input signals of the adder. For fast integration switch-off a manual switch "s1" is used. This structure provides a stable performance of the system, and easy selection of settings using different methods. One of the methods used for setting the controller parameters was RWC method (that method will be discussed later), the same as used for settings the observer's parameters.

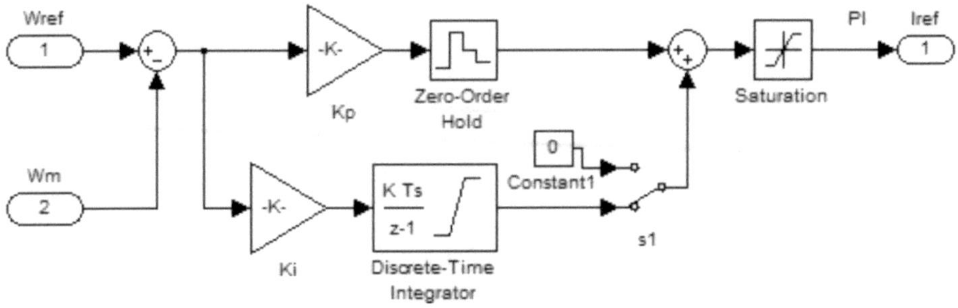

Figure 6. The speed controller structure

4. PMSM model

Assuming ordinary simplified assumptions, the general form of the PMSM model in $\alpha\beta$ stationary orthogonal coordinates can be expressed as follows:

$$\begin{aligned} \frac{di_\alpha}{dt} &= -\frac{R}{L}\cdot i_\alpha - \frac{1}{L}\cdot e_\alpha + \frac{1}{L}\cdot v_\alpha \\ \frac{di_\beta}{dt} &= -\frac{R}{L}\cdot i_\beta - \frac{1}{L}\cdot e_\beta + \frac{1}{L}\cdot v_\beta \end{aligned} \tag{1}$$

and the mechanical part:

$$\begin{aligned} \frac{d\omega}{dt} &= \frac{1}{J}\cdot\left(\Psi_\beta\cdot i_\alpha - \Psi_\alpha\cdot i_\beta - T_L\right) \\ \frac{d\theta}{dt} &= \omega \end{aligned} \tag{2}$$

The motor model with state variables i_α, i_β ω and Θ is non-linear. All state variables are measurable but in a concept without mechanical sensor ω and Θ should be estimated. The symbols i_α, i_β, Ψ_α, Ψ_β, e_α, e_β are stator current, stator flux linkage and induced back EMF in $\alpha\beta$ coordinates. Symbols v_α, v_β are the components of input stator voltage, R and L are the stator windings resistance and inductance. The symbols ω and Θ are the rotor speed and the position, J is the moment of inertia and T_L is the load torque treated as an external disturbance. Such model formula is used for easy derivation of the observer structure. The observer is prepared as a $\alpha\beta$ model because there is no need of conversion of the coordinates systems for calculation of the output values.

After simple conversion of the motor model, we get the model in the coordinates system rotating with the rotor - dq – electrical part:

$$\begin{aligned} u_d &= R\cdot i_d + L_d\frac{di_d}{dt} - \Psi_q\cdot\omega \\ u_q &= R\cdot i_q + L_q\frac{di_q}{dt} + \Psi_d\cdot\omega \end{aligned} \tag{3}$$

$$\begin{aligned} \Psi_d &= L_d \cdot i_d + \Psi_f \\ \Psi_q &= L_q \cdot i_q \end{aligned} \tag{4}$$

and the mechanical part:

$$\begin{aligned} T_e &= \frac{3}{2}\left[\Psi_d \cdot i_q - \Psi_q \cdot i_d\right] \\ T_e - T_L &= J\frac{d\omega}{dt} \end{aligned} \tag{5}$$

where u_d, u_q means the components of input voltage, i_d, i_q, L_d, L_q mean currents and inductance of the motor in the *dq*-axis respectively, Ψ_d,Ψ_q,Ψ_f means flux in the *dq*-axis respectively and flux excited by permanent magnet. The electromagnetic torque is represented by a symbol T_e .

Such structure gives a possibility to ease analyze of the decoupled *dq* values of the currents and introduction of different forms of the nonlinear flux distribution. It should be noted that such simple model does not take into account the variable number of pole pairs.

Based on such general model, in simulation PMSM block expanded on nonlinearities in distribution of the flux, current measurement noise addition with control and simple model of friction are used. Model prepared in *dq*-axis gives simple solution to simulate salient pole motor by use the different values of the axis inductance. The *dq* model is equipped with external conversion modules, to get inputs and outputs as voltages and currents in *ABC* phases. It gives possibility to test the drive under various conditions. Outside the PMSM model in axis *dq*, the model is equipped with conversion block into *ABC* coordinates systems used to supply and measurement (Fig 2). As a measurement noise source a uniform random number function may be used.

5. Observer structure

Proposed observer system calculates position information from back EMF estimated in $\alpha\beta$ coordinates (stator based). This coordinates system was chosen because of its simple form, and there is no need to convert the coordinate system by using the (estimated) shaft position. The sine and cosine of shaft position is calculated from back EMF values, and based on their modulus, is calculated the motor speed (Fig. 7). The inner structure of the observer depends on the correction function. As is shown in figure 7, the observer consists of the electrical part of the PMSM model and an additional correction loop. Different forms of correction functions are shown in the following equations.

According to the method presented in [13] it is convenient to use only first two electrical equations (1), in which the back EMF components are considered as disturbances. In such a case we can prepare an extended state formula, which can be described as:

$$\dot{\mathbf{x}}_E = \mathbf{A}_E \mathbf{x}_E + \mathbf{B}_E \mathbf{u}, \qquad \mathbf{y} = \mathbf{C}_E \mathbf{x}_E \tag{6}$$

where

$$\mathbf{x}_E = \begin{bmatrix} i_\alpha \\ i_\beta \\ e_\alpha \\ e_\beta \end{bmatrix}, \quad \mathbf{y} = \begin{bmatrix} i_\alpha \\ i_\beta \end{bmatrix}, \quad \mathbf{u} = \begin{bmatrix} v_\alpha \\ v_\beta \end{bmatrix} \tag{7}$$

For presented system it is possible to use ordinary Luenberger observer with correction based on error between measured and calculated currents value. Assuming that derivative of disturbances is equal zero one can write the equations describing observer (8).

$$\begin{aligned}
\frac{d\hat{i}_\alpha}{dt} &= -\frac{R}{L}\hat{i}_\alpha - \frac{1}{L}\hat{e}_\alpha + \frac{1}{L}v_\alpha + K_{i\alpha}\left(i_\alpha - \hat{i}_\alpha\right) \\
\frac{d\hat{i}_\beta}{dt} &= -\frac{R}{L}\hat{i}_\beta - \frac{1}{L}\hat{e}_\beta + \frac{1}{L}v_\beta + K_{i\beta}\left(i_\beta - \hat{i}_\beta\right) \\
\frac{d\hat{e}_\alpha}{dt} &= +K_{e\alpha}\left(i_\alpha - \hat{i}_\alpha\right) \\
\frac{d\hat{e}_\beta}{dt} &= +K_{e\beta}\left(i_\beta - \hat{i}_\beta\right)
\end{aligned} \tag{8}$$

or in matrix form

$$\dot{\hat{\mathbf{x}}}_E = \mathbf{A}_E \hat{\mathbf{x}}_E + \mathbf{B}_E \mathbf{u} + \mathbf{K}\left[\Delta \mathbf{i}\right] \tag{9}$$

where **K** is a correction factor.

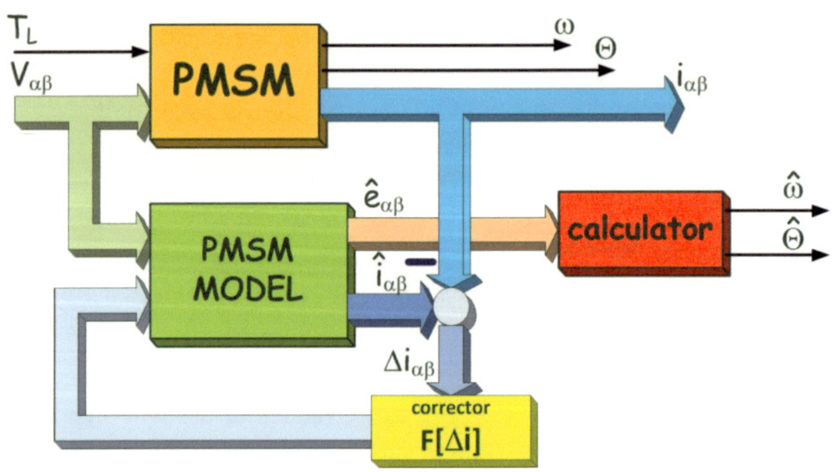

Figure 7. General structure of observer

Such solution generates acceptable observer's performance, however, a more accurate model was also taken into account [14].

The cost of that simplicity is required of the change of the observer's corrector parameters settings due to operating point (*gain scheduling*). Modifying the observer's parameters as a function of velocity only is sufficient at this case. Its proper change is very important in the case where the speed range is wide. At that case (low speed), the corrector parameters may be constant. Otherwise a scheduling mechanism based on the fuzzy logic or artificial neural network should be used [14]. Because observer estimates back EMF values, to achieve position and speed information one can use that transformation:

$$\sin\hat{\Theta} = -\frac{\hat{e}_\alpha}{|\hat{e}|} \qquad \cos\hat{\Theta} = \frac{\hat{e}_\beta}{|\hat{e}|} \tag{10}$$

where

$$|\hat{e}| = \sqrt{\hat{e}_\alpha^2 + \hat{e}_\beta^2} \qquad |\hat{\omega}| = \frac{|\hat{e}|}{k_e} \tag{11}$$

Multiplication of observer error by constant coefficient **K** (9) gives the observer structure with proportional correction equation. To modify observer operation it can be proposed a more complex function of observer error **F[Δi]** instead of a proportional one. By analogue to designing ordinary controller of P, PI and PID structure, one can propose instead of proportional correction more complex operation like PI or PID. This leads to a new general concept of observer, which formula can be written as:

$$\dot{\hat{\mathbf{x}}}_E = \mathbf{A}_E\hat{\mathbf{x}}_E + \mathbf{B}_E\mathbf{u} + \mathbf{F}[\Delta\mathbf{i}] \tag{12}$$

where **F[Δi]** is a function of observer corrector. So, the correction function may be a sliding mode corrector [15], an integrated sliding mode corrector [16] or e.g. any other correction function based on integration. Such idea of the observer structure may be used for position estimation also in other types of motor, e.g. SRM [17].

In the case of the proportional-integral (PI) correction the observer equations take the following form:

$$\mathbf{F}_1[\Delta\mathbf{i}] = \mathbf{K}_p[\Delta\mathbf{i}] + \mathbf{K}_i\int[\Delta\mathbf{i}]\,dt \tag{13}$$

On the basis of many simulation tests a more complex corrector structure with proportional-double integral (PII²) correction was proposed [16]:

$$\mathbf{F}_2[\Delta\mathbf{i}] = \mathbf{K}_p[\Delta\mathbf{i}] + \mathbf{K}_i\int[\Delta\mathbf{i}]\,dt + \mathbf{K}_{ii}\int\left[\int[\Delta\mathbf{i}]\,dt\right]dt \tag{14}$$

The advantage of introducing integral and double integral components of the observer corrector is that they ensure the astatic character of observation (parameters estimation) even during the transient speed process, in which fast changes of speed and reference currents occur – when the back EMFs waveforms are not in sinusoidal shape. The estimation of back EMF signals by the observer enables the calculation of the new values of the rotor speed and position from (10) and (11) at each step of algorithm realization. In fact, the observed signals (back EMFs) are still changing its values (sinusoidal wave) when motor isn't at standstill and the astatic character of observer corrector is very important to follow up the position with small estimation error and small phase shift. The structure of the observer's parameters vector consists of six different elements due to symmetry of the equation (14) for current and back EMF calculation and the additional seventh k_e, which is used to scaling back EMF's estimated amplitude into speed value (11). The observer's structure is identical in both α and β component.

6. Observer parameters setting

The choice of observer parameters is an important task and should take into account dynamics in closed loop system as well as good accuracy of observation. The simulated drive is a compound object. Motor nonlinearity, discontinuity caused by the inverter structure and discrete structure of the control loop make it difficult to calculate the parameters of the observer. The solution presented in this paper is based on the special algorithm, which is used for automatic supervising the calculations, and after a certain number of cycles generates the results in form of the observer parameter set. The process of parameter synthesis was optimised by means on the base of random weight change (RWC) procedure [18] (Fig. 8). This algorithm is fast and insensitive to the local minimum of the optimized criterion. Depending on the value of the search step parameters, the effects of the algorithm performance that we get are like for gradient algorithm or evolutionary algorithm (Fig. 9), the possibility to quickly find a local minimum or in longer calculations the searching and finding the global minimum. The searching process is supervised by the quality index. The quality function of observer optimization is formulated as:

$$Q = \int_{t_1}^{t_1+\tau} e_{\Theta}^{2}(t)\,dt + \Delta e_{\Theta}(\tau) \tag{15}$$

where e_Θ is the position estimation error, Δe_Θ is the range of the error value changes of the estimated position during the transient process, t_1 and $t_1 + \tau$ are the time boundaries of the integral calculation. The meaning of those parameters is explained in figure 10.

The optimization procedure is performing *off-line* by simulating a transient process (can also be performed *on-line* using real system, while motor drive is operating, in a case of significantly reduced range of coefficients change). According to the RWC procedure a new set of corrector settings is randomly selected at each step but only the set which gives estimation improvement (for quality index defined by (15) means smaller quality index

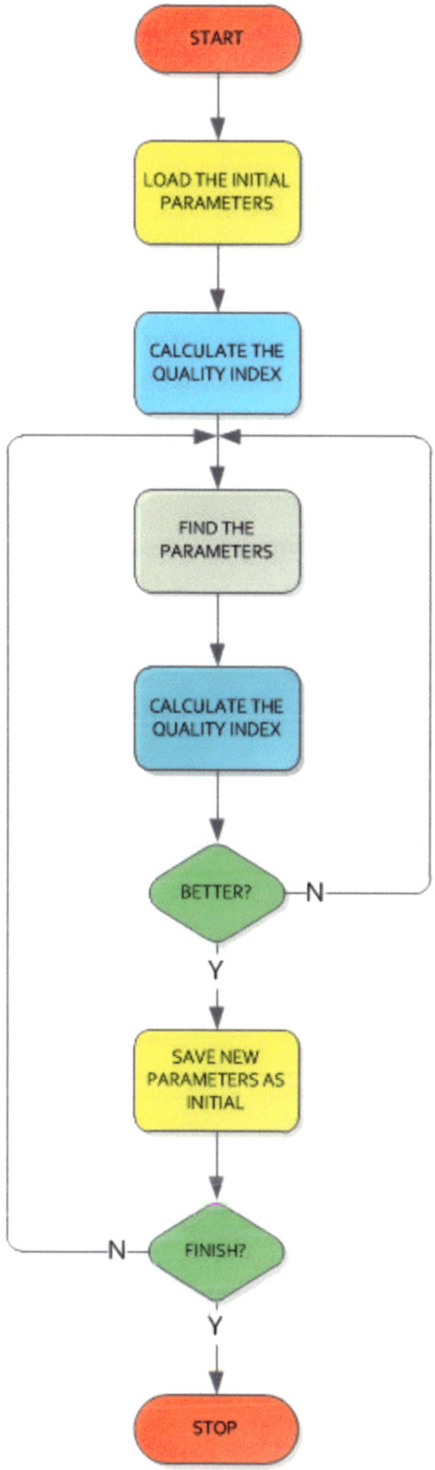

Figure 8. Adaptation of the RWC algorithm to the parameter selection of the observer procedure

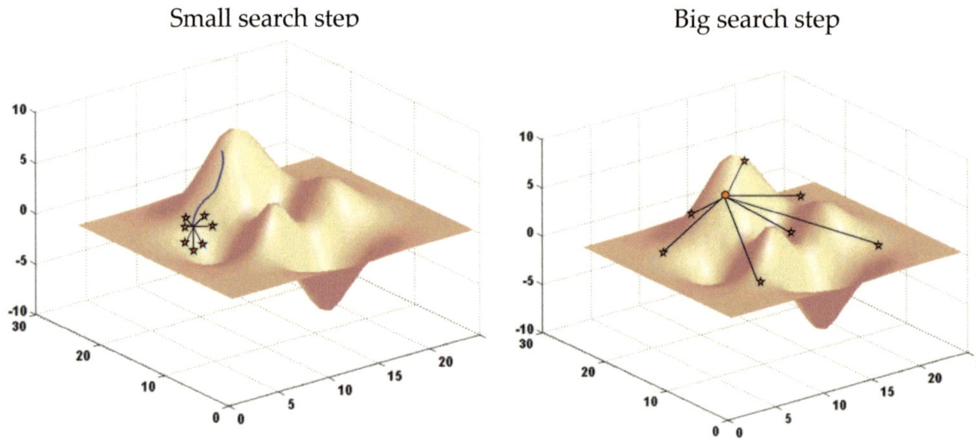

Figure 9. Features of the algorithm, depending on the search step value

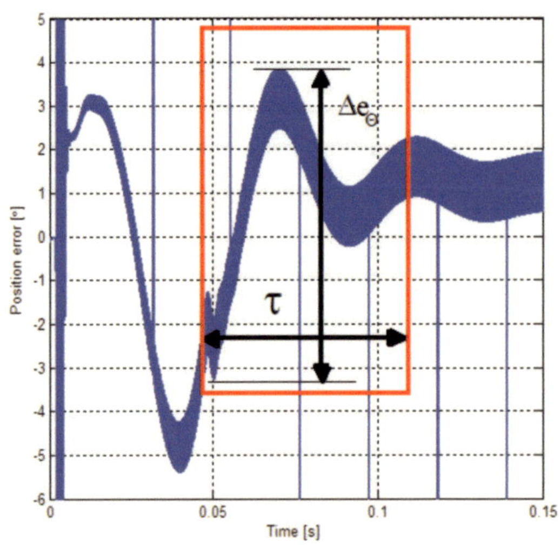

Figure 10. Explanation of the equation (15) parameters

value) is saved. In the procedure a dimension of search area (a range of randomly change of coefficient values) must be determined at each step. In the presented solution a wide area was assumed at the beginning of optimization process for fast quality index reduction and next at the final stage its dimension was reduced to achieve better accuracy. As a result of such *off-line* optimization a set of optimal values of corrector coefficients is found for the analyzed point of operation. If the speed is changed in a wide range, the modifying of the parameter set is needed. This procedure depends on search parameters, may be fast and insensitive to the local minimum of the optimized criterion. The optimization procedure may be performed *off-line* by simulating a transient process. The optimization procedure should be repeated for different points of operation, which were determined by the steady state speed value. At each step of optimization the transient process of the step response to speed reference changes in the selected point of operation was simulated, and during this process the value of the criterion was calculated. According to the RWC procedure a new set of corrector settings is randomly selected at each step but only the set which gives estimation improvement (smaller criterion value) is stored. In the procedure a dimension of search area (a range of randomly change of coefficient values) must be determined at each step. In the presented solution a wide area was assumed at the beginning of optimization process and next at the final stage its dimension was reduce to achieve better accuracy.

Because the optimization procedure of the observer parameters is based on random numbers generation, it is important to take care on proper initiation of that generator. It is very important to initiate generating values using such code:

```
rand('state', sum(100*clock))
```

It is used to eliminate the generation of the same values sequence, each time you start MATLAB.

7. Simulation results

The model of the PMSM control system was carried out in MATLAB Simulink ® environment. The motor was modeled with ordinary simplifying assumptions such as constant resistance and inductance in stator windings, symmetry of windings, and isotropic properties of motor (3, 4, 5). The motor model was connected with a model of a control system, which includes a vector control system of stator currents, a speed controller and a model of the analyzed observer (Figure 1). Drive model contains also a *d*-axis current control loop because even that current value is considered during sensorless mode operation.

The model of the observer was used as an element of feedback sending detected signals of rotor position and speed. The motor model was calculated with a very small step of integration, which simulates its continuous character. The step value was within the range of 0.02÷20 μs, depending on the simplification level of the inverter model. To reduce simulation time, the inverter may be neglected and calculation step 20 μs may be used. Contrary to that, the model of the control system with the observer was calculated with much higher step values (50÷200 μs), simply because it enables a better simulation of how the control system works on a signal processor with a real value of the sampling period. Presented waveforms are achieved for observer's parameter settings prepared for reference speed 5 rad/s.

Selected waveforms of speed, currents and position error are presented below. These images well illustrate the operation of observer compared with sensor mode. These waveforms were obtained as responses to the step change of speed reference, generated in the form of a step sequence starting from zero speed to 10 rad/s and to 5 rad/s at time 0.1 s. Motor load changes from zero to motor's nominal load value at time 0.16 s. In addition, figures 11 and 12 show ±2 % range of reference value. Waveform 11 and 12 prove the well performance of sensorless mode drive at low speed – even at 5 rad/s. That drive still remains robustness on disturbance (rapid reference speed and load change). Enlarged part of figure 11 (Fig. 12) shows clearly the setpoint achieving process. Figures 13 and 14 show waveforms of currents in *q*-axis and *d*-axis respectively obtained for test such as at figure 11. One can notice the *d*-axis current value in sensorless mode isn't close zero at transients – it is determined by temporary ripple in position estimation signal but the ripple quickly fades away. Figure 15 shows waveforms of the calculated position error (observer estimates only sine and cosine of the position). The steady state position error does not depend on motor load (which is seen at time 0.1÷0.2 s of that figure) but the operating point (determined as a motor speed). Presented in figure 16 sine and cosine of the estimated position waveforms proves that observer operates well at longer simulating time. Figures 17 and 18 present drive performance for additional difficulty: disruption of the "measured" phase currents by injection of the random signal. Reliable performance is considered even for such disturbance. Then observer was tested to determine its robust on inaccurate estimation of the motor parameters. Results are shown in figure 19 and table 1. For such system the parameters lower deviation range is about ±10 %. Motor parameters were stationary, only the observer's parameters were changed with factors presented below. Certain robust on inaccuracy parameter estimation is noticed.

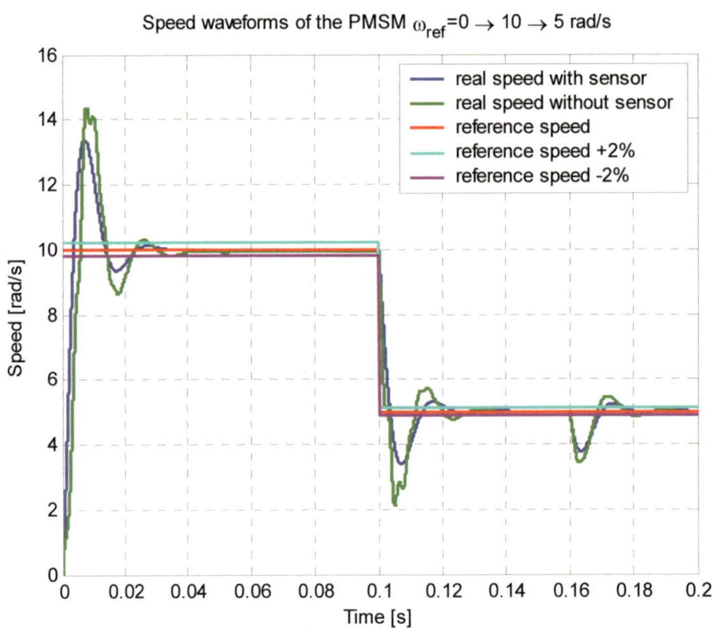

Figure 11. Waveforms of real and estimated speed involved by step changes of reference 0→10→5 rad/s
at t=0.16 s load changes from 0 to its nominal value

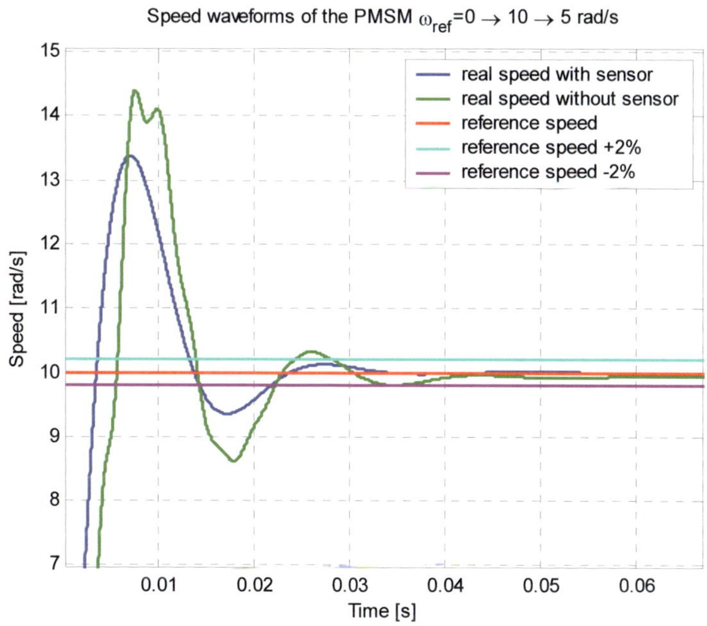

Figure 12. Waveforms of real and estimated speed involved by step change of reference 0→10 rad/s – enlarged part of fig. 11.

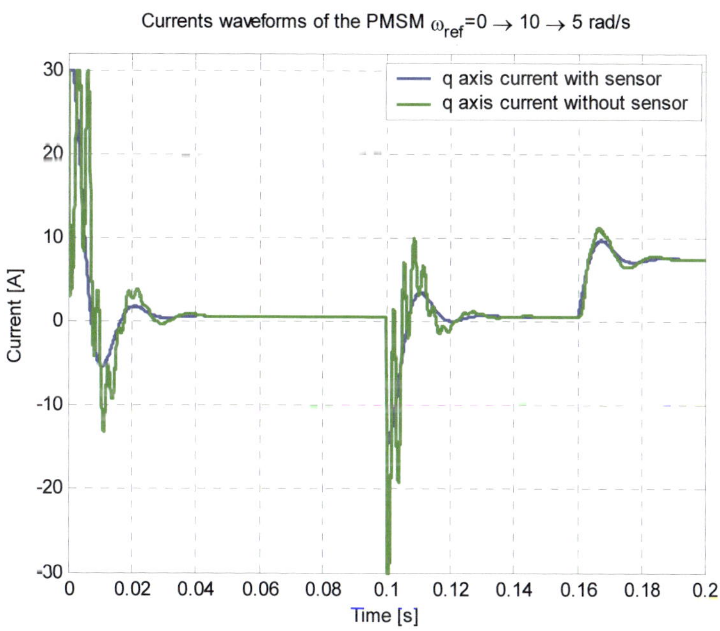

Figure 13. Waveforms of q-axis current in sensor and sensorless mode; step changes of reference speed 0→10→5 rad/s as shown in fig. 11. At t=0.16 s load changes from 0 to its nominal value

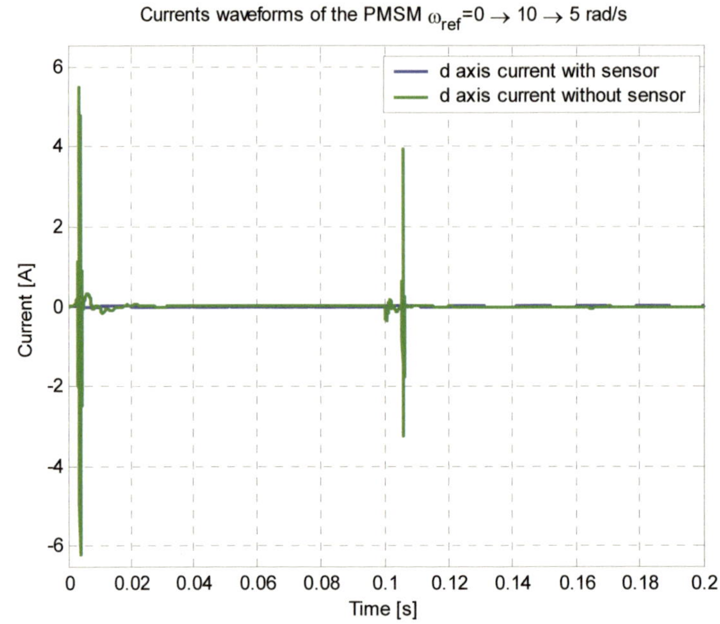

Figure 14. Waveforms of *d*-axis current in sensor and sensorless mode; step changes of reference speed 0→10→5 rad/s as shown in fig. 11. At t=0.16 s load changes from 0 to its nominal value

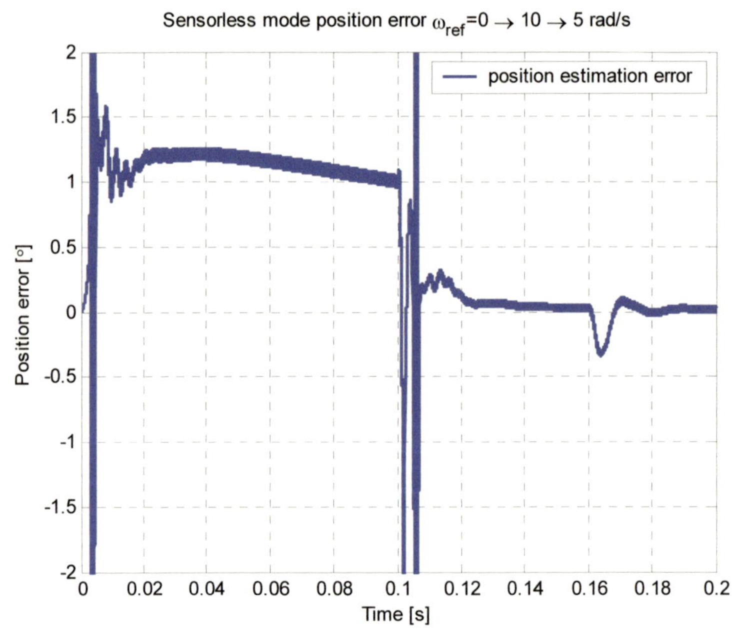

Figure 15. Waveform of position estimation error involved by step changes of reference speed 0→10→5 rad/s as shown in fig. 11
at t=0.16 s load changes from 0 to its nominal value

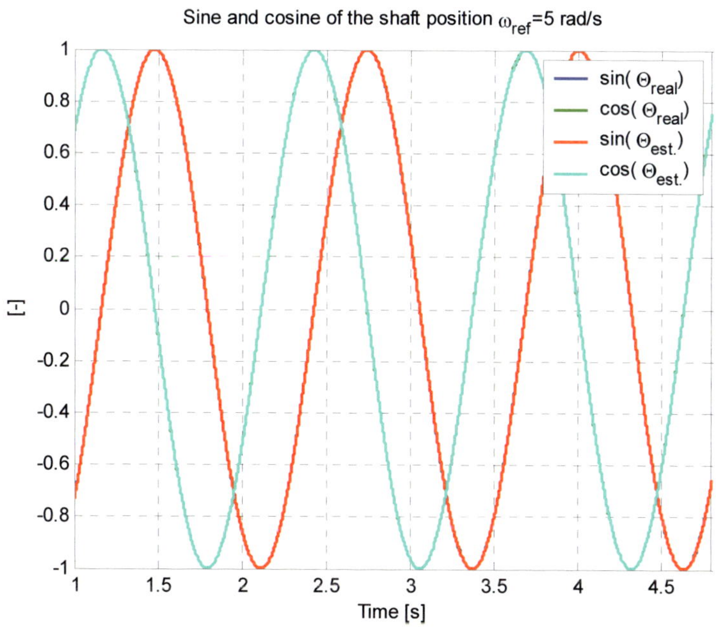

Figure 16. Waveforms of sine and cosine of the estimated and real position at reference speed 5 rad/ at steady state

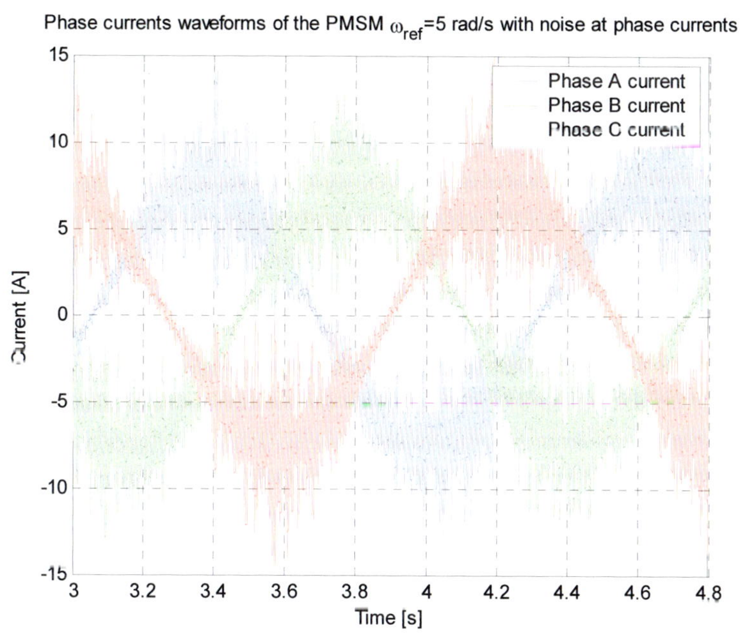

Figure 17. Waveforms of phase currents in sensorless mode for reference speed 5 rad/s with "measuring" noise at phase currents

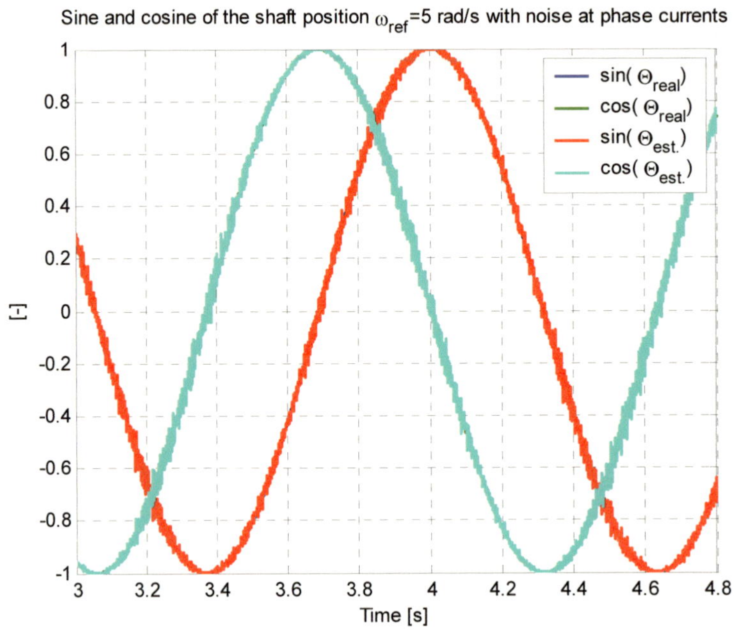

Figure 18. Waveforms of sine and cosine of the estimated and real position at reference speed 5 rad/s at steady state with "measuring" noise at phase currents as shown in fig. 17

In observer		Position error [°]		
R factor	L factor	loaded 5 rad/s	unloaded 5 rad/s	unloaded 10 rad/s
1	1	0.08	0.08	0.5
1.2	1	0.1	0.1	0.5
0.9	1	0.06	0.08	0.5
1	0.91	-0.2	0.05	0.5
1.1	0.91	-0.2	0.06	0.5

Table 1. Position error according to motor parameter inaccuracy

The final test was prepared to determine the robustness to the incorrect estimate of the initial position. The question was how big may be position difference between estimated and the real one, to prevent the motor startup. Tests have shown, that the possible range of the initial position error, for which the engine will start correctly, it is 80 degrees of arc (Fig. 24). Figures 20-23 show the sine and cosine waveforms of the estimated and the real shaft position. Corresponding to sine and cosine waveforms from figures 20-23, figure 24 shows the "measured" speed waveforms. The robustness on initial position error estimation is proven.

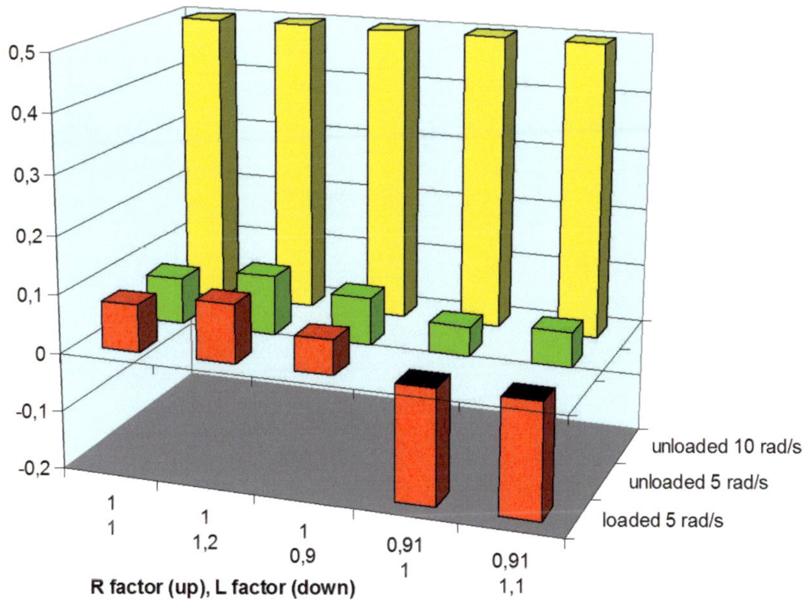

Figure 19. Position error [°] according to motor parameter inaccuracy

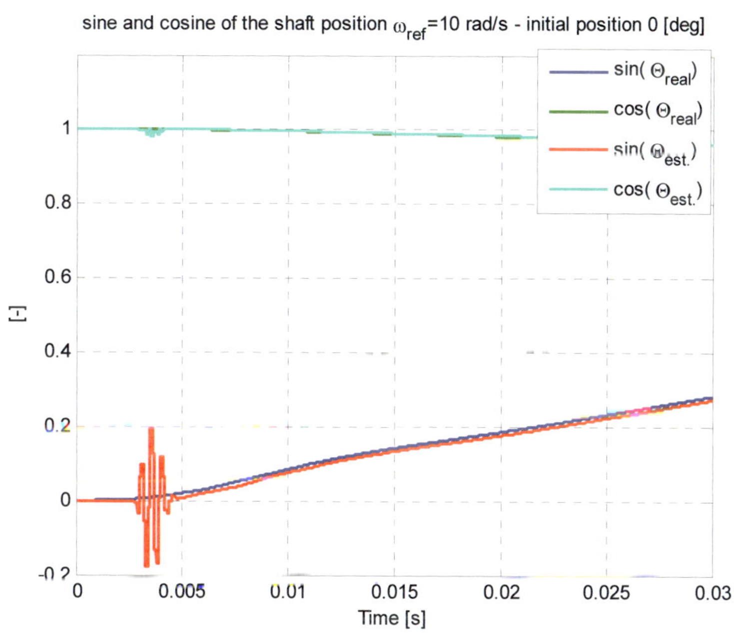

Figure 20. Waveforms of sine and cosine of the estimated and real position at reference speed 10 rad/s during startup – shaft initial position equal the estimated one

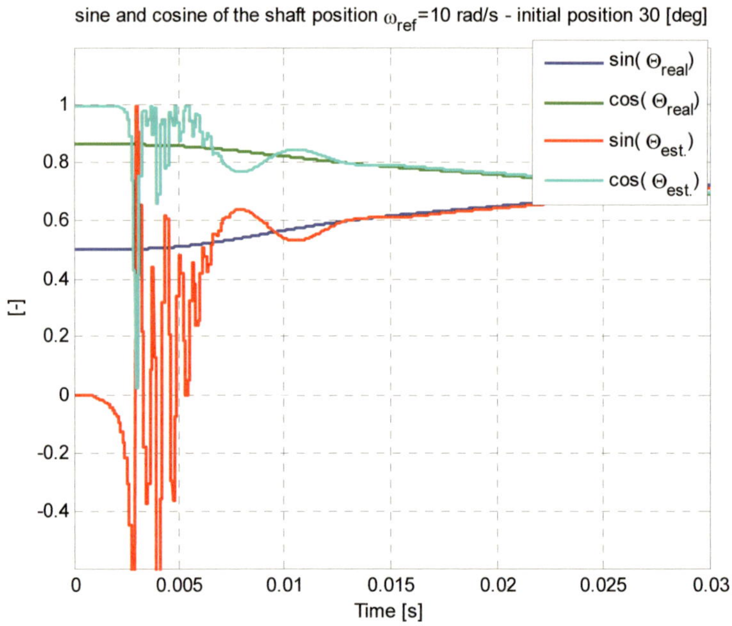

Figure 21. Waveforms of sine and cosine of the estimated and real position at reference speed 10 rad/s during startup – shaft initial position different than estimated one: 30 °

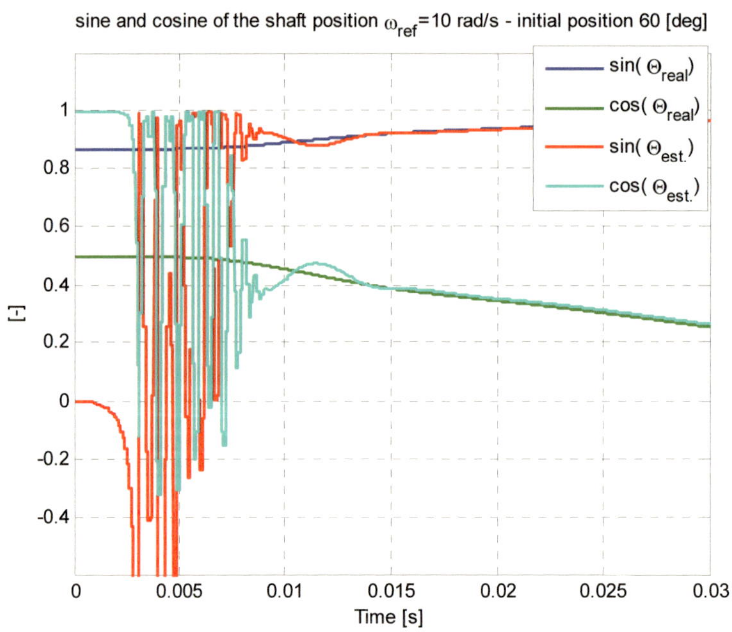

Figure 22. Waveforms of sine and cosine of the estimated and real position at reference speed 10 rad/s during startup – shaft initial position different than estimated one: 60 °

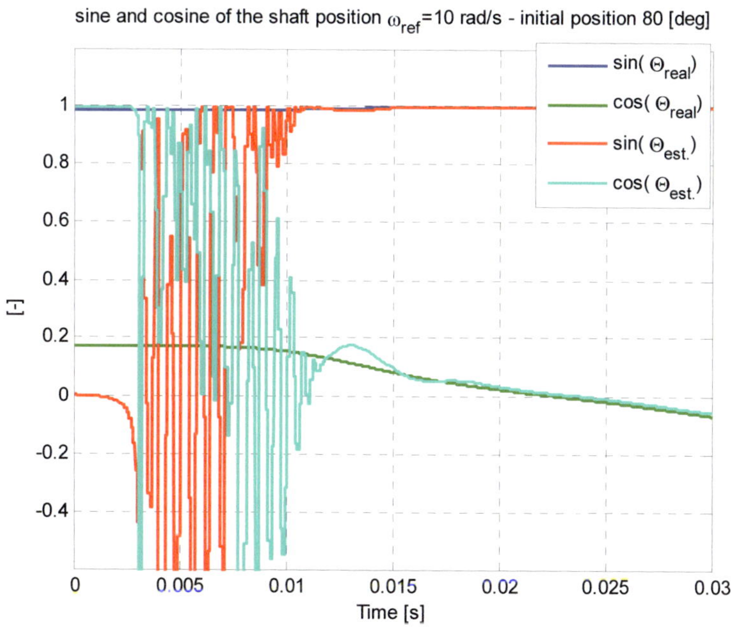

Figure 23. Waveforms of sine and cosine of the estimated and real position at reference speed 10 rad/s during startup – shaft initial position different than estimated one: 80 °

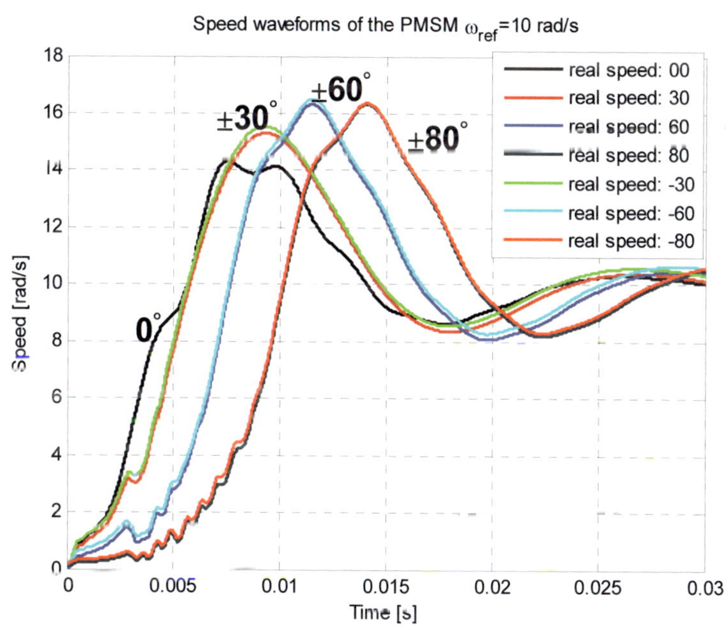

Figure 24. Robustness to the incorrect estimate of initial position during startup – speed waveforms for 0→±80 ° position variance

8. Conclusions

Stable performance of the sensorless drive with PMSM at low speed was noticed in the closed loop mode. Small position error and robust on inaccuracy motor parameter estimation were proven. The resistance tolerance is about 20 %, whereas inductance error tolerance is below 9 %. A wider range of resistance change could be achieved by using resistance observation. A test for robustness on the disturbance in the measured signal was passed: even a disruption of the phase currents by injection of the random signal does not disturb the performance of the sensorless drive. Such drive can achieve high dynamics according to the definition presented in abstract. Robustness to the incorrect estimate of initial position was also tested. The used PI controller discrete implementation gives possibility to use the same speed controller settings in both operating mode – sensor and sensorless. The sensorless drive using modified Luenberger observer gives possibility of the high performance of the high dynamic drive, where the "high dynamic" definition is introduced in this chapter. An additional effect of this work is to present the outline of how to create and how to operate the complex models of electrical motor drives in the context of the selection of model components of varying complexity which affect the calculation time and quality and accuracy of the results.

Notice

Motor parameters:

- stator inductance: $L = 5.7$ mH
- stator resistance per phase: $R = 0.7\ \Omega$
- total moment of inertia: $J = 0.007273\ \text{kg}\cdot\text{m}^2$

Author details

Konrad Urbanski
Institute of Control and Information Engineering, Poznan University of Technology, Poznan, Poland

Acknowledgement

This work was supported by grant N N510 325937.Appendix

9. References

[1] J. Liu, S. Hao, R. Ma, and M. Hao, "Research on Integer State Observer in Current Control for PMSM," 2008, pp. 228–231.
[2] L. A. Jones and J. H. Lang, "A state observer for the permanent-magnet synchronous motor," *IEEE Transactions on Industrial Electronics*, vol. 36, no. 3, pp. 374–382, Aug. 1989.

[3] T.-F. Chan, P. Borsje, and W. Wang, "Application of Unscented Kalman filter to sensorless permanent-magnet synchronous motor drive," presented at the Electric Machines and Drives Conference, IEMDC, 2009, pp. 631–638.

[4] S.-M. Gu, F.-Y. He, and H. Zhang, "Study on Extend Kalman Filter at Low Speed in Sensorless PMSM Drives," presented at the 2009 International Conference on Electronic Computer Technology, 2009, pp. 311–316.

[5] F. Parasiliti, R. Petrella, and M. Tursini, "Sensorless speed control of a PM synchronous motor based on sliding mode observer and extended Kalman filter," 2001, vol. 1, pp. 533–540.

[6] J. Vittek, P. Bris, M. Stulrajter, P. Makys, V. Comnac, and M. Cernat, "Chattering free sliding mode control law for the drive employing PMSM position control," 2008, pp. 115–120.

[7] A. B. Kulkarni and M. Ehsani, "A novel position sensor elimination technique for the interior permanent-magnet synchronous motor drive," *IEEE Transactions on Industry Applications*, vol. 28, no. 1, pp. 144–150, Feb. 1992.

[8] U. H. Rieder and M. Schroedl, "A simulation method for analyzing saliencies with respect to enhanced INFORM-capability for sensorless control of PM motors in the low speed range including standstill," in *Power Electronics and Applications, 2005 European Conference on*, 2005, p. 8–pp.

[9] Y. Ying, Z. Jianguo, G. Youguang, and J. Jianxun, "Numerical simulation of a PMSM model considering saturation saliency for initial rotor position estimation," in *Control Conference, 2008. CCC 2008. 27th Chinese*, 2008, pp. 114–118.

[10] F. Genduso, R. Miceli, C. Rando, and G. R. Galluzzo, "Back EMF Sensorless-Control Algorithm for High-Dynamic Performance PMSM," *IEEE Transactions on Industrial Electronics*, vol. 57, no. 6, pp. 2092–2100, Jun. 2010.

[11] K. Urbanski, "Sensorless control of PMSM high dynamic drive at low speed range," in *2011 IEEE International Symposium on Industrial Electronics (ISIE)*, 2011, pp. 728–732.

[12] D. Luenberger, "An introduction to observers," *IEEE Transactions on Automatic Control*, vol. 16, no. 6, pp. 596– 602, Dec. 1971.

[13] Germano, F. Parasiliti, and M. Tursini, "Sensorless Speed Control of a PM Synchronous Motor Drive by Kalman Filter," in *Proc. of the 1994 International Conference on Electrical Machines*, 1994, vol. 2, pp. 540–544.

[14] K. Urbanski and K. Zawirski, "Adaptive observer of rotor speed and position for PMSM sensorless control system," *COMPEL: Int J for Computation and Maths. in Electrical and Electronic Eng.*, vol. 23, no. 4, pp. 1129–1145, 2004.

[15] F. Parasiliti, R. Petrella, and M. Tursini, "Sensorless speed control of a PM synchronous motor by sliding mode observer," in *Industrial Electronics, 1997. ISIE'97., Proceedings of the IEEE International Symposium on*, 1997, pp. 1106–1111.

[16] K. Urbanski and K. Zawirski, "Rotor speed and position detection for PMSM control system," in *Proceedings of 9th Int. Conference and Exhibition on Power Electronics and Motion Control*, Kosice, 2000, vol. 6, pp. 239–243.

[17] K. Urbanski and K. Zawirski, "Sensorless control of SRM using position observer," in *2007 European Conference on Power Electronics and Applications*, 2007, pp. 1–6.

[18] B. Burton, F. Kamran, R. G. Harley, T. G. Habetler, M. A. Brooke, and R. Poddar, "Identification and control of induction motor stator currents using fast on-line random training of a neural network," *IEEE Transactions on Industry Applications*, vol. 33, no. 3, pp. 697–704, Jun. 1997.

Chapter 10

Digital Differential Protection of Power Transformer Using Matlab

Adel Aktaibi and M. Azizur Rahman

Additional information is available at the end of the chapter

http://dx.doi.org/10.5772/48624

1. Introduction

Power system development is reflected in the development of all the power system devices generators, transformers with different sizes, transmission lines and the protection equipment. Modern power transformer is one of the most vital devices of the electric power system and its protection is critical. For this reason, the protection of power transformers has taken an important consideration by the researchers. One of the most effective transformer protection methods is the differential protection algorithm. Typically, transformer protection is focused on discriminating the internal faults from the magnetizing inrush currents in the power transformers and overcoming the CTs related issues [1 -5].

2. Conventional differential protection scheme

This scheme is based on the principle that the input power to the power transformer under normal conditions is equal to the output power. Under normal conditions, no current will flow into the differential relay current coil. Whenever a fault occurs, within the protected zone, the current balance will no longer exist, and relay contacts will close and release a trip signal to cause the certain circuit breakers (CBs) to operate in order to disconnect the faulty equipment/part. The differential relay compares the primary and secondary side currents of the power transformer. Current transformers (CTs) are used to reduce the amount of currents in such a way their secondary side currents are equal. Fig. 1 shows the differential relay in its simplest form. The polarity of CTs is such as to make the current circulate normally without going through the relay, during normal load conditions and external faults.

Current transformers ratings are selected carefully to be matched with the power transformer current ratings to which they are connected so as the CTs secondary side currents are equal. However, the problem is that the CTs ratios available in the market have standard ratings. They are not available exactly as the desired ratings. Therefore, the primary ratings of the CTs are usually limited to those of the available standard ratio CTs. Commonly the primary side of the current transformer has only one turn (1) and the secondary side has many turns depending on the transformation ratio (N) of the CT, which is selected to match the ratings of the power transformer. Since the transformation ratio of transformers is the ratio between the number of turns in the primary side to the number of the turns in the secondary side. Therefore, the turn ratio of the primary current transformer is $\frac{1}{N_1}$ and the turn ratio of the secondary side current transformer is $\frac{1}{N_2}$. The secondary current of the CT located in the primary side of the power transformer is [2], [6-7];

$$I_1 = \frac{I_p}{N_1} \tag{1}$$

Where:

I_p : the primary side current of the power transformer,
I_1 : the secondary side current of CT_1.
N_1 : the number of turns in the secondary side of CT_1

In the same manner for the CT located at the secondary side of the power transformer, the CT secondary current is:

$$I_2 = \frac{I_s}{N_2} \tag{2}$$

Where:

I_s : secondary side current of the power transformer,
I_2 : secondary side current of CT_2.
N_2 : number of turns in the secondary side of CT_2

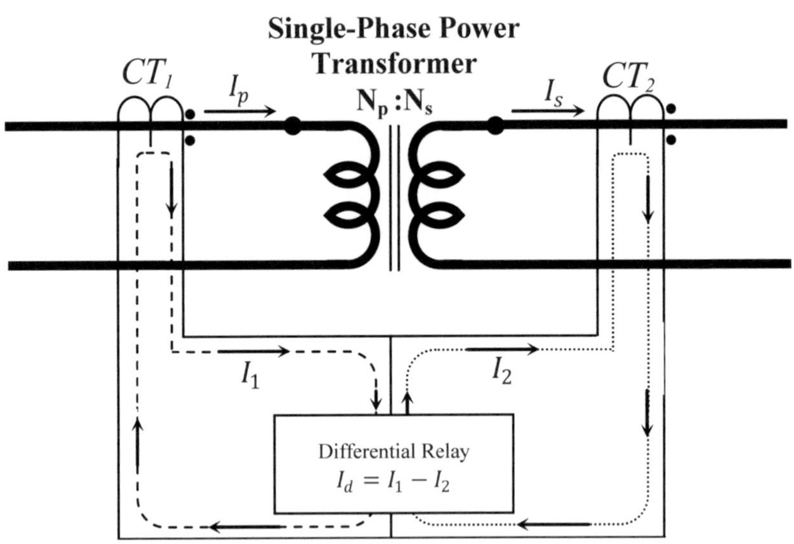

Figure 1. Differential protection for single phase two winding transformer

Since the differential current is: $I_d = I_1 - I_2$, then, from equation (1) and equation (2) the differential current flowing in the relay operating coil current I_d can be calculated as;

$$I_d = \frac{I_p}{N_1} - \frac{I_s}{N_2} \tag{3}$$

If there is no internal fault occurring within the power transformer protected zone, the currents I_1 *and* I_2 are assumed equal in magnitude and opposite in direction. That means the differential current $I_d = 0$ as shown in figure 2. The primary and secondary side current of the power transformer are related to each other by equation (4);

$$\frac{I_p}{I_s} = \frac{N_s}{N_p} \tag{4}$$

Where:

N_p and N_s: primary and secondary side turns of the power transformer, respectively

$\frac{N_p}{N_s}$: power transformer transformation ratio.

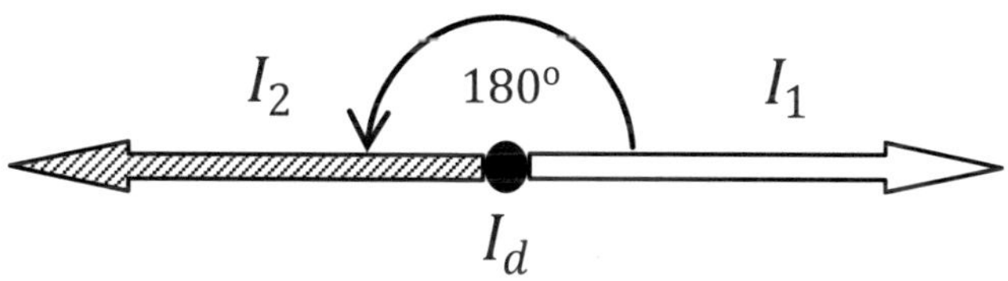

Figure 2. Output currents of the CTs are equal in magnitude and opposite in direction

If there is any fault in the power transformer protected zone, the currents I_1 *and* I_2 are no longer equal in magnitude and opposite in direction. That means the differential current $I_d = I_d\angle\theta$ has a significant value as shown in figure 3.

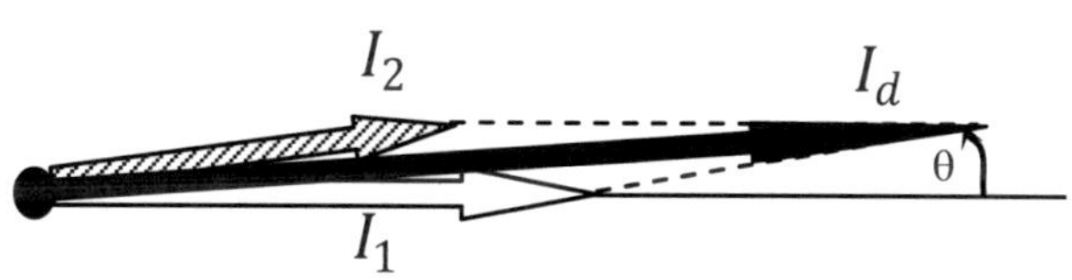

Figure 3. Output currents of the CTs are not equal in magnitude and not opposite in direction

The amount of current $I_d = I_d\angle\theta$ induces the relay operating coil to operate in order to send a trip signal to the circuit breakers to isolate the transformer.

From equation (4) the secondary current with respect to the primary current of the power transformer is [2], [6-7];

$$I_s = \frac{I_p \times N_p}{N_s} \tag{5}$$

Therefore, by manipulating equations (3) and (5),

$$I_d = \frac{I_P}{N_1} - \frac{I_P \times (N_p/N_s)}{N_2}$$

$$I_d = \frac{I_P}{N_1}\left(1 - \frac{N_p/N_s}{N_2/N_1}\right) \quad (6)$$

$$\lambda = \left(1 - \frac{N_p/N_s}{N_2/N_1}\right)$$

From equation (6) it is obvious that the term λ must be equal to zero in order to make $I_d = 0$

$$\left(1 - \frac{N_p/N_s}{N_2/N_1}\right) = 0$$

$$\frac{N_2}{N_1} = \frac{N_p}{N_s} \quad (7)$$

Equation (7) gives the condition for the security of the differential relay, which means the reciprocal of the ratio of the secondary side turns of the CTs must equal to the turns ratio of the power transformer.

In power transformers, the input power is equal to the output power. However, the voltage and the current in both the primary and secondary sides are different depending on whether the transformer is step up or step down. For instance, if the transformer is step up that means; the input voltage of the power transformer is low and the current is high, meantime the voltage in the secondary side is high and the current is low. This action makes both the input and output power equal. Due to this nature the CTs in the primary and the secondary sides of the power transformer do not have same turn ratio. However, they are carefully selected, in terms of turn ratio and magnetizing characteristics, so that they have the same output current at normal conditions of operations. If identical CTs are not available, the closer ones are chosen and then the mismatch between them is compensated by using the interposing CTs. The interposing CTs can fix the mismatch in the CTs; however they add their own burden to the output of the main CTs.

The same argument is applied for three phase (3ϕ) transformers, except some extra issues may appear in polyphase transformers. Figure 4 shows the schematic diagram of the 3ϕ differential protection.

In some cases, of 3ϕ power transformer connections as shown in figure 5, a 30° phase shift between primary and secondary currents is taking place. This phase shift occurs in the Y-Δ or Δ-Y connected transformers due to the transformation of the current from Y-Δ or Δ-Y as illustrated in the figure 4. This phase shift can be corrected easily by connecting the CTs secondary circuits in opposite way to the way that the power transformer phases are connected. I.e. if the transformer windings are connected in Y-Δ the CTs secondary windings should be connected in Δ-Y and vice versa [20]. As shown in figure 4 the relation between the line-to-line voltage (V_{LL}) to the phase voltage (V_{ph}) can explain the phase shift between the Δ-Y transformer connection. The following equation gives the relationship between the line-to-line voltage (V_{LL}) to the phase voltage (V_{ph}) [2], [3], [6], [7]:

$$\frac{V_{ab}}{2} = V_{an}\cos$$

$$\frac{V_{ab}}{2} = V_{an}\frac{\sqrt{3}}{2} \tag{8}$$

$$V_{ab} = \sqrt{3}\,V_{an}$$

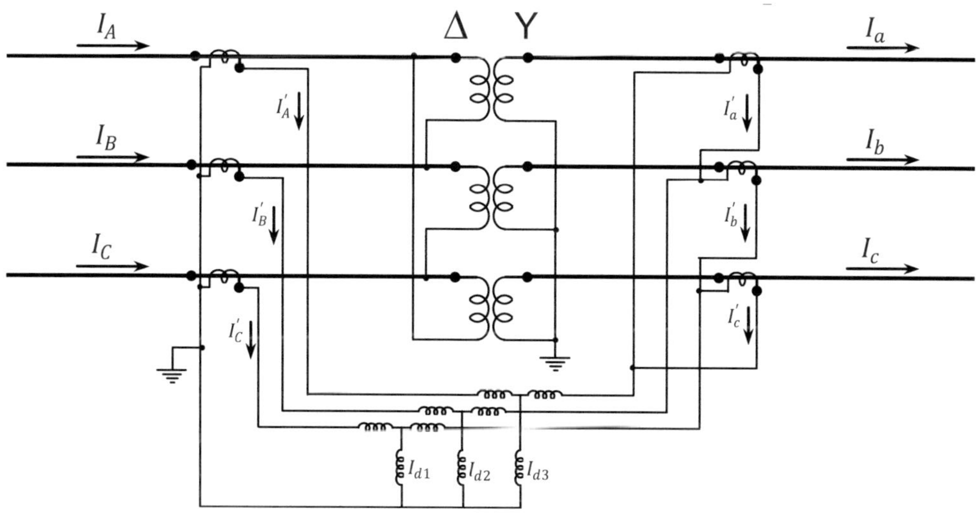

Figure 4. Connection of differential protection of 3-phase Δ-Y transformer

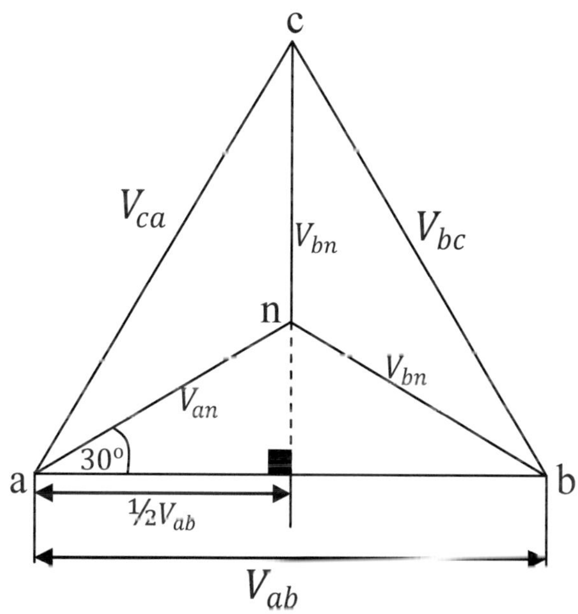

Figure 5. The relationship between line to line voltage and the phase to neutral voltage and the phase shift between them which reflects the phase shift in Y-Δ or Δ-Y connected transformers

3. Differential protection difficulties

Generally, three main difficulties handicap the conventional differential protection. They induce the differential relay to release a false trip signal without the existing of any fault. These complications must be overcome in order to make the differential relay working properly [2], [3]:

- Magnetizing inrush current during initial energization,
- CTs Mismatch and saturation,
- Transformation ratio changes due to Tap changer.

3.1. Magnetizing inrush current

This phenomenon, the transient magnetizing inrush or the exciting current, occurs in the primary side of the transformer whenever the transformer is switched on (energized) and the instantaneous value of the voltage is not at 90^0. At this time, the first peak of the flux wave is higher than the peak of the flux at the steady state condition. This current appears as an internal fault, and it is sensed as a differential current by the differential relay. The value of the first peak of the magnetizing current may be as high as several times the peak of the full load current. The magnitude and duration of the magnetizing inrush current is influenced by many factors, some of these factors are [2], [6], [7];

- The instantaneous value of the voltage waveform at the moment of closing CB,
- The value of the residual (remnant) magnetizing flux,
- The sign of the residual magnetizing flux,
- The type of the iron laminations used in the transformer core,
- The saturation flux density of the transformer core,
- The total impedance of the supply circuit,
- The physical size of the transformer,
- The maximum flux-carrying capability of the iron core laminations,
- The input supply voltage level,

The effect of the inrush current on the differential relay is false tripping the transformer without of any existing type of faults. From the principle of operation of the differential relay, the relay compares the currents coming from both sides of the power transformer as explained above. However, the inrush current is flowing only in the primary side of the power transformer. So that, the differential current will have a significant value due to the existence of current in only one side. Therefore, the relay has to be designed to recognize that this current is a normal phenomenon and to not trip due to this current.

3.2. False trip due to C.T characteristics

The performance of the differential relays depends on the accuracy of the CTs in reproducing their primary currents in their secondary side. In many cases, the primary ratings of the CTs, located in the high voltage and low voltage sides of the power transformer, does not exactly match the power transformer rated currents. Due to this discrepancy, a CTs mismatch takes place, which in turn creates a small false differential current, depending on the amount of this mismatch. Sometimes, this amount of the differential current is enough to operate the differential relay. Therefore, CTs ratio correction has to be done to overcome this CTs mismatch by using interposing CTs of multi taps [8].

Another problem that may face the perfect operation of the CTs is the saturation problem. When saturation happens to one or all CTs at different levels, false differential current appears in the differential relay. This differential current could cause mal-operation of the differential relay. The dc component of the primary side current could produce the worst case of CT saturation. In which, the secondary current contains dc offset and extra harmonics [9], [10].

3.3. False trip due to tap changer

On-Load Tap-Changer (OLTC) is installed on the power transformer to control automatically the transformer output voltage. This device is required wherever there are heavy fluctuations in the power system voltage. The transformation ratio of the CTs can be matched with only one point of the tap-changing range. Therefore, if the OLTC is changed, unbalance current flows in the differential relay operating coil. This action causes CTs mismatches. This current will be considered as a fault current which makes the relay to release a trip signal [11], [12].

4. Digital differential protection

Many digital algorithms have been used so far after the invention of the computer. These algorithms do the same job with different accuracy and speed. The acceptable speed according to IEEE standard for transformer protection is 100 msec. All modern algorithms are faster than this IEEE standard. Nowadays, there are some algorithms performs their function in less than 10 msec. In this chapter, a fast algorithm is introduced. Its speed is in the range of 1 to 15 msec. This algorithm is based on the Fast Fourier algorithm (FFT) This algorithm is not new, however, significant changes has been introduced to make it much faster.

The proposed digital differential relay is designed using a simulation technique in Matlab Simulink environment. The design is implemented to protect the power transformer against internal faults and prevent interruption due to inrush currents.

This algorithm is built on the principle of harmonic-current restraint, where the magnetizing-inrush current is characterized by large harmonic components content that are not noticeably present in fault currents. Due to the saturated condition of the transformer iron, the waveform of the inrush current is highly distorted. The amplitude of the harmonics, compared with the fundamental is somewhere between 30% to 60% and the third harmonic 10% to 30%. The other harmonics are progressively less [3] [6], [13]. Fast Fourier Transform (*FFT*) is used to implement this approach. In general, any periodic signal $f(t)$ can be decomposed to its sine and cosine components as follows:

$$f(t) = \frac{a_0}{2} + \sum_{k=1}^{\infty} C_k \cos(kwt) + S_k \sin(kwt)$$

Where: a_0 is the DC component of the f (t), and C_k, S_k are the cosine and sine coefficients of the frequencies present in $f(t)$, respectively. The discrete forms of the coefficients C_k, S_k are expressed in the following equations:

$$C_k = \frac{2}{N} \sum_{n=1}^{N-1} x(n) \cos\left(\frac{2kwt}{N}\right)$$

$$S_k = \frac{2}{N} \sum_{n=1}^{N-1} x(n) \sin\left(\frac{2kwt}{N}\right)$$

The Fourier harmonic coefficients can be expressed as [13]:

$$F_k = \sqrt{S_k^2 + C_k^2}$$

Where: $F_k$is the kth harmonic coefficient for k = 1, 2,...,N and $x(n)$ is the signal $f(t)$ in its discrete form. The *FFT* produces exactly the same results as the *DFT*; however, the *FFT* is much faster than DFT, where the speed of calculation is the main factor in this process [13-16].

Fig 6 illustrates the flow chart of the designed digital Fourier Transform based logic technique algorithm. In this algorithm the output currents of the *CTs* undergo over two analysis processes, amplitude comparison process and harmonic content calculation process. The amplitude comparison between the *RMS* values of the *CTs* output currents ($|I_{d1}$ - $I_{d2}|$) is in the left hand side of the flowchart, and the harmonic calculation is in the right hand side of the flowchart.

The software is implemented according to the following steps [15-17]:

Step 1. Reading data from the *CTs*.
Step 2. Data calculation, which is given as follows;

For the amplitude calculation, if the absolute difference ($|I_{d1}$ - $I_{d2}|$) between the *CTs* output currents is greater than zero the logic (1) takes place, which indicates the case of an inrush current or an internal fault. Otherwise, the logic (0) takes place, which indicates a detection of an external fault.

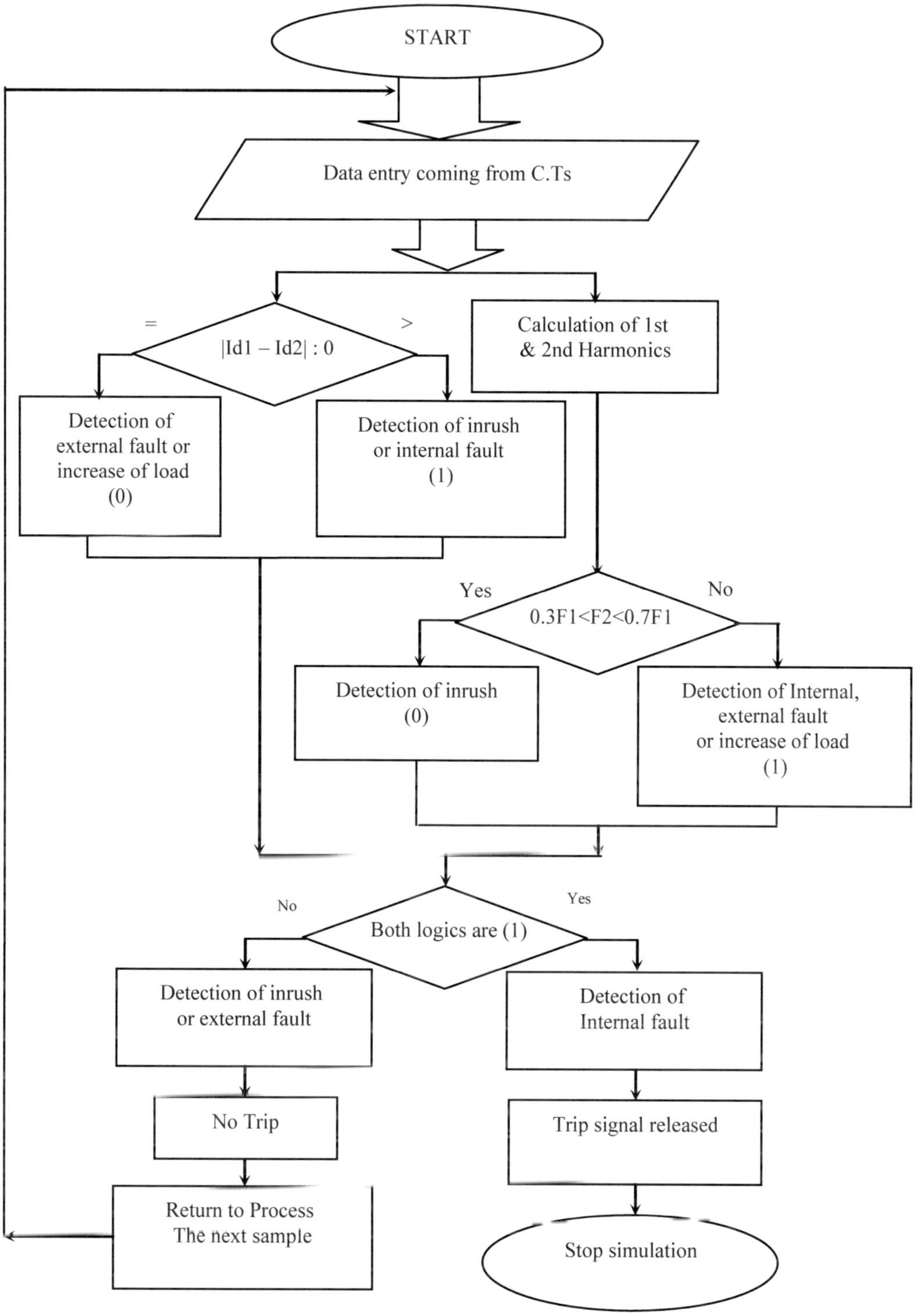

Figure 6. Flow chart of the proposed Digital Differential Relay Scheme

In the meantime, the harmonic calculation is performed. If the percentage value of the second harmonic amplitude is in the range of (0.3 to 0.6) of the fundamental component amplitude, then the logic (0) occurs, that means recognition of inrush current. Otherwise, the logic (1) takes place, which indicates a detection of an internal or external fault.

Step 3. Taking the final decision:

If the logic cases received from both cases (a & b) in step two are both (1), that indicates a detection of an internal fault. Then a trip signal is released to stop the simulation.

For the other logic options of (0,1) means an external fault, (1,0) means an inrush current, or (0,0) indicate an occurrence of an inrush current or an external fault, and the simulation goes back to step two to start the calculation again for the next sample.

5. Implementation of the digital differential protection using matlab

This implementation is done using Matlab/Simulink environment. Figure 7 shows the simulated power system built in Matlab/Simulink environment. In which a three phase, 250MVA, 60Hz, (735/315) kV, Y/Δ power transformer is used in this system. The contents of each designed block are illustrated in separate figs. 8 to 12.

There are some coefficients are kept hidden for the reader to find them. These coefficients can change the behavior of the design.

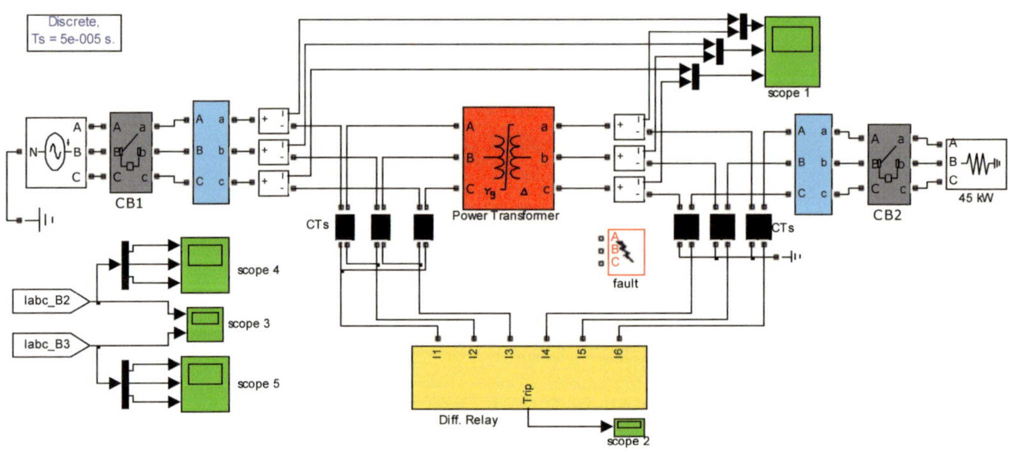

Figure 7. Matlab/Simulink Model of the proposed system

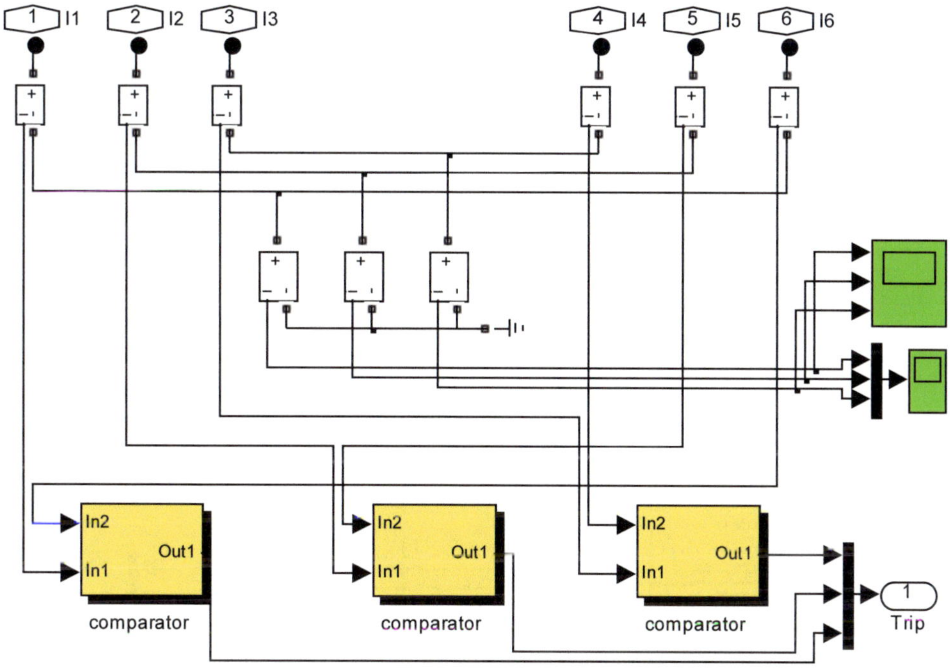

Figure 8. The differential relay block contents

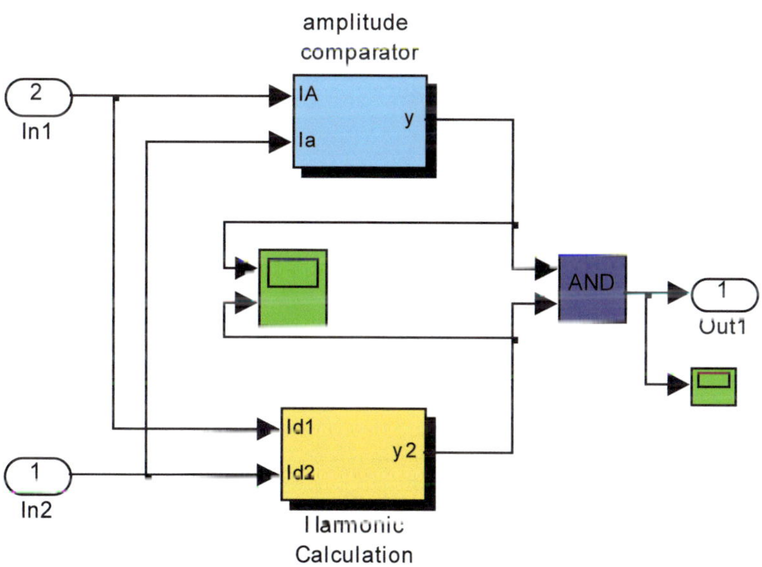

Figure 9. The comparator block contents

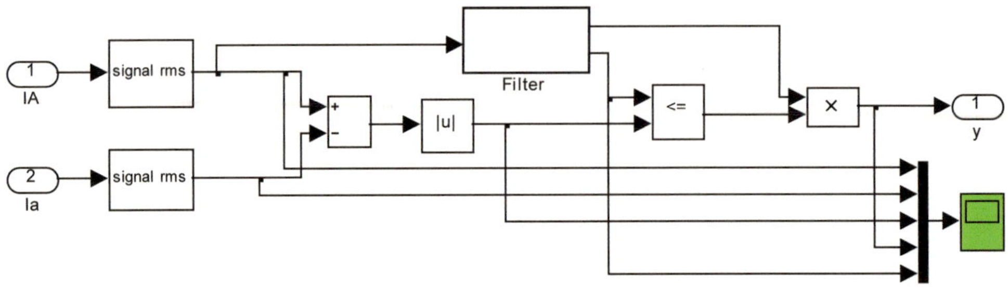

Figure 10. The amplitude comparator block contents

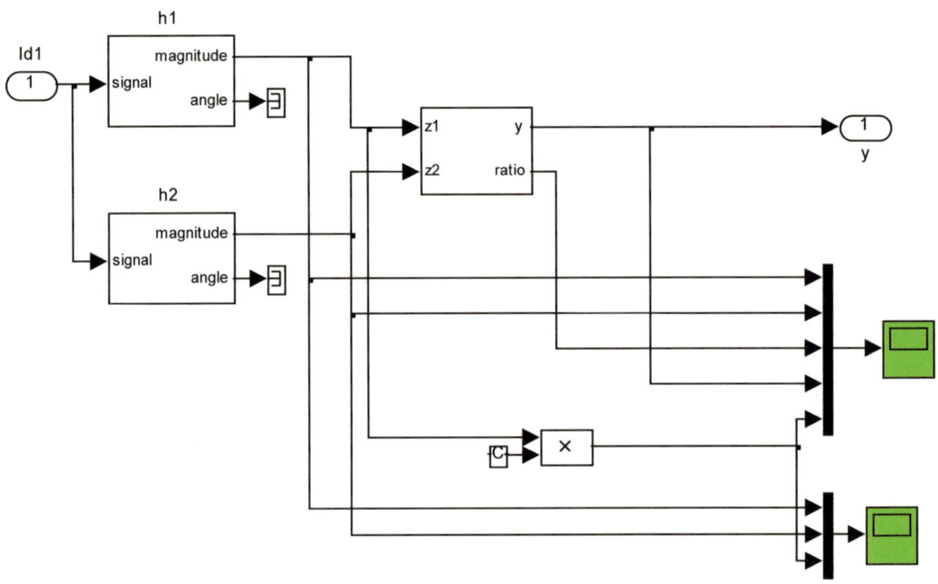

Figure 11. The harmonic comparator block contents

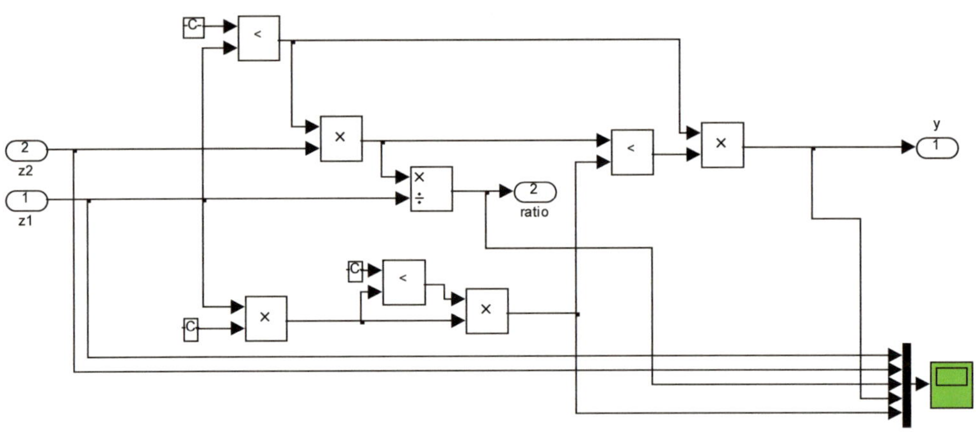

Figure 12. The ratio block contents

6. The results and discussions

The results will be given for different cases:

Case 1: magnetizing inrush current,
Case 2: magnetizing inrush with adding load,
Case 3: Three phase to ground fault at loaded transformer,
Case 4: Phase A to ground external fault at loaded transformer,

Other cases of different types of faults and inrush currents such as single line to ground fault, line-to-line fault, line to line to ground fault and three phase fault in both cases loaded and unloaded transformer are illustrated.

Case 1: Magnetizing inrush current:

In this section of simulation, when the primary side CB1 is closed at 0.1 sec, only the inrush current flows in the primary circuit of the power transformer and no current passes through the power transformer to the secondary side as shown in Fig. 13. The harmonic comparator shows in Fig. 14 that the value of the 2nd harmonic is higher than 0.3 of the fundamental component.

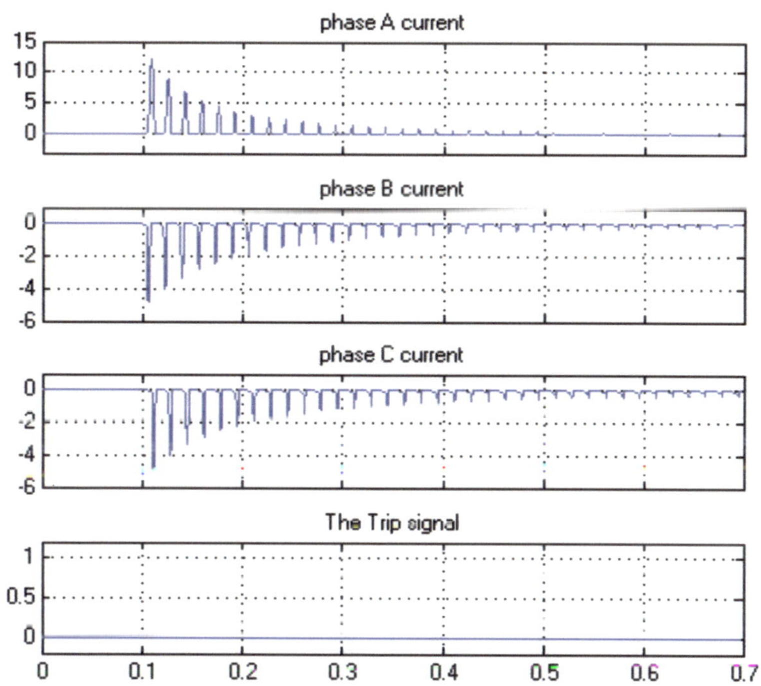

Figure 13. Inrush currents waveforms of the three phases at the primary side of the power transformer.

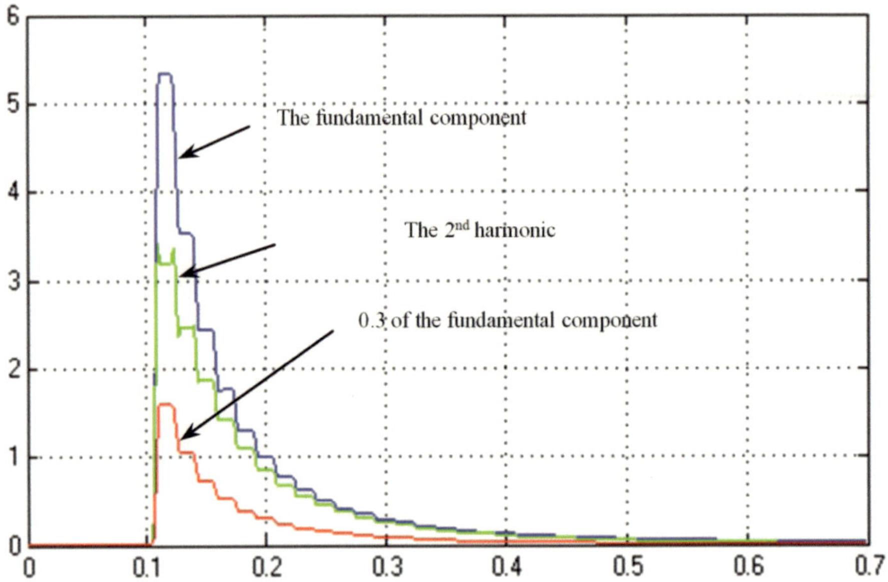

Figure 14. Harmonic comparator result: the 2nd harmonic and the fundamental component for the 1st case.

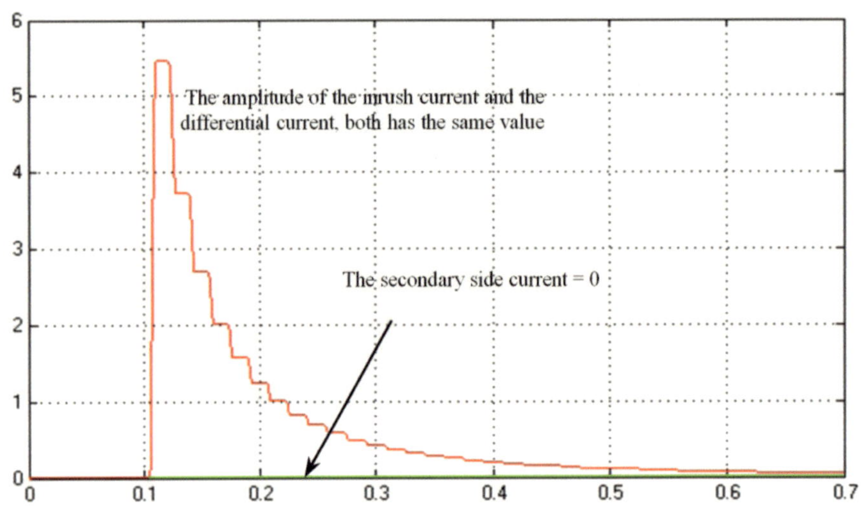

Figure 15. Amplitude comparator results for the 1st case.

In this case the harmonic calculation part released logic (0) but the amplitude comparator showed in Fig. 15 that the differential current is equal to the inrush current, where both curves are drown over each other, then the amplitude comparator release logic (1). For this logic coordination (0,1) no trip signal is released.

Case 2: Magnetizing inrush with adding load:

This test is carried out after the energization of the power transformer by switching ON the CB1 at 0.1sec and CB2 at 0.3 sec from the beginning of the simulation to see the effect of load excursion on the accuracy of the designed approach. Therefore, a 500W resistive load is added to the system at 0.3 sec. Consequently, the inrush current disappeared and load current started to flow in the primary and secondary circuits of the transformer according to the transformation ratio of the power transformer as shown in Fig. 16. However, the amplitude of the output currents of the primary and secondary CTs are equal due to the proper selection of the transformation ratio of the primary and secondary CTs, which can obviously noticed in Fig. 18. Where, before the time 0.3 sec the differential current was equal to the inrush current, but after the swathing ON of the load the differential current went to zero and the primary and secondary currants became equal.

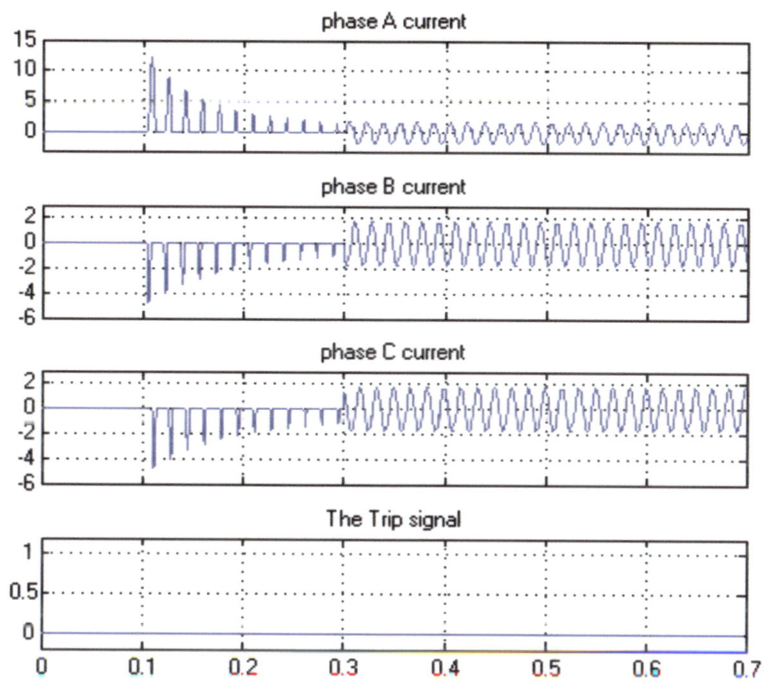

Figure 16. Normal load current starts flowing at 0.3sec.

As shown in Fig. 17, after the switching of CB2, the value of the 2nd harmonic become lower than 0.3 of the fundamental component. Accordingly, the harmonic calculation part released logic (1) but the amplitude comparator released logic (0). Consequently, for this logic coordination (1,0) no trip signal is released. Figure 18 shows the amplitude comparator results.

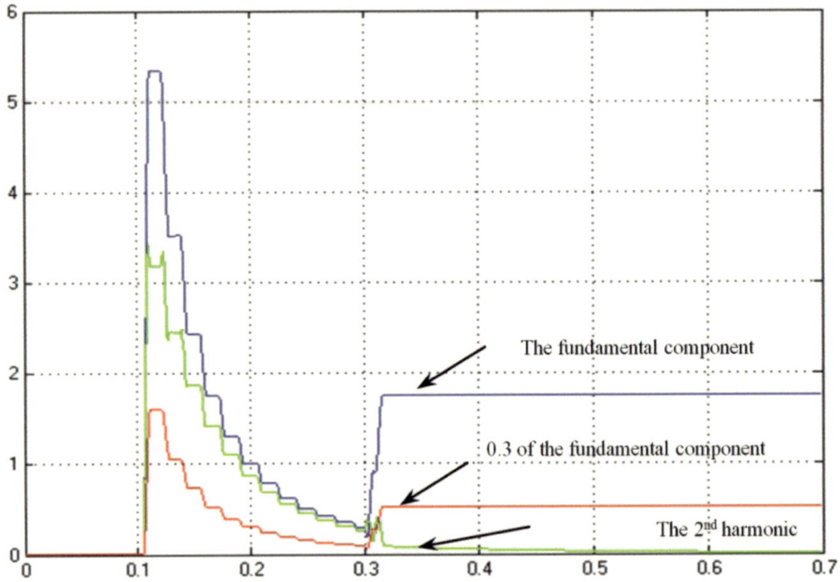

Figure 17. 2nd harmonic and the fundamental component for the 2nd case.

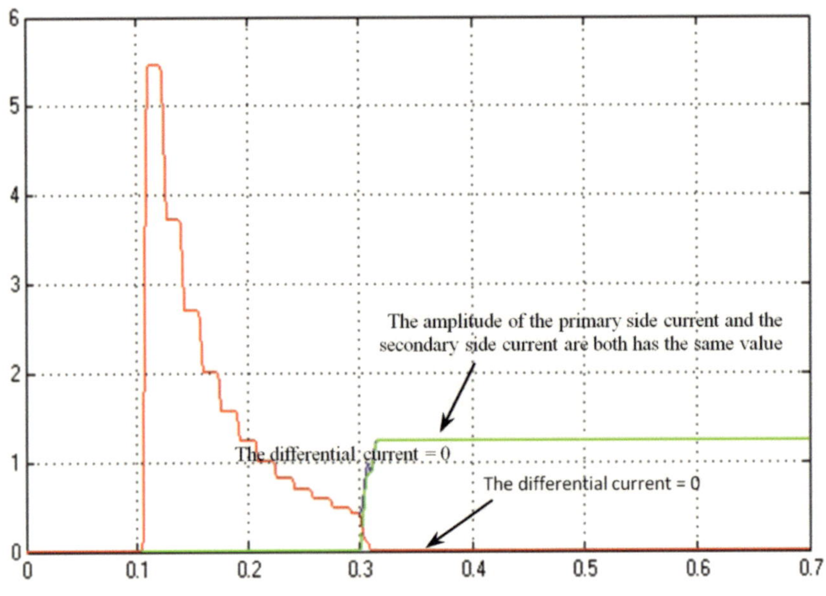

Figure 18. Amplitude comparator results for the 2nd case.

Case 3: Three phase to ground fault at loaded transformer:

In this section, a three phase to ground fault is created to test the security of the algorithm. After the switching of CB1 at 0.1sec, an internal fault is created at 0.5 sec at the secondary side of the power transformer by connecting the three phases A, B and C of the secondary side of the power transformer to the ground. In this case, a significant increase of the primary current takes place due to the fault occurrence inside the protected zone at 0.5 sec as shown in Fig. 19. The relay detected this increase using the harmonic and amplitude comparators and realized it as an internal fault. Consequently the transformer is isolated from the grid. Also it is obvious from Fig. 20 that the relay has released a trip signal after 0.57 msec after the occurrence of the fault, which can be considered as a very good speed to isolate the transformer.

As shown in Fig. 21, after the occurrence of the fault at time 0.5 sec, the value of the 2nd harmonic increased during the transient time and then decreased rapidly to a value lower than 0.3 of the fundamental component once the steady state is achieved. Accordingly, the harmonic calculation part released logic (1). Also from Fig. 22 which shows the result of the amplitude comparator the value of the differential current is no longer equal to zero. Accordingly the amplitude comparator released logic (1). Therefore, for this logic coordination (1,1) a trip signal is released in order to isolate the power transformer from the grid.

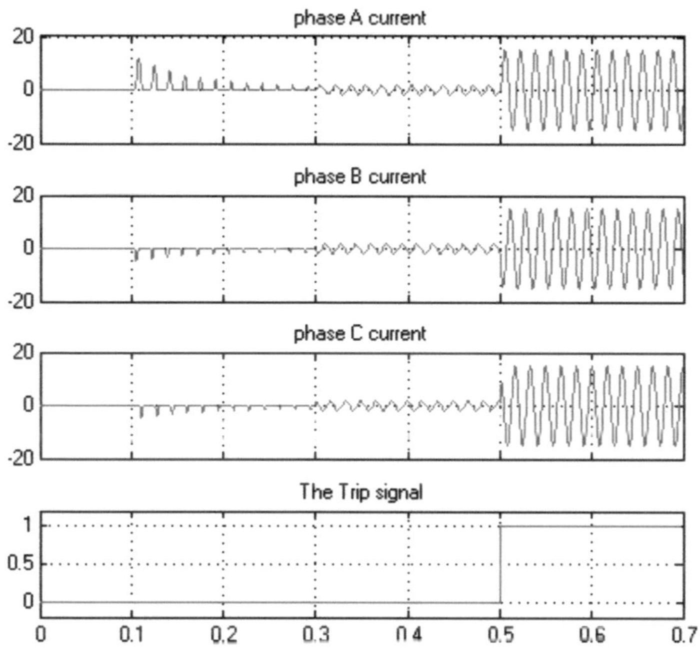

Figure 19. Increase of phase A, B & C currents due to the occurrence of the fault at 0.5 sec for loaded transformer

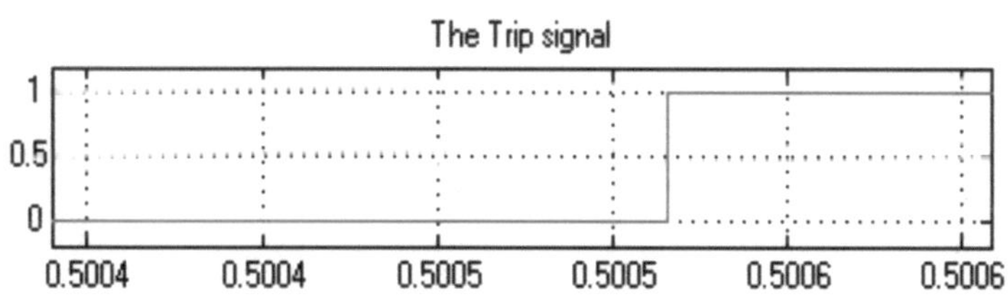

Figure 20. Zoomed trip signal, trip time is around 0.57 msec

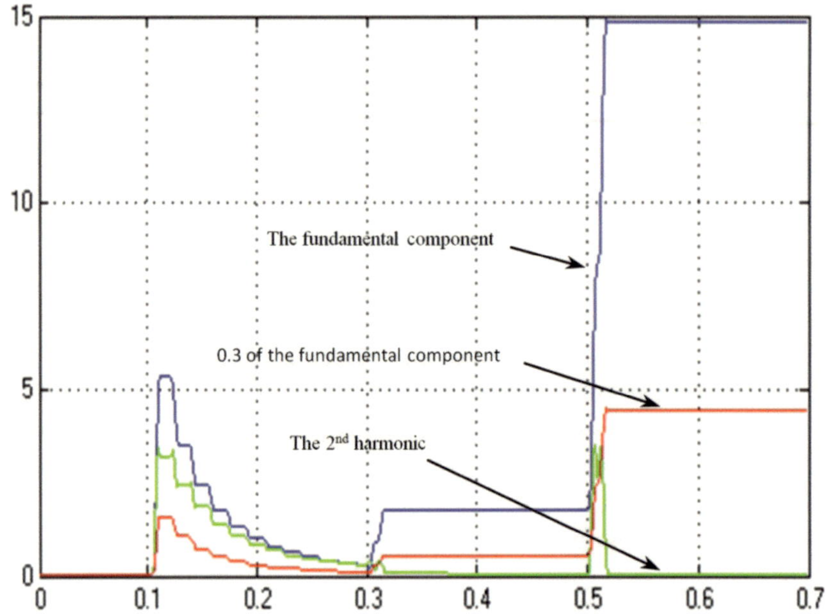

Figure 21. 2nd harmonic and the fundamental component for the case of three phase to ground fault at loaded transformer.

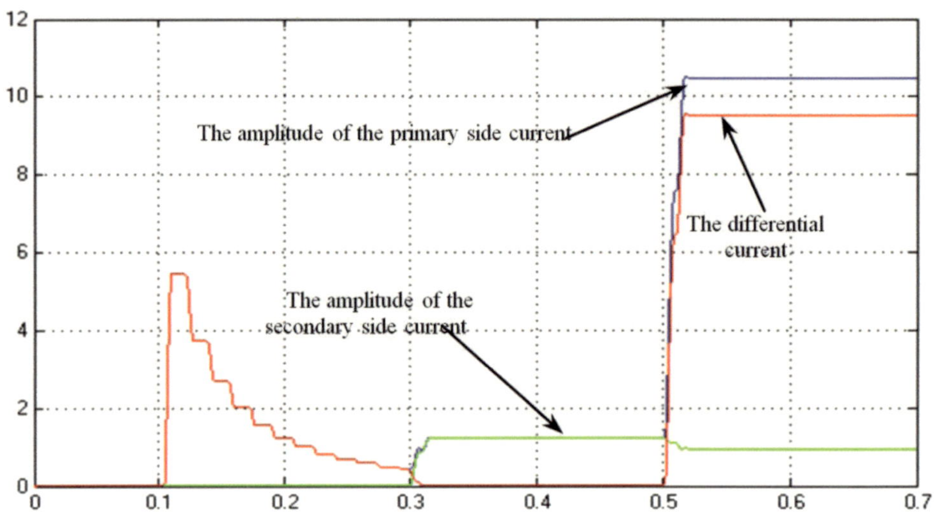

Figure 22. Amplitude comparator result for the 3rd case.

Case 4: Phase A to ground external fault at loaded transformer.

This case is similar to case 2, where the occurrence of the fault current outside the protected zone leaded to the increase of fault currents in both sides of the power transformer. Therefore the relay considered this case as a sever increase in load currents. Fig. 23 shows the increase in phase A currant and no trip signal is released

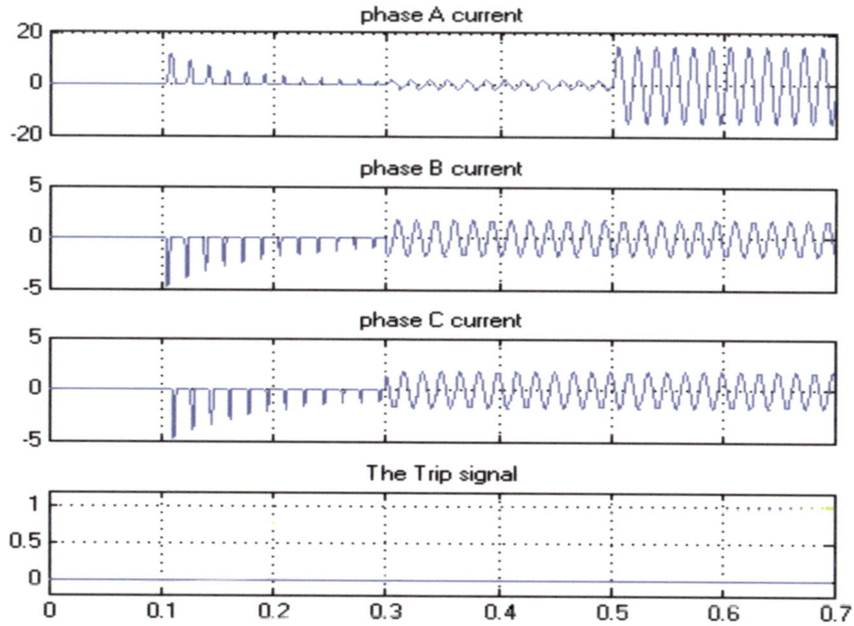

Figure 23. Increase of phase A current due to the occurrence of the fault at 0.5 sec for loaded transformer

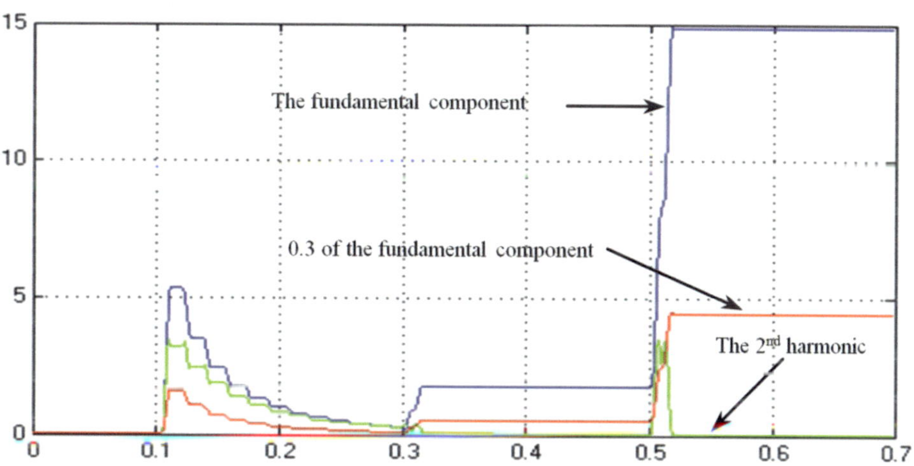

Figure 24. 2nd harmonic and the fundamental component for the Case for the 4th case.

As illustrated in Fig. 24, after the occurrence of the external fault at 0.5 sec, the value of the 2nd harmonic decreased to a value less than 0.3 of the fundamental component. Accordingly, the harmonic calculation part released logic (1) but the amplitude comparator released logic (0) because the differential current is almost zero as it can be seen from Fig. 25. Consequently, for this logic coordination (1,0) no trip signal is released.

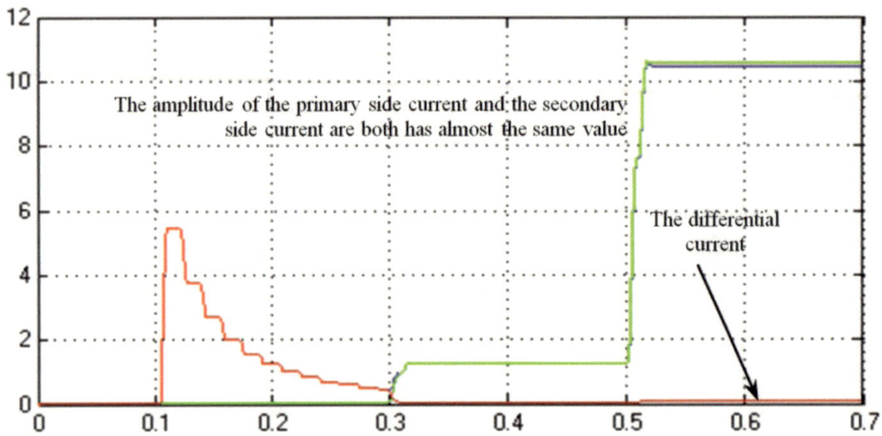

Figure 25. Amplitude comparator result for the 4th case.

Similarly, the relay is tested for all other cases of different types of faults such as single line to ground, line to line, line to line to ground and three phase faults in both cases loaded and unloaded transformer. In all cases the relay has successfully released a trip signal in each case. The results of some of these different types of faults are shown in Figs (26 - 30).

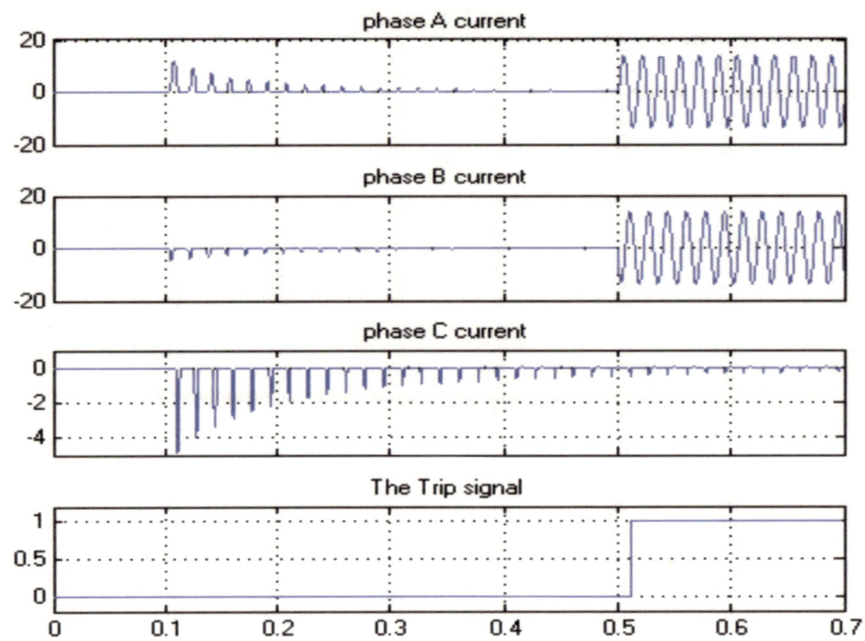

Figure 26. Increase of phase A & B currents due to the occurrence of the fault at 0.5 sec, for unloaded transformer

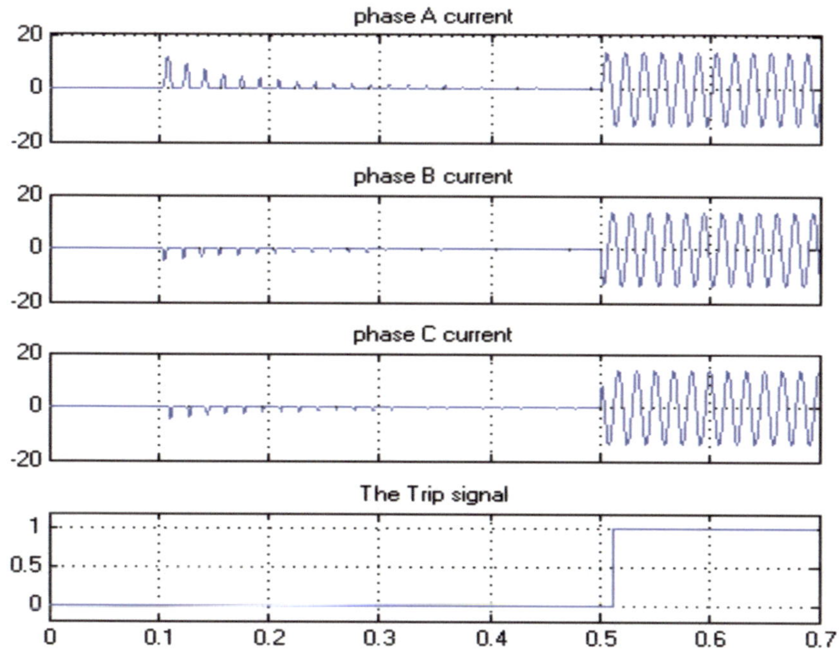

Figure 27. Increase of phase A , B & C currents due to the occurrence of the fault at 0.5 sec, for unloaded transformer

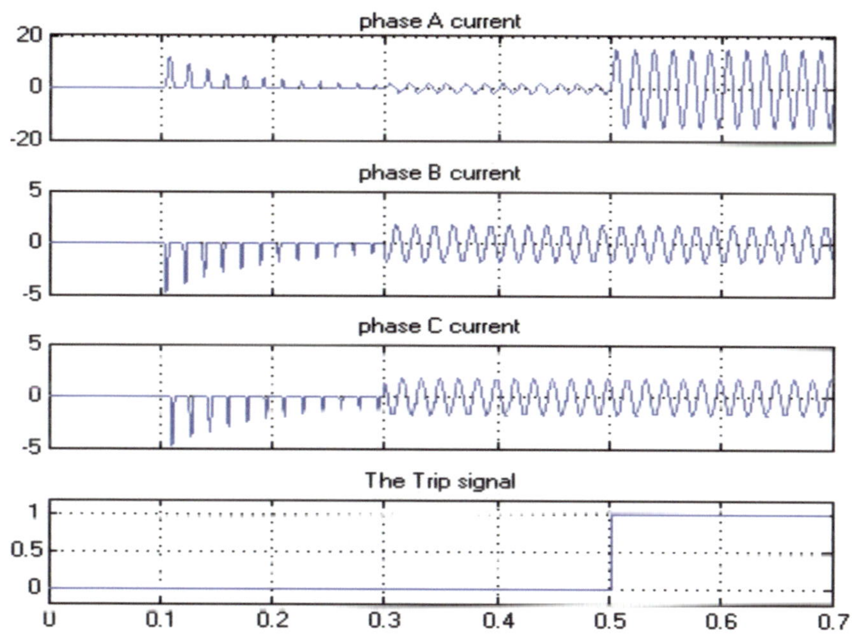

Figure 28. Increase of phase A current due to the occurrence of the fault at 0.5 sec for loaded transformer

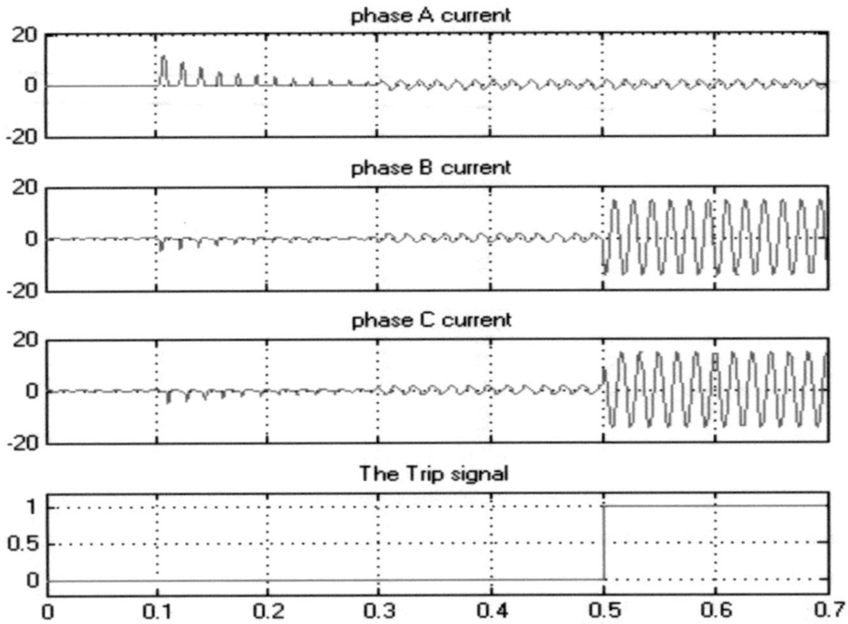

Figure 29. Increase of phase B & C currents due to the occurrence of the fault at 0.5 sec for loaded transformer

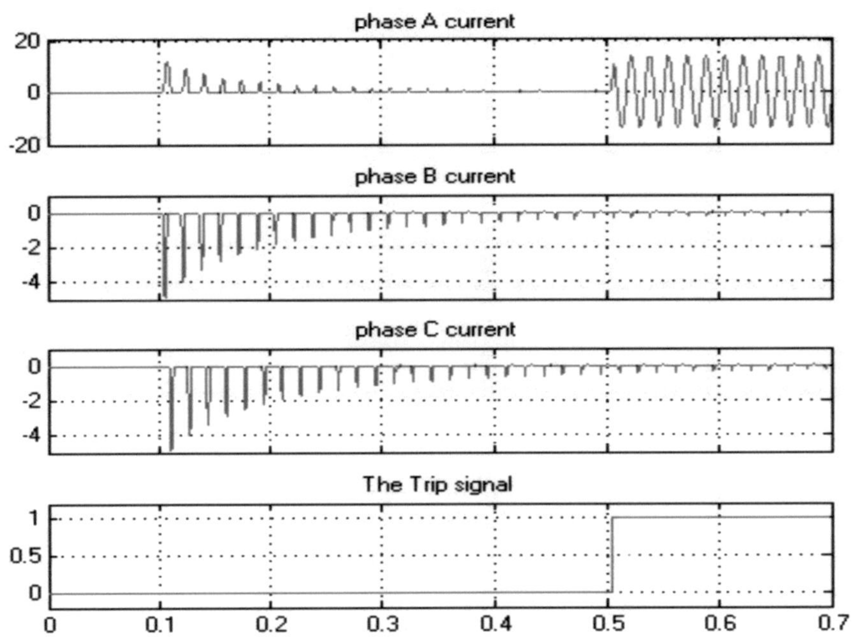

Figure 30. Increase of phase A current due to the occurrence of the fault at 0.5 sec, for unloaded transformer

7. Summary of all tested cases

case type	Relay response	Trip signal release time (m sec)	
		Loaded	unloaded
Phase A to ground	Trip	1.7	4.7
Phase B to ground	Trip	0.6	12
Phase C to ground	Trip	0.6	15
Phase A to phase B	Trip	0.8	12.2
Phase B to phase C	Trip	0.6	12.2
Phase A to phase C	Trip	1.3	14.6
Phase A to phase B to ground	Trip	0.6	12
Phase B to phase C to ground	Trip	0.6	12
Phase A to phase C to ground	trip	0.6	13.2
Three phase to ground	Trip	0.6	0.57
Three phase	Trip	0.6	12
Inrush current	Restrain	No trip signal	
Load current	Restrain	No trip signal	
External fault	Restrain	No trip signal	

Table 1. Summary of the performance of the designed differential relay at different types of disturbances that may occur to the power transformer

8. Conclusions

This chapter is talking about the implementation and simulation of a small power system with a differential protection for the power transformer. The implementation is shown in step by step. This simulation is tested for various cases and for all cases it gave satisfactory results. All the tests gave satisfactory results. There are some difficulties are faced in the implantation of this system such as the lack of some toolbox in the Sim-power-system. For example, there is no current transformer in the toolbox. In this case, there are two choices to solve this problem. The first one is to use a regular single phase and make some changes in its specification to fit the current transformer specifications. The second one is to use a current measurement, but this one will not simulate the problems of the CTs.

Author details

Adel Aktaibi and M. Azizur Rahman
Memorial University of Newfoundland, Canada

9. References

[1] M. A. Rahman and B. Jeyasurya, "A state-of-the-art review of transformer protection algorithms", IEEE Trans. Power Delivery, vol. 3, pp. 534–544, Apr. 1988.

[2] P. M. Anderson, "Power System Protection", Piscataway, NJ: IEEE Press, 1999.

[3] C. D. Hayward, "Harmonic-Current Restrained Relays for Transformer Differential Protection", AIEE trans., vol. 60, pp 276, 1941.

[4] M. S. Sachdev, T. S. Sidhu, H. C. Wood, "A Digital Relaying Algorithm for Detecting Transformer Winding Faults", IEEE Transactions on Power Deliver, vol. 4, No. 3. July 1989.

[5] K. Yabe, "Power Differential Method for Discrimination between Fault and Magnetizing Inrush Current in Transformers", IEEE Transactions on Power Delivery, Vol. 12, No. 3, July 1997.

[6] A. R. Van C. Warrington, "Protective Relays Their Theory and Practice", vol. 1, Chapman Hall Press, 3rd edition, 1985.

[7] J. Duncan Glover and Mulukutla Sarma, "power system analysis and design", PWS publishing company, 2nd ed., 1994.

[8] AREVA, "KBCH 120, 130, 140 Transformer Differential Protection Relays Service Manual", KBCH/EN M/G11, France, 2001.

[9] W. Rebizant, T. Hayder, L. Schiel, "Prediction of C.T Saturation Period for Differential Relay Adaptation Purposes", web site, 2004.

[10] A. G. Zocholl, G. Benmouyal and H. J. Altuve, "Performance Analysis of Traditional and Improved Transformer Differential Protective Relays", web site, 2000.

[11] Y. Marty, W. Smolinski, and S. Sivakumar, "Design of a digital protection scheme for power transformer using optimal state observers," IEE Proceedings Vol. 135,pt. C, No.3 May 1988.

[12] ABB relays, "Power transformer protection application guide", AG03-5005E, 1998.

[13] M. A. Rahman, Y.V.V.S. Murthy and Ivi Hermanto, "Digital Protective Relay for Power Transformers", U.S. Patent No. 5,172,329, December 1992.

[14] P.K. Dash and M.A. Rahman, "A New Algorithm for Digital Protection of Power Transformer", Canadian Electrical Association Transactions, Vol. 26, Part 4, 1987, pp. 1-8, (87-SP-169), 1987.

[15] A. Gangopadhay, M.A. Rahman, B. Jeyasurya, "Simulation of Magnetizing Inrush Currents in Single Phase Transformers", International Journal of Energy Systems, Vol. 7, No. 1, 1987, pp. 34-38.

[16] M.A. Rahman and A. Gangopadhay, "Digital Simulation of Magnetizing Inrushes Currents in Three-Phase Transformers", IEEE Transactions on Power Delivery, Vol. PWRD-1, No. 4, October 1986, pp. 235-242. (Over 100 citations)

[17] Adel Aktaibi and M. A. Rahman, "A Software Design Technique for Differential Protection of Power Transformers", International Electric Machines & Drives Conference (IEMDC 2011), IEEE, 15-18 May 2011, Page(s): 1456–1461.

PH Control Using MATLAB

Mostefa Ghassoul

Additional information is available at the end of the chapter

http://dx.doi.org/10.5772/46454

1. Introduction

Wastewater neutralization plays an important part in a wastewater treatment process. It provides the optimum environment for microorganism activity between pH 6.5 and 7.5{1}, and the right water discharge to the public sewage as mandated by the Department of Environment of between pH 5 and 9 (Environmental Quality Act, 1974) {2}. Wastewater of pH below 4.5 and above 9 may greatly reduce the activity of the microorganisms which treat the water and may not support their life at all {3}.

For a number of years, Hydrogen chloride (HCL) acid was used in wastewater treatment facilities to control alkalinity. It's a product that works, but it also has many potential problems. HCL acid can be difficult to apply and control. Correcting the pH of alkaline wastewater is usually required either for discharge to sewer, in preparation to further biological, physical/chemical treatment or direct discharge to the environment. Strong acids such as hydrochloric acid have traditionally been used to neutralize alkaline waste streams prior to discharge {4}.

On the control side, It is well known that controlling pH is very difficult, and specially neutralization in industry, due to the high non linearity of the system. In fact the pH dynamics are not only time variant, but change with each pH value and becomes oscillatory around the 7 mark as well. Even by placing the pH probe in the proximity of a mixer or in a turbulent flow could result in a big change in the pH. It has been reported in literature that researchers have been trying for ages to control the pH with a tuned classical PID controller with many additional restrictions; but experience has shown that this is not satisfactory because of the changing of dynamics hence the transfer function where when the PID is tuned for a certain characteristics, it becomes completely un-tuned for the next. To overcome this problem, we (here at the chemical engineering department University of Bahrain) have engaged in finding a solution to the problem. One of the option possible is the use of fuzzy logic. For the last fifty years, since Zadeh {5} introduces his famous paper on fuzzy logic and control, fuzzy logic control has been widely implemented successfully in many industrial applications ranging from home appliances such as washing machines to heavy industries such as loading and unloading very heavy loads in ports efficiently by minimizing the action time. Certainly its use in controlling pH is feasible.This is due two reasons:

1. The fuzzy control does not require any transfer function, nor any tedious mathematical analysis. So there is no need to model the system continuously, with each pH space, so the change of the pH characteristic does not influence the control strategy.
2. The membership space of the pH is restricted between zero and fourteen where pH between zero and seven is acid and between seven and fourteen is base. This space is divided into a limited number of memberships, and the control for each membership could be easily tuned separately. To apply this strategy we had to look for the best possible solution. And luckily, we find the solution in MATLAB, through SIMULINK fuzzy control blocksets. The choice of SIMULINK fuzzy control blocksets was considered very carefully for several reasons.
    1. The huge number of rule one could implement. In fact, we have currently applied more than 125 rules and still the margin is open.
    2. The simplicity of MATLAB fuzzy control, where the SIMULINK blocksets could be used directly. This saves a lot of computing time. On top of that, those blocksets are already optimized.
    3. Though MATLAB was originally designed as a simulator platform, for the last few years, several companies have developed several interfacing cards to interface online different processes to the MATLAB platform, such as HUMUSOFT MF 624 multifunction I/O card and National Instrument card NI PCI-6221 data acquisition card. Hardware interface to the process in question, real time, where this has been done with a relative ease thank's to National Instrument NI PCI- 6221 data acquisition card.

But before discussing how SIMULINK is used, we first have to highlight the pH apparatus used. Luckily, we found an obsolete pH control apparatus made by ARMFIELD UK (PC5 PH control RIG) which was made back in the early eightees, with the following components: framework assembly complete with pump set, two storage tanks, two flow meters, with a completely irreparable pH probe, pneumatically operated valve driven with a current to pressure converter, air filter regulator, glass vessel, clamps , stirrer together with obsolete three term PID electronic controller, slide indicator and chart recorder. The control was developed around a dedicated classical PID controller where the user only sets up the PID parameters through a number of knobs. The response is either given through slide indicator or chart recorder. (see figure (1)). This procedure was no use, where advanced control is not possible. So this controller was completely isolated and replaced by a modern SIMULINK based controller built for this purpose. The process is as follows. Two tanks are used ; one filled with an acidic liquid and the other with base liquid. The acidic liquid is controlled manually and the base liquid is controlled through a 3 to 15 PSI proportional control valve. The pressure is generated by controlling a pressure gauge through a current to pressure converter. Unfortunately, the output from MATLAB to the acquisition card is only in volts, whereas the valve driving signal is in milliamperes. This has lead to the design of a 0 - 5V voltage to 4-20mA current converter to drive the valve. The control voltage is generated by SIMULINK as a result of the control strategy developed around the fuzzy control blocksets. The control signal produced by the blockset is outputted through the NI card to the hardware. The beauty of this control is that the process could be monitored through MATLAB virtual instrument online.

1.1. PH control

PH is an important variable in production fields such as chemical and petrochemical industries where tons of toxic products are pumped into environment due to contaminated chemical waste. Most of those product wastes are mainly alkaline. This will certainly harms the environment in particular sea life as well as agricultural products which in turn reflects on the human life quality. So it is essential to treat those wastes to neutralize their pH to an acceptable level, ideally around 7. So what is pH. The PH of a solution is defined as the negative of the logarithm to the base of 10 of the hydrogen ion concentration.

$$PH = -\log 10 \left[H+\right]$$

Most of the factories waste is mainly alkaline; this certainly harms the environment by poisoning life onshore or offshore, including humans either through contaminated food and water or through breathing. This is witnessed by the increased rate of cancer cases in the world. So it is a must to neutralize the industry waste by neutralizing the pH. This is quantitavely done by bringing the pH to around the magic value of seven. In industry, the pH could vary between any value between 2 and 10. Here in our lab, we are using PC5 Armfield obsolete PH control apparatus. Its PI & D diagram is shown in figure(1).

The neutralization process basically follows the following reaction:

$$(NCL+NAOH \rightarrow NACL+H_2O)$$

This reaction results in salt and water which do not present any harm to nature. (The process system is shown in figure(2)). The system basically consists of two liquid circuits; one feeding the acidic substance and the other feeds the base liquid. The added liquid is controlled by a proportional control valve whereas the base liquid is manually operated.

To make the mixture homogeneous, a variable speed mixer is used. The pH is picked up with the aid of a probe placed into the mixing vessel close to the outlet. Unlike the PID controller where many restrictions are imposed, fuzzy controller only requires the probe to be out off the flow turbulence way next the outlet. The probe reading is conditioned and fed to the controller through the NI PCI-6221 card of the E series, and at the same time, fed to the pH meter for confirmation. The card has 16 analogue input channels which could be connected as differential or single ended, sixteen bit resolution and two output analogue channels. The signal conditioning is no more than an instrumentation amplifier (figure(3)) of type INA114. This type of amplifier is very precise. The output of the amplifier is then fed to

NI card, to be read into SIMULINK to be analyzed using the fuzzy controller. Once the signal has been treated, the resulting control variable is outputted through the output port of the NI card to drive the control valve. Unfortunately this output is in volts, whereas the driving signal required by the control valve is in milliamperes(current). This requires the design of a voltage to current converter. It should be mentioned here that the control valve used is of proportional type where it closes linearly from fully closed to fully open by using a current to pressure converter which converters a 4-20mA to 3-15PSI pressure. The Valve controls the acid flow rate of type HCL. So by varying the valve opening, the flow rate changes so does the pH. The base flow is manually controlled. The output of the pH sensor is fed to an instrumentation amplifier as mentioned earlier, to condition it, and at the same time to the NI6221 acquisition card, through which it is read into the SIMULINK fuzzy controller. The output of the controller is applied to the voltage to current converter, which in turn drives the current to pressure converter. This action adjusts the flow rate of the HCL, thus the input to the controller is the pH reading of the waist (NAOH) which is compared against the required set point. At the same time the output obtained from the controller is used to control the valve. (1- convert the output voltage to current. 2- convert the current to pressure which drives the valve) and the valve in turn controls the percentage the valve opening to control the HCL flow rate. This output tends to maintain the pH value of the waist (NAOH) to a target value.

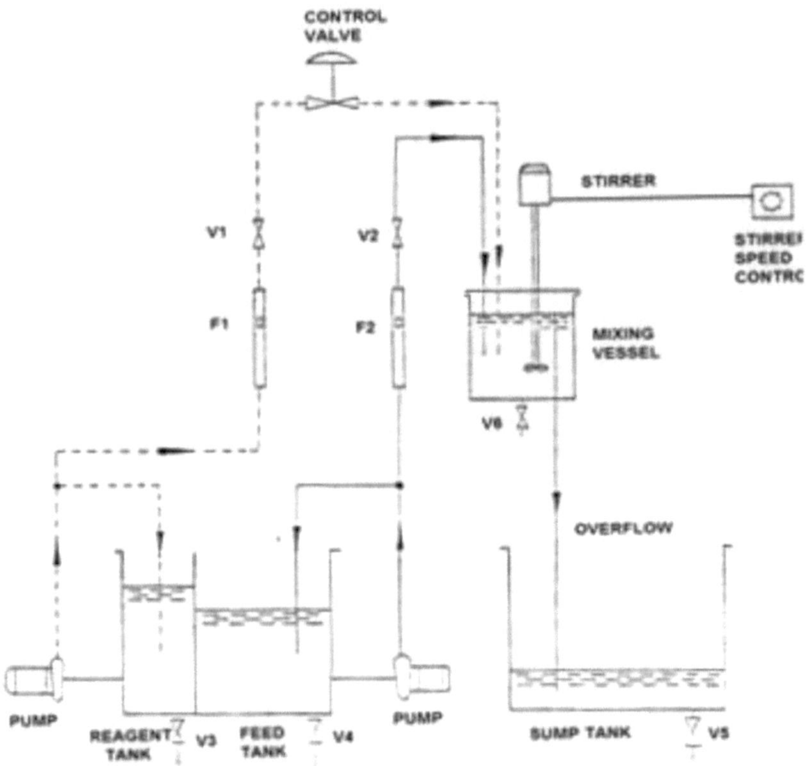

Figure 1. PI & D of the PH control system

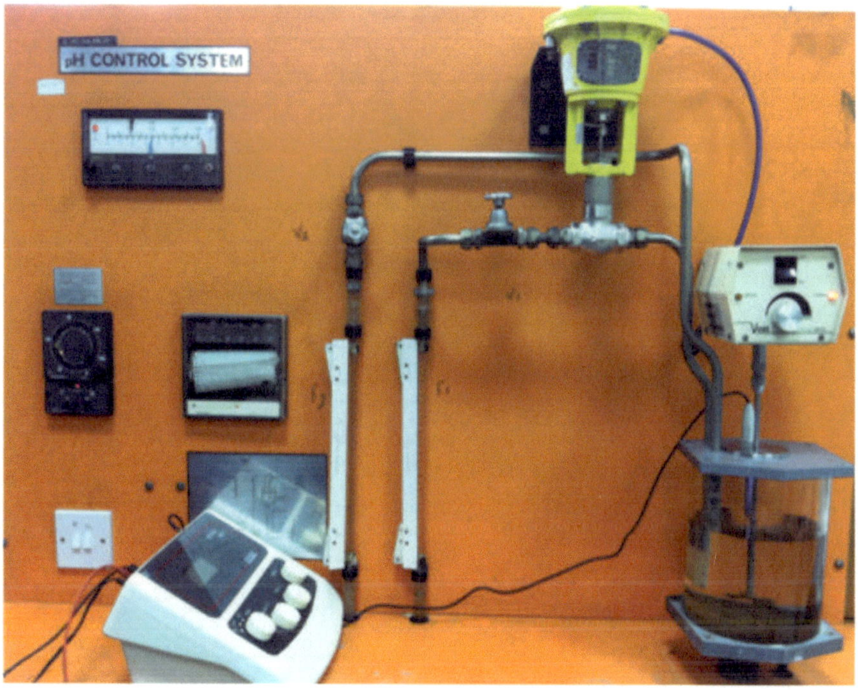

Figure 2. The PH control system

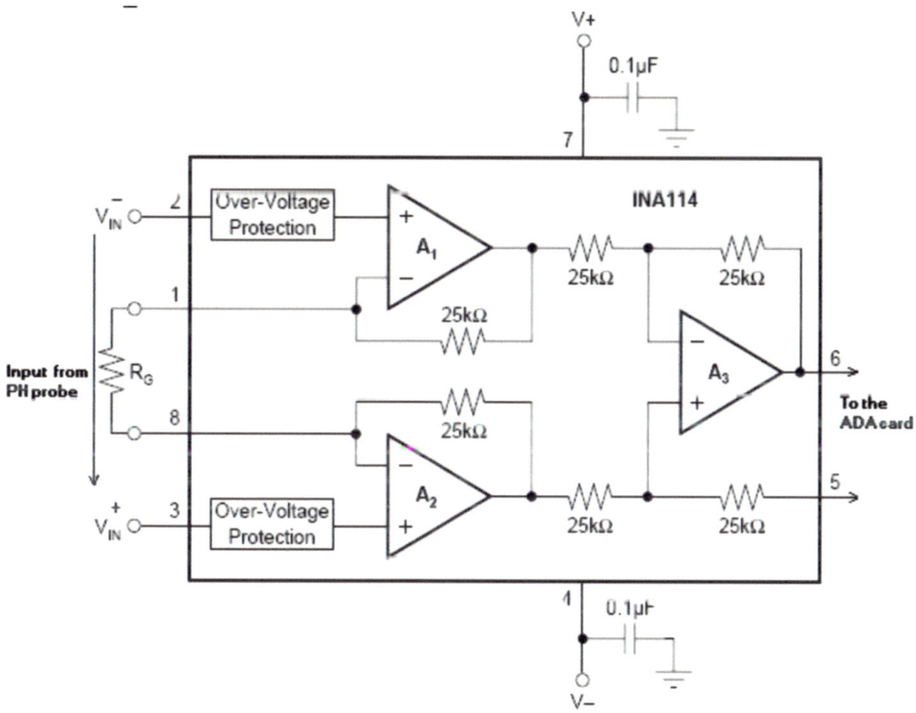

Figure 3. Signal amplifier of type INA114

2. Data acquisition

The National Instrument Data Acquisition Toolbox™ provides functions for connecting MATLAB® to data acquisition hardware. The toolbox supports a variety of DAQ hardware.

With it, one could configure data acquisition hardware to read data into MATLAB or SIMULINK for immediate analysis. One can also send out data over analogue or digital output channels provided by data acquisition hardware. Depending on which card is used, one can configure several channels, as input or output, digital or analogue. The card is interfaced to the process through a screw type connectors SCB-68 Quick Reference Label. Figure(4) shows the real connector board.

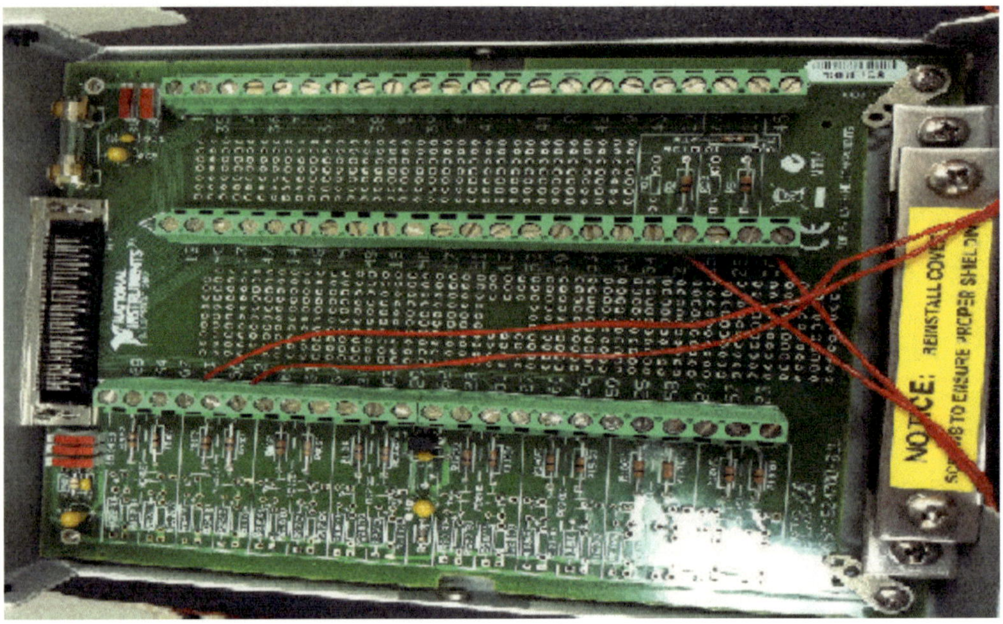

Figure 4. Interfacing connecting card to PCI 6221

Data Acquisition Toolbox lets you make a variety of measurements directly to MATLAB or SIMULINK, without the need to convert the data, so one can directly read the pH from the probe through the signal conditioning circuitry. In our case, only analogue input channel0 and output channel0 are used.

2.1. Voltage to current converter "V/I" circuit

A voltage to current converter is basically a circuit which delivers a constant current with a variable voltage. The voltage changes with the change of load. The circuit used here is the XTR105 from Texas Instruments, which converts the 0 to 5 volts to a 4 to 20 milliamperes through the setting of the gain resistor R_G. This is the perfect signal to drive the control valve. R_G, the gain resistor is given by:

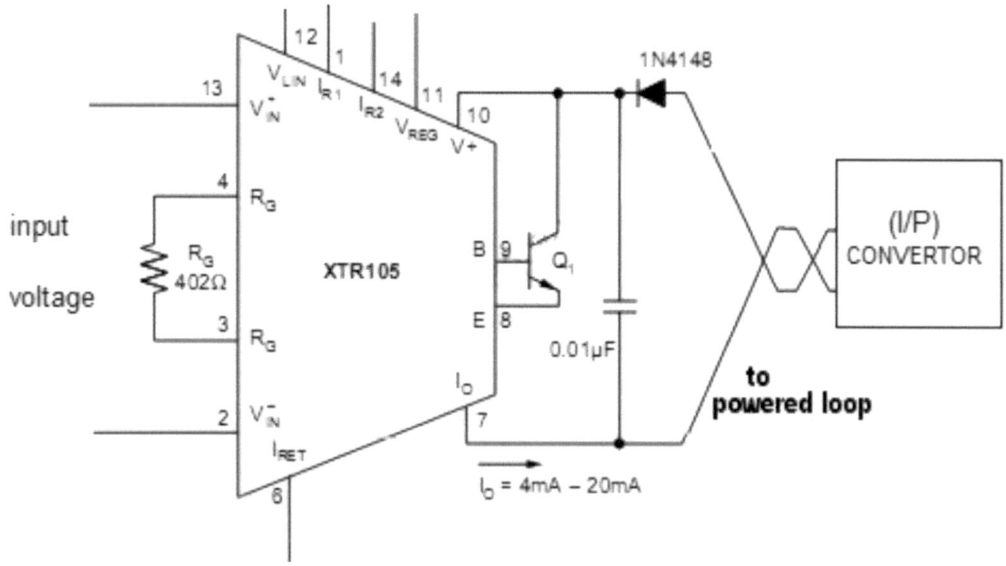

Figure 5. Voltage to current circuit

$$R_G = \frac{2R_1(R_2+R_Z)-4(R_2R_Z)}{R_2-R_1}$$

And the load current I_O is given by:

$$I_O = 4mA + V_{IN} * (40/R_G)$$

Where V_{IN} is the input differential voltage in volts applied between pin 13 and pin2 and R_G is the gain resistor in Ohms. It could be noticed that with no input voltage, the output current is 4mA. Transistor Q_1 conducts the majority of the signal dependent4-20mA loop current. Using an external transistor isolates the majority of the power dissipation from the precision input and reference circuitry of the XTR105, maintaining excellent accuracy.

The output current of the XTR105 is directly fed to current to pressure converter (I/P) which in turn controls the opening and closing of the control valve.

2.2. Control valve

The valve is opened and closed according to controlling action according to the added desirable HCL solution. The calibration of the valve opening to the input current is shown in table(1); and Its behavior is shown in figure (6). It is clear that the relationship is linear.

Voltage	Current	Opening Valve (%)
0	4	100 %
1	7.2	80 %
2	10.4	60 %
3	13.6	40 %
4	16.8	20 %
5	20	0 %

Table 1. Output current in terms of input voltage

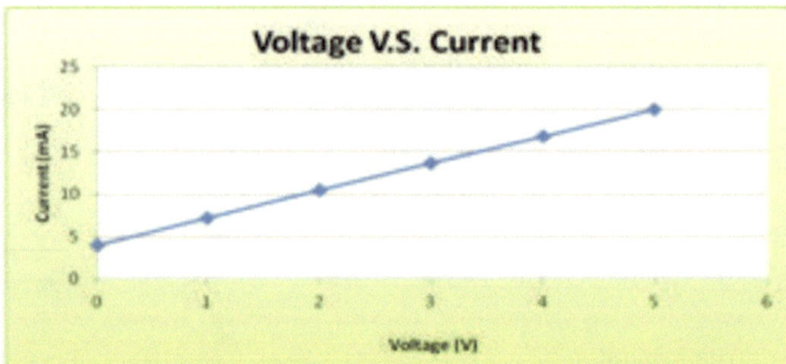

Figure 6. Voltage to current conversion

2.3. Software

After discussing the hardware required and the calibration of the equipment, we devote the rest of this chapter to the software development. In this project we develop the pH control strategy using SIMULINK fuzzy controller and compare it with the PID controller using different currently available tuning techniques. But before going into that, let's see first the behaviour of the pH.

2.3.1. PH behaviour

Before the fuzzy controller is discussed, a major problem inherent into the pH is highlighted. That is the severe non linearity inherent into the pH . Though the PH changes linearly from zero to two and from nine to fourteen, but unfortunately, it oscillates between two and nine. This is known as titration curve. This renders any linear control strategy inefficient, including the three term controller. This explains the complete deficiency of the PID controller, no matter how small is the gain chosen. (See figure (7)).

Figure (8) shows online titration curve. When reagent flow first starts, the pH only changes minimally. This results in a low process gain. But, as more reagent is added, the pH suddenly changes by a large amount, resulting in a high process gain. This titration curve shows the degree of difficulty of controlling the pH . So due to this high non linearity, it is extremely difficult to use any linear technique to control the pH . This has open the door to look at other alternatives, one of them is the use of fuzzy control as it was mentioned earlier.

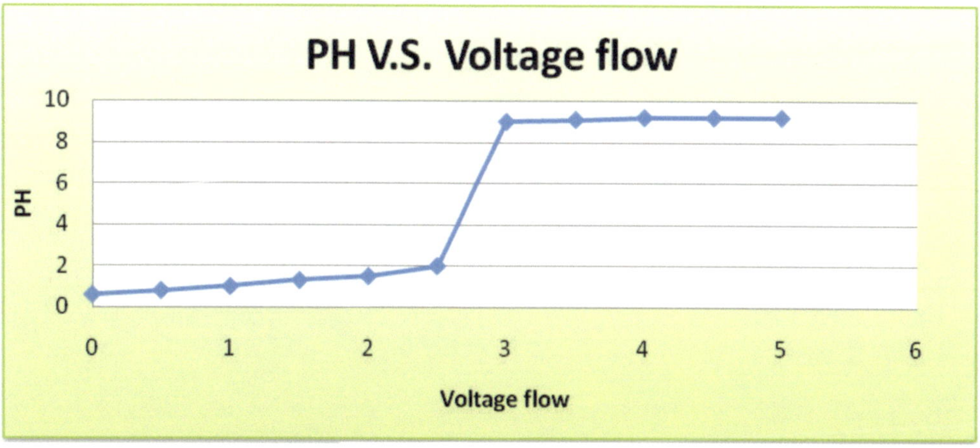

Figure 7. Titration curve obtained experimentally

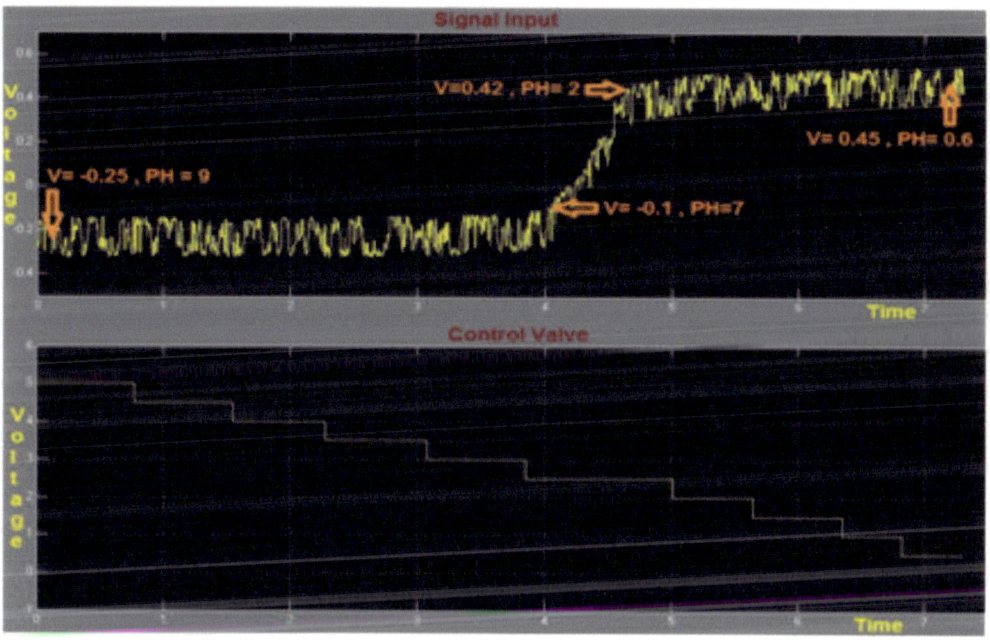

Figure 8. Titration curve test online

It is also worth mentioning here that the relationship between the output voltage and the pH is linear, where a cretin voltage corresponds to a cretin pH level. This is shown in figure (9). This curve has been obtained experimentally. It shows that the output voltage varies between -0.5V and 0.5V for full pH swing. The relationship is given by:

$$Y = -0.0126X + 7.0119$$

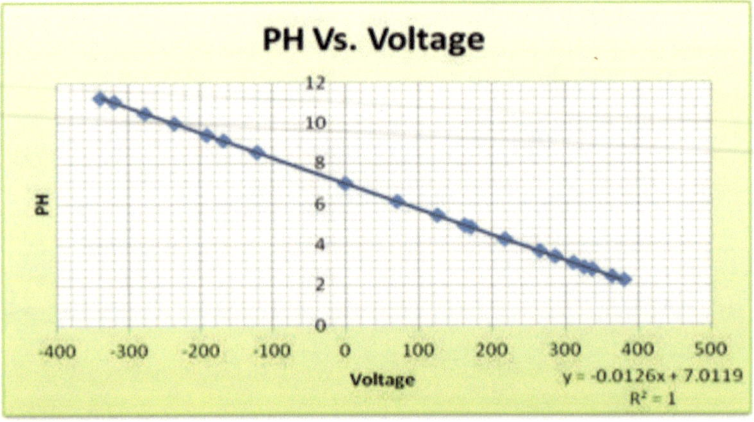

Figure 9. PH vs. Voltage

2.4. MATLAB

MATLAB is a high-performance language for technical computing where it integrates computation, visualization, and programming in an easy-to-use environment where problems and solutions are expressed in familiar mathematical notation. In Addition it has easy to use drivers to interface applications through standard interfacing cards such as NI-PCI 6221 card. On top of that the MATLAB SIMULINK platform incorporates a wide range of signal processing tools. This include easy to use fuzzy control block sets.

2.5. Configuration of acquisition card NI-PCI 6221 using SIMULINK

After MATLAB is installed, together with NI DAQmax drivers, the data acquisition card is configured. This is summarized as shown in the following slides. (Refer to figures from 10.a to 10.c).

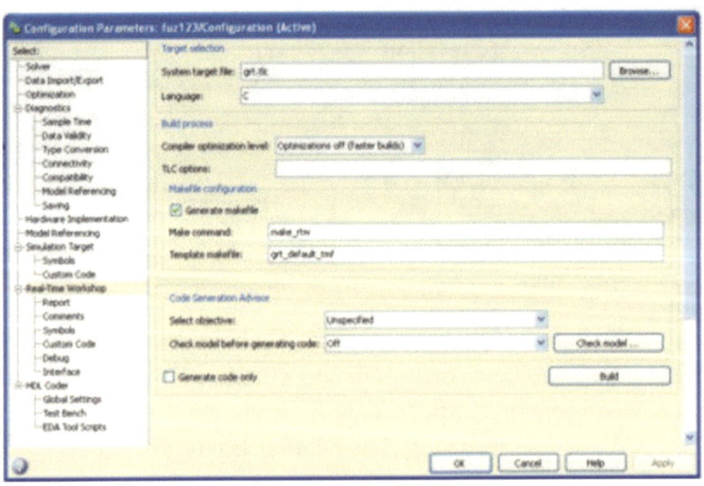

A

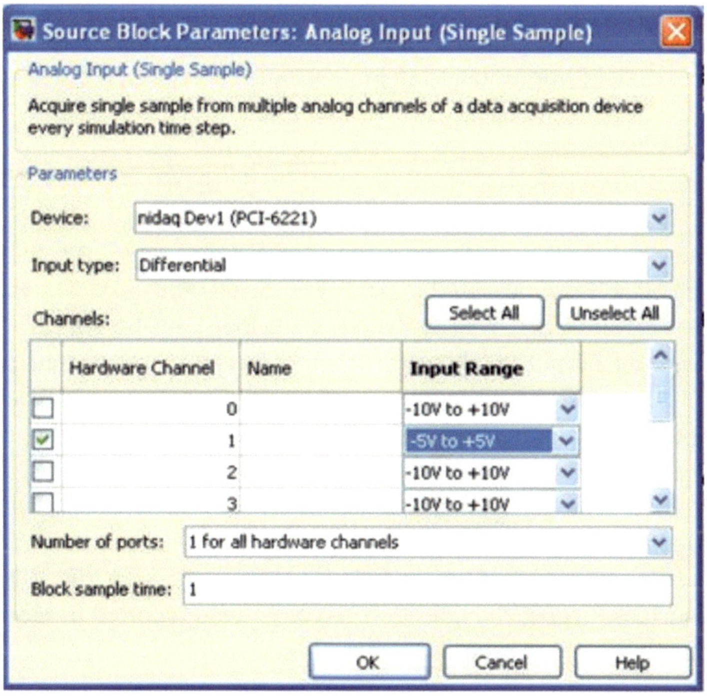

B

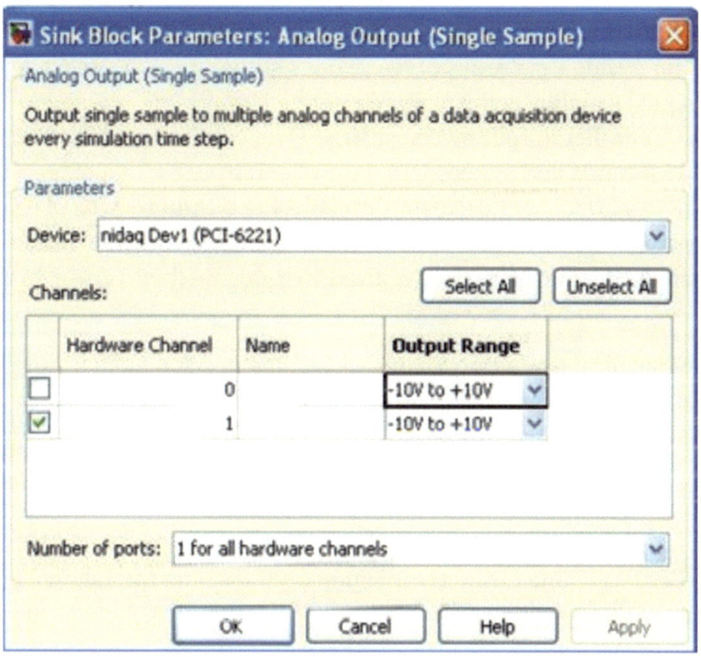

C

Figure 10. a: configure Parameters, b: configure input, c: configure output

2.5.1. PID control

The three term controller (Proportional-Integral-Deriavative) is well defined as:

$$u(t) = K\left(e(t) + \frac{1}{T_i}\int_0^t e(\tau)d\tau + T_d \frac{de(t)}{dt} \right)$$

Where e(t) is the error signal, which represents the difference between the desired value known a set point SP and the measured variable MV. So e(t) =SP –MV. T_i is the integral time constant, T_d is the derivative time constant and K is the loop gain. So basically the role of this controller is to force the output to follow the input, as fast as the parameters permit, with an acceptable overshoot and without steady state error. This requires very careful choosing of the parameters (known as tuning) with a considerable gain without driving the system into non stability. The PID controller algorithm is used for the control of almost all loops in the process industries, and is also the basis for many advanced control algorithms and strategies. In order for control loops to work properly, the PID loop must be properly tuned. Standard methods for tuning loops and criteria for judging the loop tuning have been used for many years such as Ziegler, though new ones have been reported in recent literature to be used on modern digital control systems.

2.5.1.1. PID tuning

- When one wants to find the parameters of PID control he needs first the transfer function for his process. G. Shinskey and J. Gerry (6) have described the pH tuning technique after setting up a series of restrictions summarized as follows((figure(11)):
- Let the pH signal stabilize in the manual mode
- Decrease the controller output by about 10%
- Wait about 15 seconds and increase the controller output by 20% of its original value.
- Wait another 15 seconds and decrease the controller output by 10% of its original value.
- Let the pH signal re-stabilize. Analysis software processes the data to optimal PID tuning variables. It could be clearly noticed that this method is near to an offline more than to online technique.

This results in the smallest upset due to the fact that the net change in the amount of reagent added is zero.

From figure(11), by reducing the control valve opening by 30% (step response), the pH response could be represented by a first order system plus a time delay model (FOPTD). The following could be noticed:

For this First Order Plus Time Delay (FOPTD) model, we note the following characteristics of its step response:

1. The response attains 63.2% of its final response at time, $t = \tau + \theta$.
2. The line drawn tangent to the response at maximum slope ($t = \theta$) intersects the y/KM=1 line at ($t = \tau + \theta$).

3. The step response is essentially complete at t=5τ. In other words, the settling time is t_s=5τ.

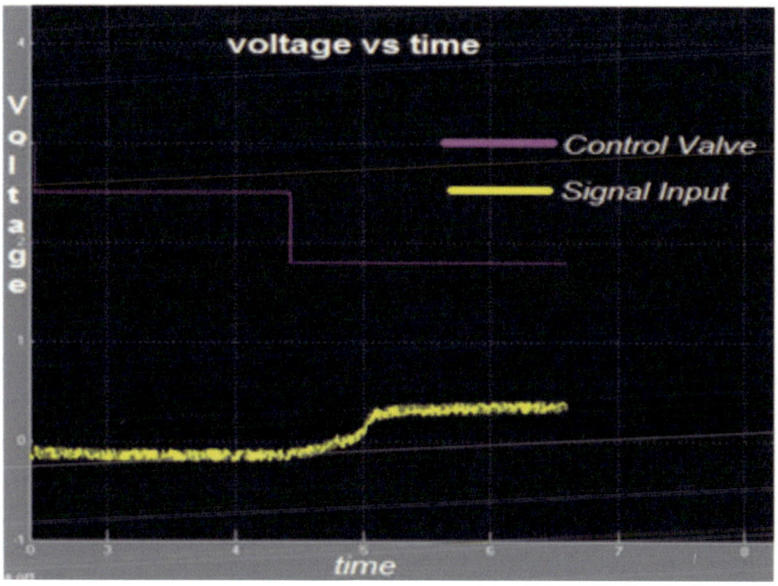

Figure 11. PH with small disturbance on the flow rate

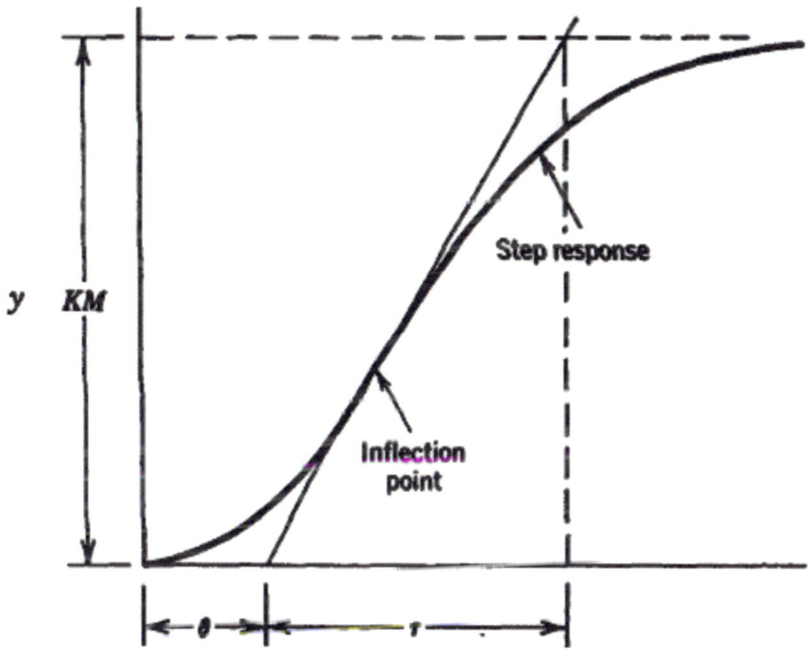

Figure 12. Graphical analysis of to pbtain parameters of FOPTD

From pervious steps the transfer function is:

$$TF = \frac{-4.67e^{-0.916}}{0.4s+1}$$

In the next section, we discuss different tuning methods to determine the PID parameters.

2.5.1.2. ITEA technique

Integral of the time –weighted absolute error (ITEA). ITEA criterion penalizes errors that persist for long period of time.

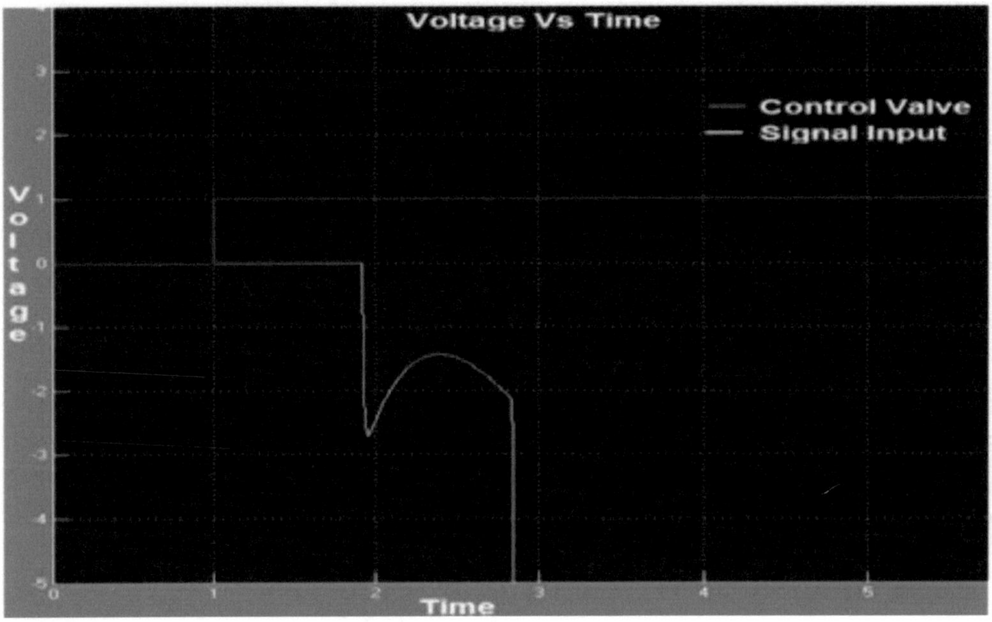

Figure 13. ITEA SIMULINK test

PROPOTIONAL:

$$Y = A\left(\frac{\theta}{\tau}\right)^{B} = 0.965\left(\frac{0.916}{0.41}\right)^{-0.85} = 0.488$$

$$KK_C = 0.488$$

$$K_C = \frac{0.488}{0.476} = -0.1045$$

INTEGRAL:

$$Y = A + B\left(\frac{\theta}{\tau}\right) = 0.796 - 0.1465\left(\frac{0.916}{0.41}\right) = 0.469$$

$$\frac{\tau}{\tau_I} = 0.469\tau_I = \frac{0.4}{0.469} = 0.876$$

DERIVATIVE:

$$Y = A\left(\frac{\theta}{\tau}\right)^{B} = 0.308\left(\frac{0.916}{0.41}\right)^{0.929} = 0.649$$

$$\frac{\tau_D}{\tau} = 0.649$$

$$\tau_D = 0.649 \times 0.4 = 0.267$$

PID equation is:

$$PID = -0.1045\left(1 + \frac{1}{0.876s} + 0.267s\right)$$

2.5.1.3. IMC

More comprehensive method model design is the Integral Model Control (IMC).

PROPOTIONAL:

$$KK_C = \frac{\tau + \frac{\theta}{2}}{\tau_c + \frac{\theta}{2}} = \frac{0.4 + \frac{0.916}{2}}{1 + \frac{0.916}{2}} = 0.588$$

$$K_C = \frac{0.858}{-4.67} = -0.126$$

INTEGRAL:

$$\tau_I = \tau + \frac{\theta}{2} = 0.4 + \frac{0.916}{2} = 0.858$$

DERIVATIVE:

$$\tau_D = \frac{\tau\theta}{2\tau + \theta} = \frac{0.4 \times 0.916}{2 \times 0.4 + 0.916} - 0.2136$$

PID equation is:

$$PID = -0.126\left(1 + \frac{1}{0.858s} + 0.2136s\right)$$

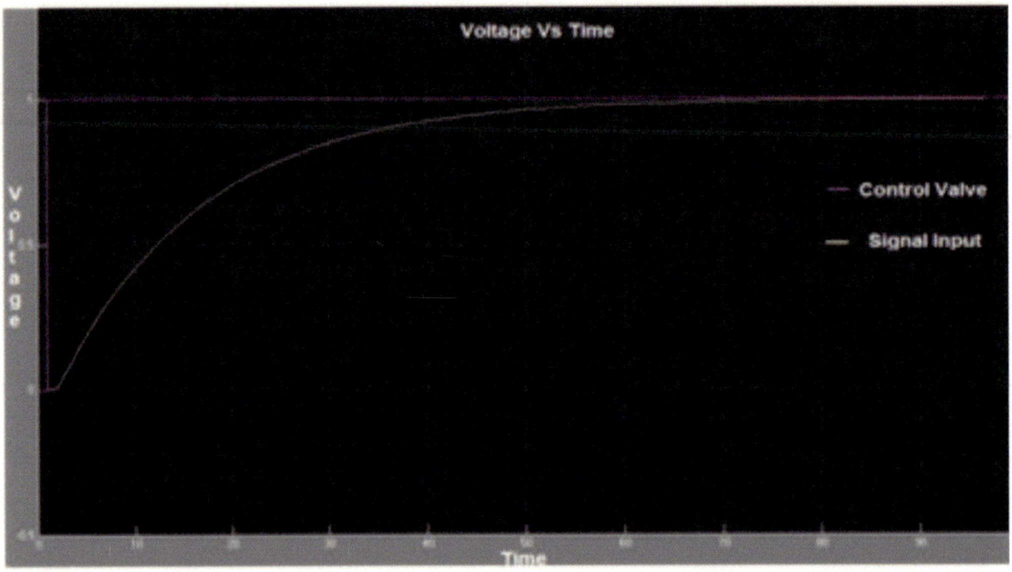

Figure 14. IMC using SIMULINK test

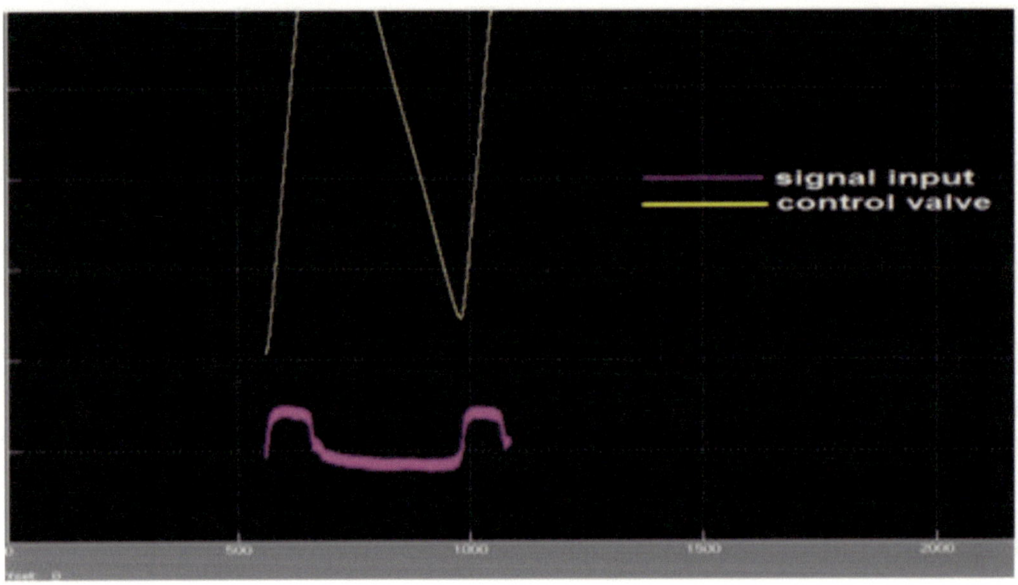

Figure 15. IMC online test

2.5.1.4. Self tuning

The SIMULINK is used to tune the PID (refer to figure(16)). The following transfer function of the self tuning PID was obtained:

$$PID = -0.16877\left(1 + \frac{1}{-0.1335s} + 0.0329s\right)$$

From figure (13-18), it could be easily noticed that neither technique, when applied to the real system, they have all produced unsatisfactory result. In fact, the best one is the self tuning, yet it has produced an oscillatory response. This has been reflected on the valve opening. (Refer to fig(18)). This is due to the fact that there are three gains. So any small change in the input results in a large change in the output. And this explains the behaviour of the titration curve. This has lead us to look for a non linear controller to control the system. This is the fuzzy logic control which is the subject of the next part.

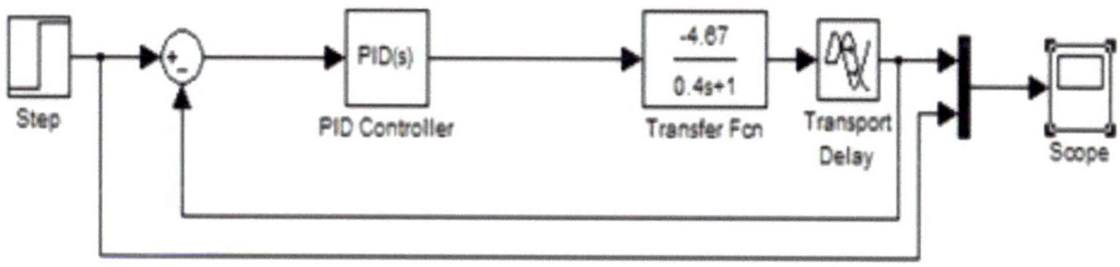

Figure 16. SIMULINK for Parameters

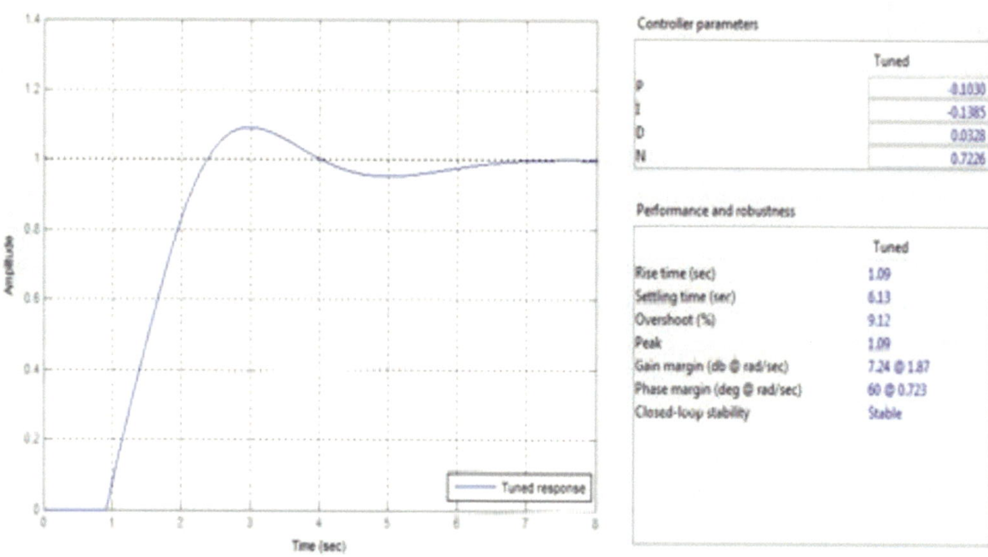

Figure 17. Self turning using SIMULINK simulation

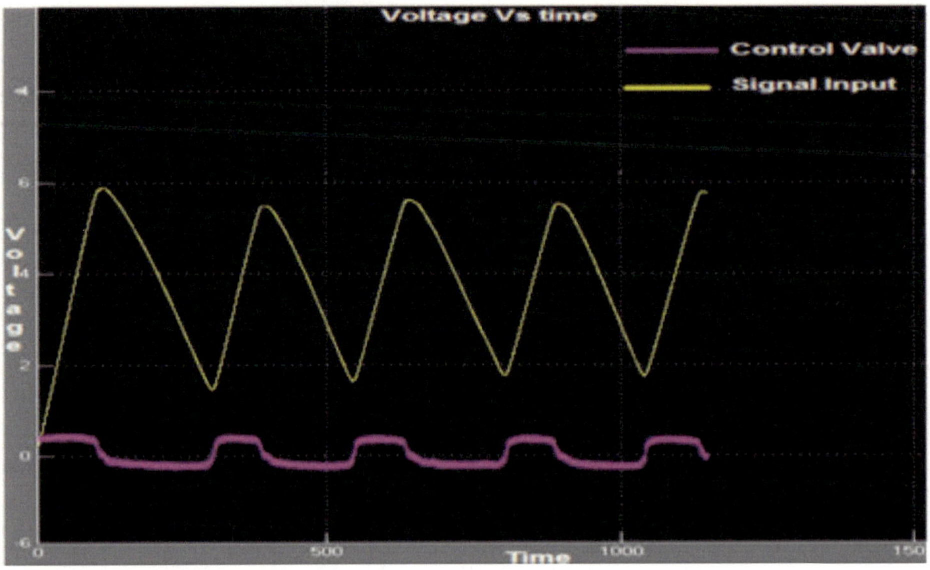

Figure 18. Self tunung online test

3. Fuzzy logic control

3.1. Introduction

In any standard book on fuzzy control, fuzzy logic control is defined to be a practical alternative for a variety of challenging control applications since it provides a convenient method for constructing non-linear controllers via the use of heuristic information. Since heuristic information may come from an operator who has acted as "a human in the loop" controller for a process. In the fuzzy control design methodology, a set of rules on how to control the process is written down and then it is incorporated into a fuzzy controller that emulates the decision making process of the human. In other cases, the heuristic information may come from a control engineer who has performed extensive mathematical modelling, analysis and development of control algorithms for a particular process. The ultimate objective of using fuzzy control is to provide a user-friendly formalism for representing and implementing the ideas we have about how to achieve high performance control. Apart from being a heavily used technology these days, fuzzy logic control is simple, effective and efficient. In this section, the structure, working and design of a fuzzy controller is discussed in detail through an in-depth analysis of the development and functioning of a fuzzy logic pH controller.

The general block diagram of a fuzzy controller is shown in figure (19). The controller is composed of four elements:

- A Rule Base
- An Inference Mechanism
- A Fuzzification Interface
- A Defuzzification Interface

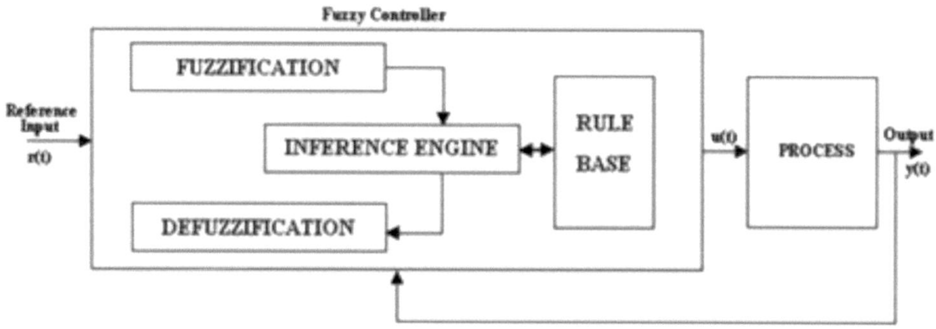

Figure 19. Fuzzy Controller

RULE BASE

This is a set of "If ……..then….." rules which contains a fuzzy logic quantification of the expert's linguistic description of how to achieve good control.

INFERENCE MECHANISM

This emulates the expert's decision making in interpreting and applying knowledge about how best to control the plant.

FUZZIFICATION INTERFACE

This converts controller inputs into information that the inference mechanism can easily use to activate and apply rules.

DEFUZZIFICATION INTERFACE

It converts controller inputs into information that the inference mechanism converts into actual inputs for the process.

SELECTION OF INPUTS AND OUTPUTS

It should be made sure that the controller will have the proper information available to be able to make good decisions and have proper control inputs to be able to steer the system in the directions needed to be able to achieve high-performance operation.

The fuzzy controller is to be designed to automate how a human expert who is successful at this task would control the system. Such a fuzzy controller can be successfully developed using high-level languages like C, Fortran, etc. Packages like MATLAB® also support Fuzzy Logic.

Fuzzy Sets and Membership Function

Given a linguistic variable Ui with a linguistic value Aij and membership function μ Aij(Ui) that maps Ui to [0,1], a 'fuzzy set is defined as

$$\text{Aij} = \left\{ \left(\text{Ui}, \mu \text{ Aij} \left(\text{Ui} \right) \right); \text{ Ui } \varepsilon \ \upsilon\text{i} \right\}$$

The above written concept can be clearly understood by going through the following example. Suppose we assign Ui="PH" and linguistic value A11="base", then A11 is a fuzzy set whose membership function describes the degree of certainty that the numeric value of the temperature, Ui ε υi, possesses the property characterized by A11. This is made even clearer by the fig (20).

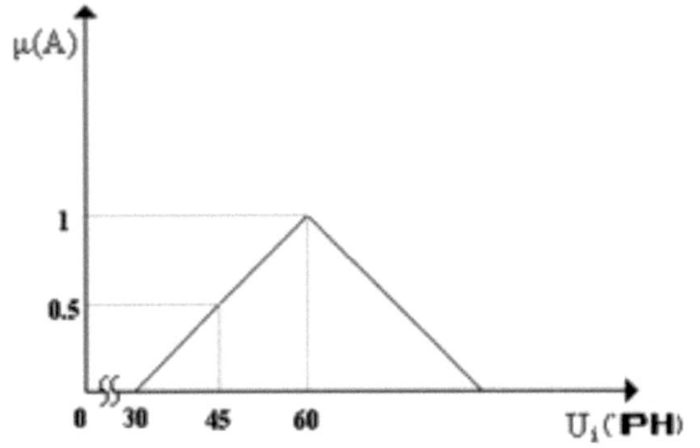

Figure 20. Membership Function

In the above example, the membership function chosen is of triangular form. There are many other membership functions like Gaussian, Trapezoidal, Sharp peak, Skewed etc. Depending on the application and choice of the designer, one could choose the shape which suits his application. Figure(21) shows just few.

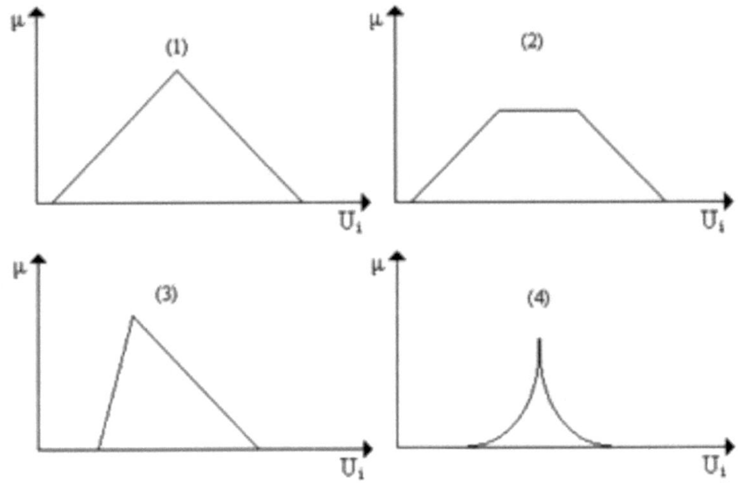

Figure 21. 1)Triangular, 2)Trapezoidal, 3)Skewed triangular, 4)Sharp peak

In the project in hand, the fuzzy controller has two inputs, the first one is the signal from the pH transmitter and the other one is the set point. The controller has a single output which goes through saturation, Quantizer and Weighted moving average. The saturation limiter is used to protect against over range of control valve and the Quantizer and Weighted moving average are used to hold the control valve(figure (22)).

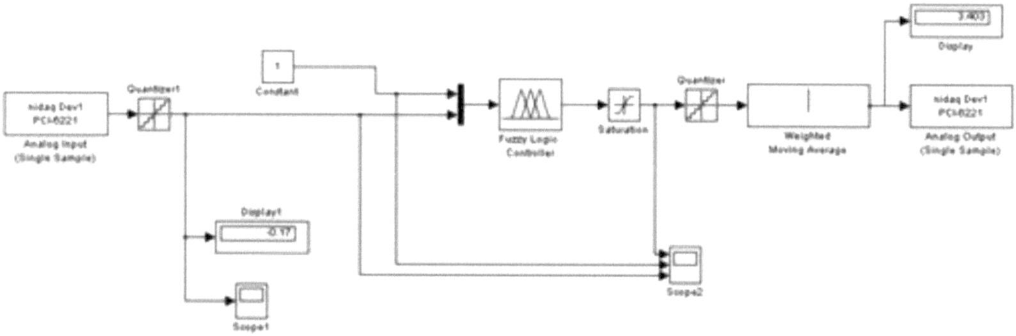

Figure 22. SIMULINK block diagram of the PH controller

A detailed description of the design and functioning of the fuzzy controller is given in the following section. The different sections in the fuzzy controller used in this PH controller are:

- Fuzzification Section
- Rule Base
- Inference Mechanism
- Defuzzification Section

3.2. Fuzzification section

The variables pH, set point and percentage of opening are selected for Fuzzification. In this section, the action performed is obtaining a value of the input variable and finding the numerical values of the membership function defined for that variable. As a result of Fuzzification, the situation currently sensed (input) is converted into such a form that, it can be used by the inference mechanism to trigger the rules in the rule base.

After fuzzification, the fuzzy sets obtained are labelled using the following term set, T={**LAD, MAD, SAD, SP, SAL, MAL, LAL, FULLY CLOSED, 3Q, M, Q, FULLY OPEN ,** #**N0**, }

3.2.1. Input 1

- S.acid – large acidic
- M.acid = medium acidic
- L.acid = small acidic
- natural = set point PH
- L.alk = law alkaline
- M.alk = medium alkaline
- S alk. = strong alkaline

3.2.2. Input 2

- #N0(1-14 PH) = SETPOINT

3.2.3. Output

- Fullyopen = 100% opening
- 3Q = 75% opening
- M = 50% opening
- Q = 25% opening
- Fullyclose =0% opening

The membership functions of input variables PH and output variable percentage opening shown in figures 23, 24 and 25 respectively. μ_i is the membership function of output. In the current work the triangular membership is chosen.

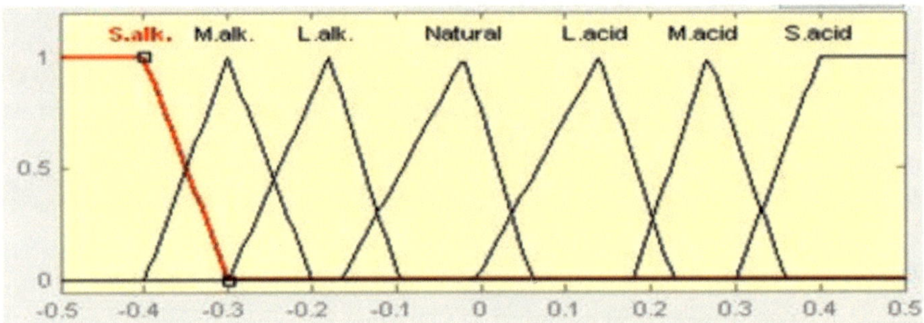

Figure 23. membership Function of input of PH

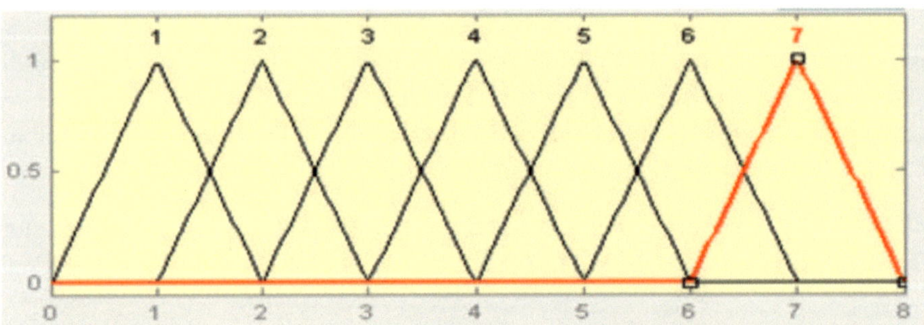

Figure 24. Membership Function of set point (input2)

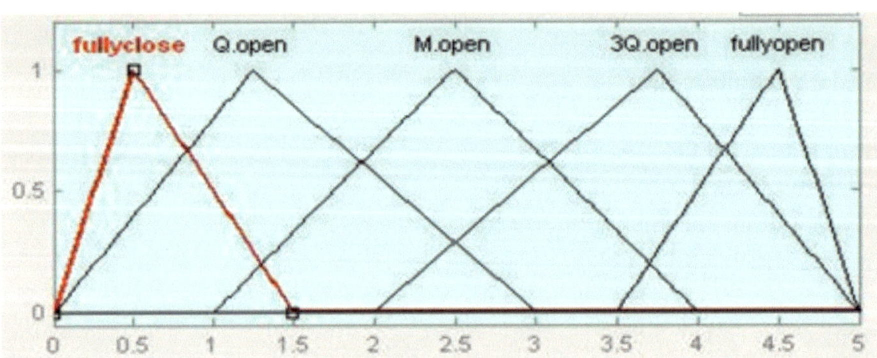

Figure 25. Membership Function of output pH

As a result of Fuzzification, we get the names of fuzzy sets to which the input belongs and to what extent they belong to these sets, their membership functions.

3.3. Rule base

Rule base stores the different rules that are to be fired or used according to the inputs. These rules are either gathered from experienced human operator or from careful study of existing PH systems. The base represents the control strategy employed in the PH control.

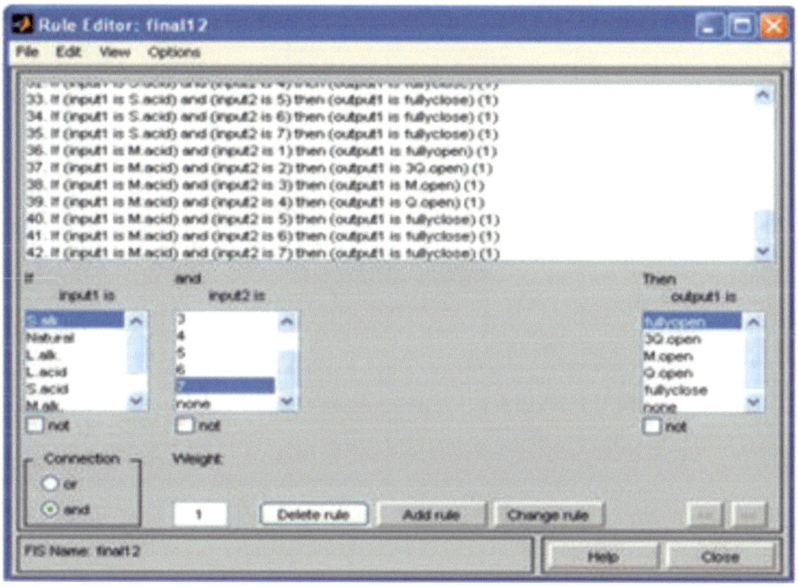

Figure 26. Fuzzy rule

The rules used have been designed based on the expertise. Those rules are carefully chosen to make the system as accurate as possible. They have been entered through the MATLAB editor. After rigoreous testing and trial, near optimum rules have been obtained. Table above gives the set of fuzzy action rules related to the application in hand.

3.4. Inference mechanism

The inference mechanism employed in pH control is based on individual rule firing. In this scheme, contribution of each rule is evaluated and overall decision is derived.

During inference process, each rule that is fired by a crisp value of pH is summed up after giving the weightages decided by the fuzzification unit. This weightage is called degree of satisfaction (DoS). DoS is decided by the fuzzification module.

In the inference mechanism, depending on which all fuzzy sets the input belongs to, the corresponding rules are fired. This describes the functioning of the three out of four blocks in the fuzzy controller. Now comes the defuzzification section.

	PH 1	PH 2	PH 3	PH 4	PH 5	PH 6	PH 7
S.acid	FULLY CLOSE	Q OPEN	M OPEN	M OPEN	M OPEN	3Q OPEN	3Q OPEN
M.acid	FULLY OPEN	3Q OPEN	M OPEN	Q OPEN	FULLY CLOSE	FULLY CLOSE	FULLY CLOSE
L.acid	FULLY OPEN	FULLY OPEN	3Q OPEN	M OPEN	M OPEN	FULLY CLOSE	FULLY CLOSE
Natural	M OPEN	M OPEN	Q OPEN	Q OPEN	Q OPEN	Q OPEN	FULLY CLOSE
L.alk.	3Q OPEN	3Q OPEN	3Q OPEN	3Q OPEN	M OPEN	M OPEN	M OPEN
M.alk.	3Q OPEN	3Q OPEN	3Q OPEN	M OPEN	M OPEN	Q OPEN	Q OPEN
S. .alk.	FULLY OPEN	FULLY OPEN	FULLY OPEN	FULLY OPEN	3Q OPEN	3Q OPEN	3Q OPEN

The Rule Base

3.5. Defuzzification

This section performs the task of converting the output of inference mechanism, the rules that are fired, and the DoS given by the fuzzification module into a signal to the control valve. For this, it uses "height defuzzification" which is computationally simple and fast.

4. Discussion and conclusions

Finally, let's conclude this chapter by discussing a real online example where it is required to bring the pH from 3 to 7. This example was chosen to show how the fuzzy controller has successfully solved oscillation due to titration curve mentioned earlier. Using all the expertise to set the membership functions as well as the rules, plus a fine tuning process, the membership function is shown in figure (27), and the pH response is shown in figure (28). It is clear that the pH has been brought from 3 to 7 in a very smooth manner. This value has been confirmed through the pH meter reading.

As a general conclusion, due to non linearity inherent in the chemical waist, the study presented here has shown that using fuzzy logic control is probably best suited to control the pH of industrial waist, despite the expertise required to fine tune the controller as well as the time required. It has also been shown that no matter how the linear controllers are tuned especially PID, including the many restrictions, plus the delays and settling time for each disturbance, their action was not satisfactory. Finally, the study has also shown that implementing the fuzzy control technique, by careful selection of memberships and setting the right rules, it is possible to bring any waist pH to neutrality smoothly in an acceptable time, regardless if the waist is strong base nature or strong acidic or not.

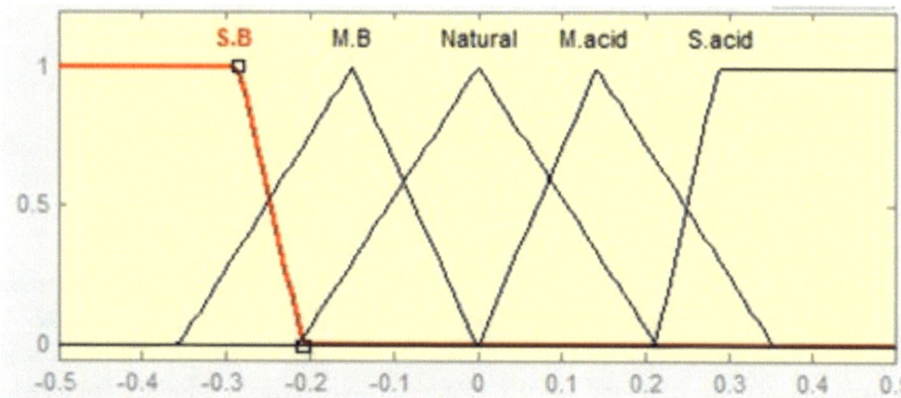

Figure 27. First membership function

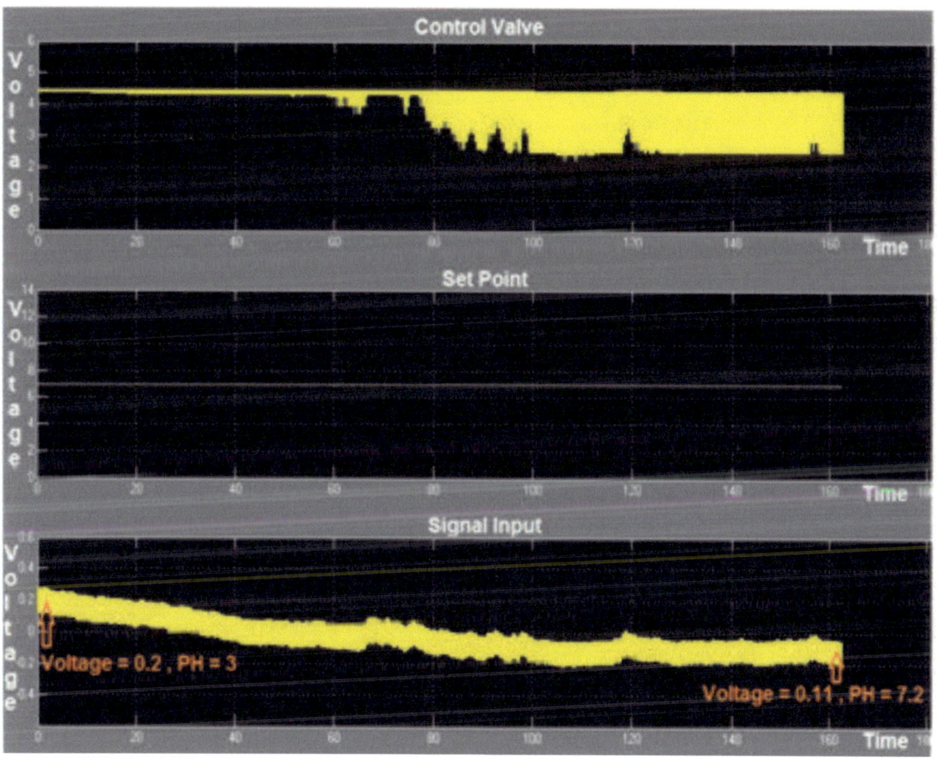

Figure 28. First test online at set point 7

Author details

Mostefa Ghassoul
Chemical Engineering, University of Bahrain, Bahrain

5. References

[1] faolex.fao.org/docs/pdf/mal13278.pdf.
[2] www.skcct.com/EQA%20Summary.htm.
[3] http://aabi.tripod.com/notes/modeling_control_neutralization_wswater.pdf.
[4] https://boc.com.au/boc_sp/.../BOC_Carbon_Dioxide_for_Water.pdf.
[5] Zadeh, L., Fuzzy sets, Information Control 8, 338–353, 1965
[6] http://www.mathworks.com/products/daq/index.html.
[7] www.eusflat.org/publications/.../295_Nortcliffe.pdf.
[8] http://discuss.itacumens.com/index.pHp?topic=27299.0
[9] Salehi S., Shahrokhi M. And Nejati M. "Adaptive nonlinear control of pH neutralization process using fuzzy approximators" Control Engineering Practice 17, (2009) 1329-1337
[10] Duan S., Shi P., Feng H., DUan Z. And Mao Z. "An on-line Adaptive Control Based on DO/pH measurements and ANN Pattern Recognition Model For Fed-Batch Cultivation" Biochemical Engineering Journal, 30 (2006) 88-86

Chapter 12

An Advanced Transmission Line and Cable Model in Matlab for the Simulation of Power-System Transients

Octavio Ramos-Leaños, Jose Luis Naredo and Jose Alberto Gutierrez-Robles

Additional information is available at the end of the chapter

http://dx.doi.org/10.5772/48530

1. Introduction

The design and operation of power systems, as well as of power apparatuses, each time depends more on accurate simulations of Electromagnetic Transients (EMTs). Essential to this is to count with advanced models for representing power transmission lines and cables. Electromagnetic Transients Program (EMTP), the most used EMT software, offer various line models. Among these, the most important ones are: 1) the Constant Parameters Line model (CP), 2) the Frequency Dependent or J. Marti Line model (FD) and 3) the Universal Line Model (ULM). The CP Line model is the simplest and most efficient one from the computational point of view. Nevertheless, it tends to overestimate the transient phenomena as it considers that line parameters are constant. Thus, it is recommended only for modeling lines on zones distant to an area where a transient event occurs. The FD Line model (Marti, 1982) evaluates multi–conductor line propagation in the modal domain and takes into account effects due to frequency dependence of the line parameters. Nevertheless, as the transformations between the modal and the phase domains are approximated by real and constant matrices, its accuracy is limited to cases of aerial lines which are symmetric or nearly symmetric. The FD model tends to underestimate the transient phenomena. ULM (Morched et al., 1999) takes into account the full-frequency dependence of line parameters. ULM works directly in phase domain, thus avoiding simplifying assumptions regarding modal–to–phase transformations. So far it is the most general model, capable to accurately represent asymmetric aerial lines as well as underground cables.

The development of ULM is fairly recent and these authors consider that it still is a subject for further research and development. The authors believe also that researchers and power system analysts will benefit considerably from the full understanding of the theoretical basis of the ULM, as well as from counting with a ULM–type code that is easy to understand and modify. One problem with this is that the theoretical basis of ULM includes various topics and subjects that are scattered through several dozens of highly specialized papers. Another difficulty with this is the high complexity of the code for a ULM–type model. This chapter aims at providing a clear and complete description of the theoretical basis for this model. Although this description is intended for power engineers with an interest in electromagnetic transient phenomena, it can be of interest also to electronic engineers involved in the analysis and design of interconnects. The chapter includes as well the description of Matlab program of a ULM–type model, along with executable code and basic examples.

2. Multi-conductor transmission line analysis

2.1. Telegrapher's Equations

Electromagnetic behavior of transmission lines and cables is described by the Modified Telegrapher Equations, which in frequency domain are expressed as follows:

$$-\frac{d\mathbf{V}}{dx} = \mathbf{ZI}. \tag{1}$$

$$-\frac{d\mathbf{I}}{dx} = \mathbf{YV}. \tag{2}$$

where $\boldsymbol{V}$ is the vector of voltages, $\boldsymbol{I}$ is the vector of currents, $\boldsymbol{Z}$ and $\boldsymbol{Y}$ are the (N X N) per unit-length series impedance and shunt admitance matrix of a given line with N conductors, repectively. To solve equations (1) and (2), let equation (1) be first differentiated with respect to x; then, (2) is used to eliminate the vector of currents at the right hand side. The resulting expression is a second order matrix ODE involving only unknown voltages:

$$\frac{d^2\mathbf{V}}{dx^2} = \mathbf{ZYV}. \tag{3}$$

In the same way, equation (2) can be differentiated with respect to x and (1) can be used to eliminate the right-hand-side voltage term. The resulting expression involves unknown currents only:

$$\frac{d^2\mathbf{I}}{dx^2} = \mathbf{YZI}. \tag{4}$$

Solution to (4) is:

$$\mathbf{I}(x) = \mathbf{C}_1 e^{-\sqrt{\mathbf{YZ}}x} + \mathbf{C}_2 e^{\sqrt{\mathbf{YZ}}x}, \tag{5}$$

where C_1 and C_2 are vectors of integration constants determined by the line boundary conditions; that is, by the connections at the two line ends. In fact, the term including C_1 represents a vector of phase currents propagating forward (or in the positive x–direction) along the line, whereas the one with C_2 represents a backward (or negative x–direction) propagating vector of phase currents. Expression (5) is an extension of the well–known solution for the single–conductor line. Note that this extension involves the concept of matrix functions. This topic is explained at section 2.2.

The solution to (3) takes a form analogous to (5) and it is obtained conveniently from (5) and (2) as follows:

$$\mathbf{V}(x) = -\mathbf{Y}^{-1}\frac{d\mathbf{I}}{dx} = \mathbf{Z}_c\left[\mathbf{C}_1 e^{-\sqrt{\mathbf{YZ}}x} - \mathbf{C}_2 e^{\sqrt{\mathbf{YZ}}x}\right] \tag{6}$$

where, $\mathbf{Z}_C = \mathbf{Y}^{-1}\sqrt{\mathbf{YZ}}$ is the characteristic impedance matrix and its inverse is the characteristic admittance matrix $\mathbf{Y}_C = \sqrt{\mathbf{YZ}}\mathbf{Z}^{-1}$.

2.2. Modal analysis and matrix functions

Matrix functions needed for multi-conductor line analysis are extensions of analytic functions of a one–dimensional variable. Consider the following function and its Taylor expansion:

$$f(x) = \sum_{k=0}^{\infty} a_k x^k \tag{7}$$

The application of $f()$ to a square matrix A of order $N{\times}N$ as its argument is accomplished as follows:

$$f(\mathbf{A}) = \sum_{k=0}^{\infty} a_k \mathbf{A}^k, \tag{8}$$

where A^0 is equal to U, the $N{\times}N$ unit matrix. Consider now the case of a diagonal matrix:

$$\mathbf{\Lambda} = \begin{bmatrix} \lambda_1 & 0 & \dots & 0 \\ 0 & \lambda_2 & \dots & 0 \\ \vdots & \vdots & \ddots & \vdots \\ 0 & 0 & \dots & \lambda_N \end{bmatrix}. \tag{9}$$

Application of (8) to Λ yields:

$$f(\mathbf{\Lambda}) = \sum_{k=0}^{\infty} a_k \mathbf{\Lambda}^k = \begin{bmatrix} \sum_k a_k \lambda_1^k & 0 & \dots & 0 \\ 0 & \sum_k a_k \lambda_2^k & \dots & 0 \\ \vdots & \vdots & \ddots & \vdots \\ 0 & 0 & \dots & \sum_k a_k \lambda_N^k \end{bmatrix} = \begin{bmatrix} f(\lambda_1) & 0 & \dots & 0 \\ 0 & f(\lambda_2) & \dots & 0 \\ \vdots & \vdots & \ddots & \vdots \\ 0 & 0 & \dots & f(\lambda_N) \end{bmatrix} \tag{10}$$

This expression thus shows that the function of a diagonal matrix is simply obtained applying the one–dimensional form of the function to the matrix nonzero elements. Consider next the function of a diagonalizable matrix ***A***; that is,a matrix ***A*** that is similar to a diagonal one ***Λ***:

$$\mathbf{A} = \mathbf{M}\boldsymbol{\Lambda}\,\mathbf{M}^{-1}. \tag{11}$$

where ***M*** is the nonsingular matrix whose columns are the eigenvectors of ***A***, while ***Λ*** is the matrix whose diagonal elements are the eigenvalues of ***A*** (Strang, 1988).

Application of *f()* as in (10) to ***A*** yields:

$$f(\mathbf{A}) = \sum_{k=0}^{\infty} a_k (\mathbf{M}\boldsymbol{\Lambda}\mathbf{M}^{-1})^k = \mathbf{M}\left(\sum_{k=0}^{\infty} a_k \boldsymbol{\Lambda}^k\right)\mathbf{M}^{-1} = \mathbf{M}f(\boldsymbol{\Lambda})\mathbf{M}^{-1} \tag{12}$$

Therefore, the function of a diagonalizable matrix is conveniently obtained first by factoring ***A*** as in (10), then by applying the function to the diagonal elements of ***Λ*** and, finally, by performing the triple matrix product as in (11) and (12).

It is clear from subsection **2.1**, that multi-conductor line analysis requires evaluating matrix functions of ***YZ***. To do so, it is generally assumed that ***YZ*** always is diagonalizable (Wedephol, 1965; Dommel, 1992). Although there is a possibility for ***YZ*** not being diagonalizable (Brandao Faria, 1986), occurrences of this can be easily avoided when conducting practical analysis (Naredo, 1986).

3. Line modelling

Figure 1 shows the representation of a multi-conductor transmission line (or cable) of length *L*, with one of its ends at $x = 0$ and the other at $x = L$. Let $\boldsymbol{I_0}$ be the vector of phase currents being injected into the line and $\boldsymbol{V_0}$ the vector of phase voltages, both at $x=0$. In the same form, $\boldsymbol{I_L}$ and $\boldsymbol{V_L}$ represent the respective vectors of injected phase currents and of phase voltages at $x=L$. Line equation solutions (5) and (6) are applied to the line end at $x=0$:

$$\mathbf{I}_0 = \mathbf{I}(0) = \mathbf{C}_1 + \mathbf{C}_2 \tag{13}$$

$$\mathbf{V}_0 = \mathbf{V}(0) = \mathbf{Z}_C[\mathbf{C}_1 + \mathbf{C}_2]. \tag{14}$$

Then, the value of C_1 is determined from (13) and (14):

$$\mathbf{C}_1 = \frac{\mathbf{I}_0 + \mathbf{Y}_C\mathbf{V}_0}{2}. \tag{15}$$

Expressions (5) and (6) are applied to the line end conditions at $x = L$:

$$\mathbf{I}_L = -\mathbf{I}(L) = -\mathbf{C}_1 e^{-\sqrt{\mathbf{YZ}}L} - \mathbf{C}_2 e^{\sqrt{\mathbf{YZ}}L} \tag{16}$$

and

$$\mathbf{V}_L = \mathbf{V}(L) = \mathbf{Z}_C\left[\mathbf{C}_1 e^{-\sqrt{\mathbf{YZ}}L} - \mathbf{C}_2 e^{\sqrt{\mathbf{YZ}}L}\right]. \tag{17}$$

After doing this, (17) is pre–multiplied by $\boldsymbol{Y}_C$ and subtracted from (16) to obtain:

$$\mathbf{I}_L - \mathbf{Y}_C\mathbf{V}_L = -2\mathbf{C}_1 e^{-\sqrt{\mathbf{YZ}}L}. \tag{18}$$

Finally, (15) is introduced in (18) rendering

$$\mathbf{I}_L - \mathbf{Y}_C\mathbf{V}_L = -e^{-\sqrt{\mathbf{YZ}}L}\left[\mathbf{I}_0 + \mathbf{Y}_C\mathbf{V}_0\right] \tag{19}$$

Expression (19) establishes the relation among voltages and currents at the terminals of a multi-conductor line section. Its physical meaning follows from realizing that the term $\boldsymbol{I}_0+\boldsymbol{Y}_C\boldsymbol{V}_0$ at its right hand side represents a traveling wave of currents leaving the line end at $x = 0$ and propagating in the positive x–axis direction, whereas $\boldsymbol{I}_L-\boldsymbol{Y}_C\boldsymbol{V}_L$ at the left hand side is the traveling wave of currents leaving the line end at $x = L$.

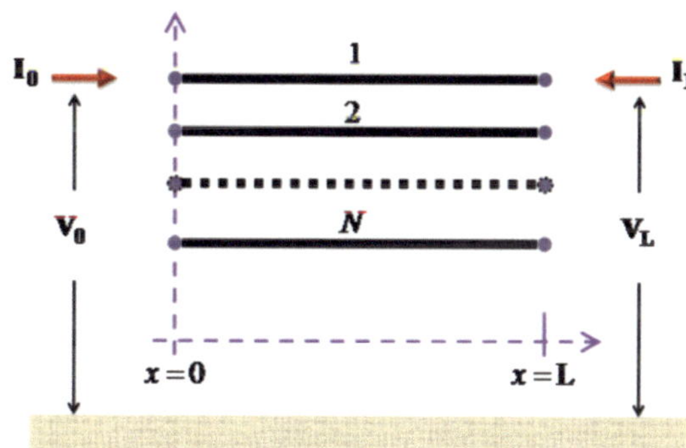

Figure 1. Multi-conductor line segment of length L.

By a similar process as the previous one for deriving (19), it is possible to show also that the following relation holds as line equation solutions (5) and (6) are applied to line end conditions at x=0:

$$\mathbf{I}_0 - \mathbf{Y}_C\mathbf{V}_0 = -e^{-\sqrt{\mathbf{YZ}}L}\left[\mathbf{I}_L + \mathbf{Y}_C\mathbf{V}_L\right] \tag{20}$$

Note however that this relation can also be obtained by simply exchanging at (19) sub–indexes $\boldsymbol{0}$ and $\boldsymbol{L}$. This exchange is justified by the input/output symmetry of the line section. Expressions (19) and (20) provide a very general mathematical model for a multi-conductor transmission line. This is a model based on traveling wave principles. Let (19) and (20) be rewritten as follows:

$$\mathbf{I}_L = \mathbf{I}_{sh,L} - \mathbf{I}_{aux,L} \tag{21}$$

where, $\boldsymbol{I}_{sh,L} = \boldsymbol{Y}_C\boldsymbol{V}_L$ is the shunt currents vector produced at terminal L by injected voltages $\boldsymbol{V}_L$. $\boldsymbol{I}_{aux,L} = \boldsymbol{H}\boldsymbol{I}_{rfl,0}$ is the auxiliary currents vector consisting of the reflected currents at terminal 0, $\boldsymbol{I}_{rfl,0}= \boldsymbol{I}_0+ \boldsymbol{Y}_C\boldsymbol{V}_0$ and the transfer functions matrix $\boldsymbol{H}=e^{-\sqrt{(\mathbf{YZ})}L}$.

In the same way as it has been previously done for (19), expression (20) is conveniently represented as follows:

$$\mathbf{I}_0 = \mathbf{I}_{sh,0} - \mathbf{I}_{aux,0} \tag{22}$$

with, $I_{sh,0} = Y_C V_0$, $I_{aux,0} = HI_{rfl,L}$,and $I_{rfl,L} = I_L + Y_C V_L$.

Expressions (21) and (22) constitute a traveling wave line model for the segment of length *L* depicted in figure 1. The former set of expressions represents end *L* of the line segment, while the latter set represents end *0*. A schematic representation for the whole model is provided by figure 2. Note that the coupling between the two line ends is through the auxiliary sources $I_{aux,0}$ and $I_{aux,L}$.

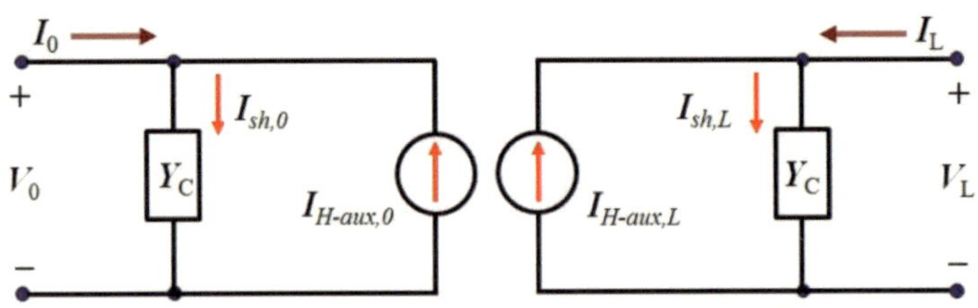

Figure 2. Frequency domain circuit representation of a multi-conductor line.

The line model defined by expressions (21) and (22) is in the frequency domain. Power system transient simulations require this model to be transformed to the time domain. For instance, the transformation of (21) to the time domain yields:

$$\mathbf{i}_0 = \mathbf{i}_{sh,0} - \mathbf{i}_{aux,0} \tag{23}$$

with

$$\mathbf{i}_{sh,0} = \mathbf{y}_C * \mathbf{v}_L \tag{24}$$

and

$$\mathbf{i}_{aux,0} = \mathbf{h} * \mathbf{i}_{rfl,0} \tag{25}$$

Note that at (23), (24), (25) the lowercase variables represent the time domain images of their uppercase counterparts at (22) and that the symbol * represents convolution. Reflected currents can be represented as

$$\mathbf{i}_{rfl,L} = 2\mathbf{i}_{sh,L} - \mathbf{i}_{aux,L} \tag{26}$$

Expressions (23)-(26) constitute a general traveling–wave based time–domain model for line end *0*. The model corresponding to the other end is obtained by interchanging sub–indexes "*0*" and "*L*" at (23)-(26). Equation (23) essentially provides the interface of the line–end *0* model to the nodal network solver that, for power system transient analysis, usually is the EMTP (Dommel, 1996). Expressions (24) and (25) require the performing of matrix–to–vector convolutions that are carried out conveniently by means of State–Space methods (Semlyen & Abdel-Rahman, 1982). State–Space equivalents of (23) and (24) arise naturally as ***Yc*** and ***H*** are represented by means of fitted rational functions (Semlyen & Dabuleanu, 1975).

4. Phase domain line model

Since rational fitting and model solutions are carried out directly in the phase domain, the model described here is said to be a phase domain line model. Rational fitting for this model is carried out using the Vector fitting (VF) tool (Gustavsen, 2008). In the case of ***Yc***, the whole fitting process is done in the phase domain, whereas for ***H*** initial poles and time delays are first calculated in the modal domain.

4.1. Rational approximation of Yc

The following rational representation has been proposed for ***Yc*** in (Marti, 1982) and (Morched et al., 1999):

$$\mathbf{Y}_C = \mathbf{G}_0 + \sum_{i=1}^{Ny} \frac{\mathbf{G}_i}{s - q_i} \tag{27}$$

where Ny is the fitting order, q_i represents the *i–th* fitting pole, $\boldsymbol{G}_i$ is the corresponding matrix of residues and $\boldsymbol{G}_0$ is a constant matrix obtained at the limit of ***Yc*** when $s=j\omega\rightarrow\infty$. Note in (27) that common poles are used for the fitting of all the elements of ***Yc*** obtained by fitting the matrix trace and finally the fitting of the matrices of residues $\boldsymbol{G}_i$ and of proportional terms $\boldsymbol{G}_0$ is done in the phase domain. Section 7 provides an overview of the VF procedure and further information is to be found in (Gustavsen & Semlyen, 1999) and (Gustavsen, 2008).

4.2. Rational approximation of H

Rational fitting of transfer matrix ***H*** is substantially more involving than the one of ***Yc*** above. To attain an accurate and compact (low order) rational representation for ***H*** it is essential to factor out all terms involving time delays (Marti, 1982). The major difficulty here is that its elements could involve a mix of up to N different delay terms due to the multimode propagation on an N–conductor line (Wedepohl, 1965). Separation of matrix ***H*** into single-delay terms is obtained from the following modal factorization (Wedepohl, 1965):

$$\mathbf{H} = \mathbf{M}\mathbf{H}_m\mathbf{M}^{-1} \tag{28}$$

where $\boldsymbol{H}_m$ is a diagonal matrix of the form

$$\mathbf{H}_m = diag[e^{-\gamma_1 L}, e^{-\gamma_2 L}, \ldots, e^{-\gamma_N L}] \tag{29}$$

and $\gamma=\sqrt{(YZ)}$ is the propagation constant of a conductor line (Wedepohl, 1965). As the triple product in (28) is performed by partitioning $\boldsymbol{M}$ in columns and $\boldsymbol{M}^{-1}$ in rows, the following expression is derived:

$$\mathbf{H} = \sum_{i=1}^{N} \mathbf{D}_i e^{-\gamma_i L} \tag{30}$$

where D_i is the rank–1 matrix obtained from pre–multiplying the *i–th* column of M by the *i–th* row of M^{-1}. Matrix D_i in fact is an idempotent (Marcano & Marti, 1997). The exponential factors at (30) can be further decomposed as follows:

$$e^{-\gamma_i L} = e^{-\tilde{\gamma}_i L} e^{-s\tau_i}; i = 1,2,\ldots,N \tag{31}$$

where $\exp\left(-\tilde{\gamma}_i L\right)$ is a minimum phase–shift function (Bode, 1945) and τ_i is the time delay associated to the velocity of the *i–th* mode. Hence:

$$\mathbf{H} = \sum_{i=1}^{N} \mathbf{D}_i e^{-\tilde{\gamma}_i L} e^{-s\tau_i} \tag{32}$$

The time delays in (32) can be initially estimated by applying Bode's relation for minimum phase complex functions (Bode, 1945) to the magnitudes of $exp(-\gamma_i L)$ in (30). Although (32) provides the desired separation of H as a sum of terms, each one involving a single delay factor, the following consideration is brought in for computational efficiency (Morched et al., 1999). Modal delays often occur in groups with almost identical values. Suppose that a number Ng of these groups can be formed and that (32) can be modified as follows:

$$\mathbf{H} = \sum_{k=1}^{Ng} \tilde{\mathbf{H}}_k e^{-s\tau_k} \tag{33}$$

where Ng is less or equal to N, and τ_k is the representative delay for the *k–th* group. Clearly, by comparing (33) and (32):

$$\tilde{\mathbf{H}}_k = \sum_{i=1}^{Ik} \mathbf{D}_i e^{-\tilde{\gamma}_i L} e^{-s\tau_i} k = 1,2,\ldots,Ng \tag{34}$$

with Ik being the number of modal terms in the *k–th* group. To determine whether a set of exponential factors can be grouped or not, the maximum phase shifts associated to their time delays are compared. The set is grouped into a single delay group if the phase shift differences are below a pre-established value typically chosen at 10° (Morched et al., 1999). Each term $\tilde{\mathbf{H}}_k$ at (34) can now be considered free of delay factors and can be fitted as follows:

$$\tilde{\mathbf{H}}_k = \sum_{i=1}^{Nh(k)} \frac{\mathbf{R}_{k,i}}{s - p_{k,i}} k = 1,2,\ldots,Ng \tag{35}$$

where $Nh(k)$ is the fitting order for the *k–th* term $\tilde{\mathbf{H}}_k$, $p_{k,i}$ represents its *i–th* fitting pole and $R_{k,i}$ is the corresponding matrix of residues. Note in (35) that common poles are being used to fit all elements at each matrix $\tilde{\mathbf{H}}_k$. As (35) is introduced in (33), the following rational form is obtained for H:

$$\mathbf{H} = \sum_{k=1}^{Ng} e^{-s\tau_k} \sum_{i=1}^{Nh(k)} \frac{\mathbf{R}_{k,i}}{s - p_{k,i}} \tag{36}$$

Initial estimates for the poles as well as time delays are obtained in the modal domain. The poles result from applying VF to the sum of the modal exponential factors conforming each delay group. The time delays proceed from Bode's formula as it has been said before. With all the poles $p_{k,i}$ and group delays τ_k of (36) being estimated in the modal domain, the overall fitting of $\boldsymbol{H}$ is completed in the phase domain by obtaining the matrices of residues $\boldsymbol{R}_{k,i}$ and recalculating the poles (Gustavsen & Nordstrom, 2008). The fitting parameters so obtained can be taken as final or can be further refined by an iterative process. VF is applied throughout all these fitting tasks and detailed descriptions of these processes can be found in (Gustavsen & Nordstrom, 2008; Gustavsen & Semlyen, 1999).

4.3. State-space analysis

With the rational representation of $\boldsymbol{Y_C}$ and $\boldsymbol{H}$ state–space forms to evaluate $\boldsymbol{i}_{sh,0}$ and $\boldsymbol{i}_{aux,0}$ arise naturally. Consider first the case of $\boldsymbol{i}_{sh,0}$. Taking (22) and introducing (27) yields

$$\mathbf{I}_{sh,0} = \mathbf{G}_0 \mathbf{V}_0 + \sum_{i=1}^{Ny} \mathbf{W}_i \tag{37}$$

where

$$\mathbf{W}_i = \frac{\mathbf{G}_i}{s - q_i} \mathbf{V}_0 \quad i = 1,2,\ldots,Ny \tag{38}$$

Application of the Inverse Laplace Transform to (37) and (38) gives the following continuous-time-state-space (CTSS) form for $\boldsymbol{i}_{sh,0}$:

$$\mathbf{i}_{sh,0} = \mathbf{G}_0 \mathbf{v}_0 + \sum_{i=1}^{Ny} \mathbf{w}_i \tag{39}$$

and

$$\frac{d\mathbf{w}_i}{dt} = q_i \mathbf{w}_i + \mathbf{G}_i \mathbf{v}_0 \quad i = 1,2,\ldots,Ny \tag{40}$$

The CTSS form to evaluate $\boldsymbol{i}_{aux,0}$, is derived now. On replacing the fitted form of $\boldsymbol{H}$ given by (36) into (22):

$$\mathbf{I}_{aux,0} = \sum_{k=1}^{Ng} \sum_{i=1}^{Nh(k)} \mathbf{X}_{k,i} \tag{41}$$

with

$$\mathbf{X}_{k,i} = \frac{R_{k,i}}{s - p_{k,i}} I_{rfl,L} e^{-s\tau_k}; \quad \begin{matrix} i = 1,2,\ldots,Ny \\ k = 1,2,\ldots,Ng \end{matrix} \tag{42}$$

Application of the Inverse Laplace Transform to (41) and (42) renders the following CTSS form:

$$\mathbf{i}_{aux,0} = \sum_{k=1}^{Ng} \sum_{i=1}^{Nh(k)} \mathbf{x}_{k,i} \tag{43}$$

$$\frac{d\mathbf{x}_{k,i}}{dt} = p_{k,i}\mathbf{x}_{k,i} + \mathbf{R}_{k,i}\mathbf{i}_{rfl,L}(t-\tau_k); \quad \begin{matrix} i = 1,2,\ldots,Ny \\ k = 1,2,\ldots,Ng \end{matrix} \tag{44}$$

CTSS forms (39), (40), (43) and (44) provide the basis for a phase domain line model (Morched et al., 1999). Nevertheless, their solution by a digital processor requires the conversion to discrete–time state–space (DTSS). This is accomplished by applying a numerical differentiation rule to the CTSS forms. The one adopted here is the mid–point rule of differentiation, which is equivalent to the trapezoidal integration rule extensively used in EMTP (Dommel, 1969, 1992). Application of this rule to (44) with Δt as the solution time step results in:

$$\mathbf{x}_{k,i} = a_{k,i}\mathbf{x}'_{k,i} + \tilde{\mathbf{R}}_{k,i}[\mathbf{i}_{rfl,L}(t-\tau_k) + \mathbf{i}'_{rfl,L}(t-\tau_k)]; \quad \begin{matrix} i = 1,2,\ldots,Ny \\ k = 1,2,\ldots,Ng \end{matrix} \tag{45}$$

where $a_{k,i}=(2+\Delta t p_{k,i})/\ (2-\Delta t p_{k,i})$ and $\tilde{\mathbf{R}}_{k,i}=(\Delta t \mathbf{R}_{k,i})/\ (2-\Delta t p_{k,i})$. $x_{k,i}$ are discrete-state variables and primed variables denote their value at one previous time step $x'_{k,i}= x_{k,i}(t\text{-}\Delta t)$. The discrete–time version of (43) maintains its original form:

$$\mathbf{i}_{aux,0} = \sum_{k=1}^{Ng} \sum_{i=1}^{Nh(k)} \mathbf{x}_{k,i}$$

Transmission line simulation of EMTs requires the use of time steps Δt smaller than any of the travel times τ_k in the line. Hence, (45) provides the update of state vectors $x_{k,i}$ using only past values of variables already available, either from initial conditions or from previous simulation time steps.

The differentiation mid–point rule is now applied to (40):

$$\mathbf{w}_i = a_i\mathbf{w}'_i + \tilde{\mathbf{G}}_i(v_0 + v'_0); i = 1,2,\ldots,Ny \tag{46}$$

where $a_i=(2+\Delta t q_i)/\ (2-\Delta t q_i)$ and $\tilde{\mathbf{G}}_i=(\Delta t \mathbf{G}_i)/\ (2-\Delta t q_i)$

Expression (46) is not a proper DTSS form, as w_i depends on the present–time value of v_0 which still is to be determined (Gustavsen & Mahseredjian, 2007). This problem is fixed here with the following redefinition of the state variable vector:

$$\mathbf{y}_i = (\tilde{\mathbf{G}}_i^{-1}\mathbf{w}_i - v_0) / (a_i + 1); i = 1,2,\ldots,Ny \tag{47}$$

Introducing (47) in (46) and (39) the following expressions are obtained:

$$\mathbf{y}_i = a_i\mathbf{y}'_i + v'_0; i = 1,2,\ldots,Ny \tag{48}$$

$$\mathbf{i}_{sh,0} = \mathbf{G}\mathbf{v}_0 + \mathbf{i}_{y-aux,0} \tag{49}$$

where

$$\mathbf{i}_{y-aux,0} = \sum_{i=1}^{Ny} \hat{\mathbf{G}}_i \mathbf{y}_i \ ; \ \hat{\mathbf{G}}_i = (a_i + 1)\tilde{\mathbf{G}}_i \ ; \ \mathbf{G} = \mathbf{G}_0 + \sum_{i=1}^{Ny} \tilde{\mathbf{G}}_i$$

Expression (48) is a proper DTSS form for the sequential evaluation of $i_{sh,0}$ at the phase domain line model.

Finally, the introduction of (43) and (49) in (23) results in:

$$\mathbf{i}_0 = \mathbf{G}\mathbf{v}_0 + \mathbf{i}_{hist,0} \tag{50}$$

with

$$\mathbf{i}_{hist,0} = \mathbf{i}_{y-aux,0} - \mathbf{i}_{aux,0} = \sum_{i=1}^{Ny} \hat{\mathbf{G}}_i \mathbf{y}_i - \sum_{k=1}^{Ng} \sum_{i=1}^{Nh(k)} x_{k,i}$$

Expression (50), along with (48) and (49), provides a discrete time–domain model for end *0* of the line segment at figure 1. The expressions for the model at end *L* are simply obtained by exchanging sub–indexes *0* and *L* at (48), (49) and (50). Obviously, state variables "y_i" and "$x_{k,i}$" of end *L* model are different from those of end *0*. Figure 3 provides a discrete–time circuit–model for the line segment of length *x*=*L*. This model is based on expression (50) and its companion for line end *L*. Note that the model consists of parallel arrangements of shunt conductances and auxiliary sources of currents comprising historic terms of ends (or nodes) *0* and *L*. Figure 3 model is thus in an appropriate form for computer code implementation. In this chapter, the Matlab environment has been chosen for this end.

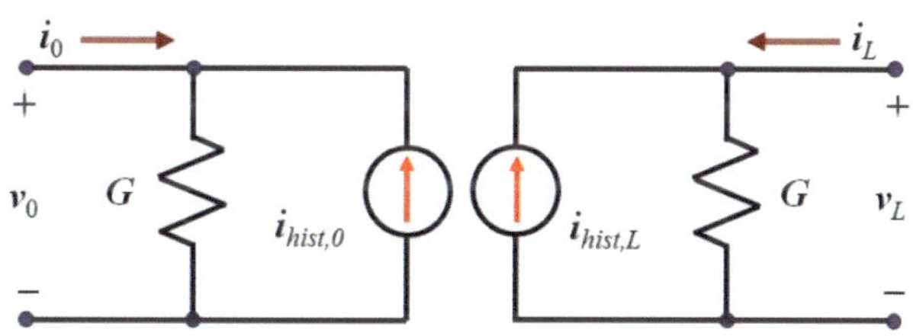

Figure 3. Discrete time domain circuit representation of a multi-conductor line.

5. Line model implementation in Matlab

The discrete–time line model depicted in figure 3 and defined by (50) has been programmed by these authors in Matlab as an M–code function (see Appendix). This function consists of two sub–blocks, one for each multi-conductor line end. This model is to be used with a nodal network solver, a complete explanation on the nodal solver can be found in (Dommel, 1969 & 1992). Expression (50) constitutes essentially the interface between the line model and the nodal solver. Each one of the two sub–blocks in the line model performs iteratively the six tasks that are described next for line–end *0* sub–block. Figure 4 provides the block diagram of the complete line/cable model, along with its interfacing with the nodal solver.

Step 1. State–variable and history–current values are assumed known, either from initial conditions or from previous simulation steps. These values are used by the nodal solver to determine line end (nodal) voltages v_0 and v_L.

Step 2. Shunt current due to the characteristic admittance of the line is calculated by (49) repeated here for convenience:

$$\mathbf{i}_{sh,0} = \mathbf{G}\mathbf{v}_0 + \mathbf{i}_{y-aux,0}$$

Step 3. Auxiliary current source value, due to the reflected traveling waves at the remote line end, is updated by (43):

$$\mathbf{i}_{aux,0} = \sum_{k=1}^{Ng} \sum_{i=1}^{Nh(k)} \mathbf{x}_{k,i}$$

Step 4. Vector of reflected currents at the local line–end (node) "$i_{rfl,0}$" is calculated for the present time by means of (26) being modified to suit line–end *0*:

$$\mathbf{i}_{rfl,0} = 2\mathbf{i}_{sh,0} - \mathbf{i}_{aux,0}$$

This vector is delivered to end *L* sub–block through a delay buffer. Although branch current vector i_0 usually is not explicitly required, it is conveniently evaluated here by (50):

$$\mathbf{i}_0 = \mathbf{G}\mathbf{v}_0 + \mathbf{i}_{hist,0}$$

Step 5. Internal states inside the line model are updated by (48) and (45):

$$\mathbf{y}_i = a_i \mathbf{y}'_i + v'_0$$

$$\mathbf{x}_{k,i} = a_{k,i}\mathbf{x}'_{k,i} + \tilde{\mathbf{R}}_{k,i}[\mathbf{i}_{rfl,L}(t-\tau_k) + \mathbf{i}'_{rfl,L}(t-\tau_k)]$$

Step 6. The vector of history currents for end (node) *0* is updated by means of (50) and the update is delivered to the nodal-network solver.

Steps ***1*** to ***6*** are iterated N_t times until $N_t\Delta t$ spans the total simulation time of interest.

5.1. Handling of line-travel delays

It follows from expressions (43) and (45) that the calculation of $i_{aux,0}$ requires the reflected currents vector $i_{rfl,L}$ being evaluated with various time delays τ_1, τ_2, …, τ_{Ng}. Recall that the delays are due to the travel time needed by a wave to travel from one line end to the other. Past values of $i_{rfl,L}$ can be obtained either from line initial conditions or from previous simulation steps; nevertheless, these values are given by samples regularly distributed Δt seconds apart. Since the involved travel times (or line delays) usually are not integer multiples of Δt, the required values of $i_{rfl,L}$ must be obtained by means of interpolations. The standard procedure for this is to interpolate linearly (Dommel, 1992) and this is adopted here.

Evaluation of the delayed values require a memory buffer spanning at least the largest travel time

$$\tau_{\max} = \max\{\tau_1, \tau_2, \ldots, \tau_{Ng}\}, \tag{51}$$

and buffer length N_b is calculated as follows:

$$N_b = \left\lfloor \frac{\tau_{\max}}{\Delta t} \right\rfloor + 1 \tag{52}$$

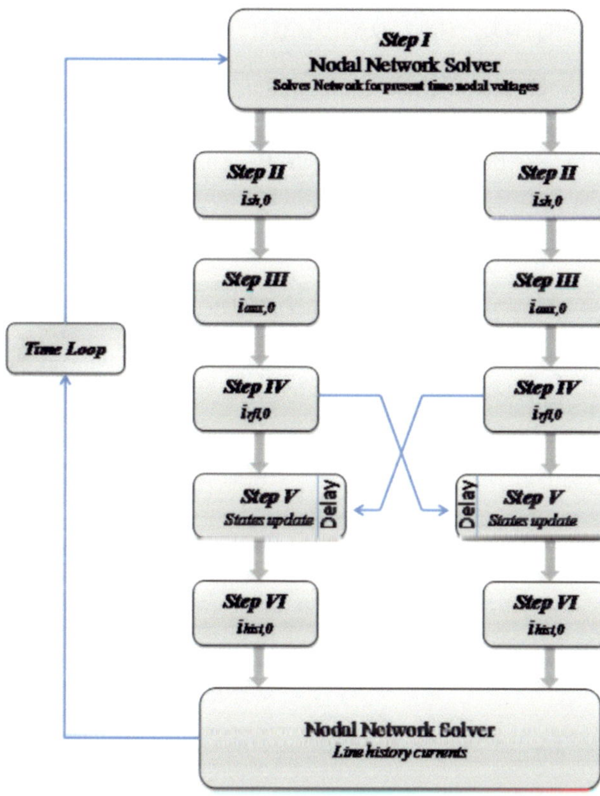

Figure 4. Line/Cable model's complete flow diagram.

If a propagation delay is an integer multiple of Δt, the required value of $\boldsymbol{i}_{rfl}$ can be readily retrieved from the memory buffer. This is illustrated by figure 5 where the simulation time step is Δt=*0.03* ms and the travel time is τ=0.10 ms. It can be seen that at simulation time *t= 0.24* ms the required history value at 0.09ms is available from the table.

On a multiphase system, nevertheless, it is highly improbable that all the propagation times can be made integer multiples of a single value of Δt suitable for transient simulations. Thus, the required values must be obtained through interpolation. Figure 6 illustrates this case, where a simulation time step Δt=*0.04* ms is assumed instead of the Δt=*0.03* ms one at figure 5. Notice that now the required history value, for a time delay of 0.09ms, is not readily available.

Suppose now that the required value $\mathbf{i}_{rfl}(t-\tau)$ is between the *k–th* and the *(k+1)–th* stored samples of $\mathbf{i}_{rfl}$. Let ζ be the fractional part of $\tau/\Delta t$, that can be obtained as follows:

$$\zeta = \frac{\tau}{\Delta t} - \left\lfloor \frac{\tau}{\Delta t} \right\rfloor, \tag{53}$$

with, $0 \leq \zeta < 1$. The estimated value of $\mathbf{i}_{rfl}(t-\tau)$ by linear interpolation is thus:

$$\mathbf{i}_{rfl,L}(t-\tau_k) \cong \mathbf{i}_{rfl,L}(t-r\Delta t) + \zeta[\mathbf{i}_{rfl,L}(t-k\Delta t) - \mathbf{i}_{rfl,L}(t-k\Delta t-\Delta t)]. \tag{54}$$

Figure 7 illustrates the memory buffer management, either for $\mathbf{i}_{rfl,0}$ or for $\mathbf{i}_{rfl,L}$. At the first simulation time step corresponding to time $t=0\times\Delta t$, calculated $\mathbf{i}_{rfl}$ is stored at memory *1*, and so on until step N_b which is the buffer size limit. Beyond this limit, memory cells *1*, *2*, *3* and on, are overwritten as figure. 7 shows, since their previously stored values are not needed any longer.

t(ms)	$i_{rfl,0}$	$i_{rfl,L}$
0.0	*	*
0.03	*	*
0.09	*	*
0.12	*	*
0.15	*	*
0.18	*	*
0.21	*	*
0.24	*	*

Figure 5. Interpolation scheme: Δt integer multiple.

t(ms)	$i_{rfl,0}$	$i_{rfl,L}$
0.0	*	*
0.04	*	*
0.08	*	*
0.12	*	*
0.16	*	*
0.20	*	*
0.24	*	*

Figure 6. Interpolation scheme: Δt non integer multiple.

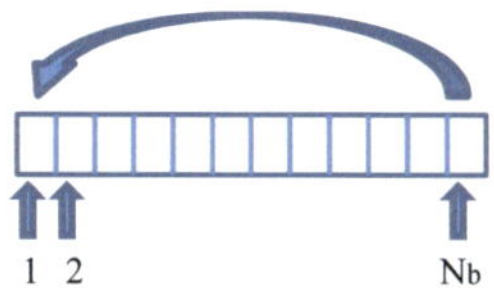

Figure 7. History buffer management.

Linear interpolation is an order 1 numerical procedure and the trapezoidal rule used for the rest of the line model is of order 2. The question arises as to whether or not the order 2 quadratic interpolation should be adopted instead. This has been investigated at (Gutierrez–Robles et al., 2011) and it has been found that the increase in accuracy is marginal.

6. Application examples

The simulation results presented as follows are obtained with the Matlab implementation of the model being described here. These results are compared against those from the phase domain line model in EMTP-RV. Two examples are presented next, first an aerial 9–conductor line and, finally, one for an underground cable. Also a basic m-code for the described phase domain line model is provided at the appendix. The code is given along with the companion routines to perform the first example presented in (Ramos- Leaños & Iracheta, 2010). The reader can readily modify the provided m-code for other applications of interest.

6.1. Aerial line case

The transversal geometry of this test case is shown in figure 8. Phase conductors are 1192.5 ASCR 54/19 and ground wires are 7 No 5 AWLD. This case consists of three coupled three–phase transmission lines. First line (or circuit 1) is composed of conductors 1 to 3, second line (or circuit 2) includes conductors 5 to 6 and the third line (or circuit 3) comprises conductors 7 to 9. The line length is 150 km. The test circuit is shown in figure 9 where the source is 169 kV, Y-grounded, source impedance is determined by its zero and positive sequence data in Ohms: R_0=2, R_1=1, X_0=22, X_1=15, and closing times are 0 s for phase a, 0.63 ms for phase b and 0.4 ms for phase c. The simulation time step is 5 μs.

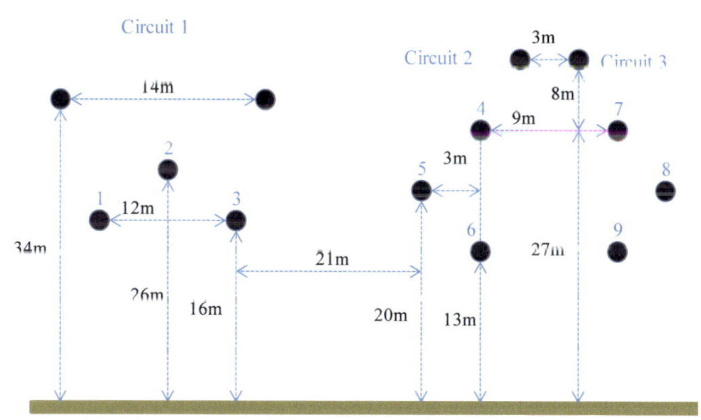

Figure 8. Aerial line transversal geometry.

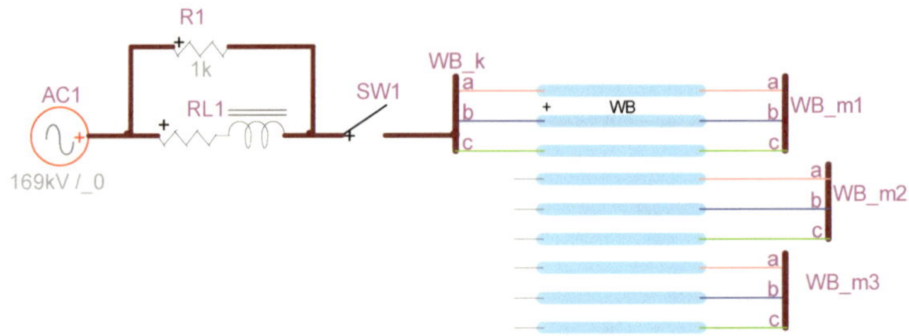

Figure 9. Test circuit for the case of a nine–conductor line.

Simulation results are presented in figure 10 where the receiving end voltage waveforms of circuit 1 are shown, those for phase a are in blue, those for phase b are in green and those for phase c are in red. A dashed line is used for waveforms obtained with EMTP-RV, while a solid line is used for the results with the line model in Matlab. Notice that the two sets of results overlap and not difference can be seen. Figure 10 provides the differences between the two sets of results. Note that the largest difference is around 3e-9.

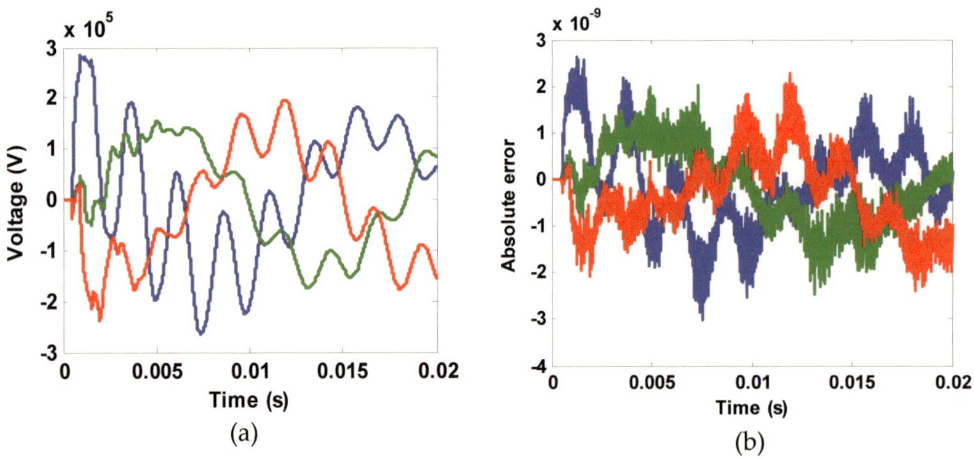

Figure 10. (a) Over voltages at receiving end for conductors 1, 2 and 3, (b) Differences between results with Matlab model and with EMTP–RV.

6.2. Underground cable case

The underground cable system used for this test consists of three single–phase coaxial cables, its transversal layout is shown in figure 11. The Corresponding connection diagram is provided in figure 12. Circuit parameters are given in table 1, the cable length is 6.67km and the time step used for the simulation is 1 μs. The applied excitation is by a 3ph 169kV ideal source.

The simulation experiment consists in the simultaneous energizing of the three cable cores. The results presented in figure 13 correspond to the core voltages at the far end. Phase a voltages are in blue, phase b voltages are in green and those for phase c are in red. A dashed line is used for the results obtained with EMTP-RV, while a solid line is used for the Matlab model results. Notice that both sets of results overlap and that no difference can be seen by eye. Figure 13 also shows the difference between the two sets of results which is around 4e-9. Compared to the 1.69e+5 amplitude of the excitation source, this difference shows the outstanding accuracy of the Matlab model.

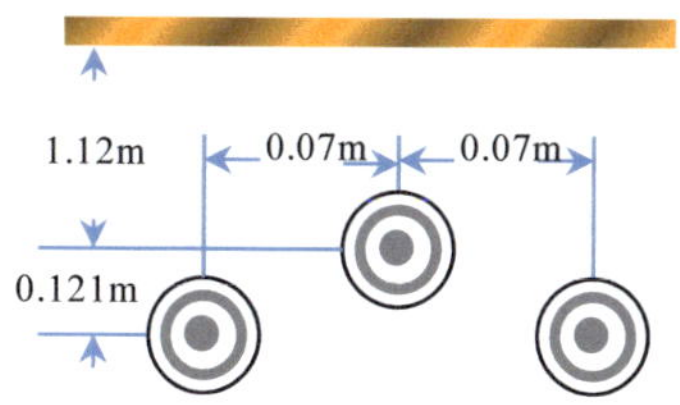

Figure 11. Cable layout.

Radius of inner solid conductor (m)	0.015
Resistivity nuclei/sheath (ohm/m)	4.25e-8/2.84e-8
Inner/Outer radius of sheath (m)	0.0258/0.0263
Relative permittivity of 1st & 2nd insulation	2.5

Table 1. Cable data.

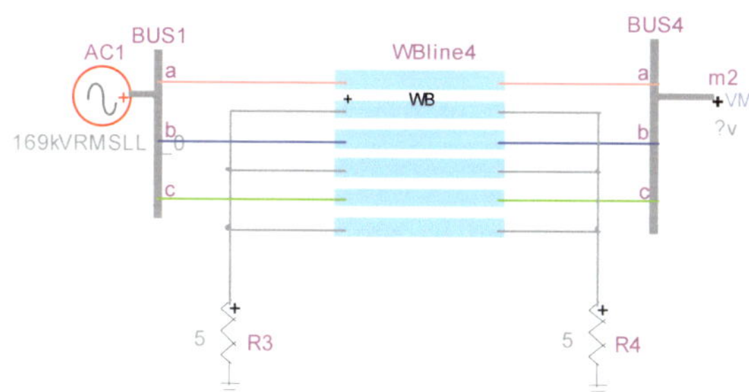

Figure 12. Cable test circuit

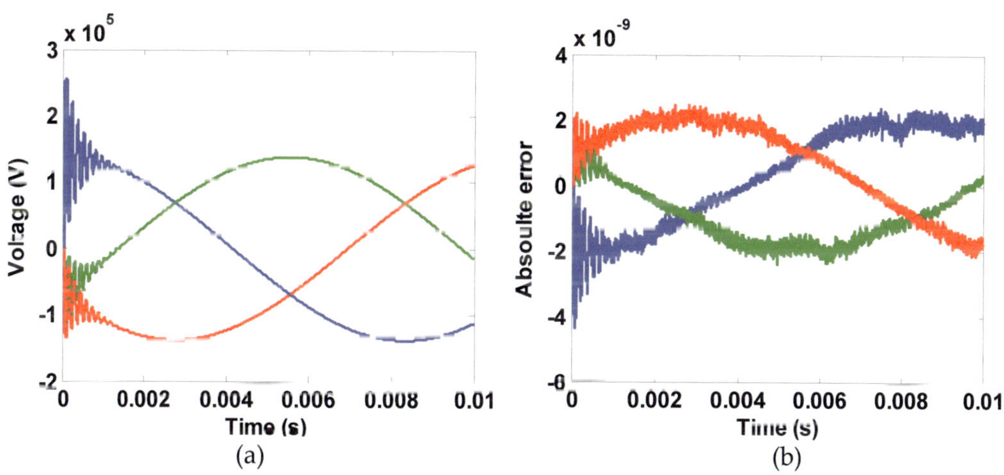

Figure 13. (a) Receivng end core voltages, (b) absolute error.

7. Vector fitting

The goal of VF is to approximate a complex function of frequency by means of a rational function; that is, a quotient of two polynomials of the frequency variable (Gustavsen & Semlyen, 1999). The function to be approximated could be trascendantal or could be specified by its values at a number of frequency points. The form of the approximation obtained with VF is that of a partial fraction expansion:

$$f(s) \cong \sum_{n=1}^{N} \frac{r_n}{s+\overline{p}_n} \tag{55}$$

VF estimates the system parameters by means of a two-stage linear least–squares procedure. First a set of initial poles for the partial fraction basis (55) is selected and relocated iteratively until a prescribed convergence criterion is attained. Then, convergence is tested by means of a second linear least–squares procedure in which the previously obtained poles are fixed and the corresponding residues are taken as the unknown parameters.

Consider the following relation (Gustavsen & Semlyen, 1999):

$$\sum_{n=1}^{N} \frac{\widehat{r}_n}{s+\overline{p}_n} \cong f(s)\left(1+\sum_{n=1}^{N} \frac{\tilde{r}_n}{s+\overline{p}_n}\right), \tag{56}$$

where, N is the order of approximation, $\overline{p}_n$ represents the unknown poles and $\hat{r}_n$ and $\tilde{r}_n$ are unknown residues. Poles are initialized by values distributed logarithmically over the frequency range of interest. Expression (56) is now rewritten as follows:

$$\sum_{n=1}^{N} \frac{\widehat{r}_n}{s+\overline{p}_n} - \left(\sum_{n=1}^{N} \frac{\tilde{r}_n}{s+\overline{p}_n}\right) f(s) \cong f(s). \tag{57}$$

An over–determined least squares equation–system is then obtained by evaluating (57) at a number M of specific frequencies, with $M>2N$:

$$\mathbf{Ax} = \mathbf{b}, \tag{58}$$

where $\boldsymbol{A}$ is the $M{\times}2N$ matrix whose elements depend on the poles, $\boldsymbol{x}$ is the $2N$–dimension vector of unknown residues and $\boldsymbol{b}$ is the M–dimension vector with the values of the function to be approximated (Gustavsen & Semlyen, 1999). Special care is taken to accommodate next to each other those complex–conjugate pairs of pole–residues that can arise. Expression (58) is solved through an iterative process represented symbolically as follows:

$$\mathbf{A}^{(j-1)}\mathbf{x}^{(j)} = \mathbf{b}, \tag{59}$$

were (j–1) and (j) represent super–indexes and j is the iteration index. $\boldsymbol{A}^{(0)}$ is obtained from the initial poles with logarithmic distribution over the frequency range of interest

(Gustavsen & Semlyen, 1999). As (59) is solved in the first iteration, a second step is to use the obtained residue values to recalculate new poles for the function to be fitted *f(s)*. This is accomplished by computing the eigenvalues of the following matrix *Q* (Gustavsen & Semlyen, 1999):

$$\mathbf{Q} = \mathbf{W} - \mathbf{g}\tilde{\mathbf{x}}^T, \tag{60}$$

where *W* is a diagonal matrix containing previously calculated poles $\overline{p}_n$, *g* is a vector of ones and $\tilde{\mathbf{x}}$ is a vector containing the $\tilde{r}$ terms only. The reason for using (60) is explained next. Let (56) be rewritten as follows:

$$\frac{\sum_{n=1}^{N} \frac{\hat{r}_n}{s+\overline{p}_n}}{\sum_{n=1}^{N} \frac{\tilde{r}_n}{s+\overline{p}_n} + 1} = \frac{\prod_{n=1}^{N'} (s+\hat{z}_n)}{\prod_{n=1}^{N} (s+\tilde{z}_n)} \cong f(s). \tag{61}$$

It is clear in (61) that the two polynomials containing the poles $\overline{p}_n$ cancel each other, and that the zeros $\tilde{z}_n$ become the poles of *f(s)*. Notice further that the denominator on the left–hand–side of (61) can be written as follows:

$$\sum_{n=1}^{N} \frac{\tilde{r}_n}{s+\overline{p}_n} + 1 = \frac{\prod_{n=1}^{N} (s+\tilde{z}_n)}{\prod_{n=1}^{N} (s+\overline{p}_n)}. \tag{62}$$

Zeros $\tilde{z}_n$ are then obtained by finding the roots of (Gustavsen & Semlyen, 1999)

$$\sum_{i=1}^{N} \left(\tilde{r}_i \prod_{n=1, n\neq i}^{N} (s+\overline{p}_n) \right) + \prod_{n=1}^{N} (s+\overline{p}_n) = 0, \tag{63}$$

which is equivalent to finding the eigenvalues of *Q* in (60) (Gustavsen & Semlyen, 1999).

The newly found set of poles is replaced in (55) to determine a new set of residues r_n. This is again an over–determined linear system. The fitting error is tested at this stage for each available sample of *f(s)*. If the error level is not acceptable, the new poles are used to restart the procedure as with (56). If the desired error limit is not met after a pre specified number of iterations, then, the order of approximation *N* is increased and the iterative procedure is restarted (Gustavsen & Semlyen, 1999).

Even in most cases where initial poles are not chosen adequately, VF is capable of finding a solution at the expense of more iterations. In some cases an iteration can produce unstable poles; these poles simply are flipped into the left–hand–side part of the complex plane (i.e., the stable part) and a new solution is searched (Gustavsen & Semlyen, 1999).

8. Conclusions

Proper design and operation of present-day power systems and apparatuses each time require accurate simulations of their electromagnetic transient performance. An important aspect of these simulations is the realistic representation of transmission lines by digital computer models. The ULM is the most general line model available today, mostly with EMTP–type programs. By being of relatively recent creation, this model still is a subject for substantial improvements in accuracy, stability and computational efficiency. It has been postulated in this work that, both, researchers and power system analysts will benefit considerably from the full understanding of the theoretical basis of the ULM, as well as from counting with a ULM–type code that is easy to understand and modify. It has been contended also that the best way to carry out ULM research and development is by providing a model version in an interpretive environment and Matlab has been the platform chosen for this. This chapter provides a comprehensive description of the theoretical basis of ULM, phase domain line model. In addition to this, full description of a ULM prototype in Matlab has been provided here, along with executable code and typical application examples.

Author details

Octavio Ramos-Leaños
École Polytechnique de Montréal, Canada

Jose Luis Naredo
Cinvestav-Guadalajara, Mexico

Jose Alberto Gutierrez-Robles
University of Guadalajara, Mexico

Appendix

CODE EXECUTION

The following code provides the line model described in the paper and it is embedded into an application example. It simulates the simultaneous energizing of a 150 km long aerial line. At the source side the three voltage sources have a 600 Ω Thevenin impedance. The program asks for the type of source (unit step or three phase sinusoids). At the load end the line is open. Figure 14 shows the geometry of the simulated line. Figure 15 shows the sending and receiving voltages for the unit step source, while Figure 16 shows the sending and receiving voltages for the sinusoidal source.

Note at Figure 15 that waveforms for phases A and C are equal and their plots are superposed. This is because the symmetry of the line and the excitation.

Main program

```
clear all
clc
 % m file to set line data
LineData
 % Per unit length parameters
[Zg,Zt,Zc,Yg,ZL,YL] = LineParameters(Mu,Eo,Rsu,Geom,Ncon,Ns,w);
 % Modal Parameters
for k=1:Ns
   [Yc(:,:,k),Vm(k,:),Hm(k,:)] = ABYZLM(ZL(:,:,k),YL(:,:,k),lenght,w(k));
end
% Characteristic Admittance Fitting
[YcPoles,YcResidues,YcConstant,YcProportional] = YcFit(Yc,f,Ns,Ncon);
 % Hk fit
[HkPoles,HkResidues,HkConstant,HkProportional,md] =
HkFitTrace(Hm,Vm,ZL,YL,f,Ns,lenght,Ncon);
% m file to execute simulation loop.
SimulationLoop
```

Code to Load LineData

```
% Line Geometry
% column 1—conductor number
% column 2-- x position of each cond in m
% column 3-- y position of each cod in m
% column 4-- radii of each conductor
% column 5-- number of conductor in bundle
% column 6-- distance between  conductors in bundle
% column 7—conductor resistivity
% column 8—conductor relative permitivity
% column 9-- line lenght in m
Geom=[1   0 20  0.0153  3  0.4  2.826e-8  1e3 150e3
          2   10 20  0.0153  3  0.4  2.826e-8 1e3 150e3
          3   20 20  0.0153  3  0.4  2.826e-8  1e3 150e3];
 lenght  = Geom(1,9);              % Line lenght
Ncon  = Geom(max(Geom(:,1)),1);  % # of cond
Rsu  = 100;               % Earth resistivity Ohm-m
Mu  = 4*pi*1E-7;            % Henry's/meters
Eo  = (1/(36*pi))*1E-9;  % Farads/meters
Rhi  = 9.09E-7;  % Ohm-m resistivity of the iron.
Ral = 2.61E-8;  % Ohm-m res of the aluminum.
Rhg  = 2.71E-7;  % Ohm-m  res of the sky wires.
Ns  = 500;                        % Number of samples
f  = logspace(-2, 6, Ns);     % Vector of log spaced Frequencies
w = 2*pi*f;  % Vector of freqs in radian/sec.
```

Function LineParameters

```
function [Zg,Zt,Zc,Yg,ZT,YT]=LineParameters (Mu,Eo,Rsu,Geom,Ncon,Ns,w)
 % Function to compute the distances between conductor
[Dij,dij,hij]=Height(Geom);
```

```
Zg  = zeros(Ncon,Ncon,Ns);
Zt  = zeros(Ncon,Ncon,Ns);
Zc  = zeros(Ncon,Ncon,Ns);
Yg  = zeros(Ncon,Ncon,Ns);
Zcd = zeros(Ncon,Ns);
Zaf = zeros(Ncon,Ns);
P  = (1./sqrt(j*w*Mu/Rsu)); % Complex depth
Pmatrix = log(Dij./dij);  % Potential Coeff. Matrix
Pinv   = inv(Pmatrix);     % Inverse of Pmatrix
% Loop to compute matrices at all frequencies
for kl = 1:Ns
  % Geometric impedance
  Zg(:,:,kl) = (j*w(kl)*Mu/(2*pi))*Pmatrix;
  % Earth impedance
  for km = 1:Ncon
    for kn = 1:Ncon
      if km == kn
        Zt(km,km,kl) = (j*w(kl)*Mu/(2*pi))*
        log(1+P(kl)./(0.5*hij(km,km)));
      else
        num  = hij(km,kn)^2 + 4*P(kl)*hij(km,kn) +
        4*P(kl)^2 + dij(km,kn)^2;
        den = hij(km,kn)^2 + dij(km,kn)^2;
        Zt(km,kn,kl) = (j*w(kl)*Mu/(4*pi))*
       log(num/den);
      end
    end
  end
  % Geometric admittance
  Yg(:,:,kl) = (j*w(kl)*2*pi*Eo)*Pinv;
end
% Conductor impedance
for kd = 1:Ncon;
  Rcon = Geom(kd,4); %  conductor radii in m.
  Nhaz = Geom(kd,5);  % # of conductor in bundle
  Rpha = Geom(kd,7); % Resistivity in Ohm-m.
  Zcd(kd,:)  = (1/Nhaz)*Rpha./(pi.*Rcon.^2);
  Zaf(kd,:)  = (1/Nhaz)*(1+j).*(1./(2.*pi.*Rcon)) .*
  sqrt(0.5.*w.*Mu.*Rpha);
  Zc(kd,kd,:) = sqrt(Zcd(kd,:).^2 + Zaf(kd,:).^2);
end
% Outputs
ZT = Zg + Zt + Zc ;  % Total impedance
YT = Yg ;            % Total admittance
```

Function ABYZLM

```
function [Yc,Vm,Hmo] = ABYZLM(Z,Y,Lo,w)
 [M, Lm] = eig(Y*Z);  % Eigenvalues of YZ
Minv = inv(M);  % Inverse of eigenvectors matrix
Yc  = inv(Z)*(M*sqrt(Lm)*Minv);  % Characteristic Admittance
```

```
Gamma   = sqrt(diag(Lm));           % Propagation constants.
Vm = w./imag(Gamma);    % Modal Velocities
Hmo = diag(expm(-sqrtm(Lm)*Lo));  % Modal propag. Matrix H
```

Function YcFit

```
function [YcPoles,YcResidues,YcConstant, YcProportional]=YcFit(Yc,f,Ns,Ncon)
% Trace of characteristic admittance matrix
for k = 1:Ns
   Ytrace(k,1) = trace(Yc(:,:,k));
end
Npol = 6;                        % Number of poles
[Ps] = InitialPoles(f,Npol);   % Set initial poles
s    = j*2*pi*f.';             % Vector of values of variable "s"
Ka=2; % 1.-Strictly proper, 2.-Proper, 3.-Improper
for khg=1:20
  % Fit the trace of Yc (Poles)
  [YcPoles]=Poles(Ytrace.',s,Ps,Ns,Ka);
  Ps=YcPoles;
end
% Residues and constant term for Yc from poles of trace of Yc
for k = 1:Ncon
  for l = 1:Ncon
    Hs(:,1) = Yc(k,l,:); % k-l term of  admittance
    [C,D,E]=Residue(Hs.',s,YcPoles,Ns,Ka);
    YcResidues(k,l,:) = C;      % k-l residues term
    YcConstant(k,l)  = D;       % k-l constant term
    YcProportional(k,l)=E; %k-l proportional term
  end
end
```

Function HkFitTrace

```
function [HkPoles,HkResidues,HkConstant, HkProportional,md]=HkFit(Hm,Vm,ZL,YL,f,Ns,
lenght,Ncon);
 % Minimum phase of each mode
md = ModeDelay(Hm.',f,lenght,Vm.',Ns,Ncon);
% Computing Idempotents
for k=1:Ns
  % Function to calculate Idempotents of Y*Z
  [Hk] = HmIdem(ZL(:,:,k),YL(:,:,k),lenght,f(k), md,Hm(k,:));
  HkIdem(:,:,:,k) = Hk; % Idempotents
end
for m = 1:3
  for k=1:Ns
    TraceHk(m,k) = trace(HkIdem(:,:,m,k));
  end
end
s = j*2*pi*f.';        % Vector of the variable "s"
Ka =1;%1.-Strictly proper,  2.-Proper,  3.-Improper
Npol = 5;                         % Number of poles
[Ps] = InitialPoles(f,Npol); % Set the initial poles
```

```
for m = 1:3
  Hk = TraceHk(m,:);
  for khg=1:10
    [HkPol]=Poles(Hk,s,Ps,Ns,Ka);
    Ps=HkPol;
  end
  HkPoles(m,:)=Ps;
end
% Residues for Idempotent matrices of
% Hm from the poles of each trace.
for m = 1:3
  for k = 1:Ncon
    for l = 1:Ncon
      Hs(:,1) = HkIdem(k,l,m,:); % k-l term
      [C,D,E]=Residue(Hs.',s,HkPoles(m,:),Ns,Ka);
      HkResidues(k,l,m,:)  = C; % k-l-m term
      HkConstant(k,l,m)  = D; % k-l-m constant
      HkProportional(k,l,m) = E; % k-l-m prop
    end
  end
end
```

SimulationLoop program

```
Ts  = 0.016;              % Observation time
Nt  = fix(Ts/Dt);         % Number of time steps
t1  = fix(md./Dt);        % Delay of H in samples
t0  = fix(max(md)./Dt);   % Maximum time delay as expressed in
% number of samples
t   = (0:Dt:(Nt+t1)*Dt-Dt);    % Vector of time
Ks = menu('CHOOSE THE TYPE OF INPUT SOURCE' , '1 -unit step' , '2 -sinusoidal');
if Ks == 1  % unit step source
   Isr  = ones(Ncon,Nt+t0);
elseif Ks ==2  % sinusoidal source
   Isr(1,:) = sin(337*t);
   Isr(2,:) = sin(337*t+2*pi/3);
   Isr(3,:) = sin(337*t+4*pi/3);
end
NpYc = length(YcPoles); % Number of poles of Yc
NpH = length(HkPoles); % Number of poles for the first
% Idempotent matrix
Ng = 3;                %Number of groups
 % Initialize the states for both nodes
ZA = zeros(Ncon,NpYc); % State variables
ZB  = zeros(Ncon,NpYc);  % State variables
YA  = zeros(Ncon,NpH,Ng);  % State variables
YB  = zeros(Ncon,NpH,Ng);   % State variables
IfarA = zeros(Ncon,t0+3);  % Current at node A
IfarB = zeros(Ncon,t0+3);    % Current at node B
VO  = zeros(Ncon,1);    % Voltage at node A
Vi  = zeros(Ncon,Nt+t0);       % Voltage at node A
```

```
VL  = zeros(Ncon,1);      % Voltage at node B
Vf  = zeros(Ncon,Nt+t0);      % Voltage at node B
IO  = zeros(Ncon,1);      % Current at node A
Ii  = zeros(Ncon,Nt+t0);      % Current at node A
IL  = zeros(Ncon,1);      % Current at node B
If  = zeros(Ncon,Nt+t0);      % Current at node B
Iri = zeros(Ncon,Nt+t0);      % Current at Y source
Irf = zeros(Ncon,Nt+t0);      % Current at Y charge
 IfarAint = zeros(Ncon,Ng); % Current at node A
IfarBint = zeros(Ncon,Ng);     % Current at node B
% Constants for the state ZA and ZB
Ai(:,1) = (1+(Dt/2)*YcPoles)./(1-(Dt/2)*YcPoles);
Au(:,1) = ((Dt/2)./(1-(Dt/2)*YcPoles));
Bi(:,1) = (Ai+1).*Au;
Gy = zeros(Ncon,Ncon);
for nm = 1:NpYc
   Di(:,:,nm)    = YcResidues(:,:,nm)*Bi(nm);
   Gy   = Gy + YcResidues(:,:,nm)*Au(nm);
end
% Constants for the states YA and YB
for k = 1:Ng
   K1(:,k) = (1+(Dt/2)*HkPoles(:,k))./(1-(Dt/2)*HkPoles(:,k));
   Ka(:,k) = (((Dt/2))./(1-(Dt/2)*HkPoles(:,k)));
   Ku(:,k) = (K1(:,k)+1).*Ka(:,k);
end
for k = 1:Ng
   for nm = 1:NpH
    K2(:,:,nm,k) =  HkResidues(:,:,nm,k).*Ka(nm,k);
    K3(:,:,nm,k) = HkResidues(:,:,nm,k).*Ku(nm,k);
   end
end
Gy  = Gy + YcConstant;  % Admitance of the Ish
Yi  = diag(eye(3)*[1/600; 1/600; 1/600]);      % Admittance of the source, connected at node A
Gys = inv(Gy + Yi);  % Impedance to calculate VO
Yr  =diag(eye(3)*[1/1e6; 1/1e6; 1/1e6]);     % Admittance of load connected at node B
Gyr = inv(Gy + Yr);  % Impedance to calculate VL
% Contants terms to perform the interpolation
tm =md - t1*Dt;  % Time for the interpolation
% Linear interpolation constants
c1 = tm/Dt;
c2 = 1-c1;
c3 = ones(Ng,1);
% Pointers for the interpolation and the buffer
h1 = t1+1;
h2 = t1+2;
h3 = t1+3;
 for k = t0+2:Nt+t0-3
       IfarA(:,1) = IL + Gy*VL + sum(ZB(:,:),2);
      IfarB(:,1) = IO + Gy*VO + sum(ZA(:,:),2);
    % Linear interpolation
```

```
    for m = 1:Ng
      IfarAint(:,m) = c2(m)*IfarA(:,t1(m)) + c3(m)*IfarA(:,h1(m)) + c1(m)*IfarA(:,h2(m));
      IfarBint(:,m) = c2(m)*IfarB(:,t1(m)) + c3(m)*IfarB(:,h1(m)) + c1(m)*IfarB(:,h2(m));
    end
    IfarA(:,2:h3) = IfarA(:,1:h2);
    IfarB(:,2:h3) = IfarB(:,1:h2);
    for m = 1:NpYc
      ZA(:,m) = Ai(m)*ZA(:,m) + Di(:,:,m)*VO;
      ZB(:,m) = Ai(m)*ZB(:,m) + Di(:,:,m)*VL;
    end
    for l = 1:Ng
      for m = 1:NpH
        YA(:,m,l) = K1(m,l)*YA(:,m,l) + K2(:,:,m,l)*IfarAint(:,l);
        YB(:,m,l) = K1(m,l)*YB(:,m,l) + K2(:,:,m,l)*IfarBint(:,l);
      end
    end
    HistO = - sum(ZA(:,:),2) + sum(sum(YA(:,:,:),3),2);
    HistL  = - sum(ZB(:,:),2) + sum(sum(YB(:,:,:),3),2);
    VO = Gys*(Isr(:,k)+HistO);
    VL = Gyr*HistL;
    IO = Gy*VO - HistO;
    IL = Gy*VL - HistL;
    Vi(:,k) = VO;
    Vf(:,k) = VL;
    Ii(:,k) = IO;
    If(:,k) = IL;
  end
  Iri = Yi*Vi;
  Irf = Yr*Vf;
  vt = (0:Dt:length(Vi(1,:))*Dt-(t0+4)*Dt)';
  N = length(vt);
  a1 = t1+1;
  a2 = Nt+t1-3;
  figure(1),plot(vt,Vi(:,a1:a2),':',vt,Vf(:,a1:a2))
  ylabel('Amplitude in volts')
  xlabel('Time in seconds')
  legend('Sending end phase A' , 'Sending end phase B' , 'Sending end phase C' , 'Receiving end phase A' ,
  'Receiving end phase B' , 'Receiving end phase C')
```

Function Height

```
function[Dij,dij,hij]=Height(Geom)
Ls  = Geom(max(Geom(:,1)),1);
Req  = zeros(Ls,1);
 % Equivalent bundle radii
k4  = sqrt(2*(Geom(:,6)/2).^2);
for nc = 1: Ls;
  if Geom(nc,5)==1
    Req(nc) = Geom(nc,4);
  else
    Req(nc) = (Geom(nc,4).*Geom(nc,5).*k4(nc).^
```

```
(Geom(nc,5)-1)).^(1./Geom(nc,5));
  end
end
% Direct and image distances among conductors
for xl = 1:Ls;
  for yl = 1:Ls;
    if xl==yl
      dij(xl,yl)=Req(xl);
      y1=Geom(yl,3);
      hij(xl,yl)=2*y1;
      Dij(xl,yl)=hij(xl,yl);
    else
      x=abs(Geom(yl,2)-Geom(xl,2));
      y=abs(Geom(yl,3)-Geom(xl,3));
      dij(xl,yl)=sqrt(x^2 + y^2);
      y1=Geom(xl,3);
      y2=Geom(yl,3);
      hij(xl,yl)=y1+y2;
      x=abs(Geom(yl,2)-Geom(xl,2));
      y=hij(xl,yl);
      Dij(xl,yl)=sqrt(x^2 + y^2);
    end
  end
end
```

Function InitialPoles

```
function [Ps]=InitialPoles(f,Npol)
 even  = fix(Npol/2); % # of complex initial poles
p_odd = Npol/2 - even; % Auxiliary variable to check if number
% of initial poles is odd
disc  = p_odd ~= 0;  %   0 for  even Nr of initial poles  &  1    for
% odd Nr.
% Set a real pole in case of disc == 1
if disc == 0    % Even Nr of initial poles
   pols = [];
else           % Odd Nr of initial poles
   pols = [(max(f)-min(f))/2];
end
% Set the complex initial poles
bet = linspace(min(f),max(f),even);
for n=1:length(bet)
  alf=-bet(n)*1e-2;
  pols=[pols (alf-j*bet(n)) (alf+j*bet(n)) ];
end
Ps = pols.';  % Column vector of initial poles
```

Function Poles

```
function [A]=Poles(Fs,s,Pi,Ns,Ka);
Np  = length(Pi);   % Length of vector  containing starting poles
CPX  = imag(Pi)~=0;  %  0 for  real pole and 1 for  complex pole
```

```
rp  = 0;  % Initialize the index for real poles
cp  = 0;  % Initialize the index for complex poles
RePole = []; % Initialize the vector of real poles
CxPole=[];%Initialize the vector of complex poles
% Loop to separate real poles and complex poles
for k = 1:Np
  if CPX(k) == 0    % Real Pole
    rp = rp + 1;
    RePole(rp) = Pi(k);
  elseif CPX(k) == 1 % Complex pole
    cp = cp + 1;
    CxPole(cp) = Pi(k);
  end
end
Lambda = Pi.';
RePole = sort(RePole);       % Sort real poles
CxPole = sort(CxPole);       % Sort complex poles
Lambda = [RePole CxPole]; % Concatenate poles
I  = diag(ones(1,Np));  % Unit  matrix
A  = [];                % Poles
B  = ones(Ns,1);        % the weight factor
C     = [];             % Residues
D     = zeros(1);       % Constant term
E     = zeros(1);       % Proportional term
KQA    = ones(Ns,1);

cpx = imag(Lambda)~=0;  %  0 if pole is real and 1 if pole is
% complex.
dix = zeros(1,Np);     % Initializes vector of pole types
if cpx(1)~=0      % If the first pole is complex
  dix(1)=1;       %  real part
  dix(2)=2;     %  imag part
  k=3;          % continue dix for third position
else
  k=2;  % If the first pole is real continue dix for the second position
end
% complete the classification of the poles
for m=k:Np
  if cpx(m)~=0        % If the pole is complex
    if dix(m-1)==1
      dix(m)=2;   % If the previous position has the real part put 2
% to identifies the imag part
    else
      dix(m)=1;   % 1 for the real part of a complex pole
    end
  end
end
% Creates matriz A  divided in four parts A = [A1 A2 A3 A4]
% A1 = Dk
% A2 = B.*ones(Ns,1)
```

```
% A3 = B.*s
% A4 = -Dk*Fs
Dk=zeros(Ns,Np); % Initialize  matrix with zeros
for m=1:Np   % Iterative cycle for all poles
  if dix(m)== 0              % For a real pole
    Dk(:,m) = B./(s-Lambda(m));
  elseif dix(m)== 1  % For the real part
    Dk(:,m)=B./(s-Lambda(m)) +
               B./(s-Lambda(m)');
  elseif dix(m)== 2  % For the imag part
    Dk(:,m) = i.*B./(s-Lambda(m-1)) -
                i.*B./(s-Lambda(m-1)');
  end
end
% Creates work space for matrix A
A1 = Dk;
A2 = B.*ones(Ns,1);
A3 = B.*s;
for col = 1:Np
  A4(:,col) = -(Dk(:,col).*Fs.');
end
% Asigns values to A
if Ka == 1
   A = [A1 A4];  % Strictly proper rational fitting
elseif Ka == 2
   A = [A1 A2 A4]; % Proper rational fitting
elseif Ka == 3
   A = [A1 A2 A3 A4]; % Improper rational fitting
else
   disp('Ka need to be 1, 2 or 3')
end
% Creates matrix b = B*Fs
b = B.*Fs.';
% Separating real and imaginary part
Are = real(A);   % Real part of matrix A
Aim = imag(A);   % Imaginary part of matrix A
bre = real(b);   % Real part of matrix b
bim = imag(b);   % Imaginary part of matrix b
An = [Are; Aim];  % Real and imaginary part of A
bn = [bre; bim];  % Real and imaginary part of b
% Routine to applies the Euclidian norm to An
[Xmax Ymax] = size(An);
for col=1:Ymax
 Euclidian(col)=norm(An(:,col),2);
 An(:,col)=An(:,col)./Euclidian(col);
end
% Solving system
Xn = An\bn;
Xn = Xn./Euclidian.';
% Put the residues into matrix C
```

```
if Ka == 1
  C = Xn(Np+1:Ymax);  % Strictly proper fitting
elseif Ka == 2
  C = Xn(Np+2:Ymax);     % Proper rational fitting
elseif Ka == 3
  C = Xn(Np+3:Ymax);% Improper rational fitting
else
  disp('Ka need to be 1, 2 or 3')
end
% C complex when the residues are complex
for m=1:Np
  if dix(m)==1
    alfa = C(m);  % real part of a complex pole
    betta = C(m+1); % imag part of a complex pole
    C(m)   = alfa + i*betta;  % the complex pole
    C(m+1) = alfa - i*betta;  % the conjugate
  end
end
% Now calculate the zeros for sigma
BDA = zeros(Np);
KQA = ones(Np,1);
% Loop to calculate the zeros of sigma which are the new poles
for km = 1:Np
  if dix(km)== 0          % For a real pole
    BDA(km,km) = Lambda(km);
  elseif dix(km)== 1  % For a cp with - imag part
    BDA(km,km)   = real(Lambda(km));
    BDA(km,km+1) = imag(Lambda(km));
    KQA(km)      = 2;
    Aux = C(km);
    C(km) = real(Aux);
  elseif dix(km)== 2 % For a cp with + imag part
    BDA(km,km)   = real(Lambda(km));
    BDA(km,km-1) = imag(Lambda(km));
    KQA(km)      = 0;
    C(km)  = imag(Aux);
  end
end
ZEROS = BDA - KQA*C.';
POLS  = eig(ZEROS).';
%Forcing (flipping) unstable poles to make them stable
uns  = real(POLS)>0;
POLS(uns) = POLS(uns)-2*real(POLS(uns));
 % Sort poles in ascending order. First real poles and then complex poles
CPX   = imag(POLS)~=0; % Set to 0 for a real pole and  to1 for a
%complex pole
rp  = 0;  % Initialize index for real poles
cp  = 0;  % Initialize index for complex poles
RePole = []; % Initialize the vector of real poles
CxPole = []; % Initialize the vector of cp
```

```
% Loop to separate real and complex poles
for k = 1:Np
  if CPX(k) == 0     % Real Pole
    rp = rp + 1;
    RePole(rp) = POLS(k);
  elseif CPX(k) == 1 % Complex pole
    cp = cp + 1;
    CxPole(cp) = POLS(k);
  end
end
RePole = sort(RePole);    % Sort real poles
CxPole = sort(CxPole);    % Sort complex poles
% For conjugate pairs store first the one with positive imag part
CxPole = (CxPole.')';
NewPol = [RePole CxPole];
A = NewPol.';  % Output
```

Function Residue

```
function [C,D,E]=Residue(Fs,s,Pi,Ns,Ka);
Np   = length(Pi);
CPX = imag(Pi)~=0;  % 0 for a rp and 1 for cp
rp    = 0;  % Initialize the index for real poles
cp    = 0;  % Initialize the index for complex poles
RePole = [];   % Initialize the vector of real poles
CxPole=[]; %Initialize the vector of complex poles
% Loop to separate real poles and complex poles
for k = 1:Np
  if CPX(k) == 0     % Real Pole
    rp = rp + 1;
    RePole(rp) = Pi(k);
  elseif CPX(k) == 1 % Complex pole
    cp = cp + 1;
    CxPole(cp) = Pi(k);
  End
end
RePole = sort(RePole);      % Sort real poles
CxPole = sort(CxPole);      % Sort complex poles
CxPole = (CxPole.')';
Lambda = [RePole CxPole];
I  = diag(ones(1,Np));  % Unit diagonal matrix
A     = [];                % Poles
B     = ones(Ns,1);        % weight factor
C     = [];                % Residues
D     = zeros(1);          % Constant term
E     = zeros(1);          % Proportional term
cpx = imag(Lambda)~=0;  % 0 for rp and 1 for cp
dix = zeros(1,Np);      % Vto identifies poles
if cpx(1)~=0          % If the first pole is complex
  dix(1)=1;          % put 1 in dix(1) for the real part
  dix(2)=2;        % put 2 in dix(2) for the imag part
```

```
  k=3;          % continue dix for the third position
else
  k=2;  % If the first pole is real continue dix for the second
% position
end
% complete classification of the poles
for m=k:Np
  if cpx(m)~=0       % If the pole is complex
    if dix(m-1)==1
      dix(m)=2;  % If the previous position has the real part, set to % 2 to identify the imag part
    else
      dix(m)=1;  % put 1 for the real part of a cp
    end
  end
end
% Output matrices:
Dk=zeros(Ns,Np);
for m=1:Np
  if dix(m)==0       % Real pole
    Dk(:,m) = B./(s-Lambda(m));
  elseif dix(m)==1   % Complex pole, 1st part
    Dk(:,m) = B./(s-Lambda(m)) + B./(s-Lambda(m)');
  elseif dix(m)==2   % Complex pole, 2nd part
    Dk(:,m) = i.*B./(s-Lambda(m-1)) - i.*B./(s-Lambda(m-1)');
  end
end
% Creates work space for matrices A and b
AA1=Dk;
AA2=B.*ones(Ns,1);
AA3=B.*s;
if Ka == 1
  AA = [AA1];  % Strictly proper rational fit
elseif Ka == 2
  AA = [AA1 AA2]; % Proper rational fit
elseif Ka == 3
  AA = [AA1 AA2 AA3]; % Improper fit
else
  disp('Ka must be 1, 2 or 3')
end
bb  = B.*Fs.';
AAre = real(AA);     % Real part of matrix A
AAim = imag(AA);  % Imaginary part of matrix A
bbre = real(bb);     % Real part of matrix b
bbim = imag(bb);     % Imaginary part of matrix b
AAn = [AAre; AAim];  % Real and imag part of A
bbn = [bbre; bbim];  % Real and imag part of b
 [Xmax Ymax] = size(AAn);
for col=1:Ymax
  Eeuclidian(col)=norm(AAn(:,col),2);
  AAn(:,col)=AAn(:,col)./Eeuclidian(col);
```

```
end
% Solving system  X
Xxn=AAn\bbn;
X=Xxn./Eeuclidian.';
% Putting residues into matrix C
C=X(1:Np);
% C is complex when the residues are complex
for m=1:Np
  if dix(m)==1
    alfa  = C(m);   % real part of a complex pole
    betta = C(m+1); % imag part of a complex pole
    C(m)  = alfa + i*betta;  % the complex pole
    C(m+1) = alfa - i*betta; % the conjugate
  end
end
% Outputs
if Ka == 1
  A  = Lambda.';   % Poles
  C  = C;          % Residues
  D  = 0;          % Constant term
  E  = 0;          % Proportional term
elseif Ka == 2
  A  = Lambda.';   % Poles
  C  = C;          % Residues
  D  = X(Np+1);    % Constant term
  E  = 0;          % Proportional term
elseif Ka == 3
  A  = Lambda.';   % Poles
  C  = C;          % Residues
  D  = X(Np+1);    % Constant term
  E  = X(Np+2);    % Proportional term
End
```

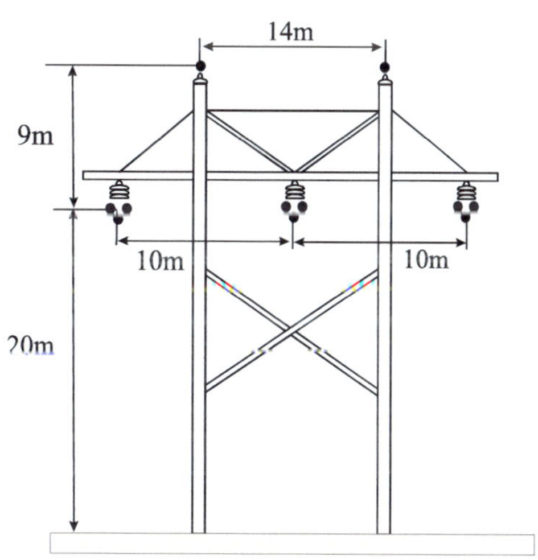

Figure 14. Transversal geometry of aerial line in example.

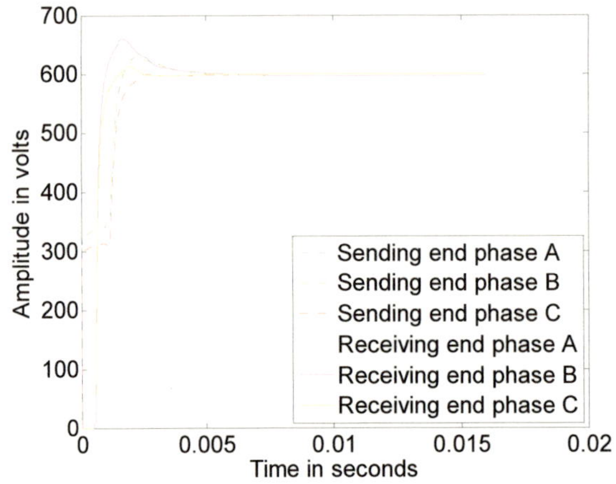

Figure 15. Voltage responses at sending and receiving ends. Unit step excitation.

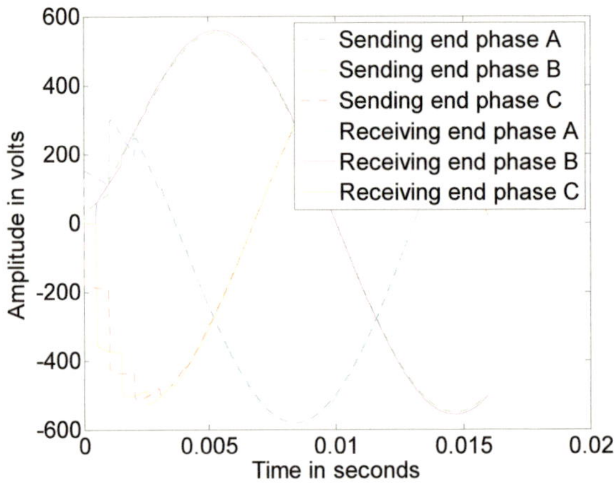

Figure 16. Voltage responses at sending and receiving ends. Sinusoidal excitation.

9. References

Bode, H. W. (1945). *Network Analysis and Feedback Amplifier Design*, D Van Nostrand Company, London, 1945.

Brandao Faria, J. A. & Borges da Silva, J. F. (1986). Wave Propagation in Polyphase Transmission Lines a General Solution to Include Cases Where Ordinary Modal Theory Fails, *Power Delivery, IEEE Transactions on*, vol.1, no.2, (April 1986), pp.(182-189).

Dommel H. W. (1969). Digital computer solution of electromagnetic transients in single and multiphase networks. *IEEE Trans. On Power App. Syst.*, Vol. 88, (July 1969), pp.(388).

Dommel, H. W. (1992). *EMTP Theory Book,* 2nd ed., Microtran Power System Analysis Corporation, Vancover, Canada, 1992.

Gustavsen B. & Semlyen A.(1998). Simulation of transmission line transients using vector fitting and modal decomposition. *Power Delivery, IEEE Trans. On,* Vol.13, No.2,(April 1998), pp.(605-614).

Gustavsen, B., Semlyen, A. (1999). Rational approximation of frequency domain responses by vector fitting, *Power Delivery, IEEE Transactions on,* vol.14, no.3, (July 1999). pp.(1052-1061).

Gustavsen, B. & Mahseredjian, J. (2007). Simulation of Internal Overvoltages on Transmission Lines by an Extended Method of Characteristics Approach, *Power Delivery, IEEE Transactions on,* vol.22, no.3, (July 2007), pp.(1736-1742).

Gustavsen, B., Nordstrom, J. (2008). Pole Identification for The Universal Line Model Based on Trace Fitting, *Power Delivery, IEEE Transactions on,* vol. 23, no. 1, (January 2008), pp. (472–479).

Gustavsen, B. (2008). "User's Guide for vectfit3.m", Available at http://www.energy.sintef.no/Produkt/VECTFIT/index.asp, Aug. 2008.

Gutierrez-Robles, J. A., Snider, L. A., Naredo, J. L. & Ramos-Leaños (2011). An Investigacion of Interpolation Methods Applied in Transmission Line Models for EMT Analysis, *Proceedings of the International Conference on Power System Transients,* IPST, Delft, The Netherlands, Jun. 2011.

Marcano, F. J. & Marti, J. R. (1997). Idempotent Line Model: Case Studies, *Proceedings of the International Conference on Power System Transients,* IPST, Seattle, USA, Jun. 1997.

Marti, J. R. (1982). Accurate modeling of frequency dependent transmission lines in electromagnetic transient simulations. *IEEE Trans. On Power App. Syst.,* Vol. 101, No. 1, (January 1982), pp. (147-155)

Morched, A., Gustavsen B. & Tartibi M.(1999).A universal model for accurate calculation of electromagnetic transients on overhead lines and underground cables. *IEEE Trans. On Power Delivery,* Vol. 14, No. 3,(July 1999), pp. (1032-1038)

Naredo, J. L., Brandao Faria, J. A., Borges da Silva, J. F. (1986). Discussion to Wave Propagation in Polyphase Transmission Lines a General Solution to Include Cases Where Ordinary Modal Theory Fails, *Power Delivery, IEEE Transactions on,* vol.1, no.2, (April 1986), pp. (188-195)

Ramos-Leaños O. & Iracheta R. (2010). Wide-Band line model implementation in MatLab for EMT analysis. *Proceedings of the North American Power Symposium,* Arlington USA, September 2010.

Strang, G. (1988). *Linear Algebra and its Applications.* Third Edition, Harcourt College, 1988.

Semlyen A. & Dabuleanu A.(1975).Fast and accurate switching transient calculations on transmission lines with ground return using recursive convolutions. *IEEE Trans. On Power App. Syst.,* Vol. 94, No. 2,(April 1975), pp. (561-571)

Semlyen, A., Abdel-Rahman, M. (1982). A state variable approach for the calculation of switching transients on a power transmission line, *Circuits and Systems, IEEE Transactions on*, vol.29, no.9, (September 1982), pp. (624-633)

Wedepohl, L. M., (1965). Electrical characteristics of polyphase transmission systems with special reference to boundary-value calculations at power-line carrier frequencies, *Electrical Engineers, Proceedings of the Institution of*, vol.112, no.11,(November 1965), pp.(2103-2112)

Chapter 13

A New Modeling of the Non-Linear Inductances in MATLAB

M. Ould Ahmedou, M. Ferfra, M. Chraygane and M. Maaroufi

Additional information is available at the end of the chapter

http://dx.doi.org/10.5772/46447

1. Introduction

In this chapter, we present a new approach for modeling the non-linear inductances by an analytic expression under the MATLAB-SIMULINK® code.

The current representation of these nonlinear inductances under MATLAB-SIMULINK® based on the introducing point by point (by a Lookup Table bloc in SIMULINK) [3]-[7] the values of Φ (i) deduced from the values of the magnetizing curve B-H and the geometric parameters of the corresponding portion of the magnetic circuit.

This new approach is based on a determination of analytic expressions of the non liner inductances deduced by a new analytic fitting of the nonlinear B-H curve. We have validate this new approach using the high voltage circuit of the power supply for magnetrons simulated by MATLAB-SIMULINK® code at the nominal state using the ferromagnetic material SF_{19}. The comparison between experimental and simulated currents and voltages shows that the simulation curves match nearly with the experimental measurements (an error approximately one percent: 1%) [6].

This approach allowed us to give a general equivalent model for an eventual HV power supply (single and three phases) of the microwaves generators with N magnetrons (N = 1, 2,... ....10) for the industrial applications. In other words, we were able to modeling a HV transformer (single and three phases) with magnetic shunts able to supplying N magnetrons on its secondary. Thus, to define a general strategy for multicriteria optimization of this HV power supply with N magnetrons. This approach can also solve many problems of modeling, simulation and optimization of the electrics machines in general [8]

To summarize, this chapter is organized as follows. In the second section, we remind of the actual modeling of the nonlinear inductances under MATLAB-SIMULINK code. Section III presents the new model based on a hybrid method of fitting the magnetizing curve B-H in order to derive analytic expressions of the nonlinear inductances. In the last one a conclusion.

2. Actual modelling of the nonlinear inductances under MATLAB-SIMULINK code

In the following of this chapter, we take as example the equivalent circuit of the HV power supply of microwaves generators used for the industrial applications. The three nonlinear inductances (primary, secondary and shunt) of the special HV power transformer of this alimentation (model in Fig.1) are function of the reluctances of the magnetic circuit portion which it represents. Each one of them is represented by its characteristic Φ (i) outcome of the relation, $L(i) = (n_2 \Phi(i) / i)$ which can be determined from the magnetization curve B (H).

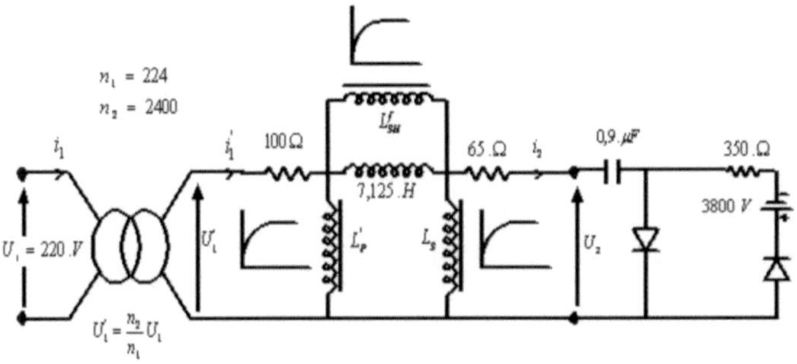

Figure 1. Equivalent circuit of HV power supply for microwaves generators

Not having analytical expression representing this B (H) curve for high values of the magnetic field H, we have introduced point by point the values of this curve using a linear interpolation between two consecutive points in the iterations of the code under SIMULINK. However, this method of interpolation can lead in case of temporal simulations including the traditional models of transformers to a numerical instability as quoted in [1]-[9]. A specific routine was elaborated in MATLAB to deduce the values couple (i, Φ) from those (H, B) and geometrical data of three inductances. The implementation of each nonlinear inductance of this circuit under SIMULINK software was realized by using the following blocks (Fig. 2):

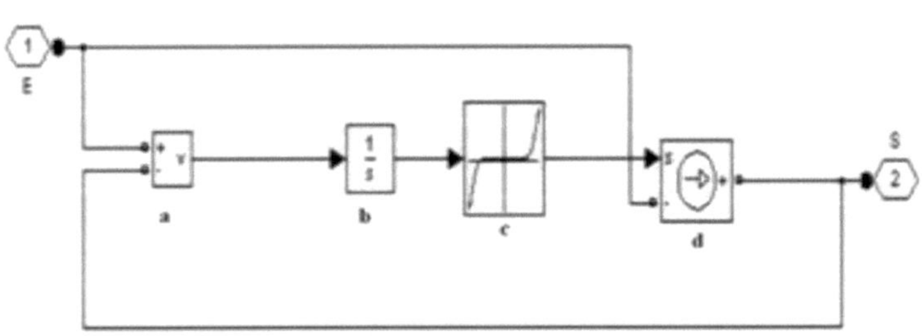

Figure 2. Implementation of each nonlinear inductance under SIMULINK, a: Voltage measurement, b: Integrator, c: Lookup Table, d: current source

- An integrator to derive the flux from the voltage.
- A Lookup Table function, which contains a big number of N points (N=100 points) relating to flux and currents deduced from the code previously quoted.
- A source of current imposed.

To ensure the convergence of nonlinear model simulation under SIMULINK, the simulation steps which is a crucial problem in the numerical simulations has been appropriately chosen Te= 0.01 ms after many trials.

We superimpose in Fig.3A, Fig.3B the simulation results obtained by SIMULINK code with those simulated by EMTP under the same conditions. These shapes resulting from the two codes under nominal operation (U1=220 V et f=50 Hz) are consistent with those obtained in

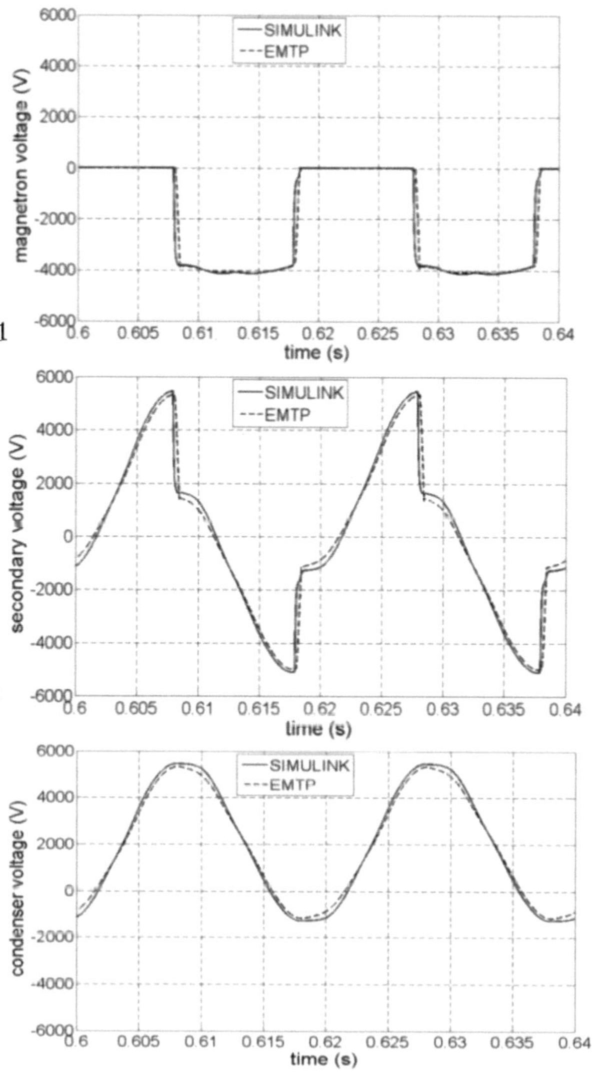

A.1

A.2

A.3

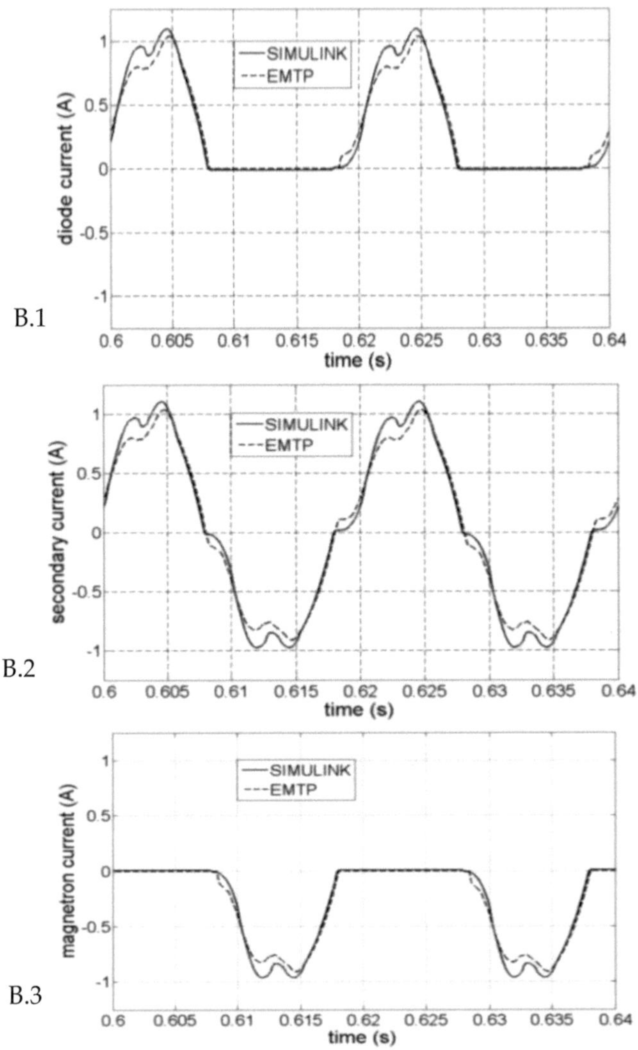

Figure 3. A. Simulation with EMTP and SIMULINK code: Forms of voltage waves (at the nominal operation); B. Simulation with EMTP and SIMULINK code: Forms of current waves (at the nominal operating)

practice (Fig.7), especially the magnetron current curves which respect the maximum current magnetron constraint (I_{peak}<1.2A) recommended by the manufacturer. Precisely, the current patterns resulting from SIMULINK are closer to practice than EMTP current patterns. Indeed, The current magnetron peak value reaches approximately -0.96 A (Fig.3.B.3) using SIMULINK code which is near -1 A from experimental results (Fig.7) while the peak value obtained from EMTP code equals -0.92 A. In general, between peak to peak values (Fig.3.A, Fig.3.B, Fig.7), the relative variations never exceed 8 % for EMTP code while those resulting from SIMULINK do not exceed 4%. The accuracy of the outcome resulting from SIMULINK can be justified by the large number of points

N=100=2x50 (including the negative values) used to feature B (H) in the table (see lookup table in Fig.2) while in our EMTP code version [18], we were limited to use a restricted number N=17. Taking into account the precision of the various data and acceptable tolerances on operation of the magnetron, modelling was considered to be satisfactory with the two codes.

3. New modelling of the nonlinear inductances

The field problem solution involving ferromagnetic materials is complicated by the nonlinear relationship between B and H. One of the problems encountered is the absence of single mathematical expression, to represent the magnetization curve characteristic over a wide range of magnetic fields, having a smooth variation of the incremental permeability. As well, in our previous works [2]-[3], the B-H curve introduced in the π old model of this special transformer of the HV power supply for magnetrons and based on a set of measurement data, is approximated under software tools (EMTP and SIMULINK) by several straight line segments connecting the points of measurements. However, the B-H curve obtained is not smooth at the joints of the segments and the slopes of the straight lines representing the permeability are discontinuous at these joints [4]-[5]. Hence, the accuracy of permeability computed using such an approximation of the B-H curve is limited by the number of the straight-line segments. In order to improve this π model of this special transformer, we present a more accurate modelling of the nonlinear B-H curve of ferromagnetic material used for fabrication (SF_{19}). In fact, the nonlinear B-H curve is represented by analytic expressions considering two parts of this curve: the first one is the linear region which is fitted by a non integer power series and the second one representing the saturation region is approximated by polynomial representation.

3.1. Fitting H-B curve by a hybrid method

A set of N discrete measurements data In and Φn or Hn-Bn of this special transformer (n=1,2,3,…N=100) is given as depicted in Fig.4. Two parts are considered for this analytic representation:

- The linear region is fitted by a non-integer power series [1]. It is based on selected powers of B (not generally integer) with positive coefficients giving a power series. This linear part of this curve can be expressed by the power curve :

$$H = \sum k_i B^{n_i} \text{ with } k_i>0,\ n_i>0\text{, for all i.} \quad (1)$$

  An adequate procedure of determining initial ki and ni values from logarithmic plots is adopted ensuring that these initial estimates of the parameters will be positive. Once an initial estimate of parameters (ki, ni) has been obtained, the parameters are optimized using regression analysis to get the best fit which is defined as corresponding to the minimum sum of squares of absolute errors. The resulting analytic expression of H is given by:

$$\text{for} H \le H_{18}\ \mathrm{H(B)} = 220.65\mathrm{B}^{0.96} + 19.5\mathrm{B}^{11} \quad (2)$$

- The saturation region is fitted by a polynomial representation based on the method of least squares [5]-[1].

$$\text{for } H > H_{18}$$

$$\mathrm{H} = \mathrm{a}_1.\mathrm{B} + \mathrm{a}_3.\mathrm{B}^3 + \mathrm{a}_5.\mathrm{B}^5 \ldots. + \mathrm{a}_{2p+1}\mathrm{B}^{2p+1} \quad (3)$$

Using the '*polyfit*' function in MATLAB boxes, we determine all parameters ai. The best fit is obtained by choosing p=3.The resulting expression of H is given as follows:

$$\mathrm{H(B)} = 62967\mathrm{B} - 59157\mathrm{B}^3 + 17475\mathrm{B}^5 - 1409\mathrm{B}^7 \quad (4)$$

The choice of a hybrid method consisting of two analytic expressions is more adequate than only one analytic expression for fitting the whole magnetizing curve of this material, according to our attempts to estimate these coefficients. It is due to the fact that the fitting is better and uses a small number of terms in analytic expressions to be identified. To illustrate the accuracy of this procedure for modelling nonlinear characteristic of this ferromagnetic material (SF_{19}), we superpose in Fig.4 the simulate curve B-H obtained by the two analytic expressions and data measurements. It shows no discrepancies between the two curves.

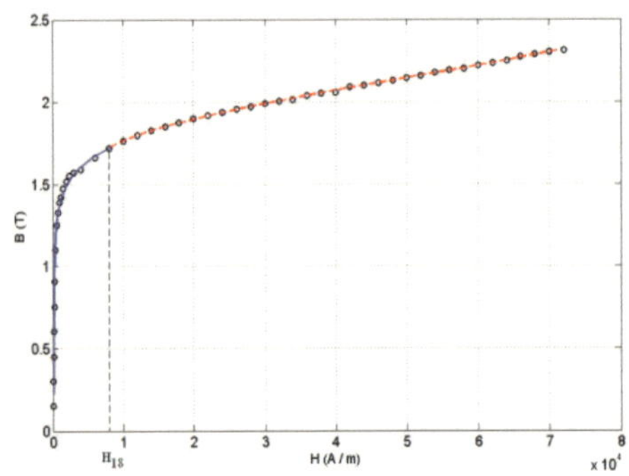

Figure 4. Magnetization curve SF_{19}: ° ° ° data measurements, —— curve represented by non integer power series, - - - - curve represented by polynomial function.

3.2. Analytic expressions of inductances

Finally, we determine the analytic expressions of inductances from this analytic approach for modelling the nonlinear characteristic B-H and the transformer data. Two analytic expressions deduced for each inductance of this new model are given using the formulae:

For B ≤ 1.7225 T

$$L'_p = L_S = \frac{n_2 \Phi_P}{i_P} = \frac{n_2^2 B S_1}{H l_P} = \frac{n_2^2 S_1}{l_P} . \frac{B}{H(B)}$$

$$L'_p = L_S = 106338{,}46 \frac{B}{220.65B^{0.96} + 19.5B^{11}} \quad (5)$$

For B ≥ 1.7225 T

$$L'_p = 106338{,}46\frac{B}{62967B - 59157B^3 + 17475B^5 - 1409B^7}$$

It is the same for the shunt inductance

For B ≤ 1.7225 T

$$L'_{Sh} = \frac{n_2\Phi_3}{i'_{Sh}} = \frac{n_2.2.\Phi_{Sh}}{Hl_{Sh}} = \frac{n_2.2(B.S_3)}{Hl_{Sh}} = \frac{2n_2B.S_3}{Hl_{Sh}}$$

$$L'_{Sh} = 138693\frac{B}{H(B)}$$

$$L'_{Sh} = 138693\frac{B}{220.65B^{0.96} + 19.5B^{11}} \quad (6)$$

For B ≥ 1.7225 T

$$L'_{Sh} = 138693\frac{B}{62967B - 59157B^3 + 17475B^5 - 1409B^7} \quad (7)$$

In the simulation of new model, the three nonlinear inductances (primary, secondary and shunt) are function of induction or flux. The implementation of each nonlinear inductance with its analytic expressions under SIMULINK software was realized by using the blocks shown in Fig.5. This model (or bloc) is valid for any nonlinear inductance. It is validated in [14], and shows a good agreement with the experimental results.

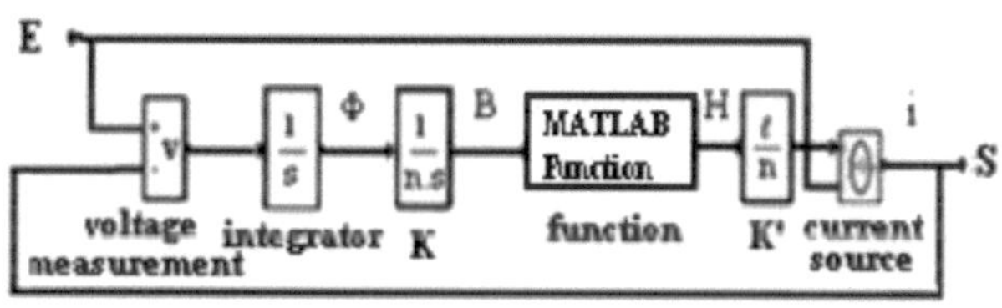

Figure 5. Implementation of the nonlinear inductance under MATLAB-SIMULINK

We superpose in Fig.6A and Fig.6B the simulation results of this new modelling, obtained by SIMULINK code with those obtained from old one by EMTP under the same conditions. These shapes resulting from the two codes under nominal operation (U1=220 V, f=50 Hz) are consistent with those obtained in practice (Fig.7), especially the magnetron current curves which respect the maximum current magnetron constraint (I_{peak} < 1.2A) recommended by the manufacturer. Precisely, the current patterns resulting from the new modelling under SIMULINK are closer to practice than EMTP current patterns issues from old modelling (Fig.2). Indeed, The current magnetron peak value reaches approximately -1 A (Fig.6.B.3) using SIMULINK code which is identical to experimental results (Fig.7) while the peak value obtained from EMTP code equals -0.92 A. In general, between peak to peak values (Fig.6.A, Fig.6.B, Fig.7), the relative variations never exceed 8 % for EMTP code (with old model) while those resulting from SIMULINK with the new model do not exceed 1%. The accuracy of the outcome resulting from SIMULINK can be justified by determining analytic inductances of this model. It leads to continuous slopes representing permeability while with the old model under EMTP introducing the B-H curve point by point and approximating it by several straight line segments, the slopes representing the permeability are discontinuous at the joints. Taking into account the precision of the various data (software) and acceptable tolerances in the operation of the magnetron, the validation of this improved modelling based on analytic inductances is considered to be more satisfactory than the old one.

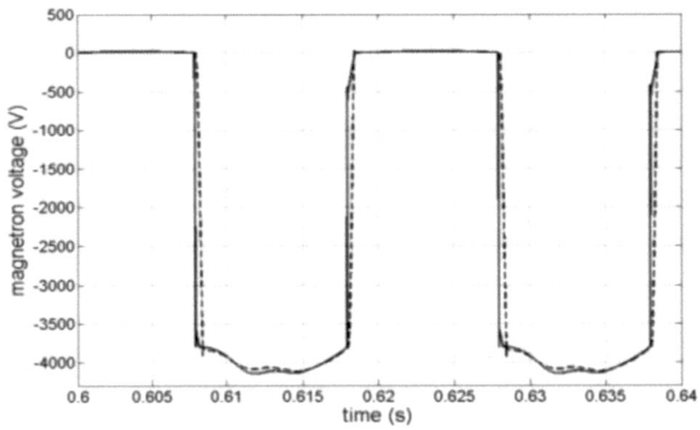

A.1

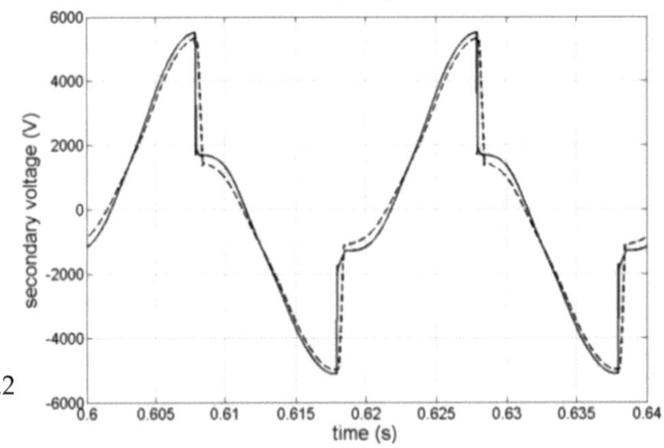

A.2

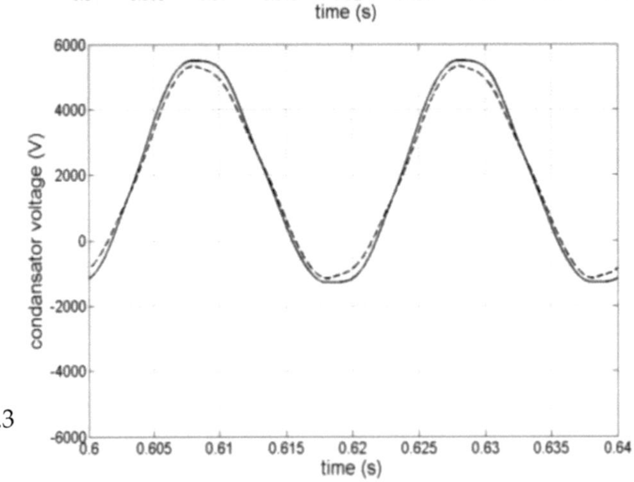

A.3

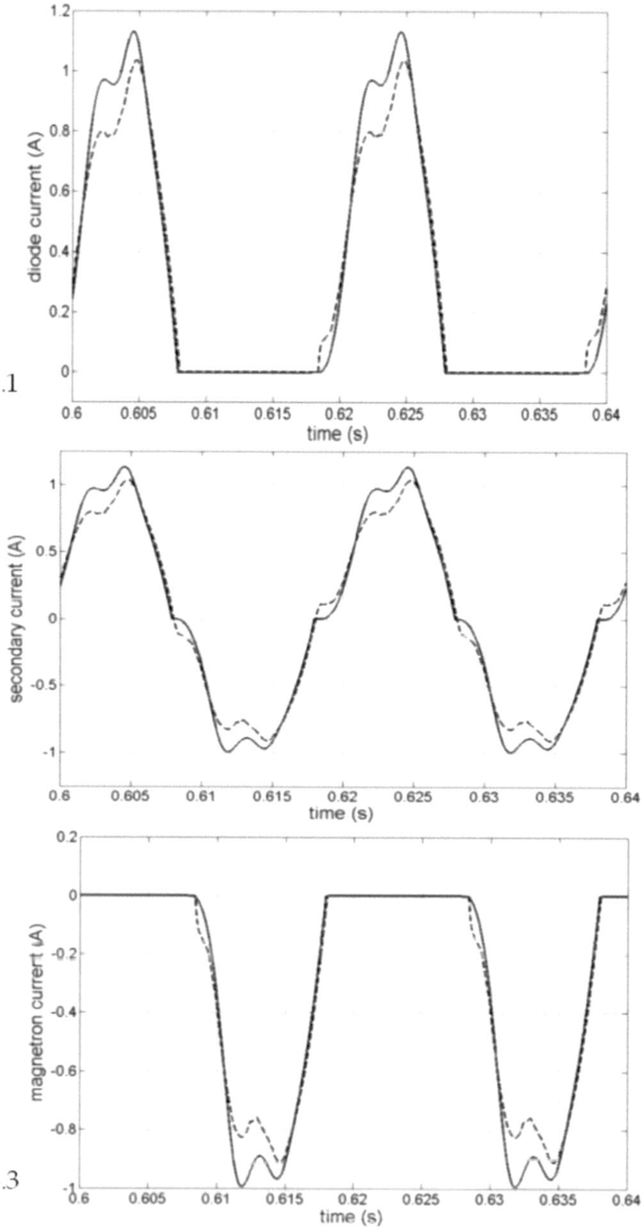

Figure 6. A. Simulation with EMTP (- - -) and SIMULINK ( ) code: Forms of voltage waves (nominal operation); B. Simulation with EMTP(- - -) and SIMULINK( ) code: Forms of current waves (nominal operating)

4. Experimental results

We sought to integrate the transformer new model (with analytic expressions of inductances) in the circuit of the HV supply from the source to the magnetron (Fig. 1), where we represented the tube microwave by the equivalent diagram deduced from its electric characteristic [2]-[3]-[6] which is formally similar to that of a diode of dynamic resistance $R = \frac{\Delta U}{\Delta I}$ neighbor of 350 Ohms and threshold voltage E of about 3800 Volts. We validate this new model by carrying out tests that have been set up previously [2] on generator microwaves composed of the following elements (Fig.1):

- A high voltage transformer with magnetic shunt ratings: f=50 Hz, S=1650 VA, U_1=220 V, and, no-load U_2=2330 V (r'_1 =100 Ω and r_2=65 Ω, for n1=224 and n_2=2400 turns).
- A cell composed of a condenser, its capacity C=0,9 μF and a diode high voltage DHV.
- A magnetron designed to operate under an approximate voltage of 4000 V. To obtain its nominal power, it needs an average current Imoy=300 mA, but without exceeding the peak current which might destroy it (Imax<1,2 A). The experimental curves are presented in Fig.6. The first three curves represent the shapes of voltage quantities while the last ones represent current patterns.

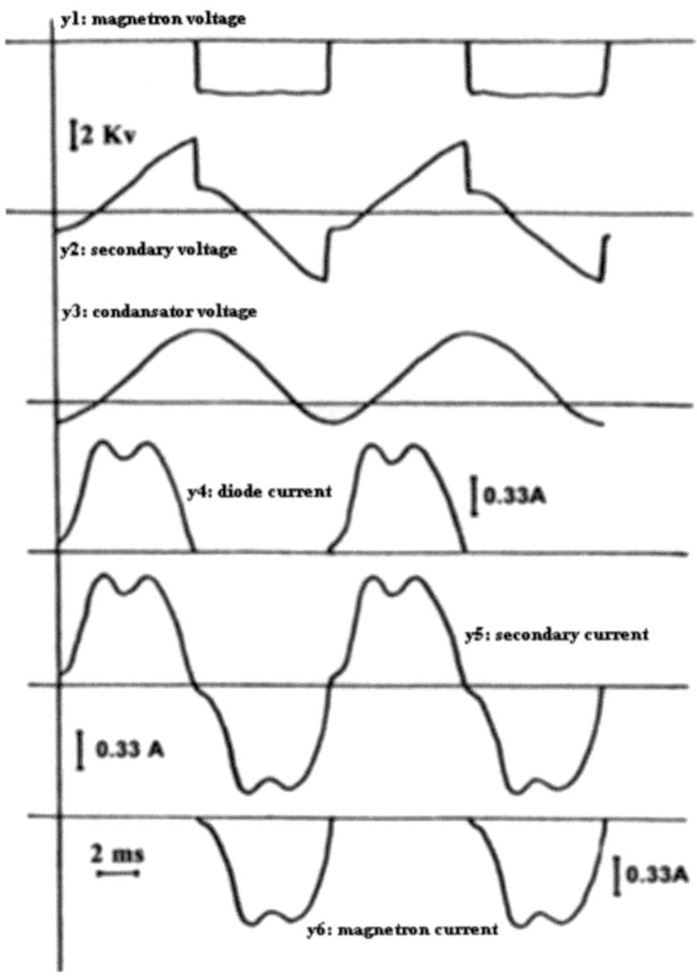

Figure 7. Experimental forms curves of the voltages and currents waves (nominal operating)

5. Conclusion

From the Simulink block modelling a non-linear inductance by introducing point by point its values, we performed a new model in two steps:

Step 1. A program M-file was developed and gives us the final results of the B-H curve fitting.
Step 2. By performing a function 'MATLAB Function' that replace us the nonlinear inductance of the current passing through this inductance as shown in Fig.4.

This approach can solve many problems of modeling, simulation and optimization of the electrical networks and electric machines also [7].

Thus, an improved procedure for modeling the nonlinear characteristic B-H of the ferromagnetic materiel (SF_{19}) of this special transformer supplying one magnetron has been presented. Starting with a discrete set of measurement data of B and H, we have obtained two analytic expressions of B-H curve in terms of non-integer power series for the linear part of this curve and polynomial representation for the saturation region. Then, these expressions have been used for improving the old modelling of nonlinear inductances into the new one based on the determination of analytic expressions of each inductance. We validate the new π model (with three nonlinear inductances) of the transformer with magnetic shunts, used in HV supply for magnetron by MATLAB-SIMULINK code in nominal mode. A comparison between the numerical results and experimental ones has shown a significant agreement.

Author details

M. Ould Ahmedou, M. Ferfra and M. Maaroufi
Mohammadia School of Engineering (Mohamed V University), Rabat, Morocco

M. Chraygane
Ibn Zohr University, Agadir, Morocco

6. References

[1] J. R. Lucas, representation of magnetization curves over a wide region using a non-integer power series, international J. Elect. Enging. Edduc – vol. 25. pp. 335 – 340. Manchester U.P. 1988. Printed in Great Britais.
[2] Chraygane M., ferfra M. & Hlimi B., Modeling of a high voltage power for microwave generators industrial in one magnetron, 3EI journal, Paris, France, vol. 41, 2005, pp. 37-47.
[3] M.Ould.Ahmedou, M.Chraygane, M.Ferfra, New π Model Validation Approach to the Leakage Flux Transformer of a High Voltage Power Supply Used for Magnetron for the Industrial Micro-Waves Generators 800 Watts. International Review of Electrical Engineering (I.R.E.E.), Vol. 5. n. 3. May-June.2010. pp. 1003-1011.
[4] B. Kawkabani, J.-J. Simond, Improved Modeling of Three-Phase Transformer Analysis Based on Magnetic Equivalent Circuit Diagrams And Taking Into Account Nonlinear B-H Curve, Journal Electromotion, Volume 13, Number 1, January-March 2006, pp. 5-10.

[5] Guanghao Liu, Xiao-Bang Xu, Improved Modeling of the Nonlinear B–H Curve and Its Application in Power Cable Analysis, IEEE Transaction on Magnetics, vol. 38, NO. 4, July 2002.

[6] Ahmedou, M.Ould., Ferfra, M., Nouri, R., Chraygane, M, "Improved π model of the leakage flux transformer used for magnetrons", 2011 International Conference on Multimedia Computing and Systems -Proceedings , art. no. 5945710

[7] MATLAB Tool Books.

[8] M.Ould.Ahmedou, M.Ferfra, N.El Ghazal, M.Chraygane, M.Maaroufi, 'Implementation And Optimization Under Matlab Code Of A Hv Power Transformer For Microwave Generators Supplying Two Magnetrons', Journal of Theoretical and Applied Information Technology pp 227 - 238 Vol 33. No. 2 – 2011.

[9] Ferfra. M, Chraygane. M, Fadel. M, Ould Ahmedou. M. "Non linear modelling of an overall new high voltage power supply for N=2 magnetrons for industrial microwave generators | [Modelisation non lineaire d'une nouvelle alimentation haute tension globale de N=2 magnetrons pour generateurs micro-ondes industriels]" Physical and Chemical News 54 , pp. 17-30, 2010.

[10] Aguili T & Chraygane M., An original power generators for microwave, General Review of Electric - France, GRE 5 (1990) 49-51.

[11] Chraygane M, Modeling and optimization of a transformer with shunt of the high voltage power supply for magnetron used as microwave generators2450MHz 800W for industrial applications, Thesis of doctorate, Claude Bernard University-Lyon I, France, n° 189 (1993).

[12] Chraygane M, Teissier M., Jammal A. et Masson J.P , Modelling of a transformer with shunts used in the HV power supply of a microwave generator in a magnetron, publication, physic III journal, France, (1994) 2329-2338.

[13] M. Chraygane, M. El Khouzaï, M. Ferfra, & B. Hlimi, Analytical study of the repartition of flux in the leakage transformer used in a power supply for magnetron 800 Watts at 2450Hz, Physical and Chemical News, PCN journal, vol. 22, 2005, pp. 65-74.

[14] M. Chraygane, M. Ferfra, & B. Hlimi, Analytical and experimental study of the distribution of flux in the transformer with shunts of a high voltage power supply for magnetron 800 Watts at 2450Hz, article, journal Physical and Chemical News, PCN, vol. 27,2006, pp. 31-42.

[15] M. Chraygane, M. Ferfra, B. Hlimi, Analytic determination of the flux and the currents of the leakage flux transformer of a high voltage power supply for magnetron used for the industrial micro-waves generators 800 Watts – 2450 Mhz. Phys. Chem. News, PCN, vol. 40, 2008, pp. 51-61.

[16] Mukerji, Saurabh Kumar; Goel, Sandeep Kumar; Basu, Kartik Prasad, Experimental determination of equivalent-circuit parameters for transformers with large series-branch impedances, International Journal of Electrical Engineering Education, vol 43, November 2006 , pp. 352-357.

[17] Jouni Pylvänäinen, Kirsi Nousiainen, Pekka Verho Studies to Utilise Calculated Condition Information and Measurements for Transformer Condition Assessment. International Review of Electrical Engineering (I.R.E.E.). Vol. 4. n. 4. june.2009. pp. 684-689.

[18] Mustafa. Kizilcay and Laszlo Prikler, "ATP-EMTP Beginner's Guide for EEUG Members, European EMTP-ATP Users Group e.V", June (2000).

Chapter 14

Dynamic Simulation of Electrical Machines and Drive Systems Using MATLAB GUI

Viliam Fedák, Tibor Balogh and Pavel Záskalický

Additional information is available at the end of the chapter

http://dx.doi.org/10.5772/48519

1. Introduction

Since the first appearance, the fields of electrical machine and drive systems have been continuously enriched by introduction of many important topics. Progress in power electronics, microcontrollers, new materials and advances in numerical modeling have led to development of new types of electrical machines and in field of electrical drives to realization of complex control algorithms. Their verification is usually done by simulation during system design, thus the effort is concentrated to development of simulation models.

MATLAB offers almost infinite possibilities for easy development of system models. MATLAB GUI (Graphic User Interface) in connection with Simulink and specialized toolboxes present a suitable and easy programmable tool for development of purpose-oriented virtual model of any dynamical system. Easy and comfortable change of parameters by control elements in MATLAB GUIDE (GUI Development Environment), such as push- and radio- buttons, text boxes, and easy visualization of results, enable to develop virtual models without deep knowledge of their substance nor without a tedious programming and debugging the models.

Well elaborated models of electrical drives and machines available on-line were developed by (Riaz, n.d.). (Saadat, 2012) presented application of MATLAB GUI for electrical engineering subjects, available online and MATLAB GUI was utilized in (Petropol-Serb et al, 2007) for development of virtual model of induction machine.

Our contribution aims to present methodology and results in development of unified series of virtual models for electrical machines and drive systems using MATLAB GUI. The organization of the contribution is as follows: after brief description of tasks at virtual models design in GUI MATLAB (chapter 2) in the third chapter we describe development of few typical GUI oriented models of (more complex) electrical machines starting from a simple outline of mathematic model, following by simulation model. Emphasis is put on development of the virtual model itself and description of its features. The fourth chapter deals with CAD of drive controllers using GUI MATLAB. Finally, in the fifth chapter we share some experiences from development of the GUIs and their utilization for training of students. In conclusion we also present ideas for our future work.

2. Design methodology for virtual models of electrical machines and drives

2.1. Tasks in design of the GUI screen

The GUI providing human-computer interaction presents one of the most important parts when working with the system model. User interacts with the computer easily, intuitively, without need for derivation, design, development, composition, and debugging the simulation model; without necessity to learn its operation, and finally, he gets required information in transparent, well-arranged form. In the fact, such GUI presents a functional virtual model, where the user sets system parameters, chooses mode of operation and required outputs to observe results. Design of GUI starts with careful planning of the following tasks:

1. Derivation of system mathematical model
2. Getting, debugging, and verification of simulation model
3. Programming GUI
4. Determination of input parameters changes (editing boxes, sliders)
5. Determination of outputs in graphical and text form
6. Design of the screen (or a set of interconnected screens)
7. Choice of calculation modes and algorithm of their control
8. Final refining and verification of functionality of the designed GUI screen

2.2. Principles of ergonomics of the GUI screen

When designing a functional GUI screen for the technical systems, designer must understand principles of good interface and screen design. Generally, the rules are described in (Galitz, 2007). We have adapted and extended them for design of virtual model – of a GUI MATLAB screen. The most important principles, when designing the placement of objects on the GUI screen, are:

- *Legibility* — saying that information should be distinguishable.
- *Facitily* —how easy is the designed GUI screen intuitively usable.
- *Readability* — how information is identifiable and interpretable.
- *Attractivity* —to attract and call attention to different screen elements (placement of control elements and outputs, using colors, …).
- *Guiding the eye* — by placement and grouping command objects by visual lines/boxes.

Further, designer should deal with user considerations, as follows:

- Visually pleasing (user friendly) *composition of the screen*.
- *Organizing screen elements* (balance, symmetry, alignment, proportion, grouping).
- Screen navigation and flow.
- Choice of implicitly *pre-setting system parameters* and their range (so that virtual models can be generally used in larger range of parameter changes).
- *Changing system parameters* by sliders or by numerical values in editing boxes.
- Finally, designer has to maintain *ergonomic of the screen* where the control elements and outputs should be organized in a legible way.

3. Virtual models for analysis of dynamical properties of electrical machines

In background of every GUI MATLAB there is working a simulation model of the system derived from its mathematical model. The same procedure is applied at development of GUI for electrical machines and drives. Let's show the GUI MATLAB development procedure on few electrical machines – the AC induction machine (asynchronous motor) and the brushless DC motor.

3.1. AC drive with 3-phase asynchronous motor

The AC drive consists of an AC machine supplied by a converter. The variables of AC machine (an asynchronous motor in our case) like electrical quantities (supply voltages and currents), magnetic variables (magnetic fluxes), and mechanical variables (motor torque and rotor angular speed) are usually to be investigated in:

- Various *reference frames* (rotating coordinate systems). In case of asynchronous motor two basic reference frames are considered:
- $\{\alpha, \beta\}$ reference frame associated with stator, whose angular speed $\omega_k = 0$
- $\{x, y\}$ reference frame rotating by synchronous angular speed $\omega_k = \omega_1$
- Various modes of supply:
- harmonic (sinusoidal voltage)
- non-harmonic (stepped voltage), PWM

3.2. Asynchronous motor model

For dynamic properties investigation of asynchronous motor (influence of non-harmonic supply to properties of the AC drive, etc.) a dynamical model of AC machine is used. The AC machine is described by set differential equations. For their derivation some generally accepted simplifications are used (not listed here) concerning physical properties, construction of the machine, electromagnetic circuit, and supply source.

In order to simplify mathematical model of the squirrel cage motor, the multiphase rotor is replaced by an equivalent three-phase one and its parameters are re-calculated to the stator. Equations describing behavior of the machine are transformed from three- to two-phase system what yields to decreased number of differential equations. The quantities in equations are transformed into reference systems.

To derive dynamic model of asynchronous motor, the three-phase system is to be transformed into the two-phase one. In the fact, this transformation presents a replacement of the three-phase motor by equivalent two-phase one. The stator current space vector having real and imaginary components is defined by the equation:

$$\overline{\mathbf{i}} = \frac{2}{3}(i_a + \mathbf{a}i_b + \mathbf{a}^2 i_c)$$

where

$$\mathrm{a} = \mathrm{e}^{\mathrm{j}120^\circ} = -\frac{1}{2} + \mathrm{j}\frac{\sqrt{3}}{2}, \quad \mathrm{a}^2 = \mathrm{e}^{\mathrm{j}240^\circ} = -\frac{1}{2} - \mathrm{j}\frac{\sqrt{3}}{2}$$

Basic equations of the AC machine with complex variables (denoted by a line over the symbol of the variable) in the reference frame rotating by general angular speed ω_k are:

$$\overline{u}_1 = R_1 \overline{i}_1 + \frac{d\overline{\Psi}_1}{dt} + j\omega_k \overline{\Psi}_1 \tag{1}$$

$$\overline{u}_2 = R_2 \overline{i}_2 + \frac{d\overline{\Psi}_2}{dt} + j(\omega_k - \omega)\overline{\Psi}_2 \tag{2}$$

$$\frac{J}{p}\frac{d\omega}{dt} = \frac{3p}{2}\,\mathrm{Im}(\overline{\Psi}_{1k}^{c}\,\overline{i}_{1k}) - m_z \tag{3}$$

where the nomenclature is as follows:

- u_1, i_1, R_1, L_1 – voltage, current, resistance and inductance of stator phase winding
- u_2, i_2, R_2, L_2 – voltage, current and resistance and inductance of rotor phase winding (re-calculated to stator quantities)
- Ψ_1, Ψ_2 – total magnetic flux of the stator and rotor (recalculated to stator side)
- ω – (rotor) mechanical angular speed
- m_z – load torque
- ω_k – angular speed of a general rotating reference frame $\omega_k = \omega_1$ or 0
- ω_1, ω – magnetic field angular speed, rotor angular speed, where $\omega = \omega_1 - \omega$
- σ – leakage factor $\sigma = (L_1 L_2 - L_h^2) / L_1^2$

For manipulation between various reference frames in the motor model the transformation formulas are used as listed in Tab. 1. All rotor parameters and variables are re-calculated to the stator side.

After inserting real and imaginary components into the complex of variables (e.g. for stator voltage $\overline{u}_1 = u_{1x} + ju_{1y}$ in synchronously rotating reference frame {*x*, *y*}), we get the AC motor mathematical model whose equations are listed in Tab. 2 and a block diagram shown in Fig. 1 where $K_1 = 1/(\sigma L_1)$, $K_2 = 1/(\sigma L_2)$, $K = L_h/(\sigma L_1 L_2)$.

Transformation	Matrix notation	Block diagram
$\{a, b, c\} \rightarrow \{\alpha, \beta\}$ from 3-phase system $\{a, b, c\}$ to 2-phase reference frame $\{\alpha, \beta\}$ fixed with the stator (Clark transform)	$\begin{bmatrix} i_\alpha \\ i_\beta \end{bmatrix} = \begin{bmatrix} 1 & 0 & 0 \\ 0 & \frac{1}{\sqrt{3}} & -\frac{1}{\sqrt{3}} \end{bmatrix} \begin{bmatrix} i_a \\ i_b \\ i_c \end{bmatrix}$	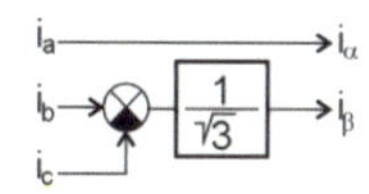
$\{\alpha, \beta\} \rightarrow \{a, b, c\}$ from 2-phase reference frame fixed with stator $\{\alpha, \beta\}$ into 3-phase system $\{a, b, c\}$ (inverse Clark transform)	$\begin{bmatrix} i_a \\ i_b \\ i_c \end{bmatrix} = \begin{bmatrix} 1 & 0 \\ -\frac{1}{2} & \sqrt{\frac{3}{2}} \\ -\frac{1}{2} & -\sqrt{\frac{3}{2}} \end{bmatrix} \begin{bmatrix} i_\alpha \\ i_\beta \end{bmatrix}$	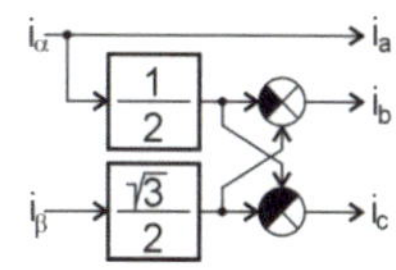
$\{x, y\} \rightarrow \{\alpha, \beta\}$ from synchronously rotating reference frame $\{x, y\}$ into the stationary frame $\{\alpha, \beta\}$ (Park transform)	$\begin{bmatrix} i_x \\ i_y \end{bmatrix} = \begin{bmatrix} \cos\rho & \sin\rho \\ -\sin\rho & \cos\rho \end{bmatrix} \begin{bmatrix} i_\alpha \\ i_\beta \end{bmatrix}$ $\rho = \omega_1 t$	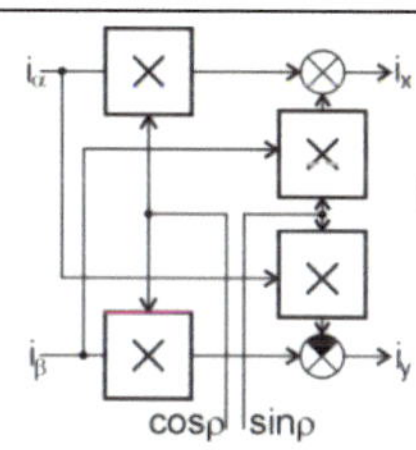
$\{\alpha, \beta\} \rightarrow \{x, y\}$ from stator reference frame $\{\alpha, \beta$ $\}$into the synchronously rotating frame $\{x, y\}$ (inverse Park transform)	$\begin{bmatrix} i_\alpha \\ i_\beta \end{bmatrix} = \begin{bmatrix} \cos\rho & -\sin\rho \\ \sin\rho & \cos\rho \end{bmatrix} \begin{bmatrix} i_x \\ i_y \end{bmatrix}$ $\rho = \omega_1 t$	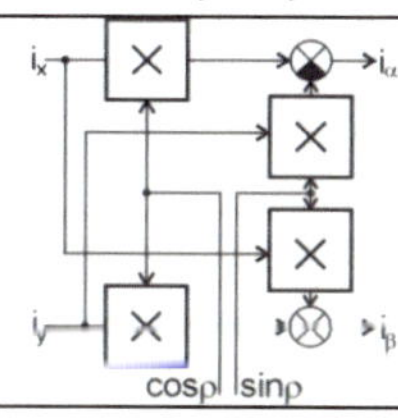

Table 1. Transformation relations between three-phase system and two-phase reference frame and between $\{x, y\}$ and $\{\alpha, \beta\}$ reference frames

	Magnetic fluxes	Relation between fluxes and currents
Stator	$\frac{d\psi_{1x}}{dt} = u_{1x} - R_1 i_{1x} + \omega_k \psi_{1y}$	$i_{1x} = K_1\psi_{1x} - K\psi_{2x}$
	$\frac{d\psi_{1y}}{dt} = u_{1y} - R_1 i_{1y} - \omega_k \psi_{1x}$	$i_{1y} = K_1\psi_{1y} - K\psi_{2y}$
Rotor	$\frac{d\psi_{2x}}{dt} = u_{2x} - R_2 i_{2x} - (\omega_k - \omega)\psi_{2y}$	$i_{2x} = K_2\psi_{2x} - K\psi_{1x}$
	$\frac{d\psi_{2y}}{dt} = u_{2y} + R_2 i_{2y} - (\omega_k - \omega)\psi_{2x}$	$i_{2y} = K_2\psi_{2y} - K\psi_{1y}$

Table 2. Equations of windings of asynchronous motor model in {x,y} reference frame

The corresponding Simulink model is drawn in Fig. 1. The model of squirrel cage motor (rotor voltages = 0) contains 4 inputs and 10 outputs (Tab. 3).

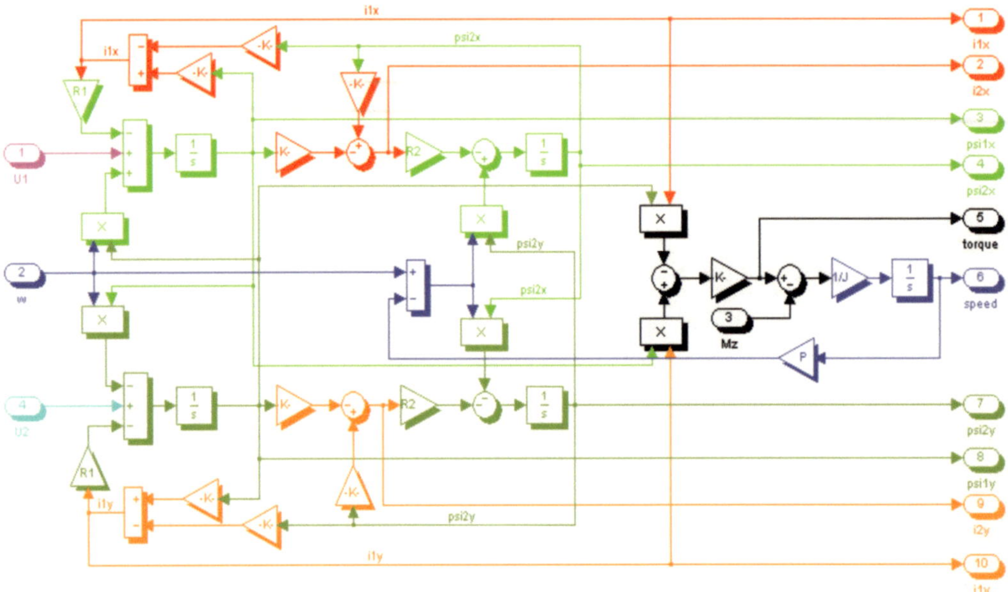

Figure 1. Simulink model of 3 phase squirrel cage asynchronous motor (the variables are denoted in the magnetic field reference frame $\{x, y\}$)

AM model inputs	AM model outputs
• U_1 input voltage (axis x or α)	• current $\bar{i}$ (4 components)
• U_2 input voltage (axis y or β)	• magnetic fluxes $\bar{\Psi}$ (4 components)
• M_z load torque	• motor torque M
• ω_k reference frame angular speed	• rotor angular speed

Table 3. Notation of inputs and outputs of the asynchronous motor model

3.2.1. Modeling of supply source

The asynchronous motor can be set into motion by various supply modes and control platforms:

- by *direct connection* to the supply network or to the frequency converter
- by *frequency starting* (with continuously increasing frequency of the supply voltage from the frequency converter)

Restrict our considerations to supply from indirect converter with the *Voltage-Source Inverter* (VSI). Based on the inverter control mode the output voltage can be:

- unmodulated (with 120 deg. switching in the power semiconductor devices)
- modulated by PWM

Developing inverter simulation schemes we have in mind two facts:

- the *constant stator flux* (i.e. fulfilling condition of constant ratio: U_1/f_1 = const.) should be preserved at all modes of motor control
- in range of very low frequency there should be kept an increased stator voltage (due to the voltage drop across the stator resistor) – so called V-curves (presenting a dependency of the supply voltage from the frequency). The V-curve can be modeled simply by a linear piecewise line.

The model of the motor supply source taking into consideration all described features is shown in Fig. 2 (signals denoted as SL and op are control signals from the GUI buttons). It has 4 inputs: supply frequency and voltage magnitude, ramp frequency and voltage (to simulate frequency starting). The switches "step/ramp" are controlled by pushbuttons from the GUI control panel.

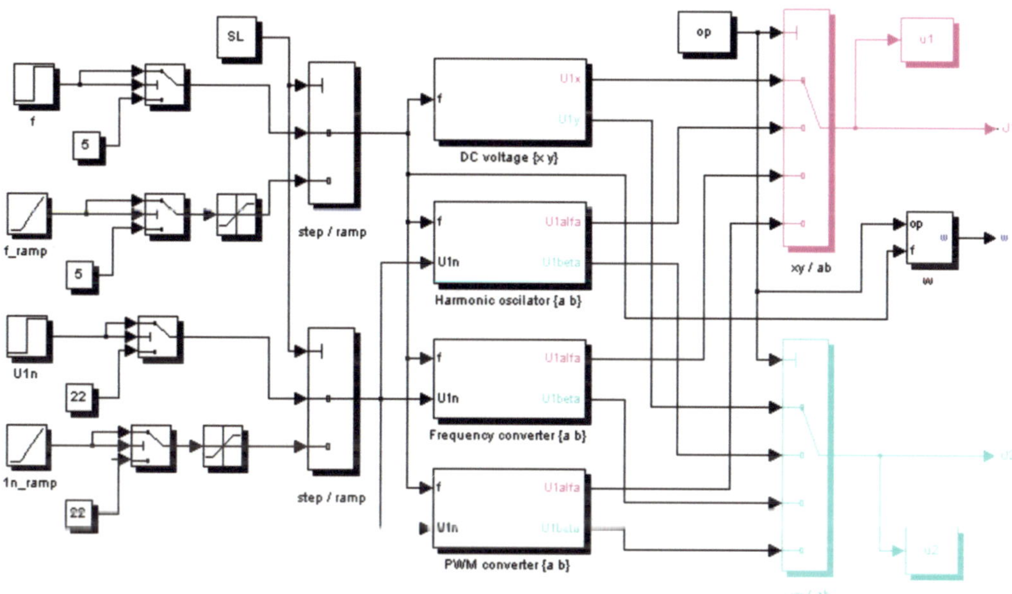

Figure 2. Simulink model of various modes of supply source (DC, harmonic, frequency converter and PWM)

Model of VSI converter (with constant output frequency)

We start to model the inverter output voltage based on a similarity of output converter voltage with the perpendicular harmonic voltages (Fig. 3a). The VSI voltage vector changes its position 6 times per period, after every 60° (Fig. 3b).

Proper switching instants are realized by comparators and switches (Fig. 4). Harmonic oscillator creates a core of the inverter model. Generation of six switching states during period of the output voltage is adjusted by comparing values of the sin/cos signals with pre-set values of *sin* 60 $=\sqrt{3}/2$ for the voltage $u_{1\alpha}$ and value of *cos* 60 = 1/2 for the voltage $u_{1\beta}$. The amplitudes of output voltage are adjusted by constants with values 1; 0,5 for $u_{1\alpha}$ and $0{,}866=\sqrt{3}/2$ for $u_{1\beta}$.

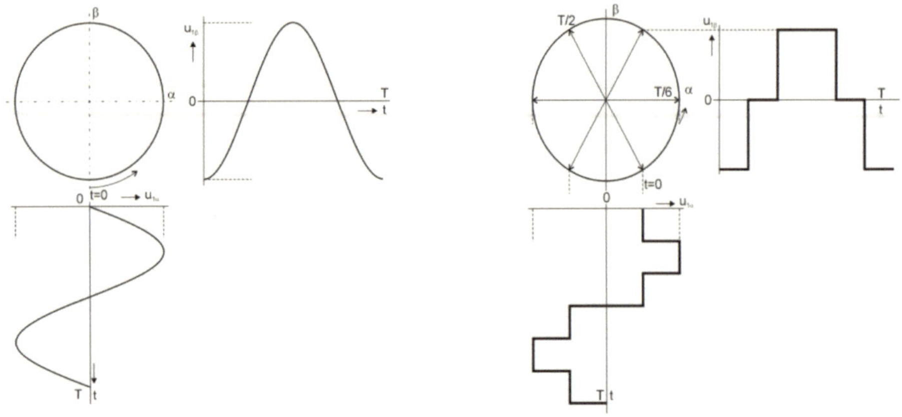

(a) (b)

Figure 3. Simulink model of inverter

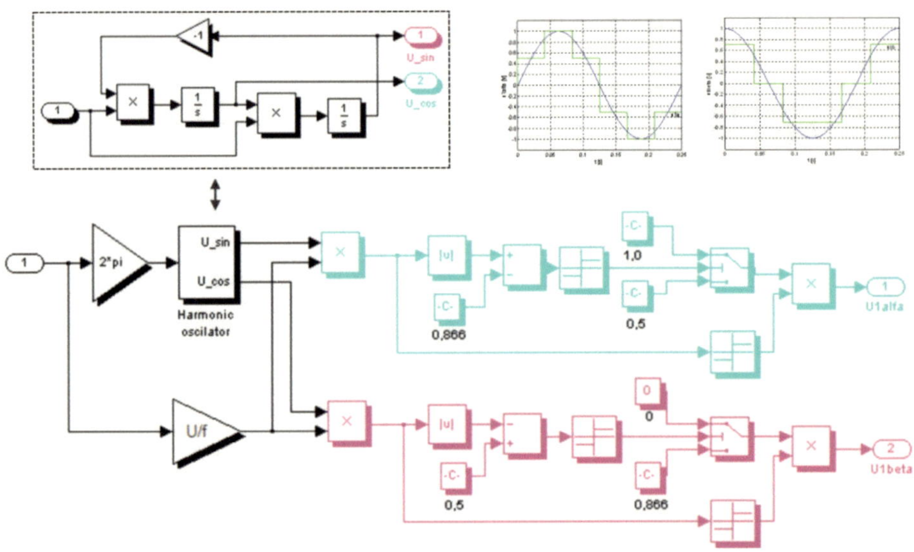

Figure 4. Simulation scheme realizing rectangle voltages $u_{1\alpha}$, $u_{1\beta}$ of the inverter

Model of PWM source

The simplest way to generate a PWM signal uses the intersective method. The three-phase PWM voltage is generated directly in two axes {α, β} as shown in Fig. 5. The courses of the inverter PWM voltages $u_{1\alpha}$ and $u_{1\beta}$ are shown in Fig. 6. In frequency starting mode of the asynchronous motor, the frequency of supply voltage increases from zero to required final value. To get the stator flux constant, the voltage across the motor has to increase linearly with frequency (U/f = const.), except of very low frequency range (due to voltage drop across the stator resistor). For this purpose, the connection must be completed by a compensating circuit which increases the value of supply voltage keeping the ratio U/f = const (Fig. 7). Up to the frequency of approx. 5 Hz the input voltage is kept constant on 10 % of its nominal value.

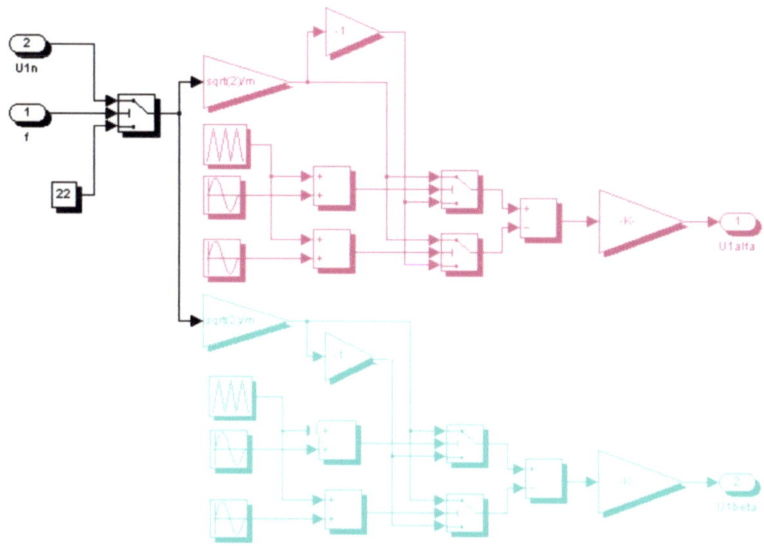

Figure 5. Model of voltages $u_{1\alpha}$ and $u_{1\beta}$ from the inverter with PWM

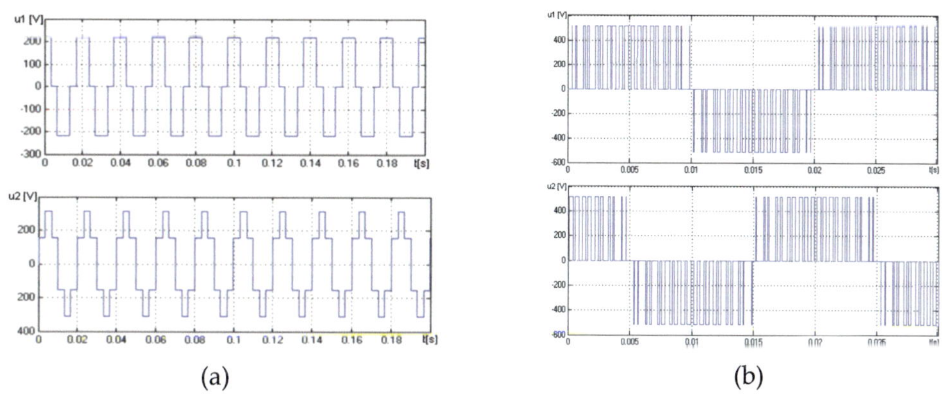

Figure 6. Output voltages and $u_{1\beta}$ and $u_{1\alpha}$ from the frequency converter: a) without and b) with PWM

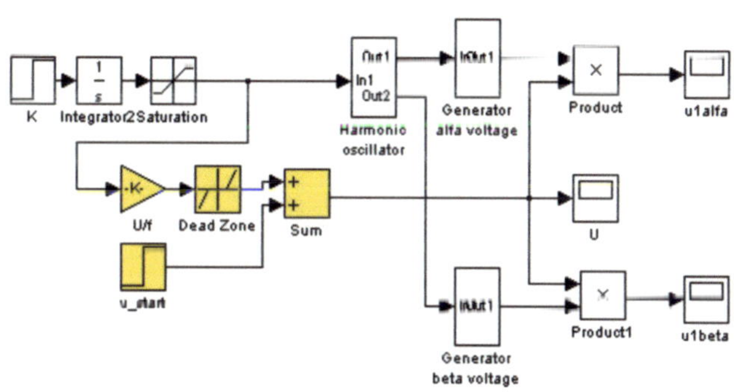

Figure 7. The model of converter realizing the frequency starting under consideration of the law of constant stator flux (U/f = const.)

The model supposes that amplitude of the DC link voltage is changed in the frequency converter. This solution is suitable for drives with low requirements to motor dynamics. The DC link contains a large capacitor what causes the DC link voltage cannot be changed step-by-step. The output inverter voltage can change faster if the PWM control is used. Output voltages of the inverter model with linear increasing frequency and voltage are shown in Fig. 8 (observe a non-zero amplitude of the voltage that at the starting what is consequence of described V-curve block).

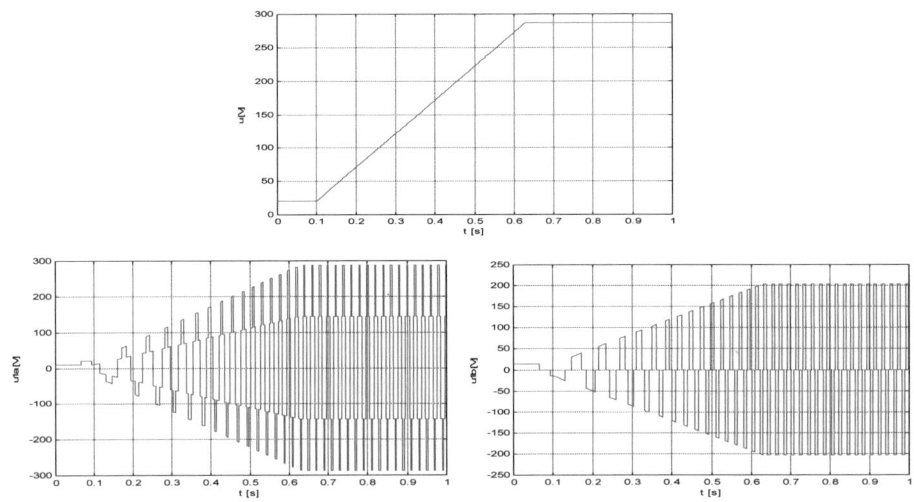

Figure 8. VSI output voltages $u_{1\alpha}$ and $u_{1\beta}$ at increased frequency (the frequency time course is on the top figure)

3.2.2. Model verification

The AC induction motor model was simulated using following motor parameters: R_1=1,8 Ω; R_2=1,85 Ω; *p*=2; *J*=0,05 kgm^2, K_1=59,35; *K2*=59,35; *K*=56,93.

Time courses of mechanical variables are shown in Fig. 10 (they are the same regardless the used reference frame). Motor dynamical characteristics $\omega = f(M)$ at various modes of supply are compared in Fig. 11.

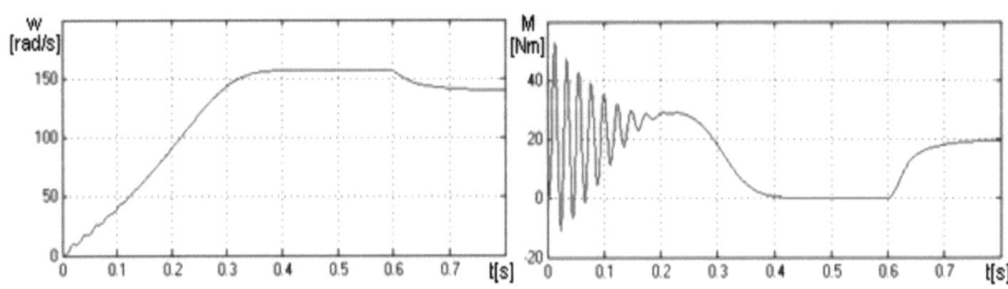

Figure 9. Time responses of asynchronous motor speed and torque at harmonic voltage supply at starting and loading the motor

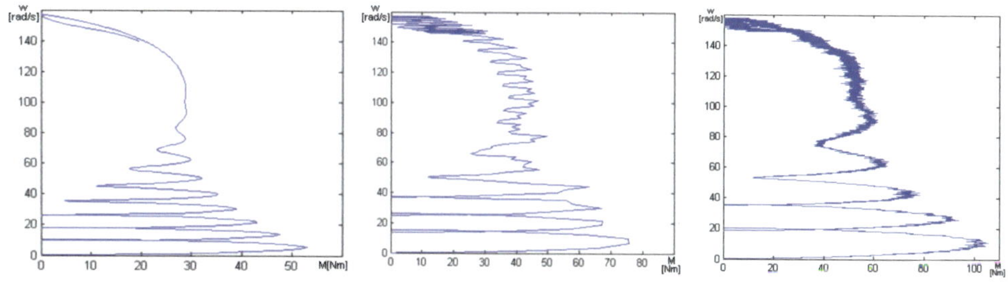

Figure 10. Dynamic characteristic of the asynchronous motor $\omega = f(M)$ supplied: a) by harmonic voltage, b) from frequency converter, c) from frequency converter with PWM

3.2.3. GUI design and realisation

After debugging the motor model (Fig. 11), development of GUI continues with careful design of the program flowchart and design of GUI screen.

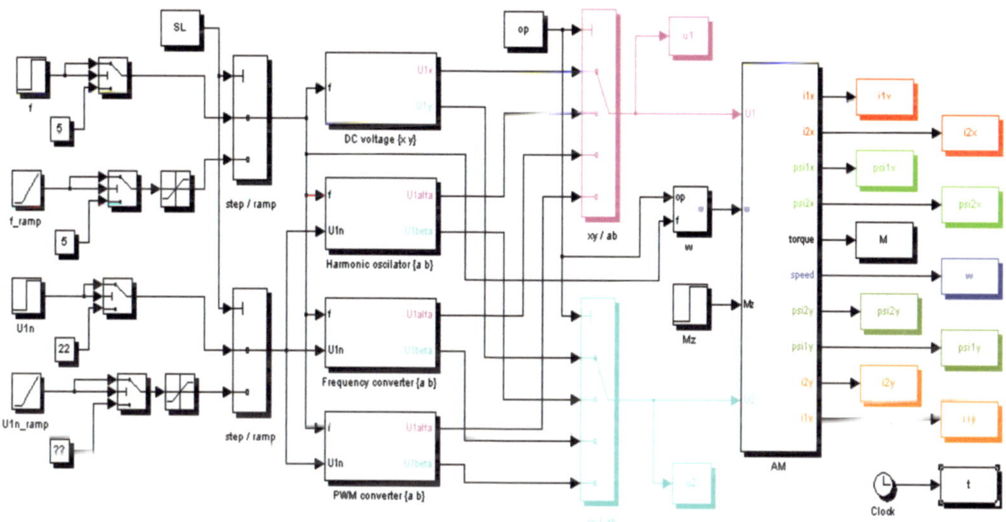

Figure 11. Arrangement of asynchronous motor subsystems in the Simulink GUI model

Description of the GUI functionality

The GUI screen (Fig. 13) consists of several panels. Their functionality is as follows:

- *Input data panel* ("Motor parameters") in the bottom left part. The panel is used to system parameters entry. Their values can be changed by inserting numeric values into editing boxes. There is a possibility to return to original (default) parameters by pushing the button Default (in the pane *Mode*).
- Choice of *Coordinate reference frame system* (the panel on the right top part) enables to display motor output variables:
    - in the synchronously rotating reference frame
    - in the reference frame associated with the stator

   - at harmonic supply
   - at nonharmonics supply from the VSI
   - at nonharmonics supply from the VSI with PWM
- *Output graphs*. Output variables are displayed in four graphs:
   - supply voltage time courses and in two coordinates
   - mechanical variables - motor torque and speed
   - stator currents or magnetic fluxes
   - rotor currents or magnetic fluxes
- The graph to be displayed can be chosen by pushing radio button in the menu *Graphs*. Time courses are chosen by the button *Time*; dependency of one variable on other is chosen by the button *Rectangular*.
- *Mode of starting* the motor can be selected in the panel *Motor supply*:
   - Direct connection to the supply – the button *Step*. The voltage U_1 (effective rms value) and frequency f_1 can be pre-set in the editing boxes.
   - Frequency starting – the button *Linear* enables to pre-set the frequency time rise starting from zero.
- Using the buttons in the panel *Mode* we start *Simulation*, at pressing *Default* (original) parameters are set, and the Simulink scheme is shown by pushing the button *Model* .

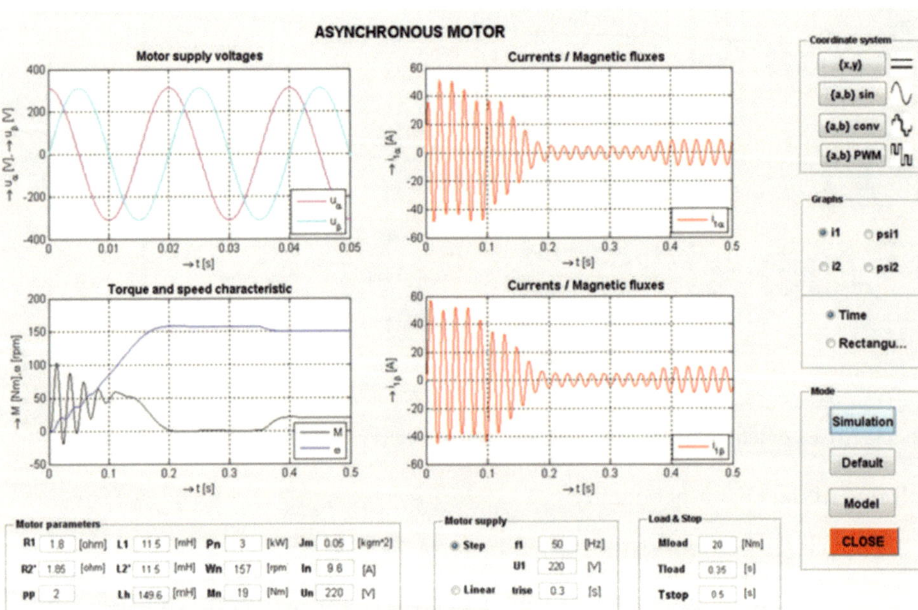

Figure 12. GUI screen of the AC drive with induction machine

Screen outputs

Samples of the screens displaying variables in the stator reference frame $\{\alpha, \beta\}$ are shown in Fig. 13:

a. time courses at supplying motor by frequency converter – button *Time*)

b. chracteristics $M = f(\omega)$, $i_{1\alpha} = f(i_{1\beta})$, $\psi_{1\alpha} = f(\psi_{1\beta})$ - button Rectangular)

c. time courses $i_{1\alpha} = f(t)$, $i_{2\alpha} = f(t)$ at supplying from the PWM frequency converter

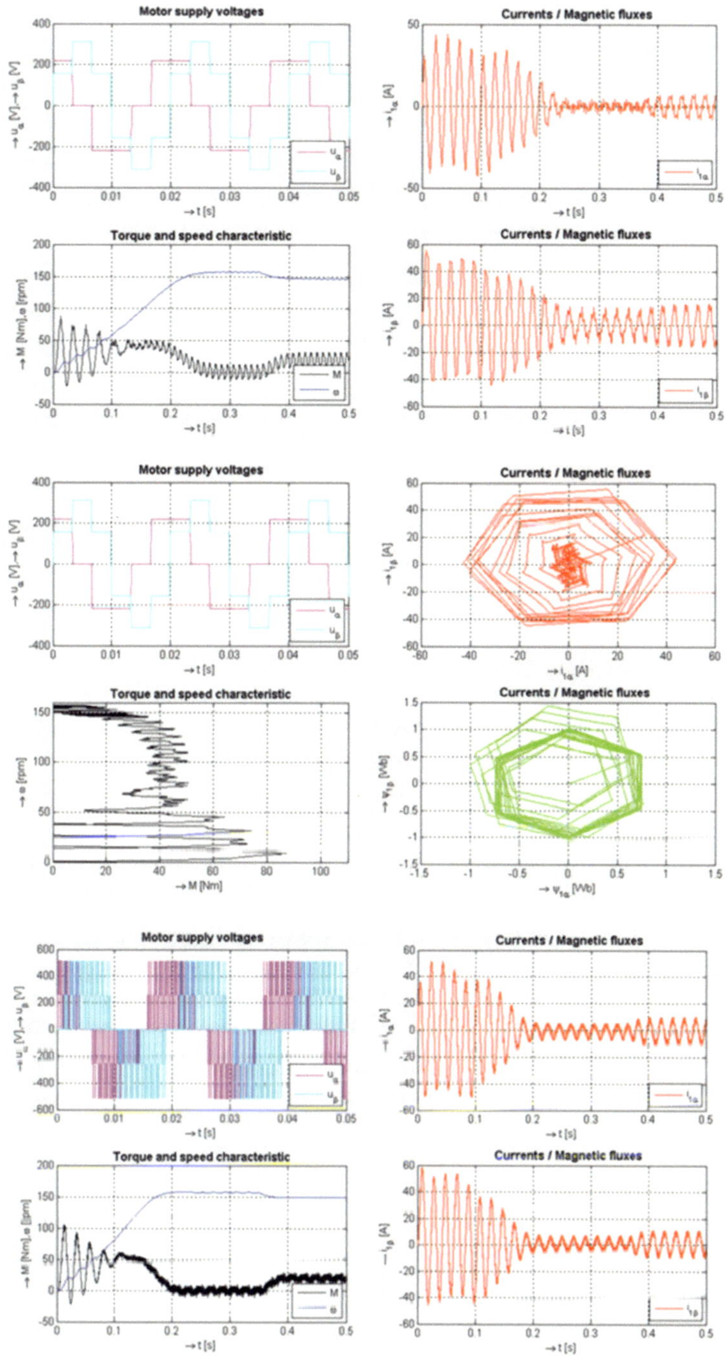

Figure 13. Examples of diplaying various graphs in the GUI for asynchronous motor

3.3. BLDC motor

The Brushless Direct Current (BLDC) motor is rapidly gaining popularity by its utilization in various industries. As the name implies, the BLDC motor do not use brushes for commutation; instead of this they are commutated electronically.

The BLDC motors have many advantages over brushed DC motors and induction motors. A few of these are: (1) Better speed versus torque characteristics; (2) High dynamic response; (3) High efficiency; (4) Long operating life; (5) Noiseless operation; (6) Higher speed ranges. In addition, the ratio of torque delivered to the size of the motor is higher, making it useful in applications where space and weight are critical factors (Indu, 2008).

The torque of the BLDC motor is mainly influenced by the waveform of back-EMF (the voltage induced into the stator winding due to rotor movement). Ideally, the BLDC motors have trapezoidal back-EMF waveforms and are fed with rectangular stator currents, which give theoretically constant torque. However, in practice, a torque ripple exists, mainly due to EMF waveform imperfections, current ripple, and phase current commutation. The current ripple follows up from PWM or hysteresis control. The EMF waveform imperfections result from variations in the shapes of slot, skew and magnet of BLDC motor, and are subject to design purposes. Hence, an error can occur between actual value and the simulation results. Several simulation models have been proposed for analysis of BLDC motor (Jeon, 2000).

3.3.1. Construction and operating principle

The BLDC motor is also referred to as an electronically commuted motor. There are no brushes on the rotor and the commutation is performed electronically at certain rotor positions. In the DC commutator motor, the current polarity is reversed by the commutator and the brushes, but in the brushless DC motor, the polarity reversal is performed by semiconductor switches which are to be switched in synchronization with the rotor position. Besides of the higher reliability, the missing commutator brings another advantage. For the DC brushed motor the commutator presents also a limiting factor in the maximal speed. Therefore, the BLDC motor can be employed in applications requiring high speed (Jeon, 2000).

The BLDC motor is usually considered as a three-phase system and thus it has to be powered by a three-phase power supply. The rotor position must be known at certain angles, in order to align the applied voltage with the back-EMF. The alignment between the back-EMF and commutation events is very important.

A simple motor model of BLDC motor consisting of a three-phase power converter and a brushless DC motor is shown in Fig. 14.

3.3.2. Mathematical model of the BLDC motor

Modeling of a BLDC motor can be developed in the similar manner as a three-phase synchronous machine. Since there is a permanent magnet mounted on the rotor, some dynamic characteristics are different. Similarly, the model of the armature winding for the BLDC motor is expressed as follows:

$$u_a = Ri_a + L\frac{di_a}{dt} + e_a \tag{4}$$

$$u_b = Ri_b + L\frac{di_b}{dt} + e_b \tag{5}$$

$$u_c = Ri_c + L\frac{di_c}{dt} + e_c \tag{6}$$

where L is armature self-inductance, R - armature resistance, u_a, u_b, u_c - terminal phase voltages, i_a, i_b, i_c - motor input currents, and e_a, e_b, e_c - motor back-EMF.

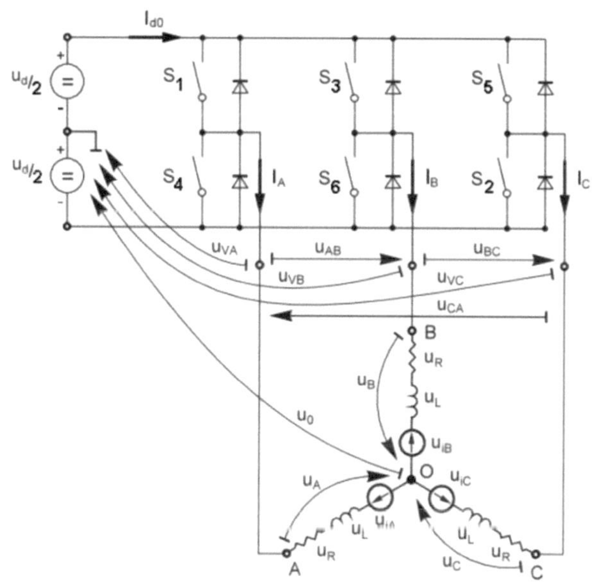

Figure 14. BLDC motor model

In the three-phase BLDC motor, the back-EMF is related to a function of rotor position and the back-EMF of each phase has 120º phase angle difference so the equation for each motor phase is as follows:

$$e_a = K_w f(\theta_e)\,\omega \tag{7}$$

$$e_b = K_w f(\theta_e - 2\pi/3)\omega \tag{8}$$

$$e_c = K_w f(\theta_e + 2\pi/3)\omega \tag{9}$$

where K_w is back EMF constant of one phase, θ_e - electrical rotor angle, ω - rotor speed. The electrical rotor angle θ_e is equal to the mechanical rotor angle θ_m multiplied by the number of poles p:

$$\theta_e = \frac{p}{2}\theta_m \tag{10}$$

Total torque output T_e can be represented as summation of that of each phase:

$$T_e = \frac{e_A i_A + e_B i_B + e_C i_C}{\omega} \tag{11}$$

The equation of mechanical part is represents as follows:

$$T_e - T_l = J\frac{d\omega}{dt} + b\omega \tag{12}$$

where T_l is load torque, J - rotor inertia, b - friction constant.

3.3.3. Simulink model of the BLDC motor

Fig. 16 shows the block diagram of the BLDC motor SIMULINK model in the rotor reference frame.

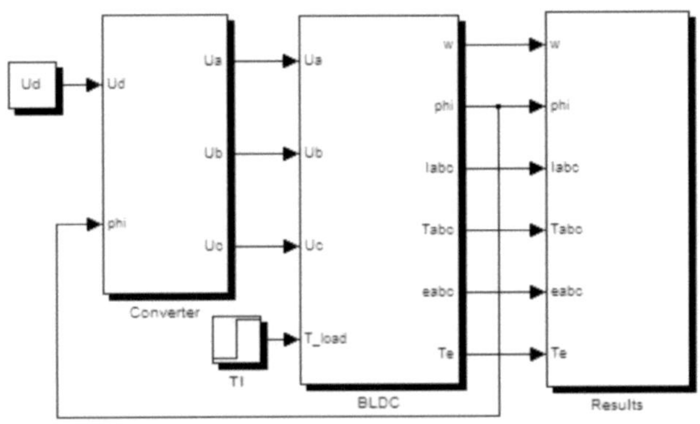

Figure 15. Simulink model of the BLDC motor

Fig. 16 shows detail of the BLDC motor block. Fig. 17a shows Simulink diagram of trapezoidal back-EMF and in Fig. 17b there is Simulink model of sinusoidal back-EMF. The trapezoidal functions and the position signals are stored in lookup tables that change their output according to the value of the electrical angle (Indu, 2008).

Unlike a brushed DC motor, the commutation of a BLDC motor is controlled electronically. To rotate the BLDC motor, the stator windings should be energized in sequences. In order to understand which winding will be energized following the energizing sequence, it is important to know the rotor position. It is sensed using Hall Effect sensors embedded into the stator. Most of the BLDC motors contain three Hall sensors embedded into the stator on the non-driving end of the motor. The number of electrical cycles to be repeated to complete a mechanical rotation is determined by rotor pole pairs. Number of electrical cycles/rotations equals to the rotor pole pairs. The commutation sequences are shown in Tab. 4.

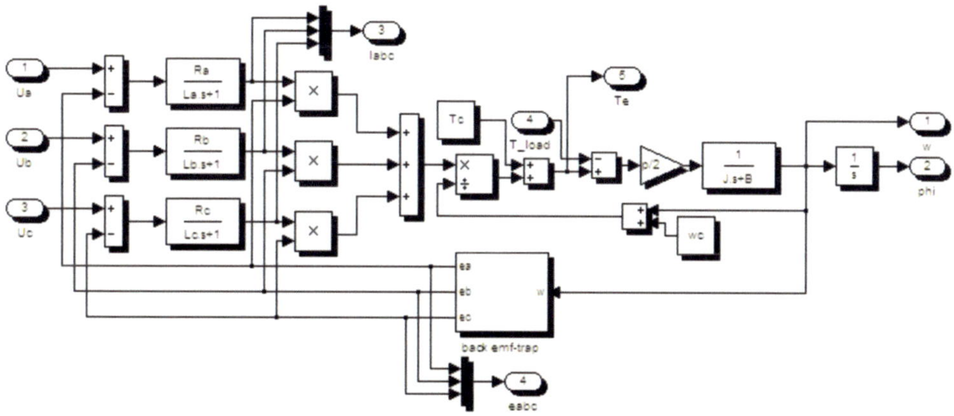

Figure 16. Detailed overview of the BLDC motor block

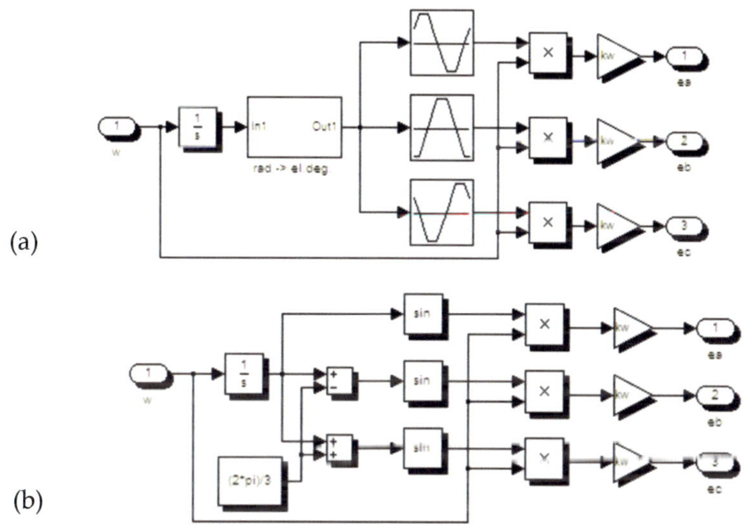

Figure 17. Trapezoidal (a) and simusoidal (b) model of the back-EMF

Electrical degree	Hall sensor value (ABC)	Phase	Switches
0º - 60º	101	A-C	S1-S2
60º - 120º	001	B-C	S2-S3
120º - 180º	011	B-A	S3-S4
180º - 240º	010	C-A	S4-S5
240º - 300º	110	C-B	S5-S6
300º - 360º	100	A-B	S6-S1

Table 4. Electrical degree, Hall sensor value and corresponding commuted phase in clockwise rotation of the rotor

3.3.4. Mathematical and simulink model of the three-phase converter

The converter supplies the input voltage for three phases of the BLDC motor. Each phase leg comprises two power semiconductor devices. Fig. 18 shows the scheme of the considered three-phase converter.

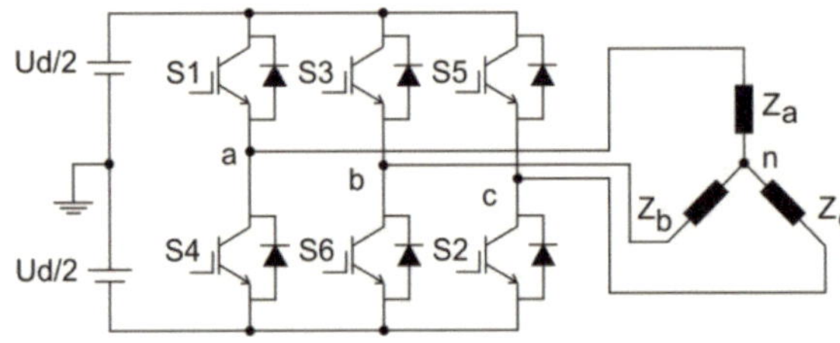

Figure 18. Modelled three-phase converter

Appropriate pairs of the switches (S1 to S6) are driven based on the Hall sensors input. Three phases are commutated in every 60° (el. degrees). The model of the converter is implemented using the equations:

$$U_{an} = S_1\frac{Ud}{2} - S_4\frac{Ud}{2} - U_f \tag{13}$$

$$U_{bn} = S_3\frac{Ud}{2} - S_6\frac{Ud}{2} - U_f \tag{14}$$

$$U_{cn} = S_5\frac{Ud}{2} - S_2\frac{Ud}{2} - U_f \tag{15}$$

where U_{an}, U_{bn}, U_{cn} are line-neural voltages, U_d – the DC link voltage, U_f – the forward diode voltage drop.

Fig. 19a shows the Simulink model of the three-phase converter block. In the simulation we assumed an ideal diode with neglected voltage drop U_f. The *Commutation sequences* block was developed based on the commutation sequence shown in Tab. 4. Converter voltage waveforms that are switched according to the commutation sequences in Tab. 4 are shown in Fig. 19b.

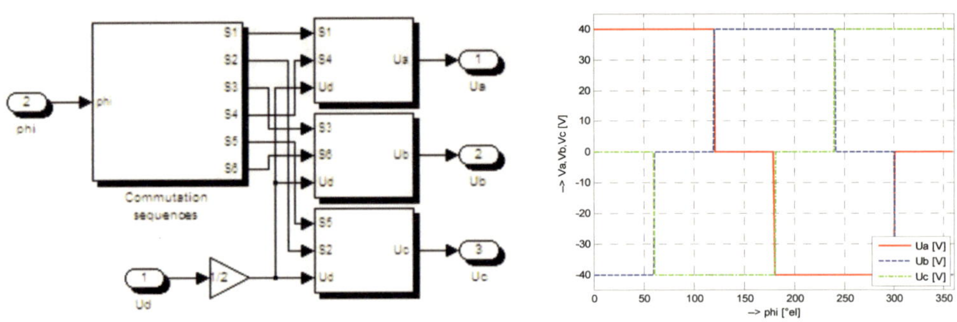

(a) (b)

Figure 19. Detailed overview of the three-phase converter (a) and voltage source waveforms (b)

3.3.5. GUI of the BLDC motor

The simulated BLDC motor is presented in a graphical user interface GUI (Fig. 20).

By the buttons in the panel *Mode* we start the *Simulation* , put *Default* (original) values and show the Simulink *Model*.

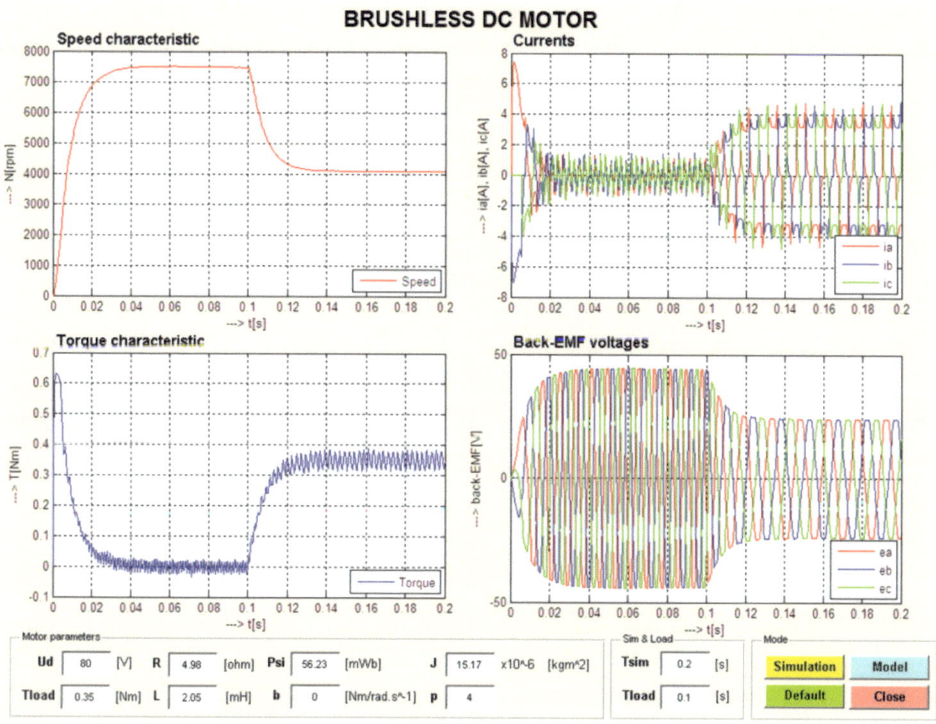

Figure 20. GUI for the BLDC motor

The default parameters of the BLDC motor for simulation are: U_d=80 V, T_l=0,35 Nm, R=4,98 Ω, L=2,05 mH, ψ=56,23.10^{-3} Wb, b=0 Nm/rad.s^{-1}, J=15,17.10^{-6} kgm^2, p=4.

4. Virtual models applied for synthesis of drive systems

MATLAB GUI presents an extremely suitable tool for development of models to support CAD design of drive controllers, whose algorithms are known. Two simple cases are presented below: design of controllers in the frequency and time domains, other cases are mentioned in the subchapter 5.1.

4.1. CAD design of controller parameters for DC motor drive in frequency domain

The DC drive controllers in the *frequency domain* are calculated mostly by using the following criteria:

1. The current controller of the PI type is calculated on basis of the *Optimum Modulus Criterion* (OMC) from the drive system parameters:

$$F_{RI} = K_{RI} + \frac{1}{sT_{iI}} \tag{16}$$

2. After calculation of the current controller parameters and current control loop simplification, the speed controller is calculated based on the *Symmetrical Optimum Criterion* (SOC). It is again of PI type having the transfer function:

$$F_{R_\omega} = K_{R_\omega} + \frac{1}{sT_{i\omega}} \tag{17}$$

Fig. 22 shows the principal block diagram of the system and in Fig. 23 there is view on the virtual GUI model of speed controlled DC drive.

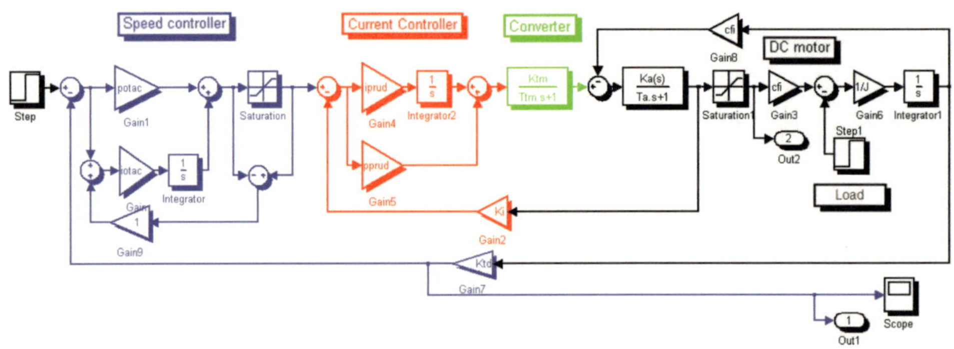

Figure 21. Control circuit of DC motor drive with current and speed controllers

Virtual model features

The user has a possibility to tune controller parameters in each design step according to displayed time response. The GUI screen consists of several panels:

- *Time response* - the graph with time courses of the motor current and speed. Immediately after change of any system parameter (motor -, drive -, or controller parameters) by a slider or inserting a numeric value into editable box the simulation starts and new time responses are drawn (like in a real drive).
- *Block diagram* - displays the block diagram of the system
- *System parameters* are changed by sliders or inserting values into the boxes.

Before starting the model, implicit parameters are set up, but they can be changed later. After pushing the button *Computed value* the parameters of controllers are calculated from the actual values of parameters. Simultaneously a small window appears there with a question whether the calculated values of controller parameters are acceptable or not (if not, user can set up own parameters and can to tune them according to the time responses of the drive). To return to starting values, the user pushes the button *Default* (similar to the system restart).

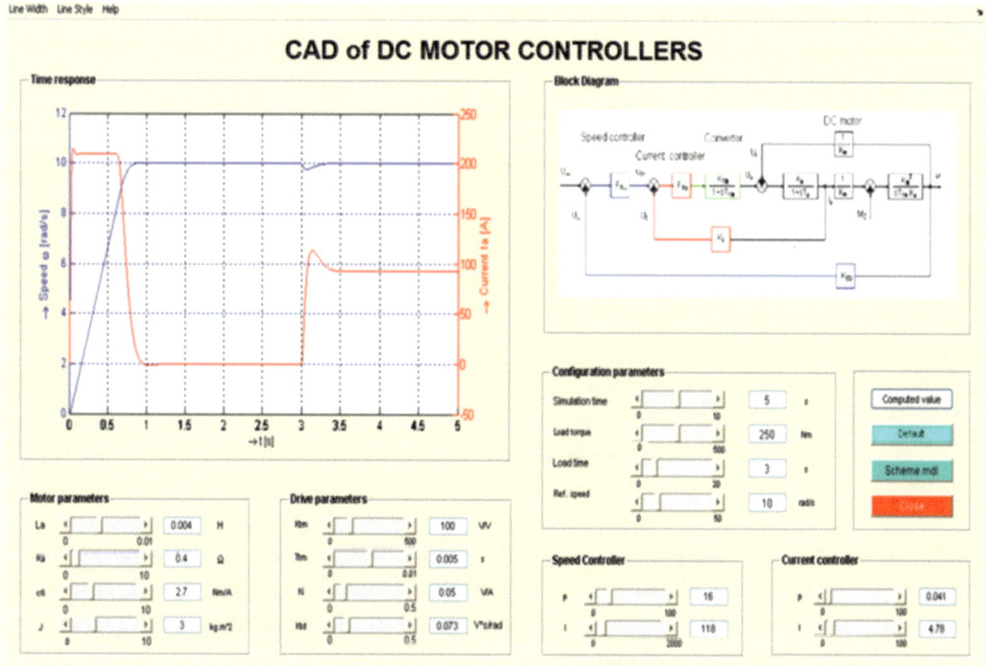

Figure 22. GUI screen for designing DC motor drive controllers in the frequency domain

4.2. CAD design of controller parameters for DC motor drive in time domain

The computing algorithm is different from calculation of the controllers in the frequency domain and the task belongs to more complex one. The computation starts from the state-space model of the DC motor having two inputs in one output, in the form of state equations:

$$\dot{\mathbf{x}} = \mathbf{A}.\mathbf{x} + \mathbf{b}.u + \mathbf{e}.z = \begin{bmatrix} 0 & \dfrac{K_m}{T_m.K_a} \\ -\dfrac{K_a}{K_m.T_a} & -\dfrac{1}{T_a} \end{bmatrix} x + \begin{bmatrix} 0 \\ \dfrac{K_T.K_a}{T_a} \end{bmatrix} u + \begin{bmatrix} -\dfrac{K_m^2}{T_m.K_a} \\ 0 \end{bmatrix} M_z \tag{18}$$

$$y = c^T x = \begin{bmatrix} 1 & 0 \end{bmatrix} x \tag{19}$$

where **A** is system matrix, **x** – state vector, **b** – input vector, $\mathbf{c}^T$ - output (row) vector **e**-disturbance vector, u – input variable, y - output variable.

The final control structure with the feedback through the state controller vector $\boldsymbol{r}^T$ is clear from the Simulink model Fig. 23. The integrator at the input serves to reject constant or slowly changing disturbances what is a common case.

The state control structure parameters: K_i , r_1 and r_2 are designed by known *pole placement method* where for a prescribed position of poles the required polynomial is compared with the system polynomial and missing parameters of the controller are calculated from a set of linear algebraic equations.

The control structure in Simulink to simulate the system is shown in (Fig. 23).

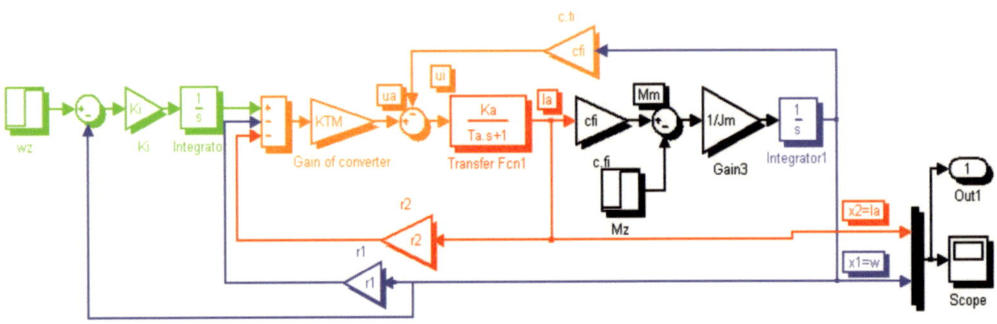

Figure 23. Simulink model of the state-space control of DC drive

Fig. 24 shows the GUI screen of the virtual model that enables to calculate state-space controller parameters and visualize time responses of the current and speed. It is a more complex GUI involving synthesis of the state-space controllers and giving the possibility to tune theoretically calculated parameters.

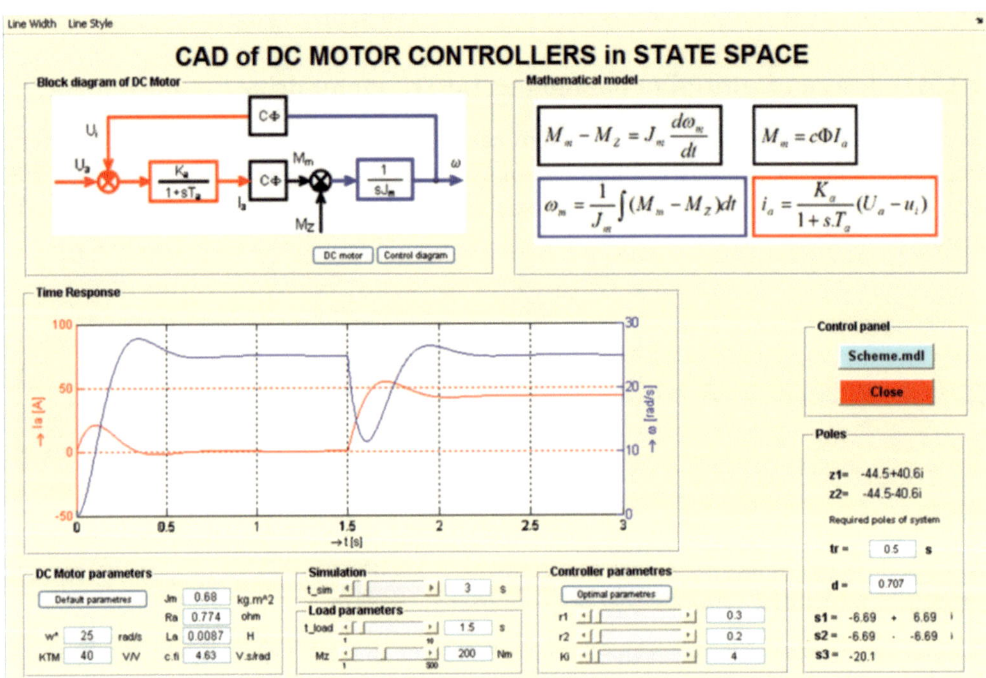

Figure 24. GUI screen for designing DC motor drive controllers in the state space domain

The panel *Controller parameters* serves to setting parameters of the state controller – by tuning or selecting the button *Optimal parameters* to calculate poles position placement.

Here:

- r_1 – feedback from state variable x_1 (motor speed),
- r_2 – feedback from state variable x_2 (motor current),
- K_i – gain of the integrator (to reject steady-state disturbances).

The state controller parameters are calculated automatically on basis of required values of control time and damping (panel *Poles*, the item *Required poles of the system*). In the upper part of the panel the real positions of poles are shown.

5. Experiences with utilization of virtual models

5.1. Utilization of virtual dynamical models

Except of the presented GUI screens of virtual models a series of tens other models from fields of electrical engineering and mechatronic systems was developed to suit institutional needs. They cover topics from Electrical Machines, Power Electronics, Electrical Actuators and Drives, Servodrives, Mechatronic Systems, Control Theory, and others. We have also developed some more complex GUIs, reported e.g. by (Ismeal & Fedák, 2012), calculating artificial intelligence algorithms - to design PID controllers using fuzzy logic and genetic algorithms with various objective functions to evaluate the best PID controller.

The developed GUIs serve as virtual models to clarify phenomena and enhance features of the systems during lectures, and to prepare students for laboratory work. In order students to get more skills and practical experiences prior entering lab their work consists of two phases:

Design and simulation – for a given system motor or drive a student has:

- to derive mathematical model,
- to compose the block diagram,
- to design control law and controllers (in case of drives),
- to verify system behavior by simulation.

Verification and analysis – a student has:

- to verify the design using a virtual reference model,
- to perform system analysis ("to play himself" with the virtual model) in order to investigate system behavior at various values of system parameters and in various working points (small experiments round working point).

5.2. Application of MATLAB compiler in virtual model development

A disadvantage of using GUI MATLAB consists in the fact, that the program can run only on a computer having installed the MATLAB program (and appropriate toolboxes containing instructions that are used in the main GUI program). This disadvantage can be suppressed by development of an executable (.exe) file from the original program. In this case the developer must install the Compiler Runtime program. The MATLAB Compiler creates a standalone executable file from the MATLAB code, which can then run in a runtime engine called *Matlab Compiler Runtime* (MCR). Once compiled, the standalone application, along with MCR, can be shared with other users for free. The only problem is that the original GUI MATLAB program cannot contain any Simulink model (mdl file). As the GUI MATLAB systems usually contain Simulink models, they have to be replaced by MATLAB programs solving mathematical model by various algorithms.

6. Conclusion

The chapter describes principles and methodology of virtual models development in GUI MATLAB for few chosen electrical machines and controlled drives. The models perform analyses of real machines and drives in various working points and they enable easily to show system performance in various working points and to analyze influence of variable system parameters, modes of supply, and control parameters to system behavior. Presented virtual models have been of various complexity – the simpler ones enable virtual analysis of electrical machines and more complex virtual models also deal with algorithms for synthesis of drive controllers.

Strong advantage of developed virtual models consists in the fact user does not need to know the complexity of dynamical system whose simulation scheme is working in the background. He changes only system parameters, selects input signals (shape and amplitude of reference values, forcing and load signals), select mode of calculations and outputs (graphs displaying). The parameters of virtual models can be changed by a slider or by editing numerical values in editable boxes.

Based on the procedure a whole series of virtual models designed in GUI MATLAB has been developed at the authors' institution in recent years which are partly accessible trough the website of the Virtual Laboratory for Control of Mechatronic Systems (KEM TU Kosice, 2010). The virtual dynamical models contribute to e-learning support at teaching and they also serve for preparation of students for laboratory experimentation. Their utilization makes more attractive lectures and considerably enhances explanation of systems properties. By simulation model students generally easier understand physical processes and they are better prepared to the laboratory work.

Shortcoming of developed models consists in the fact they run on computers having installed the MATLAB program. To overcome this, recently our work was concentrated to applications of the MATLAB Compiler to develop excecutable files. It should be noted that this application enables to run MATLAB operation without simulation (i.e. without a Simulink scheme), without 3D virtual reality views and without animation. The advantage on one side makes development of virtual models more difficult using more complex mathematical subroutines. Also some known problems with GUI MATLAB should be noted - cross platform appearance may not be the same and during the GUI development, often must be used tricks and somehow unfriendly techniques.

Author details

Viliam Fedák and Pavel Záskalický
Technical University of Košice, Slovakia

Tibor Balogh
Magneti Marelli, Electronic Systems Division, Industrial Park Kechnec, Slovakia

Acknowledgement

The financial support of the Slovak Research and Development Agency under the contract No. APVV-0138-10 is acknowledged. The work was also supported by Slovak Cultural and Educational Agency of the Ministry of Education of Slovak Republic under the contract KEGA 042TUKE-4/2012 "Teaching Innovation in Control of Mechatronic Systems".

7. References

Galitz, W. O. (2007). The Essential Guide to User Interface Design. An Introduction to GUI Design Principles and Techniques, *Wiley Publishing, Inc.*, ISBN 978-0-470-05342-3, Indianapolis, Indiana

Hill, S. (2011). How to Make an Executable From MATLAB Code, Date of access: Mach 31, 2011, <http://www.ehow.com/how_8686360_make-executable-matlab-code.html>

Indu, B., Ashly, R. & Tom, M. (2008). Dynamic Simulation of Brushless DC Drive Considering Phase Commutation and Backemf Waveform for Electromechanical Actuator. *IEEE TENCON,* Hyderabad 2008. ISBN: 978-1-4244-2408-5

Ismeal G.A. & Fedák V. (2012). Overview of Control Algorithms for DC Motor Drive as a Basis for Development of GUI in MATLAB. *XXVI. microCAD International Scientific Conference,* Miskolc, 2012, 9 p., ISBN 978-963-661-773-8

Jeon, Y.S., Mok, H.S., Choe, G.H., Kim, D.K. & Ryu, J.S. (2000). A New Simulation Model of BLDC Motor with Real Back EMF waveforms. *IEEE CNF on Computers in Power Electronics*, COMPEL 2000, pp. 217 – 220, July 2000

KEM TU Kosice (2010). Virtual Laboratory of Mechatronic Systems Control. , In: Date of access: March 31, 2012, Available from <http://andromeda.fei.tuke.sk/> (in Slovak)

MathWorks (n.d.). Deploytool - R2012a Documentation MATLAB Compiler http://www.mathworks.com/help/toolbox/compiler/deploytool.html

Parspour, N. & Hanitsch, R. (1994). Fuzzy Controlled Brushless DC Motor For Medical Applications. *Industrial Electronic, Control and Instrumentation IECON, IEEE,* Bologna, 1994, ISBN: 0-7803-1328-3

Petropol-Serb, G.D.; Petropol-Serb, I.; Campeanu, A. & Petrisor, A. (2007). Using GUI of Matlab to create a virtual laboratory to study an induction machine. EUROCON, 2007. *The International Conference on Computer as a Tool,* ISBN 978-1-4244-0813-9, Warsaw, September 9-12, 2007

Riaz, M. (n.d.): Simulation of Electric Machine and Drive Systems Using MATLAB and Simulink. University of Minnesota. www.ece.umn.edu/users/riaz/

Saadat, H. (2012). MATLAB Graphical User Interface for EE Students. Date of access: March 31, 2012, Available from <http://people.msoe.edu/~saadat/matlabgui.htm

Section 2

Image and Signal Processing

Chapter 15

Image Reconstruction Methods for MATLAB Users – A Moore-Penrose Inverse Approach

S. Chountasis, V.N. Katsikis and D. Pappas

Additional information is available at the end of the chapter

http://dx.doi.org/10.5772/45811

1. Introduction

In the last decades the Moore-Penrose pseudoinverse has found a wide range of applications in many areas of Science and became a useful tool for different scientists dealing with optimization problems, data analysis, solutions of linear integral equations, etc. At first we will present a review of some of the basic results on the so-called Moore-Penrose pseudoinverse of matrices, a concept that generalizes the usual notion of inverse of a square matrix, but that is also applicable to singular square matrices or even to non-square matrices.

The notion of the generalized inverse of a (square or rectangular) matrix was first introduced by H. Moore in 1920, and again by R. Penrose in 1955, who was apparently unaware of Moore's work. These two definitions are equivalent, (as it was pointed by Rao in 1956) and since then, the generalized inverse of a matrix is also called the Moore-Penrose inverse.

Let A be a $r \times m$ real matrix. Equations of the form $Ax = b, A \in \mathbb{R}^{r \times m}, b \in \mathbb{R}^r$ occur in many pure and applied problems. It is known that when T is singular, then its unique generalized inverse $A^{\dagger}$ (known as the Moore- Penrose inverse) is defined. In the case when A is a real $r \times m$ matrix, Penrose showed that there is a unique matrix satisfying the four Penrose equations, called the generalized inverse of A, noted by $A^{\dagger}$.

An important question for applications is to find a general and algorithmically simple way to compute $A^{\dagger}$. There are several methods for computing the Moore-Penrose inverse matrix (cf. [2]). The most common approach uses the Singular Values Decomposition (SVD). This method is very accurate but also time-intensive since it requires a large amount of computational resources, especially in the case of large matrices. Therefore, many other methods can be used for the numerical computation of various types of generalized inverses, see [16]; [25]; [30]. For more on the Moore-Penrose inverse, generalized inverses in general and their applications, there are many excellent texbooks on this subject, see [2]; [30]; [4].

The Moore-Penrose pseudoinverse is a useful concept in dealing with optimization problems, as the determination of a Şleast squaresŤ solution of linear systems. A typical application of the Moore-Penrose inverse is its use in Image and signal Processing and Image restoration.

The field of image restoration has seen a tremendous growth in interest over the last two decades, see [1]; [5]; [6]; [14]; [28]; [29]. The recovery of an original image from degraded observations is of crucial importance and finds application in several scientific areas including medical imaging and diagnosis, military surveillance, satellite and astronomical imaging, and remote sensing. A number of various algorithms have been proposed and intensively studied for achieving a fast recovered and high resolution reconstructed images, see [10]; [15]; [22].

The presented method in this article is based on the use of the Moore-Penrose generalized inverse of a matrix and provides us a fast computational algorithm for a fast and accurate digital image restoration. This article is an extension of the work presented in [7]; [8].

2. Theoretical background

2.1. The Moore-Penrose inverse

We shall denote by $\mathbb{R}^{r\times m}$ the algebra of all $r \times m$ real matrices. For $T \in \mathbb{R}^{r\times m}$, $R(T)$ will denote the range of T and $N(T)$ the kernel of T. The generalized inverse $T^{\dagger}$ is the unique matrix that satisfies the following four Penrose equations:

$$TT^{\dagger} = (TT^{\dagger})^{*}, \qquad T^{\dagger}T = (T^{\dagger}T)^{*}, \qquad TT^{\dagger}T = T, \qquad T^{\dagger}TT^{\dagger} = T^{\dagger},$$

where T^{*} denotes the transpose matrix of T.

Let us consider the equation $Tx = b, T \in \mathbb{R}^{r\times m}, b \in \mathbb{R}^{r}$, where T is singular. If T is an arbitrary matrix, then there may be none, one or an infinite number of solutions, depending on whether $b \in R(T)$ or not, and on the rank of T. But if $b \notin R(T)$, then the equation has no solution. Therefore, another point of view of this problem is the following: instead of trying to solve the equation $\|Tx - b\| = 0$, we are looking for a minimal norm vector u that minimizes the norm $\|Tu - b\|$. Note that this vector u is unique. So, in this case we consider the equation $Tx = P_{R(T)}b$, where $P_{R(T)}$ is the orthogonal projection on $\mathcal{R}(T)$. Since we are interested in the distance between Tx and b, it is natural to make use of $\|T\|_2$ norm.

The following two propositions can be found in [12].

Proposition 0.1. *Let $T \in \mathbb{R}^{r\times m}$ and $b \in \mathbb{R}^{r}, b \notin R(T)$. Then, for $u \in \mathbb{R}^{m}$, the following are equivalent:*

(i) $Tu = P_{R(T)}b$

(ii) $\|Tu - b\| \leq \| Tx - b\|, \forall x \in \mathbb{R}^{m}$

(iii) $T^{*}Tu = T^{*}b$

Let $\mathbb{B} = \{u \in \mathbb{R}^{m} | T^{*}Tu = T^{*}b\}$. This set of solutions is closed and convex; it therefore has a unique vector u_0 with minimal norm. In fact, $\mathbb{B}$ is an affine manifold; it is of the form $u_0 + \mathcal{N}(T)$. In the literature (c.f. [12]), $\mathbb{B}$ is known as the set of the least square solutions.

Proposition 0.2. *Let $T \in \mathbb{R}^{r \times m}$ and $b \in \mathbb{R}^r, b \notin R(T)$, and the equation $Tx = b$. Then, if $T^\dagger$ is the generalized inverse of T, we have that $T^\dagger b = u$, where u is the minimal norm solution defined above.*

We shall make use of this property for the construction of an alternative method in image processing inverse problems.

2.2. Image restoration problems

The general pointwise definition of the transform $\tau(u, v)$ that is used in order to convert an $r \times r$ pixel image $s(x, y)$ from the spatial domain to some other domain in which the image exhibits more readily reducible features is given in the following equation:

$$\tau(u,v) = \frac{1}{r} \sum_{x=1}^{r} \sum_{y=1}^{r} s(x,y) g(x,y,u,v) \tag{1}$$

where u and v are the coordinates in the transform domain and $g(x, y, u, v)$ denote the general basis function used by the transform. Similarly, the inverse transform is given as:

$$s(x,y) = \frac{1}{r} \sum_{u=1}^{r} \sum_{v=1}^{r} \tau(u,v) h(x,y,u,v) \tag{2}$$

where $h(x, y, u, v)$ represents the inverse of the basis function $g(x, y, u, v)$.

The two dimensional version of the function $g(x, y, u, v)$ in Equation (1) can typically be derived as a series of one dimensional functions. Such functions are referred to as being 'separable', we can derive the separable two dimensional functions as follows: The transform been performed across x

$$\tau'(u,y) = \frac{1}{\sqrt{r}} \sum_{x=1}^{r} s(x,y) g(x,u) \tag{3}$$

Moreover we transform across y:

$$\tau(u,v) = \frac{1}{\sqrt{r}} \sum_{y=1}^{r} \tau'(u,y) g(y,u) \tag{4}$$

and using Equation (3) we have

$$\tau(u,v) = \frac{1}{r} \sum_{x=1}^{r} \sum_{y=1}^{r} s(x,y) g(x,u) g(y,u) \tag{5}$$

We can use an identical approach in order to write Equation (1) and its inverse (Equation 2) in matrix form , using the standard orthonormal basis:

$$T = GSG^T, \quad S = HTH^T \tag{6}$$

in which T, S, G and H are the matrix equivalents of τ, s, g and h respectively. This is due to our use of orthogonal basis functions, meaning the basis function is its own inverse. Therefore, it is easy to see that the complete process to perform the transform, and then invert it is thus:

$$S = HGSG^T H^T \tag{7}$$

In order for the transform to be reversible we need H to be the inverse of G and H^T to be the inverse of G^T, i.e. , $HG = G^T H^T = I$.

Given that G is orthogonal it is trivial to show that this is satisfied when $H = G^T$. Given H is merely the transpose of G the inverse function for $g(x, y, u, v)h(x, y, u, v)$ is also separable.

In the scientific area of image processing the analytical form of a linear degraded image is given by the following integral equation :

$$x_{out}(i, j) = \int\int_D x_{in}(u, v)h(i, j; u, v)dudv$$

where $x_{in}(u, v)$ is the original image, $x_{out}(i, j)$ represents the measured data from where the original image will be reconstructed and $h(i, j; u, v)$ is a known Point Spread Function (PSF). The PSF depends on the measurement imaging system and is defined as the output of the system for an input point source.

A digital image described in a two dimensional discrete space is derived from an analogue image $x_{in}(u, v)$ in a two dimensional continuous space through a sampling process that is frequently referred to as digitization. The two dimensional continuous image is divided into r rows and m columns. The intersection of a row and a column is termed a pixel. The discrete model for the above linear degradation of an image can be formed by the following summation

$$x_{out}(i, j) = \sum_{u=1}^{r} \sum_{v=1}^{m} x_{in}(u, v)h(i, j; u, v) \tag{8}$$

where $i = 1, 2, \ldots, r$ and $j = 1, 2, \ldots, m$.

In this work we adopt the use of a shift invariant model for the blurring process as in [11]. Therefore, the analytically expression for the degraded system is given by a two dimensional (horizontal and vertical) convolution i.e.,

$$x_{out}(i, j) = \sum_{u=1}^{r} \sum_{v=1}^{m} x_{in}(u, v)h(i - u, j - v) = x_{in}(i, j) * *h(i, j) \tag{9}$$

where $**$ indicates two dimensional convolution.

In the formulation of equation (8) the noise can also be simulated by rewriting the equation as

$$x_{out}(i, j) = \sum_{u=1}^{r} \sum_{v=1}^{m} x_{in}(u, v)h(i, j; u, v) + n(i, j) = x_{in}(i, j) * *h(i, j) + n(i, j) \tag{10}$$

where $n(i, j)$ is an additive noise introduced by the system.

However, in this work the noise is image related which means that the noise has been added to the image.

2.3. The Fourier Transform, the Haar basis and the moments in image reconstruction problems

Moments are particularly popular due to their compact description, their capability to select differing levels of detail and their known performance attributes (see [3]; [9];[17]; [18]; [19]; [20]; [26]; [27]; [28]. It is a well-recognised property of moments that they can be used to reconstruct the original function, i.e., none of the original image information is lost in the projection of the image on to the moment basis functions, assuming an infinite number of moments are calculated. Another property for the reconstruction of a band-limited image using its moments is that while derivatives give information on the high frequencies of a signal, moments provide information on its low frequencies. It is known that the higher order moments capture increasingly higher frequencies within a function and in the case of an image the higher frequencies represent the detail of the image. This is also consistent with work on other types of reconstruction, such as eigenanalysis where it has been found that increasing numbers of eigenvectors are required to capture image detail ([23],) and again exceed the number required for recognition. Describing images with moments instead of other more commonly used image features means that global properties of the image are used rather than local properties. Moments provide information on its low frequency of an image. Applying the Fourier coefficients a low pass approximation of the original image is obtained. It is well known that any image can be reconstructed from its moments in the least-squares sense. Discrete orthogonal moments provide a more accurate description of image features by evaluating the moment components directly in the image coordinate space.

The reconstruction of an image from its moments is not necessarily unique. Thus, all possible methods must impose extra constraints in order to its moments uniquely solve the reconstruction problem.

The most common reconstruction method of an image from some of its moments is based on the least squares approximation of the image using orthogonal polynomials ([19]; [21]). In this paper the constraint that introduced is related to the bandwidth of the image and provides a more general reconstruction method. We must keep in mind that this constraint is a global, for a local one a joint bilinear distribution such as Wigner or wavelet must be used.

2.3.1. The Fourier Basis

In view of the importance of the frequency domain, the Fourier Transform (FT) has become one of the most widely used signal analysis tool across many disciplines of science and engineering. The FT is generated by projecting the signal on to a set of basis functions, each of which is a sinusoid with a unique frequency. The FT of a time signal $s(t)$ is given by

$$\tilde{s}(\omega) = \frac{1}{\sqrt{2\pi}} \int_{-\infty}^{+\infty} s(t)exp(-i\omega t)dt$$

where $\omega = 2\pi f$ is the angular frequency. Since the set of exponentials forms an orthogonal basis the signal can be reconstructed from the projection values

$$s(t) = \frac{1}{\sqrt{2\pi}} \int_{-\infty}^{+\infty} \tilde{s}(\omega)exp(i\omega t)d\omega$$

Following the property of the FT that the convolution in the spatial domain is translated into simple algebraic product in the spectral domain Equation (8) can be written in the form

$$\tilde{x}_{out} = \tilde{x}_{in}\tilde{H} \tag{11}$$

In a discrete Fourier domain the two-dimensional Fourier coefficients are defined as

$$F(m,n) = \frac{1}{\sqrt{XY}} \sum_{x=1}^{X} \sum_{y=1}^{Y} S_{XY} exp(-2\pi i(\frac{(x-1)(m-1)}{X} + \frac{(y-1)(n-1)}{Y})) \tag{12}$$

rearranging the above equation leads to

$$F(m,n) = \frac{1}{\sqrt{XY}} \sum_{x=1}^{X} exp(-2\pi i \frac{(x-1)(m-1)}{X}) \sum_{y=1}^{Y} S_{XY} exp(-2\pi i \frac{(y-1)(n-1)}{Y}))$$

thus, $F(m,n)$ can be written in matrix form as:

$$F(m,n) = K_S(x,m) S_{XY} K_S(y,n)^*$$

where $K_S(y,n)^*$ denotes the conjugate transpose of the forward kernel $K_S(y,n)$.

Using the same principles but writing Equation (12) in a form where the increasing indexes correspond to higher frequency coefficients we obtain

$$F(m,n) = \frac{1}{\sqrt{XY}} \sum_{x=1}^{X} \sum_{y=1}^{Y} S_{XY} \cdot \exp[-2\pi i(\frac{(x-1)(m-\frac{(k-1)}{2}-1)}{X} + \frac{(y-\frac{(l-1)}{2}-1)(n-1)}{Y})]$$

The Fourier coefficients can be seen as the projection coefficients of the image S_{XY} onto a set of complex exponential basis functions that lead to the basis matrix:

$$B_{kl}(m,n) = \frac{1}{\sqrt{k}} exp[-2\pi i \frac{(m-1)(n-\frac{(l-1)}{2}-1)}{k}]$$

The approximation of an image S_{XY} in the least square sense, can be expressed in terms of the projection matrix P_{kl} :

$$P_{kl} = (B_{Xk})^T S_{XY} B_{Yl}$$

as

$$\begin{aligned} S'_{XY} &= B_{Xk}(B_{Xk}^T B_{Xk}^T)^{-1} P_{kl} (B_{Yl}^T B_{Yl})^{-1} B_{Yl}^T \\ &= (B_{Xk})^- P_{kl} (B_{Yl})^\dagger \end{aligned}$$

where $()^T$ and $()^{-1}$ denote the transpose and the inverse of the given matrix. The operations $()^-$ and $()^\dagger$ stand for the left and right inverses, both are equal to the Moore-Penrose inverse, and are unique. Among the multiple inverse solutions it chooses the one with minimum norm. When considering image reconstruction from moments, the number of moments required for accurate reconstruction will be related to the frequencies present within the original image. For a given image size it would appear that there should be a finite limit to the frequencies that are present in the image and for a binary image that limiting frequency will be relatively low. As the higher order moments approach this frequency the reconstruction will become more accurate.

2.3.2. The Haar basis

The reconstruction of an image from its moments is not necessarily unique. Thus, all possible methods must impose extra constraints in order to its moments uniquely solve the reconstruction problem. In this method the constraint that introduced is related to the number of coefficients and the spatial resolution of the image. The Haar basis is unique among the functions we have examined as it actually defines what is referred to as a 'wavelet'. Wavelet functions are a class of functions in which a 'mother' function is translated and scaled to produce the full set of values required for the full basis set. Limiting the resolution of an image means eliminating those regions of smaller size than a given one. The Haar coefficients are obtained from the projection of the image onto the discrete Haar functions $B_{k,l}(m)$ for k a power of 2, and are defined as

$$B_{k,l}(m) = \frac{1}{\sqrt{k}},$$

in the case $l = 1$, and for $l > 1$

$$B_{k,l}(m) = \begin{cases} +\sqrt{\frac{q}{k}}, \; if & p \leq m < p + \frac{k}{2q} \\ -\sqrt{\frac{q}{k}}, \; if & p + \frac{k}{2q} \leq m \leq p + \frac{k}{q} \\ 0, \quad otherwise & \end{cases}$$

with $q = 2^{[log_2(l-1)]}$ and $p = \frac{k(l-1-q)}{q} + 1$, where $[.]$ stands for the function fix(x), which rounds the elements of x to the nearest integer towards zero.

3. Restoration of a blurry image in the spatial domain

This work introduces a new technique for the removal of blur in an image caused by the uniform linear motion. The method assumes that the linear motion corresponds to a discrete number of pixels and is aligned with the horizontal or vertical sampling.

Given x_{out}, then x_{in} is the deterministic original image that has to be recovered. The relation between these two components in matrix structure is the following :

$$Hx_{in} = x_{out}, \tag{13}$$

where H represents a two dimensional $(r \times m)$ priori knowledge matrix or it can be estimated from the degraded X-ray image using its Fourier spectrum ([24]). The vector x_{out}, is of r entries, while the vector x_{in} is of $m(= r + n - 1)$ entries, where $m > r$ and n is the length of the blurring process in pixels. The problem consists of solving the underdetermined system of equations (Eq. 13).

However, since there is an infinite number of exact solutions for x_{in} that satisfy the equation $Hx_{in} = x_{out}$, an additional criterion that finds a sharp restored vector is required. Our work provides a new criterion for restoration of a blurred image including a fast computational method in order to calculate the Moore-Penrose inverse of full rank $r \times m$ matrices. The method retains a restored signal whose norm is smaller than any other solution. The computational load for the method is compared with the already known methods.

The criterion for restoration of a blurred image that we are using is the minimum distance of the measured data, i.e.,

$$\min(\|x_{in}^* - x_{out}\|),$$

where x_{in}^* are the first r elements of the unknown image x_{in} that has to be recovered subject to the constraint $\|Hx_{in} - x_{out}\| = 0$. In fact, zero is not always attained, but following Proposition 0.1(ii) the norm is minimized.

In general, the PSF varies independently with respect to both (horizontal and vertical) directions, because the degradation of a PSF may depend on its location in the image. An example of this kind of behavior is an optical system that suffers strong geometric aberrations. However, in most of the studies, the PSF is accurately written as a function of the horizontal and vertical displacements independently of the location within the field of view.

3.1. The generalized inverse approach

A blurred image that has been degraded by a uniform linear motion in the horizontal direction, usually results of camera panning or fast object motion can be expressed as follows, as desribed in Eq. (13):

$$\begin{bmatrix} k_1 & \dots & k_n & 0 & 0 & 0 & 0 \\ 0 & k_1 & \dots & k_n & 0 & 0 & 0 \\ 0 & 0 & k_1 & \dots & k_n & 0 & 0 \\ \vdots & \vdots & \vdots & \vdots & \vdots & \vdots & \vdots \\ 0 & 0 & 0 & \dots & k_1 & \dots & k_n \end{bmatrix} \cdot \begin{bmatrix} x_{in\_1} \\ x_{in\_2} \\ x_{in\_3} \\ \vdots \\ x_{in\_m} \end{bmatrix} = \begin{bmatrix} x_{out\_1} \\ x_{out\_2} \\ x_{out\_3} \\ \vdots \\ x_{out\_r} \end{bmatrix} \tag{14}$$

where the index n indicates the linear motion blur in pixels. The element $k_1, \dots, k_n$ of the matrix are defined as: $k_l = 1/n \quad (1 \le l \le n)$.

Equation (3) can also be written in the pointwise form for $i = 1, \dots, r$,

$$x_{out}(i) = \frac{1}{n} \sum_{h=0}^{n-1} x_{in}(i+h)$$

that describes an underdetermined system of r simultaneous equations and $m = r + n - 1$ unknowns. The objective is to calculate the original column per column data of the image.

For this reason, given each column $[x_{out\_1}, x_{out\_2}, x_{out\_3}, \dots x_{out\_r}]^T$ of a degraded blurred image x_{out}, Eq. (3) results the corresponding column

$[x_{in\_1}, x_{in\_2}, x_{in\_3}, \dots, x_{in\_m}]^T$ of the original image.

As we have seen, the matrix H is a $r \times m$ matrix, and the rank of H is less or equal to m. Therefore, the linear system of equations is underdetermined. The proper generalized inverse for this case is a left inverse, which is also called a {1,2,4} inverse, in the sense that it needs to satisfy only the three of the four Penrose equations. A left inverse gives the minimum norm solution of this underdetermined linear system, for every $x_{out} \in \mathcal{R}(H)$. The Moore-Penrose Inverse is clearly suitable for our case, since we can have a minimum norm solution for every $x_{out} \in \mathcal{R}(H)$, and a minimal norm least squares solution for every $x_{out} \notin \mathcal{R}(H)$.

The proposed algorithm has been tested on a simulated blurred image produced by applying the matrix H on the original image. This can be represented as

$$x_{out}(i,j) = \frac{1}{n} \sum_{h=0}^{n-1} x_{in}(i,j+h)$$

where $i = 1, \ldots, r \quad j = 1, \ldots, m$ for $m = r + n - 1$, and n is the linear motion blur in pixels.

Following the above, and the analysis given in Section 3, there is an infinite number of exact solutions for x_{in} that satisfy the equation $Hx_{in} = x_{out}$, but from proposition 2.2, only one of them minimizes the norm $\|Hx_{in} - x_{out}\|$.

We shall denote this unique vector by $\hat{x}_{in}$. So, $\hat{x}_{in}$ can be easily found from the equation :

$$\hat{x}_{in} = H^{\dagger} x_{out}$$

The following section presents results that highlight the performance of the generalized inverse.

4. Experimental results

In this section we apply the proposed method on an boat picture and present the numerical results.

The numerical tasks have been performed using Matlab programming language. Specifically, the Matlab 7.4 (R2007b) environment was used on an Intel(R) Pentium(R) Dual CPU T2310 @ 1.46 GHz 1.47 GHz 32-bit system with 2 GB of RAM memory running on the Windows Vista Home Premium Operating System.

4.1. Recovery from a degraded image

Figure 1(a) provides the original boat picture. In Figure 1(b), we present the degraded boat picture where the length of the blurring process is equal to $n = 60$. Finally, in Figure 1(c) we present the reconstructed image using the Moore- Penrose inverse approach. As we can see, it is clearly seen that the details of the original image have been recovered.

The Improvement in Signal to Noise Ratio (ISNR) has been chosen in order to present the reconstructed images obtained by the proposed algorithm. It provides a criterion that has been used extensively for the purpose of objectively testing the performance of image processing algorithms expressed as:

$$ISNR = 10 \log_{10} \left\{ \frac{\sum_{i,j} \left[x_{in}(i,j) - x_{out}(i,j) \right]^2}{\sum_{i,j} \left[x_{in}(i,j) - \tilde{x}_{in}(i,j) \right]^2} \right\},$$

Figure 1. (a) Original Image (b) Blurred image for a length of the blurring process n = 60 (c) Restoration of a simulated degraded image with a length of the blurring process n = 60.

where x_{in} and x_{out} represent the original deterministic image and degraded image respectively, and $\hat{x}_{in}$ is the corresponding restored image. Figure 2(a) shows the corresponding ISNR values. for increasing the number of pixels in the blurring process $n = 1, \ldots, 60$.

The second set of tests aimed at accenting the reconstruction error between the original image x_{in} and the reconstructed image $\hat{x}_{in}$ for various values of linear motion blur, n. The calculated quantity is the normalized reconstruction error given by

$$E = \frac{1}{\sqrt{\sum_{i=1}^{r}\sum_{j=1}^{m}[x_{in}(i,j)]^2}}\sqrt{\sum_{i=1}^{r}\sum_{j=1}^{m}[x_{in}(i,j) - \hat{x}_{in}(i,j)]^2}$$

using the generalized inverse reconstructed method.

Figure 2(b) shows the reconstruction error by increasing the number of pixels in the blurring process $n = 1, \ldots, 60$.

4.2. Recovery from a degraded and noisy image

Noise may be introduced into an image in a number of different ways. In Equation (10) the noise has been introduced in an additive way. Here, we simulate a noise model where a number of pixels are corrupted and randomly take on a value of white and black (*salt and pepper* noise) with noise density equal to 0.02. The image that we receive from a faulty transmission line can contain this form of corruption. In Figure 3(b), we present the original boat image while a motion blurred and a salt and pepper noise has been added to it.

Image processing and analysis are based on filtering the content of the images in a certain way. The filtering process is basically an algorithm that modifies a pixel value, given the original value of the pixel and the values that surrounding it. Accordingly, Figure 4(a) provides a graphical representation for the ISNR of the reconstructed and filtered image for different values of n. Moreover, Figure 4(b) shows the reconstruction error by increasing the number of pixels in the blurring process $n = 1, \ldots, 60$.

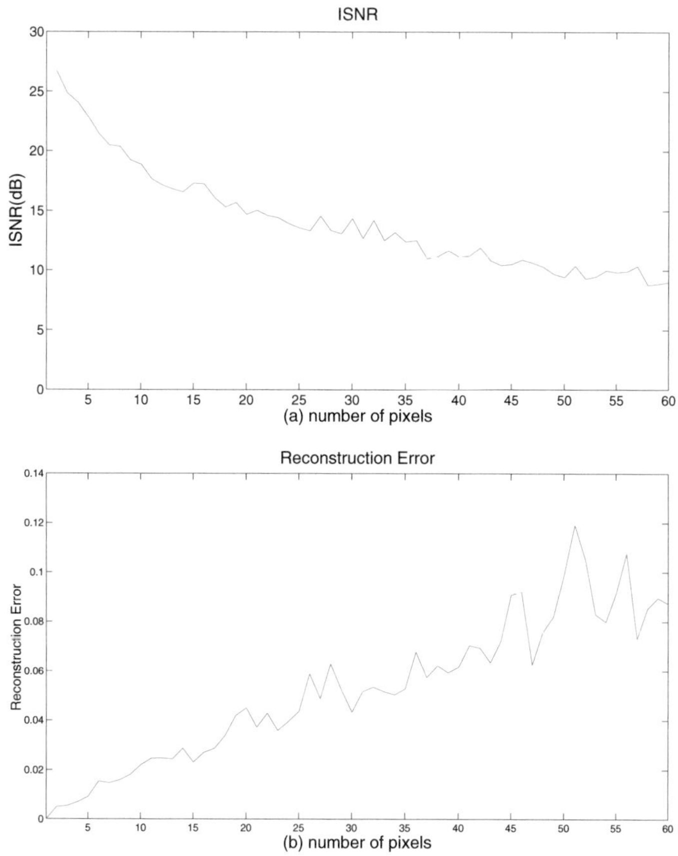

Figure 2. (a) ISNR and (b) Reconstruction Error calculations vs number of pixels in the blurring process $(n = 1, \ldots, 60)$.

Figure 3. (a) Noisy Image (b) Blurred and noisy (salt and pepper) image for length of the blurring process n = 60 (c) Restoration of a simulated degraded (n = 60) and noisy (salt and pepper) image.

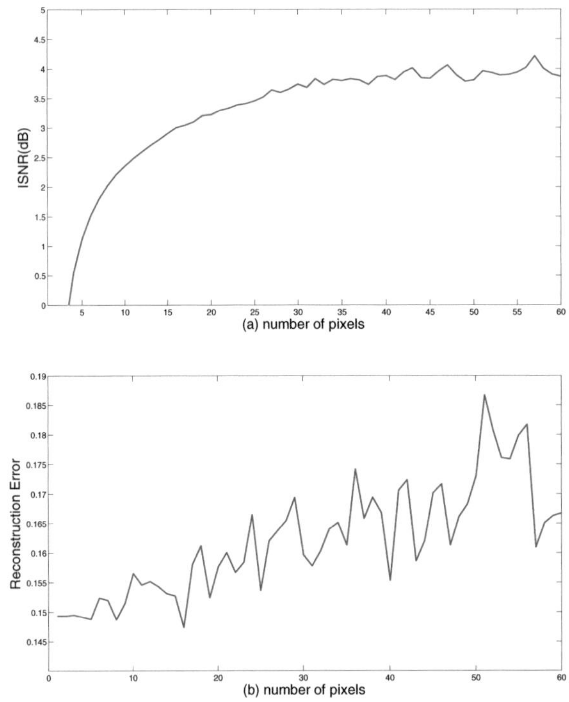

Figure 4. (a) ISNR and (b) Reconstruction Error calculations for a noisy and blurred image vs number of pixels in the blurring process $(n = 1, \ldots, 60)$.

5. Deblurring in the spatial and spectral domain: Application of the Haar and Fourier moments on image reconstruction.

As mentioned before, images can be viewed as non-stationary two-dimensional signals with edges, textures, and deterministic objects at different locations. Although non-stationary signals are, in general, characterized by their local features rather than their global ones, it is possible to recover images by introducing global constrains on either its spatial or spectral resolution. The objective is to calculate the inverse matrix of the blurring kernel H and then applied back (simple multiplication in the spectral domain) to the degraded blurred image xout. Figure 5 shows the spectral representation of the degraded image obtained using Equation (11).

In order to obtain back the original image, Equation (13) is solved in the Fourier space

$$\tilde{x}_{in} = \tilde{x}_{out}\tilde{H}^{\dagger}$$

The reconstructed image is the inverse Fourier transform of $\tilde{x}_{in}$. By using our method not only we have the advantage of fast recovery but also provide us with an operator $\tilde{H}^{\dagger}$ that exists even for not full rank non square matrices. In this section the whole process of deblurring and restoring the original image is done in the spatial domain by using the Haar basis moments and in the spectral domain by applied the Fourier basis moments on the image. It provides us the ability of fast recovering and algorithmic simplicity. The former, obtained by using directly the original image and analysed that on its moments. The method is robust in the presence of noise, as can be seen on the results. In the latter, From the reconstruction point of view the basis matrix is applied to both original image and blurring kernel transforming these into spectral domain. After the inversion of the blurring kernel, its product with the degraded image is applied to inverted basis functions for the reconstruction of the original image. The method provides almost the same robustness for the case of degradation and noise presence as for the spatial moment analysis case.

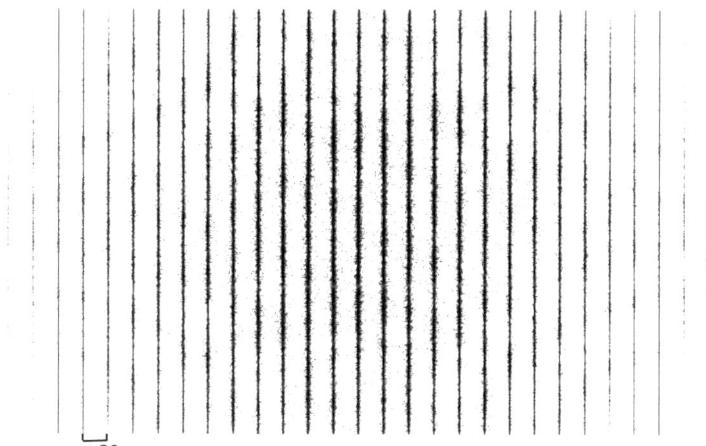

Figure 5. Spectral representations of the degraded image for n=30.

Figures $6(a), 6(b)$ and $6(c)$ present the reconstructed image using the Fourier basis,for the cases of $k = l = 30, k = l = 100$ and $k = l = 450$, respectively.

Figure 6. Fourier based moment reconstructed images for (a) k = l = 30 (b) k = l = 100 and (c) k = l = 450.

From the reconstruction point of view the basis matrix is applied to both original image and blurring kernel transforming these into spectral domain. After the inversion of the blurring kernel, its product with the degraded image is applied to inverted basis functions for the reconstruction of the original image.

Figures $7(a), 7(b)$ and $7(c)$ present the reconstructed image using the Haar basis,for the cases of $k = l = 30, k = l = 100$ and $k = l = 450$, respectively.

Figure 7. Haar based moment reconstructed images for (a) k = l = 30 (b) k = l = 100 and (c) k = l = 450.

Figures 8(a) and 8(b) show the ISNR and the Reconstruction Error accordingly, for various lengths of the blurring processes. Graphical representations on these Figures correspond to

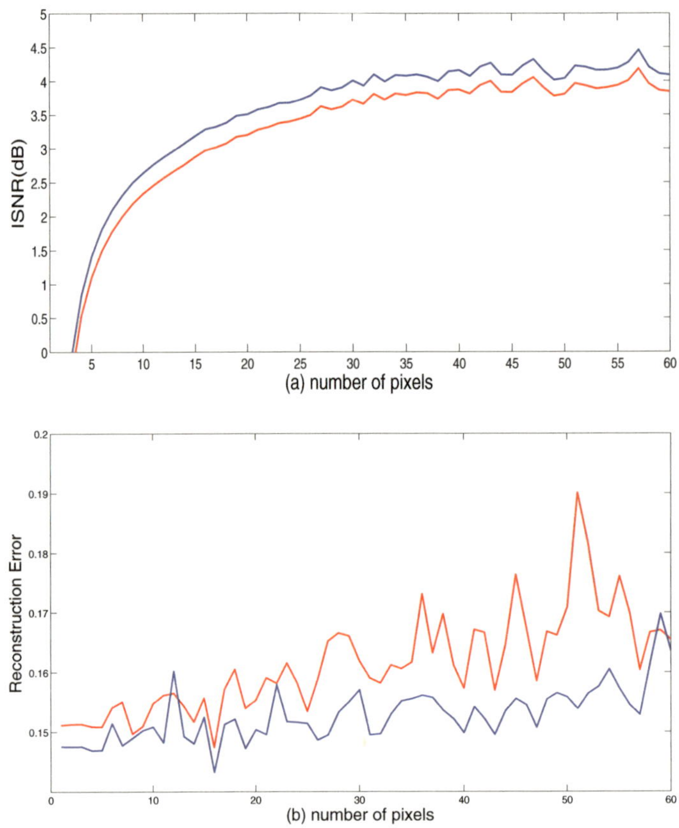

Figure 8. (a) ISNR and (b) Reconstruction Error calculations for a noisy and blurred image vs number of pixels in the blurring process ($n = 1, \ldots, 60$). The blue and red lines indicate the usage of Fourier and Haar based moment analysis of the image, respectively.

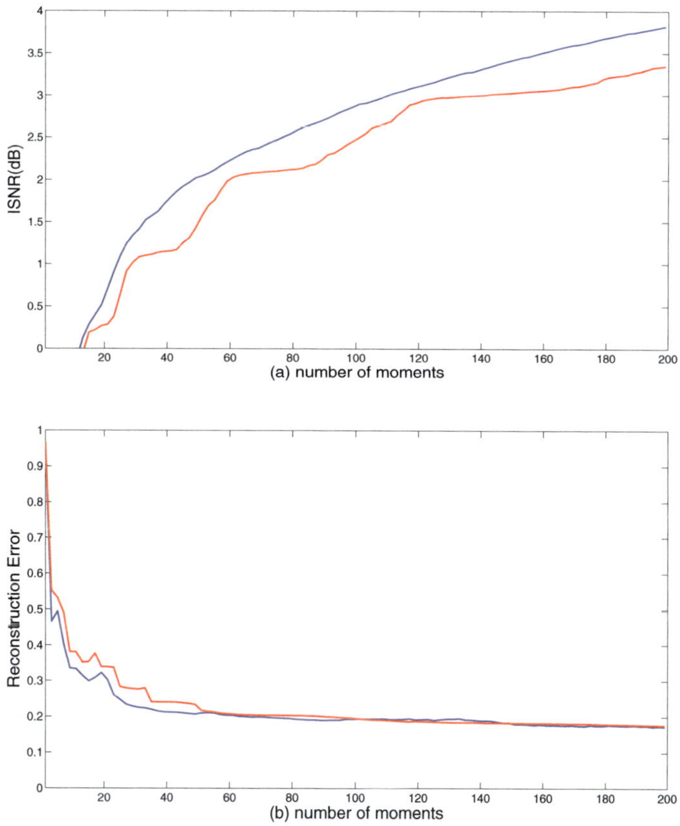

Figure 9. (a) ISNR and (b) Reconstruction Error calculations for a noisy and blurred image vs number of moments ($k = l = 1, \ldots, 200$). The blue and red lines indicate the usage of Fourier and Haar based moment analysis of the image, respectively.

moment values $k = l = 450$ (blue line for the Fourier moment and red line for the Haar moment case). The image is corrupted with white and black (salt and pepper) noise with noise density equal to 0.02. After the moment analysis took place a low pass rotationally symmetric Gaussian filter of standard deviation equal to 45 were applied. Finally, on Figures 9(a) and 9(b) we present the ISNR and the Reconstruction Error respectively, for a number of moments, $k = l = 1, \ldots, 200$ and keeping the number of blurring process at a high level equal to $n = 60$. Similarly, to the previous cases the value of the black and white noise density is equal to the 0.02 and a low-pass Gaussian filter was used for the filtering process.

6. Conclusions

In this study, we introduced a novel computational method based on the calculation of the Moore-Penrose inverse of full rank $r \times m$ matrix, with particular focus on problems arising in image processing. We are motivated by the problem of restoring blurry and noisy images via well developed mathematical methods and techniques based on the inverse procedures in order to obtain an approximation of the original image. By using the proposed algorithm, the resolution of the reconstructed image remains at a very high level, although the main advantage of the method was found on the computational load that has been decreased considerably compared to the other methods and techniques. The efficiency of the generalized inverse is evidenced by the presented simulation results. In this chapter the results presented were demonstrated in the spatial and spectral domain of the image. Orthogonal moments have demonstrated significant energy compaction properties that are desirable in the field of image processing, especially in feature and object recognition. The advantage of representing and recovered any image by choosing a few Haar coefficients (spatial domain) or Fourier coefficients (spectral domain), is the faster transmission of the image as well as the increased robustness when the image is subject to various attacks that can be introduced during the transmission of the data, including additive noise. The results of this work are well established by simulating data. Besides digital image restoration, our work on generalized inverse matrices may also find applications in other scientific fields where a fast computation of the inverse data is needed.

The proposed method can be used in any kind of matrix so the dimensions and the nature of the image do not play any role in this application

Author details

S. Chountasis
Hellenic Transmission System Operator, Greece

V. Katsikis
Technological Education Institute of Piraeus, Petrou Ralli & Thivon 250, 12244 Aigaleo, Athens, Greece

D. Pappas
Department of Statistics, Athens University of Economics and Business, Greece

Appendix

In this section we provide the interested readers with the Matlab codes used in this article.

The following Matlab functions where used to calculate the Fourier and the Haar basis coefficients, and the blurring matrix of the images used.

Function that calculates the Fourier Basis Coefficients (FBC) of an image.

```
%****************************%
%   General  Information.   %
%****************************%
% Synopsis:
% FB= FBC (b_r,b_c)
%Input:
%   b_r :  rows of FB,
%   b_c : columns of FB
```

```
%
%Output: FB: Fourier base


function FB= FBC (b_r,b_c)

FB=zeros(b_r,b_c); i=(b_c-1)/2;
  for j=1:b_c
    l=(j-i-1);
    for k=1:b_r
      FB(k,j)=exp(-j*2*pi*((k-1)*l)/b_r);
    end
  end
FB=(1/sqrt(b_r))*FB;
```

Function that calculates the Haar Basis Coefficients (HBC) of an image.

```
%**************************%
%   General  Information.   %
%**************************%
% Synopsis:
% HB=HBC(h_r,h_c)
%Input:
%   h_r : rows of HB,
%   h_c : columns of HB
%
%Output: HB: Haar base matrix

function HB=HBC(h_r,h_c)

 if (fix(log2(h_r))~=log2(h_r))
    error('The number of rows must be power of 2');
 end
  HB=zeros(h_r,h_c);
  for i=1:h_r
    HB(i,1)=1;
  end
   for l=2:h_c
    k=2^fix(log2(l-1));
    length=h_r/k;
    start=((l-1)-k)*length+1;
    middle=start+length/2-1;
    last=start+length-1;
    v=sqrt(k);
```

```
    for j=start:middle
      HB(j,l)=v;
    end
     for j=middle+1:last
       HB(j,l)=-v;
     end
    end
  HB=(1/sqrt(h_r))*HB;
```

Function that calculates the blurring matrix of an image.

```
%***************************%
%   General  Information.   %
%***************************%
% Synopsis:
% H = buildH(Fo,h)
%Input:
%   Fo : original image,
%   h : array of blurring process
%
%Output: H: blurring Matrix

function H = buildH(Fo,h)

n = length(h);
N=size(Fo,2);
M=N + n - 1;
H=zeros(N,M);
for j =1:N
H(j,j:j+n-1) = h;
end
```

7. References

[1] Banham M. R. & Katsaggelos A. K., (1997) "Digital Image Restoration" *IEEE Signal Processing Magazine*, 14, 24-41.

[2] Ben-Israel A. & Grenville T. N. E (2002) *Generalized Inverses: Theory and Applications*, Springer-Verlag, Berlin.

[3] Bovik A. (2009) *The essential guide to the image processing*, Academic Press.

[4] Campbell S. L. & Meyer C. D. (1977) *Generalized inverses of Linear Transformations*, Dover Publ. New York.

[5] Castleman K. R. (1996), Digital Processing, Eglewood Cliffs, NJ: Prentice - Hall.

[6] Chantas J., Galatsanos N. P. & Woods N. (2007), Super Resolution Based on Fast Registration and Maximum A Posteriori Reconstruction, *IEEE Trans. on Image Pro-*

cessing, 16, 1821-1830.

[7] Chountasis S.,Katsikis V. N., D. Pappas D. (2009) *Applications of the Moore-Penrose inverse in digital image restoration, Mathematical Problems in Engineering*, Volume 2009, Article ID 170724, 12 pages doi:10.1155/2009/170724.

[8] Chountasis S., Katsikis V. N. & D. Pappas D.(2010) *Digital Image Reconstruction in the Spectral Domain Utilizing the Moore-Penrose Inverse, Math. Probl. Eng.*, Volume 2010, Article ID 750352, 14 pages doi:10.1155/2010/750352.

[9] Dudani S.A., Breeding K.J. & McGhee R.B. (1977) Aircraft identification by moment invariants, *I*EEE Trans. on Computers C-26 (1), 39-46.

[10] El-Sayed Wahed M.(2007) Image Enhancement Using Second Generation Wavelet Super Resolution, *International Journal of Physical Sciences*, 2 (6), 149-158.

[11] Gonzalez R., P. Wintz (1987) Digital Processing, U.S.A., 2nd Ed. Addison - Wesley Publishing Co.

[12] Groetsch C.(1977), Generalized inverses of linear operators, Marcel Dekker.

[13] Hansen P. C., Nagy J. G. & O'Leary D. P. (2006) *Deblurring images: matrices, spectra, and filtering, SIAM, Philadelphia.*

[14] Hillebrand M. & Muller C. H. (2007) Outlier robust corner-preserving methods for reconstructing noisy images, *The Annals of Statistics.* 35, 132-165.

[15] Katsaggelos A. K., Biemond J., Mersereau R.M.& Schafer R. W. (1985), A General Formulation of Constrained Iterative Restoration Algorithms, *IEEE Proc. ICASSP*, Tampa, FL, 700-703.

[16] Katsikis V. N., Pappas D. & Petralias A.,(2011) *An improved method for the computation of the Moore-Penrose inverse matrix, Appl. Math. Comput.* **217**, 9828-9834.

[17] Martinez J., Porta J.M. & Thomas F.,(2006) *A* Matrix-Based Approach to the Image Moment Problem, *J*ournal of Mathematical Imaging and Vision, 26 , 1-2, 105-113.

[18] Milanfar P., Karl W.C. & Willsky A.S. (1996) *A* moment-based variational approach to tomographic reconstruction *I*EEE Trans. on Image Processing 5 (3), 459-470.

[19] Mukundan R., Ong S. H. & Lee P. A. (2001) Image analysis by Tchebychef moments. *I*EEE Trans. on Image Processing, 10(9) 1357-1364.

[20] Nguyen T.B. and Oommen B.J. (1997) Moment-Preserving piecewise linear approximations of signals and images. *I*EEE Trans. on Pattern Analysis and Machine Intelligence, 19 (1) 84-91.

[21] Pawlak M.(1992) On the reconstruction aspects of moment descriptors, *I*EEE Trans. on Information Theory, 38, 1698Ű1708.

[22] Schafer R. W., Mersereau R. M. & Richards M.A. (1981) "Constrained Iterative Restoration Algorithms," *Proc. IEEE*, 69, 432-450, .

[23] Schuurman D.C. , Capson D.W. (2002) Video-rate eigenspace methods for position tracking and remote monitoring, *F*ifth IEEE Southwest Symposium on Image Analysis and Interpretation, 45-49.

[24] Sondhi, M. (1972) Restoration: The Removal of Spatially Invariant Degradations, Proc IEEE, 60, no. 7, 842-853.

[25] Stanimirović I.P. & Tasić M.B.,(2011) Computation of generalized inverses by using the *LDL** decomposition, *Appl. Math. Lett.*, doi:10.1016/j.aml.2011.09.051.

[26] Teague M.R., (1980)Image analysis via the general theory of moments. *J*ournal of the Optical Society of America, vol.70 (8), 920-930.

[27] Teh C. H., Chin, R. T. (1988) On image analysis by the methods of moments. IEEE Trans. Pattern Anal. Machine Intell, 10, 496-513.

[28] Trussell H.J. & S. Fogel,(1992) Identification and Restoration of Spatially Variant Motion Blurs in Sequential Images, IEEE Trans. Image Proc., 1, 123-126.

[29] Tull D. L & Katsaggelos A.K.,(1996) Iterative Restoration of Fast Moving Objects in Dynamic Images Sequences, *Optical Engineering*, 35(12), 3460-3469.

[30] Wang G., Wei Y. & Qiao S. (2004) *Generalized Inverses: Theory and Computations*, Science Press, Beijing/New York.

Chapter 16

Artificial Human Arm Driven by EMG Signal

Mohammed Z. Al-Faiz and Abbas H. Miry

Additional information is available at the end of the chapter

http://dx.doi.org/10.5772/48531

1. Introduction

This chapter presents the anatomy of Electromyography (EMG) signal, measurement, analysis, and it's processing. EMG is the detection of the electrical activity associated with muscle contraction. It is obtained by measurement of the electrical activity of a muscle during contraction. EMG signals are directly linked to the desire of movement of the person.

Robot arms are versatile tools found in a wide range of applications. While the user moves his arm, (EMG) activity is recorded from selected muscles, using surface EMG electrodes. By a decoding procedure the muscular activity is transformed to kinematic variables that are used to control the robot arm. EMG signals have been used as control signals for robotics devices in the past. EMG signals, which are measured at the skin surface, are the electrical manifestations of the activity of muscles. It provides an important access to the human neuromuscular system. It has been well recognized as an effective tool to generate control commands for prosthetic devices and human-assisting manipulators. Up to the present, a number of EMG-based human interfaces have been proposed as a means for elderly people and the disabled to control powered prosthetic limbs, wheelchairs, teleoperated robots, and so on. The core part of these human–robot interfaces is a pattern classification process, where motions or intentions of motions are classified according to features extracted from EMG signals. Commands for device control are then generated from the classified motions (Bu et al., 2009).

It has been proposed that the EMG signals from the body's intact musculature can be used to identify motion commands for the control of an externally powered prosthesis. Information extracted from EMG signals, represented in a feature vector, is chosen to minimize the control error. In order to achieve this, a feature set must be chosen which maximally separates the desired output classes. The extraction of accurate features from the EMG signals is the main kernel of classification systems and is essential to the motion command identification (Park &Lee, 1998).

2. EMG signal fundamentals

EMG is the recording of the electrical activity produced within the muscle fibers. The relation of surface EMG to torque makes EMG an attractive alternative to direct muscle tension measurements, necessary in many physical assessments. However, the complexity of the EMG signal origin has been a barrier for developing a quantitative description of this relation. The EMG signal origin and character is necessary background to understand the difficulty of establishing a relationship between surface EMG and torque.

The nervous system controls the voluntary movement of various body parts in humans by contracting and relaxing various skeletal muscles. To instantiate a contraction, a neuron generates a small electrical potential on the surface of the muscle fiber. This electrical potential causes depolarization of the muscle fiber tissue and a following depolarization waveform. This waveform travels the length of the muscle fiber and is known as the Action Potential (AP). Fig. 1 depicts the generation of electric fields in muscle fibers.

Muscle fibers are excited by nerve branches by one motoneuron in groups known as motor units. These motor units are defined as the fundamental unit of contraction and can range from a few muscle fibers for small muscles such as those in the hand and fingers, to thousands of muscle fibers in large muscles such as those in skeletal muscle. Because each motor unit contains a number of muscle fibers that are attached to the motor neuron at various points, the electrical signal of a motor unit is the summation of the action potential of each muscle fiber, which may be phase shifted from the other muscle fibers in that unit (Perry & Bekey,1981).

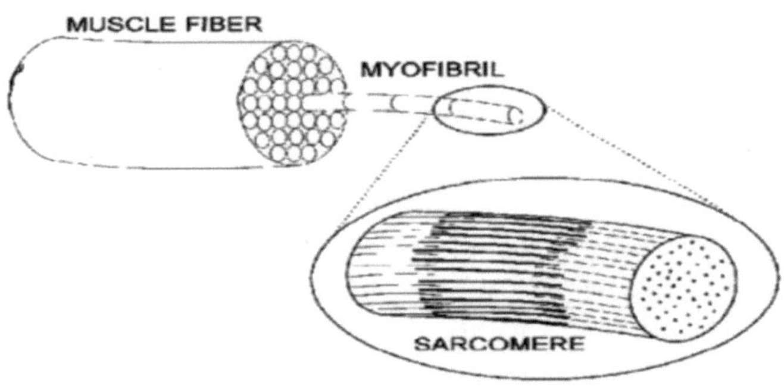

Figure 1. Muscle Fibers Composition

This notion is reinforced in Fig. 2. The electrical potential due to contraction of all fibers in a motor unit during a single activation is referred to as the Motor Unit Action Potential (MUAP). This MUAP can be recorded by using electrodes placed on the surface of the skin above the muscle. Also, a muscle is not typically excited by only one action potential. In order to hold a contraction for any length of time, the motor units must be repeatedly activated. This repeated activation gives rise to a series of MUAPs that can be modeled as a pulse train in classical signal processing terms. This series of MUAPs that is produced is referred to as a Motor Unit Action Potential Train (MUAPT). When the electromyography measured using a surface electrode, the electromyography can be defined as the superposition of numerous MUAPTs firing asynchronously. Fig. 3 reinforces the notion that the superposition of motor unit action potentials gives rise to surface EMG. The surface electromyography signal typically does not exceed 5-10 mV in amplitude with the majority of signal information being contained between the frequencies of 15 and 400 Hz. As a result, the amplitude of the EMG contains a great deal of the signal information which can be modeled as a Gaussian random process. The EMG amplitude can thus be defined as the time-varying standard deviation of the EMG signal and is a measure of the activity level of the muscle under observation.

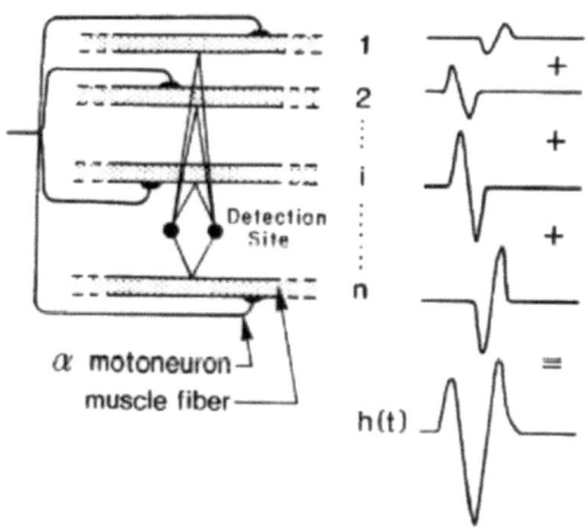

Figure 2. MUAP with Phase shifted from the other muscle fibers

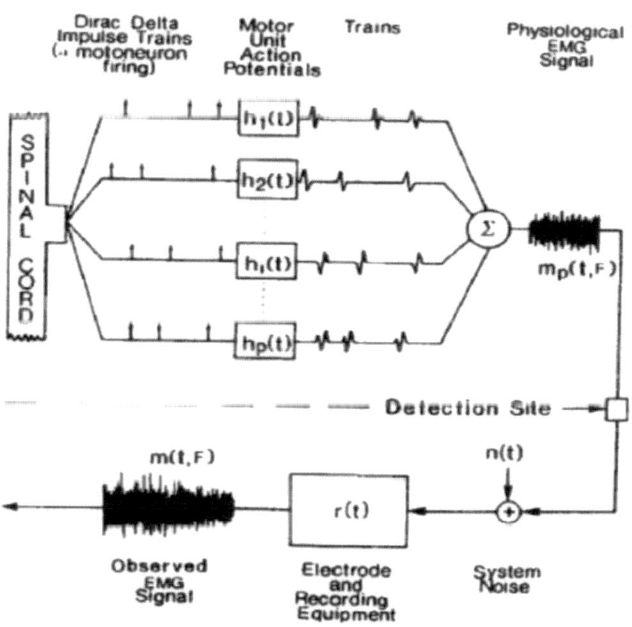

Figure 3. Superposition of Motor Unit Action Potential Gives Rise to Surface EM

3. Prosthetic limb developments

As previously discussed EMG signals provide a non-invasive measure of ongoing muscle activity. Therefore, EMG signals can be potentially used for controlling robotic prosthetic devices. Most prosthetic devices that are currently available usually only have one degree-of-freedom. As a result, these devices provide nowhere near the amount of control as the original limb which they are intending to replace. Through clinical research, it has been shown that amputees and partially paralyzed individuals typically have intact muscles that they can exercise varying degrees of control over. As a result, research is being conducted in regards to utilizing the signals from these intact muscles to control robotic devices with multiple degrees of freedom (Beau 2005). The EMG has been used in two manners in the area of prosthetic limb development. The first approach is for the subject to exert a force with a particular muscle. This force results in a steady-state EMG signal amplitude estimate. A degree of freedom of a robotic limb is then moved in proportion to the EMG amplitude. This described approach is used in the control of a standard prosthetic gripper that has one degree-of-freedom (Beau 2005).

The second manner that EMG signals are used involves discrete actions. When a discrete action is performed, such as the quick movement of the hand or arm, the surface EMG is obtained from various muscle cites. The temporal structure of the transient EMG activity is then analyzed. Upon analyzing the transient EMG activity, various movements can be classified. Hence, EMG signals can be used in the development of advanced prosthetic devices that have various degrees-of-freedom.

4. Muscle anatomy

Agonist-antagonist muscles exist in many human joint. Such human joint is usually activated by many muscles .The following is a summary of the muscles that are responsible for the movement of the arm, wrist, and hand. Abduction of the arm is performed by the deltoid. Human elbow is mainly actuated by two antagonist muscles: biceps and triceps, although it consists of more muscles. Consequently, biceps and a part triceps are bi-particular muscles. By adjusting the amount of force generated by these muscles, the elbow angle and impedance can be arbitrary controlled (Kiguchi et al., 2001). Contraction of the biceps brachii flexes the elbow. Contraction of triceps brachii extends the elbow. Most of the muscles that move the forearm and hand originate within the forearm. The extensor carpi radialis produces extension and abduction of the wrist. The flexor carpi ulnaris flexes and adducts the wrist (Elliott,1998).

5. Feature parameters

EMG classification is one of the most difficult pattern recognition problems because there exist large variations in EMG features. Especially, it is difficult to extract useful features from the residual muscle of an amputee. So far, many researches proposed many kinds of EMG feature to classify posture and they showed good performance. However, how to select a feature subset with the Best discrimination ability from those features is still an issue for classifying EMG signals (Huang et al., 2003). The success of any pattern classification system depends almost entirely on the choice of features used to represent the raw signals. It is desirable to use multiple feature parameters for EMG pattern classification since it is very difficult to extract a feature parameter which reflects the unique feature of the measured signals to a motion command perfectly. But the inclusion of an additional feature parameter with a small separability may degrade overall pattern recognition performance. The feature parameters of EMG signal are listed in Table .1 .

Feature Parameters (Phinyomark & Baraani ,2009)	
1. Integrated EMG	$IEMG=\sum_{n=1}^{N}\lvert h_n\rvert$
2. Mean Absolute Value	$MAV=\frac{1}{N}\sum_{n=1}^{N}\lvert h_n\rvert$
3. Modified Mean Absolute Value	$MMAV=\frac{1}{N}\sum_{n=1}^{N}\lvert h_n\rvert W_n \qquad W_x=\begin{cases}1 & 0.25N\le n\le 0.75N\\ 0.5 & otherwise\end{cases}$
4. Variance of EMG	$VAR=\frac{1}{N-1}\sum_{n=1}^{N}h_n^2$
5. Waveform Length	$WL=\sum_{n=1}^{N-1}\lvert h_{n+1}-h_n\rvert$
6. Wilson Amplitude(WAMP)	$WAMP=\sum_{n=1}^{N-1}f(\lvert h_{n+1}-h_n\rvert),\ f(x)=\begin{cases}1 & x\ge threshold\\ 0 & otherwise\end{cases}$

Table 1. Feature Parameters of EMG signal

The MATLAB code of this action is:

```
%% program of Building Data Base
function data_base =build_data_base
global mscl1 mscl2 mscl3 mscl4 mscl5
ths=50;interval=1600;
IIEMGT=IEMGT';IIEMGT=IIEMGT(:);
VVARR=VARR';VVARR=VVARR(:);
MMAV=MAV';MMAV=MMAV(:);
MMMAVT1=MMAV1';MMMAVT1=MMMAVT1(:);
WWAMPT=(WAMP(ths))';WWAMPT=WWAMPT(:);
WLTT=WL'; WLTT=WLTT(:);
data_base =[IIEMGT';VVARR';MMAV';MMMAVT1';WWAMPT';WLTT'];
```

6. K-nearest neighbor (KNN) algorithm

The K-nearest neighbor (KNN) classification rule is one of the most well-known and widely used nonparametric pattern classification methods. Its simplicity and effectiveness have led it to be widely used in a large number of classification problems. When there is little or no prior knowledge about the distribution of the data, the KNN method should be one of the first choices for classification. It is a powerful non-parametric classification system which bypasses the problem of probability densities completely.

Nearest Neighbor (NN) is a "lazy" learning method because training data is not preprocessed in any way. The class assigned to a pattern is the class of the nearest pattern known to the system, measured in terms of a distance defined on the feature (attribute) space. On this space, each pattern defines a region (called its Voronoi region). When distance is the classical Euclidean distance, Voronoi regions are delimited by linear borders. To improve over 1-NN classification, more than one neighbor may be used to determine the class of a pattern (K-NN) or distances other than the Euclidean may be used. The KNN rule classifies χ by assigning it the label most frequently represented among the K nearest samples; this means that, a decision is made by examining the labels on the K-nearest neighbors and taking a vote KNN classification was developed from the need to perform discriminate analysis when reliable parametric estimates of probability densities are unknown or difficult to determine (Parvin et al., 2008).

K-NN is the most usable classification algorithm. This algorithm operation is based on comparing a given new record with training records and finding training records that are similar to it. It searches the space for the k training records that are nearest to the new record as the new record neighbors. In this algorithm nearest is defined in terms of a distance metric such as Euclidean distance. Euclidean distance between two records (or two points in n-dimensional space) is defined by:

If χ_1=($\chi_{11}, \chi_{12}, \ldots, \chi_{1n}$) and χ_2=($\chi_{21}, \chi_{22}, \ldots, \chi_{2n}$) then

$$dist(\chi_1, \chi_2) = \sqrt{\sum_{i=1}^{n} (\chi_{1i} - \chi_{2i})^2} \tag{1}$$

Where χ_1 and χ_2 are two records with n attributes. This Formula measures the distance between two patterns χ_1 and χ_2 (Moradian & Baraani, 2009). The K-nearest neighbor classifier is a supervised learning algorithm where the result of a new instance query is classified based on majority of the K-nearest neighbor category. The training samples are described by n-dimensional numeric attributes. Each sample represents a point in an n-dimensional pattern space. In this way, all of the training samples are stored in an n-dimensional pattern space.

The following discussion introduces an example demonstrating the general concept of this algorithm in detail. The K nearest neighbor algorithm is very simple. It works based on minimum distance from the query instance to the training samples to determine the nearest neighbors. After we gather K nearest neighbors, we take simple majority of these K-nearest neighbors to be the prediction of the query instance. The data for KNN algorithm consists of several multivariate attributes names that will be used to classify the object Y. Suppose that the K factor is set to be equal to 8 (there are 8 nearest neighbors) as a parameter of this algorithm. Then the distance between the query instance and all the training samples is computed. Because there are only quantitative , the next step is to find the K-nearest neighbors. All training samples are included as nearest neighbors if the distance of this training sample to the query is less than or equal to the Kth smallest distance. In other words, the distances are sorted of all training samples to the query and determine the Kth minimum distance. The unknown sample is assigned the most common class among its k nearest neighbors. As illustrated above, it is necessary to find the distances between the query and all training samples. These K training samples are the closest k nearest neighbors for the unknown sample. Closeness is defined in terms of Euclidean distance (Bawaneh et al., 2008).

Let us consider a set of patterns $\chi = \{\chi_1, ..., \chi_N\} \subseteq R^P$ of known classification where each pattern belongs to one of the classes $CR = \{CR_1, CR_2, ..., CR_S\}$. The nearest neighbor (NN) classification rule assigns a pattern Z of unknown classification to the class of its nearest neighbor, where $\chi_i \in \chi$ is the nearest neighbor to Z if

$$Dist(\chi_i, Z) = \min\left\{Dist(\chi_l, Z) \quad l = 1, 2, ..., N\right\} \tag{2}$$

Dist is the Euclidean distance between two patterns in R^P. This scheme is called the 1-NN rule since it classifies a pattern based on only one neighbor of Z. The k-NN rule considers the k-nearest neighbors of Z and uses the majority rule. Let t_l where l=1, 2,..,s be the number of neighbors from class l in the k-nearest neighbors of Z (Pal & Ghosh, 2001).

$$\sum_{l=1}^{s} t_l = k \tag{3}$$

Then Z is assigned to class j if

$$t = \underset{1}{\mathrm{Max}}\{t_1\} \tag{4}$$

Here is step by step on how to compute KNN algorithm:

1. Determine parameter K – number of nearest neighbors.
2. Calculate the distance between the query-instance and all the training samples
3. Sort the distance and determine nearest neighbors based on the K-th minimum distance.
4. Gather the category Y of the nearest neighbors.
5. Use simple majority of the category of nearest neighbors as the prediction value of the query instance.These steps are summarized in Fig.4.

The MATLAB program of K-NN is :

```
%%%% main program of KNN
Dst=dist(IF,DB);nn=6;[a ,b]=sort(Dst);
st=floor(b/nn)+1;
kk=15;y=st(1:kk)';x=ones(length(y),1);
a1= y ==1;b1=sum(x(a1));
a2= y ==2;b2=sum(x(a2));
a3= y ==3;b3=sum(x(a3));
a4= y ==4;b4=sum(x(a4));
a5= y ==5;b5=sum(x(a5));
bb=[b1 b2 b3 b4 b5];
[a ,b]=sort(bb);af=fliplr(a);bf=fliplr(b);
result=bf(1)
```

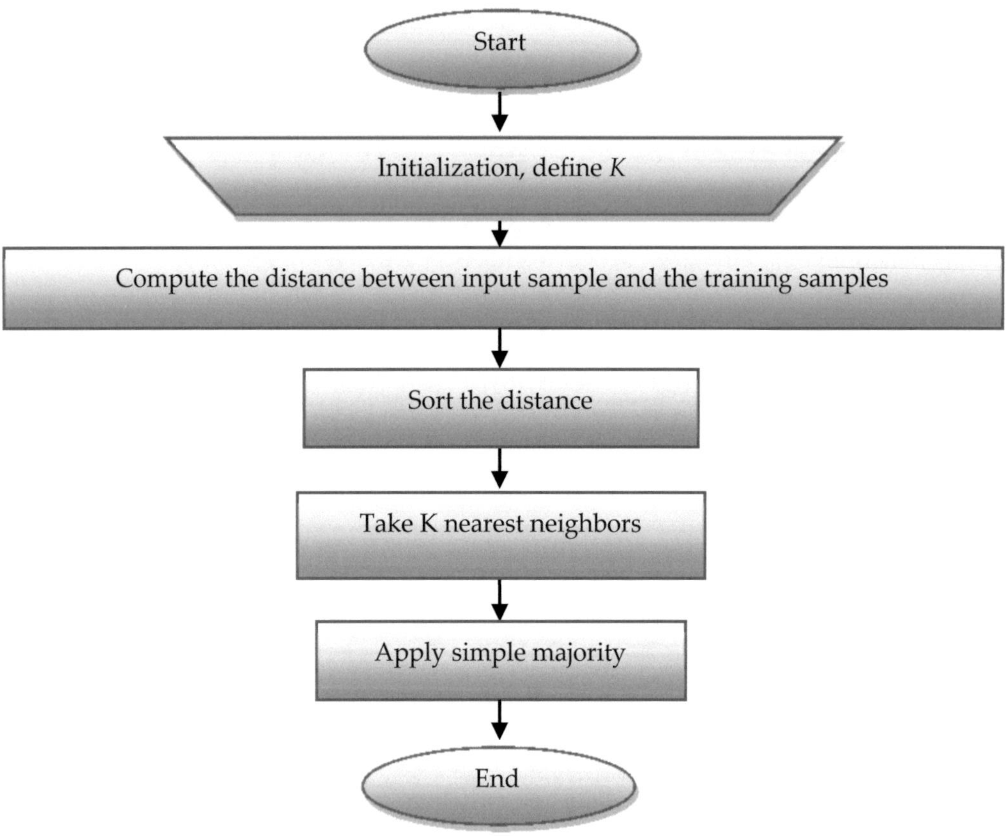

Figure 4. Flowchart for the K- nearest neighbors

7. Measurement of Real EMG signal

EMG signal has two main sources, one of them is measured real EMG and the other one is generated EMG by EMG Simulator. Every one of them has advantage and disadvantage with respect to accuracy and reliability. There are many problems in real measurement system as follows: The first stage is the sensor of EMG signal (electrodes), there are two problems related with the considered structure. The first problem related with the electrode types, that is a needle type. This problem can be summarized as follows: the procedure for using this type by inserting the needle in proper placement on muscle to touch the fiber and sensing the EMG signal. One disadvantage of this needle type is caused high pain to human and it has side affect if using for long times, and it is used only with up normal muscle to check the activity or response of nerve that supply this muscle. Another problem is fixing the needle on the skin, where at any movement of muscle the needle will go out. To overcome the above mentioned problems, the needle may be replaced by either surface electrode or integral surface electrode. The main advantage for using the needle electrode is the amplitude of measured signal where it is better than using another types. In the needle case, the EMG signal is measured directly from MU. The second problem of obtaining EMG signals measured by a needle is only one channel exist for measuring in the same time. This is huge problem in the design where it needs number of channels equal to number of muscles that caused the required recognized movements. If one likes to recognize the wrist joint movement he needs four channels. To overcome the problems in real measuring system, the user can use the generation of EMG signal by EMG simulator.

8. Simulation for EMG signal generation (EMG simulator)

The best modeling of clinical EMG signals was achieved in algorithm by A. Hamilton and D. W. Stashuk at 2005 (Hamilton & Stashuk ,2005). This algorithm is simulated by using MATLAB software and using the GUI approach to get full mathematical simulated model for generating real EMG signal of a specific human arm muscle as shown in Fig. 5 .

This simulator has many options used with rearrangement to generate EMG signal for human arm muscle. The option of the simulator can be summarized as:

Muscle: This popup shows the muscle being simulated. One can select from the list (which adding for human arm muscles), of already defined muscles or select "Custom." to define a new one. Clicking the edit button allows one to modify the muscle parameters. Helping for specification of human arm muscles is added to this window to help the user to generate EMG data more nearest to clinical data, Fig. 6 shows the window for this option.

Electrode: This popup shows the electrode being simulated. The user can select from the list of already defined electrodes or select "Custom..." to define a new one. Clicking the edit button allows the user to modify the electrode parameters. The "Electrode" panel allows the user to save new or modified sets of electrode parameters. Selecting "Multiple Electrodes" allows the user to simulate simultaneous recordings from more than one electrode. Select "Add" from the number popup to add a new electrode. Each electrode can be of a different type. If the user specifies multiple electrodes, then the program creates separate data files for each electrode. The signal from the first electrode is still named filename.dat, and the signals from the other electrodes are named filenameI.dat, where "I" is the electrode number. Fig .7 shows the window for this option.

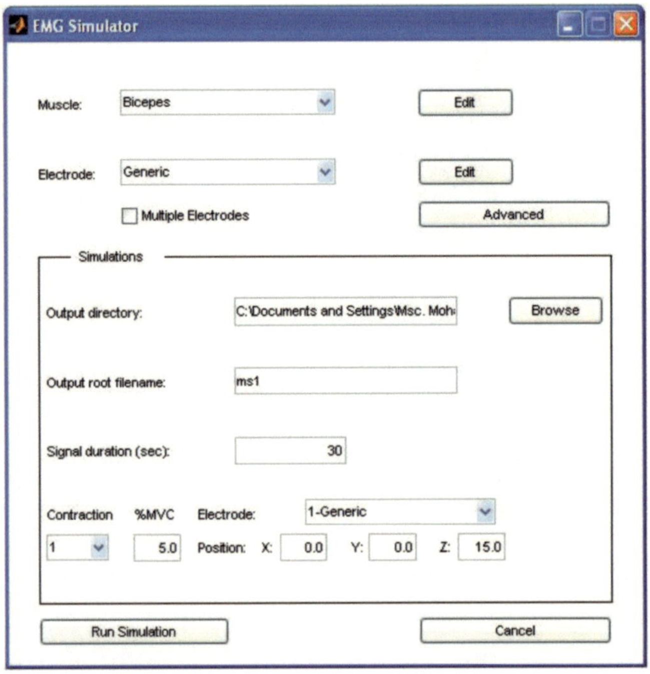

Figure 5. The EMG Signal Simulator.

Advanced: This allows the user to specify some advanced simulation preferences. Include all units: This causes the firing patterns of all the active motor units to be included in the annotation file, not just the ones closest to the electrode.

Output directory: Specifies the directory in which to write the data files. The default directory is the data subdirectory in the simulator directory.

Output root filename: Specifies the root filename for the output files.

Signal duration: Specifies the length of each signal, in seconds.

Contraction: Selects a contraction. To add additional contractions select "Add" from the popup.

%MVC: Specifies the contractile level for the selected contraction.

Position: Specifies the x, y, and z electrode locations (in mm) for the selected contraction. The z coordinate is the distance from the muscle endplate along the muscle axis. Use the "electrode" popup to specify locations for multiple electrodes. Note that you can specify different locations for each electrode in each contraction.

Delete: Deletes the current contraction.

Run Simulation. Runs the specified set of simulations (one simulation per electrode per contraction). The simulations can take a fair amount of time, depending on the specified signal duration. The trace statements from the simulation routines are displayed in the command window.

Cancel. Quits the simulator and returns to MATLAB.

After press the " Run Simulation " button , each simulation may take a minute or more. The program creates the following files for each contraction:

Filename.dat →→ EMG signal, Filename.hea →→ header file (allows signals to be read by software).,Filename.eaf. →→ annotation file, These files can be used to analysis the EMG signal. The real value of the muscle parameters can be obtained by studying the anatomy of muscles in detail. Depending on the practical data obtained from medical table and consultation with the specialist, the muscle parameters adopted are as shown in table 2. Fig.5 represents the generation of EMG signal by EMG simulator. There are two choices to get the EMG data. The first one is by EMG simulator with specified values for the parameters of the muscle as shown in figure 6. The second choice is used to produce data of EMG signal by selecting a specific muscle of the human arm as shown in figure 7. The data are calculated by selecting the specification of normal human body as given in table 2

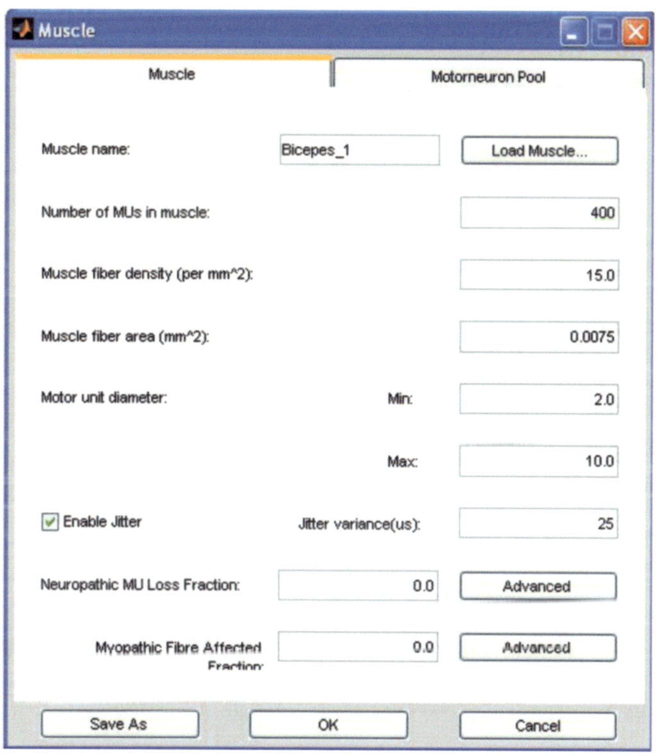

Figure 6. Window for the Selection or Design of Human arm Muscle

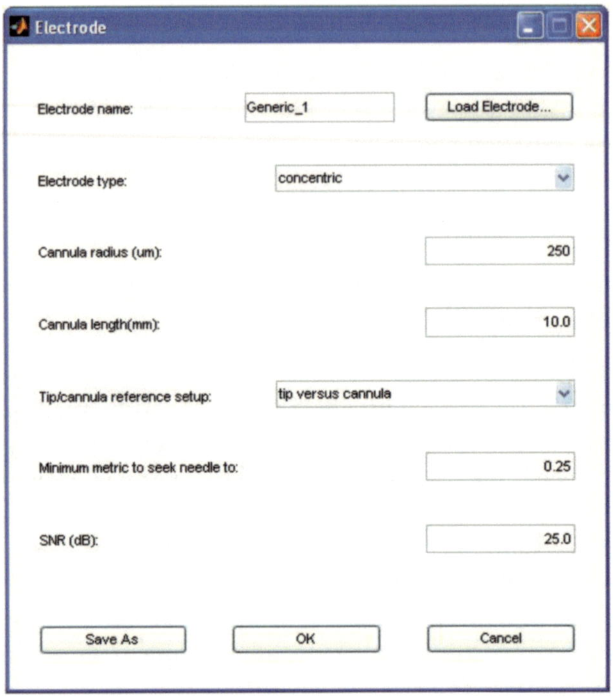

Figure 7. Window for Selecting the Type of Electrode

Muscle name	No. of MU	Fiber Density (per mm^2)	Fiber Area (mm^2)	Range MU diameter (mm)
biceps	400	15	0.0075	2 - 10
triceps	350	10	0.0055	2 – 9
deltoid	450	20	0.0085	3 - 11
extensor carpi radial	250	8	0.0035	1.5 – 8
flexor carpi ulna	100	5	0.0015	2 – 6

Table 2. Standard Parameters of Muscle Human Arm

9. Simulation for reading EMG signals generated by EMG simulator (EMG Lab)

The program, which explains the graphic of the files obtained from the EMG simulator, is called EMGlab (EMGLAB software,2008). This program is built in MATLAB software and the description of run EMGlab in MATLAB command window as follows. The program runs in a single MATLAB window, which is divided into five panels: At the top is the signal panel, which displays a segment of the EMG signal. Below that is the template panel, which displays the MUAP templates. Below that on the left is the firing panel, which displays the firing patterns of the identified MUs. To the right is the close-up panel, which displays a section of the EMG signal at an expanded scale. At the very bottom is the navigation panel which displays a thumbnail of the EMG signal. The buttons on the edges of the panels are used to change the display characteristics .

Fig. 8 shows the output of EMGlab with data of EMG signal. It receives the data that are generated by EMG simulator and the practical measured data and explain the decomposition of the signal and register the data of this signal. The inserted symbols in the window are:

+, - zoom in or out vertically

<, > scroll left or right, and I I, I I zoom in or out horizontally

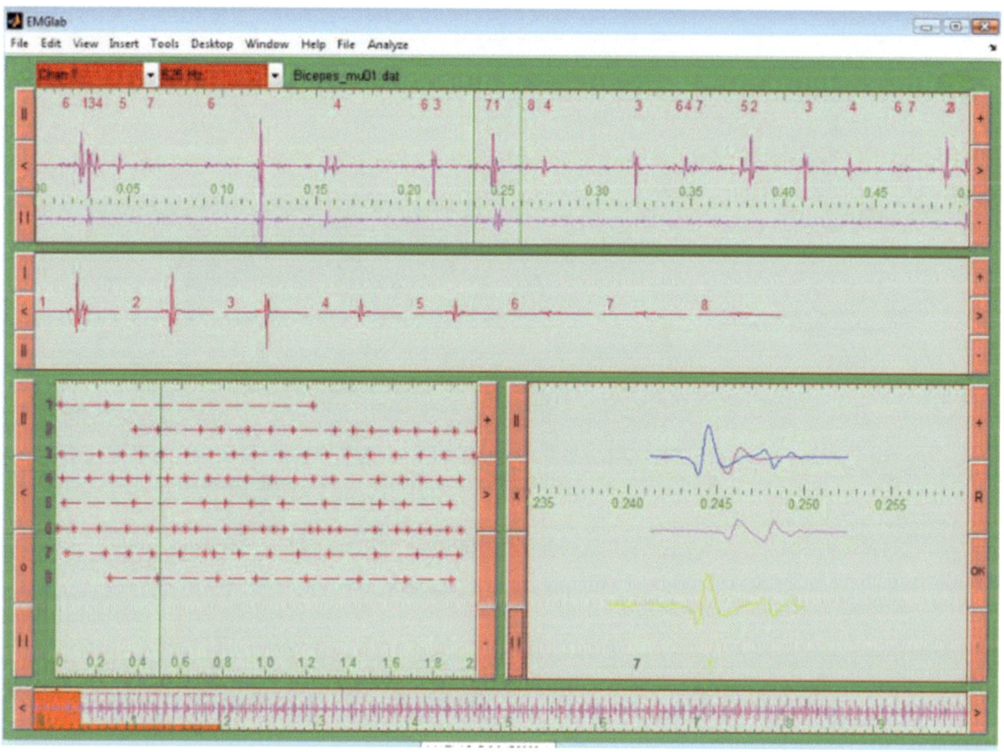

Figure 8. The Output of EMGlab for EMG Signal

10. Human arm movements recognition based on k-nearest neighbor algorithm

The discrimination of the EMG signal into the correct class of movement is a fundamental element of the system. The precision of a classifier lies on its capability to give the correct answers in spite of some inaccuracies that may occur during the process of detection of the EMG signal.

To improve precision of a classifier with decrease of the training time, a recognition system based K-NN algorithm is used. The success of any pattern classification system depends almost entirely on the choice of features used to represent the raw signals. In the proposed system multiple feature parameters for EMG pattern classification are used since it is very difficult to extract a feature parameter which reflects the unique feature of the measured signals to a motion command perfectly.

Five kinds of arm motion are recognized: Abduction of the arm, flexion the elbow, extension the elbow, extension and abduction of the wrist and flexes and adducts the wrist .These motions are produced by contraction of five muscles. Therefore ,if the EMG signal of muscle is recognized then the specified motion of this muscle is recognized. The proposed method is outlined in Fig. 9 and the stages of proposed system are discussed below:

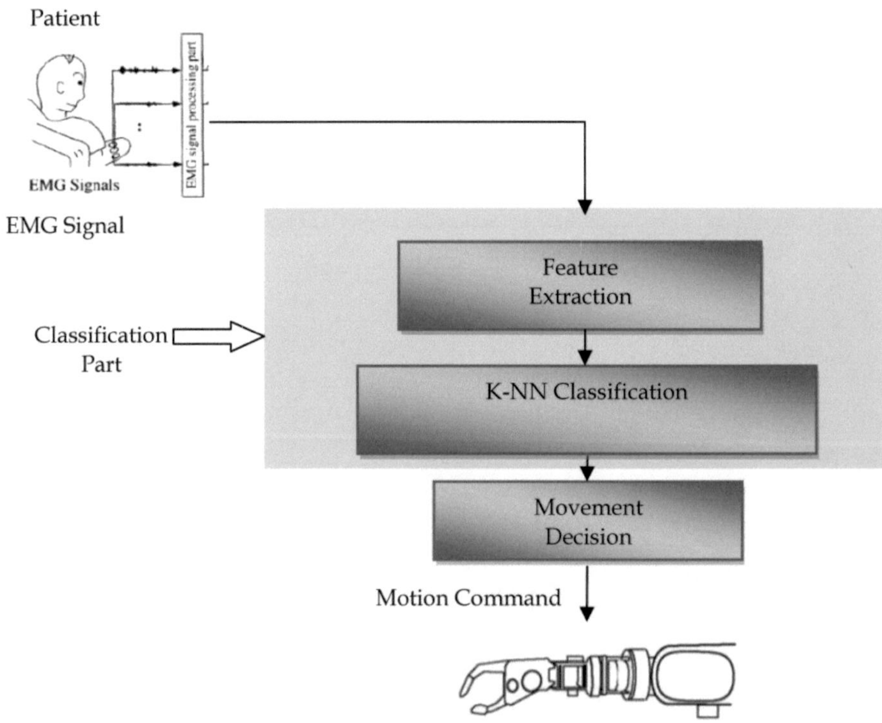

Figure 9. Structure of the Recognition system based on K-NN classifier

10.1. Data bases building with multiple feature parameters

Training of the system involves the partitioning of the feature space to represent different classes of separable motions. In this state, data base is constrained with five muscles (biceps, triceps, deltoid, extensor carpi radialis and flexor carpi ulnaris). This stage has the following steps:

Step 1. Take six frames from each muscle as shown in Fig. 10 to produce thirty frames.

Step 2. Six features (which were introduced in section (4)) are extracted from each frame. In this step thirty vectors are billed as a basic Data Base, each vector has six elements. See Fig.11.

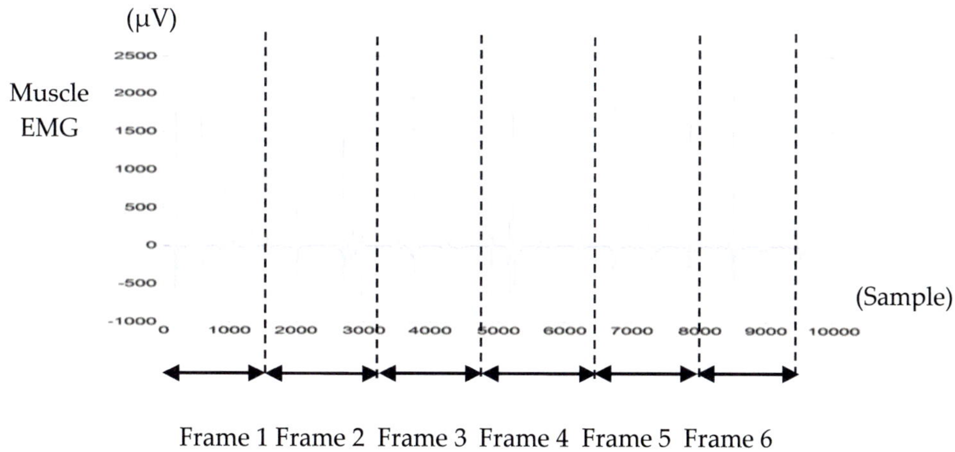

Figure 10. EMG Signal frames.

$$DB_{ij}=\{IEMG_{ij}\ MAV_{ij}\ MMAV_{ij}\ VAR_{ij}\ WAMP_{ij}\ WL_{ij}\} \quad (5)$$

i=1,…,30 ,j=1,…,6

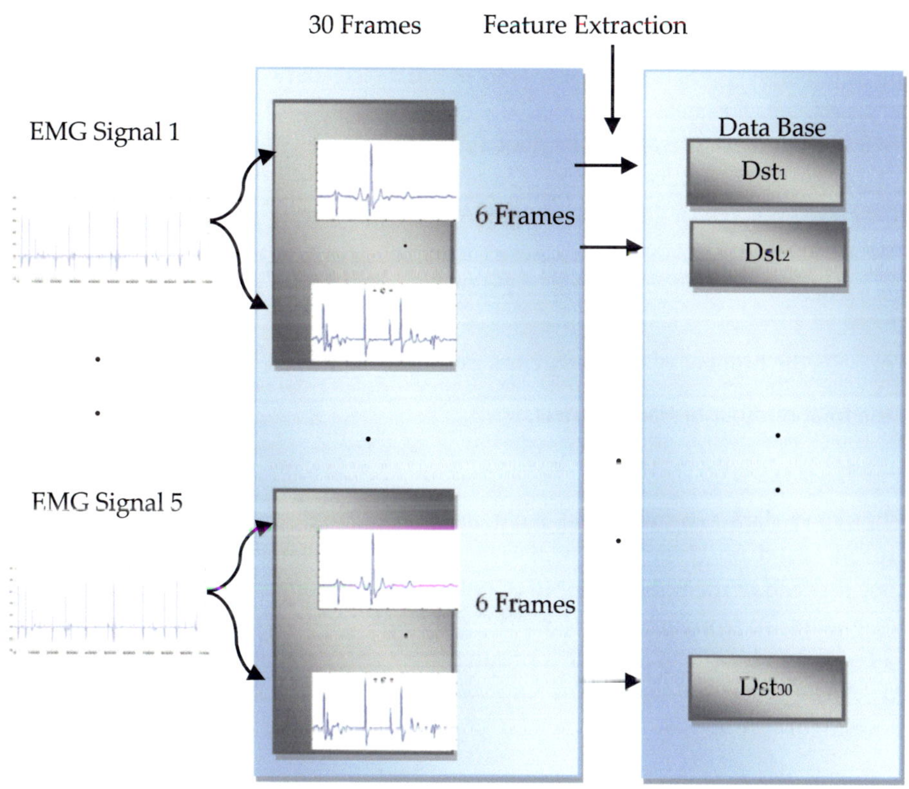

Figure 11. Building Data Base from EMG signals

10.2. Recognition of EMG signals based on k-nearest neighbor algorithm

The data for EMG are generated by EMG simulator then processing will be applied to this signal such as feature extraction.

The recognition system of EMG patterns consists of the following steps:

Step 3. In this step take the feature extraction of input signal to produce Input Feature (IF) which has six elements. Now, there is one vector and it is required to be classified to which type of EMG signal included with thirty frame found in data base, step 2-6 represent K-NN algorithm as shown in Fig. 12.

Step 4. Take Euclidean distance between IF and DB to produce set of distance elements ($Dst_1, Dst_2, \ldots, Dst_{30}$)

$$Dst_i = \{ Dist(DBi, IF) \;\; i=1,2,\ldots,30\} \tag{6}$$

Step 5. Take the nearest neighbors to IF by sorting the distance elements ascendant to produce sorted elements ($S_1, S_2, \ldots, S_{30}$), where S_1 is nearest element to IF.

Step 6. Take the first K^{th} elements from sorted elements ($S_1, S_2, \ldots, S_K$).

Step 7. Assign sorted elements to its original frames of EMG signals.

Step 8. Apply Majority Rule (Which EMG signals has largest number of neighbors from input signal in the K-Nearest Neighbors frames?). The input signal is assigned the most common class of EMG signal among its k nearest neighbors.

As illustrated above, it is necessary to find the distances between the query and all training samples and the closeness is defined in terms of Euclidean distance. Each muscle have specified motion therefore after recognize the EMG signal the command is sent to prosthetic arm to perform the motion of this muscle. The performance index for the Recognition Accuracy (RA) is given by (Momen et al.,2008):

$$RA = \frac{co}{tn} x100 \tag{7}$$

Where: co is the number of correctly classified EMG signals.

tn is the total number of EMG signals.

Case study:

The simulated data are generated from an EMG signal simulator. Several motions are recognized based on classification of five input EMG signals. In the present study, the accuracy for each participant is simply calculated by averaging the performance indices over all movements. To simulate real noise, different noise is considered, i.e. random noise. The noise is added to EMG signals which produce new EMG signal with lower SNR. Now some noised EMG signals are classified using Artificial Neural Network (ANN) and k-Nearest Neighbor algorithm.

Table 3 gives the comparison results of the K-NN with different K values with the back propagation neural network (BP-NN). The structure of BP-NN is (6-20-5). Where the input nodes equal to the number of the features and output nods equal to the number of classified EMG signals.

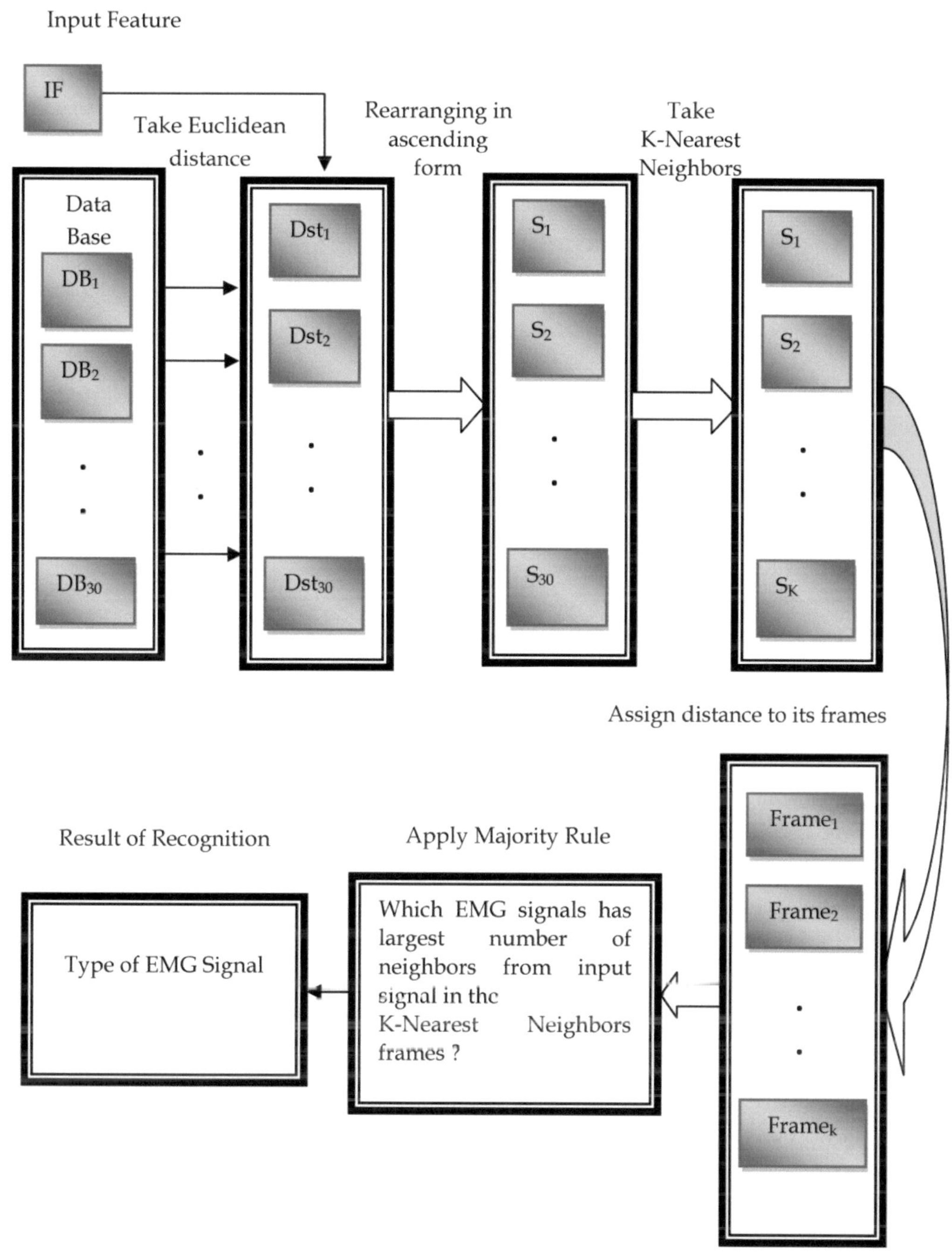

Figure 12. K-NN Classification Process

SNR (dB)	ANN	K-NN K=7	K-NN K=9	K-NN K=13	K-NN K=15	K-NN K=17
25	83%	100%	100%	100%	100%	100%
11	66%	100%	100%	100%	100%	100%
9	66%	100%	100%	100%	100%	100%
7	66%	80%	83%	88%	90%	83%
5	50%	70%	73%	80%	83%	80%

Table 3. Recognition Accuracy of Neural Network and K-NN Method with Noisy Signal.

The MATLAB program is given below:

```
%%%%%% main program of EMG recognition
clear
clc
load mscl2
%--------------------
% test signal
%-------------------
 interval=1600;
ths=50;v=120;
DB=build_data_base;
%%%%%%%%% chose second EMG signal as test signal with added noise
x=mscl2(1,:);
xold=x;
x = x'+v*randn(size((x')));
r = SNR(x, xold');
 %--------------------
% featur extraction
%-------------------
 mx=mean(abs(x));
vx=var(abs(x));
mavx=mean(abs(x))/interval;
w=.5*ones(1,interval);w(1,.25*interval:.75*interval)=1;
mmavt1=mean((w.*abs(x'))')/interval;
wwamp=WAMPsingle(x',ths);
wl=Wlsingle(x');
IF=[mx vx mavx mmavt1 wwamp wl];
```

```
%--------------------
% apply k-nn
%--------------------
Dst=dist(IF,DB);
nn=6;
[a ,b]=sort(Dst);
st=floor(b/nn)+1;
kk=15;
Frame=st(1:kk)';
x=ones(length(Frame),1);
a1= Frame ==1;
b1=sum(x(a1));
a2= Frame ==2;
b2=sum(x(a2));
a3= Frame ==3;
b3=sum(x(a3));
a4= Frame ==4;
b4=sum(x(a4));
a5= Frame ==5;
b5=sum(x(a5));
bb=[b1 b2 b3 b4 b5];
[a ,b]=sort(bb);
af=fliplr(a);bf=fliplr(b);
result=bf(1)
```

11. Proposed model and vr simulation for artificial human arm

The simulator was built using MATLAB with Virtual Reality Toolbox. MATLAB provides powerful engineering tool including frequently used mathematical functions. It is easy to implement control algorithm including visualization of data used in the algorithm. In addition, by using Virtual Reality Toolbox, it is convenient to treat 3D objects defined with Virtual Reality Modeling Language (VRML). Thus, it is possible to build a simulator within a relatively short period. virtual reality is a system which allows one or more users to move and react in a computer generated environment. The basic VR systems allow the user to visual information using computer screens. The simulation contain two part ,first ,building model for human arm in VRML, second, call and run the model of human arm using virtual reality toolbox in the MATLAB.

To realize the VRML model for Human arm save the file as HumanArm.wrl file, which is the file format for Virtual Reality software, the VRML model of the human arm is designed in V-Realm Builder 2.0 . Fig.13 presents the VRML model of the human arm.

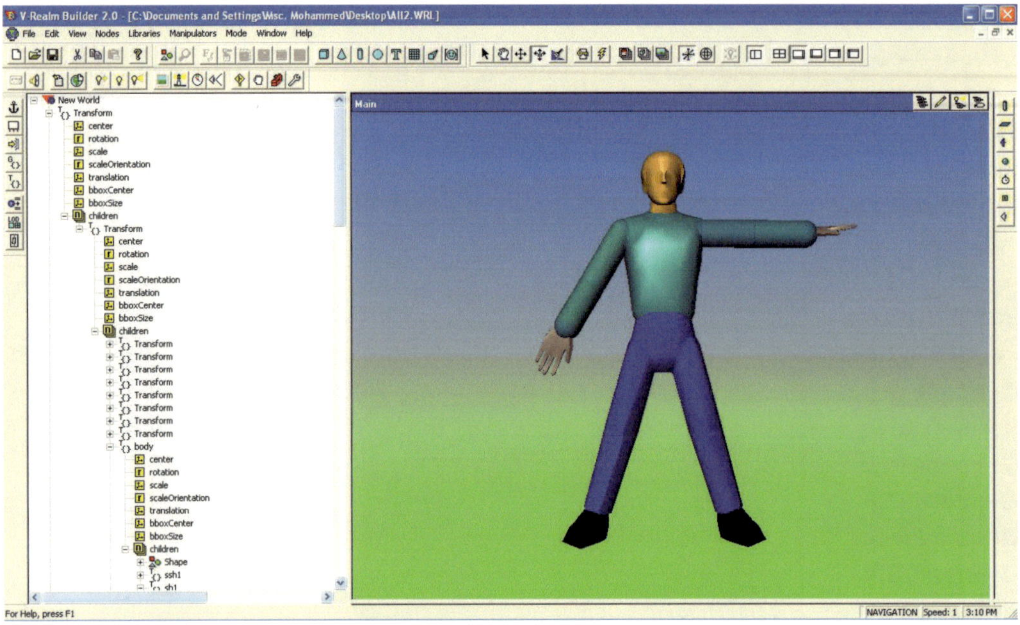

Figure 13. The VRML model of the Human arm

The MATLAB program is given as:

```
%% control of human arm as MATLAB code
world=vrworld('HumanArm.wrl', 'new');
open(world);
fig=vrfigure(world);
elbow=vrnode(world, 'elbow');
k=0;
for theta=pi/2:-pi/100:0
 k=k+1;
 x(k)=theta;
 pause(0.05)
 elbow.rotation=[0 0 theta theta];
 vrdrawnow;
end
```

12. EMG simulator based GUI

The method of recognition based K-NN algorithm and technique of virtual reality are introduced, now the simulation which connect between the EMG recognition system and virtual reality is presented.

From MATLAB, the user can set the positions and properties of VRML objects, create callbacks from Graphical User Interfaces (GUI), and map data to virtual objects. The user can also view the world with a VRML viewer, determine its structure, and assign new values to all available nodes and their fields. The Virtual Reality Toolbox includes functions for retrieving and changing the virtual world properties and for saving the VRML files corresponding to the actual structure of a virtual world. MATLAB provides communication for control and manipulation of virtual reality objects using MATLAB objects.

This part concerns with the simulation of human arm movement using EMG Signal as shown in the fig 14 .

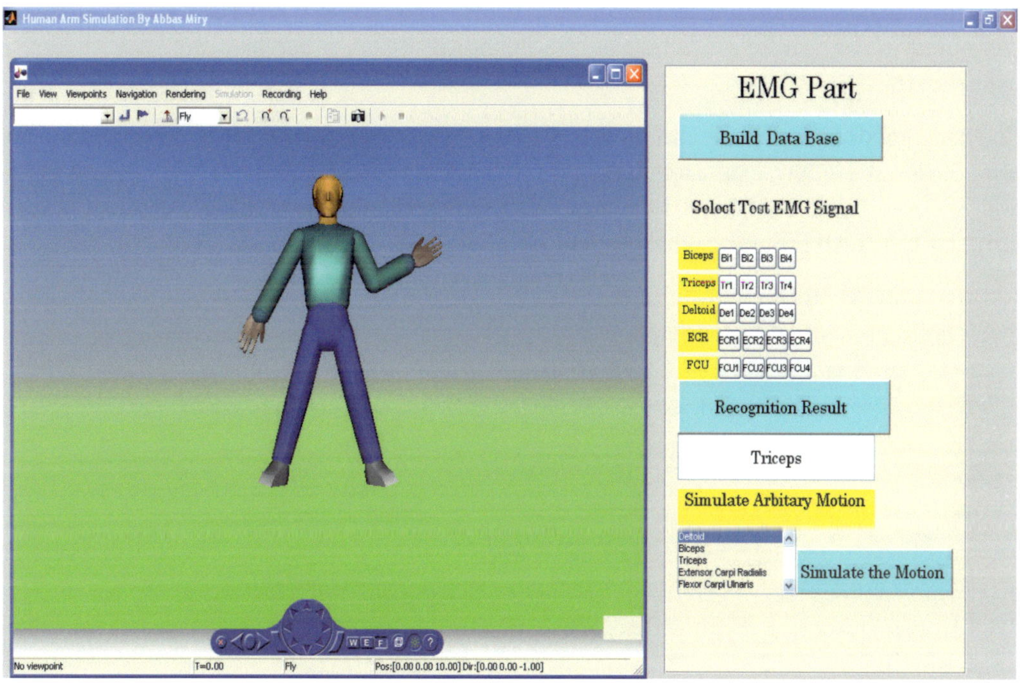

Figure 14. Recognition Result Windows

It has the following stages:

6. **Build Data Base**: This stage represents the training state in which data base is constrained with five muscles (biceps, triceps, deltoid, extensor Carpi radialis and flexor carpi ulnaris). More details found in subsection (10.1).
7. **Select Test EMG Signal**: Select the type of EMG signal to recognize with added noise to test the equality of proposed method with different noise level. Five muscle are tested (biceps,triceps, deltoid, extensor carpi radialis and flexor carpi ulnaris)are tested with four level of noise to produce four noised EMG signals for each muscle.

8. **Recognition Result:** In this stat the K-NN algorithm is applied to recognize the EMG signal in order to produce the motion provided by this EMG signal in virtual reality. The details of this stage can be found in subsection (10.2).
9. **Simulate Arbitrary Motion:** In this part of simulation any motion can be chosen by selecting the muscles which produce this motion.
10. **Simulate the Motion:** After pressing on this button the human arm is moves in the virtual reality.

The recognition algorithm consists of following steps. Firstly, a nearest neighbor algorithm is applied to compute the distance between the feature extraction of input motion to be recognized and each of the 30 feature extraction representing the recognizable motions, which were collected in a Data Base. The algorithm then sorts the motion indexes starting from the nearest candidate in descending order. The distance between two patterns is computed in the feature extraction as the Euclidean distance between the two vectors of feature extraction.

The basic motions types are executed to test the model's performance: a Abduction of the arm, flexion the elbow, extension the elbow, extension and abduction of the wrist and flexes and adducts the wrist. For all motions, the system will receive an EMG signal of human arm.The MATLAB program, which executes this algorithm, is given as:

```
function EMGGUI(hObject,eventdata)
 fh2 = figure('MenuBar','none','Name',' Artificial Human Arm Driven by EMG Signal
','NumberTitle','off','Position',[0 0 1300 800]);
 v1=10;
v2=20;
v3=30;
v4=200;
ph = uipanel('Parent',fh2,'Position',[.65 .05 .3 .9]);
e1 = uicontrol(fh2,'style','text','string','EMG Part','Position',[875 625 250
75],'FontName','Century Schoolbook','FontSize',24);
database = uicontrol(fh2,'style','pushbutton','string','Build Data Base
','BackgroundColor','c','Position', [850 600 260 50],'callback',@Data_Base,'FontName','Century
Schoolbook','FontSize',14);
 e2 = uicontrol(fh2,'style','text','string','Select Test EMG Signal ','Position',[850 500 250
60],'FontName','Century Schoolbook','FontSize',14);
 XX7=480;
e3 = uicontrol(fh2,'style','text','string','Biceps','Position',  [850 XX7 50
25],'BackgroundColor','Y','FontName','Century Schoolbook','FontSize',10);
e4 = uicontrol(fh2,'style','pushbutton','string','Bi1','Position', [900 XX7 25
25],'callback',@Biceps1);
e5 = uicontrol(fh2,'style','pushbutton','string','Bi2','Position', [925 XX7 25
25],'callback',@Biceps2);
```

```
e6 = uicontrol(fh2,'style','pushbutton','string','Bi3','Position', [950 XX7 25
25],'callback',@Biceps3);
e7 = uicontrol(fh2,'style','pushbutton','string','Bi4','Position', [975 XX7 25
25],'callback',@Biceps4);
 XX1=XX7-30;
e8 = uicontrol(fh2,'style','text','string','Triceps','Position',  [850 XX1 50
25],'BackgroundColor','Y','FontName','Century Schoolbook','FontSize',10);
e9 = uicontrol(fh2,'style','pushbutton','string','Tr1','Position', [900 XX1 25
25],'callback',@Triceps1);
e10 = uicontrol(fh2,'style','pushbutton','string','Tr2','Position', [925 XX1 25
25],'callback',@Triceps2);
e11 = uicontrol(fh2,'style','pushbutton','string','Tr3','Position', [950 XX1 25
25],'callback',@Triceps3);
e12 = uicontrol(fh2,'style','pushbutton','string','Tr4','Position', [975 XX1 25
25],'callback',@Triceps4);
 XX2=XX1-30;
 e13 = uicontrol(fh2,'style','text','string','Deltoid','Position', [850 XX2 50
25],'BackgroundColor','Y','FontName','Century Schoolbook','FontSize',10);
e14 = uicontrol(fh2,'style','pushbutton','string','De1','Position', [900 XX2 25
25],'callback',@Deltoid1);
e15 = uicontrol(fh2,'style','pushbutton','string','De2','Position', [925 XX2 25
25],'callback',@Deltoid2);
e16 = uicontrol(fh2,'style','pushbutton','string','De3','Position', [950 XX2 25
25],'callback',@Deltoid3);
e17 = uicontrol(fh2,'style','pushbutton','string','De4','Position', [975 XX2 25
25],'callback',@Deltoid4);
 XX3=XX2-30;
 e18 = uicontrol(fh2,'style','text','string','ECR','Position',    [850 XX3 50
25],'BackgroundColor','Y','FontName','Century Schoolbook','FontSize',10);
e19 = uicontrol(fh2,'style','pushbutton','string','ECR1','Position', [900 XX3 30
25],'callback',@ECR1);
e20 = uicontrol(fh2,'style','pushbutton','string','ECR2','Position', [930 XX3 30
25],'callback',@ECR2);
e21 = uicontrol(fh2,'style','pushbutton','string','ECR3','Position', [960 XX3 30
25],'callback',@ECR3);
e22 = uicontrol(fh2,'style','pushbutton','string','ECR4','Position', [990 XX3 30
25],'callback',@ECR4);
 XX4=XX3-30;
 e23 = uicontrol(fh2,'style','text','string','FCU','Position',    [850 XX4 50
25],'BackgroundColor','Y','FontName','Century Schoolbook','FontSize',10);
e24 = uicontrol(fh2,'style','pushbutton','string','FCU1','Position', [900 XX4 30
25],'callback',@FCU1);
```

```
e25 = uicontrol(fh2,'style','pushbutton','string','FCU2','Position', [930 XX4 30
25],'callback',@FCU2);
e26 = uicontrol(fh2,'style','pushbutton','string','FCU3','Position', [960 XX4 30
25],'callback',@FCU3);
e27 = uicontrol(fh2,'style','pushbutton','string','FCU4','Position', [990 XX4 30
25],'callback',@FCU4);
 result1 = uicontrol(fh2,'style','pushbutton','string','Recognition Result
','BackgroundColor','c','callback',@test,'Position',[850 300 270 60],'FontName','Century
Schoolbook','FontSize',14);
result2 = uicontrol(fh2,'style','edit','Position',[850 250 250 50],'FontName','Century
Schoolbook','FontSize',14,'BackgroundColor','W');
e28 = uicontrol(fh2,'style','text','string','Simulate Arbitary Motion
','BackgroundColor','y','Position',[850 200 250 40],'FontName','Century
Schoolbook','FontSize',14);
e29 = uicontrol(fh2,'Style','listbox','String',{'Deltoid','Biceps','Triceps','Extensor Carpi
Radialis','Flexor Carpi Ulnaris'},'Max',5,'Min',0,'Value',[1],'Position',[850 125 150 70]);
e30 = uicontrol(fh2,'style','pushbutton','string','Simulate the Motion
','callback',@simulat_motion,'BackgroundColor','c','Position',[1000 125 200
50],'FontName','Century Schoolbook','FontSize',14);
 end
```

After execution of this program, its results will be given as in Fig. 14 .

As an examples the progress of the Abduction of the arm can be observed in Fig. 15.

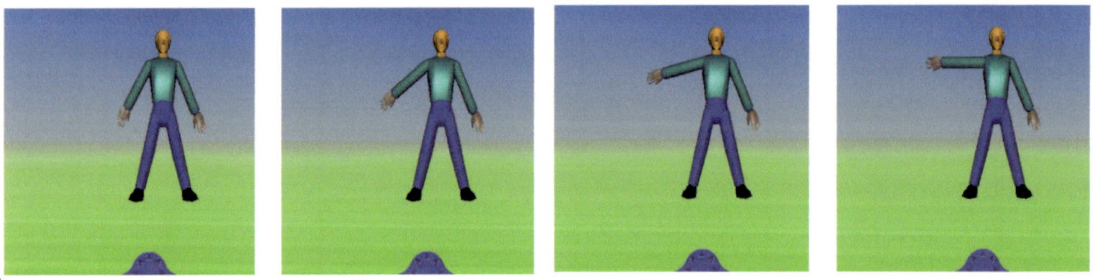

(0 sec) (0.1 sec) (0.3 sec) (0.5 sec)

Figure 15. Abduction of the arm movements

The execution of the elbow flexion can be observed in Fig. 16 along with several of the arm states. At the initial position, the human arm is in extension. When flexion begins, the human arm opposition angle is controlled to the right position for the elbow flexion. After receiving the elbow flexion signal, the structure of the arm causes its joints to flex in a natural motion

The block diagram of the package for the human arm simulator is shown in Fig. 17. It enables testing of different control algorithms. The simulator uses MATLAB as this language both provides a virtual reality toolbox and an extensive mathematical library.

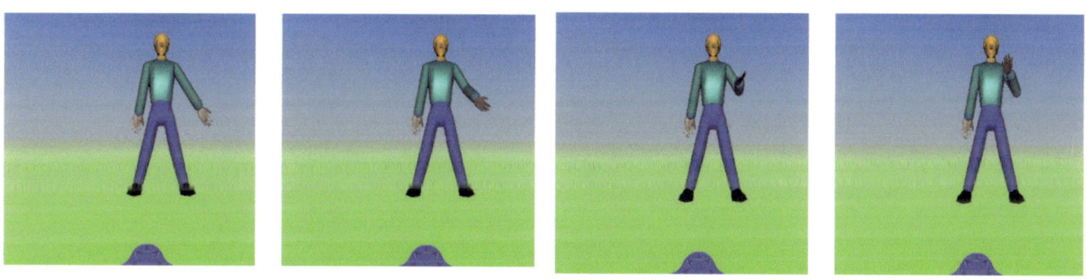

(0 sec) (0.1 sec) (0.3 sec) (0.5 sec)

Figure 16. Flexion of the elbow movements.

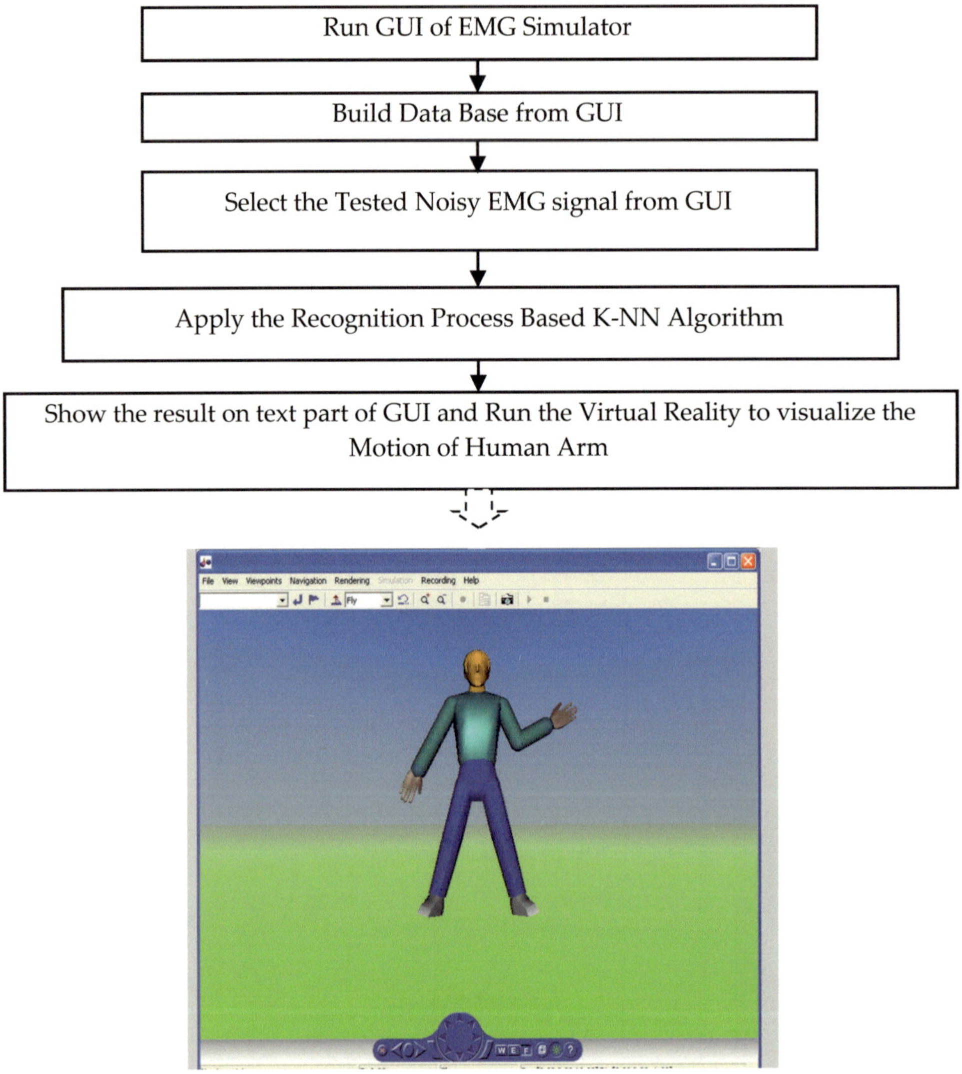

Figure 17. Block diagram for Human Arm Movement based EMG signal

13. Conclusions

In this chapter the motion classification simulations are carried out, in order to evaluate classification performance of the human arm movements recognition based on k-Nearest Neighbor algorithm. The simulated data were generated from an EMG signal simulator. Several motions are recognized based on classification of five input EMG signals. In the present study, the accuracy for each participant was simply calculated by averaging the performance indices over all movements.

The results illustrate that the recognition using K-NN presents better results than artificial neural network in term of recognition accuracy as shown Table 2. This table shows the result of recognition with noisy signal having lower SNR for the neural network and different values of k. It can be found that the K-NN method with the value of k=15 achieves better performance than neural network method and K-NN with the other values of k. The reason of successful of K-NN algorithm that, the input signal may be similar to other frames of EMG signal due to the effect of the noise, therefore ,it is necessary to check the input EMG signal with more frames of EMG signal to give good recognition result .

The possible reason for the poor results of ANN may be due to the simple decision function realized by this method. EMG signal has variation with time therefore necessary to check the input signal with more frame for each muscle as shown in K-NN which provides more accuracy in the recognition. The choice multiple features provide more information about the input signal, failer one of these features can be repaired by the other features.

This chapter also presents the simulation of human arm motion in virtual reality to test the algorithm of EMG recognition. It can be concluded that, The Virtual Reality is useful to test the viability of designs before the implementation phase on a virtual reality prototype. It found that, MATLAB a convenient platform for development of computational algorithms, and with the visualization functions of MATLAB Ver.R2009a a reasonable amount of visualization techniques are available.

Author details

Mohammed Z. Al-Faiz
Computer Engineering Department, Al-Nahrain University, Baghdad, Iraq

Abbas H. Miry
Electrical Engineering Department, AL-Mustansiriyah University, Baghdad, Iraq

14. References

Bawaneh, M.; Alkoffash, M. & Rabea, A.(2000). Arabic Text Classification using K-NN and Naive Bayes, *Journal of Computer Science*. ISSN 1549-3636, Vol.4 No.7, pp: 600-605.

Beau C. (2005), Real-Time Classification of Electromyographic Signals for Robotic Control, *Technical Report No. 2005-03-05, Department of Computer Science, University of Washington*

Bu, N.; Okamoto, M. & Tsuji, T. (2009).A Hybrid Motion Classification Approach for EMG-Based Human–Robot Interfaces Using Bayesian and Neural Networks, *IEEE Trans. on Robot*. Vol. 23, No. 3, pp. 502–511.

Elliott, R. (1998).Feature Extraction Techniques for Grasp Classification ", *Master Thesis, University of Canterbury*.

EMGLAB software Version 0.9 User's Guide, "The MathWorks, at www.mathworks.com, 2008.

Hamilton, A. & Stashuk, D. W. (2005).Physiologically based simulation of clinical EMG signals, *IEEE Trans. Biomed. Eng.*, Vol. 52, No. 2, PP:171-183, 2005.

Huang, H.; Liu, Y. & Wong, C.(2003).Automatic EMG Feature Evaluation for Controlling a Prosthetic Hand Using a Supervised Feature Mining Method :An Intelligent Approach, *International Conference on Robotics & Automation, Taiwan, IEEE,* pp:220-225, 2003.

Kiguchi, K.; Watanabe, S.; Izumi, K. & Fukuda, T. (2001).An Exoskeletal Robot for Human Elbow Motion Support—Sensor Fusion, Adaptation, and Control, *IEEE Trans on System, Man and Cybernetics,* Vol. 31, No.3, pp:353-361.

Momen K.; Krishnan, S. & Chau, T. (2007). Real-Time Classification of Forearm Electromyographic Signals Corresponding to User-Selected Intentional Movements for Multifunction Prosthesis Control, *IEEE Trans on Neural System and Rehabilitation Engineering,* Vol. 15, No. 4, pp:535-542.

Moradian, M. & Baraani, A.(2009). KNNBA: K-Nearest-Neighbor-Based-Association Algorithm. *Journal of Theoretical and Applied Information Technology,* Vol.6. No. 1, pp 123 – 129.

Pal, N. & Ghosh, S. (2001).Some Classification Algorithms Integrating Dempster–Shafer Theory of Evidence with the Rank Nearest Neighbor Rules, *IEEE Trans on Systems, Man, and Cybernetics—Part A,* Vol. 31, No. 1, pp: 59-66.

Park, S. & Lee, S. (1998). EMG Pattern Recognition Based on Artificial Intelligence Techniques, *IEEE Trans on Rehabilitation Engineering,* Vol. 6, No. 4, pp:400-405.

Parvin, H; Alizadeh, H. & Bidgoli, B. (2008). MKNN: Modified K-Nearest Neighbor, *Proceedings of the World Congress on Engineering and Computer Science,* pp:831-834.

Perry, J.; Bekey, G. (1981).EMG-force relationships in skeletal muscle." *CRC Critical Rev. in Biomed. Eng.,* pp. 1-22.

Phinyomark, A.; Limsakul, C. & Phukpattaranont, P.(2009). A Novel Feature Extraction for Robust EMG Pattern Recognition, *Journal of Computing,* ISSN: 2151-9617, Vol.1, No. 1, pp:71-80.

Chapter 17

Analysis and Modeling of Clock-Jitter Effects in Delta-Sigma Modulators

Ramy Saad, Sebastian Hoyos and Samuel Palermo

Additional information is available at the end of the chapter

http://dx.doi.org/10.5772/46453

1. Introduction

The quest for higher data rates in state-of-the-art wireless standards and services calls for wideband and high-resolution data-converters in wireless transceivers. While modern integrated circuits (IC) technologies provide high cut-off frequencies (f_T) for transistors and hence allow the operation at higher speeds, the main limitation against increasing speed of operation of data-converters is the problem of clock-jitter. Clock-jitter is a common problem associated with clock generators due to uncertainty in the timing of the clock edges caused by the finite phase-noise (PN) in the generated clock waveform. Particularly, noise components induced by several noise sources in the system providing the clock (e.g. phase-locked loop, PLL) add to the clock waveform and cause uncertainty in the timing of the zero-crossing instants from cycle to cycle. Figure 1 shows a survey chart of the analog-to-digital converter (ADC) implementations reported in IEEE International solid-state circuits conference (ISSCC) and VLSI Symposium since 1997 [1]. The straight lines show the limitation on the achievable signal-to-noise ratio (SNR) by clock-jitter for jitter root-mean square (rms) values of 1ps and 0.1ps. As can be seen from the chart, the performance of most ADCs falls below the line corresponding to 1ps rms jitter, few ADCs reside in the range between 1ps and 0.1ps, and almost all ADC implementations reported so far are beyond the 0.1ps rms jitter line. This means that the main limitation on increasing the ADC performance in terms of SNR and speed is the specification on the clock-jitter of 0.1ps.

Delta-sigma ($\Delta\Sigma$) ADCs are the convenient choice in low power and state-of-the-art multi-standard wireless receivers for two main reasons. First, they trade DSP for relaxed analog circuit complexity. Particularly, $\Delta\Sigma$ ADC implementations span analog and digital domains ($\Delta\Sigma$ pulse density modulation + digital decimation and filtering, as shown in Figure 2) and hence exploit DSP to relax hardware requirements on analog blocks. Thus, the simplified analog part ($\Delta\Sigma$ modulator) and the digital filtering can be efficiently reconfigured to fulfill performance requirements of different standards at minimum power consumption. Second, ΔΣ modulators use oversampling and hence trade speed for resolution. Specifically, for a given ΔΣ modulator and channel bandwidth (BW), higher effective number of bits (ENOB) can be achieved by increasing the oversampling ratio (OSR). This qualifies ΔΣ ADCs to benefit from increasing speeds of operation offered by advanced deep submicron CMOS technologies (maximum cutoff-frequency $f_T > 300\,GHz$ in 45nm [2]) to meet higher resolution requirements for modern and future wireless services at minimum power overhead.

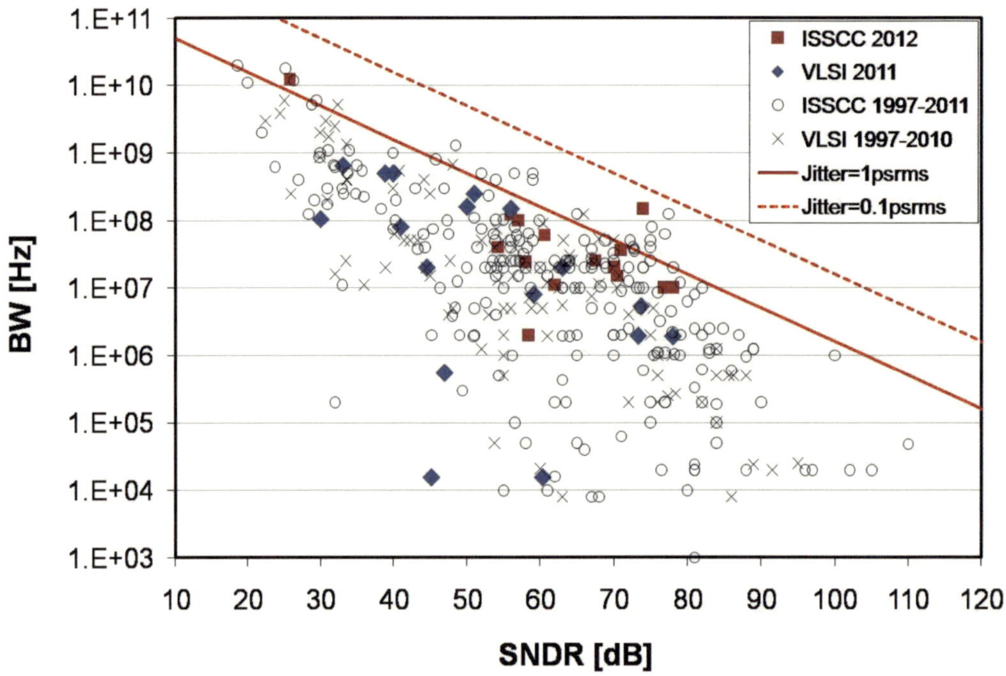

Figure 1. ADC Performance Survey 1997-2012 [1]

Continuous-time (CT) ΔΣ ADCs are widely used in wideband low power wireless receivers [3, 4]. The CT operation of the loop filter relaxes the requirements on the gain-bandwidth product (GBW) of the adopted amplifiers and hence allows the operation at higher speeds or lower power consumption compared to discrete-time (DT) implementations. Also, CT loop filters offer inherent anti-aliasing and thus save the need for explicit anti-aliasing filter before the ADC. The requirements on the sample-and-hold (S/H) circuitry are also relaxed because the sampling is performed after the loop filter and hence the sampling errors experience the maximum attenuation offered by the loop (similar to quantization noise). However, CT ΔΣ modulators suffer from high sensitivity to clock-jitter in the sampling-clock of the digital-to-analog converters (DACs) in the feedback.

In this context, this chapter is intended to provide a comprehensive background and study for the effects of clock-jitter in the sampling-clocks of ΔΣ modulators. Also, Matlab/Simulink models for additive errors induced by clock-jitter in ΔΣ modulators are given so that to help designers characterize the sensitivities of various types of ΔΣ architectures to clock-jitter. The material in this chapter is organized as follows. Section 2 gives a general background about the types of errors caused by clock-jitter in different classes of switched circuits and signal waveforms. The critical sources of jitter induced errors in a ΔΣ loop are identified for DT and CT ΔΣ modulators and a comparison between the two types, in terms of sensitivity to clock-jitter, is done in Section 3. Section 4 provides detailed sensitivity analysis for CT ΔΣ modulators to clock-jitter in the feedback DAC sampling-clock. In Section 5, Simulink models, based on the analysis of Section 4, for the additive errors generated by clock-jitter in CT ΔΣ modulators are shown and the robustness of these models is verified by CT simulations in Matlab/Simulink. Simulations results show good agreement with the theoretical expectations. Finally, conclusions are drawn in Section 6.

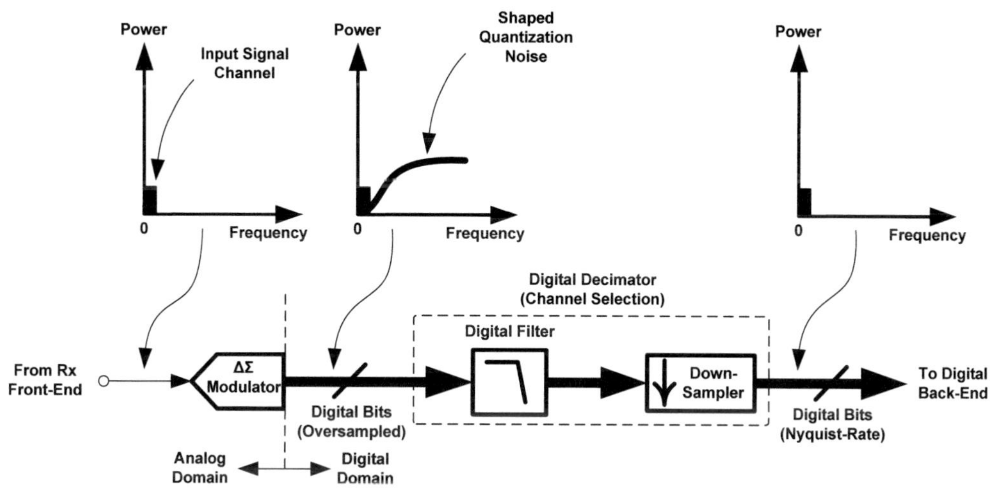

Figure 2. ΔΣ ADC (ΔΣ pulse density modulation + digital decimation and filtering).

2. Jitter problems: Background

Since digital data is always available in DT form, then any process of converting information from analog form to digital bit-stream or vice versa entails sampling. However, the clock signals driving sampling switches suffers clock-jitter due to the noise components that accompany the clock waveform. Figure 3 shows the PN density in a typical voltage-controlled oscillator (VCO)[1]. In the time-domain, the integrated effect of these noise components results in random variations in the phase of the generated clock signal. In data-converters, the problem of clock-jitter is a very critical issue and can significantly deteriorate the achievable SNR by several dBs. The problems resulting from clock-jitter are classified as follows:

[1] The design of clock generators and the mechanisms of PN generation in PLLs are not within the scope of the material given in this chapter.

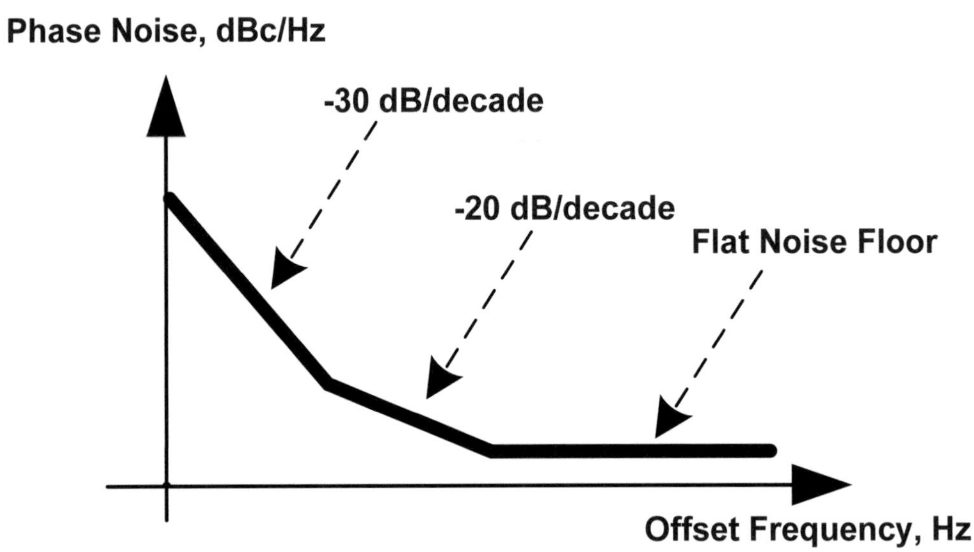

Figure 3. Typical Phase-Noise profile in a VCO.

2.1. Aperture jitter: Voltage sampling errors

In ADCs, it is desirable to convert CT voltage signals into DT form. Figure 4(a) shows a common track-and-hold (T/H) circuit based on a switch driven by a clock signal (sampling-clock) and a sampling capacitor C_S. Errors in the sampled voltage (during the tracking phase) value is one of the most common problems resulting from timing uncertainty Δt (clock-jitter) in the sampling-clock. Particularly, on sampling an input voltage signal, random variations in the timing of the clock edges can result in an incorrect sampled signal, as illustrated in Figure 4(b). This effect is called aperture jitter. The noise induced by aperture jitter can be illustrated as follows. Suppose that a sinusoidal signal $A\, sin(\omega t)$, where A is the amplitude and ω is the angular frequency, is to be sampled using a T/H circuit. Then, the error in the nth sample of the sampled signal due to a timing error $\Delta t(n)$ is given by

$$e(n\, T_s) = A\, \{sin[\omega(n\, T_s + \Delta t(n))] - sin(\omega\, n\, T_s)\}$$

$$\approx A\, \omega\, \Delta t(n)\, cos(n\, T_s). \qquad (1)$$

where T_s is the sampling-period. If σ_j^2 is the variance of the timing error Δt, then the error power is given by

$$\sigma_e^2 = E(e^2) = \frac{(A\, \omega\, \sigma_j)^2}{2} \qquad (2)$$

Since the signal power of the sinusoid is given by $A^2/_2$, the SNR due to aperture jitter is given by

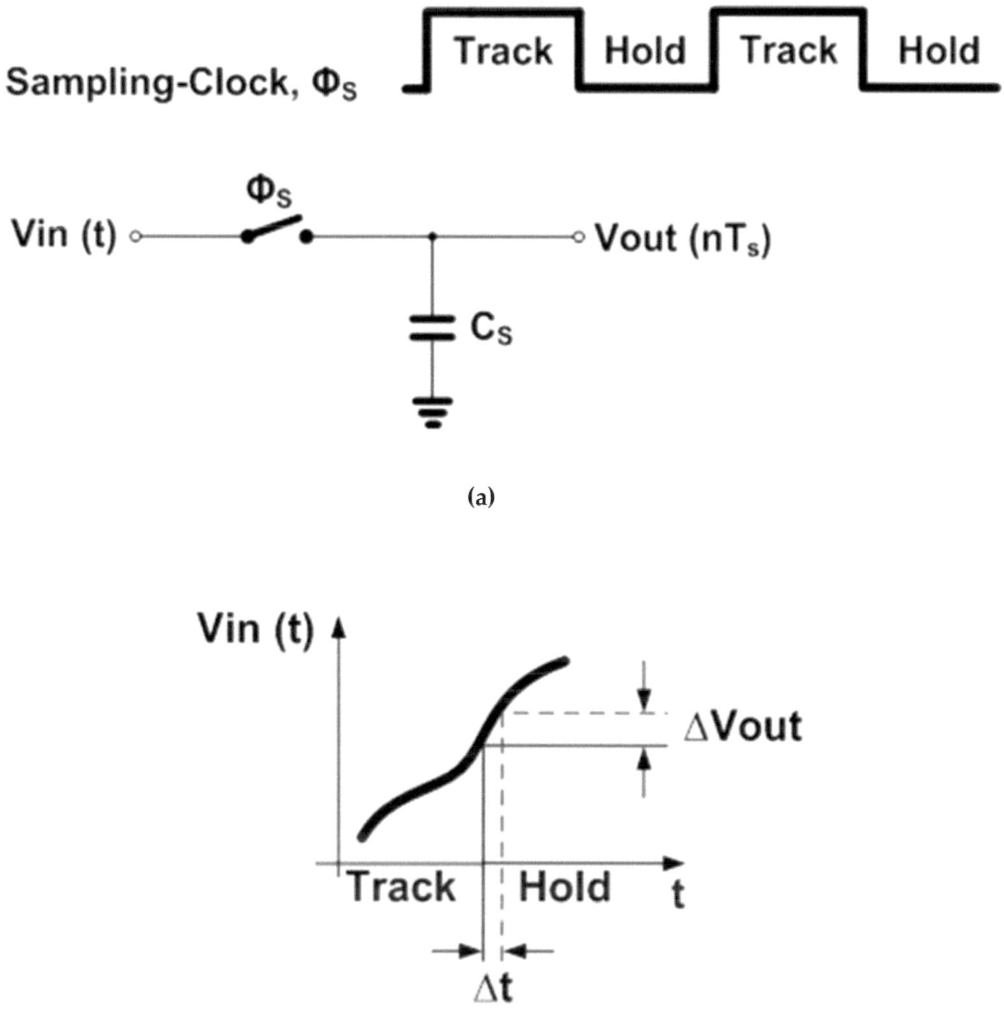

Figure 4. T/H Circuit. (a) Schematic view and clock waveform. (b) Effect of aperture jitter on sampled values.

$$SNR|_{Due\ to\ aperture\ jitter} = 10\ Log\left(\frac{1}{\omega^2\sigma_j^2}\right) = 10\ Log\left(\frac{1}{4\,\pi^2 f^2\sigma_j^2}\right) \quad (3)$$

where $f = \omega/2\pi$ is the frequency. From (3) the SNR has the worst value at the edge of the signal band (largest value of frequency, f_{max}). The plots in Figure 5 show the limitation on the achievable SNR vs. the signal frequency due to aperture jitter for different values of the rms jitter σ_j.

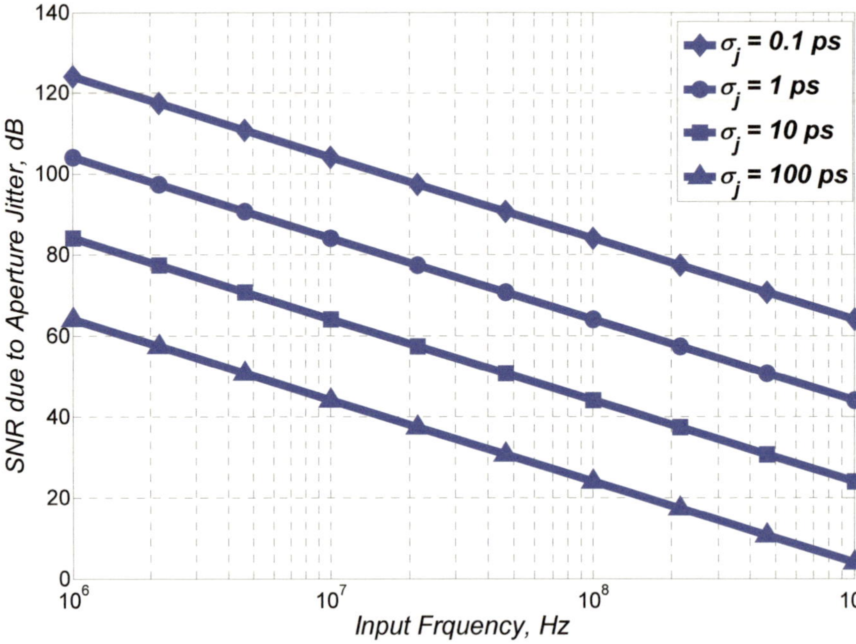

Figure 5. SNR variation with the input frequency due to aperture jitter for different rms jitter values.

2.2. Charge transfer jitter

Another effect of clock-jitter, called charge transfer jitter, shows up in circuits whose operation is based on charge transfer by switching. In particular, switched-capacitor (SC) circuits commonly used in DT ADCs and DACs suffer from charge transfer errors due to clock-jitter in the sampling clocks. Consider the simple non-inverting SC integrator in Figure 6(a). As shown by the time-domain waveforms in Figure 6(b), during integrating phase $\emptyset_2$, the charge stored in a sampling capacitor C_S is transferred to an integrating capacitor C_I through the ON resistance (R_{ON}) of the switch. The discharging of C_S takes place in an exponentially-decaying rate.

For a given clock-cycle n, the instantaneous exponentially-decaying current $I_n(t)$ resulting from the charge transfer from C_S to C_I can be derived as follows:

$$I_n(t) = \begin{cases} I_P \, e^{\frac{-(t-\alpha)T_S}{\tau}} & , \quad \alpha T_s < t < \beta T_s, 0 \leq \alpha \leq \beta \leq 1 \\ 0 & , \quad otherwise \end{cases} , \tag{4}$$

where I_P is the value of the peak current at the beginning of the pulse, α and β are the start and end times of the exponentially-decaying pulse normalized to the sampling period T_s and τ is the discharging time-constant and is given by the product $R_{ON}C_S$. The values of α and β are determined by the duty-cycle of the clock. In typical SC circuits, $\alpha = 0.5$ and $\beta =$

1. Recall that the input voltage is sampled on C_S during the first clock half-cycle (when $\emptyset_1$ is high) and then the charge on C_S is transferred to C_I during the second clock half-cycle (when $\emptyset_2$ is high). For a total charge of Q_n to be transferred during $\emptyset_2$ of clock-cycle n,

$$Q_n = \int_{\alpha T_s}^{\beta T_s} I_n(t)\, dt = \int_{\alpha T_s}^{\beta T_s} I_P\, e^{\frac{-(t-\alpha)T_s}{\tau}} dt = -\tau\, A\, e^{\frac{-(t-\alpha)T_s}{\tau}}\Big|_{\alpha T_s}^{\beta T_s} = \tau\, A \left(1 - e^{\frac{-(\beta-\alpha)T_s}{\tau}}\right) \tag{5}$$

Thus,

$$I_P = \frac{Q_n}{\tau\left(1 - e^{\frac{-(\beta-\alpha)T_s}{\tau}}\right)}. \tag{6}$$

Substituting with (6) in (4) yields

$$I_n(t) = \begin{cases} \dfrac{Q_n}{\tau\left(1 - e^{\frac{-(\beta-\alpha)T_s}{\tau}}\right)} e^{\frac{-(t-\alpha)T_s}{\tau}}, \alpha T_s < t < \beta T_s, 0 \leq \alpha \leq \beta \leq 1. \quad (7) \\ 0\,, otherwise. \end{cases} \tag{7}$$

However, in presence of timing error $\Delta t(n)$ in the pulse-width of the discharging phase $\emptyset_2$, the resulting error in the integrated charge in the nth clock-cycle is given by

$$e_j(n) = \frac{Q_n}{\tau\left(1 - e^{\frac{-(\beta-\alpha)T_s}{\tau}}\right)} \int_{\beta T_s}^{\beta T_s+\Delta t(n)} e^{\frac{-(t-\alpha)T_s}{\tau}} dt = \frac{-Q_n}{\left(1 - e^{\frac{-(\beta-\alpha)T_s}{\tau}}\right)} e^{\frac{-(t-\alpha)T_s}{\tau}}\Bigg|_{\beta T_s}^{\beta T_s+\Delta t(n)}$$

$$= \frac{Q_n}{\left(1 - e^{\frac{-(\beta-\alpha)T_s}{\tau}}\right)} \left[e^{\frac{-(\beta-\alpha)T_s}{\tau}} - e^{\frac{-(\beta-\alpha)T_s-\Delta t(n)}{\tau}}\right]$$

$$= \frac{Q_n}{\left(1 - e^{\frac{-(\beta-\alpha)T_s}{\tau}}\right)} e^{\frac{-(\beta-\alpha)T_s}{\tau}} \left[1 - e^{-\frac{\Delta t(n)}{\tau}}\right], \tag{8}$$

which for $\Delta t_n \ll \tau$ can be approximated by

$$e_j(n) \approx \frac{Q_n}{\tau\left(1 - e^{\frac{-(\beta-\alpha)T_s}{\tau}}\right)} e^{\frac{-(\beta-\alpha)T_s}{\tau}} \Delta t(n). \tag{9}$$

If σ_j^2 the variance of the timing error $\Delta t(n)$, then the error power is given by

$$\sigma_e^2 = E(e^2) = \left(\frac{Q_{rms}}{\tau\left(1 - e^{\frac{-(\beta-\alpha)T_s}{\tau}}\right)} e^{\frac{-(\beta-\alpha)T_s}{\tau}}\right)^2 \sigma_j^2, \tag{10}$$

where Q_{rms} is the rms charge sampled on the sampling capacitor C_S. Thus, the SNR due to charge transfer jitter caused by charge transfer jitter is given by

$$SNR|_{Due\ to\ charge\ transfer\ jitter} = 10\ Log\left(\frac{{Q_{rms}}^{2}}{\left(\frac{Q_{rms}}{\tau\left(1-e^{\frac{-(\beta-\alpha)T_s}{\tau}}\right)}\,e^{\frac{-(\beta-\alpha)T_s}{\tau}}\right)^{2}\sigma_j^2}\right)$$

$$= 10\ Log\left(\frac{\tau^2\left(1-e^{\frac{-(\beta-\alpha)T_S}{\tau}}\right)^{2}}{\left(e^{\frac{-(\beta-\alpha)T_S}{\tau}}\right)^{2}}\frac{1}{\sigma_j^2}\right). \quad (11)$$

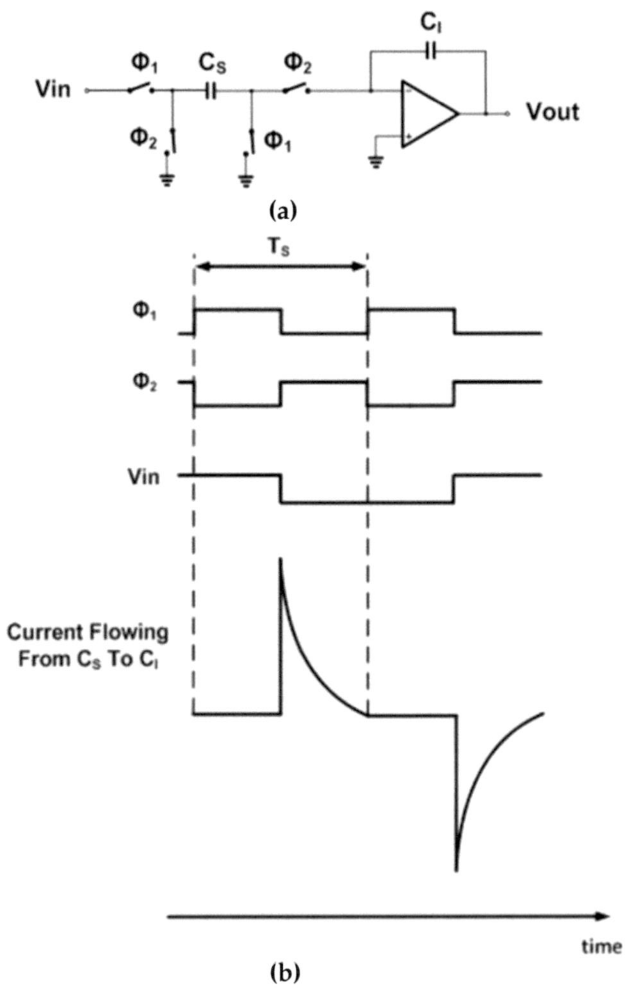

Figure 6. (a) Non-inverting switched-capacitor discrete-time integrator. (b) Time-domain waveforms for clock phases, input signal, and charge flow from C_S to C_I.

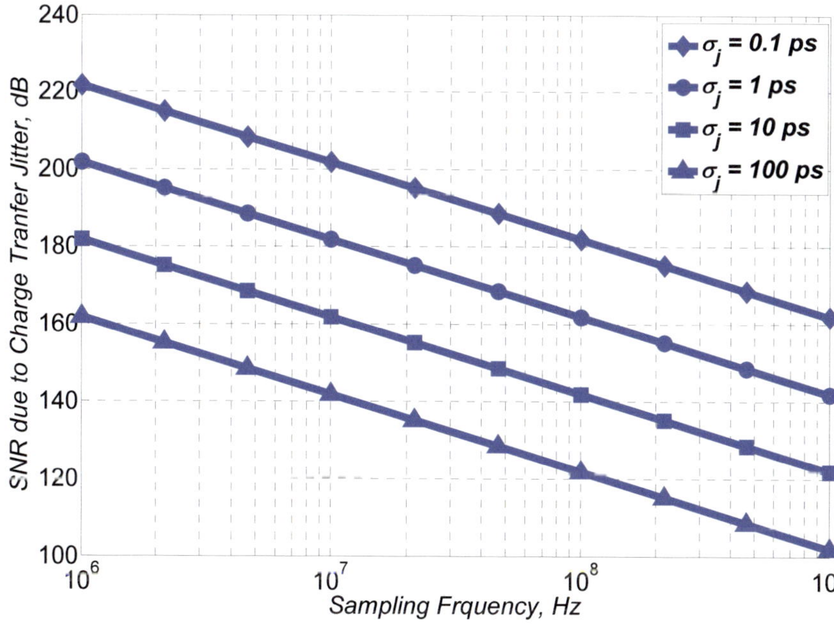
σj = 0.1 ps
σj = 1 ps
σj = 10 ps
σj = 100 ps
SNR due to Charge Tranfer Jitter, dB
Sampling Frquency, Hz

(a)

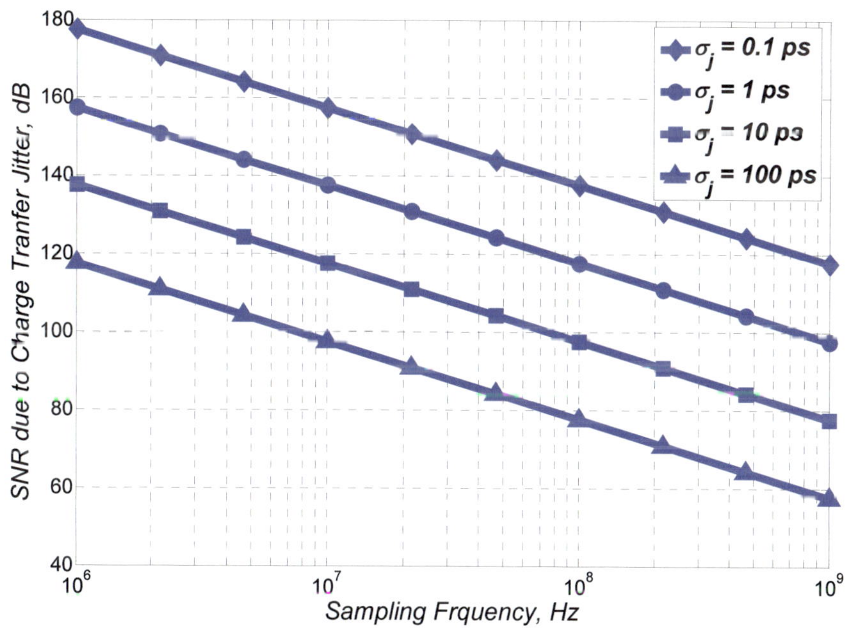
σj = 0.1 ps
σj = 1 ps
σj = 10 ps
σj = 100 ps
SNR due to Charge Tranfer Jitter, dB
Sampling Frquency, Hz

(b)

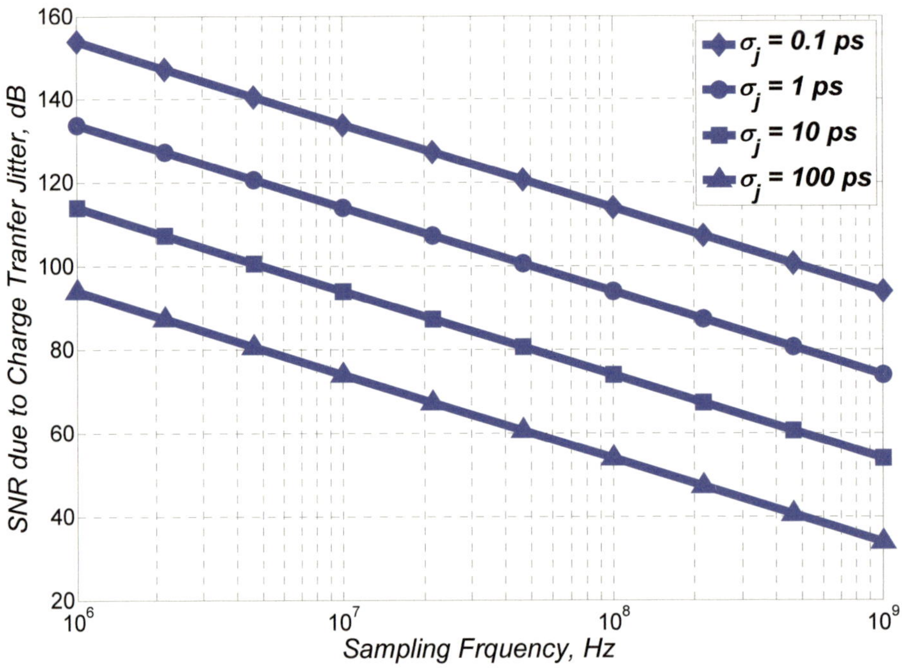

(c)

Figure 7. SNR variation with the input frequency due to charge transfer jitter for different rms jitter values. (a) $\boldsymbol{\tau = 0.05\, T_s}$. (b) $\boldsymbol{\tau = 0.1\, T_s}$. (c) $\boldsymbol{\tau = 0.2\, T_s}$.

The plots in Figure 7 show the limitation on the achievable SNR vs. the signal frequency due to charge transfer jitter for different values of the rms jitter σ_j. Typical values of $\alpha = 0.5$ and $\beta = 1$ have been considered. The results are provided for $\tau = 0.05\, T_s, 0.1\, T_s$, and $0.2\, T_s$. As can be seen from the plots in Figure 7, for a given clock frequency, the SNR limitation due to charge transfer jitter is much more relaxed compared to the aperture jitter error (Figure 5). This result was expected because from equation (11), the effect of the jitter induced noise is reduced by an exponential factor indicating that charge transfer error in SC circuits should be less critical. This also can also be explained intuitively by noting that for the exponentially-decaying waveform in Figure 8, the amplitude of the pulse is rather low at the end of the clock-cycle and hence the amount of charge that varies over one clock period due to jitter is significantly reduced. However, for a given rms jitter and sampling frequency, the SNR limitation due to charge transfer jitter degrades as the discharging time-constant τ increases. This is because the value of the charge transfer current at the end of the clock-cycle (discharge phase) is varying exponentially with τ, thus for a given timing error Δt, the error in the amount of charge transferred is higher.

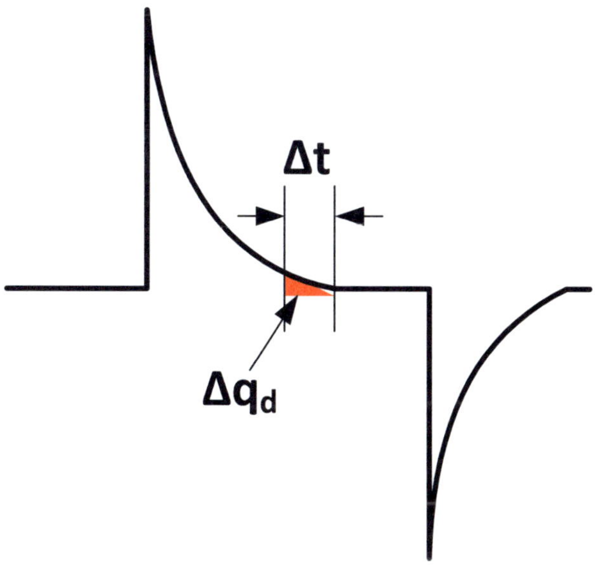

Figure 8. Jitter-tolerant exponentially-decaying waveform.

2.3. Pulse-width jitter

Continuous-time current-steering DAC, shown in Figure 9(a), is used to convert digital signals into CT analog pulses. Clock-jitter in the sampling-clock of a CT DAC modulates the pulse-width of the waveform at the DAC output. Called pulse-width jitter (PWJ), this problem generally shows up in circuits whose operation is based on current-switching, e.g. current-steering DACs, charge sampling circuits, and charge pumps. In systems using CT DACs (e.g. audio transmitters and CT ΔΣ modulators), the DAC is loaded by a CT filter stage that integrates the output current pulse from the DAC. The error in the amount of integrated charges is directly proportional to the timing error Δt in the pulse-width, as illustrated by the time-domain waveform in Figure 9(b). If the clock-jitter causes timing errors Δt with variance σ_j^2 and the switched-current levels are $\pm I_S$, the variance of the charge transferred per clock-cycle T_s is

$$\sigma_e^2 = \sigma_j^2 \, {I_S}^2. \tag{12}$$

For a sinusoidal signal, the maximum signal power in terms of the integrated charge signal per clock-cycle is given by

$$\sigma_{signal}^2 = \frac{{I_S}^2 \, {T_S}^2}{2}. \tag{13}$$

Thus, the maximum SNR against PWJ is given by

$$SNR|_{Due\ to\ pulse-width\ jitter} = 10\ Log\left(\frac{{T_s}^2}{2\,\sigma_j^2}\right), \tag{14}$$

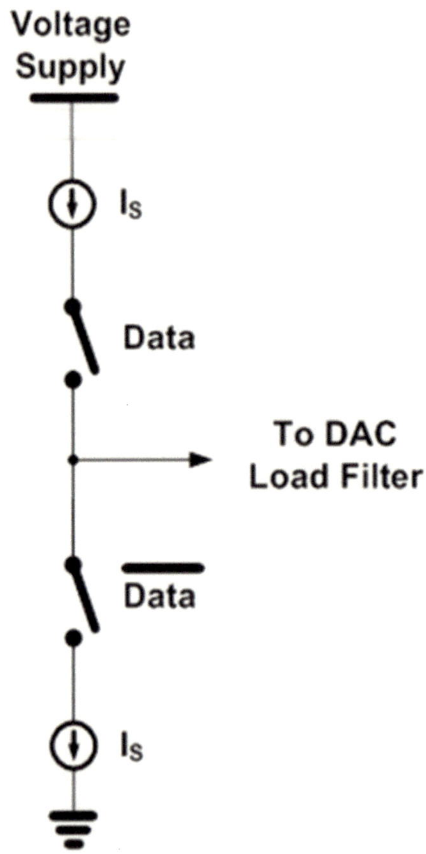

(a)

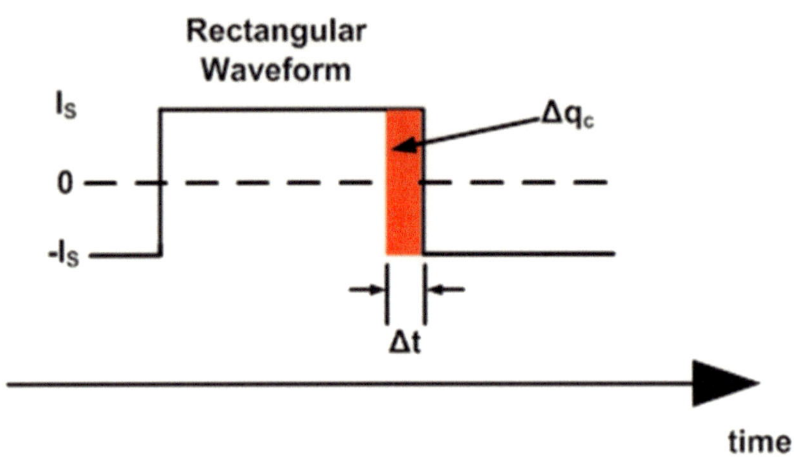

(b)

Figure 9. Pulse-width jitter in switched-current circuits.

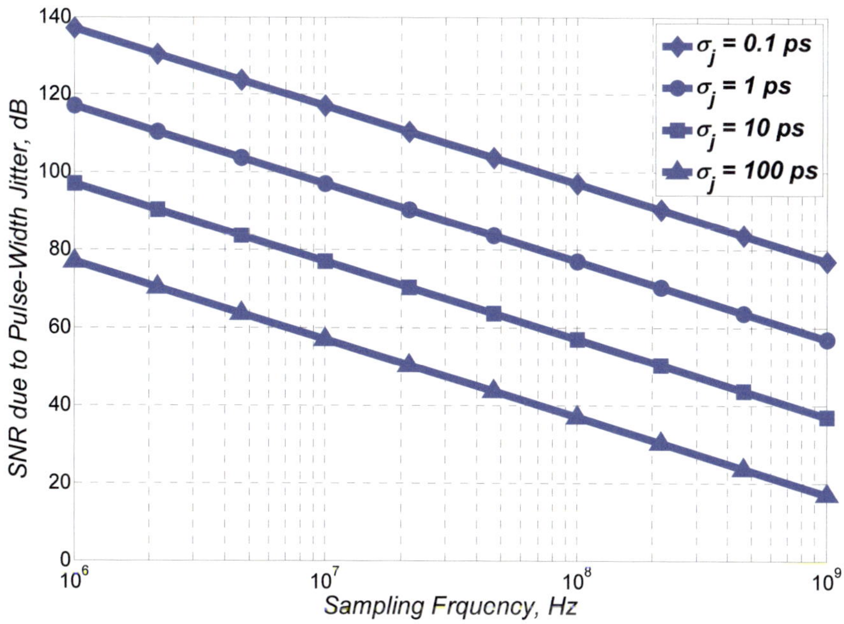

Figure 10. SNR variation with the input frequency due to pulse-width jitter for different rms jitter values.

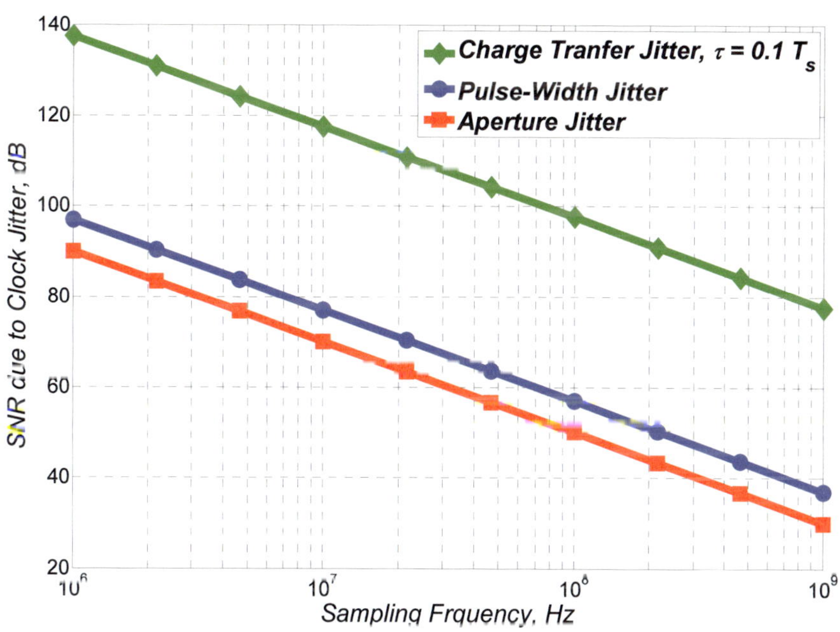

Figure 11. SNR variation with the sampling frequency due to different types of jitter induced errors for a rms jitter of 10 ps.

Thus, the SNR degradation by PWJ is less than that of the aperture jitter by a factor of $2\pi^2$. The plots in Figure 10 show the limitation on the achievable SNR vs. the signal frequency due to PWJ problem for different values of the rms jitter σ_j.

Figure 11 provides a comparative insight about the SNR limitation imposed by each one of the clock-jitter induced problems discussed above. It is worth noting that these plots are for Nyquist-rate sampling; however the foregoing analysis and results can be easily extended to include the effect of oversampling in oversampled circuits. As can be observed from the plots in Figure 11, for a given sampling frequency, the maximum limitation on the achievable SNR is caused by aperture jitter. However, the charge transfer jitter limits the SNR at very high frequencies; for example for an SNR of 80 dB, the charge transfer jitter starts to limit the achievable SNR at sampling frequency $F_s \geq 1\,GHz$ for $\tau = 0.1\,T_s$, and as mentioned before more robustness to charge transfer jitter at high frequencies can be obtained by reducing the discharging time-constant τ.

3. Sensitivity of ΔΣ modulators to clock-jitter

The purpose of this section is to address the effects of clock-jitter in the two main classes of ΔΣ modulators, shown in Figure 12, and provide a comparison between them in terms of sensitivity to clock-jitter. In order to determine the performance sensitivity to clock-jitter in DT and CT modulators, the critical sources of jitter induced errors in the loop should be identified in each one. The most critical clock-jitter errors in a ΔΣ modulator are those generated at the modulator input and in the feedback path through the outermost DAC feeding the first stage in the loop filter (recall that errors generated at inner nodes in the loop are suppressed by the previous stages of the loop filter).

The feedback signal is carrying a digital data (coming from the loop quantizer) and hence it is robust to aperture jitter[2]. However, depending on the type of the adopted feedback DAC, the feedback signal in a ΔΣ loop can suffer one of the other two kinds of jitter induced errors (namely, charge transfer jitter and PWJ). The effect of feedback jitter can be further discussed in the frequency domain with the aid of Figure 13 as follows. Recall that the modulator feedback signal includes the in-band desired signal (input signal) and the high-pass shaped noise. Since the sampling process ideally is a multiplication in time, the spectra of the analog input signal and the clock signal convolve. Thus, the error generated by DAC clock PN has two main components, as illustrated by Figure 13. First, the clock PN components close to the clock frequency modulates the in-band desired signal resulting in signal side-bands in the same manner like the PN of an upfront sampler [5]. Second, the wideband clock PN, modulates the high-pass shaped noise components and the modulation products fall over the desired band and hence elevate the in-band noise level.

---

[2] Since the digital data coming in the feedback is usually sampled at the middle of the clock-cycle, sampled signal in the feedback can suffer aperture jitter only if the clock-jitter is $\geq \boldsymbol{T_s/2}$.

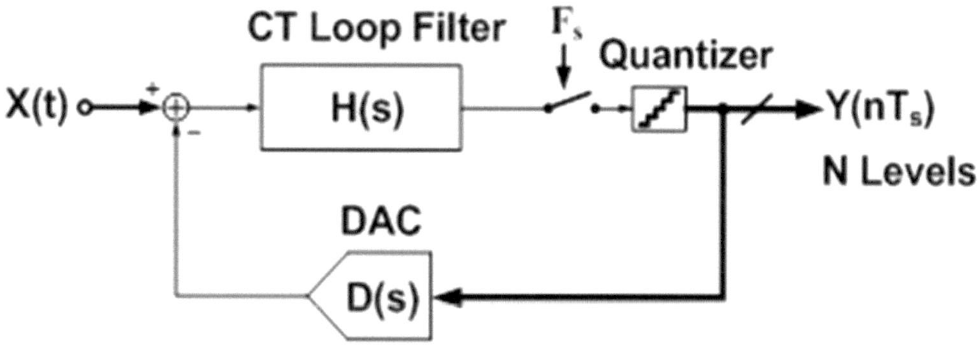

(a)

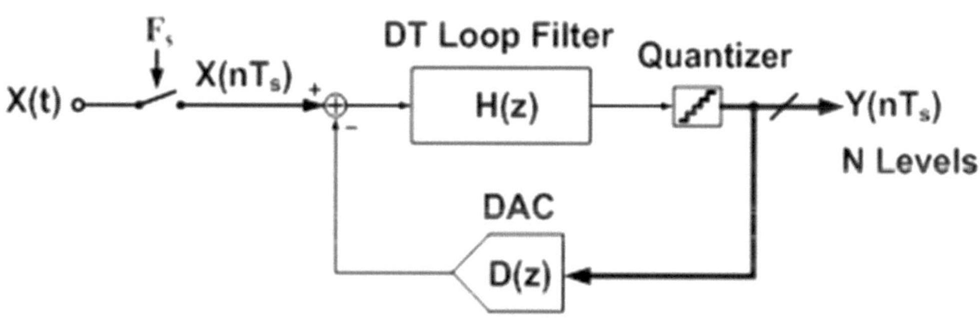

(b)

Figure 12. ΔΣ Modulators. (a) Continuous-Time. (b) Discrete-Time.

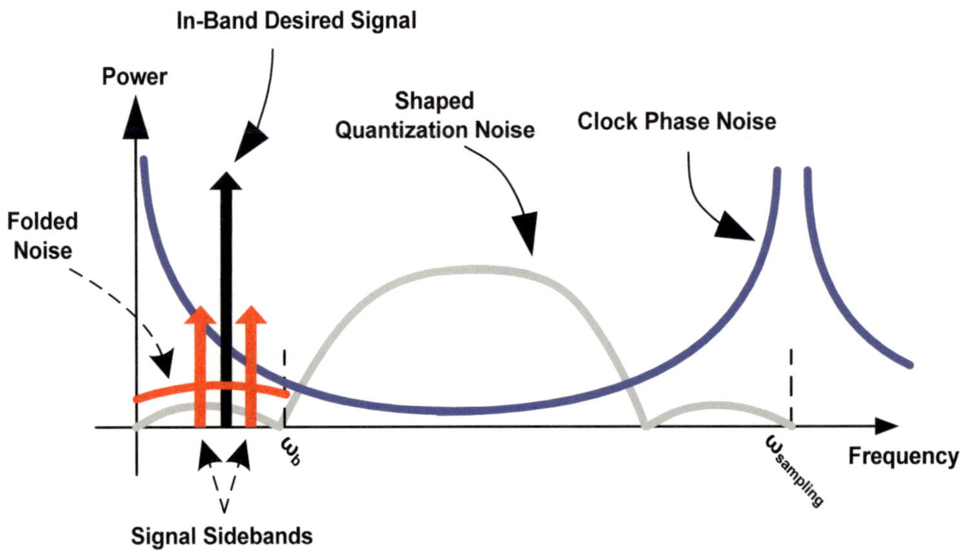

Figure 13. Modulation of in-band desired signal and shaped quantization noise by phase-noise in the DAC sampling clock.

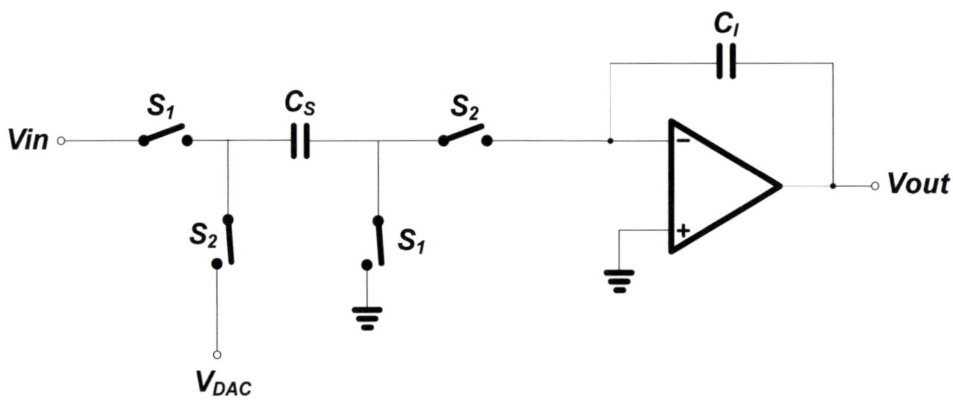

Figure 14. Non-inverting switched-capacitor discrete-time integrator.

3.1. DT ΔΣ modulators

In DT ΔΣ modulators, the sampling takes place at the modulator input. The SC integrator in Figure 14 is commonly used as an input stage for DT loop filters in ΔΣ modulators. The sampling aperture jitter errors due to the sampling switch (S_1) will be added to the signal at the input and hence will directly appear at the modulator output without any suppression. As mentioned earlier, the feedback signal (V_{DAC}) doesn't experience aperture jitter because the feedback signal is DT and also it has discrete amplitude levels. Thus, timing errors cannot result in a sampled value that is different from the original feedback one. Timing errors at switch S_2 cause charge transfer jitter errors being added at the input stage. However, the charge transfer jitter errors at S_2 are very small owing to the high robustness of the exponentially-decaying waveform to clock-jitter and moreover R_{ON} of the switches are usually very small resulting in a small time-constant τ which gives more jitter robustness to the waveform (recall the analysis given in the previous section).

According to the above discussion, the jitter induced noise in DT ΔΣ modulators is mainly dominated by the aperture error at S_1. At a given sampling speed, the only way to improve the performance of DT ΔΣ modulators is to improve the jitter performance of the clock generator which translates into significant increase in the total power consumption in case of ΔΣ ADCs targeting high resolution. On the other hand, for a given rms jitter, if the sampling frequency is reduced for the sake of improving tolerance to jitter errors, then to achieve high resolution at the resulting low OSR, the filter order and/or the quantizer levels need to be increased. This translates into significant power penalty too. Moreover, this approach wouldn't work for state-of-the-art wireless standards with continuously increasing channel bandwidths.

3.2. CT ΔΣ modulators

In CT ΔΣ modulators, sampling occurs after the loop filter and hence sampling errors including aperture jitter are highly suppressed when they appear at the output because this is the point of maximum attenuation in the loop. However, CT ΔΣ implementations suffer from jitter errors added to the feedback signal. Particularly, in a CT ΔΣ modulator the DAC converts the quantizer output DT signal into CT pulses. The waveform coming from the CT DAC is fed to the loop filter to be integrated in the CT integrator stages. Thus, PWJ in the DAC waveform causes uncertainty in the integrated values at the outputs of the loop filter integrators. Rectangular waveform DACs are commonly used in CT ΔΣ structures due to their simple implementation and the relatively relaxed slew-rate (SR) requirement they offer for the loop filter amplifiers. Return-to-zero (RZ) DACs are the most sensitive to feedback PWJ because the random variations are affecting the rising and falling edges of the waveform at every clock-cycle. The jitter sensitivity can be slightly reduced by using a NRZ DAC because in this case, the clock-jitter will be effective only during the clock edges at which data is changing. The equivalent input-referred errors induced by clock jitter in RZ and NRZ waveforms for a certain sequence of data are illustrated in Figure 15.

As mentioned earlier, clock-jitter errors added in the feedback path are the most critical because they entail random phase-modulation that folds back high-pass shaped noise components over the desired channel. For typical wideband CT ΔΣ modulators with NRZ current steering DACs in the feedback, the error induced by the PWJ in the DAC waveform can be up to 30% - 40% of the noise budget [3, 4, 6].

Convenience for low power implementations: CT ΔΣ modulators have gained significant attention in low power and high speed applications because they can operate at higher speed or lower power consumption compared to DT counterparts. Recall the relaxed gain bandwidth (GBW) product requirements they add on the loop filter amplifiers compared to DT implementations in which the loop filter is processing a DT signal and hence a GBW requirement on the amplifier is typically in the range of five times the sampling frequency.

Moreover, sensitivity of CT ΔΣ modulators to DAC clock-jitter can be minimized by processing the DAC pulse or modifying its shape so as to alleviate the error caused by the DAC clock jitter [7]. That is, the achievable SNR of a CT ΔΣ modulator can be improved against clock-jitter without having to improve the jitter performance of the clock generator or to reduce the sampling speed and increase the order of the loop filter or the quantizer resolution. This definitely translates into power savings because it avoids increasing the complexity of the clock generator or the ΔΣ modulator and hence avoiding extra power penalties[3].

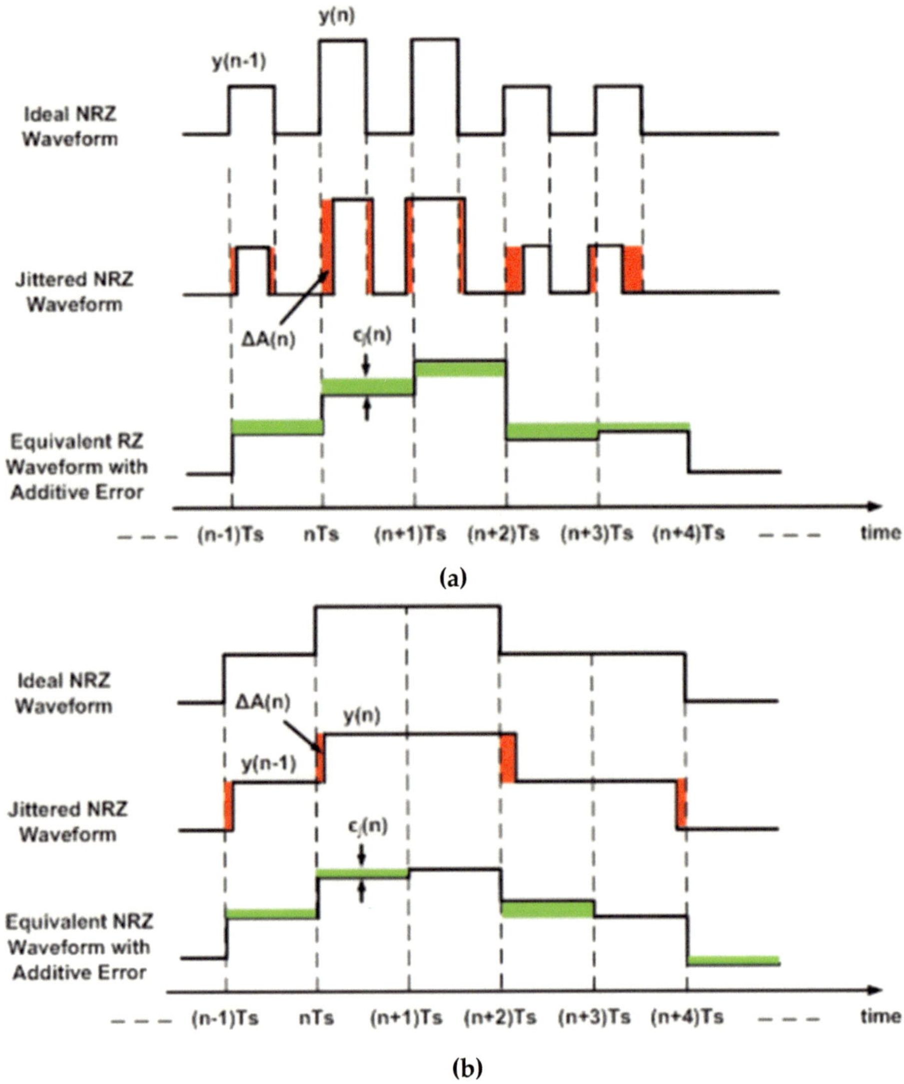

Figure 15. Equivalent input referred error induced by pulse-width jitter [7]. (a) RZ DAC. (b) NRZ DAC.

[3] This is provided that the solution adopted to improve the DAC tolerance to clock jitter errors is not adding high power overhead and thus not increasing the total power consumption.

4. Analysis of jitter effects in CT ΔΣ modulators

This section provides detailed analysis for the effects of DAC clock-jitter on the performance of CT ΔΣ modulators for the most commonly used DAC types.

4.1. Return-to-zero DAC waveforms

Return-to-zero DAC waveforms are known to be robust to even-order nonlinearities resulting from mismatch between rise and fall times, as well as less sensitive to excess loop delay in the quantizer compared to NRZ waveforms [3]. However, as mentioned in previous section, they are the most sensitive to PWJ because the additive jitter induced errors are linearly proportional to the random timing errors at the rise and fall edges every clock-cycle, as illustrated in Figure 15(a). The equivalent error induced by PWJ in a RZ DAC waveform is given by

$$\epsilon_j(n) = \frac{\Delta A(n)}{T_s} = y(n)\frac{T_s}{T_C}\frac{\left(\Delta t_r(n)+\Delta t_f(n)\right)}{T_s}, \tag{15}$$

where $\Delta A(n)$ is the area difference resulting from the error in the total integrated charge per one clock period T_s between the ideal and the jittered waveforms, $y(n)$ is the modulator output at the nth clock cycle, T_C is the duty-cycle of the RZ pulse, and $\Delta t_r(n)$ and $\Delta t_f(n)$ are the random timing errors in the rise and fall edges, respectively, of the nth DAC pulse. The amplitude of the DAC pulse varies inversely proportional with the pulse duty-cycle so that to supply a constant amount of charge (determined by Full-Scale (FS) voltage level of the quantizer) to the loop filter per clock-cycle. Following the procedure in [7], for a single tone $V_{sig} \cdot sin(\omega_{sig}t)$ at the input of the ΔΣ modulator, the integrated in-band jitter-induced noise power (IBJN) for a RZ DAC is given by

$$IBJN|_{RZ} = \frac{2}{OSR}\left(\frac{\sigma_j}{T_C}\right)^2\left[\frac{V_{sig}{}^2}{2} + \frac{\Delta^2}{12}\cdot\frac{1}{2\pi}\int_{-\pi}^{\pi}\left|NTF\left(e^{j\omega}\right)\right|^2 d\omega\right]. \tag{16}$$

where σ_j is the rms jitter in the DAC sampling-clock, OSR is the oversampling ratio of the modulator, Δ is the quantization step of the loop quantizer, and NTF is the noise transfer-function of the modulator. From equation (16), the expressions for the IBJN due to input signal and shaped quantization noise can be written as follows

$$IBJN|_{RZ,due\ to\ input\ signal} = \frac{V_{sig}{}^2}{OSR}\left(\frac{\sigma_j}{T_C}\right)^2. \tag{17}$$

$$IBJN|_{RZ,due\ to\ shaped\ noise} = \frac{1}{OSR}\left(\frac{\sigma_j}{T_C}\right)^2\frac{\Delta^2}{12\pi}\int_{-\pi}^{\pi}\left|NTF(e^{j\omega})\right|^2 d\omega. \tag{18}$$

From the expression in (16), it is evident that the IBJN decreases proportionally with the OSR and the duty cycle of the DAC pulse. Particularly, 1) as the OSR increases, the power spectral density (PSD) of the PWJ induced errors is reduced and hence the resulting integrated in-band noise is decreased accordingly, 2) the additive error in the amount of integrated charge in the loop filter varies linearly with the PWJ at the rise and fall edges by a factor roughly equal to the pulse amplitude (Figure 15(a)), which is inversely proportional to T_C. The IBJN due to in-band signal component, given in (17), causes sidebands of the input signal to appear in the desired band. Also, from (18), PWJ randomly modulating shaped noise results in noise folding back over the desired band and hence elevating the in-band noise level. In (16) and (18), the effect of the quantizer resolution is implicitly included in Δ^2.

4.2. Non-return-to-zero DAC waveforms

Non-return-to-zero DACs are known to be highly sensitive to excess loop delay and also they result in even-order nonlinearities due to mismatch between rise and fall times, in contrast to RZ DAC waveforms. However, they are commonly used in CT ΔΣ modulators due to their simple implementation, relaxed SR requirement on the integrating amplifiers, and lower sensitivity to clock-jitter compared to RZ DACs. As illustrated by Fig. 15(b), in NRZ waveforms the clock-jitter will be effective only during the clock edges at which data is changing. Equivalent error induced by clock-jitter in a NRZ waveform is given by

$$\epsilon_j(n) = \frac{\Delta A(n)}{T_s} = (y(n) - y(n-1))\frac{\Delta t(n)}{T_s}, \tag{19}$$

where $\Delta t(n)$ is the random timing error in the clock edge of the nth clock-cycle. From [7], for a single tone $V_{sig} \cdot sin(\omega_{sig}t)$ at the input of the ΔΣ modulator, the total IBJN for a NRZ DAC is given by

$$IBJN|_{NRZ} = 4 \cdot OSR \cdot BW^2 \cdot \sigma_j^2 \cdot \left[\frac{\pi^2}{2}\left(\frac{{V_{sig}}^2}{{OSR_{sig}}^2}\right) + \frac{\Delta^2 \cdot {\sigma_{NTF,RMS}}^2}{12}\right]$$

$$\leq 2\pi^2 \frac{{V_{sig}}^2 \cdot BW^2 \cdot \sigma_j^2}{OSR} + \frac{OSR \cdot BW^2 \cdot \Delta^2 \cdot {\sigma_{NTF,RMS}}^2 \cdot \sigma_j^2}{3}. \tag{20}$$

where BW is the input signal bandwidth, OSR_{sig} is the ratio of the sampling frequency to double the input signal frequency, and ${\sigma_{NTF,RMS}}^2 = \frac{1}{\pi}\int_{-\pi}^{\pi}\left[\left|NTF(e^{j\omega})\right|^2 \cdot (1-\cos\omega)\right] d\omega$. Thus, the expressions for the IBJN due to input signal and shaped quantization noise can be written as follows

$$IBJN|_{NRZ,due\ to\ signal} \leq 2\pi^2 \frac{{V_{sig}}^2 \cdot BW^2 \cdot \sigma_j^2}{OSR}. \tag{21}$$

$$IBJN|_{NRZ,due\ to\ shaped\ noise} = \frac{OSR \cdot BW^2 \cdot \Delta^2 \cdot {\sigma_{NTF,RMS}}^2 \cdot \sigma_j^2}{3}. \tag{22}$$

From the expression in (21), the IBJN due to signal is inversely proportional with the OSR because, intuitively, as the OSR increases, less signal-related transitions will occur at the modulator output and hence less additive jitter noise will be generated. This note is applicable only to transitions at the modulator output in the frequency range of the input signal. For example, in case of DC inputs, the modulator output will exhibit limit cycles and yields discrete tones at the output spectrum [8]; however, these transitions at the output waveform are due to the shaped quantization noise and not the input signal. On the other hand, from (22), the IBJN due to shaped noise increases proportionally with the OSR because a higher OSR means more OOB shaped noise components will be modulated and fold back over the desired channel by the PN components at their respective frequencies. Therefore, the OSR needs to be optimized for better robustness to PWJ according to the contribution of each component (in-band signal and shaped noise). Also, the IBJN due to shaped noise is proportional to $\sigma_{NTF,RMS}{}^2$, and thus to minimize the PWJ, the aggressiveness of the NTF needs to be relaxed. This gives a trade-off between quantization noise suppression and sensitivity to PWJ and hence a compromise is needed.

4.3. Switched-capacitor-resistor DACs with exponentially-decaying waveforms

A commonly used solution to alleviate DAC sensitivity to PWJ is the switched-capacitor-resistor (SCR) DAC with exponentially-decaying waveform, shown in Figure 16. The exponentially-decaying waveform (Figure 8) of the SCR DAC makes the amount of charge transferred to the loop per clock-cycle less dependent on the exact timing of the DAC clock-edges [4, 9].

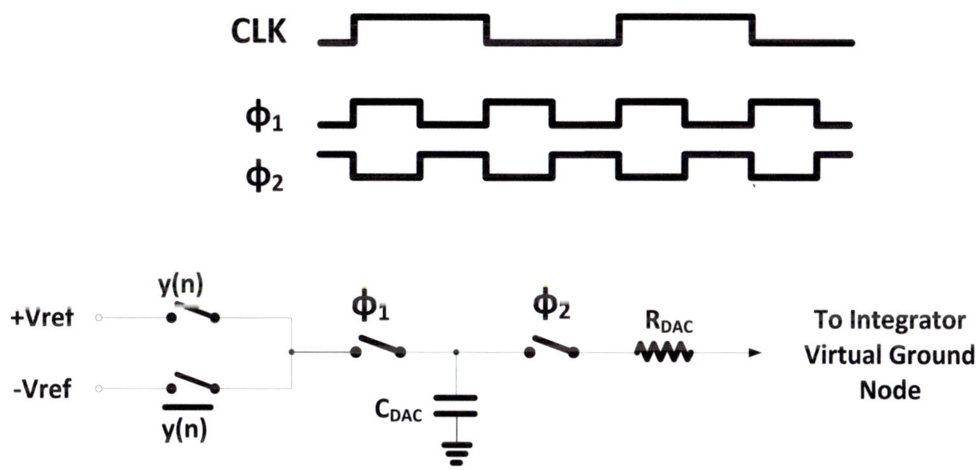

Figure 16. SCR DAC.

For a given clock-cycle n, the instantaneous exponentially-decaying current $I_n(t)$ resulting from the charge transfer is given by equation (4). Recall that the feedback value is sampled on C_{DAC} during the first clock half-cycle (when $\emptyset_1$ is high) and then the sampled voltage is transferred to loop filter during the second clock half-cycle (when $\emptyset_2$ is high). For a total integrated charge of $k_{DAC} \cdot y(n) \cdot T_S$ to be delivered by the SCR DAC during $\emptyset_1$ of clock-cycle n,

$$k_{DAC} \cdot y(n) \cdot T_S = \int_{\alpha T_s}^{\beta T_s} I_P \; e^{\frac{-(\beta-\alpha)T_s}{\tau}} \, dt = \tau \, I_P \left(1 - e^{\frac{-(\beta-\alpha)T_s}{\tau}}\right). \qquad (23)$$

where k_{DAC} is the feedback DAC gain coefficient. Therefore,

$$I_P = \frac{k_{DAC} \cdot y(n) \cdot T_S}{\tau\left(1 - e^{\frac{-(\beta-\alpha)T_S}{\tau}}\right)}. \tag{24}$$

However, in presence of timing error $\Delta t(n)$ in the pulse-width of the discharge phase $\emptyset_2$ in the nth clock cycle, the equivalent input-referred additive error in the integrated charge is given by

$$\epsilon_j(n) = \frac{1}{T_S} \frac{k_{DAC} \cdot y(n) \cdot T_S}{\tau\left(1 - e^{\frac{-(\beta-\alpha)T_S}{\tau}}\right)} \int_{\beta T_s}^{\beta T_s + \Delta t(n)} e^{\frac{-(t-\alpha)T_S}{\tau}} dt$$

$$= \frac{k_{DAC} \cdot y(n)}{\left(1 - e^{\frac{-(\beta-\alpha)T_S}{\tau}}\right)} e^{\frac{-(\beta-\alpha)T_S}{\tau}} \left[1 - e^{-\frac{\Delta t(n)}{\tau}}\right], \tag{25}$$

which for $\Delta t(n) \ll \tau$ can be approximated by

$$\epsilon_j(n) \approx \frac{k_{DAC} \cdot y(n)}{\tau\left(1 - e^{\frac{-(\beta-\alpha)T_S}{\tau}}\right)} e^{\frac{-(\beta-\alpha)T_S}{\tau}} \Delta t(n). \tag{26}$$

If σ_j^2 is the variance of the timing error $\Delta t(n)$, then for a single tone $V_{sig} \cdot sin(\omega_{sig} t)$ at the input of the $\Delta\Sigma$ modulator, the power of the input-referred IBJN is given by

$$IBJN|_{SCR} = \frac{1}{OSR} \cdot \left[\frac{e^{\frac{-(\beta-\alpha)T_S}{\tau}}}{\tau\left(1 - e^{\frac{-(\beta-\alpha)T_S}{\tau}}\right)}\right]^2 \cdot \sigma_j^2 \cdot \left[\frac{V_{sig}{}^2}{2} + \frac{\Delta^2}{12} \cdot \frac{1}{2\pi} \int_{-\pi}^{\pi} \left|NTF(e^{j\omega})\right|^2 d\omega\right]. \tag{27}$$

The expressions for the IBJN due to input signal and shaped quantization noise are given by

$$IBJN|_{SCR,due\ to\ input\ signal} = \frac{1}{OSR} \cdot \left[\frac{e^{\frac{-(\beta-\alpha)T_S}{\tau}}}{\tau\left(1 - e^{\frac{-(\beta-\alpha)T_S}{\tau}}\right)}\right]^2 \cdot \sigma_j^2 \cdot \frac{V_{sig}{}^2}{2}. \tag{28}$$

$$IBJN|_{SCR,due\ to\ shaped\ noise} = \frac{1}{OSR} \cdot \left[\frac{e^{\frac{-(\beta-\alpha)T_S}{\tau}}}{\tau\left(1 - e^{\frac{-(\beta-\alpha)T_S}{\tau}}\right)}\right]^2 \cdot \sigma_j^2 \cdot \frac{\Delta^2}{12} \cdot \frac{1}{2\pi} \int_{-\pi}^{\pi} \left|NTF(e^{j\omega})\right|^2 d\omega. \tag{29}$$

As expected, the sensitivity of SCR DACs to PWJ, given by (27)-(29) is the same as the RZ DAC case (16)-(18) but exponentially reduced. However, the increased peak current of the SCR DAC, given by (28), adds higher requirements on the SR and the GBW of the loop filter integrator [4, 10]. Moreover, CT $\Delta\Sigma$ modulators using SCR DACs have poor inherent anti-aliasing compared to those using current-steering DACs [11] due to the loading of the SCR DAC on the integrating amplifier input nodes. The hybrid SI-SCR DAC solution in [12] provides suppression to PWJ noise equivalent to that offered by SCR DACs without adding extra requirements on the SR or GBW of the integrating amplifier.

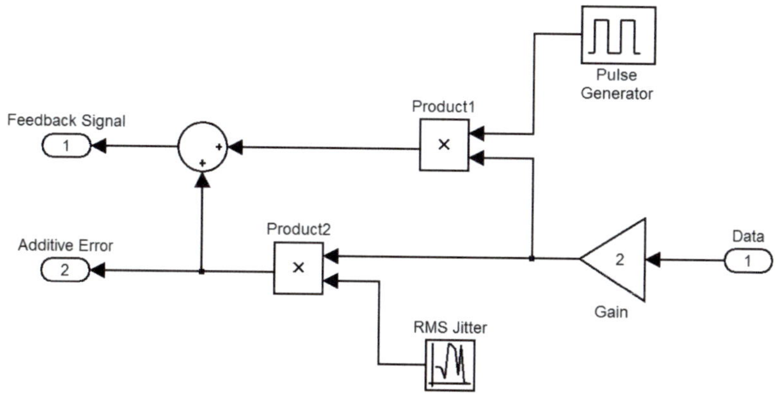

(a)

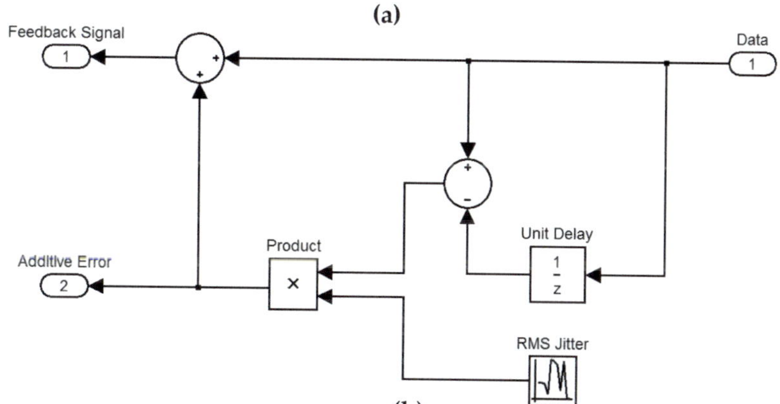

(b)

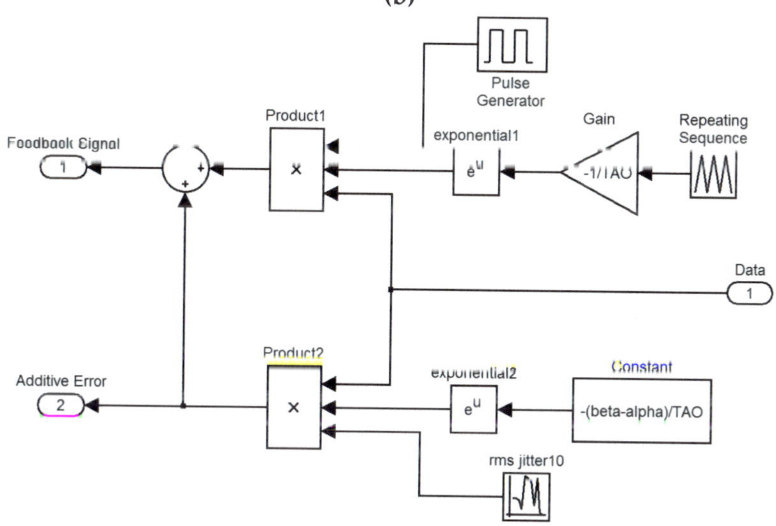

(c)

Figure 17. Simulink Modeling for DACs and jitter induced additive errors in the feedback of a CT ΔΣ modulator. (a) RZ DAC. (b) NRZ DAC. (c) SCR DAC.

5. Modeling and simulation of Jitter effects in CT ΔΣ modulators using Matlab/Simulink

In this section, Matlab/Simulink models for the jitter induced errors in different DAC types are shown. The models are based on the expressions of the additive jitter errors developed in the previous section and will be verified by simulations. Figure 17 shows the Simulink models for RZ, NRZ and SCR DACs, including the additive jitter errors based on the expressions in (15), (19), and (25), respectively. Note that these additive errors in the feedback should be multiplied by the gain coefficient of their respective feedback path. These models are examined through simulations in Matlab/Simulink to verify their accuracy and compliance with the developed analysis. The feed-forward third-order single-bit CT ΔΣ modulator in Figure 18 is used as a test vehicle for the system-level simulations. The modulator operates at an OSR of 100 with a target ENOB of 13 bits over a baseband channel bandwidth of 1.92 MHz for the WCDMA standard. The noise budgeting for the ADC to achieve the required ENOB is given in Table 1. Table 2 lists the specifications and summary of the achievable performance of the modulator when an SCR DAC model is used with DAC time-constant $\tau = 0.1\,T_S$. Recall that an SCR DAC is a convenient option to provide robustness to clock-jitter and maintain the low percentage of the jitter induced noise in the noise budget. The dynamic-range (DR) and PSD plots of the modulator are given in Figure 19 and Figure 20. The maximum signal-to-noise-plus-distortion ratio (SNDR) is calculated as 80dB.

To examine the sensitivity of the modulator to clock-jitter for different DAC types by simulations, the appropriate model for the feedback DAC including the additive jitter errors is chosen from the ones in Figure 17, according to the adopted DAC type (RZ, NRZ, or SCR), and is added to the Simulink model of the complete modulator. The plots in Figure 21 imply that for sufficiently large rms jitter in the DAC sampling-clock, the IBJN increases significantly and dominate the total in-band noise (IBN). For the SCR DAC, it can be seen from the plots in Figure 21(c) that the robustness to clock-jitter degrades proportionally with the DAC time-constant τ, as discussed earlier in the analysis. To compare the robustness to clock-jitter in the three DAC types, IBJN plots are combined together in Figure 22, and it is evident that the SCR DAC is the most tolerant to DAC jitter while RZ DAC is the most sensitive.

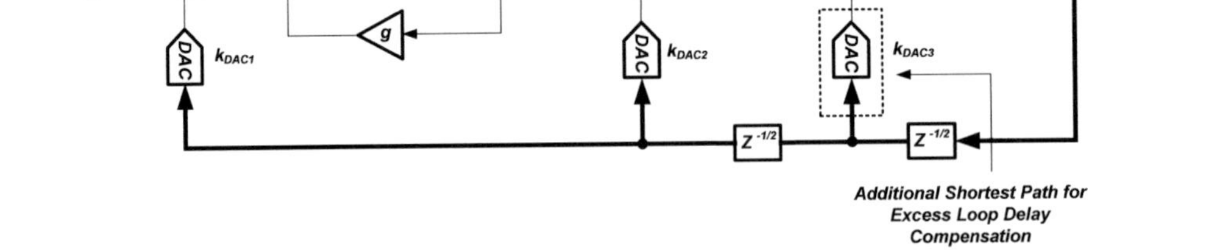

Figure 18. Adopted modified feed-forward CT single-bit ΔΣ modulator.

Noise/Distortion Source	Noise Budget	Signal-to-Noise-Ratio (SNR)
Quantization Noise	10%	90 dB
Thermal Noise	50%	83 dB
Jitter Induced Noise	10%	90 dB
Nonlinearity induced Distortion	20%	87 dB
Others	10%	90 dB

Table 1. Modulator noise budget

Property	Value
Sampling Frequency	384 MHz, RMS Jitter 10 ps
Signal Bandwidth	1.92 MHz
Oversampling Ratio (OSR)	100
ENOB	13
Peak SNDR	80 dB
Dynamic Range	84 dB
SFDR	83 dB

Table 2. Modulator specifications and performance summary

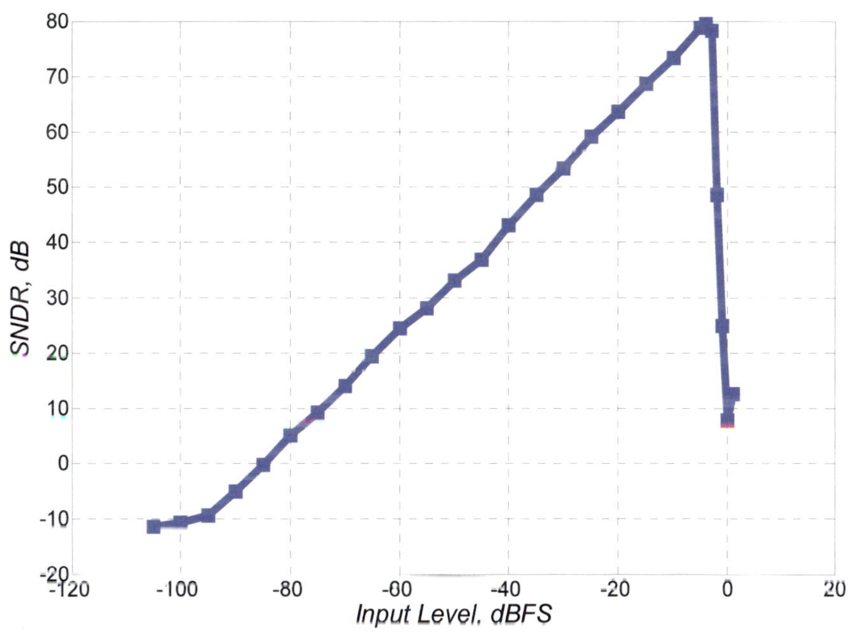

Figure 19. Dynamic-range of the adopted ΔΣ modulator.

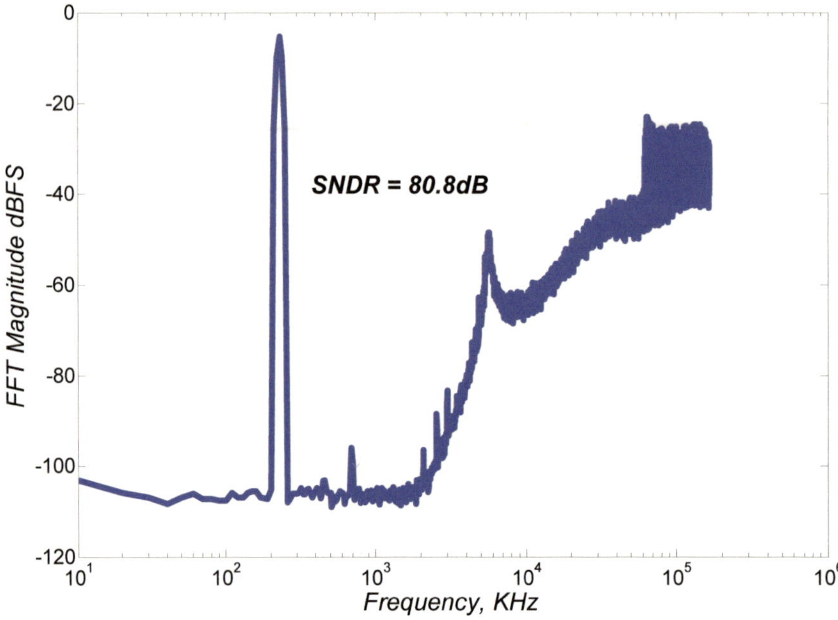

Figure 20. PSD at the modulator output calculated using 32768 FFT points with 16 averages. $\boldsymbol{Signal\ Amplitude = -4\ dBFS,\ Signal\ Frequency = 270\ KHz}$.

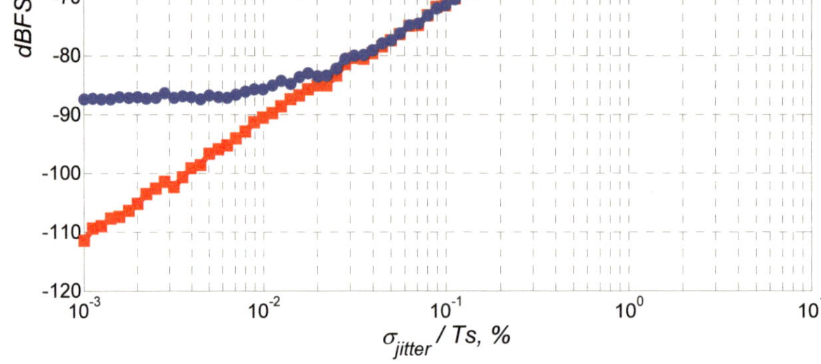

(a)

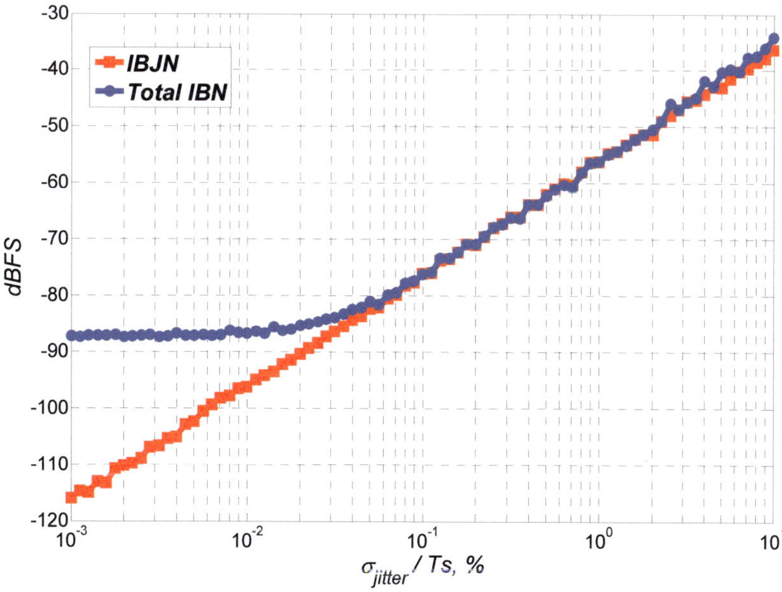

(b)

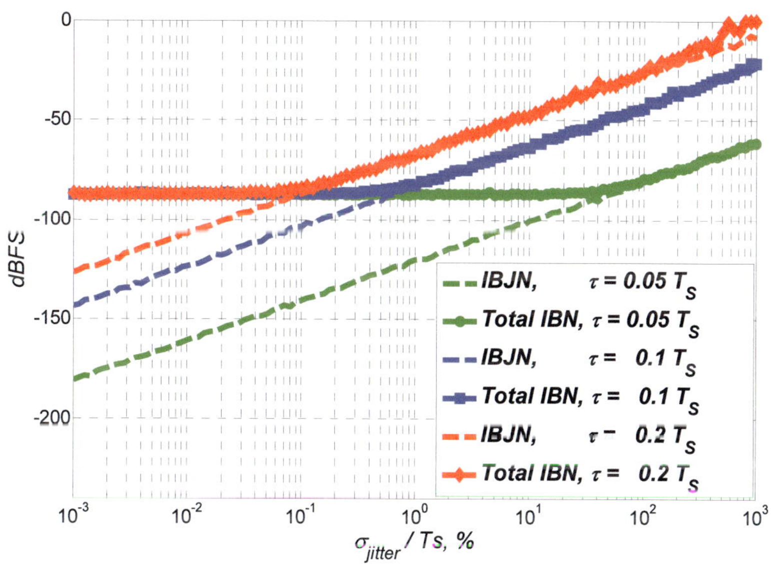

(c)

Figure 21. Sensitivity plots of the ΔΣ modulator in Figure 18 to clock-jitter in the DAC. $\boldsymbol{Signal\ Amplitude = -4\ dBFS,\ Signal\ Frequency = 1.9\ MHz}$. (a) RZ DAC. (b) NRZ DAC. (c) SCR DAC.

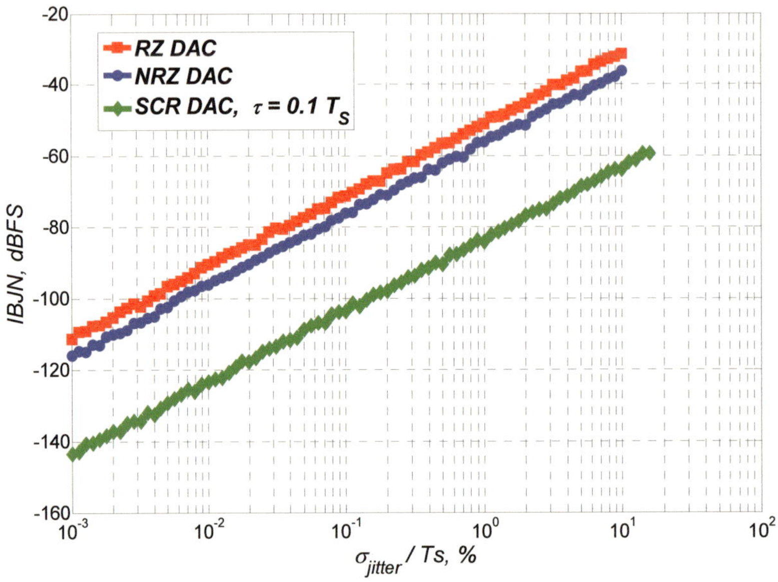

Figure 22. IBJN plots for the ΔΣ modulator in Figure 18 using different DAC types.
$\boldsymbol{Signal\ Amplitude = -4\ dBFS, Signal\ Frequency = 1.9\ MHz}$.

6. Conclusion

In this chapter, the effects of clock-jitter in the sampling-clocks of ΔΣ modulators are analyzed and studied in details. The critical sources of jitter induced errors in a ΔΣ loop are discussed for ΔΣ modulators with DT and CT loop filters. The comparison between DT and CT modulators showed that CT architectures are more sensitive to clock-jitter than DT counterparts due to PWJ in the feedback signal caused by clock-jitter in the DAC sampling-clock. In essence, PWJ in the feedback waveform entails random phase-modulation that folds back high-pass shaped noise components over the desired channel bandwidth. Thus, a detailed analysis for the sensitivities of various signal waveforms provided by different types of CT DACs to clock-jitter is given thereafter. Also, efficient Matlab/Simulink models for additive errors induced by clock-jitter in the feedback DACs are shown so that to help designers characterize the sensitivities of various types of CT ΔΣ architectures to clock-jitter and obtain the specification requirement on the rms jitter of the sampling-clock for a given target performance. Furthermore, modeling of jitter induced errors is beneficial for system-level simulations adopted in the process of developing efficient solutions and modulator or DAC architectures that can remedy the effects of clock-jitter on the ΔΣ modulator performance. The robustness of these models is verified by CT simulations in Matlab/Simulink and simulations results show good agreement with the theoretical expectations.

Author details

Ramy Saad, Sebastian Hoyos, and Samuel Palermo
Department of Electrical and Computer Engineering, Texas A&M University, College Station, Texas, USA

Acknowledgement

The authors would like to thank Semiconductor Research Corporation (SRC) for funding their research work in this topic under Grant 1836.013. Also, thanks should be expressed to the reviewers for their valuable feedback and helpful comments about the material given in this chapter.

7. References

[1] Murmann B. "ADC Performance Survey 1997-2012" [Online]. Available: http://www.stanford.edu/~murmann/adcsurvey.html.
[2] International Technology Roadmap for Semiconductors 2007. Radio Frequency and Analog/Mixed-Signal Technologies for Wireless Communities. Available: http://public.itrs.net.
[3] Cherry J. A. and Snelgrove W. M. (2000) Continuous-Time Delta-Sigma Modulators for High-Speed A/D Conversion. Norwell, MA: Kluwer Academic.
[4] Ortmanns M., Gerfers F., Manoli Y. (2005) A continuous-time Sigma Delta modulator with reduced sensitivity to clock jitter through SCR feedback. IEEE Trans. Circuits Syst. I. 52: 875–884.
[5] Mitteregger G., Ebner C., Mechnig S., Blon T., Holuigue C., Romani E. (2006) A 20-mW 640-MHz CMOS Continuous-Time ΣΔ ADC With 20-MHz Signal Bandwidth, 80-dB Dynamic Range and 12-bit ENOB. IEEE Journal of Solid-State Circuits. 41: 2641–2649.
[6] Chen X., Wang Y., Fujimoto Y., Lo Re P., Kanazawa Y., Steensgard J., Temes G. (2007) A 18mW CT ΔΣ Modulator with 25MHz Bandwidth for Next Generation Wireless Applications. Proc. IEEE Custom Integrated Circuits Conf. (CICC). 73–76.
[7] Chen X. (2007) A Wideband low-power continuous-time Delta-Sigma modulator for next generation wireless applications. Ph.D. dissertation, Sch. Elect. Eng. Comp. Sci., Oregon State Univ., Corvallis, OR.
[8] Gray R. (1989) Spectral analysis of quantization noise in a single-loop sigma-delta modulator with dc input. IEEE Transactions on Communications. 37: 588-599.
[9] Anderson M., Sundström L. (2007) A 312 MHz CT ΔΣ modulator using SC feedback with reduced peak current. Proc. 33rd European Solid-State Circuits Conf., ESSIRC 2007, München, Germany: 240–243.
[10] Anderson M., Sundström L. (2009) Design and Measurement of a CT ΣΔ ADC With Switched-Capacitor Switched-Resistor Feedback. IEEE Journal of Solid-State Circuits. 44: 473–483.

[11] Pavan S. (2011) Alias Rejection of Continuous-Time ΔΣ Modulators with Switched-Capacitor Feedback DACs. IEEE Trans. Circuits Syst. 58: 309–318.

[12] Saad R., Hoyos S. (2011) Feed-Forward Spectral Shaping Technique for Clock-Jitter Induced Errors in Digital-to-Analog Converters. IET Electronics Letters, 47: 171–172.

Chapter 18

Matlab-Based Algorithm for Real Time Analysis of Multiexponential Transient Signals

Momoh-Jimoh E. Salami, Ismaila B. Tijani,
Abdussamad U. Jibia and Za'im Bin Ismail

Additional information is available at the end of the chapter

http://dx.doi.org/10.5772/50006

1. Introduction

Multiexponential transient signals are particularly important due to their occurrences in many natural phenomena and human applications. For instance, it is important in the study of nuclear magnetic resonance (NMR) in medical diagnosis (Cohn-Sfetcu et al., 1975)), relaxation kinetics of cooperative conformational changes in biopolymers (Provencher, 1976), solving system identification problems in control and communication engineering (Prost and Guotte, 1982), fluorescence decay of proteins (Karrakchou et al., 1992), fluorescence decay analysis (Lakowicz, 1999). Several research work have been reported on the analysis of multicomponent transient signals following the pioneer work of Prony in 1795 (Prony, 1975) and Gardner et al. in 1959 (Gardner, 1979). Detailed review of several techniques for multicomponent transient signals' analysis was recently reported in (Jibia, 2010).

Generally, a multiexponential transient signal is represented by a linear combination of exponentials of the form

$$S(\tau) = \sum_{k}^{M} A_k \exp(-\lambda_k \tau) + n(\tau) \quad (1)$$

where M is the number of components, A_k and λ_k respectively represent the amplitude and real-valued decay rate constants of the kth component and $n(\tau)$ is the additive white Gaussian noise with variance σ_n^2. The exponentials in equation (1) are assumed to be separable and unrelated. That is, none of the components is produced from the decay of another component. Therefore, in determination of the signal parameters, M, A_k and λ_k from equation (1), it is not sufficient that equation (1) approximates data accurately; it is also important that these parameters are accurately estimated.

There are many problems associated with the analysis of transient signals of the form given in equation (1) due to the nonorthogonal nature of the exponential function. These problems include incorrect detection of the peaks, poor resolution of the estimated decay and inaccurate results for contaminated or closely-related decay rate data as reported in (Salami et.al., 1985). These problems become increasingly difficult when the level of noise is high. Although Gardner transform eliminated the nonorthogonality problem, it introduced error ripples due to short data record and nonstationarity of the preprocessed data. Apart from these problems, analysis of multiexponential signal is computationally intensive and requires efficient tools for its development and implementation in real-time.

To overcome these problems, modification of Gardner transform has been proposed recently with Multiple Signal Classification (MUSIC) superposition modeling technique (Jibia et al., 2008); with minimum norm modeling technique (Jibia and Salami, 2007), with homomorphic deconvolution, with eigenvalues decomposition techniques, and the Singular Value Decomposition (SVD) based-Autoregressive Moving Average (ARMA) modeling techniques (Salami and Sidek, 2000; Jibia, 2009). As reported in (Jibia, 2009), performance comparison of these four modeling techniques has been investigated. Though, all the four techniques were able to provide satisfactory performances at medium and high signal-to-noise ratio (SNR), the SVD-ARMA was reported to have the highest resolution, especially at low SNR.

Hence, the development of SVD-ARMA based algorithm for multiexponential signal analysis using MATLAB software package is examined in this chapter.

MATLAB provides computational efficient platform for the analysis and simulation of complex models and algorithms. In addition, with the aid of inbuilt embedded MATLAB Simulink block, it offers a tool for the integration of developed algorithm/model in an embedded application with little programming efforts as compared to the use of other programming languages (Mathworks, 2008). This functionality is explored in integrating the developed MATLAB-based algorithm into National Instrument (NI) Labview embedded programming tool. Hence, an integrated MATLAB-Labview software interface is proposed for real-time deployment of the algorithm. To this end, the analytical strength of MATLAB together with simplicity and user-friendly benefits of the National Instrument (NI), Labview design platforms are explored in developing an efficient, user-friendly algorithm for the real-time analysis of multiexponential transient signal.

The rest of the chapter is organized as follows. Section 2 provides brief review of techniques for multiexponential signal analysis. The MATLAB algorithm development for the signal analysis is presented in section 3. The development of an integrated MATLAB-Labview real-time software interface is then examined in section 4. Section 5 presents sample real-time data collection together with results and analysis. The chapter is concluded in section 6 with recommendation for future study.

2. Techniques of multiexponential transient signal analysis

Several techniques have been reported for the analysis of transient multiexponential signal. They are classified as: (i) time domain or frequency domain, and (ii) parametric or nonparametric techniques. The main objective of these techniques in analyzing the multiexponentially decaying signals is to estimate the signal parameters as accurately as possible and to get better display of the signal spectra. Time-domain techniques constitute the oldest methods of multiexponential signal analysis prior to the advent of Gardner transformation technique (Gardner et al, 1959; Salami, 1985). Gardner transformation is one of the most important methods of the transient signal analysis based on spectral analysis. Generally, spectral analysis involves transformation of a time-domain signal to a frequency domain so that certain features of the signals that characterized them are easily discerned such as its decay constant, λ_k and amplitude, A_k. In other words, it is the process of obtaining the frequency content (spectrum) of a signal (Proakis and Manolakis 1996). The spectral analysis approach is further categorized into nonparametric and parametric techniques. Nonparametric technique is a frequency-domain technique that obtains the signal spectra directly from the deconvolved data, while the parametric technique obtains the signal spectra indirectly by determining a finite set of parameters that defines a closed form mathematical model for the deconvolved data. Therefore the techniques of multiexponential transient signal analysis are sub-divided into time-domain, nonparametric frequency domain and parametric frequency domain techniques as shown in Figure 1 with their associated methods.

Among the earliest time-domain technique is the peeling technique. However, this technique produces poor results when $S(\tau)$ contains more than two components. Other time-domain techniques such as Prony's method and its variants produce better performance than the peeling technique, however they are very sensitive to noise (Smyth, 2002; Salami, 1995). The nonlinear least squares technique (Smyth, 2002) is computationally inefficient and the solution sometimes fails to converge, which means the estimate of the signal parameters cannot be accurately obtained.

The nonparametric techniques of spectral analysis are introduced to overcome some limitations of the time-domain techniques. The Gardner transformation technique produces error ripples which obscure the real peaks of the spectrum due to the cutoff points. This technique is good in analyzing signal with high SNR. The fast Fourier transform (FFT) technique, which is an improvement over the original Gardner transformation produces improved resolution. However, the problem of error ripples still exists. The extension of this technique involving the use of digital signal processing and Gaussian filtering is sensitive to noise and its data range has to be limited to get accurate estimates of the signal parameters. Whilst the modified FFT technique is better than the previous methods, it often fails to estimate λ_k correctly especially when the peaks are closely related. The differential technique (Swingler, 1977) provides some improvements over the existing techniques such as better resolution display but it is not suitable for analyzing noisy signal. Furthermore, modifying the FFT technique by incorporating integration procedure (Balcou,1981) does not produce better results as compared to the previous digital technique and the modified FFT technique. Moreover, this technique is still affected by error ripples.

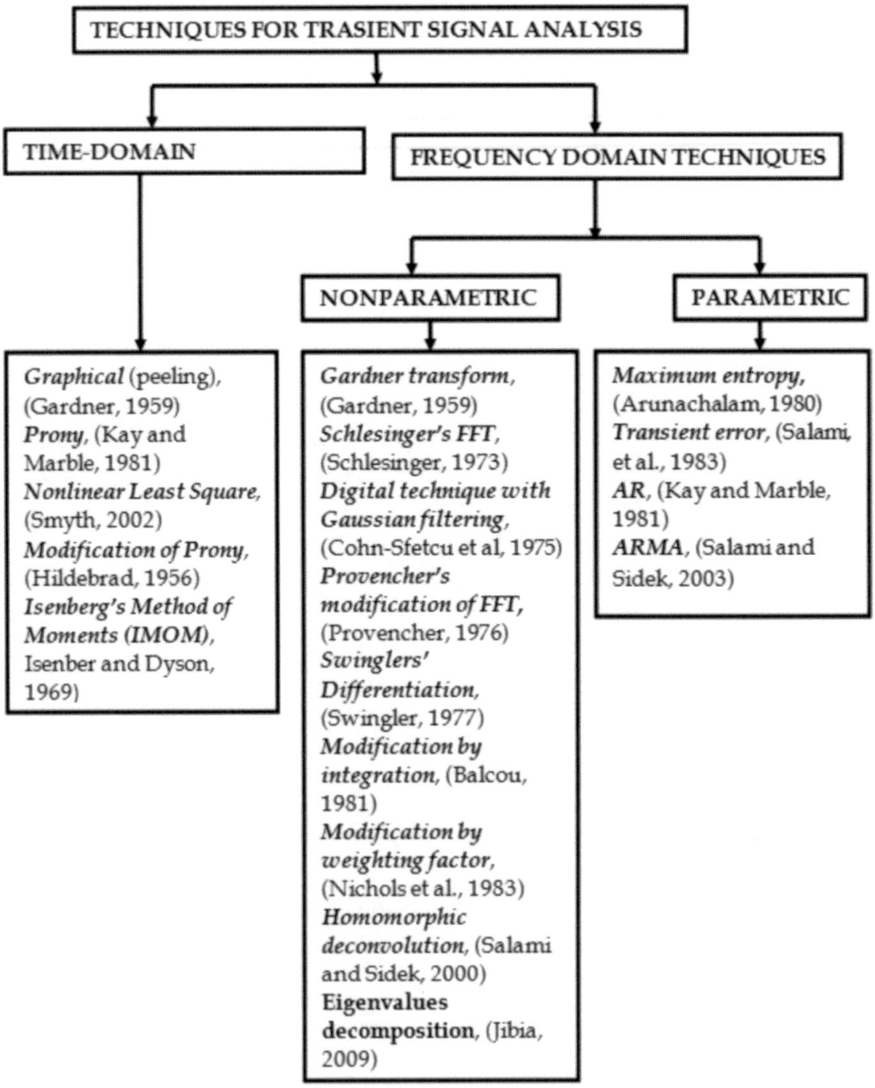

Figure 1. Overview of Techniques for Multiexponential signal analysis

Parametric techniques such as Autoregressive (AR), Moving Average (MA) and ARMA models are introduced to the analysis of multiexponential signals to alleviate the drawbacks of the nonparametric techniques. The AR modeling technique requires less computation than the ARMA modeling technique as its model parameters are relatively easy to estimate. However, it is sensitive to noise due to the assumed all-pole model. On the other hand, MA parameters are difficult to estimate and the resultant spectral estimates have poor resolution. Although, the ARMA modeling technique is much better in estimating noisy signal than the AR modeling technique, it requires a lot of computation. A detailed review of these techniques can be obtained in (Jibia, 2009; Salam and Sidek, 2000).

3. MATLAB-based Algorithm development

The systematic process involved in the development of the MATLAB-based SVD-ARMA algorithm for multiexponential transient signal analysis suitable for real-time application is discussed in this section. Apart from performance evaluation and signal generation, the algorithm consists of five major steps: obtaining convolution integral of the exponential signal using modified Gardner transformation; signal interpolation using spline technique; generation of deconvolved data; SVD-ARMA modeling of the deconvolved data; and power spectrum computation to finally estimate the transient signal parameters. A brief summary of the steps involved are as shown in Figure 2, and briefly highlighted as follows:

Step 1. Signal generation

Generate the required signal, $S(\tau)$ from MATLAB or from the fluorescence substances. For simulation data, MATLAB inbuilt function is used to generate the white Gaussian noise and the DC offset.

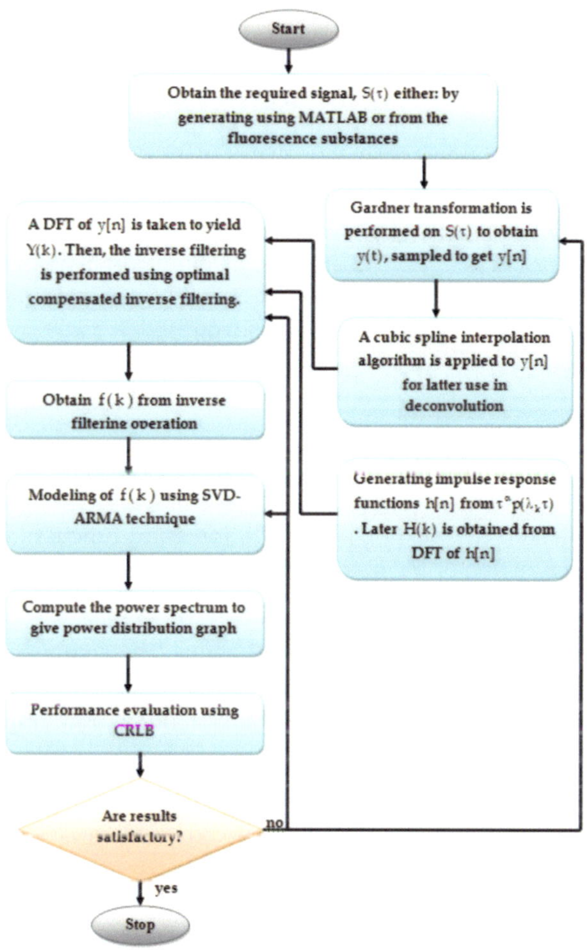

Figure 2. Flowchart of the MATLAB-based algorithm for Multicomponent transient signal analysis

Step 2. Signal preprocessing via Gardner transformation:

This involves the conversion of the measured or generated signal $S(\tau)$ and $p(\tau)$ to y(t) and h(t) respectively using modified Gardner transformation (Salami and Sidek, 2003). This yields a convolution integral as subsequently described.

In general, equation (1) is expressed as

$$S(\tau) = \sum_{k=1}^{M} A_k p(\lambda_k \tau) + n(\tau), \tag{2}$$

where the basis function, $p(\tau) = \exp(-\tau)$. This equation can also be expressed as

$$S(\tau) = \int_0^\infty g(\lambda) p(\lambda \tau) d\lambda + n(\tau), \tag{3}$$

where $g(\lambda) = \sum_{k=1}^{M} A_k \delta(\lambda - \lambda_k)$.

Both sides of equation (3) are multiplied by τ^α in the modified Gardner transformation instead of only τ in the original Gardner transformation. The value of the modifying parameter, α is carefully chosen based on the criteria given by Salami (1995) to avoid poor estimation of the signal parameters because α modifies the amplitude of the signal. Salami (1995) suggested to use $0 < \alpha \le 1$ in the analysis of multiexponential signals. According to Salami (1985), the choice of α can lead to improved signal parameters estimation as it produces noise reduction effect. The nonlinear transformation $\lambda = e^{-r}$ and $\tau = e^t$ are applied to equation (3), resulting in a convolution integral of the form

$$y(t) = \int_{-\infty}^{\infty} x(\lambda) h(t - \lambda) d\lambda + v(t), \tag{4}$$

where the output function, $y(t) = \exp(\alpha t)\, S\{\exp(t)\}$, the input function, $x(t) = \exp\{(\alpha\text{-}1)t\} g(e^{-t})$, the impulse response function of the system, $h(t) = \exp(\alpha t) p(e^t)$ and the additive noise, $v(t) = \exp(\alpha t) n(e^t)$.

The discrete impulse response function, $h[n]$ is obtained by sampling $\tau^\alpha p(\lambda_k \tau)$ at $1/\Delta t$ Hz. Later, $H(k)$ is obtained from the discrete Fourier transform (DFT) of $h[n]$. Next, equation (4) is converted into a discrete-time convolution. This is done by sampling $y(t)$ at a rate of $1/\Delta t$ Hz to obtain

$$y[n] = \sum_{m=-n_{\min}}^{n_{\max}} x[m] h[n-m] + v[n], \tag{5}$$

where the total number of samples, N equals $n_{max} - n_{min} + 1$, both n_{max} and n_{min} represent respectively the upper and lower data cut-off points. The criteria for the selection of these sampling conditions have been thoroughly discussed by Salami (1987) and Sen (1995) and these are not discussed further here. Equation (5) forms the basis of estimating the signal parameters since ideally $x(n)$ can be recovered from the observed data by deconvolution. It is necessary to interpolate the discrete time convolution of $y[n]$ since the log samples, $\tau_n = \exp(n\Delta t)$ are not equally spaced.

Step 3. Cubic spline Interpolation

The discrete-time signal y[n] obtained in (5) consists of non-equally spaced samples which would be difficult to digitally process. A cubic interpolation is therefore applied to y[n] using MATLAB function 'spline' to obtain equally spaced samples of y[n].

Step 4. Generation of deconvolved data

In this stage, deconvolved data is generated from y[n] using optimally compensated inverse filtering due to its ability to handle noisy signal when compared to conventional inverse filtering (Salami,1995).

Conventionally, this is done by taking the DFT of equation (5) to produce:

$$Y(k) = X(k)H(k) + V(k) \tag{6}$$

The deconvolved data, $\hat{X}(k)$ can be obtained by computing $Y(k)/H(k)$, that is

$$\hat{X}(k) = \frac{Y(k)}{H(k)} = X(k) + \frac{V(k)}{H(k)} \quad for\ 0 \le k \le N-1 \tag{7}$$

where $Y(k)$, $X(k)$, $H(k)$ and $V(k)$ represent the discrete Fourier transform of $y(n)$, $x(n)$, $h(n)$ and $v(n)$ respectively. This inverse filtering operation is called the conventional inverse filtering. It yields deconvolved data with decreasing SNR for increasing values of k. Therefore, the accuracy of $\hat{X}(k)$ deteriorates when the noise variance level is high.

To overcome this problem, an optimally compensated inverse filtering is introduced. In this approach, $H(k)$ is modified by adding an optimally selected value, μ into it. This procedure is done according to Riad and Stafford (1980) by initially designing a transfer function, $H_T(k)$ that yields a better $\hat{X}(k)$ in equation (7), where $H_T(k)$ is given by:

$$H_T(k) = \frac{H^*(k)}{\left[|H(k)|^2 + \mu \right]}, \tag{8}$$

where * denotes the complex conjugate. Substituting equation (8) into equation (7) yields

$$\hat{X}(k) = \frac{Y(k)H^*(k)}{\left[|H(k)|^2 + \mu \right]}, \tag{9}$$

which is referred to as the optimally compensated inverse filtering. It is noted that a small value of μ has a very little effect in the range of frequency when $|H(k)|^2$ is significantly larger than μ. However, if $|H(k)|^2$ is very small, the effect of μ on the deconvolved data is quite substantial, that is μ tends to make $\hat{X}(k)$ less noisy. Therefore, μ puts limit on the noise amplification because the denominator becomes lower bounded according to Dabóczi and Kollár (1996). The parameter μ is carefully selected according to the SNR of the data to obtain good results. The choice of the optimum value of μ according to Salami and Sidek (2001) is best determined by experimental testing.

Equation (9) shows one-parameter compensation procedure, however, multi-parameter compensation is considered in this study. Thus, a regularization operator L(k) is introduced into (8), that is

$$F(k) = \frac{H^*(k)}{\left[|H(k)|^2 + \alpha|L(k)|^2\right]} \tag{10}$$

where α is the controlling parameter and the regularization operator, $L(k)$ is the discrete Fourier transform of the second order backward difference sequence. $|L(k)|^2$ is given as

$$|L(k)|^2 = 16\sin^4\left(\frac{\pi k}{N}\right), \tag{11}$$

where N is the number of samples. Using both the second and fourth order backward difference operations in equation (10) yield

$$F(k) = \frac{H^*(k)}{\left[|H(k)|^2 + \mu + \alpha|L(k)|^2 + \beta|L(k)|^4\right]} \tag{12}$$

where $|L(k)|^4$ denotes the fourth order backward difference operator and μ, α and β are the varied compensation parameters to improve the SNR of the deconvolved data.

Unwanted high frequency noise can still be introduced by this optimally compensated inverse filtering which can make some portion of $\hat{X}(k)$ unusable. Therefore, a good portion of $\hat{X}(k)$ denoted as $f(k)$, is given as

$$f(k) = \sum_{i=1}^{M} B_i \exp(j2\pi k\Delta f \ln\lambda_i) + V(k), \tag{13}$$

where $1 \le k \le 2N_d+1$, $B_i = A_i/\lambda_i^{\alpha}$, $N_d \le (N/2)-1$, N_d is the number of useful deconvolved data points, N is the number of data samples and $V(k)$ is the noise samples of the deconvolved data. Equation (13) is interpreted as a sum of complex exponential signals. The number of deconvolved data points, N_d is carefully selected to produce good results from $f(k)$.

Step 5. Signal parameters estimation using SVD-ARMA modeling

SVD-ARMA algorithm is applied to f(k) to estimate the signal parameters M and λ_k as it provides consistent and accurate estimates of AR parameters with minimal numerical problem which is necessary for real-time application. In addition, it is a powerful computational procedure for matrix analysis especially for solving over determined system of equations. The detailed mathematical analysis of this algorithm is reported in (Salami, 1985).

Generally, the ARMA model assumes that $f(k)$ satisfies the linear difference equation (Salami 1985)

$$f(k) = -\sum_{i=1}^{p} a(i) f(k-i) + \sum_{i=1}^{q} b(i) V(k-i) \tag{14}$$

where V(k) is the input driving sequence, *f(k)* is the output sequence, *a*[i] and *b*[i] are the model coefficients with AR and MA model order of p and q respectively. Usually, the white Gaussian noise becomes the input driving sequence in the analysis of exponentially decaying transient signals.

One of the most effective procedures for estimating these model parameters is by solving a modified Yule-Walker equation (Kay and Marple 1981). This procedure is subsequently discussed.

Equation (14) is multiplied by $f^*(k-m)$ and taking the expectation yields:

$$R_{ff}(k) = -\sum_{n=1}^{p} a[n] R_{ff}(k-n) + \sum_{n=0}^{q} b[n] h(k-m), \tag{15}$$

where $R_{ff}(k)$ is the autocorrelation function of $f(k)$ and $h(k)$ is the impulse response function of the ARMA model. Next, considering the AR portion of equation (15) leads to the modified Yule-Walker equation

$$R_{ff}(k) + \sum_{n=1}^{p} a[n] R_{ff}(k-n) = 0; k \geq q+1. \tag{16}$$

Equation (16) may not hold exactly in practice because both p and q are unknown prior to analysis and $R_{ff}(k)$ has to be estimated from noisy data. This problem is solved by using an SVD algorithm. This algorithm is used by first expressing equation (16) in matrix form as **Ra** = **e** with **R** having elements $r(i,l) - R_{ff}(q_e + 1 + i - l)$, where $1 \leq i \leq r$; $1 \leq l \leq p_e + 1$. Note that both p_e and q_e are the guess values of the AR and MA model order respectively, **a** is a $p_e \times 1$ and **e** is a $r \times 1$ error vector with $r > p_e$. The SVD algorithm is applied to **R** to produce

$$\mathbf{R} = \mathbf{U \Sigma V}^T = \sum_{n=1}^{p_e} \sigma_n u_n v_n^H \tag{17}$$

where the $r \times (p_e+1)$ unitary matrix $\mathbf{U} = [u_1\ u_2 \ldots u_{p_e+1}]$, $(p_e+1) \times (p_e+1)$ unitary matrix $\mathbf{V} = [v_1\ v_2 \ldots v_{p_e+1}]$ and Σ is a diagonal matrix with diagonal elements $(\sigma_1, \sigma_2 \ldots \sigma_{p_e+1})$. These diagonal elements are called singular values and are arranged so that $\sigma_1 > \sigma_2 > \ldots > \sigma_{p_e+1} > 0$. Only the first M singular values will be nonzero so that $\sigma_{M+1} = \sigma_{M+2} = \ldots = \sigma_{p_e+1} = 0$. However, $\sigma_{M+1} \neq \sigma_{M+2} \neq \ldots \neq \sigma_{p_e+1} \neq 0$ due to noise contamination. The problem is solved by constructing a lower rank matrix $\mathbf{R_L}$ from $\mathbf{R}$ using the first M singular values, that is

$$\mathbf{R_L} = \mathbf{U_M \Sigma_M V_M}^H = \sum_{n=1}^{M} \sigma_n u_n v_n^{\ H}, \tag{18}$$

where $\mathbf{U_M}$, $\mathbf{\Sigma_M}$ and $\mathbf{V_M}$ are the truncated version of $\mathbf{U}$, $\mathbf{\Sigma}$ and $\mathbf{V}$ respectively. The AR coefficients are then estimated from the relation $\mathbf{a} = -\mathbf{R_L}^{\#}\mathbf{r}$, where $\mathbf{r}$ corresponds to the first column of $\mathbf{R_L}$ and $\mathbf{R_L}^{\#}$ is given as

$$\mathbf{R_L}^{\#} = \sum_{n=1}^{M} \sigma_n^{-1} u_{\ n}^{H} v_n. \tag{19}$$

The estimated AR coefficients are then used to generate the residual error sequences:

$$\beta(k) = \sum_{l=0}^{p_e} \sum_{m=0}^{p_e} a[l] a^*[m] R_{ff}(k+m-l) \tag{20}$$

from which the actual MA parameters are obtained directly from equation (20). However, MA spectra can be obtained from the DFT of the error sequences, $\beta(k)$. An exponential window is applied to $\beta(k)$ to ensure that the MA spectra derived from the error sequences are positive definite. Next, the ARMA spectrum is computed from

$$S_f(z) = \frac{\sum_{k=-p_e}^{p_e} \beta(k) z^{-k}}{|A(z)|^2} \tag{21}$$

and the desired power distribution of $x(t)$, denoted as $P_x(t)$ is obtained by evaluating $S_f(z)$ on the unit circle $z = \exp\left\{2\pi j \frac{t}{N\Delta t}\right\}$, that is:

$$P_x(t) = S_f(z)\Big|_{z=\exp\left\{\frac{j2\pi t}{N\Delta t}\right\}} = \sum_{k=1}^{M} B_k^2 \delta(t - \ln \lambda_k). \tag{22}$$

Eventually, M and $\ln \lambda_k$ are obtained from $P_x(t)$.

Step 6. Graphical presentation of output

Power distribution graph has been used to display the results of multiexponential signal analysis. This is computed from the power spectrum of the resulting output signal from SVD-ARMA modeling method as shown in equation (21).

Step 7. Performance evaluation

The efficiency of the algorithm with SVD-ARMA modeling technique in estimating λ_k correctly is determined by the Cramer-Rao lower bound (CRLB) expressed as:

$$\text{CRLB}(\lambda_k) = \frac{6(1+0.7(\lambda_k N)^{3/2})^2}{N^3 SNR}, \quad (23)$$

where N is the number of data points, the CRB(λ_k) is the CRLB for estimating λ_k and SNR equals to A_k^2 divided by the variance of the white Gaussian noise.

The Cramer-Rao lower bound will determine whether the estimator is efficient by comparing the variance of the estimator, $var(\hat{\lambda}_k)$ with the Cramer-Rao lower bound. Variance that approaches the CRLB is said to be optimal according to Kay and Marple (1981) and Sha'ameri (2000). Consequently, the closer the variance of the estimator is to the CRLB, the better is the estimator.

A MATLAB-mfile code has been written to implement the steps 1 to 6 described above, details of this have been thoroughly discussed in (Jibia, 2009).

4. Integrated MATLAB-labview for real-time implementation

This section discusses the development of proposed integrated Labview-MATLAB software interface for real-time (RT) implementation of the algorithm for multicomponent signal analysis as described in section 3. Real-time signal analysis is required for most practical applications of multicomponent signal analysis. In this study, reference is made to the application to fluorescence signal analysis. A typical multicomponent signal analyzer comprises optical sensor which is part of the spectrofluorometer system, signal conditioning/data acquisition system, embedded processor that runs the algorithm in real-time, and display/storage devices as shown in Figure 3. National Instrument (NI) real-time hardware and software are considered for the development of this system due to its ease of implementation.

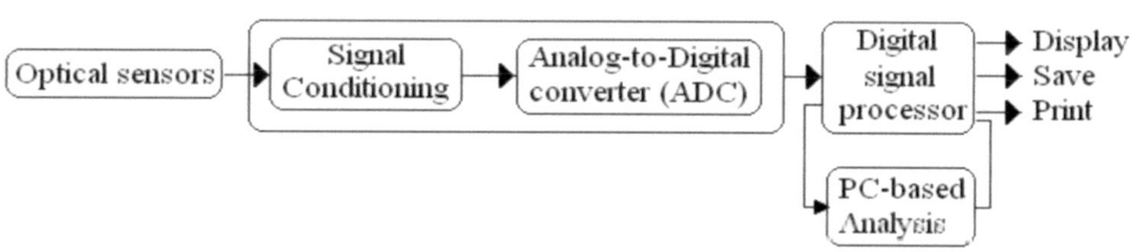

Figure 3. Block diagram of the multicomponent signal analyzer prototype.

4.1. Labview real-time module and target

The Labview real time module (RT-software) together with NI sbRIO-9642 (RT-hardware) has been adopted in this study. The Labview Real-Time software module allows for the creation of reliable, real-time applications which are easily downloaded onto the target hardware from Labview GUI programming tool.

The NI sbRIO-9642 is identical in architecture to CompactRIO system, only in a single circuit board. Single-Board RIO hardware features a real-time processor and programmable FPGA just as with CompactRIO, and has several inputs and outputs (I/O) modules as shown in Figure 4.

System development involves graphical programming with Labview on the host Window computer, which is then downloaded and run on real-time hardware target. Since the algorithm has been developed with MATLAB scripts, an integrated approach was adopted in the programme development as subsequently described.

Figure 4. NI sbRIO-9642 for real-time hardware target

4.2. MATLAB-labview software integration

The developed algorithm with MATLAB scripts was integrated inside Labview for real-time embedded set-up as shown in Figure 5. Labview front-panel and block diagrams were developed with inbuilt Labview math Scripts to run the MATLAB algorithm for the analysis of multicomponent signals. The use of Labview allows for ease of programming, and real-time deployment using the Labview real-time module described in section 4.1. Also, it provides a user friendly software interface for real-time processing of the fluorescence signals.

As shown in Figure 5, the sampled data produced by the spectrofluorometer system are pre-processed by the NI-DAQ Cards. These signals are then read by the embedded real-time software, analyze the signals and display the results in a user friendly manner. The user is prompted to enter the number of samples to be analyzed from the front-panel using the developed SVD-ARMA algorithm.

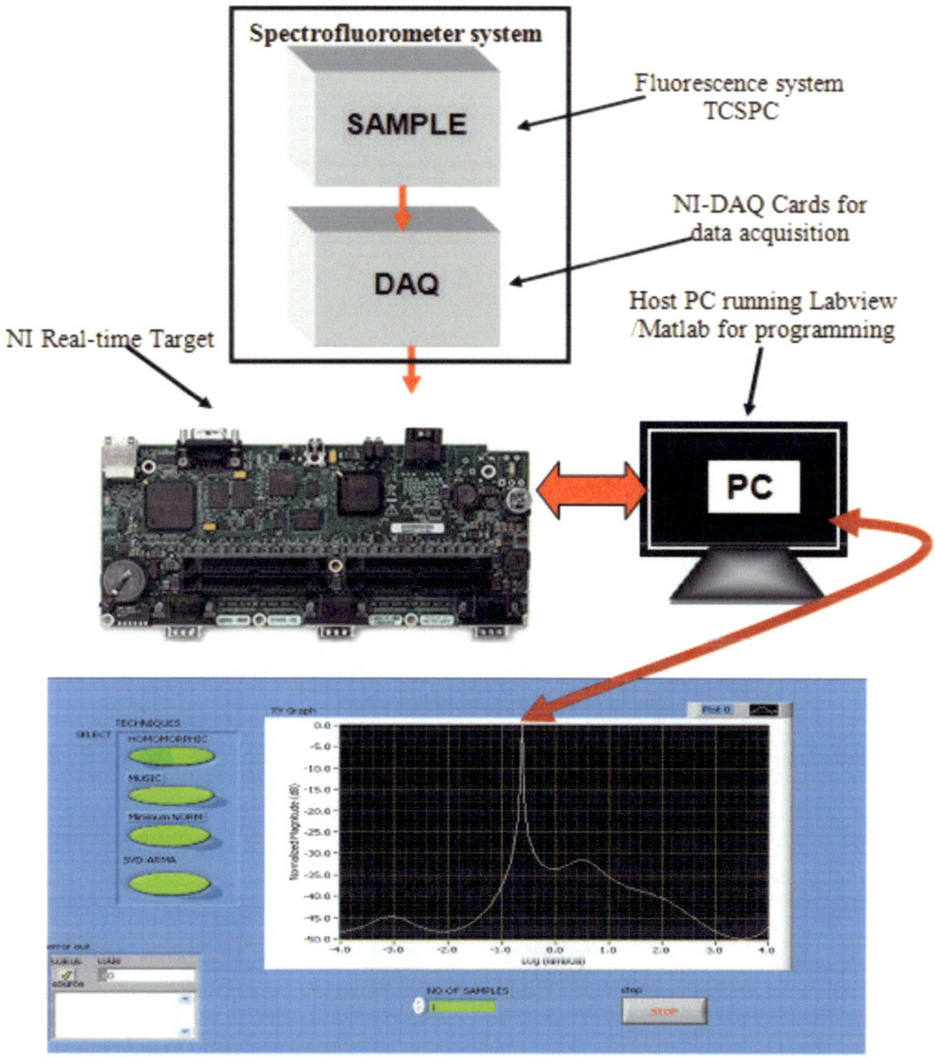

Figure 5. Block Diagram of the real-time set-up

Generally, the developed algorithm with MATLAB scripts was integrated inside Labview for real-time embedded set-up as follows:

i. Pre-simulation of the MATLAB algorithm inside embedded MATLAB Simulink block: this requires re-structuring of the codes to be compatible for embedded Simulink implementation, and hence deployment inside Labview MathScript. Figure 7 shows the MATLAB Simulink blocks configuration with embedded MATLAB function together with cross-section of the algorithm. The DATA with time vector is prepared inside the workspace and linked to the model input. Figure 10 (a-f) shows the simulation results with experimental data described in section 5.

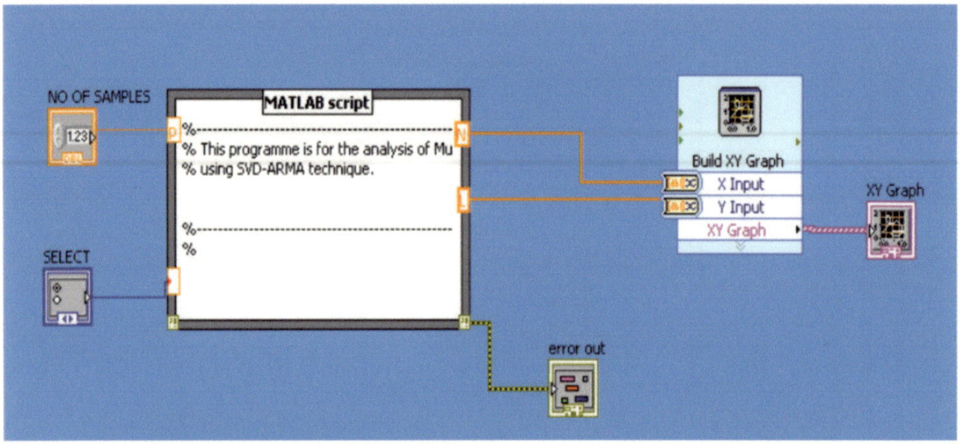

Figure 6. Lab view Block Diagram

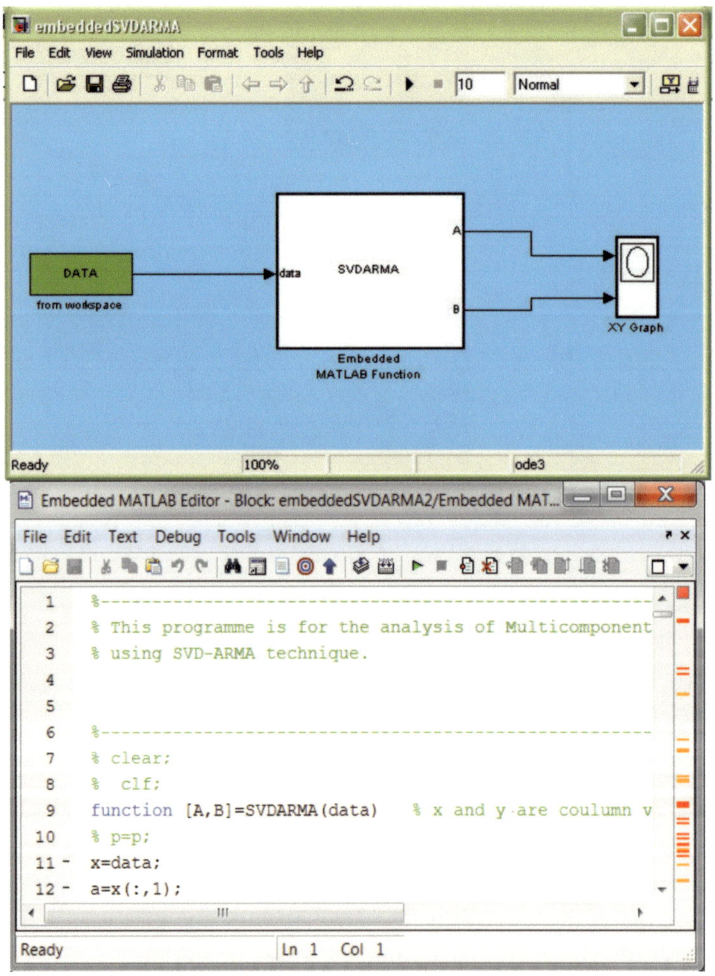

Figure 7. Embedded MATLAB set-up for algorithm simulation

ii. Labview programming: Development of Labview front-panel and block diagram is as shown in Figure 4. In the block diagram programming, the Labview MathScript node is employed to integrate the MATLAB codes in the overall Labview programme. The script (Figure 8) invokes the MATLAB software script server to execute scripts written in the MATLAB language syntax

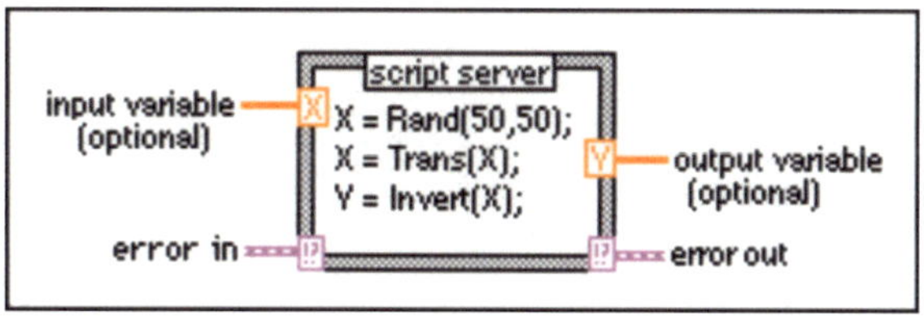

Figure 8. NI Labview MATLAB script nodes

iii. The integrated software interface is evaluated with the real-time fluorescence data collected from a spectrofluorometer.

5. Sample collection, results and discussion

Due to unavailability of spectrofluorometer system that can be directly linked with the set-up, sampled data collected from fluorescence decay experiment conducted using Spectramax Germini XS system were used to test the performance of the integrated system. The schematic diagram of the spectrofluorometer operation is shown in Figure 9, and itemized as follows:

Step 1. The excitation light source is the xenon flash lamp.

Step 2. The light passes through the excitation cutoff wheel. This wheel reduces the amount of stray light into the movable grating.

Step 3. The movable grating selects the desired excitation wavelength. Then, this excitation light enters a 1.0 mm diameter fiber.

Step 4. This 1.0 mm diameter fiber focuses the excitation light before entering the sample in the micro-plate well. This focusing prevents part of the light from striking adjacent wells.

Step 5. The light enters the wheel and if fluorescent molecules are present, the two mirrors focus the light from the well into a 4.0 mm optical bundles.

Step 6. The movable, focusing grating allows light of chosen emission wavelength to enter the emission cutoff wheel.

Step 7. This emission cutoff wheel will further filter the light before the light enters the photomultiplier tube.

Step 8. The photomultiplier tube detects the emitted light and passes a signal to the instrument's electronics which then send the signal to the data acquisition system inside the spectrofluorometer.

Three intrinsic fluorophores (Acridine Orange; Fluorescein Sodium and Quinine) were used in the experiment. The details of the substances are given in Table 1.

	Acridine Orange	Fluorescein Sodium	Quinine
Molecular formula	$C_{17}H_{12}ClN_3$	$C_{20}H_{10}Na_2O_5$	$C_{20}H_{24}N_2O_2$
Manufacturer	Merck	Merck	Merck
Molecular weight	301.8g/mol	376.28	324.43
Purity by HPLC	99.1%	Extra pure	Extra pure
Form	Solid	Solid	Powder,
Colour	Orange red	Reddish brown	White
Solubility in water	28g/l	500g/l	0.5g/l
Solutility in ethanol	Soluble	140g/l	1200g/l

Table 1. Characteristics of the fluorophores samples

The simulation results for Acridine orange, Fluorescein Sodium, Quinine, Quinine plus Arcridine, Fluorescein Sodium plus Acridine orange, and Fluorescein Sodium plus Acridine orange plus Quinin in water are shown in Figure 10 (a-f) respectively.

Figure 11 to Figure 13 show the sample of results obtained from the integrated MATLAB-Labview real-time software which has been developed. Both results of simulation and real-time software interface yield accurate estimates of the fluorescence data as shown in Figure 10-Figure 13, and presented in Table 2. The singular values for each of the samples combination are given in Table 3. The results indicate accurate determination of the constituent samples

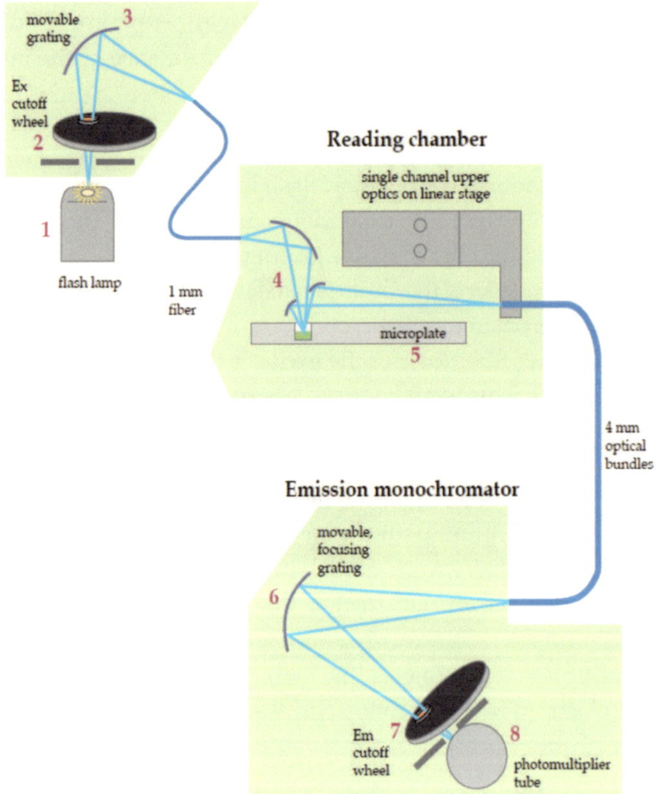

Figure 9. Schematic diagram of the SPECTRAMAX Gemini Spectrofluorometer operation (SPECTRAmax®)

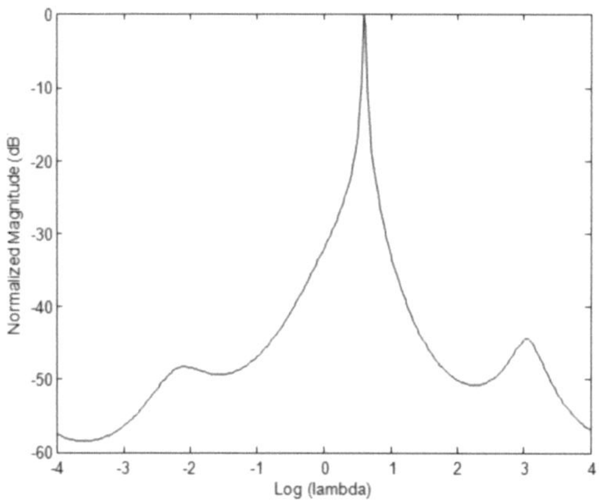

(a) Acridine orange

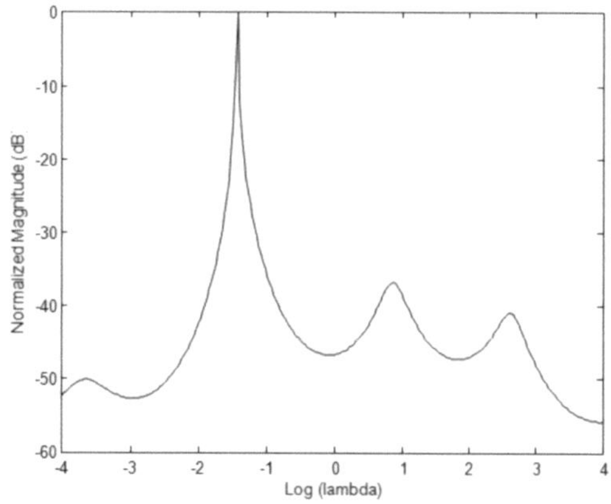

(b) Fluorescein Sodium

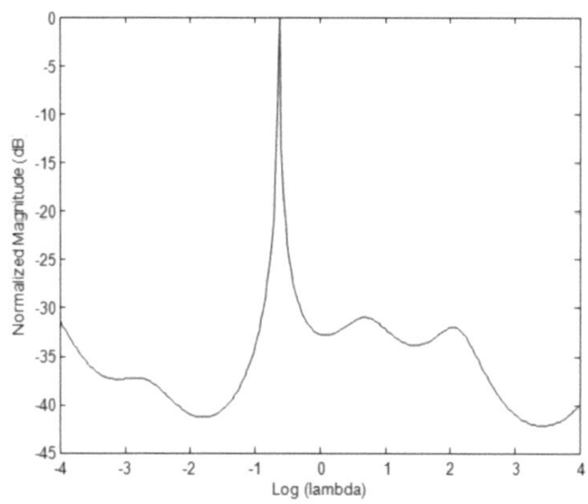

(c) Quinine

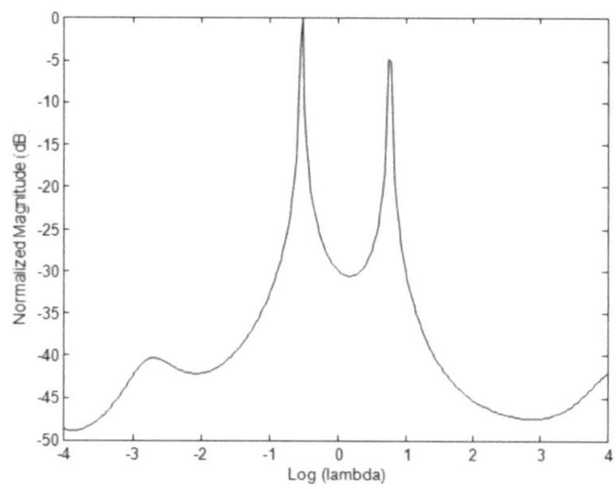

(d) Quinine plus Arcridine

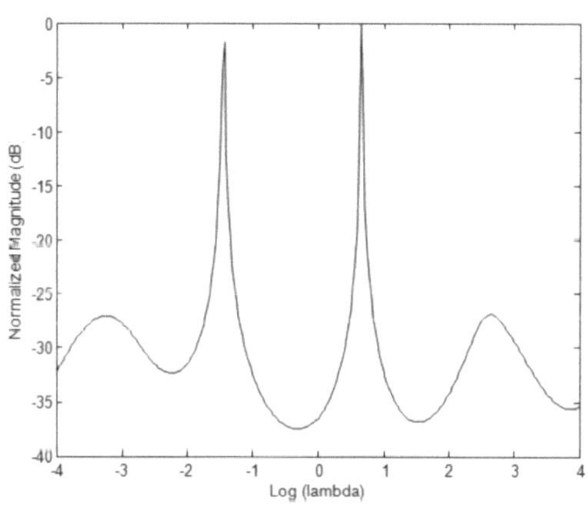

(e) Fluorescein Sodium plus Acridine

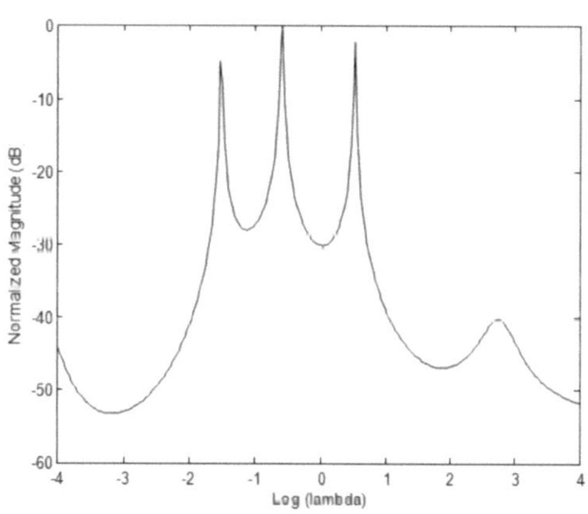

(f) and Fluorescein Sodium plus Acridine plus Quinin

Figure 10. Sample simulation results with embedded MATLAB function

6. Conclusion/Future study

The development of MATLAB-based algorithm for real-time analysis of multicomponent transient signal analysis based on SVD-ARMA modeling technique has been presented in this chapter. To enhance real-time interface and rapid prototyping on target hardware, complementary benefits of MATLAB and Labview were explored to develop real-time software interface downloadable into single board computer by NI Labview. In the absence of the spectrofluorometer system, the developed user friendly software for real-time deployment was validated with the collected real-time data. The obtained results indicate the effectiveness of the proposed integrated software for practical application of the proposed algorithm.

Future direction of this research will be directed towards development of customized spectrofluorometer sub-system that can be directly integrated to the overall system. This will eventually facilitate direct application of the developed algorithm in practical applications involving transient signal analysis. Also, other algorithms based on homomorphic and eigenvalues decomposition developed by the authors in similar study are to be made available as option on the user interface.

Mixture	Expected value	SVD-ARMA	Percentage error
Acridine orange	0.5978	0.625	4.55
Fluorescein Sodium	-1.4584	-1.438	1.40
Quinine	-0.6419	-0.625	2.63
AcridineOrange +	0.6539	0.6563	0.37
Fluorescein Sodium	-1.4584	-1.438	1.40
AcridineOrange	0.7750	0.761	1.81
+Quinine	-0.5539	-0.5313	4.08
	0.5105	0.5325	4.31
Acridine Orange + Fluorescein Sodium	-0.6152	-0.5938	3.48
+Quinine	-1.5260	-1.533	0.46

Table 2. Estimated Log of decay rates and percentage error from fluorescence decay experiment ($In\lambda$)

Singular values for Acridine Orange +Fluorescein Sodium (MPD)	Singular values for Acridine orange and Quinine (MPD)	Singular values for Acridine Orange +Fluorescein Sodium + Quinine (MPD)
1.4539e+005	1.784e+005	1.9659e+005
1742.9	14341	15247
1.8877e-011	2.7015e-011	1753.9
5.8244e-012	6.348e-012	3.4341e-011
5.2379e-012	6.0042e-012	8.2283e-012
4.9242e-012	5.6011e-012	7.3577e-012
4.5305e-012	4.9272e-012	6.899e-012
4.267e-012	4.8779e-012	6.5831e-012
3.891e-012	4.6323e-012	5.6838e-012
3.5599e-012	4.0781e-012	5.3607e-012
3.1474e-012	3.8214e-012	5.0667e-012
3.0647e-012	3.73e-012	4.5693e-012
2.6685e-012	3.4865e-012	4.1823e-012
2.4369e-012	3.3531e-012	3.859e-012
2.1072e-012	2.9901e-012	3.6511e-012
1.8205e-012	2.4538e-012	3.1307e-012
1.7258e-012	2.1495e-012	3.0133e-012
1.5546e-012	1.6585e-012	2.4723e-012
1.3322e-012	1.5298e-012	1.9237e-012
1.1956e-012	1.3568e-012	1.8882e-012

Table 3. Singular values for SVD-ARMA using experimental data

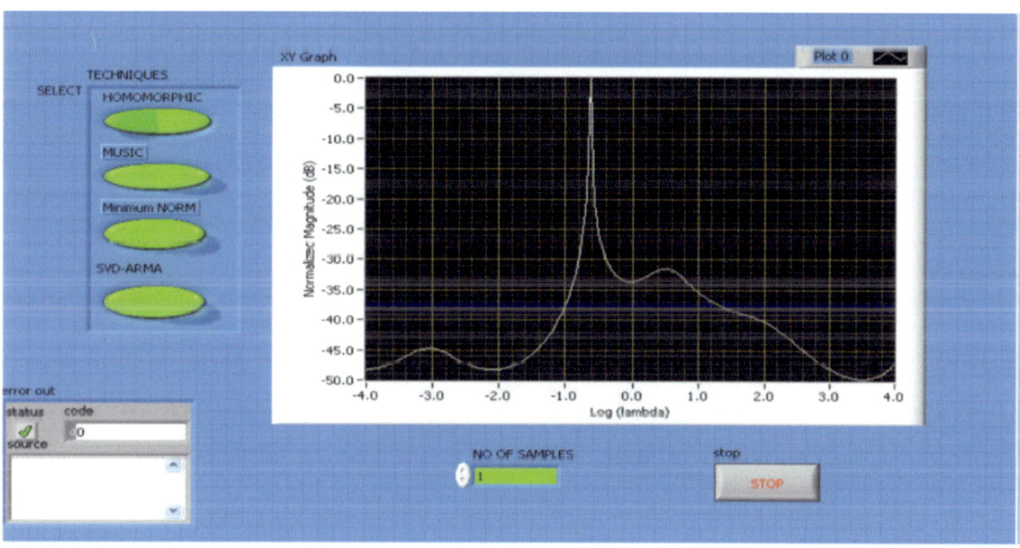

Figure 11. Power distributions for Quinine in water

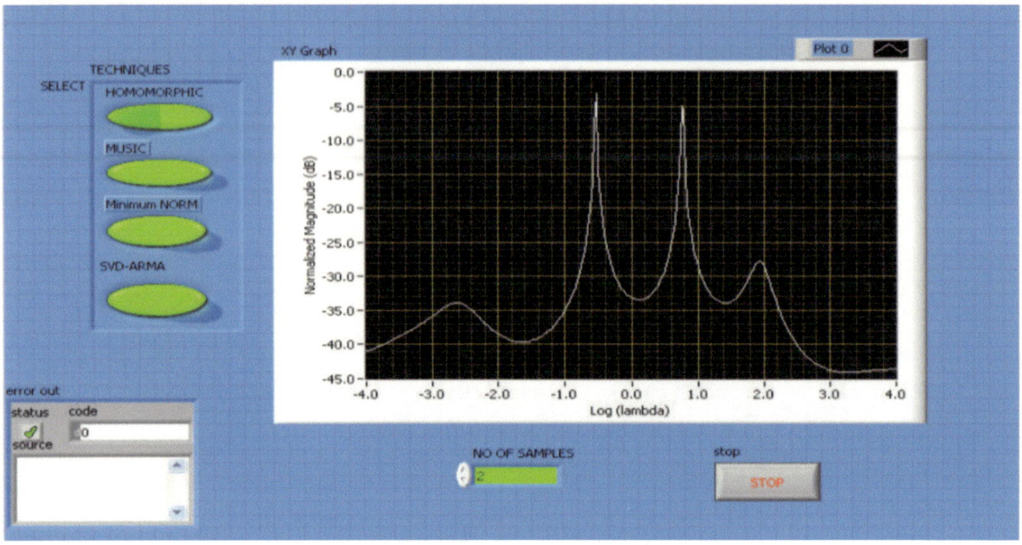

Figure 12. Power distribution Quinine plus Arcridine Sodium in water

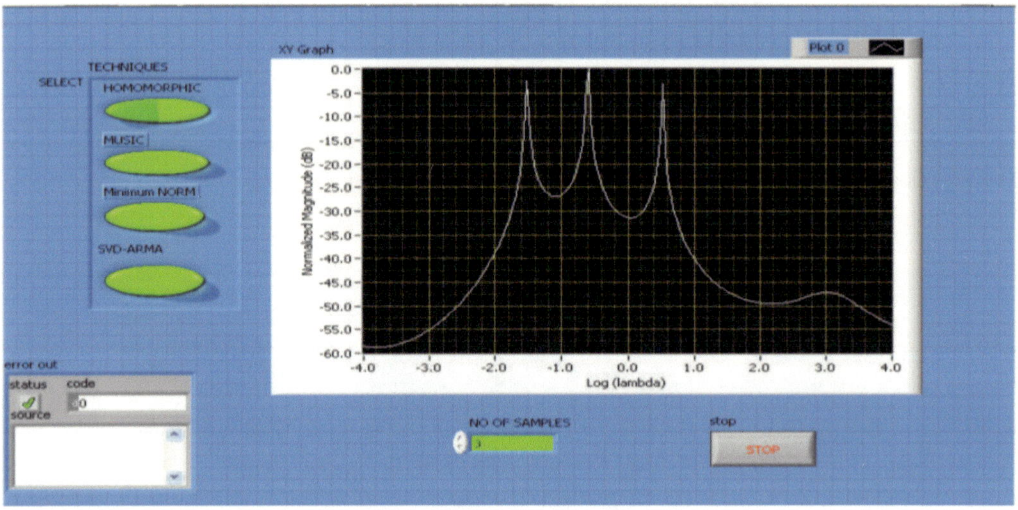

Figure 13. Power distribution for Acridine Orange + Fluorescein + Sodium and quinine in water

Author details

Momoh-Jimoh E. Salami, Ismaila B. Tijani and Za'im Bin Ismail
Intelligent Mechatronics Research Unit, Department of Mechatronics, International Islamic University Malaysia, Gombak, Malaysia

Abdussamad U. Jibia
Department of Electrical/Electronic Engineering, Bayero University Kano, Kano, Nigeria

7. References

Abdulsammad Jibia,2010."Real Time Analysis of Multicomponent Transient Signal using a Combination of Parametric and Deconvolution Techniques", A PhD thesis submitted to Department of ECE, IIUM, Malaysia.

Arunachalam, V. (1980). Multicomponent Signal Analysis. PhD dissertation, Dept. of Electrical Engineering, The University of Calgary, Alberta, Canada.

Balcou, Y. (1981). Comments on a numerical method allowing an improved analysis of multiexponential decay curves. *International journal of modelling and simulation. 1* (1), 47-51.

Cohn-Sfetcu, S., Smith, M.R., Nichols, S.T. & Henry, D.L. 1975. A digital technique for analyzing a class of multicomponent signals. *Processings of the IEEE.* 63(10): 1460-1467.

Embedded MATLAB User guide, 2008. Ww.mathworks.com, accessed date: Jan., 2011

Gardner, D.G., Gardner, J.C. & Meinke, W.W. 1959. Method for the analysis of multicomponent exponential decay curves. *The journal of chemical physics.* 31(4): 978-986.

Gutierrez-Osuna, R., Gutierrez-Galvez, A., & Powar, N. (2003). Transient response analysis for temperature-modulated hemoresistors. *Sensors and Actuators Journal B (Chemical), 93* (1-3), 57-66.

Hildebrad, F.B., (1956). *Introduction to numerical analysis.* New York: McGraw-Hill.

Istratov, A. A., & Vyvenko, O. F. (1999). Exponential Analysis in Physical Phenomena. *Rev. Sci. Instruments, 70* (2), 1233-1257.

Isernberg, I., & Dyson, R. D. (1969). The analysis of fluorescence decay by a method of moments. *The Biophysical Journal, 9* (11), 1337-1350.

Jibia, A.U., Salami, M.J.E., & Khalifa, O.O. (2009). Multiexponential Data Analysis Using Gardner Transform . (a draft ISI review journal paper)

Jibia, A.U. & Salami, M.J.E. (2007). Performance Evaluation of MUSIC and Minimum Norm Eigenvector Algorithms in Resolving Noisy Multiexponential Signals. *Proceedings of World Academy of Science, Eng. and Tech* Vol. 26, Bangok, Thailand. 24-28

Karrakchou, M., Vidal, J., Vesin, J.M., Feihl, F., Perret, C. & Kunt, M. 1992. Parameter estimation of decaying exponentials by projection on the parameter space. *Elsevier Publishers B.V.* 27: 99-107.

Kay, S.M. &Marple, S.L. (1981). Spectrum analysis – A modern perspective. Labview usr manual,2010. www.ni.com/pdf/manuals. accessed Jan., 2011

Lakowicz, J.R. 1999. *Principles of fluorescence spectroscopy.* 2nd Ed. New York: Kluwer Academic/Plenum Publishers.

Nichols, S.T., Smith, M.R. & Salami, M.J.E. (1983). *High Resolution Estimates in Multicomponent Signal Analysis* (Technical Report). Alberta: Dept. of Electrical Enginering, University of Calgary.

Provencher, S.W. 1976. A Fourier method for the analysis of exponential decay curves. *Biophysical journal.* 16: 27-39.

Prost, R. & Goutte, R. 1982. Kernel splitting method in support constrained deconvolution for super-resolution. Institut National des Science, France.

Prony, R. (1795). Essai Experimentals et Analytique. *J. ecole* Polytech., Paris, 1, 24- 76.

Proakis, J.G. & Manolakis, D.G. (2007). *Digital signal processing: Principles, algorithms, and applications.* New Jersey: Prentice-Hall.

Prony, R. (1795). Essai Experimentals et Analytique. *J. ecole Polytech., Paris,* 1, 24-76.

Provencher, S.W. (1976). A Fourier method for the analysis of exponential decay curves. *Biophysical journal,* 16, 27-39.

Salami, M.J.E. (1985).Application of ARMA models in multicomponent signal analysis. Ph.D. Dissertation, Dept. of Electrical Engineering, University of Calgary, Calgary, Canada

Salami, M.J.E. (1995). Performance evaluation of the data preprocessing techniques used in multiexponential signal analysis. *AMSE Press. 33* (2), 23-38.

Salami, M.J.E. (1999). Analysis of multicomponent transient signal using eigen-decomposition based methods.*Proc. Intern. Wireless and Telecom. Symp.,3* (5), 214-217.

Salami, M.J.E., & Bulale, Y.I. (2000). Analysis of multicomponent transient signals: A MATLAB approach. 4th International Wireless and Telecommunications Symposium/Exhibition, 253-256.*Proceedings of the IEEE, 69* (11), 1380-1419.

Salami M.J.E. & Ismail Z. (2003). Analysis of multiexponential transient signals using interpolation-based deconvolution and parametric modeling techniques. *IEEE International conference on Industrial Technology,* 1, 271-276.

Salami M.J.E. and Sidek S.N. (2000). Performance evaluation of the deconvolution techniques used in analyzing multicomponent transient signals. *Proc. IEEE Region 10 International Conference on Intelligent System and Technologies for the New Millennium (TENCON 2000),* 1, 487-492.

Sarkar, T.K., Weiner, D.D. & Jain V.K. (1981). Some mathematical considerations in dealing with the inverse problem. *IEEE transactions on antennas and propagation, 29* (2), 373-379.

Schlesinger, J. (1973). Fit to experimental data with exponential functions using the fast Fourier transform. *Nuclear instruments and methods.* 106, 503-508.

Sen, R. 1995. On the identification of exponentially decaying signals. *IEEE Transaction Signal Processing.* 43(8): 1936-1945.

Smyth, G.K. (2002). Nonlinear regression. *Encyclopedia of environmetrics.* 3, 1405-1411.

SPECTRAmax® GEMINI XS product literature. http://www.biocompare.com/Product-Reviews/41142-Molecular-Devices-8217-SPECTRAmax-GEMINI-XS-Microplate-Spectrofluorometer/ accessed on December, 2008.

Swingler, D.N. (1999). Approximations to the Cramer-Rao lower bound for a single damped exponential signal. . *Signal Processing, 75* (2), 197-200.

Trench, W.F. (1964). An algorithm for the inversion of finite Toeplitz matrices. *J. SIAM, 12* (3), 515-522.

Ulrych, T.J. (1971). Application of homomorphic deconvolution to seismology. *Geophysics, 4* (36), 650-660.

Chapter 19

Digital FIR Hilbert Transformers: Fundamentals and Efficient Design Methods

David Ernesto Troncoso Romero and Gordana Jovanovic Dolecek

Additional information is available at the end of the chapter

http://dx.doi.org/10.5772/46451

1. Introduction

Digital Hilbert transformers are a special class of digital filter whose characteristic is to introduce a $\pi/2$ radians phase shift of the input signal. In the ideal Hilbert transformer all the positive frequency components are shifted by $-\pi/2$ radians and all the negative frequency components are shifted by $\pi/2$ radians. However, these ideal systems cannot be realized since the impulse response is non-causal. Nevertheless, Hilbert transformers can be designed either as Finite Impulse Response (FIR) or as Infinite Impulse Response (IIR) digital filters [1], [2], and they are used in a wide number of Digital Signal Processing (DSP) applications, such as digital communication systems, radar systems, medical imaging and mechanical vibration analysis, among others [3]-[5].

IIR Hilbert transformers perform a phase approximation. This means that the phase response of the system is approximated to the desired values in a given range of frequencies. The magnitude response allows passing all the frequencies, with the magnitude obtained around the desired value within a given tolerance [6], [7]. On the other hand, FIR Hilbert transformers perform a magnitude approximation. In this case the system magnitude response is approximated to the desired values in a given range of frequencies. The advantage is that their phase response is always maintained in the desired value over the complete range of frequencies [8].

Whereas IIR Hilbert transformers can present instability and they are sensitive to the rounding in their coefficients, FIR filters can have exact linear phase and their stability is guaranteed. Moreover, FIR filters are less sensitive to the coefficients rounding and their phase response is not affected by this rounding. Because of this, FIR Hilbert transformers are often preferred [8]-[15]. Nevertheless, the main drawback of FIR filters is a higher complexity compared with the corresponding IIR filters. Multipliers, the most costly elements in DSP implementations, are required in an amount linearly related with the length of the filter. A linear phase FIR Hilbert transformer, which has an anti-symmetrical impulse response, can be designed with either an odd length (Type III symmetry) or an even length (Type IV symmetry). The number of multipliers m is given in terms of the filter length L as $m \approx C \cdot L$, where $C = 0.25$ for a filter with Type III symmetry or $C = 0.5$ for a filter with Type IV symmetry.

The design of optimum equiripple FIR Hilbert transformers is usually performed by Parks-McClellan algorithm. Using the MATLAB Signal Processing Toolbox, this becomes a straightforward procedure through the function `firpm`. However, for small transition bandwidth and small ripples the resulting filter requires a very high length. This complexity increases with more stringent specifications, i.e., narrower transition bandwidths and also smaller pass-band ripples. Therefore, different techniques have been developed in the last 2 decades for efficient design of Hilbert transformers, where the highly stringent specifications are met with an as low as possible required complexity. The most representative methods are [9]-[15], which are based in very efficient schemes to reduce complexity in FIR filters.

Methods [9] and [10] are based on the Frequency Response Masking (FRM) technique proposed in [16]. In [9], the design is based on reducing the complexity of a half-band filter. Then, the Hilbert transformer is derived from this half-band filter. In [10], a frequency response corrector subfilter is introduced, and all subfilters are designed simultaneously under the same framework. The method [11] is based on wide bandwidth and linear phase FIR filters with Piecewise Polynomial-Sinusoidal (PPS) impulse response. These methods offer a very high reduction in the required number of multiplier coefficients compared to the direct design based on Parks-McClellan algorithm. An important characteristic is that they are fully parallel approaches, which have the disadvantage of being area consuming since they do not directly take advantage of hardware multiplexing.

The Frequency Transformation (FT) method, proposed first in [17] and extended in [18], was modified to design FIR Hilbert transformers in [12] based on a tapped cascaded interconnection of repeated simple basic building blocks constituted by two identical subfilters. Taking advantage of the repetitive use of identical subfilters, the recent proposal [13] gives a simple and efficient method to design multiplierless Hilbert transformers, where a combination of the FT method with the Pipelining-Interleaving (PI) technique of [19] allows getting a time-multiplexed architecture which only requires three subfilters. In [14], an optimized design was developed to minimize the overall number of filter coefficients in a modified FT-PI-based structure derived from the one of [13], where only two subfilters are needed. Based on methods [13] and [14], a different architecture which just requires one subfilter was developed in [15].

In this chapter, fundamentals on digital FIR Hilbert transformers will be covered by reviewing the characteristics of analytic signals. The main connection existing between

Hilbert transformers and half-band filters will be highlighted but, at the same time, the complete introductory explanation will be kept as simple as possible. The methods to design low-complexity FIR filters, namely FRM [16], FT [17] and PPS [11], as well as the PI architecture [19], which are the cornerstone of the efficient techniques to design Hilbert transformers presented in [9]-[15], will be introduced in a simplified and concise way. With such background we will provide an extensive revision of the methods [9]-[15] to design low-complexity efficient FIR Hilbert transformers, including MATLAB routines for these methods.

2. Complex signals, analytic signals and Hilbert transformers

A real signal is a one-dimensional variation of real values over time. A *complex signal* is a two-dimensional signal whose value at some instant in time can be specified by a single complex number. The variation of the two parts of the complex numbers, namely the real part and the imaginary part, is the reason for referring to it as two-dimensional signal [20]. A real signal can be represented in a two-dimensional plot by presenting its variations against time. Similarly, a complex signal can be represented in a three-dimensional plot by considering time as a third dimension.

Real signals always have positive and negative frequency spectral components, and these components are generally real and imaginary. For any real signal, the positive and negative parts of its real spectral component always have even symmetry around the zero-frequency point, i.e., they are mirror images of each other. Conversely, the positive and negative parts of its imaginary spectral component are always anti-symmetric, i.e., they are always negatives of each other [1]. This conjugate symmetry is the invariant nature of real signals.

Complex signals, on the other hand, are not restricted to these spectral conjugate symmetry conditions. The special case of complex signals which do not have a negative part neither in their real nor in their imaginary spectral components are known as *analytic signals*or also as quadrature signals [2]. An example of analytic signal is the complex exponential signal$x_c(t)$, presented in Figure 1, and described by

$$x_c(t) = e^{j\omega_0 t} = x_r(t) + jx_i(t) = \cos(\omega_0 t) + j\sin(\omega_0 t). \tag{1}$$

The real part and the imaginary part of the analytic signal are related trough the *Hilbert transform*. In simple words, given an analytic signal, its imaginary part is the Hilbert transform of its real part. Figure 1 shows the complex signal $x_c(t)$, its real part $x_r(t)$ and its imaginary part, $x_i(t)$. Figure 2 presents the frequency spectral components of these signals. It can be seen that the real part $x_r(t)$ and the imaginary part $x_i(t)$, both real signals, preserve the spectral conjugate symmetry. The complex signal $x_c(t)$ does not have negative parts neither in its real spectral component nor in its imaginary spectral component. For this reason, analytic signals are also referred as one-side spectrum signals. Finally, Figure 3 shows the Hilbert transform relation between the real and imaginary parts of $x_c(t)$.

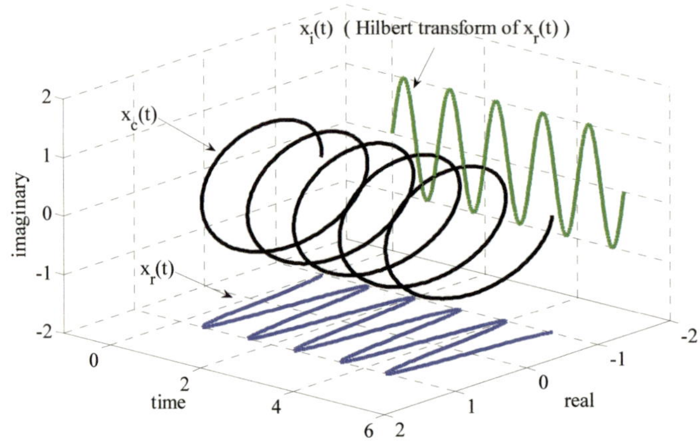

Figure 1. The Hilbert transform and the analytic signal of $x_r(t) = \cos(\omega_0 t)$, $\omega_0 = 2\pi$.

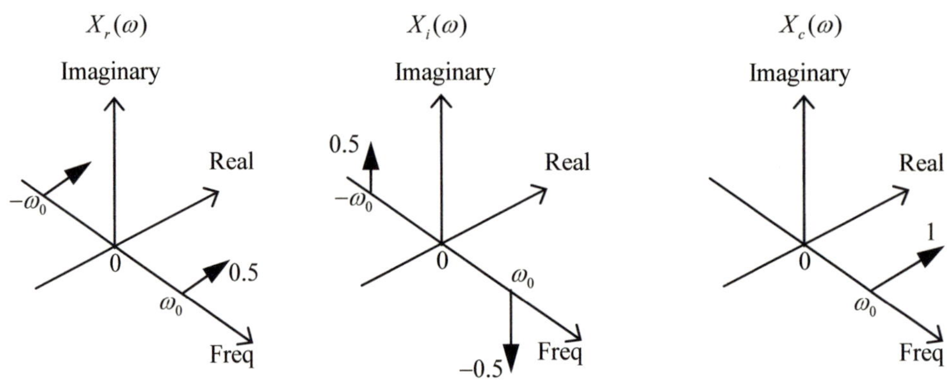

Figure 2. From left to right, frequency spectrum of $x_r(t)$, $x_i(t)$ and $x_c(t)$.

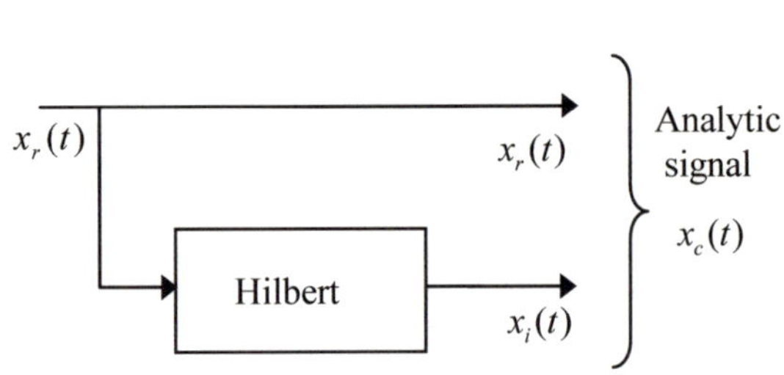

Figure 3. Hilbert transform relations between $x_r(t)$ and $x_i(t)$ to generate $x_c(t)$.

The motivation for creating analytic signals, or in other words, for eliminating the negative parts of the real and imaginary spectral components of real signals, is that these negative parts have in essence the same information than the positive parts due to the conjugate symmetry previously mentioned. The elimination of these negative parts reduces the required bandwidth for the processing. For the case of DSP applications, it is possible to form a complex sequence $x_c(n)$ given as follows,

$$x_c(n) = x_r(n) + jx_i(n), \tag{2}$$

with the special property that its frequency spectrum $X_c(e^{j\omega})$ is equal to that of a given real sequence $x(n)$ for the positive Nyquist interval and zero for the negative Nyquist interval, i.e.,

$$X_c(e^{j\omega}) = \begin{cases} X(e^{j\omega}) & \text{for } 0 \le \omega < \pi, \\ 0 & \text{for } -\pi \le \omega < 0. \end{cases} \tag{3}$$

Although analyticity has no formal meaning for sequences [2], the same terminology, i.e., analytic sequence, will be applied for complex sequences whose frequency spectrum is one-sided, like in (3).

If $X_r(e^{j\omega})$ and $X_i(e^{j\omega})$ respectively denote the frequency spectrums of $x_r(n)$ and $x_i(n)$, then

$$X_c(e^{j\omega}) = X_r(e^{j\omega}) + jX_i(e^{j\omega}). \tag{4}$$

The spectrums of $x_r(n)$ and $x_i(n)$ can be readily deduced as

$$X_r(e^{j\omega}) = \tfrac{1}{2}[X_c(e^{j\omega}) + X_c^*(e^{-j\omega})], \tag{5}$$

$$jX_i(e^{j\omega}) = \tfrac{1}{2}[X_c(e^{j\omega}) - X_c^*(e^{-j\omega})], \tag{6}$$

where $X_c^*(e^{j\omega})$ is the complex conjugate of $X_c(e^{j\omega})$. Note that (6) gives an expression for $jX_i(e^{j\omega})$, which is the frequency spectrum of the imaginary signal $jx_i(n)$. Also, note that $X_r(e^{j\omega})$ and $X_i(e^{j\omega})$ are both complex-valued functions in general. However, $X_r(e^{j\omega})$ is conjugate symmetric, i.e., $X_r(e^{j\omega}) = X_r^*(e^{-j\omega})$. Similarly, $jX_i(e^{j\omega})$ is conjugate anti-symmetric, i.e., $jX_i(e^{j\omega}) = -jX_i^*(e^{-j\omega})$. These relations are illustrated in Figure 4.

From (5) and (6) we obtain

$$X_c(e^{j\omega}) = 2X_r(e^{j\omega}) - X_c^*(e^{-j\omega}), \tag{7}$$

$$X_c(e^{j\omega}) = 2jX_i(e^{j\omega}) + X_c^*(e^{-j\omega}), \tag{8}$$

and since $X_c^*(e^{-j\omega}) = 0$ for $0 < \omega < \pi$ (see Figure 4b), eqs. (3), (7) and (8) give

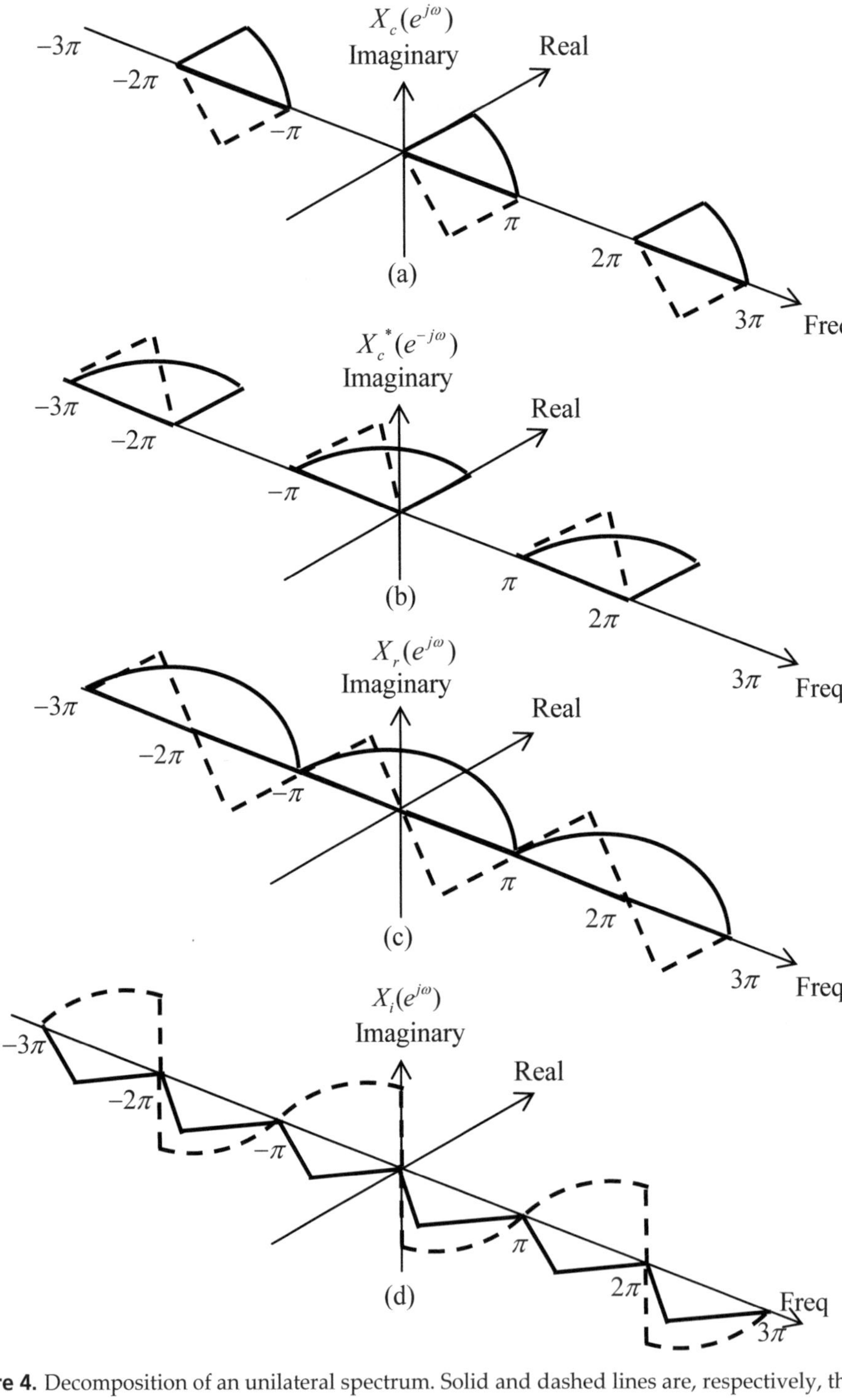

Figure 4. Decomposition of an unilateral spectrum. Solid and dashed lines are, respectively, the real and imaginary parts.

$$X_c(e^{j\omega}) = \begin{cases} 2X_r(e^{j\omega}) & \text{for } 0 \le \omega < \pi, \\ 0 & \text{for } -\pi \le \omega < 0. \end{cases} \tag{9}$$

$$X_c(e^{j\omega}) = \begin{cases} 2jX_i(e^{j\omega}) & \text{for } 0 \le \omega < \pi, \\ 0 & \text{for } -\pi \le \omega < 0. \end{cases} \tag{10}$$

Thus

$$X_i(e^{j\omega}) = -jX_r(e^{j\omega}) \quad \text{for } 0 \le \omega < \pi. \tag{11}$$

On the other hand, from (4), and since $X_c(e^{j\omega}) = 0$ for $-\pi \le \omega < 0$, we have

$$X_i(e^{j\omega}) = jX_r(e^{j\omega}) \quad \text{for } -\pi \le \omega < 0. \tag{12}$$

Therefore, (11) and (12) can be expressed as

$$X_i(e^{j\omega}) = \begin{cases} -jX_r(e^{j\omega}) & \text{for } 0 \le \omega < \pi, \\ jX_r(e^{j\omega}) & \text{for } -\pi \le \omega < 0, \end{cases} \tag{13}$$

or

$$X_i(e^{j\omega}) = H(e^{j\omega})X_r(e^{j\omega}), \tag{14}$$

where

$$H(e^{j\omega}) = \begin{cases} -j & \text{for } 0 \le \omega < \pi, \\ j & \text{for } -\pi \le \omega < 0. \end{cases} \tag{15}$$

According to (14), $x_i(n)$ can be obtained by processing $x_r(n)$ with a linear time-invariant discrete-time system whose frequency response $H(e^{j\omega})$ is given in (15). This frequency response has unity magnitude, a phase angle of $-\pi/2$ radians for $0 < \omega < \pi$, and a phase angle of $\pi/2$ radians for $-\pi < \omega < 0$. A system of this type is commonly referred to as *Hilbert transformer* or sometimes as 90-degree phase shifter.

The impulse response $h(n)$ of a Hilbert transformer is [2]

$$h(n) = \begin{cases} \dfrac{2}{n\pi}\sin^2\left(\dfrac{n\pi}{2}\right) & \text{for } n \ne 0, \\ 0 & \text{for } n = 0. \end{cases} \tag{16}$$

This impulse response is not absolutely summable and thus the frequency response of (15) is ideal. However, approximations to the ideal Hilbert transformer can be obtained with IIR or FIR systems. Thus, Hilbert transformers are considered a special class of filter.

IIR Hilbert transformers have phase error as well as magnitude error in approximating the ideal frequency response. Basically, these filters can be designed by using two all-pass systems whose phase responses differ by approximately $\pi/2$ over some well-defined portion of the band $0 < |\omega| < \pi$. By taking the outputs of the two all-pass filters as the real and imaginary parts of a complex signal it can be found that the spectrum of such signal nearly vanishes over much of the negative frequency interval. As such, the outputs of the two all-pass filters are quite nearly a Hilbert transformer.

FIR Hilbert transformers with constant group delay can be easily designed. The $\pi/2$ phase shift is realized exactly, with an additional linear phase component required for a causal FIR system. By evaluating (16) over some positive and negative values of n, it can be seen that the impulse response is anti-symmetric. Therefore, FIR Hilbert transformers are based on either Type III (i.e., anti-symmetric impulse response with odd length L) or Type IV (i.e., anti-symmetric impulse response with even length L) symmetry. Filters with Type III symmetry have amplitude equal to zero in $\omega = 0$ and $\omega = \pi$ and filters with Type IV symmetry have amplitude equal to zero only in $\omega = 0$. Thus, the FIR approximation is acceptable over a given range of frequencies (a pass-band region) which does not include these extremes.

The exactness of the phase of Type III and Type IV FIR systems is a compelling motivation for their use in approximating Hilbert transformers. Additionally, whereas IIR Hilbert transformers can present instability and they are sensitive to rounding error in their coefficients, FIR filters have guaranteed stability, are less sensitive to the coefficients rounding and their phase response is not affected by this rounding. Because of this, FIR Hilbert transformers are often preferred [8]-[15]. The rest of this chapter will be focused on the design of FIR Hilbert transformers.

2.1. Basic design of FIR Hilbert transformers with MATLAB

Since the phase requirement in FIR Hilbert transformers is accomplished, the design of a FIR Hilbert transformer consists on finding the impulse response $h(n)$, for $n = 0$ to $L–1$, which satisfies the following magnitude response specification,

$$(1-\delta) \le \left|H(e^{j\omega})\right| \le (1-\delta) \qquad \text{for } \omega_L \le \omega \le \omega_H, \tag{17}$$

where δ is the allowed pass-band ripple, ω_L is the lower pass-band edge and ω_H is given as $\omega_H = \pi - \omega_L$ if the desired Hilbert transformer is a Type III filter or $\omega_H = \pi$ if it is Type IV. The values ω_L and ω_H can be made to approach 0 and π, respectively, as closely as desired by increasing the length L of the filter. For Hilbert transformers, the value $\omega_L/2\pi$ is considered the transition band.

The design of optimum equiripple Type III and Type IV FIR linear phase Hilbert transformers is usually performed by Parks-McClellan algorithm. With the MATLAB Signal Processing Toolbox this becomes a straightforward procedure through the function `firpm`. The order of the filter, $L–1$, must be estimated in advance. A useful formula to estimate L, presented in [10], is

$$L \approx \varphi(\delta,\ \omega_L) = \Big[0.002655\big(\log_{10}(\delta)\big)^3 + 0.031843\big(\log_{10}(\delta)\big)^2 - \ldots \\ 0.554993\log_{10}(\delta) - 0.049788\Big] / \left(\tfrac{\omega_L}{2\pi}\right) + 1. \tag{18}$$

Example 1. The following code example illustrates the design of a Type III Hilbert transformer with δ= 0.01, ω_L= 0.1π and ω_H= π− ω_L= 0.9π using the MATLAB Signal Processing Toolbox. From (18), L is estimated as $L \approx 24.3266$. For convenience, we use L = 4k+3 with k integer and the closest value for L, higher than the estimated value, is chosen. In this case we use L = 4*6+3 = 27.

```
d = 0.01; w_L = 0.1*pi; w_H = 0.9*pi; L = 27;
h = firpm(L-1,[w_L/pi w_H/pi],[1 1],'hilbert');
[H w] = freqz(h,1);
figure; stem(0:length(h)-1, h,'fill')
figure; plot(w/pi, abs(H))
```

Figure 5a shows the impulse response and Figure 5b shows the magnitude response of the obtained Hilbert transformer.

As we mentioned earlier, the most expensive elements in digital filters are multipliers. For a Type III Hilbert transformer, the number of multipliers, m, is $(L+1)/4$ if $L = 4k+3$, or $(L-1)/4$ if $L = 4k+1$, with k integer. In this last case the impulse response values $h(0)$ and $h(L-1)$ are zero. For a Type IV Hilbert transformer, the number of multipliers is $L/2$. This number can be simplified as

$$m \approx C \cdot L, \tag{19}$$

where C = 0.25 for a Type III Hilbert transformer or C = 0.5 for a Type IV Hilbert transformer.

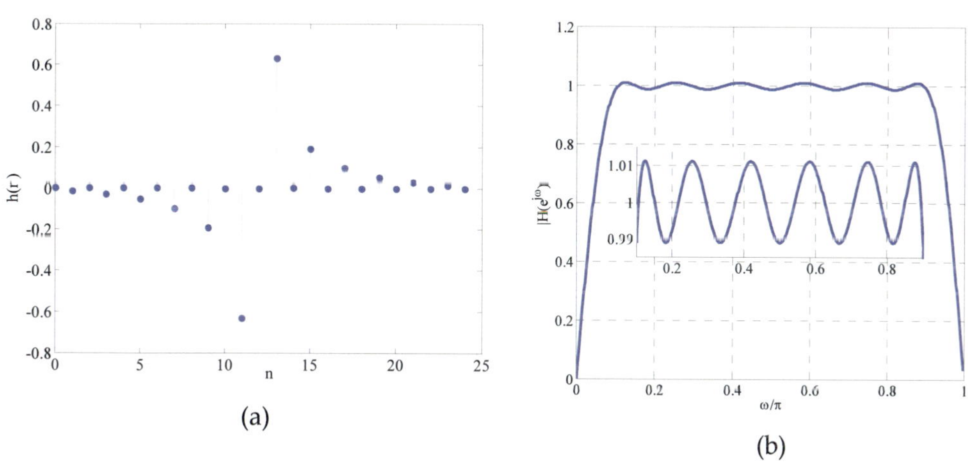

Figure 5. (a) Impulse response and (b) Magnitude response of a digital FIR Hilbert transformer.

It is worth highlighting the following point. A Type III Hilbert transformer can be derived from a Type IV Hilbert transformer by adding one zero-valued impulse response sample between each two impulse response samples of the Type IV Hilbert transformer. This is equivalent to replacing each z^{-1} in the transfer function of this filter by z^{-2}. The opposite procedure can be straightforwardly followed to derive a Type IV Hilbert transformer from a Type III Hilbert transformer.

From (18), it can be seen that the length L increases inversely proportional with the transition band $\omega_L/2\pi$. Hence, for cases with narrow transition band and small ripple the implementation cost becomes very high. As a simple example, the estimated length for a Hilbert transformer withδ= 0.001 and ω_L= 0.001π is $L \approx 3661.2$. It implies approximately 915.3 multipliers, which is impractical. Therefore, the design of FIR Hilbert transformers with strict specifications requires specialized techniques to reduce the number of multipliers and the computational complexity of the filter. Before of the revision of these techniques, in the next section we will highlight the relation between Hilbert transformers and half-band filters because this relation is crucial for developing the specialized techniques to design low-complexity FIR Hilbert transformers.

3. The Hilbert transformer and its relation with the half-band filter

Half-band filters have their transfer function given by

$$H_{Hb}(z) = \sum_{n=0}^{2M} h_{Hb}(n) z^{-n}, \tag{20}$$

where $h_{Hb}(n)$ is the impulse response, M is an odd integer and $2M$isthe filter order [21]. The coefficients are symmetric with respect to the central coefficient $h_{Hb}(M)$, namely, they accomplish the following relation,

$$h_{Hb}(2M-n) = h_{Hb}(n) \quad \text{for} \quad n = 0,1,...,2M. \tag{21}$$

The length of the filter, L, is an odd number given as $L = 2M + 1$ with $M = 1, 3, 5\dots$ etc. In a lineal phase half-band filter, almost a half of the coefficients are zero. Figure 6 shows the procedure to design a half-band filter. It starts with the transfer function of a Type II lineal phase filter, i.e., a filter with symmetric impulse response whose length is even. For this filter we have,

$$Q(z) = \sum_{n=0}^{M} q(n) z^{-n} \quad \text{for} \quad q(M-n) = q(n). \tag{22}$$

First, samples with value zero are introduced between the $q(n)$ impulse samples (see Figure 6a and 6c). This generates a transfer function with Type I symmetry, whose order is $2M$, given by

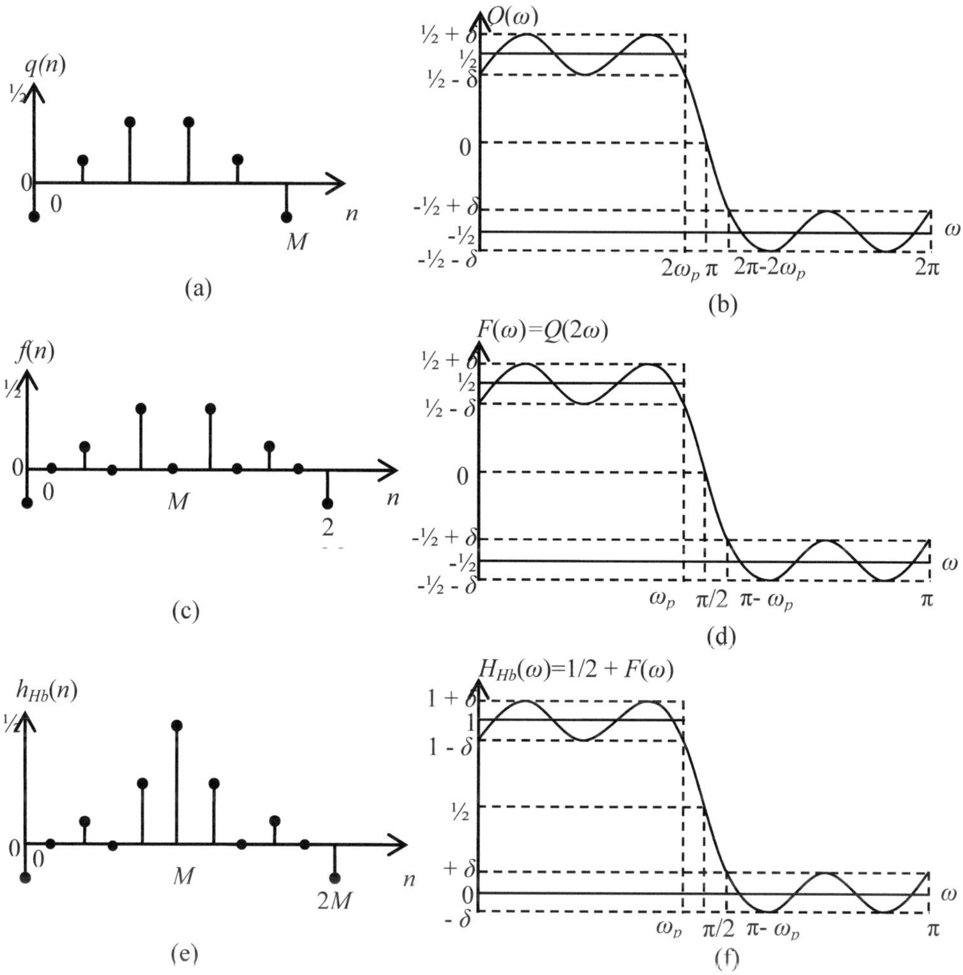

Figure 6. Low-pass half-band filter design. (a) Impulse response of a Type II filter with order M, $q(n)$. (b) Zero-phase frequency response of the Type II filter with order M, $Q(\omega)$. (c) Impulse response of a Type I filter with order $2M$, $f(n)$. (d) Zero-phase frequency response of the Type I filter with order $2M$, $F(\omega)$. (e) Impulse response of a half-band filter, $h_{Hb}(n)$. (f) Zero-phase frequency response of the half-band filter, $H_{Hb}(\omega)$.

$$F(z)=\sum_{n=0}^{2M} f(n)z^{-n}=Q(z^2)=\sum_{n=0}^{M} q(n)z^{-2n}. \tag{23}$$

Then, the zero-valued sample with index $n = M$ is replaced by the value 1/2 (See Figure 6e). Thus we obtain

$$H_{Hb}(z)=\frac{1}{2}z^{-M}+F(z)=\frac{1}{2}z^{-M}+\sum_{n=0}^{M} q(n)z^{-2n}. \tag{24}$$

The coefficients of the half-band filter are obtained from (20) and (24) as

$$h_{Hb}(M) = \frac{1}{2}, \quad h_{Hb}(n) = q\left(\frac{n}{2}\right) \text{ for } n \text{ even,} \tag{25}$$

$$h_{Hb}(n) = 0, \text{ for } n \text{ odd and } n \neq M, \tag{26}$$

and the zero-phase frequency response of $H_{Hb}(z)$ is

$$H_{Hb}(\omega) = \frac{1}{2} + Q(2\omega) = \frac{1}{2} + F(\omega). \tag{27}$$

Based on the previous relations, the design of a half-band low-pass filter with pass-band frequency ω_p and pass-band ripple δ can be carried out by designing the $Q(z)$ filter, such that its zero-phase frequency response, $Q(\omega)$, oscillates within $1/2 \pm \delta$ over the range of frequencies $[0, 2\omega_p]$ (See Figure 6b). Since $Q(z)$ has a Type II transfer function, it presents a fixed zero in $z = -1$ ($\omega = \pi$). Note from Figure 6b that $Q(\omega)$ oscillates within $-1/2 \pm \delta$ over the range of frequencies $[2\pi - 2\omega_p, 2\pi]$. The corresponding zero-phase frequency response of the filter $F(z)$, given as $F(\omega) = Q(2\omega)$, remains within $1/2 \pm \delta$ over the range of frequencies $[0, \omega_p]$ and within $-1/2 \pm \delta$ over the range of frequencies $[\pi - \omega_p, \pi]$ (See Figure 6d). Finally, $H_{Hb}(\omega)$ oscillates around 1 over the range of frequencies $[0, \omega_p]$ with tolerance δ and around 0 over the range of frequencies $[\pi - \omega_p, \pi]$ with the same tolerance δ (See Figure 6f). Note that, as a low-pass filter, the half-band filter has the relations $\omega_s = \pi - \omega_p$ and $\delta_p = \delta_s$.

Example 2. The following code example illustrates the design of a half-band filter with $\delta_p = \delta_s = 0.005$, $\omega_p = 0.4\pi$ and $\omega_s = \pi - \omega_p = 0.5\pi$ using the MATLAB Filter Design Toolbox. Eq. (18) can be applied to estimate the filter length L, by substituting $\omega_L = (\pi/2) - \omega_p$ and $\delta = 2\delta_p$. The length L is estimated as $L \approx 24.3266$. Since L must be represented as $L = 2M+1$ with M odd to avoid zero-valued impulse response samples in the left and right extremes of the impulse response, we use $L = 2*13 + 1 = 27$.

```
dp = 0.005;w_p = 0.4*pi;w_s = 0.5*pi; L = 27;
h_half = firhalfband(L-1, w_p/pi);
[H_half w] = freqz(h_half,1);
figure; stem(0:length(h_half)-1, h_half,'fill')
figure; plot(w/pi, abs(H_half))
```

3.1. Hilbert transformer derived from a half-band filter

A Hilbert transformer filter can be designed from a half-band filter. First,the sample with value 1/2, located in the index $n = M$, is replaced by the value 0 (See Figures 7a and 7d). Thus we obtain

$$\tilde{H}(z) = H_{Hb}(z) - \frac{1}{2}z^{-M}. \tag{28}$$

The subtraction of this coefficient, drawn in Figure 7d, causes the zero-phase frequency response of the half-band filter to be shifted downwardly, as illustrated in Figure 7c. The filter $\tilde{H}(\omega)$ must be shifted by $\pi/2$ on the horizontal direction in the frequency domain. This is accomplished by multiplying the remaining coefficients, $\tilde{h}(n)$, by $(j)^{-n}$. The effect of this action produces a Hilbert transformer with odd length and a pass-band gain equal to 0.5. Therefore, a Hilbert transformer with unitary gain will be obtained by scaling all the coefficients by 2. This is illustrated in Figure 8. The transfer function of the Hilbert transformer given in terms of the transfer function of a half-band filter is

$$H(z) = 2\left[H_{Hb}(jz) - \frac{1}{2}(jz)^{-M} \right] = 2\sum_{\substack{n=0 \\ n\neq M}}^{2M} h_{Hb}(n)(jz)^{-n} . \quad (29)$$

The impulse response of the Hilbert transformer is related with the impulse response of the half-band filter through the following expression,

$$h(n) = \begin{cases} 0; & n = 2k+1, \\ 2(-1)^{k-1} h_{Hb}(n); & n = 2k \quad \text{with} \quad k = 0,1,2,...,M. \end{cases} \quad (30)$$

It was mentioned earlier that the useful bandwidth in a Hilbert transformer is restricted to some range given as $0 < \omega_L \leq \omega \leq \omega_H < \pi$, where $\omega_H = \pi - \omega_L$. The relation of the low-pass edge frequency ω_L with the band-edge frequencies of the half-band filter, ω_p and ω_s, is given by

$$\omega_L = (\pi/2) - \omega_p , \quad (31)$$

$$\omega_L = \omega_s - (\pi/2) , \quad (32)$$

where $\omega_s = \pi - \omega_p$.

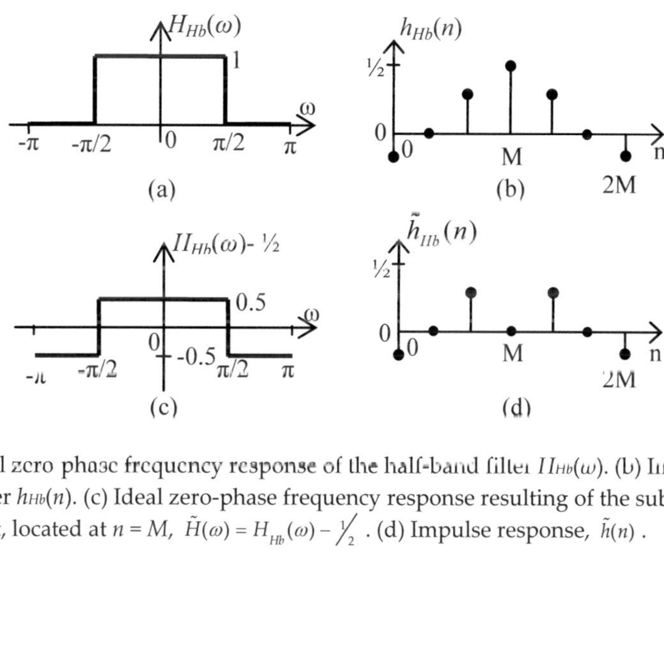

Figure 7. (a) Ideal zero phase frequency response of the half-band filter $H_{Hb}(\omega)$. (b) Impulse response of the half-band filter $h_{Hb}(n)$. (c) Ideal zero-phase frequency response resulting of the subtraction of the central coefficient, located at $n = M$, $\tilde{H}(\omega) = H_{Hb}(\omega) - 1/2$. (d) Impulse response, $\tilde{h}(n)$.

Hilbert transformers designed from half-band filters have odd length. In these cases, there is a coefficient of value zero between each coefficient of its impulse response. Thus, a Hilbert transformer with even length can be obtained by eliminating these zero-valued coefficients.

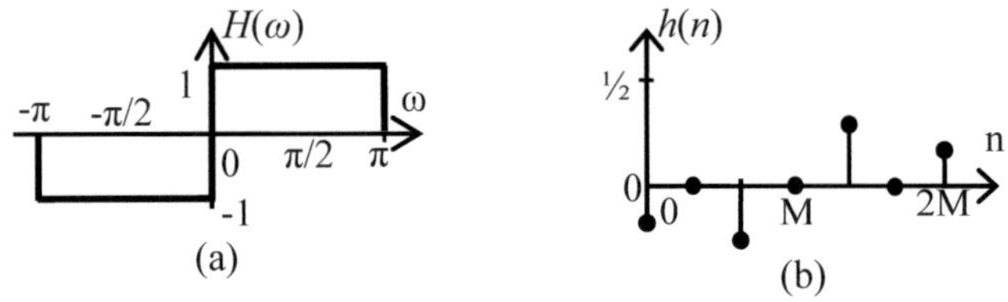

Figure 8. Hilbert transformer design, (a) Ideal zero-phase frequency response of the Hilbert transformer obtained from $H_{Hb}(\omega)$. (b) Impulse response $h(n)$.

Example 3. The following code example illustrates a simple way to obtain the impulse response of a Hilbert transformer from the impulse response of a half-band filter. If we consider that the code of Example 2 has been previously run, it can be assumed that `h_half` and `L` are already defined. The resulting Hilbert transformer coefficients in `h` are the same as the ones obtained in Example 1, since the half-band filter generated in Example 2 accomplish the relations $\omega_L = (\pi/2) - \omega_p$ and $\delta = 2\delta_p$with regard to the specifications in Example 1.

```
index = [1:L];
middle_sample = [zeros(1,(L-1)/2) 1/2 zeros(1,(L-1)/2)];
m = (ones(1,L)*i).^(-(index-1));
h = 2*(h_half.*m - middle_sample.*m);
```

4. Efficient methods to design FIR filters

It is known that the complexity of FIR digital filters increases in an inverse proportion with the transition bandwidth. A simple example in Sub-section 2.1 was given for the case of a Hilbert transformer with small ripple and bandwidth. Several efficient techniques have been developed to efficiently design FIR filters with strict specifications, such that the resulting filter accomplishes the desired specification with a lower complexity than the direct design obtained with the Parks-McClellan algorithm. For Hilbert transformers, however, these methods have been specially adapted, since Hilbert transform filtering has special characteristics as we saw in Section 2. Prior to starting the review of the special methods to design FIR Hilbert transformers with low complexity, we will briefly introduce in this section the general techniques which are the origin of these methods. These techniques are Frequency-Response Masking (FRM), Frequency Transformation (FT) and Piecewise Polynomial Sinusoidal (PPS).

4.1. Frequency-Response Masking technique

The FRM technique, introduced in [16], uses the so-called expanded-by-M filters as basic building blocks, where the transfer functions have the form $G(z^M)$. In general, a filter $G(z)$ becomes expanded-by-M by replacing every of its elements z^{-1} by z^{-M} or, in other words, by inserting M–1 zero-valued impulse response samples between two of its original impulse response samples. The periodic frequency response of these filters has M periods in the frequency range [0, 2π].

Figures 6a to 6d show how a filter $F(z) = Q(z^2)$ has a compressed-by-two frequency response in comparison with the original filter $Q(z)$, whose impulse response is depicted in Figure 6a. The zero-phase frequency response of $Q(z)$, presented in Figure 6b, shows a period that covers the frequency range [0, 2π]. On the other hand, the filter $F(z)$ has a very similar zero-phase frequency response, with the only difference that its period covers the frequency range [0, π]. The transition bandwidth of this expanded-by-2 filter $F(z)$ is a half of the transition bandwidth of the filter $Q(z)$. However, now this expanded filter has a replica of the frequency response of $Q(z)$ (which covers the range of frequency [2π, 4π]) over the range [π,2π]. The number of multipliers of $F(z)$ is the same as the one of $Q(z)$. This can be seen in Figure 6c, where several impulse response samples are zero-valued.

The main idea of the FRM technique is using an expanded filter $G(z^M)$ and its complementary filter, $G_c(z^M)$, to form the transition band of a desired filter $H(z)$. Because of that, these filters are so-called band-edge shaping filters. The complementary filter is given as

$$G_c(z) = z^{-(L_G-1)/2} - G(z), \tag{33}$$

where L_G is the length of the filter $G(z)$. Since the frequency response of these filters is periodical, two non-periodic masking filters, $H_{Ma}(z)$ and $H_{Mc}(z)$, are respectively cascaded with $G(z^K)$ and $G_c(z^K)$ to eliminate the unwanted periodic replicas of frequency response. The overall filter formed with the FRM technique is given as

$$H(z) = G(z^M)H_{Ma}(z) + [z^{-M(L_G-1)/2} - G(z^M)]H_{Mc}(z)\,. \tag{34}$$

Extensive information about the basic FRM method can be found in [16] and [23].

4.2. Frequency Transformation technique

The FT technique, first studied in [22] and then generalized in [17], is based on the repetitive use of an identical simple subfilter $G(z)$. Let us consider $G(\omega)$ as the zero-phase frequency response of $G(z)$ and an amplitude change function $Q(x)$ given as

$$Q(x) = \sum_{k=0}^{M} q(k)x^k\,. \tag{35}$$

The function $Q(x)$ allows changing the values $x = G(\omega)$to new values $y = Q(x)$. Basically, the new amplitude values $y = Q(x)$ must approximate the desired values $d = D(x)$ for $x \in X_p \cup X_s$, where X_p is the range of values $[x_{p,l}, x_{p,u}]$ and X_s is the range of values $[x_{s,l}, x_{s,u}]$, such that the zero-phase frequency response of the overall filter $H(z)$ achieves the desired values d with a maximum absolute pass-band deviation δ_p over the pass-band region Ω_p, as well as a maximum absolute stop-band deviation δ_s over the stop-band region Ω_s. This characteristic is reached if the following conditions are simultaneously met,

$$D(x) - \delta_p \le Q(x) \le D(x) + \delta_p, \text{ for } x_{p,l} \le x \le x_{p,u}, \tag{36}$$

$$D(x) - \delta_s \le Q(x) \le D(x) + \delta_s, \text{ for } x_{s,l} \le x \le x_{s,u}, \tag{37}$$

$$x_{p,l} \le G(\omega) \le x_{p,u}, \text{ for } \omega \in \Omega_p, \tag{38}$$

$$x_{s,l} \le G(\omega) \le x_{s,u}, \text{ for } \omega \in \Omega_s \tag{39}$$

Usually, $D(x) = 1$ for $x \in X_p$ and $D(x) = 0$ for $x \in X_s$. Basically, two problems can be solved from this approach:

Problem 1. Given M, the number of subfilters, find the optimal coefficients of $Q(x)$ and the optimal coefficients of $G(z)$ to meet the conditions (36) to (39) with the minimum length L_G (which must be odd).

Problem 2. Given the subfilter $G(z)$, find the optimal coefficients of $Q(x)$ to meet the conditions (36) to (39) with the minimum value M.

The overall filter formed with the FT technique is given as

$$H(z) = \sum_{k=0}^{M} q(k) z^{-(M-k)(L_G-1)/2} \left[G(z)\right]^k . \tag{40}$$

Detailed information about the FT method can be found in [16] and [23].

4.3. Piecewise Polynomial Sinusoidal technique

In the PPS technique, introduced in [24] for wide-band Type I filters, extended in [25] for Hilbert transformers and detailed in [11] for both cases, the idea is to divide the impulse response of a wideband filter into sub-responses and to generate each sub-response with polynomials with a given degree. For wideband linear-phase filters, the impulse response has a narrow main lobe and the side lobes have very rapid change in sign. Therefore, it is taken advantage of sinusoids in such a way that the polynomial pieces follow the polynomial-sinusoidal shapes to decrease the number of polynomial pieces and, as a consequence, to reduce the number of coefficients.

The overall transfer function $H(z)$ for a desired Type I filter with length $2N+1$ is constructed with M parallel branches connected and delayed with z^{-N_m} in order to keep the center of symmetry at the same location for all the sub-impulse responses. These sub-responses are modulated with a sinusoidal function and finally an arbitrary number of separately generated filter coefficients is added as follows,

$$H(z) = \sum_{m=1}^{M} z^{-N_m} H_m(z) + z^{-\hat{N}} \hat{H}(z), \tag{41}$$

where,

$$H_m(z) = h_m(N - N_m) z^{-(N-N_m)} + \sum_{n=0}^{(N-N_m)-1} h_m(n)[z^{-n} + z^{-(2(N-N_m)-n)}]. \tag{42}$$

The integers N_m in the delay terms z^{-N_m} satisfy $N_1 = 0$ and $N_{m+1} > N_m$ for $m = 1, 2, \ldots, M-1$, and the order of $H_m(z)$ is $2(N - N_m)$. The impulse response is given as

$$h_m(n) = \sum_{r=0}^{L} a_m^{(L)}(r) n^r \times \sin[\omega_c(n - (N - N_m))]. \tag{43}$$

In addition, $z^{-\hat{N}} \hat{H}(z)$ is a conventional direct-form transfer function with non-zero impulse response coefficients $\hat{h}(n)$, with $n = N-c+1, N-c+2, \ldots, N-c+T$, where $c = \lceil T/2 \rceil$ and T is the number of additional coefficients at the center of the filter. Given the values N_m for $m = 1, 2, \ldots, M-1$, M and L, the objective is finding the polynomial coefficients such that the error with respect to a desired amplitude characteristic is minimized. An extensive explanation on this method can be reviewed in [11].

4.4. Pipelining-Interleaving architecture

The Pipelining-Interleaving (PI) technique developed in [19] provides efficient structures of FIR digital filters to avoid the repetitive use of an identical filter. Suppose that we have two sequences of independent signals, $x_1(n)$ and $x_2(n)$, that are filtered by two identical filters $H(z)$. Thus, two corresponding sequences of independent outputs, $y_1(n)$ and $y_2(n)$, are obtained. An alternative form for this purpose is the multirate implementation using $H(z^2)$ as shown in Figure 9. This structure uses a single filter to implement two identical filters. The clock rate for this implementation must be twice the data rate [19]. If only one sequence of input signal is filtered, it is possible to connect the first output sequence $y_1(n)$ to the second input $x_2(n)$. In this way, $H(z^2)$ is used to implement $H^2(z)$.

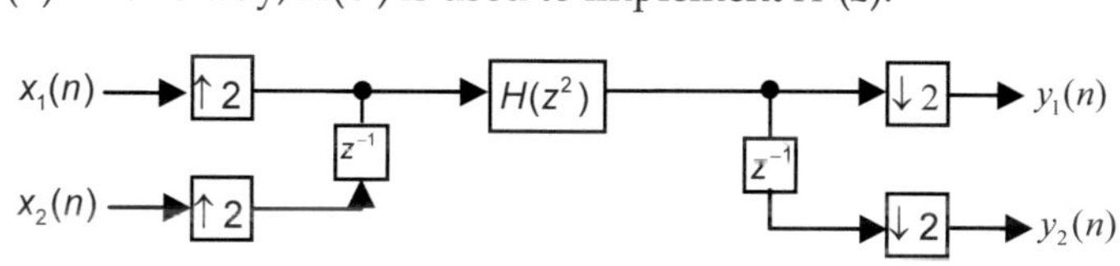

Figure 9. Filtering of two independent sequences using one filter.

The PI structure of the Figure 9 can be extended to implement the filtering of K different signals, each one filtered by an identical filter $H(z)$, with K being an arbitrary positive integer. From this, it is possible to implement the filtering of one signal with K identical filters in cascade. Figure 10a presents the general structure to filter a signal using one filter $H(z^K)$. Figure 10b shows the equivalent structure, which consists of the filtering of a signal by a cascade of K identical filters $H(z)$ [19].

In the structure shown in Figure 10a, the clock rate of $H(z^K)$ must be K times the data rate. Clearly, for high data rate applications, K must be chosen as a relatively small integer, otherwise a very high clock rate will be required. More details on this time-multiplexed architecture can be found in [19].

5. Efficient Methods to design FIR Hilbert transformers

It has been mentioned earlier that the design of low-complexity FIR Hilbert transformers with stringent specifications requires special efficient methods. In the following we will review the most representative and useful methods, which are based on the techniques revised in the previous section.

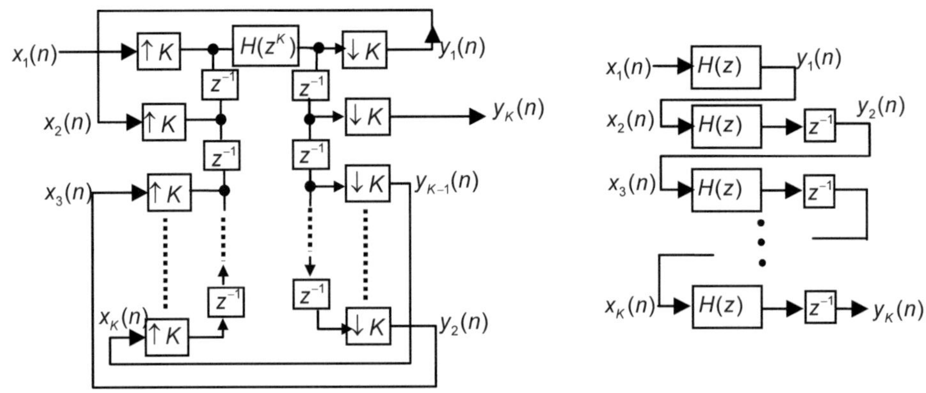

Figure 10. Filtering of a sequence with K identical cascaded filters, (a) PI architecture with only one filter, (b) equivalent single-rate structure.

5.1. Hilbert transformer design based on Frequency Response Masking

This method, proposed in [9], relies on the special case of FRM for the synthesis of a half-band filter $H_{Hb}(z)$ [26]. Consider a half-band filter $H_a(z)$ as a band-edge shaping filter whose transfer function is given by

$$H_a(z) = \tfrac{1}{2} z^{-2K+1} + A(z), \tag{44}$$

$$A(z) = \sum_{k=1}^{K} a(2k-1+2K-1)\left[z^{2k-1-2K+1} + z^{-2k+1-2K+1} \right], \tag{45}$$

where $L_a = 4K - 1$ is the length of $H_a(z)$, with K being an integer greater than zero, and $a(n)$ is the impulse response of $H_a(z)$. Replacing $G(z)$ by $H_a(z)$ in (34) we have

$$H_{Hb}(z) = H_a(z^M) H_{Ma}(z) + [z^{-M(2K-1)} - H_a(z^M)] H_{Mc}(z). \tag{46}$$

We can express the transfer function of the overall half-band filter as

$$H_{Hb}(z)=\left[\tfrac{1}{2}z^{-M(2K-1)}+A(z^M)\right]H_{Ma}(z)+\left[\tfrac{1}{2}z^{-M(2K-1)}-A(z^M)\right]H_{Mc}(z). \tag{47}$$

If M is odd, then either $[\frac{1}{2}z^{-M(2K-1)}+A(z^M)]$ or$[\frac{1}{2}z^{-M(2K-1)}-A(z^M)]$ has a transition band centered at $\pi/2$, just as desired for a half-band filter.

If M is given by the form

$$M=4k+1, \quad \text{with } k=\{0,1,2,...\}, \tag{48}$$

then the pass-band of $H_{Ma}(z)$ is greater than the pass-band of $H_{Mc}(z)$. With ω_p and ω_s denoting the band-edge frequencies of $H_{Hb}(z)$, these values can be express as [26]

$$\omega_p=\frac{2\pi m+\theta}{M}, \qquad \omega_s=\frac{2\pi m+\phi}{M}, \tag{49}$$

where m is an integer less than M. The values m, θ and φ can be calculated as

$$m=\left\lfloor\frac{\omega_p M}{2\pi}\right\rfloor, \qquad \theta=\omega_p M-2\pi m, \qquad \phi=\omega_s M-2\pi m \tag{50}$$

where $\lfloor x \rfloor$ represents the integer part of x, whereas θ and φ are the pass-band and stop-band edges of $H_a(z)$. The pass-band and stop-band edge frequencies of the masking filter $H_{Ma}(z)$, θ_{Ma} and φ_{Ma}, as well as the pass-band and stop-band edge frequencies of the masking filter $H_{Mc}(z)$, θ_{Mc} and φ_{Mc}, are given by

$$\theta_{Ma}=\omega_p=\frac{2\pi m+\theta}{M}, \phi_{Ma}=\frac{2\pi(m+1)-\phi}{M}, \theta_{Mc}=\frac{2\pi m-\theta}{M}, \phi_{Mc}=\omega_s=\frac{2\pi m+\phi}{M} \tag{51}$$

If M is given by the form

$$M=4k+3, \quad \text{con } k=\{0,1,2,...\}. \tag{52}$$

then the passband of $H_{Mc}(z)$ is greater than the pass-band of $H_{Ma}(z)$. In this case the frequencies ω_p and ω_s are given by

$$\omega_p=\frac{2\pi m-\phi}{M}, \omega_s=\frac{2\pi m-\theta}{M}, \tag{53}$$

To calculate m, θ and φ we use the following relations,

$$m=\left\lceil\frac{\omega_s M}{2\pi}\right\rceil, \theta=2\pi m-\omega_s M, \phi=2\pi m-\omega_p M, \tag{54}$$

where $\lceil x \rceil$ represents the rounding operation to the closest integer greater than x. The values, θ_{Ma}, φ_{Ma}, θ_{Mc} and φ_{Mc}, are given by

$$\theta_{Ma} = \frac{2\pi(m-1)+\phi}{M}, \; \phi_{Ma} = \omega_s = \frac{2\pi m-\theta}{M}, \; \theta_{Mc} = \omega_p = \frac{2\pi m-\phi}{M}, \; \phi_{Mc} = \frac{2\pi m+\theta}{M}. \tag{55}$$

If $H_{Ma}(z)$ is a Type I filter with length $L_{Ma} = 4k + 1$, where k is an integer, we can write

$$H_{Ma}(z) = h_{Ma}\left((L_{Ma}-1)/2\right) + \sum_{k=1}^{(L_{Ma}-1)/2} h_{Ma}\left(k+(L_{Ma}-1)/2\right)\left[z^{k-(L_{Ma}-1)/2} + z^{-k-(L_{Ma}-1)/2}\right]. \tag{56}$$

Now we define the transfer functions $B(z)$ and $C(z)$ as

$$\begin{aligned} B(z) = {} & h_{Ma}\left(1+(L_{Ma}-1)/2\right)\left[z^{1-(L_{Ma}-1)/2} + z^{-1-(L_{Ma}-1)/2}\right] + \\ & h_{Ma}\left(3+(L_{Ma}-1)/2\right)\left[z^{3-(L_{Ma}-1)/2} + z^{-3-(L_{Ma}-1)/2}\right] + \ldots \end{aligned} \tag{57}$$

$$\begin{aligned} C(z) = {} & h_{Ma}\left((L_{Ma}-1)/2\right) + \\ & h_{Ma}\left(2+(L_{Ma}-1)/2\right)\left[z^{2-(L_{Ma}-1)/2} + z^{-2-(L_{Ma}-1)/2}\right] + \\ & h_{Ma}\left(4+(L_{Ma}-1)/2\right)\left[z^{4-(L_{Ma}-1)/2} + z^{-4-(L_{Ma}-1)/2}\right] + \ldots \end{aligned} \tag{58}$$

with $h_{Ma}(n)$ as coefficients of the filter $H_{Ma}(z)$. Replacing (57) and (58) in (56), we have

$$H_{Ma}(z) = B(z) + C(z) \cdot \tag{59}$$

In the half-band filter design, the masking filters are related by

$$H_{Mc}(z) = z^{-(L_{Ma}-1)/2} - H_{Ma}(-z) \cdot \tag{60}$$

From (59) and (60), and noting that $B(-z) = -B(z)$ and that $C(-z) = C(z)$, we have

$$H_{Mc}(z) = z^{-(L_{Ma}-1)/2} + B(z) - C(z) \cdot \tag{61}$$

Once known the transfer function of the masking filters from (59) and (61), the overall transfer function of the half-band filter can be obtained by substituting (59) and (61) in (47). Finally, we obtain

$$H_{Hb}(z) = \tfrac{1}{2} z^{-[M(2K-1)+(L_{Ma}-1)/2]} + z^{-M(2K-1)} B(z) + A(z^M)[2C(z) - z^{-(L_{Ma}-1)/2}]. \tag{62}$$

The half-band filter with desired deviation δ and pass-band edge frequency ω_p can be designed with the FRM technique by applying the following steps:

1. Get the optimal value of M, using the following approximation,

$$M_{opt} \approx \frac{1}{2}\sqrt{\frac{2\pi}{\omega_s - \omega_p}} \cdot \tag{63}$$

Note that the obtained value must be rounded to an odd integer.

2. Find if M can be expressed either as in (48) or (52). Then obtain the pass-band and stop-band edge frequencies of the band-edge shaping filter $H_a(z)$, θ and φ, as well as the ones of the masking filter $H_{Ma}(z)$, θ_{Ma} and φ_{Ma}, using (50) and (51) if M is expressed as in (48), or (54) and (55) if M is expressed as in (52).Design these filters with a ripple approx. 15% less than the desired ripple.
3. Obtain $A(z)$ from $H_a(z)$ using (44) and (45). Then obtain $B(z)$ and $C(z)$ from $H_{Ma}(z)$ using (56), (57) and (58).
4. Synthesize the overall structure of (62) in terms of $A(z^M)$, $B(z)$ and $C(z)$.

A Hilbert transformer can be derived from a unity gain half-band filter by subtracting the constant ½ from its transfer function and then modulating the remaining coefficients by $e^{-j\pi n/2}$ (see section 3.1). The transfer function of the Hilbert transformer $H(z)$ is given by [9]

$$H(z) = 2(jz)^{-M(2K-1)}B(jz) + 2A\left((jz)^M\right)[2C(jz) - (jz)^{-(L_{Ma}-1)/2}]. \tag{64}$$

It is worth highlighting that the filter in (64) does not need complex-number arithmetic processing because of the following reasons. First, note that the filter $A(j^M z^M)$ has only real coefficients since the imaginary unit generated by $(jz)^{-n}$ with n odd is eliminated by zero-valued coefficients in these indexes n. Second, note that all the coefficients in $[2C(jz) - (jz)^{-(L_{Ma}-1)/2}]$ are real and all the coefficients in $B(jz)$ are imaginary when L_{Ma} is expressed as $4k$+1, with k integer. Third, the term $(jz)^{-M(2K-1)}$ is always imaginary, since its exponent is always odd. From these reasons, we have that if $B(jz)$ has imaginary coefficients, the term $(jz)^{-M(2K-1)}$ makes them real and the overall filter has real coefficients.

The Hilbert transformer from (64) can be seen as a parallel connection of two branches. In the first branch we have $H_b(z) = 2(jz)^{-M(2K-1)}B(jz)$ and in the second branch we have the cascade of $H_1(z^M)$ and $H_M(z)$, where $H_1(z^M) = 2A(j^M z^M)$ and $H_M(z) = [2C(jz) - (jz)^{-(L_{Ma}-1)/2}]$. This structure is presented in Figure 11. Let us review a different point of view of the FRM technique, presented in [10].

The filter $H_b(z)$ can be seen as a low-order Hilbert transformer, the filter $H_1(z^M)$ as a band-edge shaping filter and $H_M(z)$ as a masking filter. The basic filter $H_b(z)$ provides a low order approximation (with wide transition bandwidth) to the desired specification. The cascaded connection of $H_1(z^M)$ and $H_M(z)$ produces a correction term to the transfer function that decreases the transition bandwidth. The transfer function for the overall filter is given by

$$H(z) = H_1(z^M)H_M(z) + H_b(z). \tag{65}$$

Let the lengths of $H_b(z)$, $H_1(z)$ and $H_M(z)$ be L_b, L_1 and L_M, respectively. The length of $H_1(z^M)H_M(z)$ is $ML_1 + L_M - M$. The delay introduced by $H_b(z)$ and the delay introduced by $H_1(z^M)H_M(z)$ must be the same; otherwise, pure delays must be introduced into the shorter-delay branch to equalize them.

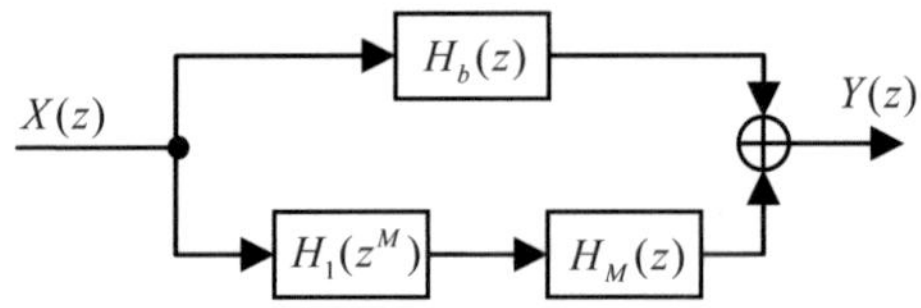

Figure 11. Structure for the synthesis of a Hilbert transformer using the FRM technique.

In order to avoid inserting half-sample delay in the implementation, the parities of L_b and of $(ML_1 + L_M - M)$ must be the same. Furthermore, $H_1(z^M)H_M(z)$must have anti-symmetrical impulse response.

Consider the magnitude response of $H_b(z)$ as $|H_b(e^{j\omega})|$, as shown in Figure 12a, where L_b is even. The computational complexity of $H_b(z)$ is low since its transition band is wide. Now consider the magnitude response of a transition band correction filter, $|H_c(e^{j\omega})|$, as shown in Figure 12b. The Hilbert transformer with sharp transition bandwidth, as shown in Figure 12c, is obtained from the parallel connection of the correction filter with $H_b(z)$.

The objective is designing a correction filter with very low complexity using FRM technique. Consider the band-edge shaping filter $H_1(z)$ with magnitude response $|H_1(e^{j\omega})|$, as shown in Figure 12d. The complexity of $H_1(z)$ is low because it has a wide transition band. Replacing each delay of $H_1(z)$ by M delays, a magnitude response $|H_1(e^{jM\omega})|$ is obtained, as shown in Figure 12e. A masking filter $H_M(z)$, with magnitude response $|H_M(e^{j\omega})|$ shown in Figure 12f, is used to mask the unwanted pass-band of $|H_1(e^{jM\omega})|$. With this masking, the magnitude response $|H_c(e^{j\omega})|$, shown in Figure 12b, is produced. $H_M(z)$ has low complexity because its magnitude response has a wide transition band.

Since the length of $H_b(z)$ is even, the length of $H_1(z^M)$ $H_M(z)$, i.e.,$MN_1 + N_M - M$, must also be even. If M is odd, $N_1$and$N_M$must have different parities. By considering the gain of $|H_M(e^{j\omega})|$ in the vicinity of $\omega = 0$, it is clear that $H_M(z)$ has symmetrical impulse response. Thus, $H_1(z)$ must have anti-symmetrical impulse response to satisfy the condition that $H_1(z^M)$ $H_M(z)$ must have anti-symmetrical impulse response.

The band-edges of $H_b(z)$ and $H_M(z)$ are the same. Let the band-edge of $H_b(z)$ be θ_b and let the band-edge of $H_1(z)$ be θ_1. It can be seen from Figure 12 that the value θ_b satisfies $\theta_b \leq (2\pi - \theta_1)/M$. For an arbitrary value θ_1, it is possible to obtain θ_b if the appropriate value of M is known, which is obtained with the objective of minimizing the overall number of coefficients. Finally, the overall filter is designed with a joint simultaneous optimization of $H_1(z^M)$, $H_b(z)$ and $H_M(z)$. For the examples in [10], the algorithm in [27] was used.

In the following we present a simple example to design an efficient FIR Hilbert transformer with stringent specifications based on the FRM technique. The approach presented in this example follows the procedure based on the four steps to design a half-band filter in terms of filter $A(z)$, $B(z)$ and $C(z)$.

The Hilbert transformer is derived using (64). Since this approach does not require a simultaneous optimization for all the filters, it is simple and straightforward. Additionally, the sensitivity to the rounded coefficients is less since every filter is designed separately [28].

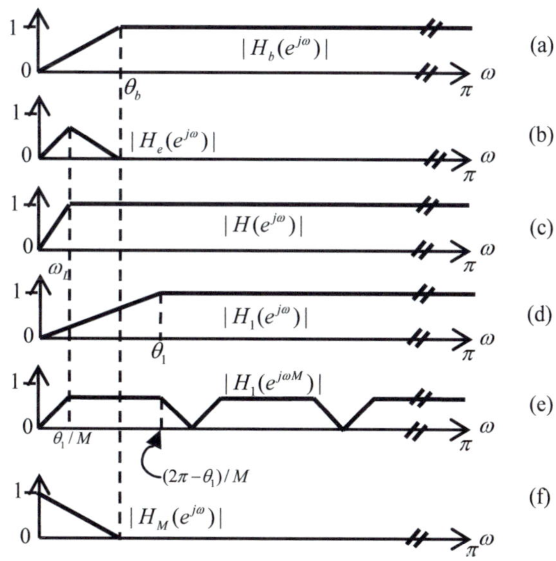

Figure 12. Magnitude responses of the subfilters for even length $H_b(z)$. Note that $\omega_L/2\pi$ is the desired transition bandwidth.

Example 4. The following code example illustrates the design of a Type III Hilbert transformer with δ= 0.0001, ω_L= 0.00125π and ω_H= π− ω_L= 0.99875π using the MATLAB Signal Processing Toolbox and the Filter Design Toolbox to generate the half-band filter. The conversion of filters with argument z into filters with argument jz is performed with the same principle illustrated in the code of example 3.

```
wL=0.00125*pi; wH=0.99875*pi; d=0.0001; % Hilbert transformer specification
wp=pi/2 - wL;  ws=pi/2 + wL;  %find the half-band band-edge frequencies
dp=d/2;        ds=d/2; %find the half-band ripple specification
%--------STEP 1. Optimum M----------
M = (1/2)*round(sqrt(2*pi/(ws-wp))); if mod(M,2)==0; M = M+1; end
%-----------------------------------
%-------STEP 2. Band-edge-Shaping and Masking Filters--------------
if mod((M-1)/4,1)==0;
    m=floor(wp*M/(2*pi));  theta=(wp*M)-(2*pi*m);   phi=(ws*M)-(2*pi*m);
    theta_Ma=wp; phi_Ma=(2*pi*(m+1)-phi)/M; theta_Mc=((2*pi*m)-theta)/M;
    phi_Mc=ws;
else
    m=ceil(ws*M/(2*pi));  theta=(2*pi*m)-(ws*M);   phi=(2*pi*m)-(wp*M);
    theta_Ma=(2*pi*(m-1)+phi)/M;  phi_Ma=ws;  theta_Mc=wp;
    phi_Mc=((2*pi*m)+theta)/M;
```

```
end
La=firpmord([theta/pi  phi/pi],[1 0], [0.85*dp 0.85*ds]);
if mod(La,2)==0; La=La+1; end
if mod((La+1)/4,1)~=0; La=La+2; end
K=(La+1)/4;
[L_Ma,fo,ao,W]=firpmord([theta_Ma/pi  phi_Ma/pi],[1 0], [0.85*dp 0.85*ds]);
if mod(L_Ma,2)==0; L_Ma=L_Ma+1; end
if mod((L_Ma-1)/4,1)~=0; L_Ma=L_Ma+2; end
ha = firhalfband(La-1,theta/pi);
h_Ma = firpm(L_Ma-1,fo,ao,W);
%------------------------------------------------------------
%--------STEP 3. Filters A(z), B(z) and C(z)---------------------
a = ha - [zeros(1,2*K-1) 1/2 zeros(1,2*K-1)];
for i=1:L_Ma; if mod(i-1,2)==0; b(i)=0; c(i)=h_Ma(i); else b(i)=h_Ma(i);
c(i)=0; end
end
delay_b = [zeros(1,M*(2*K-1)) 1 zeros(1,M*(2*K-1))];
delay_c = [zeros(1,(L_Ma-1)/2) 1 zeros(1,(L_Ma-1)/2)];
%------------------------------------------------------------
%--------STEP 4. Form the Hilbert transformer (or half-band filter)-------
a_M = upsample(a,M); a_M = a_M(1:end-(M-1));
index_a_M = [1:length(a_M)];
m_a_M = (ones(1,length(a_M))*j).^(-(index_a_M-1));
index_b = [1:length(b)];
m_b = (ones(1,length(b))*j).^(-(index_b-1));
index_c = [1:length(c)];
m_c = (ones(1,length(c))*j).^(-(index_c-1));
index_delay_b = [1:length(delay_b)];
m_delay_b = (ones(1,length(delay_b))*j).^(-(index_delay_b-1));
index_delay_c = [1:length(delay_c)];
m_delay_c = (ones(1,length(delay_c))*j).^(-(index_delay_c-1));
h = 2*conv(delay_b.*m_delay_b, b.*m_b) +...
    2*conv(a_M.*m_a_M,(2*c.*m_c - delay_c.*m_delay_c));
[H w] = freqz(h,1,10000);
figure; plot(w/pi, abs(H))
%--------------------------------------------------------
```

Figure 13 shows the magnitude response of the obtained Hilbert transformer. The overall structure requires 148 coefficients in total, i.e., 69 for $A(j^M z^M)$, 39 for $B(jz)$ and 40 for $C(jz)$. Clearly, the FRM-based design is a very efficient method comparing to a direct design, like the one presented in example 1, where the estimated length is 4017 and which would require approximately 1005 coefficients.

5.2. Hilbert transformer Design based on Frequency Transformation

The Frequency Transformation (FT) method, developed in [12] to design FIR Hilbert transformers, allows designing FIR Hilbert transformers using a tapped cascaded interconnection of repeated simple basic building blocks constituted by two identical subfilters. To this end, two simple filters are required, namely, a prototype filter and a subfilter. The number of times that the subfilter is used, as well as the coefficients used between each cascaded subfilter, depends on the prototype filter. Both, the prototype filter and the subfilter are Hilbert transformers. The former is always a Type IV filter whereas the latter can be a Type III or Type IV filter according to the type of the desired Hilbert transformer [12].

The prototype filter must be a Type IV FIR filter, i.e., with even length given as $L_P = 2N$ and anti-symmetric impulse response of the form $p(2N-1-n) = -p(n)$. Its frequency response is expressed as

$$P(e^{j\Omega}) = e^{-j((2N-1)\Omega/2 - \pi/2)} P(\Omega), \tag{66}$$

where $P(\Omega)$, the zero-phase term, is given by

$$P(\Omega) = j \cdot \sin\left(\frac{\Omega}{2}\right) \sum_{n=0}^{N-1} \tilde{d}(n) \cos(\Omega n), \tag{67}$$

and Ω denotes the frequency domain of the prototype filter. The coefficients $\tilde{d}(n)$ can be obtained directly from the impulse response $p(n)$ [1].

Using the equivalence $\cos(\Omega n) = T_n\{\cos(\Omega)\}$ [17], where $T_n\{x\}$is the nth-degree Chebyshev polynomial defined with the following recursive formulas,

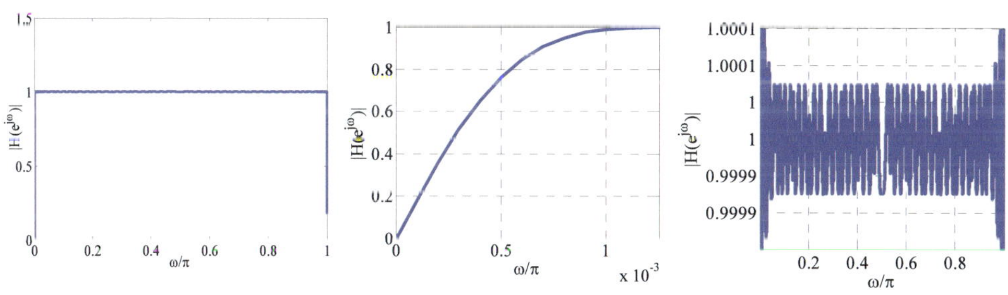

Figure 13. Magnitude responses of the FRM-based Hilbert transformer. From left to right: overall magnitude response, transition bandwidth detail and passband ripple detail.

$$T_0\{x\}=1,\ T_1\{x\}=x \ \text{ and } \ T_n\{x\}=2xT_{n-1}\{x\}-T_{n-2}\{x\}, \tag{68}$$

the zero-phase term can be rewritten as

$$P(\Omega)=j\cdot\sin\left(\tfrac{\Omega}{2}\right)\sum_{n=0}^{N-1}\alpha(n)\left[\cos\left(\Omega\right)\right]^{n}, \tag{69}$$

where $\alpha(n)$ are obtained from $\tilde{d}(n)$ using the coefficients of the Chebyshev polynomials. Based on the equivalence given as

$$\cos\left(2x\right)=1-2\sin^2\left(x\right)=1+2\left(j\cdot\sin x\right)^2, \tag{70}$$

the zero-phase term can be expressed by

$$P(\Omega)=j\cdot\sin\left(\tfrac{\Omega}{2}\right)\sum_{n=0}^{N-1}\alpha(n)\left[1+2\left(j\cdot\sin\left(\tfrac{\Omega}{2}\right)\right)^2\right]^{n}. \tag{71}$$

Consider the case of a Type III subfilter with odd length given as $L_G = 2M + 1$ and anti-symmetric impulse response of the form $g(2M - n) = -g(n)$. Its frequency response is expressed as

$$G(e^{j\omega})=e^{-j(2M\omega/2)}G(\omega), \tag{72}$$

where $G(\omega)$ is the zero-phase term, given by

$$G(\omega)=j\cdot\sum_{n=1}^{M}c(n)\sin(\omega n). \tag{73}$$

The coefficients $c(n)$ can be obtained directly from $g(n)$ [1]. Note that the term $G(\omega)$ can be put in (71) by using the following expression,

$$j\cdot\sin\left(\tfrac{\Omega}{2}\right)=j\cdot\sum_{n=1}^{M}c(n)\sin(\omega n), \tag{74}$$

resulting in

$$H(\omega)=j\cdot\sum_{n=1}^{M}c(n)\sin(\omega n)\sum_{n=0}^{N-1}\alpha(n)\left[1+2\left(j\cdot\sum_{n=1}^{M}c(n)\sin(\omega n)\right)^2\right]^{n}, \tag{75}$$

where $H(\omega)$ is the zero-phase term of the overall filter. Therefore, the frequency transformation is obtained from (74) and is given by

$$\Omega=2\sin^{-1}\left[\sum_{n=1}^{M}c(n)\sin(\omega n)\right]. \tag{76}$$

Equation (76) implies that the magnitude response of the prototype filter is preserved, but its frequency domain is changed by the subfilter.

The transfer function of the overall Hilbert transformer is given as

$$H(z) = G(z)\sum_{n=0}^{N-1} z^{-2M(N-1-n)}\alpha(n)\left[H_1(z)\right]^n, \; H_1(z) = z^{-2M} + 2G^2(z) \tag{77}$$

with $G(z)$ being the transfer function of the subfilter.

For a desired Hilbert transformer specification expressed as in (17), the magnitude response $|P(\Omega)|$ of the prototype filter must satisfy the following condition,

$$(1-\delta) \le \left|P(\Omega)\right| \le (1+\delta), \quad \text{for } \Omega_L \le \Omega \le \pi, \tag{78}$$

with Ω_L being the lower band-edge frequency of the prototype filter. The magnitude response of the subfilter, $|G(\omega)|$, must fulfill simultaneously

$$v_d - \delta_G \le \left|G_0(\omega)\right| \le 1, \quad \text{for } \omega_L \le \omega \le \pi - \omega_L, \tag{79}$$

$$v_d = \tfrac{1}{2} + \tfrac{1}{2}\sin\left(\tfrac{\Omega_L}{2}\right), \; \delta_G = \tfrac{1}{2} - \tfrac{1}{2}\sin\left(\tfrac{\Omega_L}{2}\right). \tag{80}$$

The design procedure proposed in [12] starts with an arbitrary prototype filter, and then the subfilter is designed accordingly.

Note that the complexity of the subfilter depends almost exclusively on its transition bandwidth, since its ripple specification is considerably relaxed. Similarly, the prototype filter is a low-complexity filter because, even though its ripple specification is strict, its transition bandwidth is relaxed. The relaxed ripple specification of the subfilter makes it suitable to be implemented as a simple, multiplierless system with rounded coefficients [13]. Additionally, it was observed in [13] that the repeated use of identical subfilters can be avoided by taking advantage of the PI technique, which has been introduced in sub-section 4.4. Therefore, a time-multiplexed design with lower area can be obtained.

Figure 14 presents the PI-based architecture proposed in [13]. This structure was straightforwardly derived from [19], where a similar example is given for the sharpening technique of [22]. Additionally, the design of the Hilbert transformer was made multiplierless by applying rounding to the coefficients of the prototype filter and the subfilter.

Instead of choosing an arbitrary prototype filter as in [12], a heuristic search was employed to select the prototype filter and the subfilter, such that the proposed architecture uses a number of coefficients less or equal to 0.25 times the estimated number of multipliers required in a direct design using the Parks-McClellan algorithm.

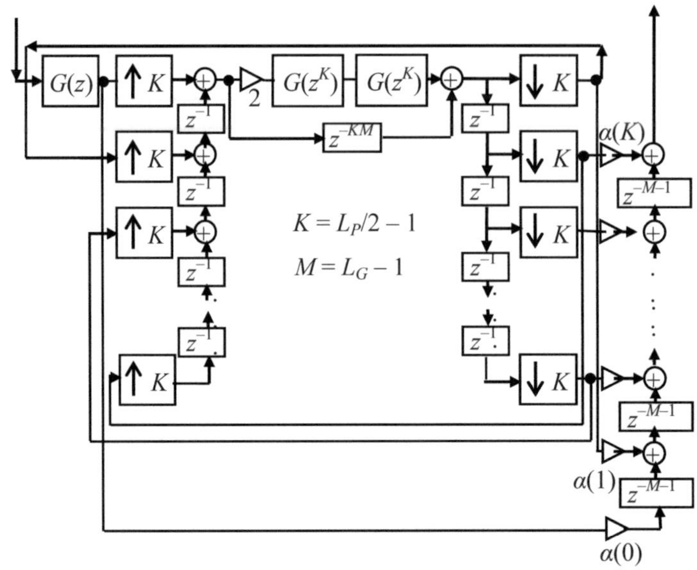

Figure 14. PI-based structure with three subfilters [13].

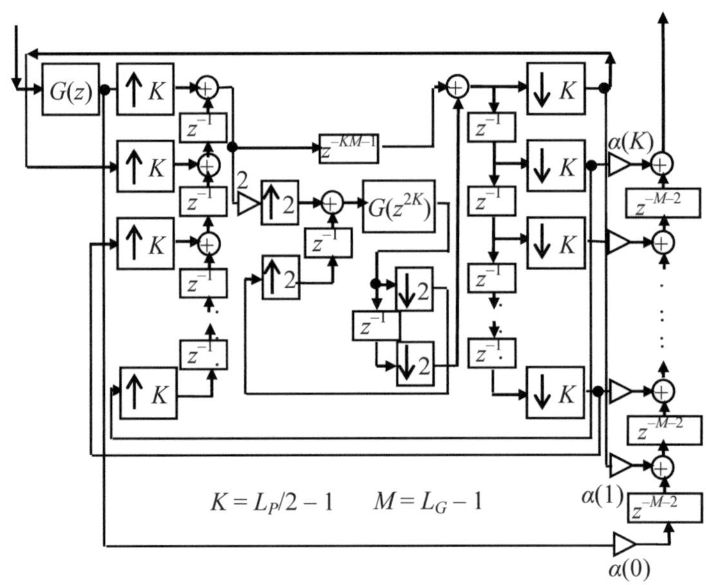

Figure 15. PI-based structure with two subfilters [14].

In [14] the authors observed that the cascaded interconnection of the two subfilters $G(z)$ required to build $H_1(z)$ can be decoupled and also implemented with the PI technique. Thus, the PI-based architecture shown in Figure 15, which only requires two subfilters, was obtained. The approach of PI-based architectures for FT designs was further developed in

[15], and a simple procedure to derive a PI-based structure from a FT-based design with identical subfilters was proposed. With this procedure, the architecture presented in Figure 16 was proposed for Hilbert transformers, where only a simple subfilter is required.

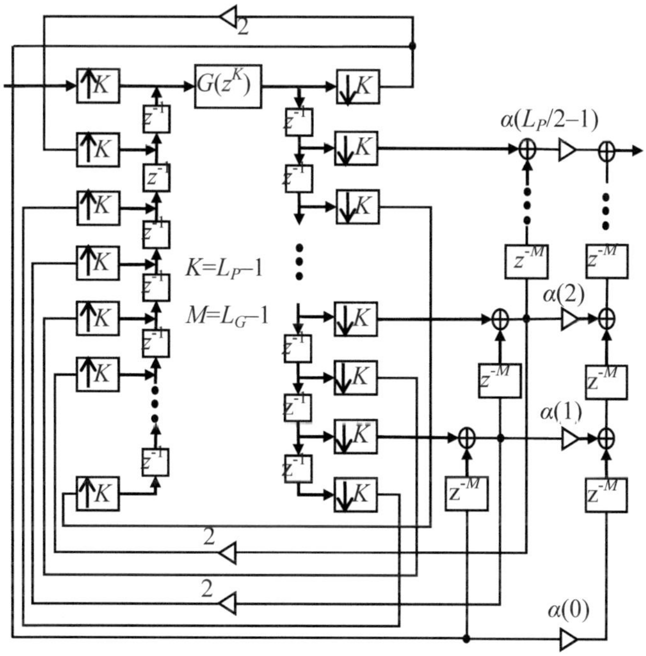

Figure 16. PI-based structure with one subfilter [15].

An important insight proposed in [14] was avoiding the arbitrary selection of the prototype filter as in [12] through the optimized search of the adequate prototype filter, such that a cost metric is minimized. Since multipliers are the most expensive elements in digital filters, reducing the overall number of coefficients is the goal. In general terms, this is equivalent to improve the original heuristic search proposed in [13]. From (78), (79) and (80) it can be observed that the prototype filter and the subfilter can be designed if the frequency Ω_L is known. The problem consists on finding the optimal frequency Ω_L.

Consider a function $\phi(\delta, \omega_L)$, which can estimate with an acceptable exactitude the length of a HT in terms of its ripple δ and its lower passband edge ω_L, such as the one presented in (18). We have, for the prototype filter and the subfilter,

$$L_G \approx \hat{L}_G = \phi(\delta_G / v_d,\ \omega_L), \tag{81}$$

$$L_P \approx \hat{L}_P = \phi(\delta,\ \Omega_L), \tag{82}$$

where $\hat{L}_G$ and $\hat{L}_P$ are the respective approximations to the lengths of the subfilter, L_G, and the prototype filter, L_P, whereas v_d and δ_G are given in (80). Clearly, $\hat{L}_G$ and $\hat{L}_P$ are given as functions of the ripple and transition band of the subfilter and of the prototype filter, respectively.

For the previously revised PI-based structures, it is always possible to express the overall number of multipliers m in terms of the numbers of multipliers of the prototype filter and the subfilter as,

$$m = f(m_G,\ m_P), \tag{83}$$

$$m_G \approx C \cdot L_G, \tag{84}$$

$$m_P = L_P / 2, \tag{85}$$

where m_P and m_G are taken from (19).

Substituting v_d and δ_G from (80) in (81), and using the approximations (81) and (82) respectively in (84) and (85) we have

$$m(\delta,\ \omega_L,\ \Omega_L) \approx f\left(C \cdot \phi\left(\tfrac{1-\sin(\Omega_L/2)}{1+\sin(\Omega_L/2)},\ \omega_L\right),\ \tfrac{1}{2} \cdot \phi(\delta,\ \Omega_L)\right). \tag{86}$$

Note that, even though $m(\delta, \omega_L, \Omega_L)$ is a function of δ, ω_L and Ω_L, the values δ and ω_L are known a priori because they are given by the problem at hand (see (17)). Therefore, since the unique unknown is Ω_L, the approach consists in finding the optimum value Ω^*_L for Ω_L, with $0 < \Omega_L < \pi$, such that $m(\delta, \omega_L, \Omega_L)$ is minimized. This optimization problem is given as

$$\begin{aligned} &\min_{\Omega_L \in \mathbb{R}} m(\delta,\ \omega_L,\ \Omega_L) \\ &\text{such that } 0 < \Omega_L < \pi, \end{aligned} \tag{87}$$

where $m(\delta, \omega_L, \Omega_L)$ is given in (86). The result obtained from (86) is an estimation which depends on the exactitude of the function $\phi(\delta, \omega_L)$.

Equation (18) was utilized in [17] as the function $\phi(\delta, \omega_L)$. However, this function does not give good length estimation for filters with a huge ripple (like the subfilters in the FT method). Using the proposal from [29] as starting point, we have recently derived the following more accurate formula,

$$\begin{aligned} \phi(\delta,\ \omega_L) = \frac{1}{2} + &\left[\frac{1.101[-\log_{10}(\delta)]^{1.1}}{\left(\frac{\omega_L}{2\pi}\right)} + 1\right] \cdot \left[\frac{2}{3\pi}\arctan\left\{\left[2.325[0.30103 - \log_{10}(\delta)]^{-0.445} \cdot \ldots\right.\right.\right. \\ &\left.\left.\left.\left(\tfrac{\omega_L}{2\pi}\right)^{-1.39}\right]\left[\frac{1}{0.5 - \left(\frac{\omega_L}{2\pi}\right)}\right]\right\} + \frac{1}{6}\right]. \end{aligned} \tag{88}$$

Thus, the FT method consists on finding the optimum value Ω_L by solving (87). With this value, the prototype filter and the subfilter are designed as given in (78) and (79). Finally, the coefficients $\alpha(n)$ are found from the prototype filter coefficients by relating (67) and (69) and the overall filter is synthesized by using any of the structures existing in literature [13]-[15] or [17].

Example 5. The following code example illustrates the design of a Type III Hilbert transformer with δ= 0.004, ω_L= 0.01π and ω_H= π− ω_L= 0.99π using the MATLAB Signal Processing Toolbox. The optimized value for Ω_L is Ω^*_L = 0.2237π and the lengths for the prototype filter and the subfilter are, respectively, L_P = 14 and L_G = 31. The value Ω^*_L has been optimized to minimize the number of coefficients in the structure of Figure 16. This code makes use of the MATLAB function ChebyshevPoly.m, which is available online [30].

```
%*********** INITIAL DATA ****************
L_g=31;  wl=0.01*pi;  L_p=14;   Om_L=0.2237*pi;
%************** SUBFILTER*********************
wH=pi-wl;    dG = (1/2) - (1/2)*sin(Om_L/2);
vd = (( 1 - sin(Om_L/2) )/2) + sin(Om_L/2);
g = firpm(L_g-1,[wl/pi wH/pi],[vd vd],'hilbert');
%*************PROTOTYPE FILTER****************
[p]=firpm(L_p-1,[Om_L/pi 1],[1 1],'hilbert');
%***************BASIC BUILDING BLOCK H1*******************
r1=2*conv(g,g);
delay=[zeros(1,L_g-1) 1 zeros(1,L_g-1)];
h1=r1+delay;
%**************ALPHA COEFFICIENTS FROM CHEBYSHEV POLYNOMIAL *************
N = L_p/2
for mm=1:N;  d(mm)=2*(p((N+1)-mm)); end
D(N)=2*d(N);
for Mm=fliplr([3:N]);  D(Mm-1)=(2*d(Mm-1))+(D(Mm));  D(1)=d(1)+((1/2)*D(2));
end
tt=0;
for nn=fliplr([0:N-1]); tk=ChebyshevPoly(nn); T(nn+1,:)=[zeros(1,tt) tk'] ;
  tt=tt+1;
end
ll=sum((D'*[ones(1,N)]).*T);
alpha=fliplr(ll);
%**************OVERALL FILTER *************
upper_branch = g;   lower_branch = g*alpha(1);  h = lower_branch;
for ii=1:N-1;
upper_branch = conv(upper_branch,h1);
lower_branch = conv(h, [zeros(1,L_g-1) 1 zeros(1,L_g-1)]);
h=lower_branch + alpha(ii+1)*upper_branch;%Overall Hilbert transformer
end
[H w]=freqz(h,1,1000);
figure
plot(w/pi,abs(H))
```

Figure 17 shows the magnitude response of the obtained Hilbert transformer. The overall structure requires only 15 coefficients in total, i.e., 7 structural coefficients, $\alpha(0)$ to $\alpha(6)$, and 8 coefficients for the subfilter $G(z)$. Compared to a direct design, where the estimated length is 287 and which would require approximately 72 coefficients, The FT-based design achieves almost a 75% of reduction in the number of distinct required coefficients.

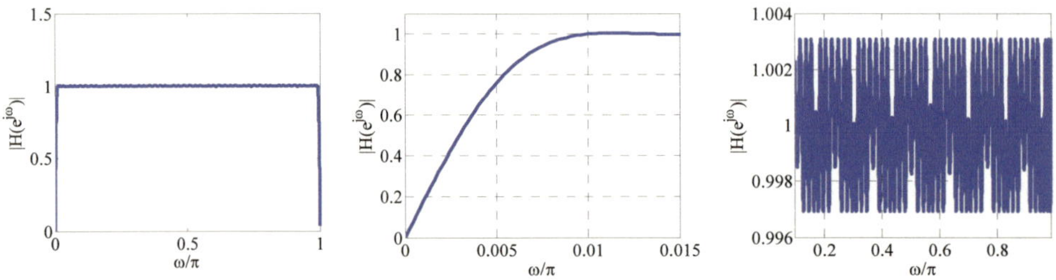

Figure 17. Magnitude responses of FT-based Hilbert transformer. From left to right: overall magnitude response, transition bandwidth detail and passband ripple detail.

5.3. Hilbert transformer design based on Piecewise Polynomial Sinusoidal technique

This method to synthesize Hilbert transformers, first proposed in [25] and then detailed in [11], is based on the previous method [31] and on a modification to the method [32]-[33]. The method stems from a windowing technique for Type III and Type IV FIR filters of order $2N$ and $2N$-1, respectively. The basic windowing technique for Type III filters is expressed as

$$h(n) = w(n)h_0(n), \tag{89}$$

where

$$h_0(n) = \begin{cases} 0 & \text{for } n \text{ odd} \\ \dfrac{1-\cos((n-N)\pi)}{(n-N)\pi} & \text{for n even} \end{cases} \tag{90}$$

is an ideal impulse response, $w(n)$ is the window function and N is odd. Similarly, an ideal odd-order impulse response can be expressed as

$$h_0(n) = \frac{1}{(n-(2N-1)/2)\pi}. \tag{91}$$

The overall transfer function can be expressed in the following way,

$$F(z) = \begin{cases} \sum_{n=0}^{2N} W(n)[1-\cos((n-N)\pi)]z^{-n}, & \text{Type III} \\ \sum_{n=0}^{2N-1} W(n)z^{-n}, & \text{Type IV} \end{cases} \tag{92}$$

with

$$W(n)=\begin{cases} w(n-N)/[\pi(n-N)], \\ w(n-(2N-1/2))/[\pi(n-(2N-1/2))]. \end{cases} \tag{93}$$

$W(n)$ is an impulse response satisfying $W(2N-n)=-W(n)$ for $n=0, 1, \ldots, N-1$, $W(N)=0$, and $W(2N-1-n)=-W(n)$ for $n=0, 1, \ldots, N$, for Types III and IV respectively. Additionally, $w(n)$ is a positive and symmetric window function for all n.

A way to generate the piecewise-polynomial-sinusoidal transfer function $F(z)$ is to consider the following transfer function:

$$G(z)=\sum_{n=0}^{N_s} W(n)z^{-n}(e^{j(n-N)\pi})=\sum_{n=0}^{N_s} W(n)\left[1-(\cos((n-N)\pi)+j\sin((n-N)\pi))\right]z^{-n}, \tag{94}$$

where N_s is $2N$ or $2N-1$ for Types III and IV, respectively. From (92) it follows that $F(z)$ can be expressed as

$$F(z)=\mathrm{Re}\left\{\sum_{n=0}^{N_s} W(n)z^{-n}+z^{-n}(e^{j(n-N)\pi})\right\}=\mathrm{Re}\left\{\sum_{n=0}^{N_s} W(n)\left[1-z^{-N\pi}(z^{-1}e^{j\pi})^{n}\right]\right\}. \tag{95}$$

In [32] a wideband FIR filter is obtained by first generating the envelope filter with $W(n)$ for $n=0, 1, \ldots, 2N$ $[2N-1]$ as the impulse-response coefficients. This impulse response is designed to become piecewise polynomial. The coefficient values of this envelope filter are modified by multiplying them with $[1-\cos(n-N)\pi]$ for Type III, which gives $F(z)$. From (92) it can be seen that for Type IV the piecewise-polynomial-sinusoidal impulse response coincides with the piecewise-polynomial impulse response, i.e., the constant part of the real part in (95).

Let us consider the simpler case Type IV filter. The overall transfer function, denoted by $H(z)$, is constructed as presented previously in sub-section 4.3. We will repeat the equation here for convenience,

$$H(z)=\sum_{m=1}^{M} z^{-N_m}H_m(z)+z^{-\hat{N}}\hat{H}(z). \tag{96}$$

Recall that the integers N_m in the delay terms z^{-N_m} satisfy $N_1=0$ and $N_{m+1}>N_m$ for $m=1, 2, \ldots, M-1$, and the order of $H_m(z)$ is $2(N-N_m)-1$. The impulse response is given for $n=0, 1, 2, \ldots, N-N_m-1$by Lth order polynomials as follows

$$h_m(n)=\sum_{r=0}^{L} a_m^{(L)}(r)n^r \tag{97}$$

Additionally, $z^{-\hat{N}}\hat{H}(z)$ is a conventional $[2N-1]$th-order Type IV direct-form transfer function with the additional impulse response coefficients at $n=N-c, \ldots, N-1$, where $c=$

$\lceil T/2 \rceil$ and T is the number of additional coefficients at the center of the filter. The delay terms in (96) are used to shift the center of the symmetry at the desired location, which occurs at $n = (2N - 1)/2$.

In order to indicate that the overall filter has a piecewise-polynomial impulse response the time interval $[0, N - 1]$ is divided into the following M subintervals:

$$X_M = [N_m, N_{m+1} - 1] \text{ for } m = 1, 2, \ldots, M - 1 \tag{98}$$

and

$$X_M = [N_M, N]. \tag{99}$$

First, we have that$X_1 = [0, N_2 - 1]$ because $N_1 = 0$, Secondly, the overall impulse response can be studied up to $n = N - 1$ because of the odd symmetry. The impulse response on X_m can be expressed as

$$h(n) = \sum_{m=1}^{M} \tilde{h}_m(n), \tag{100}$$

where

$$\tilde{h}_M(n) = \sum_{k=1}^{m} \left[\sum_{r=0}^{L} \left[a_k^{(L)}(r)(n - N_M)^r \right] \right] \tag{101}$$

for $m = 1, 2, \ldots, M - 1$ and

$$\tilde{h}_M(n) = \sum_{k=1}^{M} \left[\sum_{r=0}^{L} \left[a_k^{(L)}(r)(n - N_M)^r \right] \right] + h'(n), \tag{102}$$

which equals the overall impulse response and where $h'(n)$is a conventional direct-form Type IV filter with nonzero coefficients for $n = N - c, \ldots, N - 1$, in which $c = \lceil T/2 \rceil$ and T is the number of separately generated additional center coefficients. The slices N_ms should be chosen so that $|N_2 - N_1| \neq |N_3 - N_2| \neq \ldots \neq |N_M - N_{M-1}|$,where $N_1 = 0$ and M is the number of subintervals in the overall impulse response.

Based on the above equations, in each X_m for $m = 1, 2, \ldots, M$, a separate piecewise-polynomial impulse response can be generated. In addition, in the X_M, there are additional center coefficients, which are of great importance for fine-tuning the overall filter to meet the given criteria.

Given the filter criteria as well as the design parameters M,N, L, N_m's, and the number of center coefficients included in $\hat{H}(z)$, the overall problem is solvable by using linear programming.

6. Conclusion

In this chapter we have studied the Hilbert transform relations existing among the real part and the imaginary part of complex analytic signals. The importance of these signals has been highlighted in terms of spectral efficiency, i.e., the analytic signals do not have spectral components in their negative-frequency side. For discrete-time sequences, this characteristic holds for the negative-frequency side in every Nyquist period.

The Hilbert transformer has been introduced as a special type of FIR filter which is the key processing system to generate analytic signals. The design of such important filter is, of course, straightforward with the aid of an important filter design tool: the MATLAB Signal Processing Toolbox. However, this direct design method, shown as a very simple and convenient MATLAB code, cannot be efficiently applied for more stringent and realistic specifications. We have presented a concise explanation of the relation of Hilbert transformers and half-band filters because this relation, as has been observed from literature, is one of the most important characteristics to overcome this problem.

The efficient methods to design low-complexity FIR Hilbert transformers with strict specifications have been detailed. Three methods have been analyzed, namely, Frequency-Response Masking (FRM), Frequency Transformation (FT) and Piecewise-Polynomial Sinusoidal (PPS). These schemes are based on three different approaches to design efficient FIR filtering. FRM is a periodical subfilter based method, FT is an identical subfilter based method and PPS is a piecewise-polynomial based method. Additionally, it has been observed that FRM and PPS are fully parallel approaches and do not take direct advantage of hardware multiplexing. On the other hand, we have shown that FT allows area-efficient architectures by multiplexing a simple subfilter.

Finally, the FRM and the time-multiplexed FT approach have been illustrated in MATLAB, with the aid of the Signal Processing Toolbox. Even though the underlying theory on the efficient techniques to design FIR Hilbert transformers is specialized, the MATLAB codes have been preserved in a simple and as clear as possible presentation. The presented codes allow a clearer understanding on such specialized techniques and, at the same time, can serve as a basis for more elaborated algorithms and further research on this fertile area.

Author details

David Ernesto Troncoso Romero and Gordana Jovanovic Dolecek
Department of Electronics, Institute INAOE, Tonantzintla, Puebla, Mexico

Acknowledgement

Special thanks to Miriam G. Cruz Jimenez for her valuable assistance in the development of this chapter.

7. References

[1] Andreas Antoniou (2006) Digital Signal Processing. McGraw Hill, USA.

[2] Alan V. Oppenheim, Ronald W. Schafer (1989) Discrete-Time Signal Processing. Prentice Hall, USA.

[3] R. L. C. Van Spaendonck, F. C. A. Fernandez, R. G. Baraniuk and J.T. Fokkema (2002) Local Hilbert transformation for seismic attributes. EAGE 64th Conference and Technical Exhibition.

[4] Jose G. R. C. Gomes and A. Petraglia (2002) An analog Sampled-data DSB to SSB converter using recursive Hilbert transformer for accurate I and Q channel matching. IEEE Trans. Circ. Syst. II, vol. 49, no. 3, pp. 177-187.

[5] Michael Feldman (2011) Hilbert transform in vibration analysis. Mechanical Systems and Signal Processing, no. 25, pp. 735-802.

[6] R. Ansari (1987) IIR discrete-time Hilbert transformers. IEEE Trans. Acoust. Speech and Signal Processing, vol. ASSP-35, no. 8, pp. 1116-1119.

[7] Ljiljana D. Milic and Miroslav D. Lutovac (1999) Approximate linear phase Hilbert transformer. IEEE International Conference on Telecommunications in Modern Satellite, Cable and Broadcasting Services, TELSIKS´99, pp. 119-124.

[8] S. Samadi, Y. Igarashi and H. Iwakura (1999) Design and multiplierless realization of maximally flat FIR digital Hilbert transformers. IEEE Trans. Signal Processing, vol. 47, no. 7, pp. 1946-1953.

[9] Yong C. Lim and Y. Yu (2005) Synthesis of Very sharp Hilbert transformer using the Frequency-Response Masking technique. IEEE Trans. on Signal Processing, vol. 53, no. 7, pp. 2595-2597.

[10] Yong C. Lim, Y. Yu and T. Saramaki (2005) Optimum masking levels and coefficient sparseness for Hilbert transformers and Half-band filters designed using the Frequency-Response Masking technique. IEEE Trans. Circuits and Sistems-I: Reg. Papers, vol. 52, no. 11, pp. 2444-2453.

[11] R. Lehto, T. Saramaki and O. Vainio (2010) Synthesis of wide-band linear-phase FIR filters with a piecewise-polynomial-sinusoidal impulse response. Circ. Syst. and Signal Process., vol 29, no. 1, pp. 25-50.

[12] Y. L. Tai and T. P. Lin (1989) Design of Hilbert transformers by multiple use of same subfilter, Electronics Letters, vol. 25, no.19, pp. 1288-1290.

[13] M. G. C. Jimenez, D. E. T. Romero and G. J. Dolecek (2010) On design of a multiplierless very sharp Hilbert transformer by using identical subfilters. In Proc. 53rd. IEEE Int. Midwest Symp. on Circ. and Syst., MWSCAS'10, pp. 757-760.

[14] D. E. T. Romero, M. G. C. Jimenez and G. J. Dolecek (2012) Optimal design of multiplierless Hilbert transformers based on the use of a simple subfilter (in Spanish). Computación y Sistemas, vol. 16, no. 1, pp. 111-120.

[15] D. E. T. Romero, M. G. C. Jimenez and G. J. Dolecek (2012) A new Pipelined-Interleaved structure for FIR Hilbert transformers based on frequency transformation technique. IEEE 5th Int. Symp. on Communications, Control and Signal Process, ISCCSP'12 (In press).

[16] Y. C. Lim (1986) Frequency-Response Masking Approach for the synthesis of Sharp Linear Phase Digital filters. IEEE Transactions on Circuits and Systems, vol. CAS-33, no. 4, pp. 357-364.
[17] T. Saramaki (1987) Design of FIR Filters as a Tapped Cascaded Interconnection of Identical Subfilters. IEEE Transactions on Circuits and Systems, vol. CAS-34, no. 9, pp. 1011-1029.
[18] S. M. M. Zanjani, S. M. Fakhraie, O. Shoaei and M. E. Salehi (2006) Design of FIR filters using identical subfilters of even length. In Proc. IEEE Int. Conf. on Microelectronics, ICM'06, pp. 83-86.
[19] Z. Jiang and A. N. Wilson (1997) Efficient digital filtering architectures using Pipelining/Interleaving. IEEE Transactions on Circuits and Systems- II: Analog and Digital Signal Processing, vol. 44, no. 2, pp. 110-119.
[20] Richard G. Lyons (2004) Understanding Digital Signal Processing. Prentice Hall.
[21] H. W. SchüBler and P. Steffen (1998) Halfband filters and Hilbert transformers. Circuits and Systems signal Processing, vol. 17, no.2, pp. 137-164.
[22] J. F. Kaiser and R. W. Hamming (1977) Sharpening the response of a symmetric non-recursive filter by multiple use of the same filter. IEEE Transactions Acoustics Speech. Signal Processing, ASSP-25, pp. 415-422.
[23] Sanjit K. Mitra, James F. Kaiser (1993) Handbook for Digital Signal Processing. John Wiley & Sons, USA.
[24] R. Lehto, T. Saramaki and O. Vainio (2007) Synthesis of wide-band linear-phase FIR filters with a piecewise-polynomial-sinusoidal impulse response. IEEE International Symp. Circuits and Systems ISCAS 2007, pp. 2052-2055.
[25] R. Lehto and O. Vainio (2008) Hilbert transformers with a piecewise-polynomial-sinusoidal impulse response, IEEE International Symp. Circuits and Systems ISCAS 2008, pp. 2450-2453.
[26] T. Saramaki, Y. C. Lim and R. Yang (1995) The synthesis of halfband filter using frequency-response masking technhique. IEEE Trans. Circuits Syst., vol. 42, no. 1, pp. 58-60.
[27] T. Saramaki, J. Yli-Kaakinen and H. Johansson (2003) Optimization of frequency-response-masking based FIR filters. Circuits, Syst. Signal Processing, vol. 12, no. 5, pp. 563-590.
[28] Y. C. Lim, Y. Yu, K. L. Teo and T. Saramaki (2007) FRM-based FIR filters with optimum finite word-length performance. IEEE Trans. Signal Processing, vol. 55, no. 6, pp. 2914-2924.
[29] K. Ichige, M. Iwaki and R. Ischii (2000) Accurate estimation of minimum filter length for optimum FIR digital filters. Circuits and Systems II: IEEE Trans. on Analog and Digital signal process, vol 47, pp. 1008-1016.
[30] Matlab Chebyshev polynomial function at http://www.mathworks.fr/matlabcentral/fileexchange/35051-2-dimensional-filter-design-using-mcclellan-transformation/content/Filter%202D%20McClellan/ChebyshevPoly.m (last accessed 7-5-2012)

[31] R. Lehto, T. Saramaki and O. Vainio (2007) Synthesis of narrowband linear-phase FIR filters with a piecewise-polynomial impulse response. IEEE Trans. Circuits and Syst. I, vol.54, no. 10, pp. 2262-2276.

[32] S. Chu and S. Burrus (1984) Efficient recursive realizations of FIR filters, Part I: The filter structures. IEEE Circuits, Syst. Signal Process. , vol. 3, no.1, pp. 2-20.

[33] S. Chu and S. Burrus (1984) Efficient recursive realizations of FIR filters, Part II: Design and applications. IEEE Circuits, Syst. Signal Process. , vol. 3, no.1, pp. 21-57.

Chapter 20

Detection of Craters and Its Orientation on Lunar

Nur Diyana Kamarudin, Kamaruddin Abd. Ghani, Siti Noormiza Makhtar, Baizura Bohari and Noorlina Zainuddin

Additional information is available at the end of the chapter

http://dx.doi.org/10.5772/48526

1. Introduction

Craters are features commonly used as research landmarks compared with the other landforms such as rocks, mountains, cliffs and many others. Because of their simple and unique geometry and relatively established appearance under different conditions, the authors decided to select craters as ideal landmarks for detection and spacecraft localization. This chapter focuses on identification of craters in terms of their characteristics and detection of these visual features of the moon to determine a safe landing site for a lunar Lander. Cheng et al. proposed using craters as landmarks for navigation purposes because the geometric model grants a robust detection under different lighting conditions. Moreover, craters appear in enough density on most planetary system bodies of interest and they are also known to have fairly stable appearance or shapes over time or under different conditions and environments. These special features make them an appropriate type of landmark to observe. Currently, there is a lot of on-going studies mainly on craters detection and optical navigation systems for the moon and these studies still adopt a complex and similar approach such as detection using the Hough transform method. To part from this limitation, the authors decided to build a simple algorithm for detecting craters on the moon's surface which will detect the craters based on two important measurements including the distance and angle measurements. The advantages of using this approach are threefold: (1) its uncomplicatedness (2) fast detection (3) can be used further in ellipse reconstruction algorithm to determine the position and orientation of the crater. This chapter will discuss the method of employing MATLAB and image processing tool on an optical image as well as the morphological image detection fundamentals. In addition, some geometrical projection analysis in reconstructing an ellipse as a disc will be evaluated in order to obtain the orientation of the disc (crater) for an autonomous optical navigation system.

1.1. Background and context

The first lunar exploration spacecraft named Luna 1 was flown to the moon on January 1959 [21]. Nonetheless, this mission did not give too much impact as it did not land on the moon itself. Due to the enthusiasm to continue the journey of previous research pioneers, Luna 2 became the first spacecraft to land on the moon's surface in late 1959 [21]. These histories of moon explorations became a motivation for a new researcher and moon explorer to find out more about Lunar and its unique features.

A crater plays a vital feature to estimate the age of the moon's surface when any sample specimen is not available [10, 11]. An autonomous crater detection algorithm will help space research scientists to reduce their laboratory works of manually identifying those craters. Previously, several automatic and semi-automatic crater detection algorithms were proposed [12], but their accuracy was not enough for craters chronology and they have yet to be fully tested for practical uses (example: spacecraft navigation). Craters chronology means the history or the sequence of events that formed the craters on the moon's surface and the variety of its features. Optical Landmark Navigation using craters on the planetary surface was first used operationally by the Near Earth Asteroid Rendezvous (NEAR) mission [15, 16]. This mission is to determine the spacecraft orbits and the range of the body for close flybys condition and low attitude orbiting [13].

Many planetary missions such as SELENE (Selenological and Engineering Explorer) and Clementine take the images of the moon's surface for on-going research. This attention to the moon exploratory especially will help us divulge the unimagined information and characteristics of planetary science specifically on the moon's surface. In 2006, a Japanese Lunar Orbiting Spacecraft was launched and was expected to bring a large amount of useful data for on-going planetary research. However, it is known that the images taken under the low sun elevation, such as those from 'Lunar Orbiter' and 'Apollo' are suitable for crater detection as mentioned before to differentiate the 'light and dark patches' for sooner analysis.

Current descent and landing technology for planetary operations, such as those of lunar, is performed by a landing error ellipse greater than 30x100 kilometres without terrain recognition or hazard avoidance capability. Most of the previous research on lunar pin point landing specifically has a limitation such that requires *a priori* reference map describing the past and future lunar imaging and digital elevation map data sets in order to detect the landmarks on a particular planetary surface. Due to this drawback, the authors propose a landmark-based detection algorithm named craters detection algorithm to detect main hazards on the moon's surface independently from those references in order to produce a reliable and repeated identification and detection system. This intelligent imagery-based algorithm will detect craters based on their pointing direction relative to the sun and classification to differentiate between the light and dark patches. Furthermore, by making a match of those detected craters with the internal lunar atlas, the Lander can further determine the spacecraft motion and velocity relative to the lunar surface.

1.2. State of the art

A spacecraft mission on the moon involving Entry, Descent and Landing (EDL) requires precise and intelligent landing techniques. There were numerous previous research efforts and various methods used to determine such landing sites that are safe for a moon Lander. Trying to get a new technique that can search for free hazards locations, this paper will propose an intelligent algorithm described as craters identification algorithm in order to recognize and detect craters consistently and repeatedly over most of the moon's surface. In addition, using geometric recognition techniques, the authors we can also determine the position, attitude, velocity and angular velocity of the spacecraft; the four important parameters used to land safely on the moon by finding a match of those detecting craters to a database containing the 3D locations of the craters (internal lunar atlas).

The lunar surface consists of several hazardous characteristics such as rocks, mountain, boulders, slopes and mainly craters. Particularly, in this paper, the authors choose craters as primary hazard detection because of its geometric shape which makes it easy to identify using image detection codes. Over the years, craters are created as a result of a continuous bombardment of objects from outer space like meteorites, asteroids and comets. All of them strike the lunar surface at various speeds, typically 20 kilometres per second. In addition, unlike the earth, there is no atmosphere on the moon to protect it from collision with other potential impactors.

Previous researchers such as Cheng and Ansar [5] proposed a feature detector and tracker algorithm for detecting craters as mapped landmarks and matched those using applications during EDL for the spacecrafts. In a sequence, one can also determine the position and velocity of the spacecraft using the desired parameters achieved by the matched craters technique mentioned above. For this approach, craters are classified based on their size and orientation of their outlining ellipses. There are databases of previously matched craters to detect the desired impact craters. Position is estimated using subset middle values of at least three matched craters in a linear pose estimation algorithm [6]. By combining the average velocity between two image based position and computed velocity by integrating the accelerometer reading, the actual velocity is dictated by the output of the image processing algorithm.

Continuously, there were preceding research on On-board hazard detection and avoidance for a safe landing which has aimed to autonomously detect the hazards near the landing site and determine a new landing site free from those hazards [7]. In order to detect the potential hazards on the moon's surface, there are specific requirements as agreed by the ALHAT project which will detect the hazards that are 0.3 meters tall or higher and slopes that are 5 degrees or greater mainly for the craters. Moreover, the requirement is not just to detect the hazards with the above mentioned criteria but also must be able to find a safe landing site with a diameter around 15 meters over most of the moon's surface. This proposed system is achieved by using the imaging LIDAR sensors to get the direct measurements of the lunar surface elevation from high altitude. Besides, the probability of the existence of a hazard free landing site is determined as a function of a Lander diameter, hazard map area and rock coverage, and together these procedures are used as guidance for LIDAR sensors and the overall Navigation and Control Architecture.

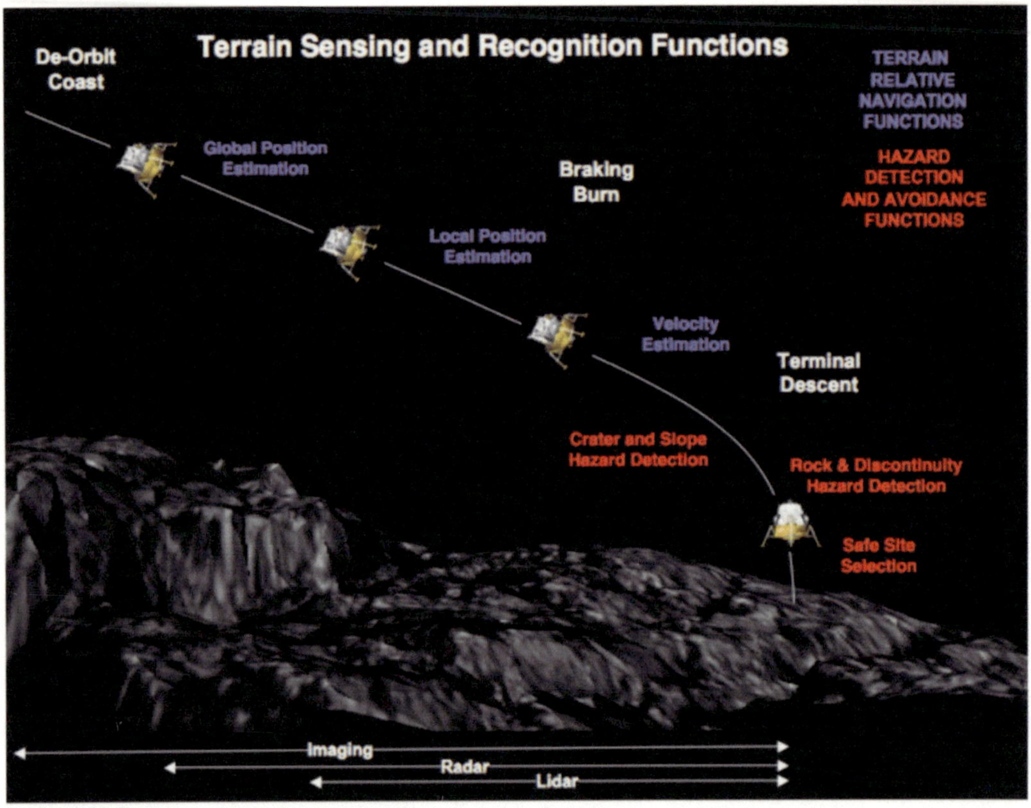

Figure 1. Terrain sensing and recognition functions for safe land site determination [5].

Hazard Detection Avoidance (HDA) and Terrain Relative Navigation (TRN) are on-board capabilities that use sensing and computing technologies to achieve optical safe and precise terrain navigation within 100 meters of a predetermined location on the lunar's surface [8]. They are based on three methods including global position estimation, local position estimation and velocity estimation as illustrated in Figure 1 above. All these functions can be realized using passive imaging or active range sensing. One of the TRN approaches is by using pattern matching which requires *a-priori* reference map describing past and future imaging and digital elevation map datasets (map-dependant system). Pattern matching approach applies landmark (Craters) matching instead of patch correlation and employs passive visible imagery system. There are several parameters required such as diameter of craters, relative distances and angles between landmarks. Craters are usually distinguished in a map of the landing site and then stored in a database. During landing process, craters are detected in descent imagery and are matched as well as compared to the database. Then only the position of the Lander is determined.

Continuous research in developing the greyscale imagery mainly on detecting landform is still being explored within these past few years. In order to detect craters of any particular planetary bodies, one of the approaches is by using the Hough Transform shape detecting assignments [9]. The proposed algorithm focuses on detection of the (sensor independent) geometric features of the impact craters (i.e centre position, craters radius) as well as identification of sensor dependant geometric features such (i.e rim height) as a following task. The use of a simple model (circular shape) for craters detection makes it possible to exploit the algorithm in different operational environments (i.e recognition of Earth and other planetary craters in the Solar System) using data attained by dissimilar sensors such as Synthetic Aperture Radar (SAR). Because of its complex algorithm, Hough Transform is not directly employed to the original image. Some pre-processing steps are necessary to obtain better result and performance of the system as illustrated in Figure 2 below. The Hough Transform has been built by Paul Hough (1962) for the identification of lines in pictures. Describing a circle represented by lines, if the radius is r and centre coordinates represent (a, b), then the parametric representation of a circle:

$$R(x, y) = \{x = a + r\cos\theta,\ y = b + r\sin\theta\} \quad (1)$$

where $\theta = [0, 2\pi]$

Each point (x, y) represents a, b and r parameter is mapped in a cone surface that has the following representation:

$$H(a, b, r) = \{a = x - r\cos\theta,\ b = y - r\sin\theta\} \quad (2)$$

where $\theta = [0, 2\pi]$

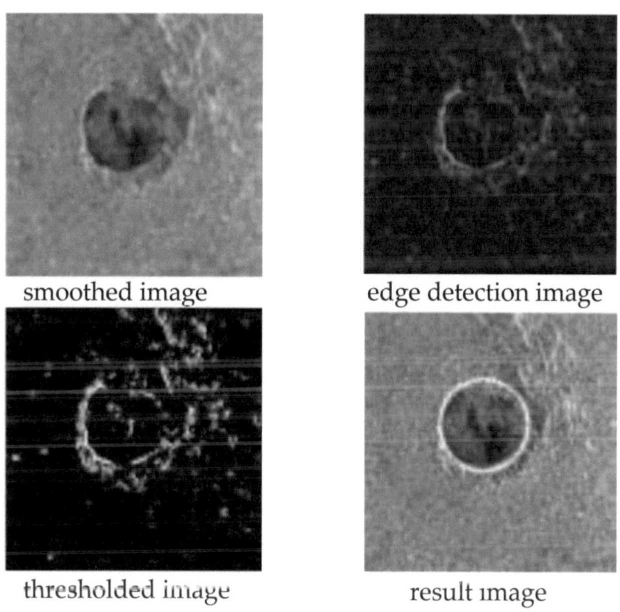

Figure 2. Result obtained using Hough Transform in SAR (Synthetic Aperture Radar) Image [7].

There is also multiple approach algorithms in detecting craters on the lunar's surface as proposed by Sawabe, Matsunaga and Rokugawa, 2005. It is known that the crater's feature changes according to its size. Small craters form a simple circle, and the larger its size, the more complex its shape becomes [3]. This change in feature poses difficult problems to detect craters with different sizes by a single approach. In their data-dependant based algorithm, they defined that a crater is a circular topographical feature in images and a minimum detection crater size is two pixels in radius [13] and it uses data from SELENE (Selenological and Engineering Explorer) to visualize the surface geological settings and the subsurface structure of the Lunar. These approaches are different to the authors' research as they consider the crater to bean ellipse for their detection algorithm. The authors also propose the data independent based algorithm. Four different methods were used with the crater detecting algorithm to find (1) 'shady and sunny' patterns in images with low sun angle, (2) circular features in edge images (3)curves and circles in thinned and connected edge lines, and (4)discrete or broken circular edge lines using fuzzy Hough transform. Besides, the detected craters are also classified by spectral characteristics derived from Clementine UV-Vis multi-spectral images [13]. The main advantages of the proposed algorithm compared to the previous one are that the detection algorithm is uncomplicated and it has an outstanding successful rate of detections. These methods of detection and their determination of accuracy will be evaluated in the experimental results afterwards.

In Landmark Based Pinpoint Landing Simulator (LAMPS) by Cheng and Ansar, a robust yet complex crater detection algorithm has been developed for autonomous spacecraft navigation. Based on their research, craters might have a random appearance based on their ages and sizes. For example, younger craters may have sharper and regular rims [14]. Spatial densities of craters also form the primary basis for assessing the relative and absolute ages of geological units on planetary surfaces [14]. However, typical craters will have ellipse shape in their rims, with a light to dark pattern that is dictated by the sun azimuth and elevation as well as its own topography. In fact, this statement is very similar to the authors' own approach in defining a crater as a composition of light and dark patch. Technically, Cheng and Ansar approach algorithm consists of five major steps which are edge detection, rim edge grouping, ellipse fitting, precision fitting and crater confidence evaluation. Another important property of landmark based detection system is the use of spacecraft pinpoint landing (PPL) for autonomous navigation method. To decrease the probability of landing on a hazard surface, one of the two safe landing proposals must be taken into account: craters hazard detection avoidance, which will detect all hazardous craters upon landing on the moon's surface or pinpoint landing which determines the Lander's position in real time and guide the spacecraft to a safe and free landing site, away from those hazards (craters).

According to recent studies on the size and frequency of the craters on a Mars' surface [17], a sufficient number of adequately sized craters for determining spacecraft position are very likely to be found in descent imagery. For an instance, if the image was taken using a camera field of 45 degrees and is taken from 8km above the surface, there will be an average of 94 craters of less than 200m in diameter. Ideally, from this situation, these craters can be used as landmarks to match a pre-existing crater database and therefore to determine the position of the Lander. This approach of pattern matching will be further used as future works in the authors' research. For the time being, the authors have proposed to use a projection geometry concept in determining the orientation and position of the spacecraft using two vital equations that were discussed later.

As in Figure (3) below, the proposed pinpoint landing is as follow. First, the landing site is pre-determined on the targeted body (moon's surface, Mars' surface, etc) on the earth using orbital imagery, and the landmarks within the landing ellipse (red ellipse) are mapped. During EDL, its preliminary position prior to the landmarks and selected landing site is determined. The Lander's position is then frequently tracked and guided using continuous updates of the Lander's position and the velocity all the way through the descent.

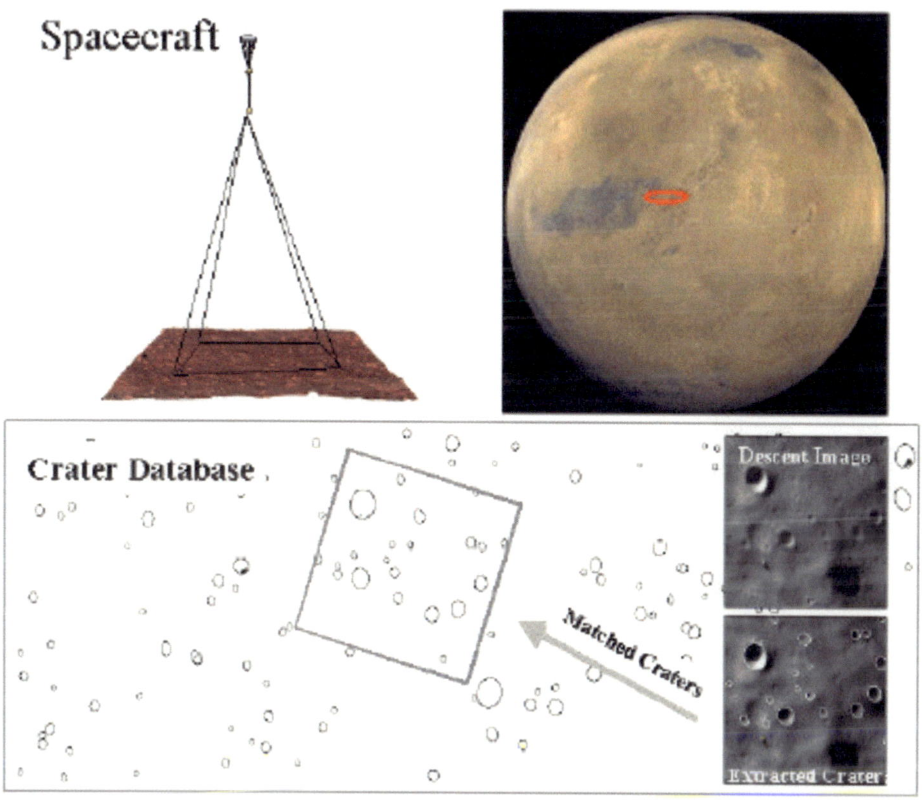

Figure 3. Craters pattern matching for position estimation of the spacecraft during EDL [14]

2. Methodology

2.1. Real time craters detection algorithm

This reliable topography-based Craters Detection Algorithm that the authors are proposing in this chapter is mainly based on a real image (optical image) analysis and morphological

Image Analysis. There are various stages of coding in order to get a satisfactory result, provided that the sun's elevation angle is known. This algorithm is suitable for any optical images taken from 'Lunar Orbiter' or 'Apollo' sources. The Algorithm flowchart is presented in Figure (4) below:

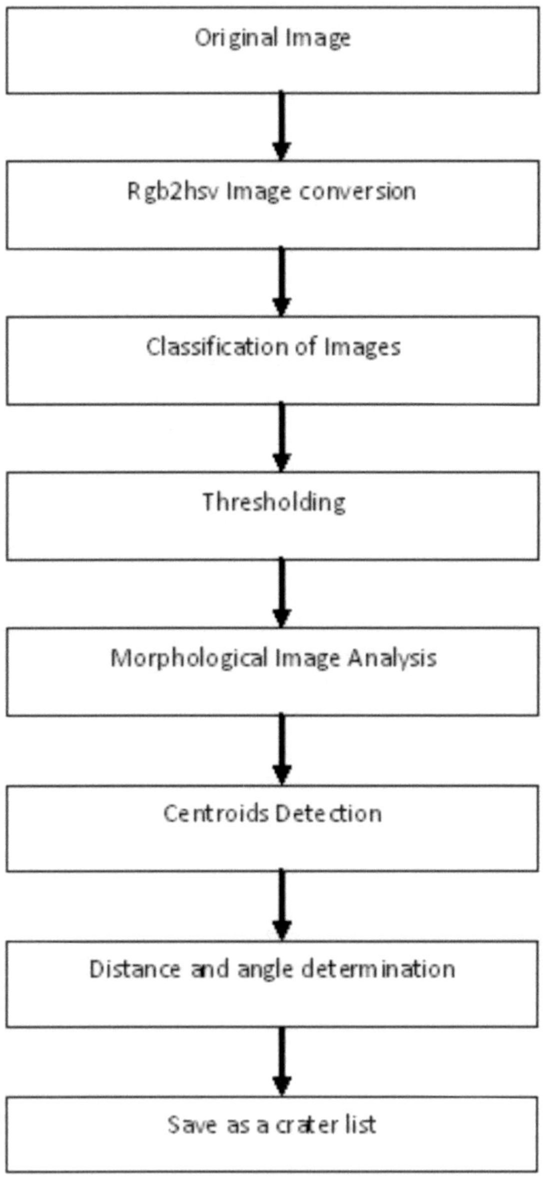

Figure 4. Flowchart of the proposed Craters Detection Algorithm

In the proposed craters detection algorithm, the authors used the original image (3D optical image) of the moon's surface. Originally, this image is a coloured image. For pre-processing step, the authors invented a colour conversion technique which started/originated from RGB (red,green,blue) image to HSV (hue,saturation,value) image using rgb2hsv function in MATLAB. Converting the RGB image to HSV image is basically the transformational of colours from RGB space into HSV space. Value (brightness) gives the amount of light in the colour; hue describes the dominant wavelength which determines the colour type while saturation indicated the vibrancy of the colour. The vital reason for this colour conversion is that the authors want to analyze only one of the entities that is Value entity in HSV component range 0(tend to be dark) to 1(tend to be light) which is then further used in the thresholding calculation. Besides, HSV plane is more popular in analyzing images because of its similarities to the way human intends to recognize colour. RGB and CMYK (Cyan, Magenta, Yellow and Black) colour models are additive and subtractive models respectively, defining colour in terms of the combination of primary colours whilst HSV encapsulates information about a colour in terms of its familiarity to the human adaptation such as; what colour is it? How light and dark the picture is? Or what is the colour vibrant?

For thresholding purposes, a similar approach as Sawabe et al's [13] has been implemented and is discussed thoroughly in the technical section. The purpose of applying a threshold is to distinguish the craters on the moon's surface to light and dark patches groups. Thresholding is the simplest method of image segmentation. This segmentation procedure is to classify the pixels into object pixel (light and dark patch) and non object pixel (background). In this classification of images, it is clearly seen that a crater is formed by two different patterns that are light and dark patches under a different angle of sun beam. The authors use this property of craters in order to analyze and detect them on a lunar's surface. These light and dark patches pattern is distinguished based on the values of pixel's intensity for both images. For an instance, alight patch is determined by a pixel value that is below the threshold brightness calculated whilst a dark patch is determined from a pixel by a pixel value that is above the similar threshold brightness calculated.

Furthermore, in morphology image analysis, erosion and dilation is applied as a combined analysis to the tested image. These two operations can be described simply in terms of adding or removing pixels from the binary image according to certain rules which depend on the pattern of neighbouring pixels. Erosion removes pixel from features in an image or equally turns pixel OFF that were originally ON [20]. Fundamentally, erosion can entirely remove extraneous pixels representing point noise or line defects which are only a single pixel wide. The image that is processed using erosion and dilation are shown in Figure (9) below for better visualization. These two methods are discussed entirely in the experimental results section (craters detection algorithm results) later. Another method is called dilation, which is widely used to add pixels. The dilation rule is that for erosion, is to add (set to ON) any background pixel which touches another pixel that is already part of a foreground region [20]. This will add a layer of pixels around the periphery of all regions which results in dimension increment and may cause images to merge or expand.

In centroid determination, the authors use 'regionprops' function to get every centre for each light and dark blob classified previously. After that, the authors then have to link the blobs together in a single picture. As a result, the final image will comprise a group of clusters or patches that correspond to craters on the moon's surface. These groups of blobs (light and dark patches) will then be used to measure the minimum distance and angle between each of them. First, the algorithm will calculate all the distances of every patch and will pick only the minimum distance. The light patches with minimum distances that are attached to the dark patches will be considered craters as a first step. Second, every angle between the known input sun vector and pairing patches vector is calculated using a scalar product or dot product. Technically, all these methods will be elaborated further in the technical section and experimental results section.

2.2. Geometrical analysis

In the geometric analysis, there are several stages that can be determined as Figure 5 below:

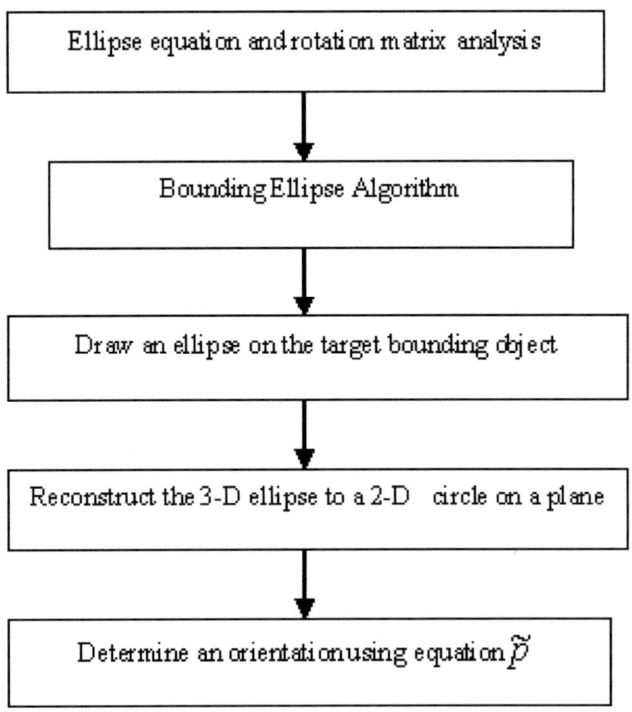

Figure 5. Flowchart of Geometrical Analysis

Users must consider a crater as an ellipse in a real image. This method of consideration will convert an ellipse in a 2D image into a circle on a plane using Conical Projection Analysis. Any ellipse will appear to be a circle from a certain point of views. In other words, an ellipse will be projected into a circle at a certain projection point. At the final stage, this method will be able to calculate the orientation and position of a crater (disc in shape) that is being detected before through the proposed detection algorithm.

2.2.1. *Fundamentals of ellipse and rotation matrix*

Mathematically, an ellipse can be defined as the locus of all points on the plane whose distances R1 and R2 (as Figure 6 below) to two fixed points added to the same constant and can be notified as:

$$R1 + R2 = 2a \tag{3}$$

where a = semi major axis and the origin of the coordinate system is at one of the foci (-c,0) and (c,0). These two focis are chosen to be identical with the bounding ellipse algorithm equation. It is sometimes defined as a conical section from cutting a circular conical or cylindrical surface with an oblique plane. There are five vital parameters in ellipse including semi-major axis denoted as **a**, semi-minor axis denoted as **b**, centre, **c** of ellipse in X-coordinate, **Xc**, centre of ellipse in Y-coordinate, **Yc**, and an angle of rotation denoted as **ω**. The ellipse with all the parameters can be illustrated as below:

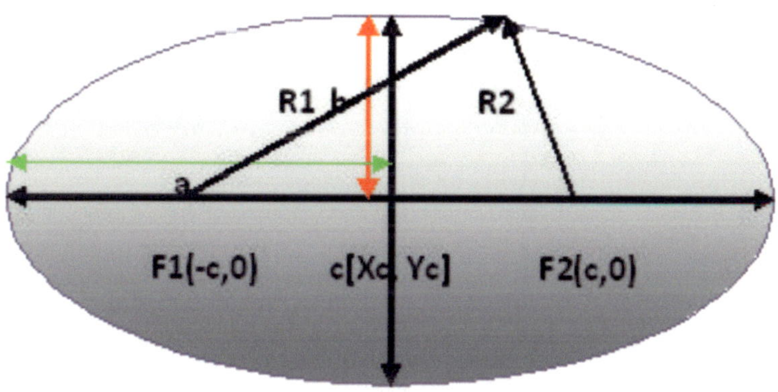

Figure 6. Ellipse

An ellipse that lies along the horizontal X-axis with foci points F1 (-c, 0) and F2(c, 0) as can be shown in Figure (6) above, will have an equation of

$$x^2/a^2 + y^2/(a^2-c^2) = 1 \text{ where } a > c \text{ for the ellipse} \tag{4}$$

For an ellipse, the distance c between the centre and a focus is less than the distance a between the centre and foci, so a^2-c^2 is positive and a new constant b>0 is introduced by setting [2]:

$$b^2 = a^2 - c^2 \text{ for ellipses} \tag{5}$$

Hence the equation of an ellipse with F1 (-a, 0) and F2 (a, 0) is simplified to

$$x^2/a^2 + y^2/b^2 = 1 \text{ where } 0 < b < a \tag{6}$$

For both the hyperbola and the ellipse, a number e, called the eccentricity is introduced by setting [2]:

$$e = c/a \text{ or } e = \sqrt{(a^2-b^2)}/a \tag{7}$$

In this mathematical and geometrical analysis, the authors started to brief in ellipse equations and rotation matrix first which are going to be analyzed soon in the bounding ellipse algorithm and for the reconstruction of ellipse to a circle on a 2-D plane. These methods are beneficial to determine the orientation and the position of the spacecraft during Entry, Descent and Landing (EDL) applications. In this case, the rotation matrix for an ellipse can be illustrated as Figure 4 below:

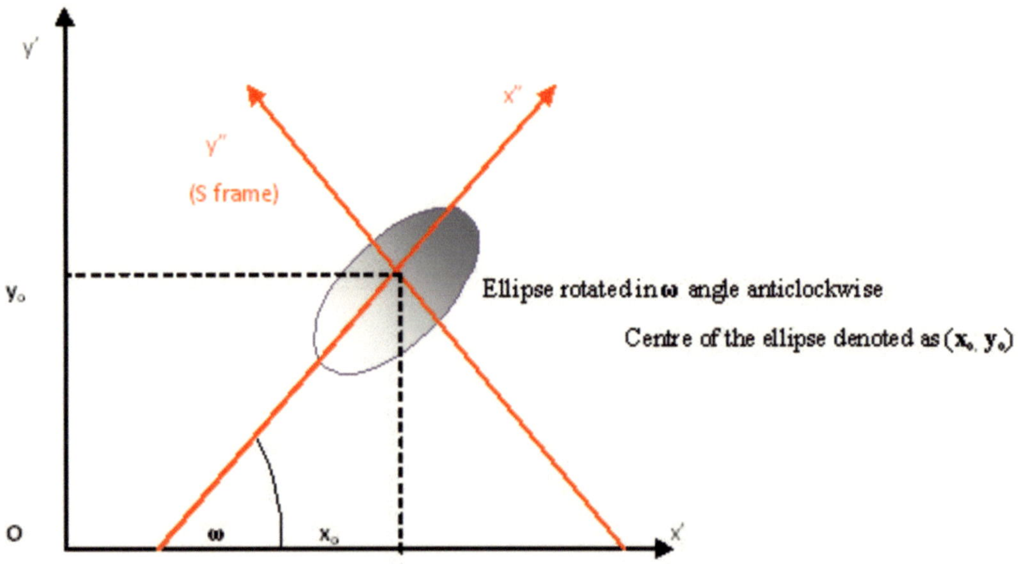

Figure 7. Rotation Ellipse

In S frame as in figure 7 above, it can be shown/demonstrated that using a standard ellipse equation, the x″ and y″ can be expressed as

$$(x'')^2/a^2 + (y'')^2/b^2 = 1 \text{ where } 0 < b < a \tag{8}$$

Where

$$\begin{pmatrix} x'' \\ y'' \end{pmatrix} = \begin{pmatrix} \cos\omega & \sin\omega \\ -\sin\omega & \cos\omega \end{pmatrix} \begin{pmatrix} x' \\ y' \end{pmatrix} \tag{9}$$

$$= \begin{pmatrix} x'\cos\omega \;\; y'\sin\omega \\ -x'\sin\omega \, y'\cos\omega \end{pmatrix} \tag{10}$$

and

$$\begin{pmatrix} x' \\ y' \end{pmatrix} = \begin{pmatrix} x - xo \\ y - yo \end{pmatrix} \tag{11}$$

After substitution of these three vital equations, new formula for the rotation ellipse, which is also the bounding ellipse equation:

$$\frac{((x-xo)\cos\omega+(y-yo)\sin\omega)^2}{a^2}+\frac{((-x+xo)\sin\omega+(y-yo)\cos\omega)^2}{b^2}=1 \tag{12}$$

Again, the rotation ellipse can also be expressed through this formula:

$$(\tilde{x}-\tilde{c})^T A(\tilde{x}-\tilde{c})=(x-xo)^2 A_{11}+((x-xo)(y-yo))(A_{21}+A_{12})+(y-yo)^2 A_{22}=1 \tag{13}$$

Where $A_{11}, A_{21}, A_{12}, A_{22}$ is the E matrix that is determined from the bounding ellipse algorithm following the form of

$$A=\begin{pmatrix} A_{11} & A_{12} \\ A_{21} & A_{22} \end{pmatrix} \tag{14}$$

Thus, by comparing the equations of 12 and 13 above, the authors express all the ellipse parameters a,b,c (Xc and Yc) and ω in terms of this $A_{11}, A_{21}, A_{12}, A_{22}$ entities when drawing the bounding ellipse around the target patch which:

$$a=\left(\frac{2\sin 2\omega}{(A_{11}+A_{22})\sin 2\omega+2A_{12}}\right)^{1/2} \tag{15}$$

$$b=\left(\frac{2\sin 2\omega}{(A_{11}+A_{22})\sin 2\omega-2A_{12}}\right)^{1/2} \tag{16}$$

$$\omega=\tan^{-1}\left(\frac{-2A_{12}}{A_{22}-A_{11}}\right)/2 \tag{17}$$

Furthermore, the other two ellipse parameters Xc and Yc values can be determined straight away from the bounding ellipse algorithm.

2.2.2. *Bounding ellipse algorithm*

This is the first method used in the geometrical analysis and the reason of using it is to get the bounding ellipse around the targeted patch. This is further used in a final stage of this section that is reconstruction or projection of the ellipse to a circle in a 2-D plane. The bounding ellipse takes five inputs of the ellipse parameters described previously, which are semi-major axis a, semi-minor axis b, centre of ellipse in x-coordinate Xc, centre of ellipse in y-coordinate Yc and rotation angle ω. These five parameters are embedded in the A matrix produced by this algorithm as an output along with the Xc and Yc values. In order to draw the bounded ellipse the authors need to express all those ellipse parameters in terms of the entities $A_{11}, A_{21}, A_{12}, A_{22}$ of the A matrix. The derivations of these terms are comprehensively described in the previous section. The results of this bounding ellipse algorithm will then be used to reconstruct this 2-D ellipse to a 2-D circle in a plane using Reconstruction Ellipse Algorithm. There are two vital equations of reconstructing a disc that will be used in this algorithm to determine the orientation of the spacecraft which is described below [18]; nonetheless in this chapter the authors will only determine the orientation:

$$\tilde{q} = \frac{B}{\sin\alpha}\left\{\cos\beta\tilde{R}_1 \pm_1 \cos\alpha\sin\beta\sqrt{\tan^2\alpha - \tan^2\beta}\tilde{R}_2\right\} \tag{18}$$

$$\tilde{p} = \pm_2 \cot\alpha\left\{\frac{\sin\beta}{\cos\alpha}\tilde{R}_1 \pm_1 \cos\beta\sqrt{\tan^2\alpha - \tan^2\beta}\tilde{R}_2\right\} \tag{19}$$

Where:

$\tilde{q}$ = is the position of the reconstructed ellipse
$\tilde{p}$ = is the orientation of the reconstructed ellipse
B = is the radius of a disc (craters that the authors model as a disc)
α= is the arc length of the semi-major axis
β= is the arc length of the semi-minor axis
$\tilde{R}_1$ = Rotation matrix of the column vector
$\tilde{R}_2$ =Rotation matrix of the column vector

This is the reconstruction or projection ellipse equations where the authors consider an ellipse as a half-length along the axis symmetry, which is taken to 0 that is **A**=0. In this case, the authors need to model the crater bounded as a disc. That is the reason for the half-length along the axis symmetry **A**, is taken to 0. **A** in this case is not the attributes of the matrix determined previously. The authors have to deal with those two equations above where as can be seen the equation $\tilde{p}$, the orientation of a disc, is independent of parameters B (the radius) which means that the authors are able to determine quickly the reconstruction algorithm in order to identify the orientation of the spacecraft relative to the moon's surface. There is the ambiguity case in equation $\tilde{p}$ which is the negative and positive case of $\pm_2$ sign. In this case, the $\tilde{p}$ equations always takes a positive value instead of negative as the crater's orientation is just pointing upward towards a camera or in other words, a disc will only be seen if its outward face points towards the camera rather than away from the camera [18]. This is a discerning case; when one considers how human calculates an object's position, its exact size is needless in finding the direction of neither its centre nor its orientation. In contrast, the equation $\tilde{q}$ is dependent on the radius of a disc, B which the authors have no knowledge of the radius of the craters and how far it is from the moon's surface. Therefore, searching for a solution q is actually an interesting future work that needs to be achieved if the authors want to find the position of the spacecraft during the EDL operations.

3. Technical sections

There are different mathematical equations and fundamentals applied during this project development. In order to make the project runs smooth as planned; the authors have divided the logical structures of the project into three different sections:

3.1. Craters detection algorithm

This project involved the development of the detection algorithm using MATLAB image processing tool and an image of the moon's surface. It is mainly based on the binary image and morphological image analysis. At the first stage, the authors introduce the concept of HSV (Hue, Saturation, and Value) as well as morphology image investigation such as dilation and erosion to exploit the real image. The Hue is expressed as an angle around a colour hexagon mainly using the real axis as 0° axis. The Value is measured along the cone and has two different conditions. If V=0, the end of the axis is represented by black and white if V=1at the end of the axis is represented by white [4]. The Saturation is the purity of the colour and is measured as the distance from the V axis looking at the hue, saturation and value hexagonal cone.

The HSV colour system is based on cylindrical coordinates. Mathematically, converting form RGB (Red, Green and Blue) image to HSV is actually developing the equation from the Cartesian coordinates to cylindrical coordinates. To reduce the complicatedness of analysis on image detection, the authors analysed a 2-D optical image. The threshold for the image is set using intelligent approach from Sawabe, Natsunaga and Rokugawa in classifying the images as can be shown in equations (20) below. By using this approach, images were classified into two components that are light and dark patches or obviously known as 'sunny and shady patches'. Ideally, these two groups of patches are easily recognizable if the image was taken under low sun elevation. These patterns of light and dark patches were detected when all these equations [13] are satisfied:

$$R_{min} < R_m - \sigma$$

$$R_{max} > R_m + \sigma \qquad (20)$$

$$P_{min} < P_{max}$$

Where R_{min} indicates the minimum pixel value, R_{max} indicates the maximum pixel value; R_m indicates the average pixel value and σ indicates the standard deviation in the small area including the targeted patches. P_{min} and P_{max} indicate the positions at the minimum and maximum value pixels from the direction of the sun radiation or sun vector [13].

Apart from that, there are two basic fundamentals on morphological operation applied in the algorithm which are dilation and erosion. Dilation is an operation that grows or expands objects in a binary image. This can be represented by a matrix of 1's and 0's but usually it is convenient to show only the 1's group. The dilation between two images A and B, is denoted by A ⊕ B and is defined as [1]:

$$A\mathring{A}B = \{z \mid (\mathbf{B})_z \cap A \neq f\} \qquad (21)$$

Nevertheless, erosion shrinks or thins objects in a binary image, which is the opposite case of the dilation operation. The mathematical definition of erosion can be expressed as [1] and the result of eroded and dilated image is shown in Figure 8 as below. This can be compared to the original image in Figure (9):

$$A \Theta B = \{z \mid (B)_z \cap A^c \neq f\} \quad (22)$$

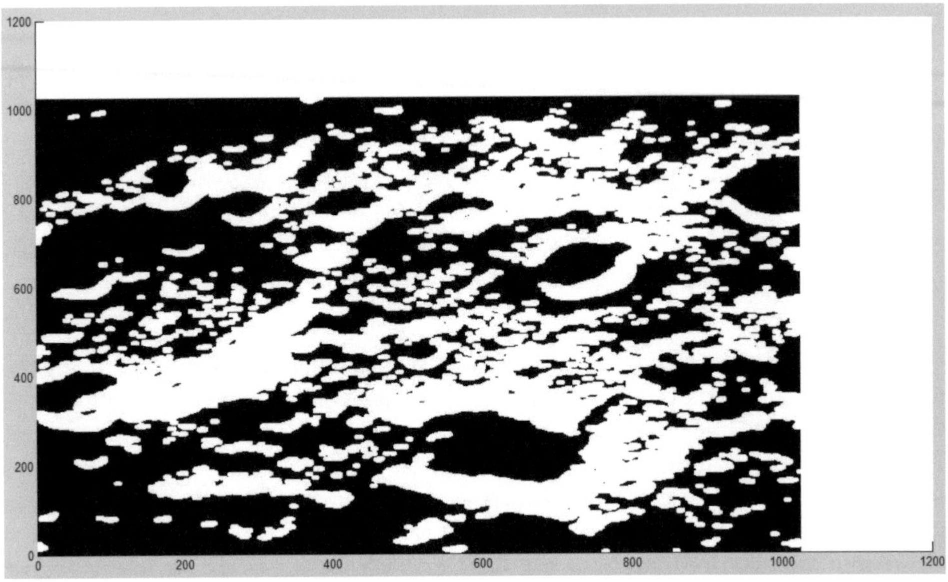

Figure 8. Image after dilation and erosion were applied

The previous stages are then followed by another image analysis methodology that is *regionprops* function and this region indicates the patch that the authors want to analyze. The reason for using this region descriptors function is to plot the centroids of each light and dark patch and gather them (light and dark patches) back together in a single picture which will then be used to further calculate the desirable minimum distance and angle between them to the known sun direction. *Regionprops* takes the labelled matrix as an input and uses axis-x and axis-y to describe horizontal and vertical coordinates respectively.

To classify and consider this region of interest as a crater, the authors proposed two ways of detection which are minimum distance measurement and angle detection based on the known sun vector. In the distance measurement, the minimum distances between each of the centroids calculated previously are determined using this formula:

$$|\mathbf{Distance}| = \sqrt{[(\mathbf{x}^2-\mathbf{x}^1)^2 + (\mathbf{y}^2-\mathbf{y}^1)^2]} = |\mathbf{r}| \quad (23)$$

where $|\mathbf{Distance}|$ is the measurement of distance between two pairing patches (light and dark), $\mathbf{x}^2$ and $\mathbf{x}^1$ are the x-component of the centroids and $\mathbf{y}^2,\mathbf{y}^1$ are the centroid's component of the y-axis respectively. In the angle determination, the authors give an input for the sun vector which is known by looking at the sunray effect at those craters (the position of the light and dark shades). This algorithm will then compute each of the angles of every pairing blob with their minimum distances to the sun vector added input using scalar product or dot product in the vector analysis which is:

$$\mathbf{r.s} = |\mathbf{r}|\,|\mathbf{s}| \cos\theta \quad (24)$$

Where **r** = vector of each pairing blobs
s = sun vector
|**r**| = distance/length of each pairing blobs
|**s**| = distance of sun vector = unit vector = 1
θ = angle between sun vector and vector of each pairing blobs

Each of the pairing blobs angle is calculated using the above equation and those who has a minimum angle to with known sun vector and has a minimum distance calculated previously will be considered and stored as a crater. Oppositely, those who are against the direction and have the maximum angles to the sun vector will be scrapped and considered noise. At the end of these two measurements (distance and angle), the authors managed to get the best eight craters using this reliable craters detection algorithm.

3.2. Geometrical analysis

3.2.1. Bounding ellipse algorithm

The geometrical part is mainly based on the mathematical analysis on vector calculus, the rotation matrix, ellipse equations and also the mathematical applications to determine two major features that is the orientation of a crater that has been modelled as a disc and the position of the disc after projection. These two features make a vital solution to have a safe landing on the moon's surface. Firstly, from the previous codes, the authors choose one of the best eight in a crater's list to run a bounding ellipse algorithm around the targeted crater. The bounding ellipse algorithm input the P matrix which is composed from the targeted crater itself. The tolerance of the bounding image is set to get more precise result. As discussed above in the methodology section, the output of this algorithm will be the A matrix and c, the centre of the ellipse. A matrix is in the form of $A = \begin{pmatrix} A_{11} & A_{12} \\ A_{21} & A_{22} \end{pmatrix}$. The reason the authors highlighted this is to show that another important parameter in ellipse is embedded in this A matrix. They are semi-major axis **a**, semi-minor axis **b**, and angle of rotation ω. As a result, the final equations (equations 13, 14 and 15) are used to draw the ellipse to bind the targeted patches as derived from the previous methodology section. The next step is to draw the ellipse using another algorithm and all those parameters above and also the centre of the ellipse that can be determined straight away from the bounding ellipse algorithm. Statistically, after the algorithm has calculated all the values of the parameter, the authors have the same value for semi-major axis **a** and semi-minor axis **b** which suggests that a circle is formed. This important knowledge tells the authors that the camera is actually pointing straight around 90 degrees vertically to the targeted crater on the moon's surface. If the authors have an ellipse instead of a circle, it means that the camera is not pointing straight 90 degrees downward away from it (crater). That is the first assumption the authors made before doing the third stage algorithm that is Reconstruction of an Ellipse to a circle in a 2-D plane.

3.2.2. Reconstruction of an ellipse on image plane

First, the input of this algorithm is the five primary parameters of the ellipse that are **a, b, Xc, Yc, ω**, the half-length of the semi major axis is denoted as capital **A**, and the half-length of the semi-minor axis is denoted as capital **B**. This reconstruction vision is to model the craters or projected ellipse as a disc. Mathematically, the concepts are adapted by taking the focal point as an origin of a camera frame and the x-axis is aligned with the focal axis of the camera and x > 0 is what the camera is looking for. Furthermore, the image plane is always assumed to be in front of the focal point rather than those in practice. Taking this objective into account, the half-length of the semi major axis **A** is taken to 0 because it is a disc. In comparison, the half-length of the semi-minor axis **B** is actually the radius of the crater or a disc. This reconstruction or projection ellipse algorithm is based on Stephen's proposed complex method on reconstruction spheroid. The authors will use the equation 17 previously to determine the orientation of a disc or crater that the authors modelled from the reconstruction algorithm.

$$\tilde{p} = \pm_2 \cot\alpha \left\{ \frac{\sin\beta}{\cos\alpha} \tilde{R}_1 \pm_1 \cos\beta \sqrt{\tan^2\alpha - \tan^2\beta} \tilde{R}_2 \right\} \tag{25}$$

$\tilde{p}$ equation describes the orientation of the reconstructed disc (crater) and equation $\tilde{q}$ describes the position of a disc (crater) after reconstruction or projection. As the above two equations, there are four possible solutions (regardless of the ambiguity case of $\pm_2$ as discussed before in the methodology section), two of them are from equation $\tilde{p}$ and another two from equation $\tilde{q}$. The equation $\tilde{p}$ is independent from the half-length semi minor axis B as can be seen from the equation. Therefore, the authors can determine the orientation of a disc straight away from the algorithm. Unfortunately, the equation $\tilde{q}$ is dependent on the half-length of semi-minor axis B which the authors are not aware of the radius of a crater because the authors are not able to determine the distance to the moon's surface. This is the main challenge. But getting the value of $\tilde{p}$ will then lead the authors to get the position of $\tilde{q}$ by some means because they are related. The position $\tilde{q}$ of the disc will then be a greater future work to be explored.

4. Experimental results and discussion

4.1. Craters detection algorithm result

In this section, some experimental results are reported which were obtained by applying craters detection algorithm. In particular, the authors choose real images (optical images) of the moon's surface and develop the codes mainly based on the binary image analysis and morphological techniques. As mentioned before, this is the independent algorithm which does not depend on the data elevation map as well as past and future imaging data, which is the advantage compared to other detection algorithms proposed previously. There are seven stages to develop this algorithm as mentioned in the methodology (refer to the flowchart). The authors will discuss the results from the first stage until the last stage by attaching the result image for a better view and understanding of the concept used for analysis.

Erosion and dilation are two fundamentals in Morphological Image Analysis. In Figures 10 and 11, the erosion and dilation are experimented in a combined process for dark patches and light patches. For an ideal result, the authors just used the eroded image for both light and dark patches by adding them together in a single picture for centroid detection later. If the authors take consideration of both the dilation and erosion process as a combined process, the image itself will produce too much noise as shown in the figure above. For centroid determination, therefore, the authors want the noise to be kept at a minimum level in order to attach valid pairing patches and in order to produce minimum small blobs or patches that do not have their pairs (light and dark patch). This is also to reduce the processing time (running time) and complexity of centroid calculation.

Figure 9. Real Image of Craters (Optical Image)

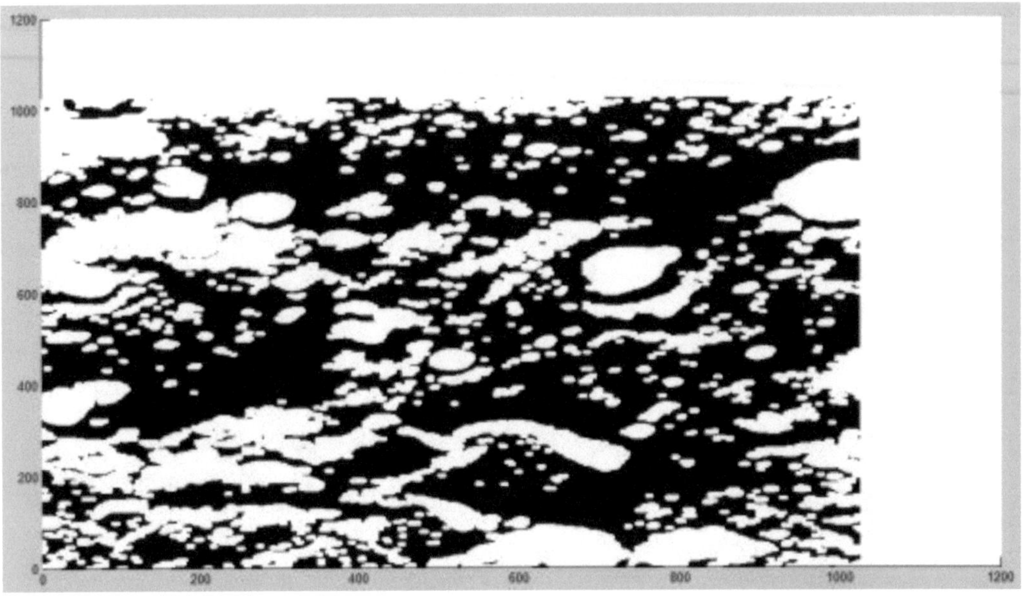

Figure 10. Erosion and Dilation for dark patches

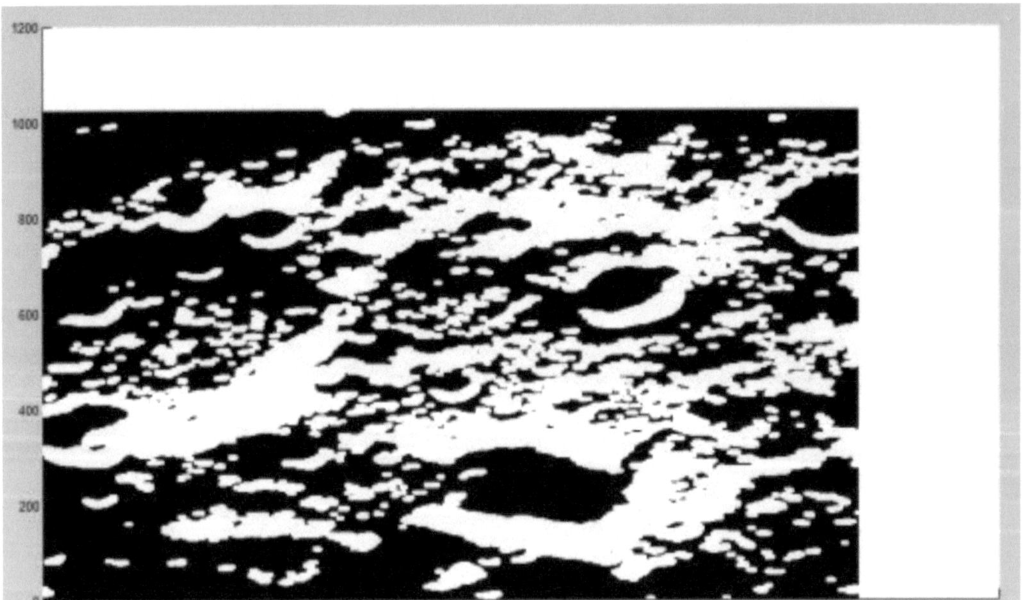

Figure 11. Erosion and Dilation for light patches

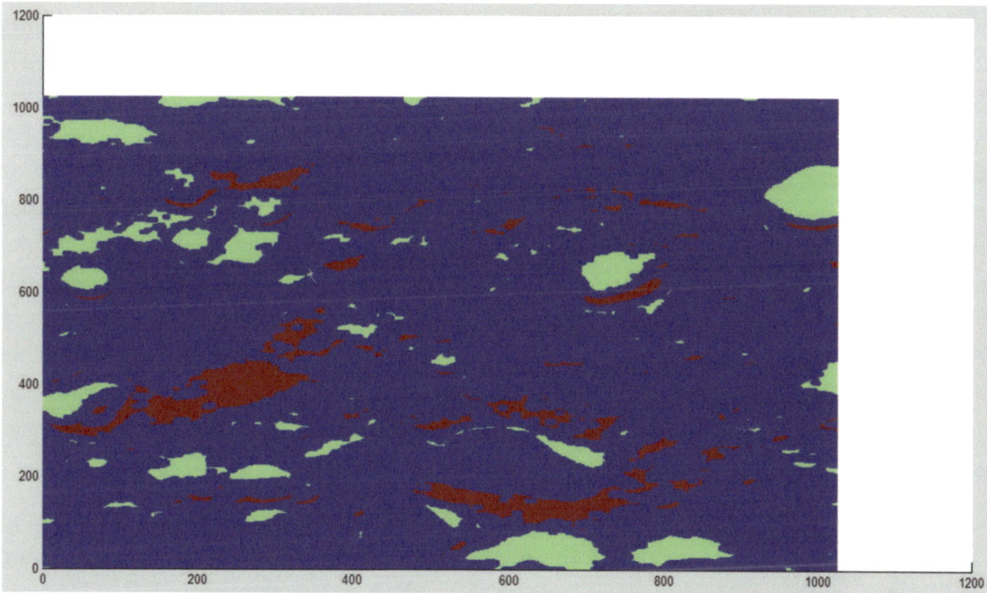

Figure 12. Threshold Image

Secondly, after converting the RGB image plane to HSV image plane and taking into consideration only the '*Value*' from the HSV image plane, thresholding is then used for image segmentation proposal. Thresholding is used firstly to differentiate the object (foreground) from the background. The targeted foreground is ideally the craters themselves that are composed by light and dark patches pattern. The light patch occurs when the pixel value is more than the calculated threshold brightness using the same approach that is fully described in the technical section. Whilst the dark patch is detected when the pixel value is less than the same threshold brightness calculated before. The threshold image can be shown in Figure (12) above.

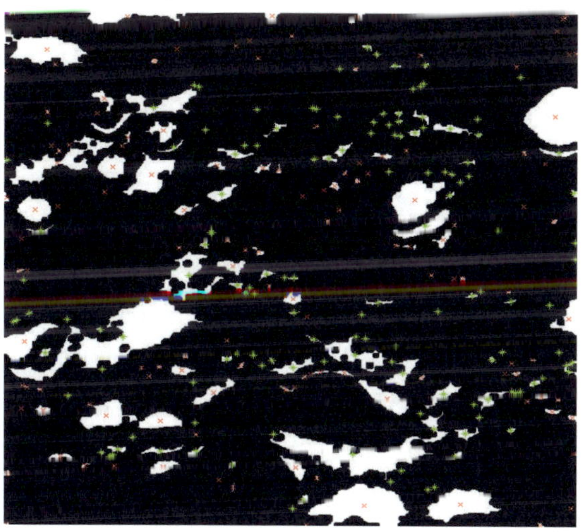

Figure 13. Centroid Determination using 'regionprops' function

Centroid determination stage is completed by using the 'regionprops' function in Matlab and this is basically to compute the desired region properties or targeted properties. This step also attached the pairing patches together to form a complete crater for further analysis. Regionprops only takes the label matrix as an input. Therefore, the authors have to pre-process the image by labelling it first using 'bwlabel' function along with regionprops function later. In MATLAB, bwlabel is used to label the connected components in binary image and bwlabel also supports the 2-D inputs only. After labeling the entire target then only the authors can use them in a memory with regionprops. Regionprops takes this labelled component as an input and return them with an image of centroid determination labelled as a cross (*) symbol as in Figure (13) above. For a smoother image, the authors apply another function in MATLAB called bwareaopen to remove all of the unnecessary objects or all connected components (objects) that are fewer than P pixels set, producing another binary image.

The final stage of this craters detection algorithm is minimum radial distance and angle calculation. The authors have tested the algorithm with two different image conditions (different sun angles and background noises). According to the algorithm, the authors can select the number of craters to be detected by the system. The users can choose how many craters to be detected by the system based on the original image taken. As for this case, it will select the eight best craters that satisfy the minimum distance and angle conditions by assuming that the sun direction is known. An image of the landing site on the moon's surface has to be captured first and the amounts of craters needs to be detected are calculated manually. Based? on the original image, the authors have assumed the sun direction by identifying the shade and sunny pattern locations that formed the craters If the image has less than eight craters, then the system will choose the maximum number of craters on the image. If one deals with the image with many craters, he/she can choose any number that he/she wants to detect based on the original image, which has to be captured first prior to the detection. Although sometimes the system will detect the craters with wrong pairing patches (light patches connected to the wrong dark patch and vice versa) the Lander should understand that one of them might still be one of the hazards that have to be avoided during landing application. The radial distance is calculated for each of the pairs detected in green lines as in Figures (14) and (15) below and using the equation (23) and, the shortest distance between adjacent pairs (light and dark patch) is chosen as a preliminary result for further angle calculations.

After the light patches were connected to the dark patches with a minimum distance between them, then the system will calculate the minimum angle by inputting the direction of the sun (assuming that the authors know the sun's angle) and later comparing it with the pairing patches angle using the dot product (equation 24) as has been thoroughly described in the methodology section. By taking into account both techniques (minimum distance and angle), the authors can determine the best craters that they want on an image. The final craters detected will be denoted in yellow lines as shown in Figures (14) and (15) below.

Ideally, this algorithm will work on any images that have a clear pattern of light and dark patches and the authors do not even have to know the important parameters such as radius, gradient and etc of the craters. Unfortunately, this algorithm will work effectively on the image that has a clear pattern of these light and dark patches only. A crater with a clear pattern in this context will have clear features of light and dark patches that constitute one crater. To determine the accuracy of the algorithm created by the authors, the authors will provide a figure taken from two separate images tested by this algorithm. The final results have to be compared with the real image in order to determine which craters are true. In a real scenario, all craters detected will be considered hazards even though they are connected to the wrong pair of light or dark patches.

Comparing the results taken from Image 1to the original image (real image of the moon's surface), there are eleven valid craters or true craters after pre-processing (after erosion and noise reduction (*bwareaopen* function), labelled by BW label). Valid craters or true craters in this context means that the craters have a clear pattern of light and dark blobs regardless of the size and other features. Over these eleven valid craters, eight of them are successfully detected using this craters detection algorithm; this suggests that the authors have a 73% successful rate. The authors have tested this craters detection algorithm into two different optical images with different sun angles which are 10 degrees, > 10 degrees and with a noisy image as mentioned below. These evaluations below are to measure the accuracy of the algorithm based on the two images proposed and how robust the algorithm is. The determination of accuracy of the algorithm is based on how often craters are detected and the calculations are shown below:

Based on the original Image 1 as can be illustrated in Figure (14) below

Sun direction: 10 degrees
Manual Detection (number of craters after pre-processed): 11
Automatic Detection (number of craters detected): 8
8/11 x 100 = **73% accuracy**

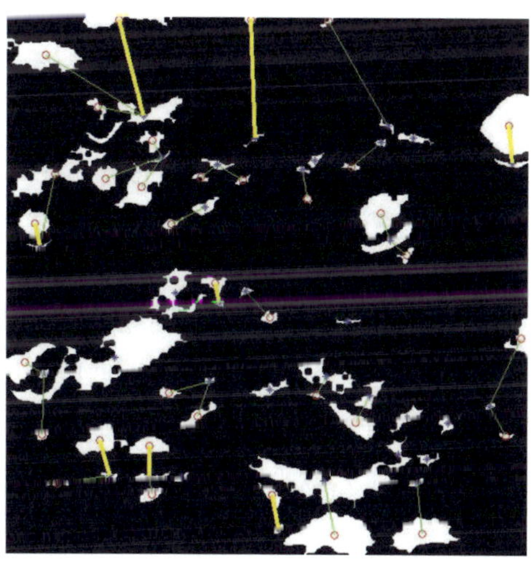

Figure 14. Craters detected from Image 1 in yellow line based on distance and angle measurements

Based on the original Image 2 as can be illustrated in Figure (15) below

Sun direction: > 10 degrees
Manual Detection (number of craters detected after pre-processed): 10
Automatic Detection (number of craters detected): 8
8/10 x 100 = **80% accuracy**

Figure 15. Craters detected from Image 2 in yellow line based on distance and angle measurements

In Figure (15) above, yellow lines, which denote as craters are detected with a minimum distance and angle detection while green lines, which denote as craters are detected with a minimum distance only prior to the minimum angle detection. This angle detection will be a final stage in defining the craters based on the light and dark patch pattern (sometimes denoted as sunny and shady parts) and the final craters are those with yellow lines. By comparison, the accuracy of the algorithm based on these two images with different types of craters, angle (Sun) and lighting condition is said to be 77% and it is quite a satisfactorily accurate.

This accuracy factor can be improved if the authors know exactly the sun elevation angle since in this research; the authors just assumed the angle and the value is not really accurate. In a real application, this sun angle can be measured separately using the satellite, altimeter or radar prior to this detection process and the value will be more accurate. Besides, this algorithm will detect the craters that are above 0.0265 meters in image size (100 pixels). This can be vouched by using the *'bwareaopen'* function where it will remove the entire blobs pixel which is less than 100 pixels.

4.2. Bounding ellipse algorithm results

In the geometrical analysis section, the authors start with the bounding ellipse algorithm using the information from the previous proposed craters detection algorithm to bound the targeted blob as shown in Figure 18 above. The blob is selected randomly from the true craters detected by the detection algorithm such as in figure (16) above by labelling the targeted output using '*bwlabel*.' This function numbers all the objects in a binary image. By using this information, the user can select the true matching pair that can be selected for further research (to determine its position and orientation) by using the function 'find' in MATLAB and this step can be repeated for all of the true matching pairs detected by the algorithm. This is the first step before the authors can draw the ellipse around the target (figure 16) to bound it and to reconstruct the crater selected as a disc using ellipse reconstruction algorithm. This reconstruction is beneficial to later determine the orientation and position of a Lunar Lander using the equation $\tilde{p}$ and $\tilde{q}$ as proposed before during EDL of the spacecraft. There are some mathematical fundamentals and equations that need to be understood before one can apply the bounding ellipse algorithm to a certain targeted object. They are fundamentals of the ellipse and also the rotation matrix fundamentals. This knowledge is used to extract the embedded entities from the output of bounding ellipse algorithm in terms of basic ellipse parameters such as **a**, **b**, **Xc**, **Yc** and **ω** which are further used to draw an ellipse around the targeted object (target patch). Generally, the authors want to express all those ellipse parameters in terms of E matrix which is the output of bounding ellipse algorithm. This E matrix takes a form of $E = \begin{pmatrix} A_{11} & A_{12} \\ A_{21} & A_{22} \end{pmatrix}$. Finally, the authors want to express the ellipse parameters in terms of $A_{11}, A_{21}, A_{12}, A_{22}$ in order to draw the bounding ellipse and further to reconstruct it as a disc.

Figure 16. Targeted blobs chosen randomly from the matched true pairs in distance and angle measurement using bwlabel function.

After the authors obtain the bounding ellipse around the targeted patch as in shown in the figure below, the next step is to reconstruct the bounded crater using ellipse reconstruction algorithm. As a result, the authors will get a circle which suggests that the camera is pointing straight vertically to the lunar's surface.

Figure 17. Bounded crater using bounding ellipse algorithm and Image plane ellipse algorithm in green circle line

As can be seen in Figure (17) above, a circle, instead of an ellipse, appeared after the authors ran the bounding ellipse algorithm along with the image plane ellipse algorithm. This is because the semi major axis **a** is actually similar to the semi minor axis **b**, so a circle is produced. In fact, this means that actually the camera is pointing down vertically straight to the moon's surface providing an angle of around 90 degrees relative to the moon's surface. Next, the reconstruction ellipse algorithm took the input of **a**, **b**, centre (Xc,Yc), A , B and produced the output of the orientation $\tilde{p}$ of the ellipse after reconstruction or projection.

4.3. Ellipse reconstruction algorithm results

This algorithm is about to model a crater as a disc and reconstruct an ellipse to a circle in 2 dimension (2-D) plane in order to determine the position and orientation of a crater relative to the spacecraft. For the first case, the authors used a real image which is an optical image. To realize the above purposes, the authors have assumed several altitudes from the spacecraft to the moon's surface. As mentioned before, after the authors performed the bounding algorithm and drew the bounding ellipse on a particular targeted crater, the authors have an image of a circle that bound a targeted crater rather than an ellipse, and therefore the authors have an assumption that the camera on the spacecraft is pointing vertically, almost 90 degrees from above in angle if measured from a flat lunar's surface. From bounding ellipse algorithm, the authors have determined the image plane ellipse parameters and the results show that the semi-major axis, $\boldsymbol{a}$ is similar to the semi minor axis, $\boldsymbol{b}$. Taking advantage of this idea, a circle will only have one solution in order to determine the position of a crater and the ambiguity case (an ellipse has 2 solutions) can be eliminated. The reconstruction algorithm [18] described in the methodology and technical sections previously is then used to reconstruct a possible disc (crater) positions and orientations after taking into account of the camera's parameters [18] below where Xc and Yc is the coordinate of the centre of an ellipse. The authors use an optical image dimension of 1024x1024 pixels.

In real applications, the lunar's surface is not flat, and the crater is not straight below the camera. In this case, the authors had determined a circle in bounding ellipse algorithm that bounds a certain target; hence the authors made this assumption as the above figure. By looking at the figure above, the focal axis line is not really parallel to the centre of the disc hence the perspective distortion would have an effect as being described further in the next section. When the authors set A = 0 it is important to bear in mind that the ellipse will become a disc and this means that $\tilde{p}$ is parallel to $\tilde{q}$ and the authors should obtain a circle. Contrary to this, if $\tilde{p}$ is perpendicular to $\tilde{q}$, the authors will get a line rather than a circle.

In a real situation, the altitude assumptions above are measured prior to the landing purposes. This altitude is usually measured by the altimeter or the satellite. Before the authors can construct the position a disc, they must determine the orientation first. This orientation and position of the disc is obtained from the equations (18) and (19) previously. As being mentioned before, the orientation equation is free from the term B and can be determined fully from the reconstruction algorithm. The orientation of the disc can be described as a unit vector that gives the direction of the centre of the disc. It is a positive value since the crater can be seen positioned upwards rather than downwards (negative side).

An ellipse will be detected on the image plane for each disc that is visible on the camera's view. For each ellipse detected, there will be two discs reconstructed in 3-D space in terms of its orientation and position as well; one is pointing away from the plane which is a true direction while the other will be pointing in the wrong direction. As can be seen in the result above, the authors have the orientations of (1.0000,-0.0000, 0.0000) and (1.0000,-0.0049,-0.0007). This ambiguity case can be removed by taking into consideration that from a camera's perspective, a disc will only be seen if they are orientated upwards (positive values) rather than downwards (negative values). So, using the information above, it is clear that the image plane is one unit away (P (1, 0, 0)) from the origin (of a camera at the spacecraft) which is the orientation of the spacecraft itself. The readers should be also reminded that in this case, the orientation vector is the unit vector that gives the direction of the centre of the crater. Hence, this orientation vector is also considered the normal vector of the crater that is pointing upward.

As can be seen in this second solution of these orientations, there is an error when the authors calculate the vector unit of this orientation which has to be 1. One of the drawbacks when the authors use MATLAB is that it will always round the value, for example 0.99995 to

1. That is why those (1.0000,-0.0049,-0.0007) values when squared, summed them all and squared root them back, the authors will have more than 1. By theory, this value should be 1 and the reason for this error is maybe due to MATLAB that has rounded the value of 1.0000 that lies on the **x** axis.

Furthermore, in order to evaluate the error of the ellipse that the authors reconstruct, the ellipse itself has an error on the image. This is because of the digitization of a real shape that has an inherent loss of information c compared with the original shape. One should notice that there is no possibility that the original ellipse can be recovered from the digital ellipse but the errors can be optimized by increasing the picture resolution of an image. If the image is unclear or has a poor resolution, the authors can pre-process the image to reduce the presence of noise in the original image by using a smoothing technique [9]. This smoothing technique is carried out by implementing the low-pass filter to the original image. The main purpose is to attenuate the high-spatial frequencies by keeping the low spatial frequencies of the signal strength [9].

Besides, what cause the error are the uncertainties that appear from hardware (altimeter, satellite, or radar), software (MATLAB) and also the landing site topography itself. In a real situation, the sensor noise that comes from the altimeter also has to be considered a noise as it will affect the accuracy of the results determined by the system.

5. Under what conditions the craters are not detected

The higher the successful detection rate is, the lesser the false alarm rate will be. When the detection rate is 80%, the false alarm rate is just 17% whereas for the detection rate of 73%, the false alarm rate increases to 25%. The authors have plotted the graph of successful rate detection versus the false alarm rate as can be shown in Figure (18) below. The FAR (False Alarm Rate) is the percentage of non-signals that were detected as signals (craters) and is calculated based on the number of false alarms and the correct-rejections which can be formulated as [19]:

$$\text{FAR} = \text{Num. Of False alarms}/(\text{Num. Of False alarms} + \text{Number of Correct-Rejections}) \quad (26)$$

The number of false alarm in this case can be referred to as a signal that was not presented but was mistakenly detected by the system whilst correct rejections can be referred to as a signal that was not presented and not detected by the system at all. The lesser false alarm rate in the system is, the better the system/algorithm will be. The main reason that brought these false alarms is the assumption of the sun angle that will lead to a faulty detection of true crater pair (true light patch connected to a true dark patch) hence will decrease the accuracy of the detection rate.

As in any true scenario, an image has to be captured first before the system can detect the safe landing sites that are free from hazards (craters). As mentioned before, this algorithm is assuming that the authors know the sun's direction and will be using the sun angle as one of the steps to detect the craters on the moon's surface. But, there will be some errors when the authors assume the sun angle without knowing its true direction. This assumption will affect the algorithm to pick up the wrong pairs (light patches will be connected to wrong dark patches and vice versa). Nowadays, the authors can obviously determine the sun elevation by many ways from the satellite system or LIDAR.

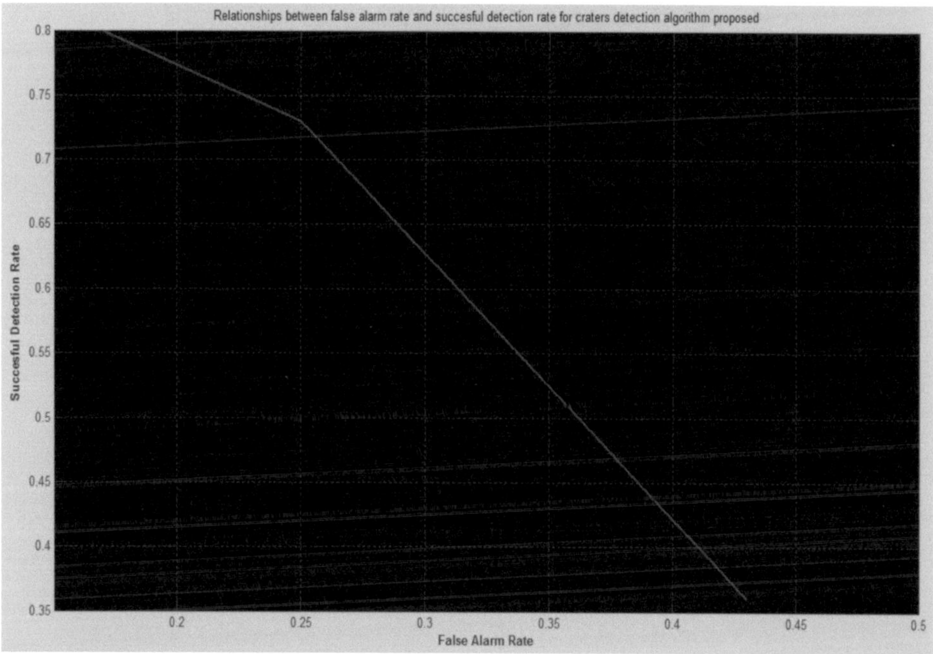

Figure 18. Relationship between successful detection rate and false alarm rate for the proposed craters detection algorithm

This algorithm is not effective on a noisy image with lots of tiny craters, undesired features that look like a crater, the craters' rims which are overlapping and segmented as well as a blurry image. Besides, an image with a too high or too low of sun elevation angle will make the system unable to differentiate the pattern (the light and the dark patches/blobs) and thus, influence the craters to be rarely detected by the system/algorithm. The algorithm will work accurately/efficiently with a sun elevation angle between 10 degrees to 50 degrees based on the experimentations under different image conditions earlier. With noisy image, the only way to reduce the tiny blobs is by using the function in MATLAB called *'bwareaopen'*. As discussed before, this function removes from a binary image all connected components (objects) that have fewer than G (set by the authors) pixels, producing another binary image. Figure (21) below is an example of the image if the algorithm does not apply the *'bwareaopen'* function to eliminate tiny blobs which makes the algorithm becomes ineffective while Figures (14) and (15) above show the detected craters after the function *'bwareaopen'* is applied. The detection rate falls to only 36% and the difference of accuracy is very obvious which is about 37%. To capture an image with a clear pattern of light and dark patches, it is vital as it is one of the most important features to improve the accuracy of the system detection.

Therefore, the image has to be taken by the spacecraft's camera under ideal sun elevation angle (not too low and too high) and a low noise image is a bonus.

Figure 19. Low detection of craters by the algorithm because of too many unnecessary blobs (tiny blobs)

However, for the advantages, the algorithm itself can detect the craters without knowing the main parameters such as the size (radius/diameter or the gradient of the craters). It is an uncomplicated detection algorithm and has a fast detection performance. Under a clear image (low noise, good lightning condition and ideal sun elevation angle) where the pattern is easily distinguishable, the accuracy will be much higher. Besides, the craters detection is independent of the shape detection whether it is a circle or an ellipse.

6. Comparison with other previous detection method

In comparison to other techniques in terms of performance, this craters detection algorithm also has an understanding performance in terms of accuracy measurement to the previous algorithm proposed by Sawabe, Matsunaga and Rokugawa in 2005. As highlighted and calculated above, it is proven that the craters detection algorithm has an accuracy detection of 77% based on the two images tested above. This understanding percentage measurement is based on how much craters are detected compared with the pre-processed image as in Figures (14) and (15) above. The detected craters are measured from groups of pairing patches (light and dark) with minimum distances and angles detection.

This proposed craters detection algorithm by the authors can be improved by introducing more approaches like edge detections of each crater and evaluating more techniques from the morphological image analysis. To experiment more with the image morphology, the authors have tested the edge detection method using *prewitt* and *canny* on the original Image 2 using the algorithm and the results are shown in Figures (22) and (23) below. As can be seen b, *canny* method has detected the edges more precisely than the *prewitt* method. There are some previous craters detection algorithms implemented in this edge detection method as proposed by Yang Cheng and Adnan Ansar in their proposed craters detection technique [5]. Edge detections are usually used in a pre-processing step to obtain better results before the shape of the crater can be detected.

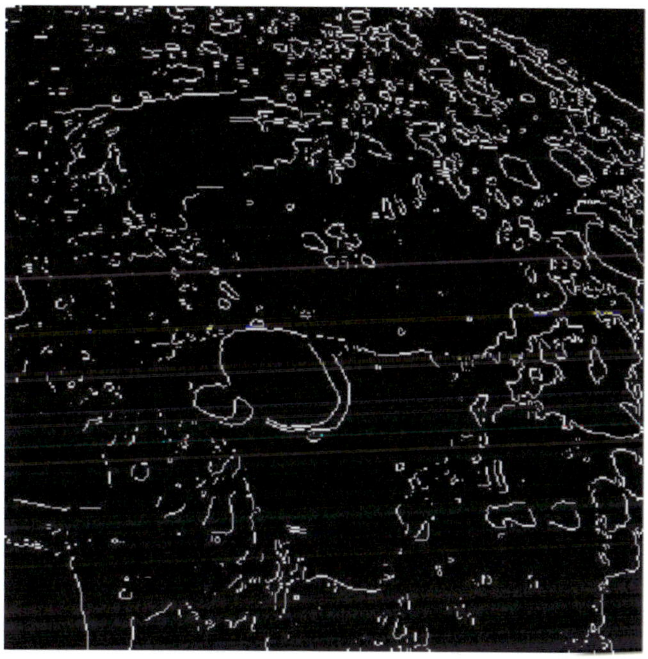

Figure 20. Edge detections using 'prewitt' detector

In comparison to the multiple approaches craters detection and automate craters classification algorithm proposed by Sawabe, Matsunaga and Rokugawa in 2005, the algorithm has an accuracy of 80%. Four approaches are implemented in the craters detection algorithm to find shady and sunny patters in images with low sun angles, circular features in edge images, curves and circles in thinned and connected edge lines and discrete or broken circular edge lines using fuzzy Hough transform. In this particular research, they have considered a crater as a circle and used circular Hough transform to detect circular feature of a crater. The detected crater is then classified by spectral characteristics derived from Clementine UV-Vis multi-spectral images. Although it has more percentage of accuracy compared with the algorithm proposed by the authors, it has a limitation such as the crater has to be assumed to be a circle before it can be used to detect a crater. If the authors have an ellipse in the image, then it will be difficult to use this method of detection.

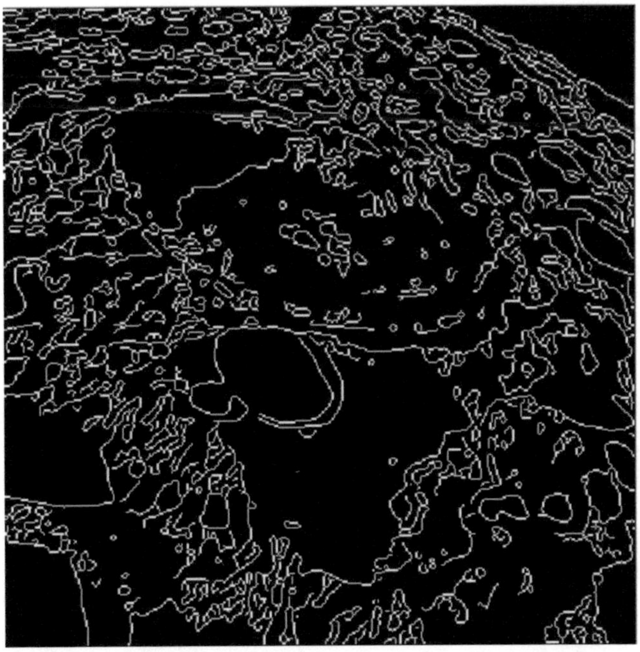

Figure 21. Edge Detection using 'canny' detector

Previously, there were quite a number of craters detection algorithms using Hough Transform especially using circular features detection as proposed by E.Johnson, A.Huertas, A.Werner and F.Montgomery in their paper [7]. As emphasized above, a camera will capture an ellipse if the image is taken from a certain angle and certain distance relative to the moon's surface. An ellipse will have five dimensions that have to be considered in the Hough algorithm when detecting shapes. An ellipse is more complicated to be detected than a circle because a circle just has 3 dimensions to be considered. It will certainly have a complex codes hence will take a longer time to construct. That is the reason why the authors have created an uncomplicated and robust algorithm in detecting hazards mainly craters on the moon's surface for easy implementation.

7. Ellipse reconstruction algorithm using artificial image

To test the algorithm with various image types, the authors have created a two dimension (2-D) image as given in Figure (22) using Adobe Photoshop with its axis of symmetry of a half-length A=0 (to model it as a disc) and degenerate axes of a half-length, B=48. The objective is to determine the position of the centre of the disc reconstructed from the reconstruction algorithm and to compare it with the known centre position determined by the Bounding Ellipse Algorithm. The ellipse created has a position of q = (168.5469, 140.0172).The image generated is 494x494 pixels. The image plane ellipse determined by the Bounding Ellipse algorithm is described as:

a = 133.998 pixels
b = 48.934 pixels
Xc = 168.5469 pixels
Yc = 140.0172pixels
omegha degrees, ω = -0.0017 degrees

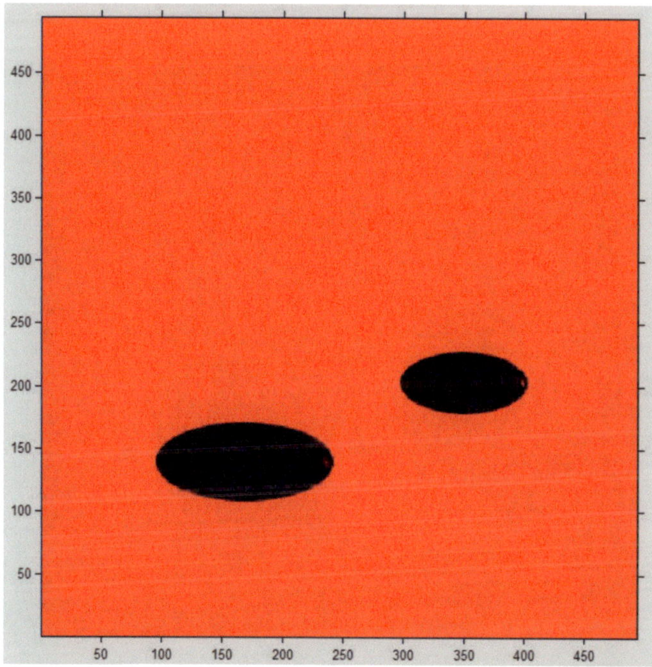

Figure 22. Artificial Image in 2-D created using Adobe Photoshop

To centralize the coordinate system and scale the image, it requires a translation of half of the image dimensions. The reconstruction algorithm is then used to determine the position and orientation of the modelled disc after taking into account the camera's parameter as below:

$Xc = (Xc_{image} - 247)/494$
$Yc = (Yc_{image} - 247)/494$
a (semi major axis) = $\mathbf{a}_{image}/494$
b (semi minor axis) = $\mathbf{b}_{image}/494$

The ellipses generated in Figure (23) above will undergo the same process as the authors performed on the real image (optical) previously using the same method of detection. For the reconstruction results, the authors will be judging two planes namely plane y and plane z to determine the position of the disc reconstructed. This is because, as being set in the algorithm, the centre coordinate of the 2-D plane is at [Zc,Yc]. Thus, the results of the position of the disc will be analyzed in two dimensions only namely Zc and Yc. This reconstructed position will be compared with the centroid's position calculated by the bounding ellipse algorithm. At the end of the experiment, the results from the reconstructed algorithm are satisfactory and similar to the results from the bounding ellipse algorithm. The positional error evaluated for both two solutions are shown in the table below. The one which has a low error will be taken as a true position. As can be seen in the results below, the positional errors are quite high from both solutions that are 8.8722 and 8.8715. Therefore, the authors take the solution 2 as a disc reconstructed position.

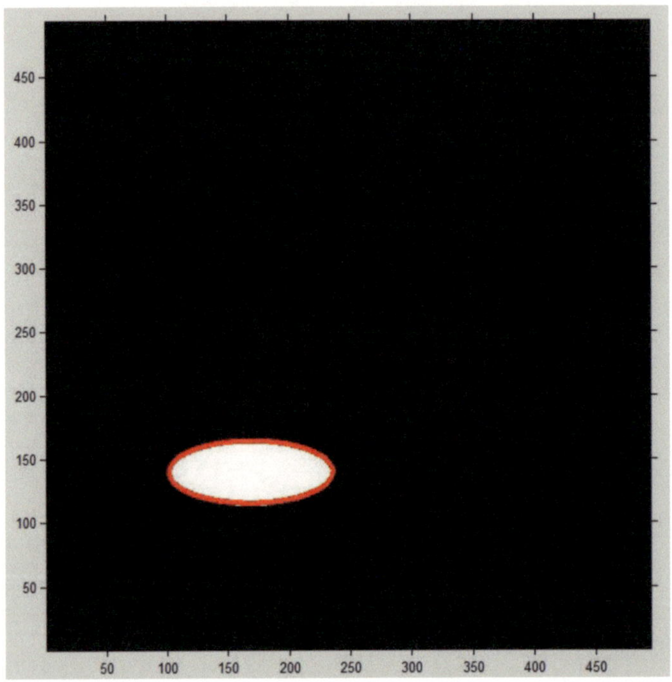

Figure 23. Artificial image of ellipse processed using minimum bounding ellipse with Khachiyan Algorithm

The positional errors are evaluated as shown in Table (3) below. Unlike before, the causes of the errors in the disc position are something similar to what were discussed in the previous 4.1.2.4 section. The positional error can be in any circumstances such as pixellation, the bounding ellipse algorithm error, MATLAB rounding figures as described before, uncertainties from the hardware and the like. These are the reasons why the authors tend to have quite a high number of errors on the position determination part. Besides, when the authors have the ellipse that is too eccentric, both the outputs of the reconstruction algorithm will become complex.

The ellipse bounding algorithm also has an error in bounding the targeted patch. As can be seen in the Figure (26) above, the targeted ellipse is not totally bounded by the red lines and this will affect the output of the image plane ellipse parameter such as semi major axis and semi minor axis. Hence, these parameters will also affect the output of the reconstruction algorithm and will cause errors in the disc's position. In practice, the way to overcome this problem is by reducing the eccentricity of the image plane ellipse or by increasing the eccentricity of the spheroid to be reconstructed. The results of this disc reconstruction algorithm are shown in the table below:

Reconstruction possible results	**Solution number 1**	**Solution number 2**
Position, q **Taken A=2;** **B = 6 ;**	Xc = 163.2225 Yc = 147.1142	Xc = 163.2224 Yc = 147.1137
Positional error	8.8722	8.8715
Orientation, p **Where A=2 and B=6**	1.0000 0.0038 0.0016	1.0000 -0.0085 -0.0036

Table 1. Reconstruction algorithm results for disc position tested in artificial image

As for the orientation part, the authors will take the positive one which has to be (1.0000, 0.0038, 0.0016) similar to those in the real optical image. As discussed before, the orientations for the crater will only be seen if they are orientated upwards (positive values) rather than downwards (negative values). Therefore, after taking into account the above condition, the authors can eliminate the negative orientation. Further, the evaluation of error in the orientation part is similar to the one with the real image as discussed in previous section.

8. Conclusion and recommendation

This paper focuses primarily on the identification and detection of craters on a lunar's surface. To realize these goals, an algorithm to detect craters which happen to be the main hazardous features on lunar is proposed. The authors divided the evaluation of this algorithm into a flowchart as presented in the methodology section. First, using the original image of craters on the moon's surface, the authors convert the RGB image plane to HSV image plane and analyze only the Value parameter of a HSV plane. Further, the thresholding is applied to the image for classification using this Value and thresholding approaches by Sawabe et al. After these classifications of images between light and dark patches, the authors have labelled them and determined the centre of each patch using 'regionprops' function. This stage is then followed by a vital stage in determining the best craters of all using two proposed methods: the minimum distance determination and angle measurement. This is a new and simple method proposed by the authors in detecting craters as main hazardous features on the moon's surface.

For precise moon landing, the authors then proposed the geometrical analysis consisted of projection or reconstruction of the ellipse to a 2-D circle on an image plane. At this stage, the authors applied the bounding ellipse algorithm as a first step in modelling a crater as a disc. The authors then calculated all the ellipse parameters using the information embedded in the output of bounding ellipse algorithm, then drew the bounding ellipse around the targeted patch. This output will then be used in ellipse reconstruction algorithm in order to get the orientation, $\tilde{p}$ and further position, $\tilde{q}$ of the disc (crater) from the camera's projection.

There are some limitations that have to be stated here for further extension and modification. For the craters detection algorithm, it is dependent on the sun angles and these assumptions will lead to an error of detecting a true pair (light and dark pairing patch). In addition, there are uncertainties as discussed before from the software (MATLAB) and the hardware itself in a real application (altimeter to measure the altitude). The Hough method seems to give more precise results but have a constraint in the shape of a crater itself. For an instance, the reconstruction needs to analyze a crater as an ellipse model instead of a circle. In Hough ellipse transformation, the authors have to analyze the ellipse in 5 dimensions instead of 3 dimensions in a circle. These limitations make the Hough Transform method to be unreliable and make its computational method a burden to use together with this craters detection algorithm

For future works, this useful research can be extended to a crater pattern matching as described in the Literature Review section above. Craters Pattern matching is proposed by previous researchers to attain the position and velocity estimation of a spacecraft and a Lander during Entry, Descent and Landing (EDL) purposes and also for autonomous precision landing purposes. By making a pattern matching, one can get the differentiation between the position determined by the pattern matching and those from the reconstruction algorithm. The errors in the crater's position between these two methods can be evaluated to determine which is better in a real application. In reality, the lunar's surface is not flat and the camera parameters will not usually estimate perfectly. The image does require scaling, but the true amount is impossible to be identified without also knowing the camera's specifications (focal length and field of view). In most cases, the picture is not usually taken straight at the centre of the image and perspective distortion will have an effect as discussed before. As none of these are true in real applications, the need of the reconstruction algorithm to find the position of the crater is high. The crater's position determination and evaluation of this reconstruction algorithm were discussed in detail in the previous section. Then, the authors can determine the velocity of the spacecraft based on the position and the orientation of the crater. The idea is, if the authors can find the position and orientation in a single frame, then the velocities are the difference from one frame to the other one. Therefore, this research has a great valuable for future works. In addition, this research is a very worthy research indeed and has valuable benefits to any spacecraft missions in order to avoid the hazardous craters (feature proposed) and for a moon Lander to have a precise landing on a Lunar. Besides, the authors can compare the position determined using equation $\tilde{q}$ and the position determined using the craters pattern matching and this will be a noble future work for new researchers.

Author details

Nur Diyana Kamarudin, Kamaruddin Abd. Ghani, Siti Noormiza Makhtar,
Baizura Bohari and Noorlina Zainuddin
National Defense University of Malaysia, Malaysia

Acknowledgement

We would like to express our gratitude to our supervisors Dr Phil Palmer and Dr David Wokes from the University of Surrey, United Kingdom for their guidance and support. This academic article is also dedicated to our new supervisor, Associate Professor Major (R) Ir. Kamaruddin Abd. Ghani, co-supervisors, our beloved families and university. This chapter is fully supported by the Department of Electrical and Electronic Engineering, Universiti Pertahanan Nasional Malaysia, Malaysia.

9. References

[1] C. Gonzalez, E. Woods, and L. Eddins (2004).*Digital Image Processing Using MATLAB*. Prentice Hall, New Jersey.

[2] Randolph J.F. (1967). *Calculus $\cup$ Analytic Geometry $\cup$ Vectors*. Dickenson Publishing Company, California.

[3] Heiken, G.H., Vaniman, D.T., French, B.M. *Lunar Source Book*. The University of Cambridge, 1991.

[4] M. Seul, Lawrence O'Gorman and J. Sammon (2000).*Practical Algorithms for Image Analysis, Description, Examples and Code*. Cambridge University Press, United Kingdom.

[5] Cheng, Y. and Ansar, A. (2005). Landmark Based Position Estimation for Pinpoint Landing on Mars. In *Proceedings of the 2005 IEEE International Conference on Robotics and Automation (ICRA),* pages 4470-4475, Barcelona, Spain.

[6] Ansar, A. And Daniilidis, K. (2003).Linear Pose Estimation from Points or Lines.*IEEE Transactions on Pattern Analysis and Machine Intelligence,* 25 (5): 578-589.

[7] E. Johnson, Andres Huertas, A. Werner and F. Montgomery (2008).Analysis of On-Board Hazard Detection and Avoidance for Safe Lunar Landing.*IEEEAC Paper*, pages 1-8, California.

[8] E. Johnson and F. Montgomery (2008).Overviewof Terrain Relative Navigation Approaches for Precise Lunar Landing.*IEEEAC Paper*, pages 1-9, California.

[9] L. Bruzzone, L. Lizzi, P.G. Marchetti, J. Earl and M. Milnes.*Recognition and Detection of Impact Craters from EO Products*. University of Trento, Italy.

[10] Neukum, G., Konig, B., Arkani-Hamed, J. A Study of Lunar Impact Crater size-distributions. The Moon 12, 201-229,1975.

[11] Neukum, G.,Ivanov, B., Hartmaan, W.K. Cratering Records in the Inner Solar System, Chronology and Evolution of Mars, vol. 55-86. Kluwer, Dordecht, 2001.

[12] Honda, R., Iijima, Y., Konishi, O. Mining of Topographic feature from heterogeneous imagery: its application to lunar craters. Progress of Discovery Science, LNAI pp. 395-407, 2002.

[13] Sawabe, Y., Matsunaga, T., Rokugawa, S. Automated detection and classification of lunar craters using multiple approaches, COSPAR (Advance in Space Research), 2005.

[14] Cheng Y., Ansar, A. A Landmark based Pinpoint Landing Simulator, Jet Propulsion Laboratory, California Institute of Technology, USA.

[15] Williams J.K. Navigation Results for NASA's Near Earth Asteroid Rendezvous Mission, AIAA/AAS Astrodynamics Specialists Conference.

[16] Miller, J.K. Determination of Shape, Gravity and Rotational State of Asteroid 433 Eros, Icarus,155, vol. 3-17,2002.

[17] Bernard, G., Golombek, M. Crater and rock hazard modelling for Mars Landing, AIAA Space 2001 Conference, Albuquerque, NM.

[18] Wokes, D.S. and Palmer, P.L. (May 2009). Perspective Projection and Reconstruction of a Spheroid onto an Image Sphere.*SIAM Journal on Imaging Science*, 2009.

[19] Coombs, C. H., Dawes, R. M., and Tversky, A. (1970) Mathematical Psychology, Englewood Cliffs, pp. 165-201, NJ: Prentice-Hall.

[20] http://www.engnetbase.com/ejournals/books/book_summary/summary.asp?id=792

[21] http://science.nationalgeographic.com/science/space/space-exploration/moon-exploration-article.html